THE SERVANT GIRL ANNIHILATORS

1885 – The Year That Changed Austin

by

D.W. Skrabanek

S & S Press
Wimberley, Texas

Copyright © 2014 by D.W. Skrabanek

All rights reserved.
No part of this publication may be reproduced, stored in a retrieval system, or transmitted in any form or by any means, electronic, mechanical, or otherwise, without the prior written permission of the author.

ISBN 13: 978-0934646161
ISBN 10: 0934646163

Published by S & S Press
The White Rabbit
Wimberley, Texas

Contents

Introduction: **City of the Violent Crown** — 5

Chapter 1: **"Bloody Work"** — 13
The Murder of Mollie Smith

Chapter 2: **"Femgerichte"** — 26
A Crime Wave Strikes Austin

Chapter 3: **"The Crimson Catalogue of Crime"** — 44
More Assaults, and Then Murder Again

Chapter 4: **"A Night of Savages"** — 59
More Murder and Mayhem

Chapter 5: **"The Long Hot Summer"** — 66
Discontent with Local Officials Grows

Chapter 6: **"The Fiend in Human Shape"** — 81
The Murders Resume

Chapter 7: **"Deeds of Dreadful Depravity"** — 91
A Massacre Near the University

Chapter 8: **"Every Effort to Ferret Out the Fiends"** — 105
The Evidence Begins to Unravel

Chapter 9: **"An Impenetrable and Fearful Mystery"** — 122
City Politics Reach the Boiling Point

Chapter 10: **"A Perfect Carnival of Gore"** — 135
The Christmas Eve Murders

Chapter 11: **"A Saturnalia of Crime"** — 146
Fury Erupts Among the Citizenry

Chapter 12: **"Worse Than Babel"** — 157
More Mischief, Theories, and Arrests

Chapter 13: **"The Bloody Enigma"** — 170
Unrest, Inquests, Surprising Arrests, and a Lynching

Chapter 14: **"Insane Passion for Blood"** — 182
Theories and Motives

Chapter 15: **"Mysterious Barefoot League of Assassins"** — 192
The Usual Suspects

Chapter 16: **"Probable Cause for Murder"?** — 209
A Tale of Three Suspects

Chapter 17: **"Base Libel"**   219
   The Swain Affair

Chapter 18: **"The Notorious Whitechapel"**   227
   The Links to Jack the Ripper

Chapter 19: **"Austin Agog"**   240
   The Trial of Jimmy Phillips

Chapter 20: **"Blood and Bob"**   255
   The Trial of Jimmy Phillips Continues

Chapter 21: **"Almost Impossible and Entirely Improbable"**   265
   The Defense Presents Its Case

Chapter 22: **"A Victim to Peculiar Circumstances"**   279
   The Outcome of the Phillips Trial

Chapter 23: **"A Whirling Mass of Confused Rubbish"**   289
   The Preliminary Trial of Moses Hancock Begins

Chapter 24: **"A Great Trial"**   298
   The Preliminary Trial of Moses Hancock Concludes

Chapter 25: **"Distressingly Conflicting Statements"**   312
   The Full Trial of Moses Hancock Begins

Chapter 26: **"Disconnected and Conflicting Circumstantial Evidence"**   323
   The Full Trial of Moses Hancock Concludes

Chapter 27: **"Revenge in Texas"**   331
   The Kenward Philp Solution

Chapter 28: **"A Dark and Profound Mystery"**   342
   Who Was the Servant Girl Annihilator?

Chapter 29: **"One Human Passion Devilish Enough"**   355
   Was Revenge the Motive?

Chapter 30: **"The Approved Capital City Style"**   371
   Did the Murders Really End?

Chapter 31: **"Villainy Which the Law Makes Possible and Permits"**   393
   What It All Means

Chapter 32: **"The Stain of Blood"**   402
   Aftermath

Sources and Resources   409
Index   424

City of the Violent Crown

Introduction

The end of 1884 marked the beginning of a mysterious series of brutal killings that left the citizens of Austin, the capital city of Texas, bewildered and terrified. By the end of 1885, the so-called servant girl murders had claimed the lives of at least five black women and girls, one black man, and two white women, most all hacked to death with an ax or a hatchet. Interspersed among these murders were numerous home attacks and other random murders and assaults. Though the servant girl murders were never officially solved, suspects included over 400 black men, Jack the Ripper, and even one of the richest and most powerful men in Austin. The circus surrounding the murders included charges of police ineptitude, municipal incompetence, social indifference, and perhaps even a conspiracy and cover-up. At the end of the year of murders, the city of Austin was stained and changed, and not necessarily for the better.

At the time of the first murder, the city was not far removed from a gunfighter marshal, Ben Thompson, who eventually was gunned down in nearby San Antonio. His replacement was Horatio Grooms Lee, the incompetent son of a founding Austin family who found himself replaced before the last murders. Austin was fueled by coal oil and violence, and the streets were little more than dirt and mud lanes. The vaunted title of "Athens of the West" was more ironic than realistic. Saloons and gambling houses lined Congress Avenue and Pecan Street, and a roiling red-light district served up prostitution, alcohol, and opium in an area near the Colorado River known as Guy Town. Most of the newspapers were little more than scandal sheets, with editors challenging other editors to duels. And even members of the state legislature brandished pistols during arguments in the capitol chambers.

A Brief History of Austin

The city of Austin was born of strong wills and politics. Mirabeau B. Lamar, the second president of the short-lived Republic of Texas, looked westward in anticipation of the expansion of Texas. He believed that the current site of Austin, on the western frontier, would help to promote that expansion. Sam Houston, the first president of the republic, looked eastward in hopes that the republic would someday become a part of the United States. Houston favored the new town named after him as the capital of the new republic. Both men had strong wills and political influence, so the location of the capital of Texas remained unsettled for decades. Houston did become the temporary capital of the republic briefly, but in 1839, a site-selection committee, appointed by the Texas Congress and goaded by then president Lamar, chose the current site of Austin for the capital city. It was surveyed and platted beginning in May 1839 by a team under the direction of Edwin Waller. By August of that year, a sale of lots took place, with some choice sites on Congress Avenue selling for thousands of dollars. Many of the prime locations on Congress Avenue became saloons. Waller and his team quickly constructed ramshackle government buildings. President Lamar arrived in Austin in October 1839, and government offices opened for business. The Texas Congress convened in Austin for the first time in November of that year. Sam Houston was not pleased with the choice of Austin as the capital. In a visit to Austin in 1841, Houston remarked, "Certainly nothing could have been more ridiculous and absurd than fixing the seat of government here." And the wisdom of that choice was challenged several times over the coming years.[1]

When Edwin Waller platted the city in 1839, the city stretched from West Avenue on the west side to East Avenue on the east side. The Colorado River was the southern boundary, with North Avenue (15th) serving as the northern boundary. The current downtown area of Austin is not much changed from the original platting. When platted, the city had north-south streets named after Texas rivers west to east geographically. The east-west streets were named after trees, with the exception of Water Street, which ran along the river, College Avenue, and North Avenue. The east-west street names were changed to numbers in the late 1880s. Some of the early settlers of Austin are still familiar names. Edwin Waller, who designed the city, was the first mayor of Austin. Other early arrivals included Jacob Harrell, Moses Johnson, Asa Brigham, Richard Bullock, Angelina Eberly, Dr. Joseph W. Robertson, and Joseph Lee and his sister, Lydia.[2]

The early years of the city were full of danger and uncertainty. Indians were known to range through the area, and the early capitol, a crude building 60 by 110 feet, was surrounded by a stockade and a moat. In May 1841, Austin almost lost one of its earliest supporters, France, in a comical skirmish called the Pig War. Richard Bullock, who ran the first hotel in the new city, had a habit of letting his pigs run loose. His pigs got into the stable and even the bedroom of Alphonse Dubois De Saligny, the French representative in Austin. De Saligny ordered his servant to kill the pigs. That action led to a strained situation between Bullock and De Saligny. Bullock beat the servant and threatened De Saligny with bodily harm. Bullock also demanded that De Saligny pay an overdue hotel bill. De Saligny called upon the nascent Texas government to punish Bullock. When no punishment came, De Saligny closed the French Legation in Austin and left. In 1841, Sam Houston again became president of the republic. He wrote a conciliatory letter and regained the graces of France. Under Houston, many feared bad times for Austin. They did not have to wait long. After Mexican troops captured San Antonio in March 1842, Houston ordered the transfer of all government records from Austin to Houston. The citizens of Austin knew if they allowed the government records to leave, the capital city was doomed. Though many of the records were moved, a hardy band of Austinites, among them Joseph Lee and Angelina Eberly, prevented the removal of the archives of the General Land Office. This conflict of citizens against their own government became known as the Archives War.[3]

In 1850, an election was held to establish the location of the capital city of the new state of Texas for the next twenty years. The contenders were Austin, Tehuacana, Huntsville, Washington-on-the-Brazos, and Palestine. Through spirited lobbying, Austin won the election, gaining twice as many votes as its nearest rival. In 1872, another election was held to determine the permanent capital of Texas. Again Austin prevailed, this time defeating Waco and Houston.[4]

The Civil War and After

Austin did not fare well during the Civil War and Reconstruction. During the Civil War, the state government for all practical purposes disbanded. Many government officials were against secession, and the more stalwart Unionists left Austin and went to Mexico, among them John Hancock and Thomas Duval. In November 1865, General George Armstrong Custer arrived in Austin to lead the Union occupation of the city. Elizabeth Custer wrote eloquently of their five-month stay in Austin. Before arriving, they camped outside the city, and Mrs. Custer described the view and commented on the people.

> We pitched our tents on rolling ground in the vicinity of Austin, where we overlooked a pretty town of stuccoed houses that appeared summery in the midst of the live-oak's perennial green. . . . There were then but one or two short railroads in operation. The one from Galveston to Brenham was the principal one, while telegraph lines were not in use. The stage to Brenham was our one means of communication with the outside world.
>
> It was hard for the citizens who had remained at home to realize that war was over, and some were unwilling to believe there ever had been an emancipation proclamation. In the northern part of the State they were still buying and selling slaves. The lives of the newly appointed United States officers were threatened daily, and it was an uneasy head that wore the gubernatorial crown. I thought them braver men than many who had faced the enemy in battle. The unseen, lurking foe that hides under cover of darkness was their terror. . . .
>
> The negroes in Texas and Louisiana were the worst in all the South. The border States had commonly sold their most insubordinate slaves into these two distant States. . . .
>
> There were a great many excellent, law-abiding citizens, but not enough to leaven the lump at that chaotic period. Even the women learned to defend themselves, as the war had deprived them of their natural protectors, who had gone either in the Northern or Southern army—for Texas had a cavalry regiment of refugees in our service. One woman, while we were there, found a teamster getting into her window, and shot him fatally. Fire-arms were so constantly about—for the men did not dress

without a pistol in their belts—that women grew accustomed to
the sight of weapons.

She noted early on in their stay that "everybody seems to be in a terrified state in this lawless land. . . . Texas was an awful country in which to live, where a man's life was not safe an hour."[5]

In the late 1860s, Austin was a cattle town. Herds followed the Chisholm Trail from San Antonio to Austin and then turned north toward Fort Worth and Oklahoma beyond. The cattle crossed the Colorado River in the area near the current site of Longhorn Dam. The Chisholm Trail was active until the early 1880s. In 1882, Texas beef was selling for $6.80 a hundredweight. But a Texas fever outbreak in 1884 kept Texas cattle quarantined from Kansas. The winter of 1884-1885 was very severe, and fully 5% of the 15,000,000 cattle in Texas perished. By 1885, the price of Texas beef had fallen to 10 cents a hundredweight. The years of 1886-1887 brought the worst drought ever in Texas, which, combined with the increasing advent of barbed wire, marked the end of the cattle drive era.[6]

In November 1869, the first bridge to span the Colorado River, supported on pontoons, opened. It washed away in a flood in October of the next year. In December 1871, the first railroad reached Austin. In July 1874, downtown Austin was first lighted with gas lamps. By January 1875, Congress Avenue had mule-drawn streetcars for the first time. And in December 1880, gunslinger Ben Thompson was elected city marshal of Austin.[7]

Austin in the 1880s

The early 1880s saw a wave of growth in Austin. In September 1881, public schools opened in Austin for the first time, with an enrollment of 942 students. In November 1881, the capitol built in 1853 was destroyed by fire, and three months later, groundbreaking took place for the new capitol, which was completed in 1888 and is still in use today. In September 1883, the University of Texas, which had been authorized in 1881, opened in the temporary capitol with 223 students. Classes first met in the Old Main Building on the UT campus in January 1884. Also that month, an iron bridge was built across the Colorado River to replace a wooden one that had collapsed the year before under the weight of a herd of cattle. The new bridge, built as a railway bridge for the International and Great Northern Railroad, also allowed foot traffic. Pedestrians paid a nickel to walk across the bridge, and horse riders paid a dime. The iron bridge, which was supposed to last forever, was replaced in 1910 by a concrete bridge.[8]

At the time of the murders, Austin was only about two miles square. The Colorado River was the general southern edge, though a few homes, brickyards and lime kilns lay on the south side of the river. The northern edge was just past the University of Texas campus, with the lunatic asylum a bit farther north. A few houses were sprinkled beyond Shoal Creek on the western side, and the eastern side was located near East Avenue, the current route of IH-35, though several communities existed east of that road. The main two streets of the city were Congress Avenue and Pecan Street. Congress Avenue was the widest street in town, platted in 1839 at 120 feet wide, but in 1885 it was little more than a dirt road lined by gas nightlights. Pecan Street, both east and west of Congress Avenue, was the location of many saloons and other businesses. Pecan and other streets were platted at 80 feet wide, and alleys were 20 feet wide.[9]

Blacks and whites for the most part did not live segregated lives in the city. Many prominent white people lived west of Congress Avenue, though some, such as Joseph W. Robertson, lived in East Austin. Robertson bought the French Legation building that Alphonse De Saligny left unfinished. That area became known as Robertson Hill. Many lawyers and judges lived in the area called Judges' Hill, located west of Congress Avenue, and bounded by 19th Street and San Gabriel, and 17th Street and West Avenue. The first house in the area belonged to Elijah Sterling Clack Robertson, a noted lawyer and politician in early Austin. The mayor during the servant girl murders, John W. Robertson, lived in that area, as did James E. Lucy, who became marshal of Austin late in 1885. Many blacks chose to live in black communities such as Wheatville north of the university, founded in 1867 by former slave James Wheat; Clarksville in West Austin, founded in 1871 by Charles Clark, a freedman; and Masontown in East Austin, founded in 1867 by Sam and Raiford Mason. Some blacks lived in shacks in downtown alleys or in shanties near the railroad tracks. Many black servants lived on the property of the person they worked for. A cook, for example, might sleep in a room in the back of the main house or in a detached small building, such as the kitchen. That very living arrangement contributed to a series of brutal murders that gripped Austin from late 1884 through Christmas 1885, the servant girl murders.[10]

In 1885, there were at least 60 sixty saloons and beer gardens in Austin. Some had gambling halls attached. Others had lunch rooms or pool halls attached. Congress Avenue was the home to at least 20 of those saloons, the most notable the Iron Front Saloon, the Crystal Saloon and Billiard Hall, and the Palace Saloon and Billiard Hall. East Pecan Street also had its share of saloons, the most notable the Black Elephant Saloon, the Puck Saloon, and the Bull's Head Saloon. Scholz's Garden was farther north, on San Jacinto between Cherry and Linden. Guy Town also had its share of saloons, the most prominent the Metz Brothers Saloon.[11]

Guy Town

Every growing city sports a red-light district, and Austin was no different. Waco had its Reservation, and Fort Worth had its Hell's Half Acre. Austin's hot spot was called Mexico by some, but it was more commonly known as Guy Town. It existed in what is now referred to as the Warehouse District in Austin. Austin's current city hall occupies part of the old Guy Town. The exact boundaries of Guy Town are debatable, but it was roughly the area bounded by Congress Avenue on the east side, Guadalupe Street on the west, the Colorado River on the south side, and Cedar (4th) or Pine (5th) to the north. Officially, it was known as the First Ward. One could obtain all sorts of pleasures in Guy Town, including liquor, prostitutes, and drugs such as opium, morphine, and cocaine. Guy Town fired up around 1870 and lasted until 1913, when it was closed by mayor A.P. Wooldridge, a man who figured prominently in the servant girl murders.[12]

In 1880, Austin had about a hundred prostitutes, or about 5% of the city's population aged 18-44. When the legislature was in session, more prostitutes were recruited to service the lawmakers. When the university opened in 1883, even more prostitutes were needed to service the college students that seemed to gravitate to Guy Town. These prostitutes needed madams, and Guy Town had its share. One of the most famous was Blanche Dumont, who was working in Guy Town almost from the time it began until its end. Her "female boarding house" was located at 211 West Cedar (4th) Street. Another famous madam was Fannie Kelley, who kept a brothel at the southeast corner of Cedar and Lavaca. Miss Carrie Smith ran a house at 312 Colorado, and Della Robinson, a widow woman, had a house on the north side of Cypress (3rd) between Nueces and Rio Grande. Eula Phillips, one of the Christmas murder victims, was said to be an occasional prostitute at Robinson's house. May Tobin, another widow woman, ran an assignation house at 103 Congress that figured prominently in Eula Phillips' murder on Christmas 1885. An assignation house provided rooms for men and women to have trysts. Along with the large-scale brothels, many prostitutes operated out of rooms and shanties along the alleys of Guy Town. At one time there were about 150 prostitutes operating in a ten square block area of Austin.[13]

Though prostitution was illegal in Texas in the late 1800s, the city officials turned a blind eye toward Guy Town, especially since many of them frequented the establishments there. If a prostitute was arrested, it was usually for disorderly behavior or vile language, not for prostitution. In 1887, the city council voted to legalize the activities in Guy Town, but the mayor, John W. Robertson, vetoed the ordinance. But even after prostitution was legalized briefly in Texas in 1907, Austin, unlike Houston and Dallas, refused to license its ladies of the night. Still, the city was content to let the ladies continue their practice as long as they did so quietly. By 1913, though, moral fervor demanded an end to such permissiveness, and A. P. Wooldridge, the mayor at the time, ordered that Guy Town be eliminated.[14]

Street Names

As mentioned earlier, when Edwin Waller platted the city of Austin in 1839, the north-south streets were named after rivers, and they are still so named today. The east-west streets were named after trees, except for Water Street by the river, College Avenue, and North Avenue, and all those east-west street names were changed in the second half of the 1880s. Just when the change occurred is debatable. Most contend the change occurred in the late 1880s or even in the late 1890s, but Eugene Bartholomew in his diary indicated that the transition began in 1886: "The streets running East & West have been recently numbered commencing at the river. Ash Street running against the South line of my place is now 9th Street." This entry was dated August 14, 1886. The 1887 Augustus Koch map included both tree names and numbers for the east-west streets.[15]

The following charts show the old and new names. For the most part, this book uses the street names that were current at the time.[16]

North-South Downtown Austin Streets
(moving west to east)

West Avenue / Rio Grande / Nueces / San Antonio / Guadalupe / Lavaca /

Colorado / Congress Avenue / Brazos / San Jacinto / Trinity / Neches /

Red River / Sabine / IH-35 (formerly East Avenue) / San Marcos

(San Marcos Street is now out of geographical order, but at one time it apparently ran parallel to Guadalupe Street west of the UT campus.)

East-West Downtown Austin Streets
(moving south to north)

Willow	North Avenue — 15th
Water — 1st	Cherry — 16th
Live Oak — 2nd	Linden — 17th
Cypress — 3rd	Chestnut — 18th
Cedar — 4th	Magnolia — 19th
Pine — 5th	Emma — 20th
Pecan — 6th	Elm — 21st
Bois d' Arc — 7th	Palmetto — 22nd
Hickory — 8th	Louisa — 23rd
Ash — 9th	Orange — 24th
Mulberry — 10th	Apple — 25th
Mesquite — 11th	Maple — 26th
College Avenue — 12th	Laurel — 27th
Peach — 13th	China — 28th
Walnut — 14th	Sycamore — 29th

(South of Cesar Chavez off Red River, Willow Street retains its original name. 1st Street was renamed Cesar Chavez Street in 1993. 19th Street was changed to Martin Luther King, Jr., Boulevard in 1975. College Avenue may also have been Rose Street. What Emma and Louisa streets are named for is unclear.)

The Book Ahead

History often applauds the positive accomplishments of a society while overlooking the negative. In the case of Austin, the servant girl murders changed the city from a sleepy frontier town into a modern burg, one with all the warts and cankers of a 20th century American city. This book chronicles the murders of late

1884 through the end of 1885 and subsequent events. The intent is to give readers the same thorough sense of the crimes Austinites might have experienced through local, state, and national media. The book is also meant as a reference source for other researchers trying to crack the servant girl case. In this volume, a hypothesis regarding the guilty parties is advanced, and a suggestion of a cover-up is made. Just why did the murders of 1885 take place?

Notes

Title: Apologies to O. Henry.

1. Humphrey, *Austin: An Illustrated History*: 10, 21, 23, 26; McComb, *Handbook of Texas Online*. (Two very small communities, Waterloo and Montopolis, already existed near the spot chosen for downtown Austin.)
2. "Mayors of Austin, Texas"; "Bullock House," *Handbook of Texas Online*; Terrell 113-128.
3. Kerr 67-68, 122, 125; Barker, *Handbook of Texas Online*; Humphrey, *Austin: An Illustrated History*: 10, 27, 32-34; Baker 315; "The Archives War."
4. Humphrey, *Austin: An Illustrated History*: 36; Humphrey, "Austin, TX (Travis County)," *Handbook of Texas Online*.
5. Marten, *Handbook of Texas Online*; Custer 136, 138, 141, 142, 144, 153; Johnson, Francis W. 549; *A Twentieth Century History of Southwest Texas*: 204; *The War of the Rebellion*: 409.
6. Worcester, *Handbook of Texas Online*; "Texas Trails: Big Boom of 1882"; "The Texas Trail"; *New York Times*, 1/26/1885.
7. Humphrey, *Austin: An Illustrated History*: 11-12.
8. Humphrey, *Austin: An Illustrated History*: 12-13; "Bridging the Colorado, an Iffy Proposition."
9. Sanborn Fire Insurance Maps. Austin, Texas, June 1885. (See also Koch's Bird's-Eye Map, 1887.)
10. "History of the French Legation"; "Central Austin Combined Neighborhood Plan," 41; Smyrl, *Handbook of Texas Online*; Thompson, "Clarksville, TX (Travis County)," *Handbook of Texas Online*; Thompson, "Wheatville, TX (Travis County)," *Handbook of Texas Online*; "Judge's Hill History."
11. *Morrison & Fourmy's General Directory of the City of Austin, 1885-1886* (See also *Legendary Watering Holes: The Saloons that Made Texas Famous*, by Richard Selcer, et. al.)
12. "Austin's Guy Town 1870-1913"; "Austin's Guy Town"; Humphrey, *Austin: An Illustrated History*: 104, 106, 108, 109, 112, 124, 167; "Texas Trails: Venturing into Hell's Half Acre."
13. *Morrison & Fourmy's General Directory of the City of Austin, 1885-1886*; *Morrison & Fourmy's General Directory of the City of Austin, 1881-1882*; Humphrey, *Austin: An Illustrated History*: 104; Humphrey, "Prostitution and Public Policy in Austin, Texas, 1870-1915": 480, 488, 489, 493.
14. "Austin's Guy Town"; Humphrey, *Austin: An Illustrated History*: 110, 124, 167; Humphrey, "Prostitution and Public Policy in Austin, Texas, 1870-1915": 484.
15. *Bartholomew Diary* 21:62, 8/14/1886. (See also Koch's Bird's-Eye Map, 1887.)
16. Pike, *Austin Plat Map, 1839*; Ford, *Austin Plat Map, 1872*; Koch, *Austin Bird's-Eye Map, 1887*; "Austin City Council Minutes, 5/6/1975"; Kerr 217-218.; "Historic Austin, Texas street names of trees."

Chapter 1

"Bloody Work"

The Murder of Mollie Smith

The glare and hiss of the gas lights on Congress Avenue fell behind them as they slowly made their way west along Pecan Street. The drunken cries from the Iron Front and the Crystal saloons slowly faded away. The rain and snow had passed, and the sky was clearing. The moon was dropping toward the distant horizon, and the night was bitterly cold. Dawn would come in a few hours.

The negro stopped the carriage on the iron bridge over Shoal Creek. The white man beside him looked back along Pecan Street to the lights of Congress Avenue and to Guy Town nearer the river. A block ahead, the moonlight on the two-story Ravy's grocery building cut a block out of the night. Just beyond Ravy's was the house of that man, Hall, across Bowie Street from the store. The Hall house was a square building with a rectangular addition jutting away from Pecan Street. This rectangular building housed the kitchen and the servant's quarters. Near the servant's quarters was the outhouse. There were several neighboring houses, but the two men did not expect to be seen at this late hour.

"No one will notice bootprints. But bare feet. That will certainly take them off their guard," the white man said, smiling at his own cleverness. He was pale, almost yellow in the light cast by the near full moon. He stroked his wiry beard as the short, heavyset negro beside him in the carriage quietly removed his boots and socks. The white man did not remove his boots or socks. They left the carriage sitting near the iron bridge and boldly walked the short distance in the bright moonlight, not even bothering to conceal themselves. The white man knew that no one would suspect a man of his position of the vile things that were sure to come.

The mud from the earlier rain and snow had frozen, and the ice sparkled in the moonlight. Ravy's grocery store was almost dark, though a candle burned in one window on the second floor. The man nodded toward the building, and the negro looked up to the candle. "Maybe that Cagle woman," the man said. "She's lucky we have no quarrel with Ravy."

The two men turned left on Bowie Street, stopping about 100 feet south of Pecan. The negro swung the single-bit ax they had brought along, its shadow in the moonlight like a clock pendulum winding down. Then it stopped altogether.

"Marse John, you know we shunt be yout here doin' these thin's," the negro said.

"We won't hurt the whites—only the coloreds, only the servants," the man said. The negro did not respond.

"Now let's get this over with. Vengeance must be done, if not by the Lord, then by us. We shall bring grief upon the heads of those who have wronged me," the white man said, and together the two moved silently through the back gate and toward the small apartment behind the Hall house. Their breath clouded the air as they stopped by the door.

The men nodded to each other, and the negro slowly opened the unlocked door. The moonlight threw a rectangular block of light on the rough wood floor. They stepped inside the small room, the sound of sleep heavy. A man and woman lay in the bed, and the white man seemed almost surprised to see a man there. He gestured toward the sleeping man, and the negro moved to that side of the bed. The white man moved silently around the side of the bed where the woman lay.

With a sharp nod from the white man, the negro landed a powerful blow with the ax head across the face of the sleeping man, just above his eye, immediately knocking him insensible. The woman roused from her sleep, and her eyes came open wide and fearful as she stared upon the white man above her. She reached for a looking glass on the table beside the bed as if to strike the man, but he slapped it away. It bounced off the wall and fell to the floor, the mirror shattering into pieces. The woman tried to get out of bed, kicking over a chair in the process, but the white man pushed her back into the bed, and she struggled no more when the negro landed a forceful blow on the side of her head, sending blood spraying upon the walls, leaving a gaping hole in the woman's skull. The woman released a puny moan, and then the room was silent again. Soon blood began to saturate the bedclothes.

"Have your fun, Nat," the white man told the other. The negro, still clinging to the ax, grabbed the motionless woman by an arm and dragged her off the bed and across the floor. He stopped at the door, dropping her arm, and grasped the doorframe as he leaned outside. All was still in the bright moonlight. He dragged her out into the yard and behind the outhouse, the trail of crimson blood in the snow glistening in the moonlight. The white man slowly followed them out, stopping in the yard. Soon the sound of ripping cloth was followed by grunts from behind the outhouse.

The white man took his time walking across the yard, the snow crunching beneath his boots. He reached the outhouse as the negro was finishing his business. He watched for a moment, his forefinger and thumb tracing the angle of his jaw. The negro offered the motionless woman to the white man, but he declined.

"Let's finish this," the white man said, and the negro began to hack the woman's body, time and again, until it barely resembled a human form. Already the pooled blood had begun to glitter with ice crystals.

"That will do," the white man said. "Finish the other one."

The negro returned to the small room and hit the gurgling man four more times. Satisfied his work was done, he tossed the ax on the bed. It bounced off the bed and landed on the floor. He surveyed the room and, with a snort, stepped outside.

The white man waited by the back gate. The bloody path to the outhouse sparkled in the bright moonlight. They passed through the gate, leaving it open, and stopped in the middle of Bowie Street.

"You go behind the houses to the creek. I'll pick you up on the road on the other side," the white man instructed the negro.

The two parted, the negro cutting through the open space behind Ravy's and another house closer to the creek. He ran heavily, making sure he left clear footprints. The white man made his way back to the carriage along the road, stopping once to look back at the Hall house and utter a curse. Reaching the bridge, he mounted the carriage and started it rolling west along Pecan Street. He turned around in the open field across from Ravy's, the carriage wheels cutting into the frozen mud. The bridge boards clattered as the carriage wheels rolled across them. He stopped at the corner of Pecan Street and West Avenue to pick up the negro, who quickly put on his socks and boots. The negro took the reins and turned the carriage left onto West Avenue, heading north out of the city. Soon their fiendish deed was behind them.

++++++++++++++++++++++++++++++++++

Did the murder of Mollie Smith occur this way? No one knows. Too much has been lost to history. We know where the murder occurred, and the results. We know the weather and when the moon rose and set. What we don't know is what was going through the mind of the killer, or killers, as the case may be. Was the motive simply rape? Was it robbery? Was it revenge? Again, no one knows, but countless theories and suspects have been dredged up in the century and more since the murder. In any case, this murder, if only of a colored servant girl, began an unparalleled string of atrocities that only grew worse as the following year unfolded.

On the morning of Thursday, January 1, 1885, the *Austin Daily Statesman* rattled the city of Austin with a sensational headline:

"BLOODY WORK. A FEARFUL MIDNIGHT MURDER ON WEST PECAN."

The accompanying article detailed the events of that dreadful evening.

> At a late hour Tuesday night there occurred one of the most horrible murders that ever a reporter was called on to chronicle—a deed almost unparalleled in the atrocity of its execution. It happened on the premises of Mr. W. K. Hall, an insurance man lately from Galveston, residing at 901 West Pecan, about a block beyond the iron bridge that spans Shoal Creek. A colored woman named Mollie Smith had been in the service of the family as a cook for a little over a month. A young colored fellow named Walter Spencer has been coming to see her for some months, and the couple, though not married, were lately living in the relation of man and wife. Between 3 and 4 o'clock Wednesday morning Mr. Thos. Chalmers, a brother of Mrs. Hall, was aroused from sleep by the entrance of Spencer. He was bleeding freely from several wounds on the head and said, "Mr. Tom, for God's sake do something to help me; somebody has nearly killed me."[1]

A *Fort Worth Daily Gazette* article gave further details about the ghastly murder of Mollie Smith.

> The bloody and horribly mutilated corpse of the woman was found on the morning of the last day of the year. Her body was lying fifty feet from the cabin in which she slept, *en dishabille*, her *abode de nuit*, as well as the corpse, were brimming with gore. A hole in the head, evidently made with a hatchet, told of how she died. Evidence went to show that the death struggle with the assassin took place IN HER APARTMENT, and that she was killed and then dragged outside. The bloody finger-prints appeared on the door-check. The furniture was broken and the mirror smashed in the death grapple before the girl yielded her life. The struggle was silent . . . but no less terrible. The pillows and sheets were soaked in blood, and the floor was red with the life-fluid of the poor victim. At the foot of the bed lay a bloody ax, the instrument of death.

And so began the year that changed Austin.[2]

The facts of the murder are clear. In the pre-dawn hours of Wednesday, December 31, 1884, likely between midnight and 3, someone entered the apartment of Mollie Smith behind the home of W.K. Hall, bludgeoned her lover and then her, and dragged the incapacitated woman outside behind the outhouse and raped her, or outraged her, as the parlance of the period went, before hacking her body to bits. The weather was bitterly cold, and snow had fallen. The moon was almost full. As noted, the facts are clear, but the perpetrator of this vile murder has never been determined. Little police action was given to the case, mostly because the parties involved were just negroes. The city marshal was Grooms Lee, "the confident but lackadaisical young son of a powerful local politician," who had become the marshal about a year before the murders began. Because the local white sentiment was that "no white man would have any reason to mutilate a black servant woman, . . . Lee focused his attention on black men." To make matters worse, there were only 12 to 15 officers on the police force for a city of 13,000 people, and several of those officers were incompetent or criminal themselves.[3]

Between 9 and 10 o'clock on Tuesday night, Walter Spencer went to Mollie Smith's room. She said she was sick and asked if Walter felt sorry for her. She also told him to wake her early the next morning. Spencer could not remember anything that happened between that time and the time he awoke to find himself injured. Sometime between 3 and 4 on the morning of December 31, Walter Spencer awoke from his stupor and entered the main house, crying for help. His entrance aroused Thomas Chalmers, the brother-in-law of William Hall. Chalmers lit a lantern and could tell quickly that Spencer was badly hurt. Spencer could not give any details of the event or the cause of his injuries, but he did say that Mollie was missing. Chalmers could not leave the house because of the sickness of one of the residents, likely his sister, who had just given birth to a daughter, Bessie. Chalmers directed Spencer to go to the doctor to have his wounds dressed. So Spencer left. He went out the back way and noticed that the back gate was open, though he had fastened it the night before. He eventually made his way to Dr. Richard Swearingen, who cleaned and bandaged his wounds, probably at his home at 311 West Pecan, about six blocks from the murder scene. Spencer returned to the Hall house around 6 A.M., but finding the front gate open, for some reason he decided to go back to town. He finally reached his brother at a restaurant on Brazos Street, and his brother took him to his mother's house at 1511 Brazos, on the southeast corner of Brazos and Cherry.[4]

Later that morning, Mollie Smith still had not been found. Around 9 o'clock, a neighbor's servant noticed "a strange looking object" behind the outhouse in the Hall's backyard. "There lay the woman, stark dead, a ghastly object to behold. A horrible hole in the side of her head told the tale." The outhouse sat just fifty steps from Mollie's room, and the trail along which she had been dragged must still have been visible, so it is a wonder no one discovered her earlier. Later in the day a reporter for the local newspaper visited the murder scene.

> He was at first shown the woman still lying in the yard, but a brief glance at the sickening sight was sufficient. She was a light-colored mulatto, apparently about twenty-five years of age. A distinct trail on the ground leading to her door showed where the inhuman fiend had dragged her. She was nearly nude when first discovered. Inside the room was evidence of a desperate struggle. A broken looking-glass, disarranged furniture, and bloody finger marks on the door showed that a fight for life, silent, and unseen save by the principals, but obstinate to the end, had taken place. The pillows and sheets were bathed in blood, and sanguinary stains were all over the floor. Beside the foot of the bed lay an ax, beyond doubt the instrument of the crime, as it, too, was blood-stained. Who used it? There lies the mystery.

Unfortunately, the mystery would remain a mystery.[5]

A few months later in the year, William Sidney Porter (better known as O. Henry), who was living in Austin at the time, gave the killers the name of the Servant Girl Annihilators. In the case of Mollie Smith, the name was appropriate. To *annihilate* means to reduce to nothing. Mollie's "body had been hacked and gashed from head to foot with an ax, and so cut to pieces that it would not hold together when it was put into a coffin." Mollie Smith was buried on January 3, 1885, in the colored ground in Oakwood Cemetery, the oldest cemetery in Austin. According to the coroner, Justice of the Peace William Von Rosenberg, Jr., the cause of death was a broken skull.[6]

As for Walter Spencer, his wounds were serious but not fatal. "He was in a pitiable light, but was able to speak, though with a somewhat indistinct utterance. There were five facial hurts—the most serious one being a puncture under the eye, fracturing the orbital bone." Dr. William J. Burt, the city physician, "had found a part of the bone pressed back into the cavity against the eye-ball, and had pulled it forward into place." Dr. Burt thought Spencer's chances of recovery were good. Dr. Burt believed, however, that Spencer's wounds were not caused by an ax. He thought that Spencer was "struck by some sharp pointed instrument—a rock or piece of iron probably." Dr. Burt's statement was curious because in some of the later murders, the victims were essentially lobotomized with an iron spike driven into their brains through their ears. Could the weapon used on Spencer have been a similar spike?[7]

"Injuries on Her Head"

Why was Mollie Smith murdered? Was the motive simply rape? Or was she the unfortunate target of an insane maniac? Was her murder some sort of revenge? Or was Mollie Smith simply the victim of a romantic relationship gone truly bad?

Though servant girls were often thought to have less than honorable reputations, Smith did not seem to fit that category. She was, however, said to possess "a high temper, and she had once spoken of nearly killing a man with a bottle." The 1880 census placed Mollie Smith as a 23-year-old servant in the Waco home of F.O. Rogers, the tax collector for McLennan County. She was born in Virginia around 1857, making her about 28 when she was murdered, not 25 as reported in a local Austin newspaper. She had been in Austin less than a year. The 1885-1886 city directory listed her as working for Frank C. Woodburn, a traveling salesman who resided at 104 West Chestnut with his widowed sister-in-law, though no address was given for Smith. So she had only been working for the Hall family for a short time.[8]

Was Mollie Smith really just a mistaken victim? She had been working for William K. Hall for less than a month. Was the intended victim really Hilda Sanberg, who was listed in the city directory as working for Mr. Hall and residing in the fateful apartment? After all, attacks on Swedish servant girls would become an alarming trend in Austin in early 1885.[9]

Was Mollie Smith an innocent victim of a larger revenge plot against Mr. Hall? Had Mr. Hall ruffled the feathers of someone because of his land and insurance deals? William K. Hall was "an insurance man lately from Galveston," but he had been in the area before. Hall was born in Kentucky in February 1856, and in October 1881, he married Julia V. Chalmers in Travis County, Texas. The Galveston city directory noted that Hall had a "substantial" insurance agency in Galveston, selling mainly fire insurance. By 1884 he had moved with his wife to Austin and was working as a land and insurance agent with an office at 816 Congress Avenue. By the late 1890s, he and his family had left Austin, and by 1900 was living in St. Louis, Missouri. Ironically, his first child, Bessie, was born in December 1884, the same month in which Mollie Smith was killed, and that childbirth was the reason Mrs. Hall needed assistance.[10]

Little physical evidence was present at the murder scene, though "there was no effort at concealment by the guilty party." A blood-stained ax was found in Mollie Smith's room, though several people stated that there was no ax on the Hall property. Bloody finger marks were left on the door frame. "There was a trail of bare footprints in the fresh snow that led from the murder scene to Shoal Creek, a block away." And of course, there were a mutilated woman and a badly injured man. Beyond those few items, all the rest of the evidence was circumstantial.[11]

Only two suspects were named, Walter Spencer and William Brooks, a man who had known Mollie Smith in Waco. The Fort Worth newspaper claimed that a black man named Walter Thompson "had been discharged by the murdered woman at the request of her paramour," Spencer, and that Thompson had been arrested, but this information seems to be a reporting error. Curiously, though, a negro named James Thompson was arrested in November 1885 in relation to a later murder.[12]

Walter Spencer, who was a laborer and about 30 years old at the time, generally lived with his mother, Cynthia Spencer, at 1511 Brazos Street. He had two younger brothers, and all three sons had been born in Texas. Walter had been courting Mollie Smith for several months, and "the kindest relations had previously existed between them. No difficulty had occurred to break off an intimacy that had lasted for months." A black nurse working for the Halls, Nancy Anderson, indicated that Mollie Smith "seemed to possess a great influence over Spencer, who generally did whatever she requested." The nurse also stated that the couple seemed to be "on the best of terms." Still, though he was severely wounded, Spencer was regarded as a suspect on the theory that Smith and Spencer had some sort of fight, and that Spencer killed Smith in his anger. Thomas Chalmers asserted that there was no ax at the place, but that Spencer had borrowed one recently "for some temporary use." But the theory suggested that Spencer "was struck first, while sleeping by the woman, and afterwards killed her." To further complicate the situation, as noted earlier, Dr. Burt told a reporter that Spencer's wounds did not appear to be caused by an ax, but by some pointed object. Was Spencer a viable suspect? Not really, unless one accepts that a man knocked insensible by an initial blow could somehow muster enough ability to quell his attacker, drag her outside in the snow to rape her, and then hack her to bits before returning to bed to pass out for an undisclosed period of time.[13]

So William Brooks, also known as Lem, was the only other person regarded as a suspect. Brooks was in his early to mid-twenties at the time, and was "employed as a bar-tender in the barrel house saloon on East Pecan." Saylor suggests in his novel that Brooks worked at the Black Elephant Saloon, run by Hugh Hancock, though at the time there were at least ten saloons on East Pecan Street. Brooks had known Mollie Smith in Waco, and he was said to be her lover there, so his motive was supposed to be jealousy. Brooks was arrested and jailed on suspicion, though he claimed innocence and provided a sound alibi. He admitted that he knew both Smith and Spencer, but that he "never had any falling out with either" and that he had nothing to do with Smith in Austin. Spencer, though, claimed that some three months prior Brooks had wanted to fight him, though his accusation may have stemmed over jealousy regarding Smith's former relationship with Brooks.[14]

Brooks' alibi seemed quite plausible. He claimed he had been the prompter at a dance at Sand Hill, near the Tillotson Normal and Collegiate Institute at the east end of Bois d'Arc Street, until 4 in the morning. Several witnesses validated his claim. But a black woman living in the house where Brooks stayed said he had arrived home between 2 and 3 o'clock in the morning. The house was located in the rear of 705 Lavaca, behind the First Presbyterian Church, which fronted on Bois d'Arc. It was about a mile and a half from the dance site to the house. The woman, Rosie Brown, claimed she was certain of the time, saying, "After he had come in and slept a while, I woke up and happened to look at the clock and noticed it was just three." If Brooks had left the dance at 4, he would not have reached the house until about 4:30. But numerous witnesses claimed Brooks had stayed through the dance and that Brown must have been mistaken about the time. Several people besides Brown and Brooks lived in the house, most of them young black women in their early twenties. Brown was about 22 at the time, based on the fact that she died of heart disease in 1897 at the age of 34. Could she have been upset with Brooks for staying out late and ignoring her? Was she hoping to get Brooks in trouble, or was she correct in her claims?[15]

Three black men, Ceasar Barrow, John Jackson, and Henry Solomon, all farm laborers around 20 years old, asserted that Brooks had been at the dance until it broke up between 3 and 4 in the morning of December 31. Then the three, along with Brooks, returned to the city before parting at Dr. Tobin's drug store at 700 Congress. Barrow and Jackson both lived with their parents in the 2400 block of San Gabriel, and Solomon apparently lived in a boarding house at 1010 Lavaca, where he worked. But later the black woman living at the house where the dance occurred said that Brooks called the dances until the affair ended just before 2 in the morning. Other witnesses said that Brooks was at the dance from 9 in the evening until it ended, and Rosie Brown was firm in her statement that Brooks got home at 2:30 that morning.[16]

Could Brooks have been the murderer? The time of the murder is not precisely known, but the dance that Brooks attended was just over two miles from the Hall house, and the house where Brooks lived was three-fourths of a mile from the Hall house. Brooks would have had to be speedy to get from the dance to the Hall house, commit the murder, and then get back to the house on Lavaca, though the timing is possible. When arrested, he had no blood on his clothing, but he had ample time to change before his arrest. Rosie Brown, though, made no mention of any blood on Brooks. The common sentiment among local blacks was that Brooks was probably guilty, but Spencer was not.[17]

An inquest into the murder was initiated on January 1, 1885. The meeting took place behind closed doors, with Justice William Von Rosenberg, Jr., using the logic that "its publication might facilitate the escape of the guilty party." The newspaper report scoffed at this logic, saying that "criminals don't wait to read the newspapers to see if they are suspected." The reporter ironically noted that the public already knew as much as the officials. The reporters were as instrumental as the detectives in finding clues, and often the reporters knew more than the detectives about the cases.[18]

So how was this inquest different? Why should this inquest be secret? Why was such a measure of confidentiality being given to an affair involving three negroes? Was William Brooks that heinous a criminal? Was the sexual nature of the crime too sensitive to publish? Was a cover-up taking place? Whatever the situation, the reporter hoped that "justice may be executed upon the inhuman slayer of the unfortunate woman."[19]

The inquest ended on January 3, 1885, and the verdict revealed "that neither court nor jury has any more knowledge of the true circumstances of the crime than outsiders." Six white men—W.W. Pace, Isaac Suares, Robert Hatch, R.S. Caperton, Thomas Walmsley, and R.M. Sojourner—concluded:

> "We, the jury of inquest over the remains of Mollie Smith find that she came to her death between ten o'clock p.m. on the night of December 30, and three a.m. of the 31st, in Austin, Texas, from injuries on her head inflicted with an ax, and we believe that said injuries were inflicted by one Lem, alias William Brooks."

The reporter for the *Austin Daily Statesman* was unimpressed by the verdict. He concluded that the "verdict is a mere expression of opinion—nothing more. It sheds no new light on the murder—reveals nothing that tends in the slightest degree toward clearing up the mystery. . . .But those readers who have kept track of it will be very slow to accept the verdict as conclusive against Brooks." The Fort Worth newspaper concurred, stating that "no light has been thrown on the affair."[20]

Was William Brooks the Servant Girl Annihilator? He was apparently not a suspect in the later murders, and suspects in the later murders were not suspects in the Mollie Smith murder. Though the inquest concluded that Brooks had the ability and motive to commit the crime, after an examining trial on January 26, 1885, he was soon released because of lack of evidence. Brooks seems to have stayed in Austin, for in the late 1880s, he was working as a cook at a boarding house at 312 Lavaca.[21]

As for Walter Spencer, little is known about what happened to him. The local newspaper kept tabs on him through January, noting on January 8 that he continued to improve. On January 17, the newspaper reported that "Walter Spencer, who was so severely hurt at the time of the murder of the colored woman on Pecan street, is recovering from his injuries. But he is still unable to say who was the midnight assassin." Almost comically, though, in late November 1885, the mayor's brother, district attorney James H. Robertson, using evidence from two Houston detectives, Hanna and Hennessey, decided to take Walter Spencer to trial. The grand jury returned an indictment of murder against Spencer, and after a two-day trial in early December, Spencer was acquitted and released. The two detectives were soon dismissed by the city. After that, little can be found about his whereabouts. In the late 1890s, he was working as a laborer and residing with his mother at 203 East 15th Street. His mother apparently died in March 1906, and Spencer simply became a footnote in history.[22]

Was Mollie Smith murdered by one person, or were two or more people involved in the crime? If one person committed the murder, could Smith have remained asleep or silent while Spencer was being bludgeoned, especially if a violent struggle on her part took place later? One suspects that both Spencer and Smith were assaulted at the same time. A further complication lies in Dr. Burt's statement that Spencer's wounds were not caused by an ax, suggesting a second weapon was used. Could one assailant have waylaid Spencer with one weapon, without arousing Smith, and then bludgeoned Smith with the second weapon, an ax? Would one assassin have carried two weapons to the crime scene?

"The Assassin's Ax"

Was the murder of Mollie Smith the beginning of a year-long evil conspiracy of murder and depravity? Or was it simply an isolated incident? In truth, the murder was not all that spectacular. Ax murders were quite common in that day and time. Axes and hatchets were common implements at most every property, and they were cheaper and quieter to use as weapons than guns and bullets. Two good examples of ax murderers were George Washington (No, not the one that killed the cherry tree.) and Richard Parmalee, and of course, one cannot forget the legendary Lizzie Borden. George Washington committed his rampage in San Antonio on December 31, 1884, the same day that Mollie Smith was murdered. Washington, "a religious lunatic who has been confined for a long time at the county poor-house," escaped early in the morning of December 31.

> Before leaving he armed himself with an ax, carved a brother lunatic in the leg, severing a large artery and causing the lunatic nearly to bleed to death. Washington walked to town, a distance of three miles and again attacked a negro family. The police were summoned and when they arrived they found the lunatic chasing Capt. Karber, the assistant marshal, around the yard, cutting at him with an ax. Fire was opened on the negro from three or four pistols and he fell, pierced by three bullets, one in the head.

Washington died from his wounds on January 3, 1885. Later in January 1885 in Boerne, near San Antonio, G. B. Humble, "a good citizen," was killed with an ax in a dispute over the ownership of some cedar poles. "The assassin's ax struck the victim in the center of his forehead and split his head wide open, scattering the brains and blood over the ground and making the most horrible sight ever witnessed in that quiet neighborhood." Not only were ax murders effective, but they were also gruesome.[23]

Richard Parmalee, also known as Richard P. Robinson, was a more well-known and notorious ax murder suspect. He was involved in the infamous murder case of Ellen Jewett in New York in 1836. Though Robinson, as he was known in his younger days, had been seeing Jewett, a prostitute at the brothel of Rosina Townsend, for a long while, he had become engaged to another woman and apparently sought to end his relationship with Jewett. He promised to meet Jewett one final time on the evening of April 9, 1836. Early the next morning, Townsend found Jewett dead from hatchet wounds to the head and her room on fire. Robinson's cloak and a hatchet used at his place of employment were found at the scene. Robinson's alibi, later disproved, was that he was at a store when the murder occurred. He said that Jewett had begged him to let her mend a rip in his cloak, and he decided to leave the hatchet, which he had taken from the store to get sharpened, at Jewett's place, too. Robinson was tried, but the jury deliberated for only eight minutes, and he was acquitted, though public sentiment regarded him as the guilty party. By August 1835, Robinson had changed his name to Parmalee and was living in Nacogdoches, Texas, where he became quite reputable. He served as clerk of the district court from 1839 until 1850, and he was elected as the city secretary of Nacogdoches in 1843. He also became a master Mason. Could Parmalee have been the Austin ax murderer? Not hardly, since he died in Kentucky in August 1855. At his death, he was still considered the likely murderer of Ellen Jewett.[24]

The murder of Mollie Smith, though brutal and unfortunate, would likely have been soon forgotten had not the assaults on servant girls increased in frequency and severity. To this day, "the doer of the damnable deed," according to the journalistic purple prose of the time, "remains utterly unknown, save to the All-Seeing eye which takes note of everything in the universe."[25]

Notes

Title: *Austin Daily Statesman*, 1/1/1885.
Map credit: Smith murder scene excerpted from Koch's *Austin Bird's-Eye Map, 1887*.

1. *Austin Daily Statesman*, 1/1/1885.
2. *Fort Worth Daily Gazette*, 11/15/1885 (*en dishabille*: partly dressed in a loose manner; *abode de nuit*: night room).
3. *Fort Worth Daily Gazette*, 12/27/1884; "Lunar calendar"; Hollandsworth, "Capital Murders"; *Morrison & Fourmy's General Directory of the City of Austin, 1885-1886*; "City of Austin Population History 1840 to 2013" (A few days earlier, Waco, a hundred miles to the north, had experienced a "severe and unexpected wave" of cold weather and the first snow of the season. The temperature was recorded as 14 degrees inside, with a colder reading outside where a stiff wind was blowing.)
4. *Austin Daily Statesman*, 1/1/1885; 1900 Federal Census; *Austin Daily Statesman*, 1/1/1885; *Morrison & Fourmy's General Directory of the City of Austin, 1885-1886*; "Swearingen, Richard Montgomery," *Handbook of Texas Online*. (The exact ages of black people at this time were hard to calculate. Few had birth records, and many dated their birthday from the issuance of the Emancipation Proclamation.); (In his interview with the paper, Spencer called the doctor Ralph Swearingen, an apparent error. At the time, Richard Montgomery Swearingen was a local physician and the state health officer. Swearingen was born in Mississippi in 1838 and married Jennie Jessie in 1864. He moved to Austin in 1875 and died of Bright's disease in Austin in 1898.)
5. *Austin Daily Statesman*, 1/1/1885.
6. O. Henry. *Rolling Stones*: 265. Letter of May 10, 1885: "Town is fearfully dull, except for the frequent raids of the Servant Girl Annihilators, who make things lively during the dead hours of the night; if it were not for them, items of interest would be very scarce, as you may see by the Statesman."; *Frederick News*, 11/20/1888; Oakwood Cemetery Database.
7. *Austin Daily Statesman*, 1/1/1885; *Austin Daily Statesman*, 1/3/1885
8. *Austin Daily Statesman*, 1/2/1885; 1880 Federal Census; *Morrison & Fourmy's General Directory of the City of Austin, 1885-1886*; Oakwood Cemetery Database.

9. *Austin Daily Statesman*, 1/1/1885; *Austin Daily Statesman*, 3/10/1885; *Morrison & Fourmy's General Directory of the City of Austin, 1885-1886*.
10. *Austin Daily Statesman*, 1/1/1885; 1900 Federal Census: 1880 Federal Census; *Morrison & Fourmy's General Directory of the City of Galveston, 1882-1883*.
11. *Trenton Times*, 2/1/1886; *Austin Daily Statesman*, 1/1/1885; *Austin Daily Statesman*, 1/2/1885; Walton, Richard H. *Cold Case Homicides*: 555.
12. *Fort Worth Daily Gazette*, 1/1/1885; *San Antonio Daily Express*, 11/15/1885
13. *Austin Daily Statesman*, 1/1/1885; *Austin Daily Statesman*, 1/2/1885; *Austin Daily Statesman*, 1/3/1885; 1880 Federal Census.
14. *Austin Daily Statesman*, 1/1/1885; Saylor, *A Twist at the End*: 122; *Morrison & Fourmy's General Directory of the City of Austin, 1885-1886*.
15. *Austin Daily Statesman*, 1/1/1885; *Morrison & Fourmy's General Directory of the City of Austin, 1885-1886*; Oakwood Cemetery Database.
16. *Austin Daily Statesman*, 1/2/1885; *Austin Daily Statesman*, 1/3/1885: 1880 Federal Census.
17. *Austin Daily Statesman*, 1/2/1885.
18. *Austin Daily Statesman*, 1/2/1885.
19. *Austin Daily Statesman*, 1/2/1885.
20. *Austin Daily Statesman*, 1/6/1885; *Fort Worth Daily Gazette*, 1/2/1885.
21. *Austin Daily Statesman*, 1/25/1885; *Morrison & Fourmy's General Directory of the City of Austin, 1889-1890*. "Servant Girl Annihilator."
22. *Austin Daily Statesman*, 1/8/1885; *Austin Daily Statesman*, 1/17/1885; *San Antonio Daily Express*, 11/22/1885; *San Antonio Daily Express*, 12/11/1885; Hollandsworth, "Capital Murders"; Galloway, *The Servant Girl Murders*: 282; *Morrison & Fourmy's General Directory of the City of Austin, 1897-1898*; Oakwood Cemetery Database.
23. *Fort Worth Daily Gazette*, 1/1/1885; *Fort Worth Daily Gazette*, 1/4/1885; *Fort Worth Daily Gazette*, 1/26/1885.
24. *New York Times* 8/29/1855; Nicklas, *Handbook of Texas Online*.
25. *Austin Daily Statesman*, 1/3/1885; *Fort Worth Daily Gazette*, 11/15/1885.

Chapter 2

"Femgerichte"

A Crime Wave Strikes Austin

During the winter months of 1885, the weather in Austin remained cold, but the crime scene heated up. The cold snap that started in December of 1884 continued into January of 1885, with temperatures across northern and central Texas dipping to the single digits, such as 5 degrees at Paris. Snow and sleet covered the ground, and many people were falling victim to pneumonia. The weather warmed some during the first of February but returned to severe cold toward the end of February. Combined with the drought that had gripped Texas since 1884, the bitter winter weather added injury to insult.[1]

Servant girls were also injured in the winter months of 1885. The recovery of Walter Spencer and the examining trial of William Brooks held the interest of Austinites through January, but the murder of Mollie Smith soon came to be regarded as the result of just another domestic or romantic spat. No greater meaning was given to the incident.

"Bloody Battle in a Smoking Car"

In February, though, a different kind of murder gripped Austin. Contrary to popular claims, Austin was not yet the "Athens of the West" just because Elisabet Ney and O. Henry lived there. It was, instead, still a town subject to outlaws and gunfights. The murder of U.S. Marshal Hal Gosling on February 21, 1885, only helped to reinforce that fact. Gosling was the U.S. marshal for the western district of Texas. A few days earlier, two members of the Pitts-Yeager-Scott-Brannon gang (Everyone wanted to be a headliner!) were tried and convicted in the U.S. District Court in Austin for mail and post office robbery. James Pitts and Charles Yeager were sentenced to life in prison for their role in the robberies. They had been in the Austin jail since January and were to be moved to San Antonio for safekeeping. The gang was still very strong, having operated in several counties west of Burnet for years, robbing stages and mail offices. Gosling was aware of the gang's reputation, and he believed an attempt would be made to rescue the prisoners from the Austin jail. When no jailbreak attempt came, Gosling did not expect trouble from the prisoners themselves.[2]

But Pitts and Yeager were bad men. An escape plot was afoot. Pitts' wife, Melissa, was related to members of the gang, the Scott father and son. She was a ruthless sort herself. "His young wife, a woman of great beauty, urged him to the deed, procured the pistol for him and stood calmly by as, to use his own words, 'he was filled full of holes.'" The plot against Gosling "was made up in the Austin jail and by Mrs. Pitts . . . who took the pistols to the jail in her bosom and showed them to the prisoners and then concealed them again for delivery on board the train." The plot was to kill Gosling and his deputies during the train ride to San Antonio.[3]

Along with his trusted deputies J.F. Manning and J.L. Loving, Gosling was going to transport the two prisoners on the International train from Austin to San Antonio. In a moment of "good-natured carelessness," Gosling allowed several friends and relatives of Yeager and Pitts to accompany the prisoners on the train. These friends and relatives had served as witnesses at the trial of the two men. Two of the men traveling with the prisoners left the smoking car with a valise and returned later, causing suspicion in Gosling. But nothing developed, and the marshal lowered his guard. Meanwhile, the prisoners and their wives "were quite affectionate in their demonstrations," but no more so than before the two men left and returned to the smoking car, so nothing seemed awry.

> The first intimation that anything wrong was going on was the sharp report of a pistol. This was followed by the rapid discharge of shots, which filled the coach with a dense smoke, in the rifts of which the prisoners were noticed to be moving toward opposite sides of seats occupied by Gosling and his deputies. The first shot evidently missed the Marshal. He was in the act of drawing his pistol, and while rising to his feet a second shot rent the air and simultaneously with the crack of the gun the gallant Marshal fell forward with his head into the aisle and his weapon drawn, pinioning Deputy Manning for a time to his seat. Before the deputy could free himself from the body of his chief, he received a ball in the neck and one in the shoulder.

A passenger and the conductor also opened fire on the escaping prisoners as they jumped from the train. Marshal Gosling was dead, shot in the back of the head. Several of the prisoners' relatives were also wounded badly, including Pitts' sister and grandmother. The grandmother eventually died.[4]

Upon reaching New Braunfels, about 45 miles southwest of Austin, Deputy Loving immediately organized a posse to find the two escaped prisoners. Pitts was easy to capture. His "dead body was found about two hundred yards from the scene of the shooting FILLED WITH BULLETS. He never gained his feet after jumping from the train, but crawled until life left his body, when Yeager took a stone and crushed the dead man's hand in order to free himself from the shackles." Later, Yeager was captured several miles away by a San Antonio posse while trying to find a place to cross the Guadalupe River. When the posse approached, Yeager returned fire, but he was hit in the neck and leg and soon surrendered. Later, Yeager claimed that he had no gun to shoot Gosling, and that Pitts had fired the killing shot. Later, though, Yeager claimed he had dropped his gun when he jumped off the train. He had afterward taken a gun from the dead Pitts. Nevertheless, Yeager was tried and given a life sentence for murdering Gosling. Yeager escaped from the Austin jail in August 1885, but was recaptured.[5]

The murder of Marshal Gosling was mourned all throughout Central Texas. In Austin, a reporter noted that "nothing that has happened in many years has cast such a gloom over this city as the murder of Hal Gosling. The killing of the brutes that took his life is poor satisfaction for the death of so good man." The gang that killed Marshal Gosling were bad men. But the gang that started an all-out assault on Austin servant girls were even worse.[6]

"Dastardly Fiends"

As early as 1884, reports streamed in of an epidemic of burglaries in Austin and Dallas, committed by a gang of thieves supposedly headquartered in one of those cities. In February 1884, a Dallas detective found an expensive set of burglars' tools, leading him to "the opinion that a gang of professionals are making Dallas their headquarters." About the same time, the Fort Worth newspaper lightheartedly compared burglars and members of the state legislature in Austin.

> After the legislature comes the burglar. Of course no one will insinuate that there is any connection between the two—only a coincidence. The average legislator, whatever his faults, knows nothing about drills and fuses and tiles. The only method he ever adopted to enter a treasury not his own was on the "be it enacted" plan. Between the two—the legislator and the burglar—citizens of Austin have always found the company of the former a great deal more satisfactory. He supports our boarding houses and saloons, and to give him his dues, goes to church regularly and throws anywhere from five cents to a quarter in the collection plate. And to crown his virtues he only goes for the state, leaving the town generally better off than he found it. The burglar is a differently-minded individual. He disturbs our slumbers, and takes without giving—except a great deal of trouble.

The article noted that the burglars in Austin had been reinforced "by a great squad of roughs, dead-beats, tramps and professionals from Chicago, St. Louis and other eastern cities." These burglars were becoming quite defiant and "entirely too familiar with the private property of our citizens." The reporter noted that recent developments implicated "an organized gang, proposing to work the state, and with headquarters at Austin. Burglaries here are almost of nightly occurrence, and reports of similar occurrences are coming in from neighboring cities very rapidly."[7]

An even worse development was that the burglars in Austin could not be convicted because they had suitable alibis. A case in the court of Justice William Von Rosenberg, Jr., dealt with three men who had entered W.B. Walker's grocery store on East Cedar Street. The men tied up the clerk, blew open the safe, and made off with $500 in cash. Three suspicious characters were later arrested, and circumstances suggested their guilt in the matter. However, the men had numerous witnesses to swear alibis for them. As it turned out, the three men were members of the stone-cutters association that had been protesting the construction of the new capitol building. The protest was a messy result of the capitol snafu. The contractor, with the aid of the state, was using prisoner labor to quarry the granite for the new capitol. In addition, the union of stone-cutters refused the wages offered by the contractor, so Scottish stone-cutters were imported. The stone-cutters union members were then out of a job, and apparently some of them had turned to crime. One of the suspects in the robbery was "the spokesman of the committee which appeared before the senate investigating committee, and has taken an active part in the effort to impeach the integrity of the contractors, and even the state officials." Others believed the convict laborers were somehow involved in the burglaries as well.[8]

In Dallas, the burglars became more bold and more brutal. In July 1884, two light-colored mulatto men, Sidney Grame and Briscoe Young, were apprehended in Dallas. Young was a porter on the railroad and was believed to be a kingpin in the burglary gang that worked up and down the railroad lines.

> Briscoe . . . had an opportunity to rob at various points along the line, and was also in a position to dispose of stolen goods. Negroes and white men in the gang lived and operated in St. Louis, Marshall, Dallas, Fort Worth and other cities along the line. If goods were stolen here Briscoe Young could sell them in Marshall or forward them to St. Louis. If stolen in Marshall they would be sold here or at Dallas.

Briscoe seems to have been just an enterprising thief. Grame, though, was worse. He was apprehended for stealing from Captain J.P. Moore on April 1. Grame had been treating his wife badly, and detectives used this mistreatment to gain incriminating evidence about Grame. Once arrested, Grame became a prime suspect in an earlier attempted rape of a black schoolteacher, Parmele Woodson. Woodson had been attacked in December 1883 at the door of her house by what she thought was a white man. She screamed, and the man was frightened. Before he left, though, he pistol-whipped the woman, "hitting the woman a terrible blow on the head, felling her to the floor." Because she was pregnant at the time, the attack left her in critical condition, and her child was still-born "with a dent on the head, as if from a pistol." Later, Woodson tried to pick her assailant from a lineup of white men but could not. After Grame's arrest, Woodson was called in for a new lineup, and she immediately identified Grame as her assailant. Grame wound up charged not only with stealing but also with assault and a second-degree murder charge for killing the child.[9]

Also in July 1884, "another horrible crime by a brutal negro on a white girl was attempted" in Dallas. This attack marked the fourth similar assault on white women, at home at night, during the summer of 1884. In this attack, a "black fiend" climbed into the bedroom of Miss Sophie Getz, aged 15, and attempted to rape her. She screamed, alerting the household, and the black man escaped through the window. Mr. Getz ("unhappily being without arms") pursued the man, but the negro boldly climbed back over the fence to retrieve his coat, which he had left in the bedroom. Again the man escaped before Mr. Getz could secure him. An unusual aspect of this assault was the assailant's use of chloroform to subdue his victim. "The smell of chloroform was very strong in the apartment as well as the most overpowering stench from his person," and a vial of chloroform was left in the bedroom, but the label had been scratched off so that the place of purchase could not be determined. The use of chloroform played a part in some of the Austin servant murders in 1885. A black man fitting the description of the assailant was apprehended and jailed, and lynching had been "resolved on" if the identity was correct. Later, both Sophie and her mother identified the captured negro as the villain. This same man was also suspected in an assault a month earlier than the Getz attack. The earlier assault was also on a white woman, the wife of the Dallas city treasurer, Mrs. W.H. Flippen, and left her in a "very critical mental condition." Chloroform was used in that assault, too. And on the day before the Getz attack, Lizzie Kent was attacked by a negro rapist named John Hoer, and she was in critical condition in the city hospital.[10]

By mid-July, passengers arriving by train in Fort Worth claimed that four negro men were lynched in Dallas for their part in the "several late efforts at rape." Tensions were running high in Dallas, and black men were falling under increasing suspicion. There arose "almost a unanimous feeling on the part of the whites that the extermination of the worst element of that race [blacks] in Dallas is all that will end the terrible deeds they are committing." And by September, the Waco newspaper opined that "the Dallas negroes might as well understand now as hereafter that they will be lynched if they attempt to rape a white woman."[11]

Back in Austin, the burglaries continued, and the brutality of the crimes also escalated. As already discussed, Mollie Smith was murdered at the end of 1884. Was her death related to the burglaries? That connection is hard to make. As in Dallas, though, the burglaries in Austin gave way to assaults, attempted rapes, and rapes on a regular basis. After the murder of Marshal Gosling, assaults on servant girls resumed in Austin. Around the beginning of March 1885, assaults and attempted assaults were perpetrated frequently, often with several residences attacked on a given night. Early in March, the *Austin Daily Statesman* opined that "Of all diabolical outrages none surpasses in fiendishness an assault by a strong man upon one of the opposite sex. Of late however there have been several instances of this particular kind of brutality. The previous assaults were among the colored portion of the community." Then the attacks spread to include white servant girls, particularly Swedish and German girls.[12]

Early in the morning of Monday, March 9, 1885, a young German girl working for a family on East Hickory Street was awakened by a white man standing by her bed. The man demanded "her money or her life," as she later recounted. The girl screamed, which troubled the man, and he proceeded to strike her on the head several times with a rock, cutting her scalp and causing a significant blood flow. A young man living in the house was roused, and he grabbed his gun and pursued the villain. He lost sight of the man, but upon returning to the house, he became the target of a rock that bounced violently off the side of the house. Later, the girl could give no clear description of the invader, and no clues could be found. The identity of the assailant remained unknown. The girl's wounds were painful but not dangerous, and she was able to return to work the next day. Unlike other attacks, names in this attempt were "suppressed to avoid further mortification." More likely, names were suppressed because of the prominence of many of the families living on East Hickory Street, among them the postmaster and assistant postmaster of Austin, an Internal Revenue agent, a judge on the Texas Court of Appeals, a druggist, an attorney or two, and the family of Joseph Lee, an early settler of Austin and a chief member of the commission in charge of the construction of the new capitol building. Could the attack, apparently committed by a white man, have been another dastardly deed by a member of the disgruntled stone-cutters association?[13]

The early morning hours of March 13, a Friday, were exceedingly busy with mischief. "Not less than four outrageous acts" were committed by the so-called "midnight marauders" intent on committing "their diabolical deeds." The notion that an organized gang was responsible for the crime wave in Austin was becoming increasingly popular, with the *Austin Daily Statesman* stating, "It seems from the sameness of the deviltry and its constant repetition that there must be a regular gang of these brutes who perambulate the city at the small hours of night to do their unholy work."[14]

The first attack that morning occurred at the residence of Dr. Wade A. Morris at 100 West Peach Street. Dr. Morris was an elderly man, about 72 at the time. His wife, Lucy, ran a boarding house and employed several black cooks and servant girls. The Morris property was a block west of the state capitol. The property actually consisted of several buildings. Of course, at the time, houses did not have indoor plumbing or running water or central heat or air conditioning, so a house was often little more than a wooden shell. As Galloway pointed out:

> The typical living arrangements of women working as domestic servants made them particularly vulnerable. At that time, domestic servants usually resided on the property at which they were employed; either in a small room adjacent to the kitchen or frequently in a small outbuilding separate from the main residence. Both offered ease of access to potential intruders. The households that employed domestic servants were generally well-to-do. When one reads the descriptions of the residences where the crimes took place, one reads the associated names of colonels, doctors, attorneys. The homes were large; several generations usually lived together, relatives, grand-parents, parents, children, sometimes boarders, and a necessary staff of servants who performed the attendant domestic requirements of a large household.

The Morris residence was no different, with quite a few boarders, many of them workers at the capitol. Other boarders included Dr. Morris's medical partner and Mayor Robertson's law partner.[15]

Sometime after midnight in the early morning hours of March 13, a black cook working for Mrs. Morris was awakened by a violent shaking of her apartment door. She screamed, awakening her husband, who grabbed a pistol and fired two times through the door. The attackers retreated to the street and threw rocks against the door and the side of the building. The frightened woman kept screaming, and several boarders were aroused. As the boarders came out to see about the commotion, the attackers disappeared into the darkness. Unlike the bright moon on the night of Mollie Smith's murder, the moon this night was just a sliver of a waning crescent, shedding no light.[16]

Were the attacks at the Morris residence directed only at the servant, especially since she roomed with her husband? Or could the attacks have been intended as a threat against some of the boarders? As noted, William Williams, the law partner of Mayor John Robertson, was a boarder at the Morris place. Could the attack have been some sort of arrogant insult against the ineffective city government that could not curb the assaults? Also boarding at the Morris residence were numerous clerks who worked at the capitol, especially clerks for the attorney-general, the comptroller, and the Supreme Court. C. Edmundson was an assistant to Attorney-General John D. Templeton. (The home in which Templeton resided was attacked several days later.) Boarders Richard Ellis and Asa Belwin were clerks in the comptroller's office, and the comptroller, William J. Swain, was implicated in one of the murders in December of 1885. Was the attack on the Morris home random, or was it purposeful?[17]

Later that morning, the residence of Major Joe H. Stewart was attacked. Stewart, a man in his mid-forties, lived at 1913 Whitis Avenue with his wife, four children, and two black servant girls, one of them likely Mamie Figures, who worked for Stewart at the time. The house was a two-story structure at the corner of Whitis and Emma, and it had a one-story section extending from the rear of it. The two servants were sleeping in this extended part when they were rudely awakened by bangs at the door and demands for entrance. They, of course, refused to open the door, and then the intruder tried to open a window on the opposite side of the room. The two girls could take no more, and they fled the room "in mad fright." The intruder followed them, catching one and throwing her to the ground. Her screams aroused the household, and the appearance of rescuers caused the intruder to flee without being captured. The girls would not return to the room that night where, curiously, "the lamp which was not lit at the time of their hasty exit was found burning."[18]

Again, was this attack random or purposeful? The Stewart home was nine blocks from the Morris home, about a half-mile north along Lavaca Street. Mr. Stewart did not have any known boarders, but he was a partner in Stewart & Habicht, directors of the German-American Bank located at 105 East Bois d'Arc. Was the attack directed against the girls or against the homeowner for some unknown transgression against some unknown party?[19]

The third attack of the night proved more brutal, and it ended in the rape of a black servant woman, Sarah Hall. Hall worked for Mrs. Mittie Parrish at 300 West Pecan Street, just over a mile south along Lavaca Street from the Stewart residence. Mrs. Parrish was a widow woman in her early sixties when the attack occurred. Sarah Hall was in her early thirties and was no relation to William K. Hall, the owner of the home where the murder of Mollie Smith took place. According to the news report,

> The room in which a colored woman was sleeping was entered and the occupant subjected to the most brutal treatment. According to her statement both her assailants were negroes, one of them a yellow man painted black. But this did not keep her from recognizing him and accordingly a mulatto barber named Abe Pearson was yesterday arrested as one of the principals in the outrage.

The case against Abe Pearson was settled quickly. He was tried in District Court in Austin and sentenced on March 31, 1885, to two years in the penitentiary for the rape of Sarah Hall. The second suspect apparently was not apprehended.[20]

A final assault that night occurred near City Hall, at the northeast corner of West Hickory and Colorado, about three blocks from the Parrish house. In this last assault, the culprit was foiled in his attack and escaped when the woman's shrieks alerted the neighborhood. After this set of attacks, the newspaper urged that vigilantes be employed to rid the city of the perpetrators. Citizens were advised to keep a "bright look-out" and a loaded shotgun by the bed. The newspaper suggested that the "killing of one or two such characters could not help but have a wholesome effect on the remainder of these night hawks." The paper proposed that the first citizen to shoot one of the assailants should receive a gold medal.[21]

"Senators Brandishing Pistols"

Violence also spilled over into the capitol on March 13. It should be kept in mind that the state legislature was in session for the duration of this winter crime wave in Austin, meeting in regular session from January 13 through March 31. On March 13, a heated discussion was taking place in the Senate chamber. A bill was on the floor to abolish the office of Commissioner of Insurance, Statistics, and History. Senator Temple Houston, the flamboyant youngest son of Sam Houston, opposed the bill. Senator William Davis favored the bill. These two senators already had bad blood between them, with Davis calling Houston the leader of a "pack of drunken fools" and Houston calling Davis "a liar" during an earlier debate. In the March 13 debate, Houston called Davis "a scoffer." In turn, Davis remarked on Houston's "turkey gobbler strut" and mocked Houston's legislative record. Houston fired back, calling Davis "a lank, scrawny, stalking, dyspeptic, jaundiced thing that took occasion to carp at everything not ordained to suit him." Insults of "coward," "cur," and "liar" followed, and finally "pistols and knives were drawn, and but for the timely entrance of Lieut.-Gov. Gibbs bloody work would doubtless have ensued." Finally, calmer heads prevailed, and the two men apologized for their "unseemly conduct," but a future confrontation between the two was predicted.[22]

"Meeting of Three Horsemen"

The wave of violence continued with the March 16th murder of Dr. James C. Stovall, a prominent Travis County physician. The journalistic purple prose of the period was in splendid form in the reporting of Stovall's death.

> The night of the 16th of March was dark, damp, misty, gloomy. Few were out of their homes, perambulated the streets or journeyed the highways unless absolutely forced by necessitating circumstances. The evening star gleamed in the hazy west, half obscured, but still serene and brilliant. That beautiful far away orb, rolling in the far away ether, beyond the triviolitis—the wickedness, the sins of this earth, and of infinitesimal man—threw its diamond rays across the shadows of the timber that skirts the steep borders of the Colorado in the vicinity of Austin. That and the other gems of the skies shone down on a quiet rural scene that was soon to be soiled by the hand of the murderer reddened with the life blood of his victim, and when stillness was to be suddenly broken by the crack of the assassin's pistol.
>
> The hands on the dingy disk of the great clock on the tower of city hall, Austin, had hardly pointed to the hour of 9 when the dim outlines of a figure on horseback came slowly into view on a somewhat lonely part of the road from Austin to Lockhart, south of the Colorado, and about five miles from the capital of the state of Texas. The nearest human habitation was a little cottage built in rural style, about 200 yards distant and occupied by an humble citizen named Gagner or Gagnan. The solitary horseman gradually emerged from the gloom of night that lay upon the prairies and timber to the northward, toward the river. His form became more distinct as the clatter of his horse's heels drew nearer. He rode erect, looking neither to the right nor to the left, and apparently utterly unconscious of the presence of danger, with no premonition of the terrible fate that he was in a few moments to meet. It was Dr. J. C. Stovall, a highly respected citizen and physician, who had a very excellent reputation among his professional brethren, and whose home—cheered by the presence of a fine family—was at a place called St. Elmo, in the immediate neighborhood.

Stovall was returning from a house call to tend to a sick child when he met two horsemen on the road.[23]

The two horsemen approached Dr. Stovall quietly, and then, without comment, one of them drew his pistol and opened fire on the unsuspecting doctor. The vivid newspaper report continued:

> A flash, almost like vivid lightning, suddenly and for a moment lit up the surrounding darkness. The next instant Dr. Stovall fell headlong from his horse, pierced by a ball that was only too well aimed and went unerringly to its mark. At the moment it was struck, the ill-fated doctor, by the flash of his murderous pistol, saw and recognized the faces of the two horsemen to be those of two of his near neighbors, Tom and Bob Pearson, brothers, whose hatred he had incurred by testimony he had given in a trial concerning the murder of a negro.

Another news report suggested the motive was because "Dr. Stovall let one of the Pearson's relatives die in childbirth and that is why they killed him." Whatever the motive, five shots were fired, two of them hitting their mark. Stovall fell from his horse, and assuming he was dead, the two horseman casually rode on.[24]

But Dr. Stovall was not yet dead. He crawled out of the road, through a hole in a fence, and across a ditch. There he was found by a man living in the nearby hut, by the name of Gagnan. After hearing the shots, Gagnan hurried toward the scene, and there he found Stovall, almost dead from loss of blood. Stovall told Gagnan the events, that he was riding home when the two men approached and without a word, opened fire on him. Stovall "was absolutely emphatic" that his assailants were Tom and Bob Pearson, brothers from nearby St. Elmo, a settlement southeast of Austin. Stovall said he did not know why he was shot. Gagnan took Stovall back to his hut and sent word to Austin. Soon Dr. Richard Swearingen arrived, and he pronounced Stovall mortally wounded. Dr. Stovall died two nights later.[25]

Bob Pearson and his family were neighbors of the Stovalls in St. Elmo. Tom Pearson was pretty much a vagrant. In June 1873, while he was living in southeastern Bastrop County on the farm of Judge Eastland, he shot and killed a negro, Wilkes Franklin, on a neighboring farm. Before dying, Franklin identified his murderer as Tom Pearson. Pearson was arrested and given a $1,000 bond. Shortly after posting bail, Pearson left the county and basically disappeared. He would have remained undiscovered, but in 1882, while working on a farm near Sherman in north Texas, he boasted that he was under indictment in Bastrop County. The proper authorities were contacted, and Pearson was apprehended for murder. He was tried and acquitted in the Austin district court in the fall of 1883. The general belief was that Stovall was shot by Tom Pearson because of testimony Stovall had given in that murder trial. In his dying statement to Justice William Von Rosenberg, Jr., Stovall identified Tom Pearson as his murderer.[26]

Bob Pearson was tried in early May of 1885. Though several members of his family testified he was at home when Dr. Stovall was killed, Pearson was given a thirty-year prison term. Because Pearson was already in his forties, the sentence was viewed as a life sentence, though many believed he should have received the death penalty for his apparent involvement in the murder, though Dr. Stovall had identified his brother Tom as the shooter. Another man, Lee Leverton, was also charged with being an accomplice in Stovall's murder. Leverton lived about a mile from where the shooting occurred. A deputy sheriff hid under the bed of Bob Pearson in the jail, and during a discussion between Leverton and Pearson, Leverton admitted that he and Tom Pearson had been the ones who killed Stovall. The new information did little to help Pearson's case, and he was convicted. Bob Pearson's case was later appealed to the Texas Court of Appeals, but the sentence was upheld.[27]

After his brother's conviction, Tom Pearson, who was being held in the Austin jail without bail, grew increasingly nervous about his fate and decided to seize the first opportunity to escape. That opportunity came on August 7, when four prisoners overpowered a careless jailor and escaped. One of those men was Tom Pearson, and two of the others were Charles Yeager and Dick Brannon, who were in jail for the murder of Marshal Gosling in February. Three of the men were captured before leaving town, but Pearson, despite a badly sprained ankle, made his way to Waller Creek and crawled undetected to the Colorado River. He crossed the river and met friends on the south side. Pearson obtained a horse and rifle, intending to leave the country, but his ankle kept him from riding well. He was recaptured about ten miles south of Austin and returned to jail. He was tried in November 1885, convicted of murder in the first degree, and sentenced to death. Upon appeal to the Texas Court of Appeals, his verdict was also affirmed.[28]

"Reign of Terror!"

Meanwhile, the assaults on Austin servant girls, both white and black, continued on an almost nightly basis. The early morning hours of Wednesday, March 18, saw attacks on at least five more homes. The first attack occurred at the home of Col. John H. Pope at 400 College Avenue at the corner of Guadalupe Street, about two blocks west of the capitol. Col. Pope was a planter and farmer in his mid-fifties. He lived in the house with his wife and four children, and he had as a boarder John D. Templeton, the Attorney-General of Texas. As noted earlier, a clerk working for Templeton boarded at the Morris home that was attacked on March 13. Col. Pope also employed several Swedish and German servant girls.[29]

Black assailants tried to break into the servants' quarters "not only to rob but also to outrage." Here the servants that were attacked were two young Swedish girls in their twenties, Clara Strand and Christine Swensen. The two girls shared an apartment attached to the kitchen in a small building connected to the main residence by a long flight of stairs. As the newspaper reporter detailed, "the girls were aroused a short while before 1 o'clock Thursday morning by a knocking at the door of their room. One of them arose, lit the lamp and was standing holding it, in the middle of the room, when a shot fired through the window on the opposite side, grazed her neck and caused her to fly screaming from the apartment." The girl, Clara, was not seriously wounded, but in fleeing, she was pursued by the assailants. "They dragged her by the head, bruised and cut her neck, and would have accomplished their diabolical purpose were it not for the appearance of Col. Templeton on the scene." Of course, the assailants fled, and all thought the attack had ended.

> In the meantime the other girl, Christine, had gone into the kitchen and was conversing with Mrs. Pope about the propriety of leaving their usual bed room, when a second shot was fired through a broke pane of glass, striking the poor girl about midway between the shoulder blade and spinal column, inflicting a dangerous wound. All sleep was banished from that household, and Dr. Taylor, who resides just opposite, was immediately summoned to attend the wounded girl. He found that she had been struck by a small bullet, 32-caliber.

Christine was also treated by Dr. Richard Swearingen, who expected her to recover satisfactorily unless infection set in.[30]

The next attack on March 18 occurred at the home of Francis (Frank) G. Morris at 102 West Walnut, just north of the capitol, where he lived with his widowed mother. Mr. Morris was the county attorney and a partner in the law firm of Carleton & Morris. He was also apparently the nephew of Dr. Wade Morris, whose home was attacked about a week earlier. According to the news report, "unknown parties" attempted to rape Mr. Morris's black servant, Mattie McDonald, who was in her mid-twenties at the time. A neighbor, John B. Hedspeath, who resided at 100 West Walnut, heard the commotion and responded, driving off the "midnight assailant" before he could do serious harm.[31]

Another attack that night occurred at the home of John W. Kelly at 104 West Walnut, next door to the Morris residence. Kelly was an agent for the Anheuser-Busch Brewing Association, which had beer vaults at the northeast corner of Lavaca and Cypress, right in the heart of Guy Town. Kelly, in his mid-thirties, lived with his wife, Mary, and two daughters, and he employed a German servant girl, Miss Annie Faist. Kelly was also the vice-president of the local chapter of the Catholic Knights of America. He did not appear to have any boarders or any other reason to be attacked, except that the attackers might have chosen his home after failing at the Morris house next door. In any case, the assault was thwarted without injury.[32]

The fourth attack occurred at the boarding house of Miss Ella Rust at 206 East College Avenue, about a block east of the capitol. The initial report noted the place was the residence of Dudley G. Wooten, a local lawyer and also the son of Dr. Thomas Wooten. The place was actually a complex of small buildings located at the corner of East College Avenue and San Jacinto Street. Many boarders lived there, notably various clerks that worked in the nearby capitol, especially clerks associated with the General Land Office. Several lawyers also lived there, among them Wooten and Gardner Ruggles, who was also a U.S. Commissioner. This attack occurred several hours after the attack on the Pope residence. According to the news report, this attack was not the first one on the residence, so the servant, probably Miss Mona Taylor, a black cook about 23 years old, was on the lookout for trouble. "The fellow first broke out several panes of glass and then tore loose a wire screen across the window, demanding all the time to be let in. Grabbing a pistol, the girl blazed away at the man. Alas! it was a self-cocking weapon that she didn't know how to manage, and so was unable to repeat the shot. The villain then coolly walked to the door and tried to push it open." The servant screamed, and Mrs. Fannie Miller, a widow woman who made her home with Miss Rust, appeared on the scene. She stood in plain view of the black intruder and told him to leave. His response was a rock thrown at the widow, followed by several more. Mrs. Miller sounded an alarm, and Mr. Wooten and Mr. Ruggles came out, pistols in hand, but the assailant had already fled before they could get off a shot.[33]

The final attack occurred at the home of Col. Adolphus S. Rutherford, a commercial trader who resided at 1712 Lavaca, about five blocks north of the capitol. He lived with his wife, Fanny, and five children. An intruder tried to rape Rutherford's servant, who was apparently Charlotte Hall, a mulatto woman about 50 years old. Hall, who was single, was apparently not related to Sarah Hall, who was raped in one of the earlier attacks. The target might also have been Hulda Rallgren, a Swedish servant about 19 years old. In any case, an alarm was given in time to prevent the assault. After this night of assaults, the attacks seemed to cease for about six weeks before resuming at the end of April.[34]

"Organized Ruffians"

This round of assaults differed somewhat from the servant girl murders. The murders were committed within a few days of the full moon, whereas these assaults occurred within a few days of the new moon. The murders were performed in a quiet and discreet manner, unlike these assaults, which were loud, boisterous, careless, too bold. As Galloway pointed out,

> Unlike the murder of Mollie Smith, the attacks on servant girls during March were not crimes of stealth. The perpetrators were careless of noise, banging on doors, breaking windows, demanding to be let in. The perpetrators were variously described by the newspapers as "ruffians, scoundrels, brutes, villains, toughs, robbers, would-be murderers, lawless libertines." Their method was to terrorize, to gain entry if possible and assault the girls inside, only relenting if other residents appeared and forced them to retreat. . . .This behavior seems defiant, juvenile, unconcerned. The perpetrators exhibited familiarity with the neighborhoods, the residences, the means of ingress and egress. They seemed confident that they would not be apprehended, roving from house to house, across backyards, along alleys, moving quickly, with agility, escaping into the darkness.

One cannot say, however, that the same group was not responsible both for the murders and the assaults, but the methods of attack were certainly different.[35]

Just who the assailants were is also in doubt. In most of the reports, the number of assailants could not be determined. In the attack on the German girl on East Hickory Street on March 9, a single white man was said to be the assailant, with the apparent motive of robbery. In the March 13 attack on Dr. Morris's home, the news report suggested more than one attacker of unknown race. In the attack that same night on Mr. Stewart's home, the news report implied one attacker of unknown race. In the attack on the Parrish home that night, two black assailants were noted, and one, Abe Pearson, was arrested, tried, and convicted of rape. In the March 18 attack on the Pope home, the news report suggested more than one black attackers were involved. In the attack on the Rust boarding house that night, one black attacker was implicated. In the attacks on the Morris, Rutherford, and Kelly homes that night, the number and race of the attackers were not determined.

In any case, the general sentiment emerged that an organized group was responsible for the assaults and that the police force was ineffectual. The story also began to spread across the state, and various newspapers chimed in on the state of affairs in Austin. The Fort Worth newspaper on February 22 asked: "Have the negroes at Austin formed a secret association, pledged to run out the Swedish and other servant girls? It looks like it. Would it not be well to drive out the bucks?" The Waco newspaper on March 22 noted that "The servant girls of Austin seem to be among the breakers, just at present," suggesting the turbulent times. The day before, the Waco newspaper summarized the events:

> Austin is laboring under great excitement, owing to a series of attempted rapes upon servant girls a la Dallas. During the past two weeks as much as fifteen attempted cases have been reported, resulting in the rape of one woman, a negress, and the fatal wounding of another, a servant girl. The perpetrators, probably negroes, are unprecedentially bold in their assaults, and often have returned a second time in the same night. Servant girls are all frightened out of their wits, and citizens are becoming tired and indignant at the inefficiency of the police force, not one offender having been brought to trial. A vigilance committee is talked of.

The report was not quite correct, as the wounded servant girl did not die, and Abe Pearson was convicted of the rape of Sarah Hall. But the *Austin Daily Statesman* did not disagree with this assessment in general, saying, "The situation greatly resembles the terrible reign of terror in Dallas last year." It called the assaults the "diabolical doings of what appears to be a regular band of organized ruffians." The report justified the conclusion, saying, "From the similarity of the offense, and the identical methods employed in nearly every case, it is evident that the foul work has been perpetrated by the same set of lawless libertines."[36]

The Fort Worth newspaper later went so far as to brand the assaults the actions of a "barefoot league of assassins" and a "godless tribunal." The headline of the article made an allusion to the Femgerichte, a name derived from the German words for *punishment* and *court of justice*. The Femgerichte were a group of secret tribunals in Germany in the Middle Ages. Both the proceedings and membership were secret, and death sentences were carried out immediately without appeal. "In the general confusion which then prevailed in Germany, when all laws, both civil and ecclesiastical, had lost their authority, and the fabric of society seemed on the point of toppling into ruins, the Femgerichte were organised for the purpose of arresting and controlling the incipient anarchy that threatened to bring chaos back again." Just like the medieval Femgerichte, the 1885 incarnation in Austin too was secret, with the number of people and their identities unknown. One can only wonder if the motives of the Austin group reflected those of the ancient tribunals.[37]

Though the white people accepted the "supposed existence of a secret negro association whose mainspring is superstition or the blind and bloody fanaticism born of ignorance," their view was not universally held. "The negroes said the strange crimes were the work of white men, and the success in eluding pursuit made everybody believe the story." Though the attitudes differed, both groups agreed that something needed to be done. The *Austin Daily Statesman* summed up this sentiment:

> Our homes seem no longer safe from the attacks of midnight robbers and would be murderers, nor is there the necessary security afforded for the legal protection of our wives, our mothers, our sisters or the female members of our families. All is uncertainty—all is or seems to be perfect chaos. Night after night the plunderer is at large and attacks of all kinds—murder, robbery, and even worse—disgrace the annals of the city. In the midst of such a horrible condition of affairs, the citizens should take prompt action. A vigilance committee, or some other similar agency, seems necessary to grapple with the criminals that now infest the capitol. The police appear unable to master the situation, and before it is too late the people should take the matter in their own hands.

The notion of vigilante committees was taking hold in the emotional turmoil of the times, and citizens were called upon to arm themselves to wage war upon the fiends who were disrupting the safety and security of the city. The *Austin Daily Statesman* reflected this growing attitude:

> Owing to the lack of protection afforded by the police, the citizens themselves should organize into committees of safety, and patrol the various wards of the city. Any man caught out after midnight, who couldn't give a satisfactory account of himself should be treated in a way that would forever discourage him from prowling around in the dark at unreasonable hours. Some seven or eight years ago Austin was infested with a lot of thieves who plundered the citizens on all sides. A few citizens resolved themselves into a band of vigilantes, and in a short while became an entirely superfluous act to lock the doors of a house, so thoroughly was the town cleaned of the light-fingered fakirs. Something of this kind must

> be done now. It is idle to rely on the police. There are not
> enough of them to watch more than half a dozen blocks.

This call to arms would seem to be the ideal recipe for a bunch of dead citizens.[38]

"Devilish Deeds"

Just what was the reason for the onslaught of assaults? What were the motives of the attackers? Were the targets random or planned? If planned, by whom and to what end? One can't know the reason for the assaults without first determining the motives. Were the attacks simply an attempt to rob or rape poor servants? Were they only "devilish deeds," mischief? Were they meant to threaten or intimidate the blacks in Austin? Were they some sort of revenge or retaliation? Or were they purely the product of insanity? The conclusion of whether the targets were planned or random depends on the choice of motive. Though at least one of the assaults ended in rape, the others were interrupted before they reached their goal. The servant girls' living arrangements certainly made them an easy target, but most of the assailants didn't get into the servants' rooms. And why would anyone rob a poor servant girl when steps away much greater riches awaited? And why would the assailants attack high-profile homes where the chance of capture and prosecution was much higher? Mischief-makers might also act in a random fashion, being destructive when the urge overtook them. And in most of the attacks, the houses attacked were in a few blocks of one another, and many were near the capitol. In fact, the attacks might have been random. Or they might have been the crazed act of a lunatic, and one seldom knows the rationale of an insane person.

The roll call of prominent citizens targeted in the assaults, especially their roles in land, business, law, and government, gives some credence to the other motive, revenge or retaliation. Would an enemy abuse the servant to get at the master? Was a secret organization involved, the Femgerichte of Austin? Who served as the judge and jury to decide the targets? Was there really a black confederacy, the league of barefoot assassins, wreaking havoc in the capital city? If so, why were the primary targets black and mulatto servant girls, with a few Swedish and German girls thrown in for good measure? Wouldn't a black conspiracy be more likely to target white victims? One would think so, unless a white man was telling them what to do.

Were the assaults the work of the singular Servant Girl Annihilator? If so, where were the names of William Brooks and Walter Spencer, the two likely suspects in the Mollie Smith murder? Shouldn't they be persons of interest in the assaults? Was Abe Pearson the culprit? He was the only assailant captured and tried, and the assaults and murders continued after he was jailed. The likely truth is that the assaults were perpetrated by a large group of people, perhaps operating under a single command. The larger the machine becomes, the more likely the chance of breakdowns, and many of the assaults seemed to be attempted by hapless ruffians and not evil villains. Of course, had the assailants not been interrupted, one does not know how brutal the assaults might have become.

The assaults in the winter months of 1885 increased anxiety in the capital city and heightened racial tensions. The murders of Marshal Gosling and Dr. Stovall, though they were not directly related to the servant girl murders, help to illustrate the climate of violence that spawned and perpetuated the servant girl assaults. And as bad as these assaults were, the worst was yet to come.

Notes

Title: *Fort Worth Daily Gazette*, 11/15/1885.

1. *Fort Worth Daily Gazette*, 1/19/1885; *Fort Worth Daily Gazette*, 2/6/1885; *Fort Worth Daily Gazette*, 2/26/1885; Dunn, *Handbook of Texas Online*.
2. *Fort Worth Daily Gazette*, 2/23/1885; *Omaha Daily Bee*, 2/23/1885.
3. *Fort Worth Daily Gazette*, 2/23/1885; *Fort Worth Daily Gazette*, 2/24/1885.
4. *Fort Worth Daily Gazette*, 2/23/1885; *Sacramento Daily Record-Union* 2/23/1885.
5. *Fort Worth Daily Gazette*, 2/23/1885; *Salt Lake Daily Herald*, 8/7/1885.
6. *Fort Worth Daily Gazette*, 2/24/1885.
7. *Fort Worth Daily Gazette*, 2/9/1884; *Fort Worth Daily Gazette*, 2/16/1884.
8. *Fort Worth Daily Gazette*, 2/16/1884; Johnson, *Handbook of Texas Online*.
9. *Fort Worth Daily Gazette*, 8/12/1884.
10. *Fort Worth Daily Gazette*, 7/12/1884; *Fort Worth Daily Gazette*, 6/28/1884.
11. *Fort Worth Daily Gazette*, 7/16/1884; *Fort Worth Daily Gazette*, 7/12/1884; *Fort Worth Daily Gazette*, 9/22/1884.
12. *Austin Daily Statesman*, 3/10/1885.
13. *Austin Daily Statesman*, 3/10/1885; *Morrison & Fourmy's General Directory of the City of Austin, 1885-1886*; Cutrer, "Lee, Joseph," *Handbook of Texas Online*.
14. *Austin Daily Statesman*, 3/14/1885.
15. 1880 Federal Census; *Morrison & Fourmy's General Directory of the City of Austin, 1885-1886*; Galloway,*The Servant Girl Murders*: 261.
16. *Austin Daily Statesman*, 3/14/1885; "Lunar calendar."
17. *Morrison & Fourmy's General Directory of the City of Austin, 1885-1886*.
18. *Austin Daily Statesman*, 3/14/1885.
19. *Morrison & Fourmy's General Directory of the City of Austin, 1885-1886*.
20. *Austin Daily Statesman*, 3/14/1885; 1880 Federal Census; *Austin Daily Statesman*, 5/1/1885.
21. *Austin Daily Statesman*, 3/14/1885.
22. *New York Times*, 3/16/1885.
23. *Fort Worth Daily Gazette*, 11/14/1885; 1880 Federal Census (In the 1880 Federal Census, Dr. Stovall was listed as James C. Stoveall.)
24. *Fort Worth Daily Gazette*, 11/14/1885; *Bastrop Advertiser* 5/2/1885.
25. *Fort Worth Daily Gazette*, 11/14/1885; *Bastrop Advertiser* 5/2/1885.
26. *Bastrop Advertiser* 5/2/1885; *Fort Worth Daily Gazette*, 11/14/1885; *Bastrop Advertiser* 3/21/1885.
27. *Bastrop Advertiser* 5/2/1885; *Fort Worth Daily Gazette*, 7/24/1885; *Reports of cases argued and adjudged in the Court of Appeals of Texas, Volume 23*.

28. *Fort Worth Daily Gazette*, 11/14/1885; *Reports of cases argued and adjudged in the Court of Appeals of Texas, Volume 21*. (In this volume, his case is referred to as Pierson vs. the State.)

29. *Austin Daily Statesman*, 3/19/1885; *Morrison & Fourmy's General Directory of the City of Austin, 1885-1886*; 1880 Federal Census.

30. *Austin Daily Statesman*, 3/19/1885; *Austin Daily Statesman*, 3/20/1885; *Fort Worth Daily Gazette*, 11/15/1885. (Hollandsworth identified one victim as Christine Martenson, not Christine Swensen. The 1885 city directory listed Christine Martenson as working for R.T. Hill at 2000 Whitis Avenue. The 1880 Federal Census listed Christine Swensen as working and living next door to John Pope residence.)

31. *Austin Daily Statesman*, 3/19/1885; *Morrison & Fourmy's General Directory of the City of Austin, 1885-1886*; 1880 Federal Census; 1900 Federal Census (In the 1880 census, Morris was identified as T.G. Morris; in the 1885 city directory, Hedspeath was identified as John Headspeth.)

32. *Austin Daily Statesman*, 3/20/1885; *Morrison & Fourmy's General Directory of the City of Austin, 1885-1886*; 1880 Federal Census.

33. *Austin Daily Statesman*, 3/19/1885; *Austin Daily Statesman*, 3/20/1885; *Morrison & Fourmy's General Directory of the City of Austin, 1885-1886*; 1880 Federal Census (In the 1880 census, Wooten was identified as W.G. Wooten instead of D.G. Wooten.)

34. *Austin Daily Statesman*, 3/19/1885; 1880 Federal Census (Hulda Rallgren was listed as a servant for A.S. Rutherford in the 1880 census, but she could not be located in sources for 1885.)

35. Galloway, *The Servant Girl Murders*: 261-262.

36. *Fort Worth Daily Gazette*, 2/22/1885; *Waco Daily Examiner*, 3/22/1885; *Waco Daily Examiner*, 3/21/1885; *Austin Daily Statesman*, 3/20/1885.

37. *Fort Worth Daily Gazette*, 11/15/1885; *Chambers's Encyclopedia: A Dictionary of Universal Knowledge for the People*: 281.

38. *Fort Worth Daily Gazette*, 11/8/1885; *Trenton Times*, 2/1/1886; *Austin Daily Statesman*, 3/19/1885; *Austin Daily Statesman*, 3/20/1885.

Chapter 3

"The Crimson Catalogue of Crime"

More Assaults, and Then Murder Again

After the March attacks, the assaults on Austin servant girls stopped for a while, but then they resumed with a vengeance. As the *Austin Daily Statesman* put it, the ruffians were "at it again." At the end of April, several more homes were attacked. These new attacks were similar to the earlier assaults for three main reasons: they seemed to revolve around robbery or rape; the homes of government officials or lawyers were mainly targeted; and the attacks occurred about the time the moon was full. Whether the same parties were involved in the new assaults is hard to say, but the details of the assaults were certainly similar. To make matters worse, on April 22, the Colorado River flooded, escaping its banks and inundating Congress Avenue as far as Pecan Street. Shoal Creek and Waller Creek also flooded, with several bridges washed away. On the night of April 23, the Colorado rose another twenty feet, flooding farms below the city and destroying crops.[1]

In the early morning hours of Wednesday, April 29, "a black ruffian entered the sleeping apartment of Mrs. Behnke," who lived with her husband, Edward Behnke, a tailor, in a small house at 308 West Walnut Street at the corner of Guadalupe Street, about three blocks west of the capitol. When the intruder entered, Mrs. Behnke was awakened, and she jumped from bed, "only to be seized by the scoundrel who threw her to the floor." A scuffle followed, which somehow did not awaken the husband sleeping in an adjoining room. The assailant covered the woman's mouth with his "huge hands" and successfully stifled her screams. She was able to wrest a knife from his grip, which he had threatened to use to kill her, or he might have dropped the knife when fleeing. In either case, the assault ended without major damage. As the news report noted, "Had not Mrs. Behnke been possessed of great strength, she would doubtless have been a victim of the brutal passion of this fiend."[2]

At about 1 o'clock that same morning, the home of John I. Callaway was attacked. Callaway, in his early fifties, was a clerk in the office of the secretary of state. He resided at 302 East Mulberry, about three blocks southeast of the capitol, with his wife, Martha, three children, and a niece. The house was a small two-story house that backed to an alley. A black cook occupied a room in the back of the house and was sleeping alone. Hanging on the clothesline in the yard were several dresses. For some unknown reason, the intruder put on one of the dresses before entering the cook's room. Before she was aware of the attacker's presence, he had a hold of her throat. He demanded money, and wielding a razor, said he would kill the woman if she screamed. About that time, two black women came into the yard and noticed the open door to the cook's room. Hearing voices, one of the women called to the cook. The presence of the women outside scared the intruder, and he rushed out, still in the dress, slashing at the women with the razor as he dashed by them. The strange sight and the attempted assault caused the women to cry out, which awoke Orlando Caldwell, a clerk in the comptroller's office, who lived next door at 300 East Walnut. He grabbed a pistol and ran into the yard just in time to see a black man trying to take off a dress, actually cutting off the sleeves with the razor. Mr. Caldwell took careful aim and pulled the trigger, but nothing happened because he had forgotten to load the weapon. The black man hopped over a back fence into the alley and disappeared. Later that morning, the "mutilated" dress was found with blood stains on it, suggesting the intruder "had cut himself in trying to cut off the unaccustomed attire." Within a couple of days, the attack on the Callaway house was credited to an insane black man named "Old John." He had been put in the lunatic asylum "on account of similar exhibitions of lunacy, but was discharged not long ago." He was also believed to have been involved in the rash of assaults in March.[3]

Soon the situation in Austin was inspiring poetry. Just as the newspaper was calling on citizens to keep their guns and pistols handy, the same sentiment was directed at servant girls.

> Get thee a gun oh! serving girl
>
> And keep it by thy bed,
>
> Take aim upon the ruffian
>
> And fill him full of lead.

Not exactly great art, but the point of the poem was clear: Austinites needed to help end the assaults by blasting the perpetrators.[4]

"Too Common to Excite"

The *Austin Daily Statesman* seemed almost bored to keep reporting the assaults. Details of each assault became skimpier, and a sense of ennui set in.

> Nocturnal outrages have become too common to excite much comment or surprise. The ruffians continue to paint the town red in their own diabolical way. It is the same old story—the room of a servant-girl or cook entered at a late hour of the night, a pistol or razor presented, screams, threats of killing, more screams, the master of the house aroused in time to see the ruffian run away, and prolonged screams.

> It is certainly a singular circumstance that not a single one of the brutes has been harmed. The *Statesman* has time and again spoken of the necessity of keeping firearms, in order to give them a warm reception, and yet, night after night, they keep up their attacks on the serving women with the utmost impunity. Their luck in escaping, so far, has not been the result of any lack of recklessness.

Little did the newspaper know that in a few days, the excitement would pick up, and the severity of the crimes would increase.[5]

The onslaught began in earnest in the pre-dawn hours of May 1, 1885, a Friday. Under a bright moon, the first attack of the night occurred at the home of John H. Robinson, Sr., at 700 Rio Grande near its intersection with Bois d'Arc Street. Robinson, about 70 years old at the time, ran a dry goods store at 504 Congress. He lived with his wife, Martha, and daughter, Laura, in a large house with several boarders, among them Hugh Harralson, a 30-year-old clerk in the General Land Office, and James D. Sheeks, an attorney about 27 years old who was a partner in a law firm with his father, David Sheeks. Several black servants worked for the Robinson household, including Lucinda Penn, who was about 28 years old. Between one and two o'clock in the morning, "some outhouses occupied by colored women were visited, window panes broken in, and the inmates frightened nearly to death. Their screams aroused the family." James Sheeks rushed out and fired twice at a man running away, without effect. A hackman living nearby, known only as Red, also "emptied his pistol at another one," also without effect. Sheeks believed that the fleeing man fired back at him.[6]

Two blocks north of the Robinson home, the home of John W. Lawrence was also attacked. Lawrence, an attorney and land agent about 65 years old, lived at 406 West Mulberry at the corner of San Antonio. He shared a large house with his wife, Louisa, and a widow woman, Ella T. Clark. The intruder created a ruckus but did little damage and escaped unharmed.[7]

Another attack occurred at the home of Richard W. Finley at 1105 Lavaca, just north of the governor's mansion and a block west of the capitol. Finley, in his mid-thirties, was a clerk in the comptroller's office and lived with his wife, Texana, and a son, Richard, Jr. He employed a black cook, Lucy Hall, who lived in an apartment separate from the main house. At about 4 o'clock in the morning, a "big black fellow" went to the cook's room and demanded entrance. Finley's bedroom overlooked the cook's quarters, and having been aroused by the noise, "he went to the window where he had a fair view of the intruder, as the moon cast a bright light over everything outside. He yelled at the fellow to leave. He should have poured some lead into him, but unluckily had no gun." Assuming the assault was over, Finley went back to bed, only to be awakened soon after by more screams from the cook. The attacker had returned and was trying again to gain entrance.[8]

Two curiosities should be noted regarding the Finley attack. Three of the victims in the various assaults were named Hall, as was the man who employed

Mollie Smith. No relation existed between W.K. Hall and the assaulted servants, Charlotte Hall, Lucy Hall, and Sarah Hall, who was raped by Abe Pearson. No common kinship could be established for the three Hall women. The second curiosity is that Lucy Hall apparently married Walter Spencer in August 1890. Spencer was the lover and a suspect in the Mollie Smith murder case.[9]

The next attack occurred right across Lavaca Street from the Finley house. The home of John Knox Donnan, 1102 Lavaca, did not escape the antics of the assailants. Donnan, in his mid-thirties, was a land agent in partnership with Rector M. Thomson. Donnan lived in the large two-story house with his wife, Jennie, two children, and his father-in-law, Gustav Johnson, a Swedish contractor. He employed Phoebe Miller, a black servant, and Alice Carlson, a Swedish servant. Soon after the attack on the Finley house, the assailants turned their attention to the Donnan house: "a huge stone was hurled at the kitchen window shattering the sash and smashing the glass to atoms." As a possible clue, a large white hat was found in a nearby alley the next morning.[10]

One of the final attacks of the night occurred at the home of James M. Brackenridge at 405 West Mesquite. The Brackenridge house was located across an alley behind the Lawrence house that was attacked earlier in the night. James Brackenridge, in his early fifties, was a cashier and director of the First National Bank of Austin. Several of his relatives, including his father, John T. Brackenridge, and his brother, Robert J. Brackenridge, were also principals in the bank. James Brackenridge lived in the house with his wife, Martha, and two of his children, John and Isabelle. Miss Bertha Kaapke, a German woman in her mid-twenties, also lived there. Willie Simmons, a black man about 20 years old, worked for Brackenridge and lived in the house. The cook may have been Willie's mother, Adaline Simmons. Mr. Brackenridge "was awakened by a noise in the yard, and looking out, saw his cook, an elderly colored woman, engaged in a struggle with a burly negro. The woman was clinging to him with desperation, but at some noise made by Mr. Brackenridge, he freed himself from her grasp and fled, leaving his coat in the hands of the cook." The coat contained $2.35, a knife, and several other items. A "rusty black hat" was also found in the yard. This ruffian was not through, though. He returned and proceeded to bombard the cook's room and the main house with rocks. The cook said the attacker had broken into her room and demanded money, threatening to kill her. She had jumped up and grabbed hold of him, leading to the struggle in the yard.[11]

More attacks occurred this morning, but as mentioned earlier, the newspaper chose not to report on all of them, stating that it was "monotonous to recount them all," and ending the report with the now standard plea to "keep loaded firearms where they can be got at handy."[12]

Police work on the May 1 assaults did produce some results, regardless of their validity. The hat and coat recovered at the Brackenridge house and the white hat recovered near the Donnan residence were "identified and claimed by Doc Tobin," a black bartender working in Guy Town. He claimed the items had been stolen from his house. Later, John Chenneville, the sergeant of police, arrested two black men, Andrew Jackson and Henry Wallace, on suspicion of their participation in the assaults. Both men were charged with vagrancy. Several men by the name of Andrew Jackson lived in Austin. The likely suspect, though, would be an Andrew Jackson born in 1863. If this is the correct man, his arrest did not seem to entail many negative effects, for he married in 1889 and had numerous children. The second man arrested was Henry Wallace. The 1880 census listed several men by that name, but the likely one was a 17-year-old black laborer living in Guy Town at the rear of 202 Lavaca. He shared a small shack near the railroad tracks with a 21-year-old black man named Primus Johnson. Whoever the men might have been, the newspaper noted that "while they may have had something to do in the deviltry, that the main perpetrator is still at large." Obviously, black men were throwing rocks and threatening residents, but no one knew who might have been pulling the strings.[13]

"A Diabolical Plot"

After the May 1 attacks, the situation in Austin grew increasingly worse. In the early morning hours of May 4, the dental office of Dr. Charles B. Stoddard at 800 Congress Avenue was invaded and set afire. The 41-year-old dentist, who resided in the office, was chloroformed and left to die. According to the Fort Worth newspaper:

> Shortly after 2 o'clock this morning some party or parties entered the dental parlors of Dr. Stoddard by cutting a hole through the door large enough to admit a person's hand, and in this way the bolt was unbarred. Once inside, the would be murderer, with a fiendishness equal to his desperate purpose, chloroformed the doctor and then deliberately piled up nine heaps of paper in as many parts of the room, each heap being thoroughly saturated with coal oil. Chairs and lounges were also covered with the same inflamable material, and all things being thus prepared the fiend LIGHTED A MATCH and set fire to the establishment. With a fearful rapidity the fire shot upward in the main parlor, filling with dense volumes of smoke the adjoining bedroom of Dr. Stoddard, where the owner lay helpless from the effect of the drugs administered.

Luckily, Officer William Howe happened by, saw the flames, and quickly sounded the alarm. Several men arrived soon, as the dentist's office was near several saloons on Congress Avenue, and rescued the unconscious doctor as the room burned around him. The fire department arrived promptly and "soon what might have turned out to be a most serious conflagration was subdued." The office, at the northwest corner of Congress Avenue and Hickory Street, was adjoined by buildings on two sides, and had the flames spread, much of the area could have been consumed. Dr. Stoddard did not regain consciousness until the night of May 4.[14]

The newspaper article went into great detail describing the lavishness of Dr.

Stoddard's office, calling it "as handsome as any that can be found in the country," and noting that "the entire outfit of three rooms . . . was worth at least $16,000." The reported damage to the office was about $2,500. The newspaper noted the relief felt that the attack was not worse. "That at least one life has not been sacrificed and a fine business block totally destroyed is due more to the intervention of Providence than any lack of diabolical intent on the part of the heartless malefactors who concocted the horrible scheme."[15]

The Stoddard case was unusual for several reasons. First, the chloroform used to sedate the doctor was apparently stolen and used in some of the later murders of servant girls. As noted earlier, chloroform was also used in at least two of the attempted rapes in Dallas in 1884. The Fort Worth newspaper seemed to attribute the attack to the servant girl murderer, saying in the headline of the article that the office was "entered by the midnight assassin." The newspaper report went further, stating that "the motive underlying the crime was private revenge, as there is no evidence whatever that robbery was the object." Detectives were already at work on the case, and "suspicion points to certain parties who have long cherished ill will towards the doctor." In a most damning comment, the report noted that "by a strange coincidence this was the day set for the hearing of nine cases for criminal libel preferred by Dr. Stoddard against W.Y. Leader of the *Evening Dispatch*. They were temporarily postponed."[16]

Col. William Y. Leader was quite a character himself. He was a politician turned editor, and he was the publisher/editor of the *Austin Dispatch* in its various forms, and also the *Weekly Mail*. His sons, William W. and Edward J. Leader, who called themselves the Leader Brothers, worked for the *Dispatch* and also published the *Southwestern Poultry Raiser*. W.Y. Leader was born in Pennsylvania in 1836, and by 1880 he was living with his family in Austin. He seemed to relish in infuriating both sides of the political spectrum, and he often found himself in legal trouble. The *Brenham Weekly Banner*, which seemed to have it out for Leader, reported in 1880 that Leader, publisher of an "obscure republican paper, . . . was expelled from the Garfield and Arthur club of that city by a vote of 90 to 1. He was charged with unjust and unwarranted attacks upon well known true and tried republicans of Travis county." In 1881, the *Weekly Banner* noted that "W. Y. Leader of the *Austin Dispatch* is again the recipient of a whipping. He can beat any editor in the state in getting up difficulties and has been whipped oftener than any man in the state." In April 1884, the *Weekly Banner* charged that Leader, who had been an editor for 30 years, was "no nearer having a competency now than when he began." A month later, the *Weekly Banner* reported that "W. Y. Leader, of the Austin Dispatch, has no less than six or seven libel suits entered against him." In June 1884, the Fort Worth newspaper noted that "Col. W. Y. Leader, editor of the Dispatch, was arrested this morning on four charges of libel preferred by Dr. C. B. Stoddard."[17]

In 1886, Leader was involved in more impropriety after he advertised for a female assistant in a St. Louis newspaper. A "young and handsome woman" was recruited, but she turned out to be a runaway wife who refused to return with her husband, "a common stupid-looking bricklayer who seems to have no spunk at all."

Leader, a married man, was then said to have been observed drinking beer in the young woman's room on Sunday while one of his female employees wore "nothing but a loose Mother Hubbard," a gown similar to a mumu. This report in the *Evening Optic*, a rival newspaper, was widely denied. "But in connection with the affair the *Evening Optic* . . . denounced Col. Leader as a lecherous scoundrel, intimating that his part with the affair was for immoral purposes, and that this had not been his first offense in Austin. In the afternoon the editors of the *Optic* and *Dispatch* passed each other on the avenue. Leader had threatened to kill Daniels, it is said, but the latter passed him without being assaulted." The troubles for Leader did not end there. In 1887, "Colonel W. Y. Leader, editor of the Evening Dispatch, who has been in jail on a charge of forgery, was released this afternoon on a bond of $300, signed by J. F. Breckenridge, Joe Nalle, and John Hancock—three of the richest men in Austin." The J. F. Breckenridge mentioned in this last report was apparently J.T. Brackenridge, a banker. Could W.Y. Leader have been involved in the attack on Stoddard or in the other assaults plaguing Austin in early 1885? It will be remembered that the home of James M. Brackenridge, son of J.T. Brackenridge, was attacked on the morning of May 1, 1885, making Leader's involvement in the assaults, at least, rather questionable.[18]

By May 6, detectives were hard at work on the Stoddard case, claiming to have a "clew which will possibly lead to an arrest." Dr. Stoddard was recovering and was able to sit up in bed. He believed that "several parties were engaged in the affair." By May 8, a grand jury was meeting to investigate "the attempted assassination and cremation of Dr. Stoddard, and rumor has it that revelations of a most damnable character" were involved. By May 9, though, the grand jury adjourned without any results. No suspects were named, and the case was turned over to a Pinkerton detective. In this case, as in the other assaults and murders, the wheels of justice ground to a halt.[19]

"Another Deed of Deviltry"

And then, in the early morning hours of Thursday, May 7, 1885, the assaults grew deadly again. On that date, the property of Dr. Lucien B. Johnson was invaded, and his black servant woman, Eliza Shelly, was murdered. Johnson, in his late fifties, was a local physician and a former state legislator, but in 1885 he was a partner in Corwin and Johnson, a real estate and land agent business located at 308 Congress Avenue. His partner, Dennis Corwin, about 50 years old, had served various roles in Austin. In the late 1870s, Corwin was a civil engineer and also served as the county sheriff for several years. As sheriff, Corwin had as a deputy sheriff and a boarder Horatio Grooms Lee, the current city marshal. In the early 1880s, Corwin ran a grocery store on Congress Avenue just north of the capitol. And then he became a land agent and partnered with Johnson. By the late 1880s, Johnson was out of the land business and was again listed as a physician, and Corwin had taken a new partner, John W. Brown, in his real estate company.[20]

Johnson lived with his wife, Ruth, at 302 East Cypress Street at the corner of San Jacinto. Their home was a neat cottage on the corner of San Jacinto and Cypress streets, in the southern part of the city, the Central railway track being immediately in front of the house. Some forty or fifty steps in the rear stood a small cabin with one room, with an alley behind, and facing towards the residence of Dr. Johnson, from which it was separated by a high fence, with a gate between them. This cabin was on the Doctor's premises, and occupied by a colored woman named Eliza Shelly, and her three small children. The woman was employed by him as a cook, and had been in the service of the family a long time.

Eliza Shelly had three little boys, the oldest about 8 years old, and all three slept in the same bed with her. According to Dr. Johnson, Shelly had "formerly lived in the country, where she also was in his service, and was an excellent woman." She was said to have a husband in prison, possibly Ike Shelly, 35, in the Huntsville penitentiary, "to whom she was greatly attached. She never had company in her cabin," according to Johnson, and his wife also noted that Shelly was a good woman, "about thirty years old, of medium size, and of unmixed African blood." She had lived in the city for about three years, and in the 1885 city directory she was listed as living at 603 East Ash in a small building with three black men, so she had apparently moved to the Johnson property only a short while before she was murdered, about a month, perhaps. A link seemed to exist between Eliza Shelly and Sarah Hall, who was raped by Abe Pearson in March. Shelly and Hall were neighbors for a while on East Ash, with Hall living at 605 East Ash.[21]

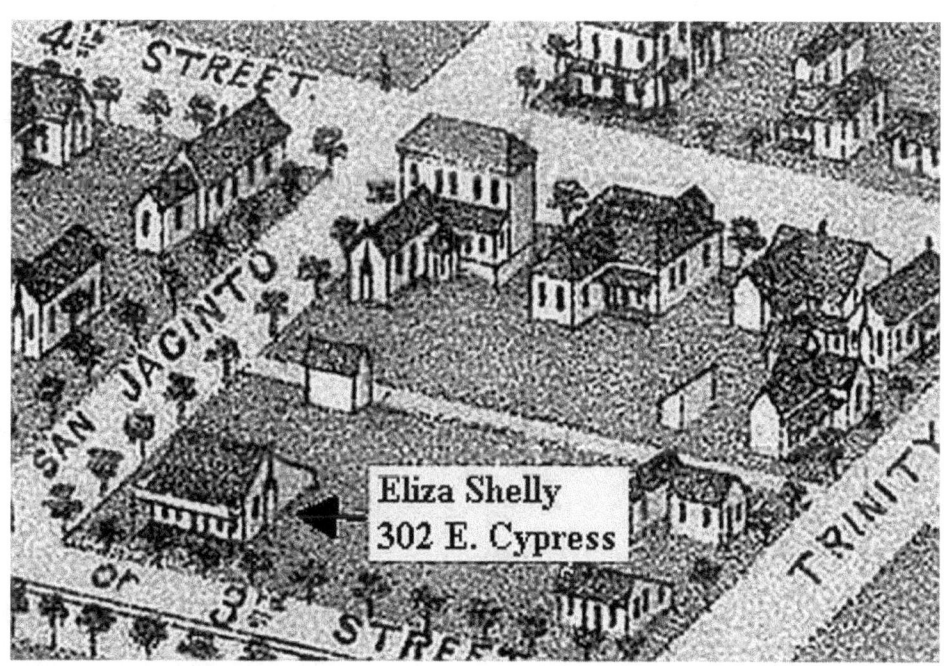

The house that Eliza Shelly lived in with her three sons on the Johnson property was little more than a one room shack near the alley. Sometime before dawn on May 7, beneath a half moon, a man entered the small shack. According to the oldest son, "A man came in the room and asked me where my mother kept her money. I told him I didn't know. He told me to cover up my head; if I didn't he would kill me. The man said he was going to St. Louis the next morning." The boy was not sure if the man was black or white, but he told the doctor's wife that the invader said he was white. The boy thought the man wore a white cloth over his face. The boy also said that "he didn't know that anything had happened to his mother in the night and that after the man left he went to sleep again." In contrast, the Fort Worth newspaper reported that the same boy said "the murderer was a negro man."[22]

But something certainly did happen to his mother. The Waco newspaper suggested that the mother screamed, which caused the man to escalate his attack. He struck the woman several times in the head, apparently killing her instantly. The *Austin Daily Statesman* provided more sordid details.

> Stretched on the floor lay the poor woman, quite dead with a gaping wound over her right eye fully two inches long and nearly that wide. It was done with some sharp instrument, probably a hatchet which cleft through the skull to the brain. It was necessarily fatal, and must have produced almost instant death. There were several minor wounds, that must have been done with some other weapon. There was a deep round hole just over the ear, and another between the eyes—both produced with some sharp instrument.

After the attack, "the pillows and sheets were saturated with blood, and the room was in great disorder." The murderer had broken open two trunks in the room and scattered the contents on the floor. He dragged the woman from the bed and placed her on a small quilt taken from the trunk, then removed the white bedspread and "deliberately wrapped it around the body. It was the coolness of a fiend," the reporter noted. Then the man left without harming the boys.[23]

None of the attack weapons was found in the room, though the weapons were similar to the ones used in the murder of Mollie Smith. Smith was hacked with an ax or hatchet, and, according to Dr. Burt, Walter Spencer was struck with some pointed instrument. Eliza Shelly was also hacked with an ax or hatchet, and some sharp instrument was used to poke holes in her head near one ear and also between the eyes. The only clue found was "the track of a bare-footed man, leading up the alley to her room and returning." The soil in that area was sandy, clearly revealing short, broad, bare footprints. Bare footprints may have been found at the scene of Mollie Smith's murder, but there, as here, no mention was made of a missing toe, a key detail later in the investigation of the series of murders.[24]

A jury of inquest was called early in the day by Justice Thomas F. Purnell. As in the Mollie Smith murder, the inquest revealed nothing new. "The verdict was in effect that Eliza Shelly came to her death by wounds from some sharp instrument, and that there was no clue to the perpetrator." There was, however, some disagreement as to the exact nature of the weapon used. "Some thought the wounds were inflicted by a sharp-edged tool like a hatchet or ax; others that they were too jagged and uneven for that and that it was done by some blunter weapon." The inquest also confirmed that no weapons were left at the murder scene to determine just what kind of instrument was used to effect the assassination.[25]

Later in the day, using the slimmest of clues, "Deputy Sheriff John Holmes arrested one Andrew Williams, said to be a half-witted colored boy, about 19 years old." He was apprehended at the home of a black woman living near the Circle Skating Rink, which was located at 611 East Mulberry at the corner of Sabine Street. That woman was possibly Nancy Scott, a midwife about 40 years old at the time, who lived a couple houses down from the skating rink at 705 East Mulberry. The young man's link to the murder was that he was barefooted at the time of his arrest. Galloway suggested that Williams was arrested because he was barefooted in the "immediate vicinity" of the crime scene. In fact, he was arrested about a half mile away. The numerous saloons on Congress Avenue and East Pecan were much closer to the crime scene than the place where Williams was arrested. The Austin reporter admitted that the link between Williams and the murder was "a slender clue" but one that might yield results, as the footprint at the scene of the crime had been measured, and Williams' footprint would be compared to those measurements. Williams seemed to be just a victim of circumstances, as he apparently did not undergo prosecution for the crime. However, in June of 1885, he was arrested again, this time for the brutal rape of a nine-year-old black girl in the area of Robertson Hill, located two blocks east of East Avenue around Mesquite Street, or about a quarter-mile from the place he was arrested in May. For this later crime, he was sentenced to life in prison.[26]

On May 9, the Fort Worth newspaper reported that "one or two negroes" were arrested in connection with the murder of Eliza Shelly. "The evidence against them is that barefoot tracks were found on the premises of the murdered woman, and the two arrested were unfortunate enough not to have shoes." The article did not name the suspects, but surely one would be Andrew Williams. The report went on to note that several more homes were attacked on the night of May 7, including the homes of L.H. Wilson and William B. Moore, a clerk in the state treasurer's office who lived at 100 East Peach. The article noted that Moore shot at the assailants, but without effect.[27]

Following the murder of Eliza Shelly, the mood in Austin was understandably grim. The Waco newspaper noted that "the colored people of Austin are terrorized over the frequency of these midnight assaults, which the authorities, so far, have been powerless to prevent and punish." The *Austin Daily Statesman* echoed this sentiment, quoting one black man who said that "he never expected to leave his house any more at night for fear his wife would be killed." The citizens of Austin, in their fright, were looking for someone to blame. The police were a popular target, but only four officers were on duty at a time, and they certainly could not be expected to patrol the entire city. The city council was also blamed for not recruiting more police officers. Citizens called for the organization of a vigilance committee. One prominent citizen suggested that the murders and assaults "must be the work of a maniac." Citizens began to pool their money to "pay several night watchmen to guard the residence portions of the city." All over, across every class, the assaults and murders were on the lips of the citizens of Austin.[28]

The *Austin Daily Statesman* did its best to fan the flames of discontent. Claiming that there were "demons in human form that lurk amidst us, singling out by day, victims for the midnight slaughter," the newspaper, under a section called "Murder and Misgovernment," waxed eloquently about the events.

> The heart sickens at these repeated details of horrid, merciless crime. The daily chronicler is sought each morning to discover who is the latest pitiless victim of the relentless murderer. . . . Since the stark, stiff form of the servant girl, Mollie Smith, was laid out upon the snow, that cold December night, to be a ghastly, grinning, startling horror of the daylight, there have been a hundred diabolical entries made into private houses in our midst, every one of which was liable to lead to murder, and before alarm was raised, in a number of instances, there has been effort to murder. Incipient bloodshed is present everywhere; it lurks at night about the windows and doors of our private residences. Insatiable, ghastly death is ever ready to claim the murderer's victim, and none of us know how soon the relentless slayer may demand a victim from among those who are the dearest, the purest and best. The shedding of woman's blood is a special feature in this murderous period, through which the weak and unprotected are passing with fear and trembling. Only once lately has an effort been made to take the life of any man, and this case was not more than chronicled before we are called upon to tell of the cold-blooded butchery of another servant woman, unmindful of danger, upon her couch at night, in the very heart of this capital city. Yes, the heart sickens, and men who cherish the loved ones of their households are called upon to protect the sacred precincts of home. Though the city is and has been overrun with crime, there seems to be no law to which the people of this municipality may appeal but that of self-preservation. . . . In Austin we pay for protection, but there is none—absolutely none. For nearly five months the city has been the home of a gang of demons incarnate, who have exercised their hellish propensities at will. The city in all this time has been given over to a misgovernment that is shameful to the age and community in which we live.

The newspaper went on to note that the city council had paid little attention to the series of crimes, with "more interest displayed one day in these misgoverning circles in favor of a bill, proposing to increase the power and pay of misgovernors, than has been shown in five months on behalf of law and order." Saying that the "condition is fearful" and the "community helpless," the article concluded with a vengeful refrain: "Death is too good, in fact, for the being who would murder, in cold blood, a mother sleeping beside her children."[29]

Certainly, something had to be done, and perhaps that realization caused the increase in arrests of black men whose only crime appeared to be their lack of shoes. Ike Plummer was one of those men. Around May 12, he was arrested and charged with the murder of Eliza Shelly. Plummer, who was considered as simple as Andrew Williams, was not even aware he was charged with murder. He thought he was being returned to jail for an earlier vagrancy charge. An examining trial was held before Justice William Von Rosenberg, Jr., to find whether ample evidence existed to continue to hold Plummer in jail. The Austin reporter described Plummer as "a tall, ungainly, ill kempt negro, with a countenance suggestive more of idiocy than brutality, and about thirty years of age." Col. John H. Pope testified on Plummer's behalf, stating that while Plummer "was commonly regarded as trifling, there was nothing of a vicious disposition about him." As discussed earlier, Pope's home was one of those attacked on March 18. The reporter also noted that "Ike did not seem uneasy during the progress of the examination but at times a half imbecile grin played over his black face."[30]

The most damning witness against Plummer was Andrew Rogers, one of the men who lived with Eliza Shelly at 603 East Ash. Rogers stated that he had known both Plummer and Shelly for about a year. He spoke of a quarrel between Plummer and Shelly that occurred around the first of April, at which time "they were living together on Red River." This claim is unclear. One can't tell if Plummer and Shelly were living together, or if Rogers and Shelly were living together. The second has been established, but Rogers and Shelly lived on East Ash, very near Red River Street, though. Possibly Plummer also lived in the small house on East Ash. In any case, Shelly's involvement with Plummer flies in the face of the earlier report of her devoted attachment to her imprisoned husband. Soon after the quarrel, Shelly went to work as a cook for Dr. Johnson. Rogers stated that as he passed by Dr. Johnson's place around 6 P.M. on May 6, he saw Plummer and Shelly together. He also claimed he overheard their conversation, in which Plummer demanded money from Shelly. She refused, saying what little money she had was for her children. She told Plummer that she didn't want him to come around anymore. Then Plummer left, saying that he would see Shelly again, if he lived. Rogers also claimed he saw "the handle of either a hammer or a hatchet protruding from Plummer's pocket." Rogers concluded his testimony by saying he lived near Plummer and was awakened by Plummer entering his room about 1 o'clock in the morning on May 7. "Plummer strongly denied his guilt" when speaking to a reporter. Could the accusations of Rogers be another case of jealousy, as was suggested as the motive in the Mollie Smith murder? Just as Walter Spencer seemed to implicate William Brooks, could Andrew Rogers be implicating Ike Plummer for the same reason?[31]

Little of import came from the examining trial. Plummer apparently was not tried for the murder, and he does not appear in connection with the later murders. There is a record of an Ike Plummer marrying an Eliza Johnson on April 11, 1892, in

Fayette County, about 80 miles east of Austin. Eliza Shelly was buried at Austin's Oakwood Cemetery on May 10, 1885, in "Colored ground." On her death certificate, the attending physician was T.J. Bennett, a partner of Dr. Wade Morris, whose home was attacked on March 13. Shelly's cause of death listed on her burial certificate at Oakwood Cemetery was a wound to the throat. Her murder was officially unsolved.[32]

Ike Plummer seems an unlikely suspect. If he had been the attacker, wouldn't Shelly's son have been able to recognize him, or at least his voice? And if Plummer only wanted money from Shelly, why did he feel compelled to kill her so brutally? Certainly, the refusal of a few dollars would not have driven a man without a violent disposition to murder the woman. Another unusual aspect of the case is the fact that Shelly's oldest boy fell asleep so quickly after the man entered the room. Could the white cloth have contained chloroform stolen from Dr. Stoddard's office, and could the cloth have been draped over the boy's face instead of the man's face, causing the boy to fall fast asleep? Were the other boys and the woman perhaps chloroformed by a second person? The boy also mentioned the assailant's plan to go to St. Louis. Could the man have been one of the gang of robbers mentioned in the preceding chapter? As noted there, the burglars in Austin had been reinforced "by a great squad of roughs, dead-beats, tramps and professionals from Chicago, St. Louis and other eastern cities." And the railroad tracks ran right in front of the Johnson house.[33]

The murder of Eliza Shelly was similar to the murder of Mollie Smith in several ways. First, similar weapons were used—an ax or a hatchet, and some sort of sharp pointed instrument. Second, at least one of the same assailants seemed to be involved in the murders, a barefooted person. Whether a second person was involved in both murders is debatable, but one would think so based on circumstances, namely the immobilization of more than one person during the attacks. Third, no viable suspect or suspects were identified, though romantic jealousy was a possibility in both murders. Fourth, at the time of the murders, both William K. Hall and Lucien B. Johnson, at whose homes the murders occurred, were working as land agents, suggesting a link between the two murders not focused on the victims themselves.

The murder of Eliza Shelly differed from the Mollie Smith murder in several significant ways. First, Eliza Shelly apparently was not raped by the assailant, as Mollie Smith was. Second, the murder of Eliza Shelly occurred under a half moon, whereas the murder of Mollie Smith occurred under a full moon. The phase of the moon seems important to several investigators of the murders. Third, if the testimony of Shelly's son is to believed, the motive in the Shelly murder was robbery, whereas the motive in the Smith murder remained unclear.

The murder of Eliza Shelly produced more questions than answers. Was the same person or persons committing the murders? Was the motive the same in both murders, or were the murders the handiwork of a motiveless maniac? Was Eliza Shelly's murder simply an escalation of the recent assaults, or was it a crime largely unrelated to the assaults? Were two different groups responsible for the assaults and the murders? Or was one group at the root of both the assaults and the murders, and was that group possibly manipulated by a white man? Were the assaults and murders an organized effort, or were they just typical crimes? The murder of two women over a period of five months does not seem that uncommon, especially in a rollicking town such as Austin. Was the ax a linking clue or just a common weapon? Were the weapons really hatchets and not axes? After all, ax murderer has a better ring than hatchet murderer. Was chloroform taken from Dr. Stoddard's office used in the Shelly murder? Finally, was the inability of the police force to find the culprits the product of design or ineptitude or a simple lack of officers? Was the mistrust in the city government well placed? Was the government truly uninterested in finding the murderer because the victims were only negroes and servant girls?

Whatever the answers to these questions might be, the following days would provide new occasions for the questions to be asked again.

Notes

Title: *Austin Daily Statesman*, 5/8/1885.

Map credit: Shelly murder scene excerpted from Koch's *Austin Bird's-Eye Map, 1887*.
1. *Austin Daily Statesman*, 4/30/1885; *Fort Worth Daily Gazette*, 4/23/1885; *Fort Worth Daily Gazette*, 4/24/1885; *Bartholomew Diary* 20:169, 4/22/1885.
2. *Austin Daily Statesman*, 4/30/1885.
3. *Austin Daily Statesman*, 4/30/1885; *Fort Worth Daily Gazette*, 4/30/1885; *Austin Daily Statesman*, 5/1/1885.
4. *Austin Daily Statesman*, 4/30/1885; *Austin Daily Statesman*, 5/1/1885.
5. *Austin Daily Statesman*, 5/2/1885.
6. *Austin Daily Statesman*, 5/2/1885; *Morrison & Fourmy's General Directory of the City of Austin, 1885-1886*; 1880 Federal Census.
7. *Austin Daily Statesman*, 5/2/1885; *Morrison & Fourmy's General Directory of the City of Austin, 1885-1886*; 1880 Federal Census.
8. *Austin Daily Statesman*, 5/2/1885; *Morrison & Fourmy's General Directory of the City of Austin, 1885-1886*; 1910 Federal Census.
9. "Texas Marriages, 1837-1973."
10. *Austin Daily Statesman*, 5/2/1885; *Morrison & Fourmy's General Directory of the City of Austin, 1885-1886*; 1880 Federal Census.
11. *Austin Daily Statesman*, 5/2/1885; *Morrison & Fourmy's General Directory of the City of Austin, 1885-1886*; 1880 Federal Census; 1900 Federal Census.
12. *Austin Daily Statesman*, 5/2/1885.
13. *Austin Daily Statesman*, 5/2/1885; *Morrison & Fourmy's General Directory of the City of Austin, 1885-1886*; 1880 Federal Census; 1900 Federal Census (The 1885 city directory listed only one Andrew Jackson, a blacksmith working and living with Mr. Risher, a blacksmith on the east side of Austin. This Andrew Jackson was about 55 years old and married for over 15 years at the time, so the suspect was likely not this man. The 1880 census also listed another Andrew Jackson of similar age and marital status. The likely suspect, though, would be an Andrew Jackson born in 1863.)
14. *Fort Worth Daily Gazette*, 5/5/1885.

15. *Fort Worth Daily Gazette*, 5/5/1885.
16. *Fort Worth Daily Gazette*, 5/5/1885.
17. *Morrison & Fourmy's General Directory of the City of Austin, 1885-1886*; 1880 Federal Census; *Brenham Weekly Banner*, 9/30/1880; *Brenham Weekly Banner*, 10/6/1881; *Brenham Weekly Banner*, 4/3/1884; *Brenham Weekly Banner*, 5/8/1884; *Fort Worth Daily Gazette*, 6/19/1884.
18. *Fort Worth Daily Gazette*, 7/23/1886; *Fort Worth Daily Gazette*, 7/24/1886; *Fort Worth Daily Gazette*, 6/5/1887.
19. *Fort Worth Daily Gazette*, 5/7/1885; *Fort Worth Daily Gazette*, 5/9/1885; *Fort Worth Daily Gazette*, 5/10/1885.
20. *Austin Daily Statesman*, 5/8/1885; 1880 Federal Census; *Morrison & Fourmy's General Directory of the City of Austin, 1885-1886*; *Mooney & Morrison's General Directory of the City of Austin, 1877-1878*; *Morrison & Fourmy's General Directory of the City of Austin, 1881-1882*; *Morrison & Fourmy's General Directory of the City of Austin, 1889-1890*.
21. *Austin Daily Statesman*, 5/8/1885; 1880 Federal Census; *Morrison & Fourmy's General Directory of the City of Austin, 1885-1886*; Oakwood Cemetery Database.
22. *Austin Daily Statesman*, 5/8/1885; *Waco Daily Examiner*, 5/9/1885; *Fort Worth Daily Gazette*, 11/15/1885.
23. *Austin Daily Statesman*, 5/8/1885; *Waco Daily Examiner*, 5/9/1885.
24. *Austin Daily Statesman*, 5/8/1885.
25. *Austin Daily Statesman*, 5/8/1885; *Morrison & Fourmy's General Directory of the City of Austin, 1885-1886*; Oakwood Cemetery Database.
26. *Austin Daily Statesman*, 5/8/1885; *Waco Daily Examiner*, 5/9/1885; *Austin Daily Statesman*, 6/24/1885; *Morrison & Fourmy's General Directory of the City of Austin, 1885-1886*; Oakwood Cemetery Database; Galloway, *The Servant Girl Murders*: 264.
27. *Fort Worth Daily Gazette*, 5/9/1885.
28. *Waco Daily Examiner*, 5/9/1885; *Austin Daily Statesman*, 5/8/1885.
29. *Austin Daily Statesman*, 5/8/1885.
30. *Austin Daily Statesman*, 5/14/1885.
31. *Austin Daily Statesman*, 5/14/1885.
32. "Texas Marriages, 1837-1973"; Oakwood Cemetery Database.
33. *Fort Worth Daily Gazette*, 2/16/1884.

Chapter 4

"A Night of Savages"

More Murder and Mayhem

The dust had barely settled on the Eliza Shelly murder when another murder rocked the city of Austin. Late in the evening of May 21, 1885, a Thursday, and into the early morning hours of May 22, the "fiends" were stirring up trouble again. The first attack of the evening came on Water Street. A ruffian "visited the house of a white lady . . . and came very near forcing his way into her room." As usual, the woman screamed, help came, and the culprit fled without causing injury. The news report did not name the woman, but there were several possibilities. A couple of widow women lived on Water Street, namely Rally Ledell at 303 East Water Street and Daisy Fowler at 1309 East Water Street. Other possibilities included a future murder victim, Sue Hancock, who lived with her husband, Moses, at 203 East Water Street. Another possibility would be the home of Charles W. Pressler, who lived at 209 East Water Street with his wife, Clara, and two sons. Pressler was the chief draftsman for the General Land Office.[1]

Later that night, under a waxing half moon, another attempt was made to enter a home in the Eighth Ward, which was an area bounded by Congress Avenue on the west, East Avenue on the east, Bois d'Arc Street on the south, and Mesquite Street on the north, or an area of about 30 square blocks. A scoundrel tried to enter a home in that area without success. The invader was fired upon by J.R. Conner, one of the city's two mounted policemen, without effect.[2]

And then the night turned brutal. Irene Cross, a mulatto servant about 33 years old, lived in the rear of 302 East Linden, across the street from Scholz's Garden, or about four blocks north of the capitol. The property was owned by Mrs. Sophie Witman (Wittman), a 53-year-old widow who lived with her son, Charles Smith (or Schmidt), an apprentice barber. In any case, the building that Irene Cross lived in was a two-room structure by the alley between Linden and Chestnut streets. She lived with her son, Washington, who was in his early twenties, and her nephew, Douglas Brown, who was about 13 at the time of the incident. If the ages in the 1880 census were correct, Irene Cross would have given birth to her son when she under 15 years old. In 1870, Irene Cross was married to Haywood Cross, and Washington was said to be nine years old. In the late 1870s, Haywood was a boot and shoe maker with a shop on Congress Avenue. After that time, he is lost from the records.[3]

Washington Cross was used to coming home late at night, so he left the doors of both rooms unlocked. The nephew slept in one of the rooms, and Irene Cross and her son slept in the other room. Sometime after midnight, in the early morning hours of May 22, the attacker entered the nephew's room and passed through into Irene's room. "Both she and the boy became awakened and set up screams of fear. The man told her to desist screaming and sprang at her with a knife inflicting two terrible gashes, one on the arm and the other across the head." Then the man rushed out without harming the boy. "On being cut, the poor woman staggered out into the yard. She was bleeding terribly. Her screams had aroused the inmates of the house, and she was assisted to a room in the residence of her employers."[4]

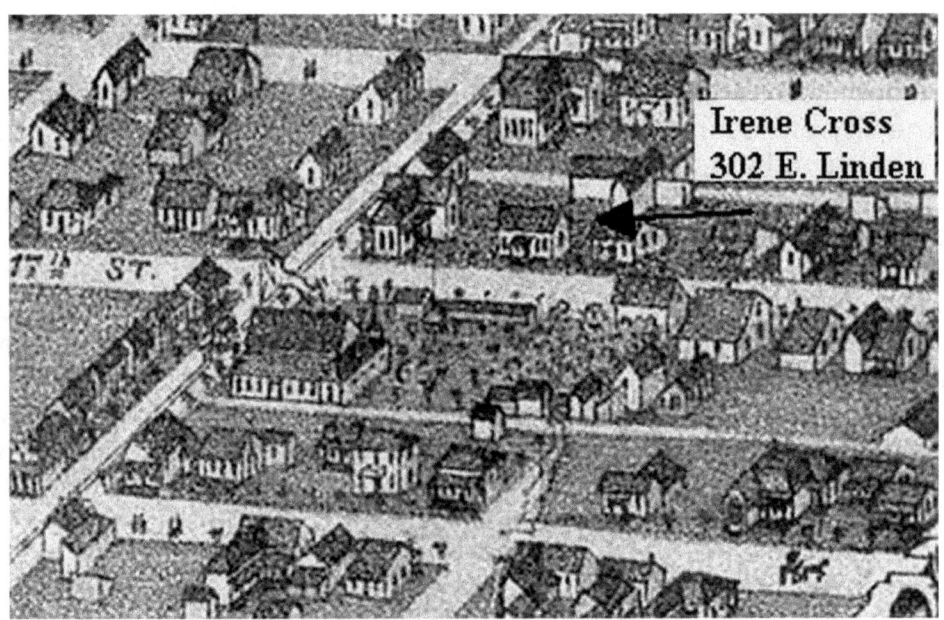

An Austin reporter soon arrived on the scene with officer Henry Brown. "Familiar as he was with repulsive sights, the reporter could not help being horrified at the ghastly object that met his view. The woman's right arm was nearly cut in two, from a gash over six inches long. A cruel cut extended over half-way around her head, commencing just above the right eye. It looked as if the intention had been to scalp her. She was moaning and writhing in pain." The reporter asked Irene Cross if she knew her attacker. She did not. Then the reporter questioned the nephew. The boy said that the attacker was a "'big, chunky negro man, bare-footed and with his pants rolled up.' He had on a brown hat and a ragged coat." When the boy cried out upon the man's entrance, the man told the boy he did not intend to harm him. The boy also said he saw a pocket knife in the man's hand. A doctor was called to treat Irene Cross, but the reporter left before the doctor's arrival.[5]

Irene Cross's injuries were worse than one might imagine. The Fort Worth newspaper noted that "the villain drew a knife and GASHED HER IN THE HEAD, and then nearly severed her right arm from the body—all except the bone. The ruptured bronchial artery spurted the blood in a terrific stream, and Irene shortly after expired from exhaustion." Irene Cross was buried at Oakwood Cemetery on May 24, 1885, in "colored ground." The coroner, Justice William Von Rosenberg, Jr., determined the cause of death as "wounds." No suspect was named in her murder.[6]

"Another Horrible Outrage"

On the same night that Irene Cross was murdered, another mulatto servant was severely wounded with a razor. The incident occurred at the home of Isaac Suares at 409 West North Avenue at the corner of San Jacinto, or about eight blocks from the place where Irene Cross was murdered. His house was also about a block from the home of Mrs. Behnke, who was attacked on April 29. Isaac Suares was a hack driver in the city, but he was also one of the members of the inquest investigating the Mollie Smith murder five months earlier. He employed a servant by the name of Mattie Sellers, about whom little is known. She was not listed in the city directory or the 1880 census. Possibly she was related to Henry Sellers, who worked as a bartender for Hugh Hancock at the Black Elephant Saloon, where William Brooks, a suspect in the Mollie Smith murder, may have been employed.[7]

Mattie Sellers lived in a small building behind the main residence. The building was by the alley between North Avenue and Walnut Street. About three o'clock in the morning of May 22, someone entered the servant's quarters. Apparently Sellers "endeavored to escape to the main residence, which was situated several yards off, but about half way the intruder caught and assaulted her with a razor. The unfortunate woman was frightfully stabbed, the left breast being nearly cut off, and receiving five or six deep slices elsewhere." She screamed, of course, and rescuers came to her aid, but the assailant escaped.[8]

The attack had all the markings of another assault by the unknown perpetrator, with the same weapon as used earlier in the evening on Irene Cross. But this attack was different. Later in the day, Mattie Sellers was conscious, but she refused to talk about the attack. In fact, she apparently knew her attacker. In the evening of May 22, "police officers arrested on suspicion a mulatto woman named Nora Johnson. It has developed since that her husband, whom she is suing for divorce, has been intimate with the injured woman, and that she has long been jealous of the latter. The shoes of the Johnson woman fitted exactly the marks made by the person who committed the assault and a key was found on her person which unlocked the door of the room in which Mattie Sellers was sleeping."[9]

Nora Johnson was born in Texas in 1862. She was married to Alexander Johnson, born in 1860. Her husband worked for Michael Butler in his brickyard. The couple had three children, Nana, born in 1879, Walter, born in 1880, and Mincie, born in 1883. One reason Mattie Sellers may not have wanted to name her attacker was to protect the husband. Though the doctors said Mattie Sellers' wounds were "not necessarily fatal," they were deemed "dangerous from the fact that she is in a delicate condition." Very likely Mattie Sellers was pregnant by Alexander Johnson, so she did not want to cause trouble. Sellers did not die from the attack. The records did not indicate what happened to the child she was carrying at the time of the attack. She did not have luck with infants, though. In February 1887, a two-day-old infant of Mattie Sellers was buried in "colored ground" in Oakwood Cemetery in Austin. The cause of death was listed as inanition, or lack of food and water. In November 1887, a four-day-old infant of M. Sellers was buried in "colored ground" in Oakwood Cemetery. The cause of death was again listed as inanition. The marriage of Nora and Alex Johnson also did not fare well. By 1900, Nora Johnson was a widow, living with her children Walter and Mincie.[10]

"More Nocturnal Crime"

The assaults and mischief spilled over into the summer months. Around four o'clock in the morning of June 2, a Tuesday, the home of Professor H. Tallichet was attacked. Tallichet served as a professor of modern literature at the University of Texas. He lived on the east side of Nueces Street between Elm Street and Palmetto Street, or about three blocks west of the campus. Jane Coleman, his family's black servant girl, was an unmarried woman in her early twenties who lived in a small apartment at the rear of the house. Coleman was sleeping near a window, which was raised slightly to allow for ventilation in the warm temperature. The daytime high temperatures were already hitting 90 degrees, and the nighttime lows were mainly in the 60s. As Coleman slept by the window, "the fiend was able to put the muzzle of his weapon within a few feet of the sleeping victim. The ball was a large one—forty-two calibre—and entering her left arm between the wrist and elbow passed into the breast, inflicting a very painful, but not fatal wound."[11]

Upon being shot, Coleman screamed, which aroused her employer. He grabbed a pistol and ran toward her room. "As he opened the door, a bullet whizzed past his head, and buried itself in the wall not four feet distant. The fellow then fled. It is not known whether he was a white or black man." Tom Bailes, the assistant chief of the Capital Detective Association, was called. He hurried to Tallichet's address, but not soon enough to catch the culprit. Dr. Thomas Wooten was called in to remove the bullet, and the young woman was said to be resting easily.[12]

At about the same time, the home of Major Joe H. Stewart, at 1913 Whitis Avenue, about three blocks from the Tallichet home, was attacked. Stewart's home had also been attacked in the early morning hours of March 13. In the earlier attack, two black servants who roomed together were scared out of their wits when someone tried to break into their room. This time, a ruffian "threw a large rock with tremendous force against the apartment occupied by a colored girl. The window was completely shattered." A black man staying with the girl rushed out, got a gun from Major Stewart, and "took after the fellow that threw the rock. The latter turned on his pursuer, after running a few feet up an alley, and fired. The other fired back and a number of shots were exchanged but none took effect. No capture." No damage or injury was reported other than the broken window.[13]

Another invasion occurred at the boarding house of Mrs. Mary A. Finnin, a widow woman living at 300 West Pine Street at the corner of Lavaca Street. Finnin's boarding house was just under a mile south of the Stewart home, but more importantly, it was located on the northern edge of Guy Town. Mrs. Finnin employed several black servants to help around the boarding house, including Jennie Johnson and Grace Lockett. Johnson was about 20 years old at the time, but little information was available for Lockett. Sometime during the early morning of June 2, a "sleek thief" entered the room of one of Mrs. Finnin's servant girls. Without waking the occupant, the thief made off with almost every possession of the young woman, including some jewelry and a little money. The reporter noted that "Why he did not shoot or cut her with a knife is a mystery. It is the first time the room of a servant woman has been entered in Austin, for the last four months, that there was no attempt at personal violence."[14]

The news report concluded by lamenting the ongoing assaults. "The above statements go to show that the era of outrage has by no means ceased in Austin. It may be expected to continue indefinitely. Why not? The authors of the deviltry go scot free. As long as they escape detection and arrest so long will they keep up their systematic course of pillage." The citizens of Austin could not rely on the police force to protect them, and the repeated advice to keep a gun handy also did not seem to do much to prevent the persistent attacks. What could be done, and when would the terror end?[15]

"A Gang of Demons Incarnate"

The three murders of servant girls in Austin so far were similar in some regards and different in other regards. The murders of Mollie Smith and Irene Cross occurred when the moon was bright, almost full, but the murder of Eliza Shelly occurred under a half moon. In the murders of Mollie Smith and Eliza Shelly, similar weapons were used, an ax or hatchet and a sharp pointed instrument. In the murder of Irene Cross, the murder weapon was a razor or knife. In all three murders, there was some indication that the primary murderer was barefooted. In the murder of Irene Cross, the murderer was definitely identified as a negro man. In the Eliza Shelly murder, there is some doubt, as the young son of Eliza Shelly apparently said the murderer was both a negro and a white man. In the murder of Mollie Smith, no determination of the race of the murderer was made. When Mollie Smith was murdered, she was dragged outside and raped. When Eliza Shelly was murdered, she was left in the room and wrapped in a bedsheet; she was not raped. When Irene Cross was slashed with a razor, she ran in the yard and raised an alarm, so one does not know what might have happened to her if the murderer had more time with her.

So the question of whether the same person was involved in all three murders and some or all of the assaults becomes more cloudy. A razor was used in the attack on the Callaway home in April, but that attack was credited to the insane black man Old John. A razor was used in the attack on Mattie Sellers, but that attack was fairly well explained as a case of romantic jealousy, with the attacker a woman. And a razor was again used in the murder of Irene Cross, but surely Old John or Nora Johnson could not have been the murderer of Irene Cross.

Could the three murders really have been the result of romantic jealousy or domestic violence, as was commonly believed? Were the three murders totally unrelated? Or was a serial killer at work in Austin? And if a serial killer was at large, was he acting alone? What was the motive? Was there a motive, or were the murders simply the handiwork of an insane man? Was there a link between the three murder victims that was not yet revealed? Or were the attacks really intended to target the homeowners, and the servant girls were simply hapless victims caught up in some nefarious plot? And if the targets were simply black women, why would the assailants risk capture and jail by attacking the homes of prominent white families?

All the questions that arose after the murder of Eliza Shelly remained unanswered, and new questions were added to the list. The continued onslaught on the sensibilities of the citizens of Austin had created an atmosphere of fear and mistrust. The police could not be trusted to solve the problem. The city government did not even seem interested in solving the problem. White people were becoming more concerned about the lack of safety after dark. The blacks in Austin "said the murders were the work of witches and they all began to wear charms against the evil eye of the voudoo."[16]

As the long, hot summer months approached, the newspapers and the citizenry kept up the cry for something to be done, but little relief came.

Notes

Title: *Fort Worth Daily Gazette*, 11/15/1885.
Map credit: Cross murder scene excerpted from Koch's *Austin Bird's-Eye Map, 1887*.

1. *Austin Daily Statesman*, 5/23/1885; *Morrison & Fourmy's General Directory of the City of Austin, 1885-1886*; 1880 Federal Census.
2. *Austin Daily Statesman*, 5/23/1885; *Morrison & Fourmy's General Directory of the City of Austin, 1885-1886*; "Lunar calendar." (This officer's name is spelled several different ways in the sources of information: Conner, Conners, Connor, and Connors. For consistency, Conner will be used, except where variant forms were used in news reports. Conner was the name given in the 1885-1886 city directory.)
3. *Austin Daily Statesman*, 5/23/1885; *Morrison & Fourmy's General Directory of the City of Austin, 1885-1886*; *Mooney & Morrison's General Directory of the City of Austin, 1877-1878*; 1870 Federal Census; 1880 Federal Census (In the newspaper reports and the city directory, Cross was named Irene. In the 1870 census, she was named Arena. In the 1880 census, she was named Irine. In her death certificate, she was named Irina. The 1870 Federal Census indicated that Irene Cross was 14 when Washington was born. Also, in the 1885-1886 city directory, Mrs. Wittman was called Witman.)
4. *Austin Daily Statesman*, 5/23/1885.
5. *Austin Daily Statesman*, 5/23/1885.
6. *Fort Worth Daily Gazette*, 11/15/1885; Oakwood Cemetery Database.
7. *Fort Worth Daily Gazette*, 5/23/1885; *Morrison & Fourmy's General Directory of the City of Austin, 1885-1886*.

8. *Fort Worth Daily Gazette*, 5/23/1885; *Fort Worth Daily Gazette*, 11/15/1885.
9. *Fort Worth Daily Gazette*, 5/23/1885.
10. *Fort Worth Daily Gazette*, 5/23/1885; 1880 Federal Census; 1900 Federal Census; Oakwood Cemetery Database.
11. *Austin Daily Statesman*, 6/3/1885; *Morrison & Fourmy's General Directory of the City of Austin, 1885-1886*; "Monthly Record of Observations Taken at Stations in the Cotton Region," Austin, June 1885.
12. *Austin Daily Statesman*, 6/3/1885; *Morrison & Fourmy's General Directory of the City of Austin, 1885-1886*.
13. *Austin Daily Statesman*, 6/3/1885.
14. *Austin Daily Statesman*, 6/3/1885.
15. *Austin Daily Statesman*, 6/3/1885.
16. *Trenton Times*, 2/1/1886.

Chapter 5

"The Long Hot Summer"

Discontent with Local Officials Grows

As the daytime temperatures increased in Austin, the nighttime assaults ceased, but the discontent with local police and government officials grew to a fever pitch. The *Austin Daily Statesman*, as well as newspapers around the state, chimed in with commentary unflattering to Austin officials. And as the summer began its slow, hot journey, still no suspects had been arrested for the murders of Mollie Smith, Eliza Shelly, and Irene Cross.

In May, the Fort Worth newspaper reported that the "Austin Statesman says misgovernment has degraded the capitol city, led to murder, arson, burglary and robbery, destroyed the fair name of Austin and made it the hospitable home of cut throats and murderers. The capitol city must be a delightful place for quiet, law-abiding people." But such criticism of the integrity of Austin and the competence of its leaders was by no means new.[1]

In January 1884, when the 18th Texas Legislature was in special session debating the fence-cutting bill, the proposal was made that all people accused of fence-cutting should be tried in Austin. Owen Brown of Johnson County, who served from 1882 through 1885 in the 17th and 18th legislatures, called the notion "monstrous." According to reports, Brown believed that

> The idea of bringing cases of this character to be tried at Austin was absurd. Why, he had been in this city now a few Sundays, and what did he see going on? He saw the ladies, (God bless them!) pretty generally going to church, but the men all turned into the saloons. (Laughter.) The saloons were all open, on Sunday and there was no use denying it. He begged the reporters not to put that down. (Laughter,) for it would disgrace the state. And this was the same city of Austin the bill would have all offenders tried in. He was opposed to it. Johnson was just as good a place to have them tried at as Austin, and the women of Johnson were just as good as those of Austin, (Laughter,) and he wanted the reporters to put that down.

A bill making fence cutting and fencing public lands illegal was passed in 1884, but the attempt to get such cases tried in Austin failed.[2]

The city council of Austin also received much criticism for excusing fines placed on those who carried pistols in public. In June 1884, the Fort Worth newspaper was especially strident in chastising the Austin city government.

> It is astonishing to read in the Statesman of the local government at Austin condoning and even encouraging pistol carrying. The city council has a penchant, so it is stated, for remitting the fines imposed by the recorder upon men who are caught with pistols secreted upon their persons. This is not done in every case, but it is done so often that the practice has become notable. Some idea of the extent to which pistol carrying prevails in Austin may be gathered from the figures on the police blotter there, which show that during the past five months the fines imposed for carrying and discharging pistols within the city limits foot up $1,629. It would seem that such a state of affairs should impel the council to cooperate with the recorder rather than negate his efforts.
>
> No city government, whether at Austin or elsewhere, can well afford to extend sympathy or leniency to that class of lawbreakers who convert themselves into walking arsenals and who are a constant menace to the lives and peace of their fellow citizens. If a poor devil gets drunk and is flued, or a fallen woman is taxed the price of her shame, it is rare, very rare, that one hears even a suggestion of leniency. The bully who struts around with a pistol in his hip pocket should be put on the same level with other violators of the law, and get the full penalty prescribed by law. If this is not done communities condoning the offence must expect to be cursed with scenes of midnight brawls, bloodshed, loss of life and general turbulency.

Ironically, when the series of murders and assaults occurred in Austin, the newspapers were singing a different tune, imploring the citizens of Austin to keep their pistols and firearms ready at a moment's notice so that any suspected assailant could be blasted on the spot.[3]

"Prowess with a Revolver"

The police force had also received its share of criticism for failing to solve the numerous murders and assaults. But the police had been lambasted for their incompetence before. The city marshal during the murders, Horatio Grooms Lee, had been appointed to the post in 1883, along with W.J. Burt as the city physician. Prior to Lee's appointment, the city marshal had been the notorious Ben Thompson, a famed gunfighter. Thompson was first elected city marshal in December 1880. He was regarded as an excellent marshal, "some claiming that he was the finest marshal that Austin had known up to that time." Because of his "honesty, loyalty, generosity, and prowess with a revolver," Thompson was re-elected in November 1881. Then things began to go bad for Thompson. While still marshal of Austin, he got into a quarrel over a card game in San Antonio. During the fracas, he shot and killed Jack Harris, the prominent owner of the Vaudeville Theater in San Antonio. Thompson was indicted for murder, and as a result, he resigned as marshal. He was later acquitted of the murder, but he returned to the Vaudeville Theater in March 1884, where he was ambushed and killed by friends of Harris.[4]

According to William. M. Walton, Thompson's attorney and first biographer, "while Thompson was city marshal, there was not a murder, not an assault to kill in the limits of the city; and as now remembered, not a solitary burglary, a single theft ... that was not detected, promptly brought to light and punished. This is no eulogy; it is not flattery, but the simple expression of truth, that all who know the facts will readily affirm." Evidence suggests that Walton's assessment was certainly exaggerated, but Thompson did maintain law and order in Austin during his two terms as marshal. Thompson tooted his own horn in a re-election ad published in the *Austin Daily Statesman*:

> I promise you, if elected, to fill the post to the best of my skill and ability. Honored by your suffrages, I entered upon the discharge of my duties without the knowledge and experience since acquired. That some minor, perhaps important, things have escaped adequate diligence and attention, I will not pretend to urge a denial; but I can truthfully affirm that I have been as faithful and vigilant as under all the circumstances I could well be. And, in this connection, I trust you will pardon me in submitting for your consideration the following extract from the official record of police matters, coming under my supervision during the ten months of my time as City Marshal and Chief of Police, dating from the 21st of December last to the 17th of October, to wit; "Number of arrests, 1200; turned over to justices court, 40 cases; dismissed, 52 cases; appealed, 18 cases. Total amount of fines and costs, $9,056. Amount of fines worked out on the streets, $2,803.75. Amount of cash collected, $6,252.25. Total amount of property and money stolen and reported to the police, $1,172; amount recovered, $912."

Thompson seemed to be effective in his job, and he could add, too.[5]

After being acquitted of the murder of Jack Harris, Thompson returned to running a gambling hall above the Iron Front Saloon in Austin. But he did not stay out of the public eye. In fact, the first big controversy in the term of Grooms Lee as the marshal came as a result of the actions of Ben Thompson. Early in January of 1884, a large group of prominent stockmen had gathered in Austin. On the night of January 11, they held a private banquet at Simon's Restaurant, located at 609 Congress Avenue, just a couple of doors up the avenue from the Iron Front Saloon, where Thompson ran his gambling hall. Around midnight, "Ben Thompson entered, flourishing a pistol, and proceeded to demolish the table furniture, brushing off the champagne bottles, glasses and dishes with his six-shooter. Several stockmen drew their pistols, but were prevented from shooting by their friends, who surrounded them and hustled them out of the room. The incident was the signal for the breaking up of the party. It is said that Thompson intended to assist a friend whom he supposed was in trouble." Likely, though, he was just looking for trouble. Even though Thompson had resigned as city marshal, he was appointed a deputy sheriff under Sheriff Malcolm Hornsby.[6]

The new marshal and the other city officials, though, did nothing to punish Thompson for his antics, causing the city of Austin to draw statewide criticism for its kid-glove treatment of Thompson. The stockmen also stated they would likely hold their next convention elsewhere. The *Brenham Weekly Banner* noted that "The Austin Statesman still hammers away at the Austin policemen. It will take a good deal of hammering to get them straightened out. They are afraid of Ben Thompson. . . . The Statesman says the chief of police and his subordinates have shown conclusively that they are not the right men, in the right place. It demands their resignations!" In another light-hearted but unflattering blow to the city, the Fort Worth newspaper reported that "much of the dissatisfaction that caused the stockmen to urge the change to Galveston arose from the advanced prices charged by the hotels and boarding houses and the conspicuous absence of the commonest sort of courtesies. They were not scared into the movement by Ben Thompson's raid on the wine party and do not want any special protection. . . . They say they are able to protect themselves against the Ben Thompsons but not against exorbitant charges for two in a bed and tough beef."[7]

The light-heartedness, though, did not mask the problems with the police force. The Fort Worth paper later reported that "the failure of the city police to secure the arrest of Ben Thompson for his extraordinary exploit in connection with the recent stockmen's banquet, and the great excitement that outrage occasioned, are bearing their appropriate fruit just now. The police were last night charged with cowardice in the matter by a resolution introduced in the city council, and the police committee of that body are now investigating charges preferred against the marshal and his sergeant for 'inefficient discharge of duty.' It is expected that at least one official head will drop into the basket as a result of the investigation. Meanwhile Ben Thompson wears his customary smile, and charges that the stockmen were more to blame than he in the little pistol encounter which brought the feast to such a sudden and unpleasant termination." The marshal, of course, was Grooms Lee, who was later chastised for his lack of efficacy in solving the servant girl murders.[8]

Thompson's shenanigans did not end at the stockmen's banquet. In early February, the *Austin Daily Statesman* published a short article about Thompson. Thompson took umbrage with the report, and early on the morning of February 2, he stormed into the *Statesman* offices, demanding to know who had written the article. Most of the editorial staff was not present, so Thompson proceeded to accost a teenaged boy who worked in the financial office, waving his pistol at the lad. The youth knew nothing about the article, so Thompson went to the composing room. The man there also knew nothing about the writer of the article, so Thompson, after vandalizing the office, left. That day, Thompson was "arrested on five affidavits preferred by Mr. Gaines and the employees of the Statesman, charging him with threatening to kill, assault and battery and carrying deadly weapons. He was arraigned in Justice Von Rosenberg's court." While bond was being determined, Thompson was taunted by a man for being under arrest, and Thompson tried to quiet the man with a chair. He was stopped before any damage could be done, but he was charged with contempt of court and fined $50. Later, Thompson admitted that he was wrong in going to the newspaper offices, but he said he did so for the sake of his family.[9]

Though seemingly apologetic about his behavior, that night Thompson returned to the *Statesman* offices. A violent quarrel broke out between Thompson and the editor of the newspaper. Thompson claimed that the *Statesman* employees were going to gun him down in the streets. As protection, Thompson said he had hired ten men with Winchester rifles, and if he was shot, those men would avenge him. The newspaper editor denied Thompson's wild claims, of course. Though all parties involved in the quarrel were heavily armed, the confrontation ended without incident when Thompson walked out. As a result of his conflict with the newspaper staff, Thompson's commission as a deputy sheriff was revoked.[10]

The police force continued to be criticized for its lack of action in restraining Thompson. The Fort Worth newspaper reported that "Officer Oberwetter has prepared charges of cowardice, etc. against Officer Brown in connection with the Ben Thompson affair, and now Brown resents the charge by making assault on Oberwetter at the city hall. It is stated that were it not for the timely interference of brother officers, the quarrel would have resulted in a tragedy, as both men are brave almost to a fault. The result of the quarrel is that Brown has been suspended by the city marshal, and you may look forward soon to rich developments in connection with the police imbroglio." But Thompson would not go away. At the end of February, the Brenham newspaper noted that "Ben Thompson has been indulging in a little innocent pastime, shooting his pistol on the Avenue in Austin. If the people of Austin can stand it, no one else should complain." Two weeks later, Thompson was killed in San Antonio, and the problem was resolved without the police doing anything. Unfortunately, the police force's inability to maintain law and order was ultimately exposed during the servant girl murders.[11]

"I Try to Do the Best I Can"

The marshal that replaced Ben Thompson, Horatio Grooms Lee, had little experience and few qualifications for the post. Granted, Lee had some law enforcement experience, but none in a leadership role. In his early twenties, Lee was a clerk in the store of his cousin, George L. Robertson, son of Joseph and Lydia Robertson, located at the northeast corner of Bois d'Arc and East Avenue in Austin. In his mid-twenties, Lee was a Texas Ranger, serving with D Company of the Frontier Battalion. His most notable engagement during that time was during the Red River War. On July 12, 1874, Lee and his comrades took part in the Lost Valley Fight near Jacksboro, Texas, northwest of Fort Worth, against Lone Wolf and about 50 warriors. The battle did not go well for the Rangers, most of them in their early twenties, and they escaped under cover of night. In the late 1870s, Lee was a deputy county sheriff under Sheriff Dennis Corwin and boarded in his home. In the early 1880s, Grooms Lee worked as a surveyor and lived at his father's home.[12]

But Grooms Lee was well-connected. He was the son of Joseph Lee and Sarah Grooms Lee. Joseph Lee was one of the earliest settlers of Austin, and he played a part in many of the major events of the early history of Austin. Lee was born in Ohio in 1810 and was admitted to the bar there in 1838. Because of poor health, he decided to move to Texas, arriving in Austin with his brother and two sisters in the spring of 1840. A year later, Travis County was organized, and Joseph Lee was made the Chief Justice of Travis County. In the winter of 1842-1843, Joseph Lee was a leader in the successful effort to prevent President Sam Houston from moving the state land archives from Austin to Houston after Mexicans threatened the frontier of Texas, a dispute that came to be called the Archives War. In October 1846, Joseph Lee married Sarah Grooms, daughter of Horatio Grooms, an army officer who was another early settler in Austin. Horatio Grooms Lee was born in 1848 or 1849, and a sister was born in 1850. Unfortunately, Sarah Lee died in that second childbirth. Two years later, Joseph Lee married Sarah J. Ogle, daughter of Jeremiah Ogle, who had settled in Austin in 1851. Together, the couple had seven more children. In 1857, Lee was elected to the Texas House of Representatives. When the Civil War came, Joseph Lee received a captain's commission but did not have a regular command in the Confederate Army. In the 1880s, he was appointed to the commission overseeing the construction of the new state capitol. Joseph Lee died of neuralgia of the heart in February 1891 at the age of 81. He was buried in Oakwood Cemetery in Austin.[13]

Grooms Lee was also related to the Robertson family in Austin. Grooms Lee's aunt, Lydia Lee, the sister of Joseph Lee, was married to Dr. Joseph William Robertson, another early settler in Austin. Joseph Robertson was born in South Carolina in February 1809. He attended Transylvania University in Kentucky and then began to practice medicine in Alabama. In Alabama, he married Ann Philips around 1835, and they had two children together. The next year, Robertson moved to Texas alone and settled in Bastrop County, becoming the first physician in that county. In 1837, he moved his family from Alabama to join him. In the early part of 1838, he was a member of the Texas Rangers. In 1839-1840, he served in the House of Representatives of the Fourth Congress of the Republic of Texas, representing Bastrop. In 1840, he moved to the new city of Austin and set up a medical practice and medical supplies business on Congress Avenue. His first wife died in 1841, and his young daughter died shortly thereafter. In September 1842, Robertson married Lydia Lee, sister of Joseph Lee, who had also moved to Austin in 1840. Together, they had ten children. Robertson was elected mayor of Austin in 1843 and served for a year. In 1846, he served as an assistant surgeon in the Mexican War. In 1848, he bought the old French Legation in east Austin and lived there with his family the rest of his life. That area became known as Robertson Hill. Joseph William Robertson died in August 1870 and was buried in Oakwood Cemetery in Austin.[14]

This relationship to Joseph William Robertson also made Grooms Lee somewhat related to the mayor of Austin during the murders, Col. John W. Robertson, and the mayor's brother, District Attorney James H. Robertson. Both the

Robertson brothers played a key role in the servant girl murders, as did Grooms Lee. The relationship between Joseph William Robertson and the Robertson brothers was rather distant, but they all descended from Scottish stock that moved to Virginia in the late 1600s. Joseph William Robertson was the son of Benoni Robertson, Sr., and Nancy Mickle Robertson. He descended from John Robertson (born ca. 1710, died ca. 1798), and his son, William Robertson (born ca. 1748, died ca. 1824). John Robertson was the son of William Robertson and Christine Ferguson Robertson. They had migrated to Virginia in the late 17th century and settled in Chesterfield County, Virginia. The Robertson brothers apparently descended from the line that included General James Robertson, the founder of Nashville, and Sterling Clack Robertson, the empresario that settled Robertson's Colony in the original land-grant period in Texas. Most of the Tennessee Robertsons apparently descended from Nicholas Robertson (born ca. 1665, died ca. 1718) and his son, Israel Robertson (born ca. 1697, died ca. 1760).[15]

John W. Robertson was born in Washington County, East Tennessee, in 1840. His parents were Dr. James R. and Mary A. (Hunt) Robertson. His father was a physician and minister. When John was five years old, the family moved to Roane County, Tennessee. In 1857 he enrolled in Hiwassee College in Madisonville, Tennessee, graduating at the top of his class in 1861. He later received a Master of Arts degree from the same institution. When war broke out, he was quick to enroll in the Confederate Army, rising to the rank of colonel after engaging in such battles as Chicamauga, Bean's Station, Walthal Station, Swift Creek, and Drury's Battle. At the fall of Petersburg in 1864, he was captured and served as a prisoner of war until June 1865. He then moved to Huntsville, Missouri, where he married Sophronia M. Austin in 1866. They moved back to Tennessee, where he served as the head of the Sweetwater Academy. In late 1867, they moved to Texas, settling first in Bryan and Calvert in the old Robertson's Colony. In 1872, the couple moved to Austin. In Austin, John Robertson served one term in the legislature and also served as District Judge for a short term. In the early 1880s, John Robertson served as the attorney for the British syndicate that constructed the new state capitol, so he must have had regular dealings with Joseph Lee, who served on the commission overseeing that construction. Robertson also served as the mayor of Austin from 1884 to 1888, the period during which the servant girl murders occurred. Though he was a loyal Confederate, he offered an interesting interpretation of the cause of the war when he delivered a memorial address for Jefferson Davis in the Texas capitol in December 1889.

> I do not believe that the war was brought upon this country by the agency of man, but I believe that the Great Ruler of nations and of man was instrumental in bringing it about, so that the doctrine of secession and the institution of slavery might be eliminated from our government and from its civilization. These were impediments to the growth, development and security of a great and powerful nation, such as this is destined to become. These ends could not be attained by legislation or by compromise, and I believe that the God of nations brought about the war to eliminate these questions from our

> government by the final and conclusive arbitrament of the sword.

John W. Robertson died in June 1892 at the age of 51. He was buried in Highland Park Cemetery, but a year later he was re-interred in Oakwood Cemetery in Austin.[16]

James Harvey Robertson was born in Roane County, East Tennessee, in 1853, also the son of Dr. James R. and Mary A. (Hunt) Robertson. When he was 20 years old, he began the study of law in Cleveland, Tennessee. The next year, 1874, he followed his brother John to Austin. He continued the study of law and was admitted to the bar in 1875. He started to practice law with his brother, but in 1876 he moved to Round Rock in Williamson County, just north of Austin. In 1878, he married Susan Marsh Townsend, and they had six children together. He was elected to the Texas legislature from Williamson County in 1882. Two years later, he was elected to the office of District Attorney of the 26th Judicial District, which included Travis and Williamson counties. Upon gaining this post, which he held until the early 1890s, he moved back to Austin. As district attorney, he was instrumental in the trials of suspected murderers in the events of 1885. James Harvey Robertson died in March 1912.[17]

This genealogical commentary is not meant as a distraction from the murders but as a tool to understand better the political situation that might have hindered the solving of the crimes. The citizens of Austin, though, were glad of any distraction that kept their minds off the murders. But the unsolved murders did not fall out of sight. The newspapers rekindled the fires of discontent throughout the summer. The tensions boiled over in early June when Marshal Lee accosted an *Austin Daily Statesman* reporter regarding an article about the "disposition of the police force." The article had questioned the placement of officers around town, and the marshal replied that "'I can dispose of the police as I see fit.'" The article wondered why so many officers were used around the saloons and in Guy Town. The marshal responded that "the necessity of it ought to be apparent to any man of sense. So that needs no reply." The article also wondered why so many officers were kept on Congress Avenue and on Pecan Street, to which the marshal replied, "This inquiry displays the ignorance of the writer. Only one policeman is stationed on each of the streets mentioned. The business interests of the city are centered there and the vast amount of property involved must be watched. Two men are insufficient for the task, but we have only two for the work." The article also questioned why more officers were not stationed in the suburbs to "catch the villains that are deprecating among the servants." Marshal Lee's response gave an insight to why the police force had largely been unable to catch the culprits. He noted that

> there are only twelve policemen, including the clerk, at the station, and one the boss of the street gang. This leaves ten men for active duty, five of whom serve half of the twenty-four hours and the other five the remainder. Now how can so small a force guard a city the size of Austin? [The reporter] says

> place them on the suburbs. Very well. Put one man on Robinson Hill, another in Wheatville, a third in Masontown, a fourth in the First Ward, and who have you got to guard to heart of the city? The truth is, the number of men is entirely too small. There should be at least one policeman to every 500 inhabitants. This is the proportion allowed by city law. Austin has at least 17,000 people, and on that basis would be entitled to thirty-four policemen. We have but little over one-third that many.

The marshal concluded his responses with a simple statement of fact: "I try to do the best I can with the few men under my control. That I have too few, with which to properly guard the city, every man who will give the subject the least attention, is bound to admit. The fault is not with the men. They are assigned to certain beats and are expected to stay on them. The trouble is the force is too small."[18]

Not quelled by the marshal's lamentations, the criticism and theories continued to swirl. At least the Texas legislature was not held at fault, for it had left town in March. In the middle of June, the Fort Worth newspaper opined that "It is hoped and believed that the killing mania among the Austin colored population has finally passed off. There can be no doubt that every murder and outrage which has been committed in the last three months was the result of marital difficulties." Three days later, though, the same newspaper mocked the situation, commenting that "Nobody has been killed at Austin within the last two weeks. It always gives us great pleasure to note substantial evidences of progress on the part of our neighbors." Were the murders really caused by marital discord? It would certainly please everyone if that explanation were valid. But if the murders were caused by marital discord, what was the cause of all the attempted home invasions? Marital discord? Surely the murders and assaults were in some way related. But almost as if to give the notion that the murders had ended more credence and at the same time to allay the criticism, it was reported on July 1 that "The officers claim to have a clew to the parties who committed the recent outrages on servant girls, and expect to run them down soon." Of course, no one was run down soon, and the mystery of the murders continued to simmer in the summer heat.[19]

Many people around town also did not accept the marital discord theory. One of those people was the famed author, O. Henry, who resided in Austin at the time. In a letter to his friend Dave Harrell, dated May 10, 1885, O. Henry noted that "Town is fearfully dull, except for the frequent raids of the Servant Girl Annihilators, who make things lively in the dull hours of the night; if it were not for them, items of interest would be very scarce, as you can see by the *Statesman*."[20] Surely the murders were the talk of the town, and surely the folks in the saloons along Congress and in Guy Town and especially on East Pecan, where Hugh Hancock oversaw operations at the Black Elephant Saloon, must have said more about the crimes than the police knew. Were the heinous crimes committed by foreigners working on the capitol, as was commonly believed? Were the murders and assaults the work of some black man run amok, perhaps cursed by voodoo? Or was someone being protected by the web of political connections at the core of the investigations? Was someone pulling the strings of a bunch of black puppets? Who could have had such influence and control? Though the murders and assaults had certainly created a healthy measure of consternation among the white people in Austin, the prevailing attitude was that the victims were only colored people, so no great urgency existed to solve the crimes.

"A Fiend's Fury"

The summer heat climbed into the upper 90s as the dog days crept along. The months of murder seemed almost an eon ago. And then, like a rainstorm in a drought, the people of Austin were distracted, at least temporarily, by the antics of a deranged fellow over near Johnson City in Blanco County, about 50 miles west of the capital city. The case of Albert Newton Lackey was peculiar from beginning to end, as one might expect of the tale of an incestuous mass murderer. Names and events were confused, and the reason for the rampage remained mysterious.

Albert Newton Lackey was born about 1838 in Texas. Albert was the son of Greenberry and Mary Harlow Lackey, and he had twelve siblings. Several of the Lackey siblings arrived in the Hickory Creek area of northern Blanco County, Texas, in 1858. In June of that same year, Albert's brother, James Lackey, married Aley Jane Pruitt (sometimes called Pruit) in neighboring Gillespie County. James would have been around 31 at the time, and Aley would have been 13, almost 14. James and Aley (or A.J. as she was often known in later events) had three children: Charles Lackey (sometimes referred to as Henry) in 1860, Mary Lackey in 1863, and James Christopher Colvin Lackey in 1865. At some point in 1865, James Lackey died from unknown causes.[21]

In April 1866, Albert Newton Lackey married his widowed sister-in-law, Aley Jane Pruitt Lackey, in Travis County, Texas. Albert and A.J. had twelve children together, two of whom were born dead. His stepchildren by his wife's marriage to Albert's brother also lived with them for a while. Albert Lackey's life began to unravel in the early 1880s. Lackey "had a stepdaughter living with him, whom, it is alleged, he seduced several years ago. Lately his own daughter has been discovered to be *enceinte* [pregnant], and his relations considered him responsible for her condition. This has been preying on his mind, and is supposed to have crazed him." The stepdaughter would be Mary Lackey, born in 1863 in Texas. His own daughter would have been Martha Susan Lackey, born about 1869 in Texas.[22]

On Monday, August 24, 1885, the day before a full moon, Albert Lackey, "maddened or demented," went on a killing rampage. The names of his victims and the exact events varied wildly in news reports of the day, but a general outline of the massacre can be developed. At some point in the mid-afternoon of August 24, Lackey "left home, intending, as he avowed to go to John Green's place to borrow a sum of money. Green and family were away. He entered the house and took Green's Winchester." Lackey also had a knife and a pistol. Lackey then went to the home of his brother, Nathaniel Greenberry Lackey. There, Albert shot and killed his brother's wife, Isabelle Adeline "Addie" Jackson Lackey. The brother fled, but about

100 yards from the house, he stumbled and fell. Albert Lackey ran up to his brother and "shot him through the head, killing him instantly." One of Berry Lackey's sons said he had heard his father plead for mercy, but Albert showed none. Lackey did spare their three year-old daughter, his niece Addie.[23]

Hearing the gunshots, a neighbor named John Nicholson rode up to investigate. Albert Lackey apparently liked Nicholson and wished him no harm. Nicholson rode with Lackey for a way, trying to talk the crazed man out of what he was doing, hoping to convince Lackey to ride to Blanco to turn himself in. Nicholson rode with Lackey to the home of James C. Stokes, a man about the same age as Lackey and the father of seven children. Lackey shot and killed Stokes. What happened to Nicholson is a matter of debate. He was either killed or likely "got away in the confusion and would later link up with the posse that was forming to bring in the killer." Whatever happened to Nicholson, Albert Lackey was not done with his murderous ways.[24]

Lackey next returned to his own home, though whom he killed there is unclear. Most reports agreed that he shot and cut the throat of Fannie Stokes Lackey, the wife of his stepson Charles (also called Henry in some reports) and the daughter of James Stokes, the man Lackey had killed a short while prior. Lackey also likely shot and killed Lucy Stokes, the wife of James Stokes, though some reports indicated he killed Lucy and Fanny at the Stokes house. Regardless, both died in the rampage. Lackey then killed his daughter, Martha Susan Lackey, who was said to be pregnant by him. Martha did not die immediately, but died later from her wounds. Before dying, she "confessed to her attending physician that her father was the author of her ruin." Next, Lackey tried to kill his own wife, Aley, but he had run out of bullets. He then tried to kill his wife and a small baby with a knife, but she was able to escape from the house and seek cover in a nearby thicket. Lackey chased Aley for some time, but he failed to catch her. After he gave up the chase, his wife "saw him slash his own throat. He seemed to back out after one deep gash had been cut; went to his horse and getting into the saddle headed in the direction of Johnson City." Whether he cut his throat in an attempt to kill himself or to pretend he had been attacked is unclear.[25]

After failing to kill his wife and then cutting his own throat, Lackey wrapped a handkerchief around the wound, mounted his horse, and began riding toward Johnson City, about four or five miles to the southeast. On the road Lackey met another neighbor, Tom Bundick. Lackey asked Bundick to ride to a nearby spring with him. "Bundick noticed that Lackey had a handkerchief to his throat but took it to be a red bandana. Lackey rode behind Bundick and shortly attacked him with his knife, and having the faster horse of the two he was able to cut his victim until he fell from his horse, and then Lackey again rode toward Johnson City." Lackey had stabbed Bundick "ten or twelve times . . . making him a cripple for life."[26]

Upon reaching Johnson City, Lackey told the sheriff that "Bundick had killed some of his family and had attacked him, but he had escaped after his throat had been cut by Bundick. A posse was formed, but before it left town a son of Lackey came in and told officers his father had committed the crimes and that he did not know how many were killed. Bundick was found and taken home where physicians attended him; he was badly cut but recovered after some weeks." Lackey was promptly arrested, and a doctor in Johnson City stitched the cut in his throat. Lackey was then taken to Blanco, at the time the county seat of Blanco County, and detained in the county jail. Curiously, the sheriff in Johnson City was Colvin Pruitt, the brother of Aley Lackey and Albert's brother-in-law.[27]

Later, Lackey's wife, Aley, told the sheriff about her escape from her husband and also witnessing him cutting his own throat. All told, Albert Lackey killed at least six people, most of them relatives, and left about 20 children as orphans. The victims were buried the next day, August 25, "in a little cemetery on Hickory Creek, some two miles below the Sandy post office."[28]

The story of Albert Lackey was not finished, however. On August 26, a large group of citizens of Blanco County decided not to wait for a trial, and they called upon the metaphorical Judge Lynch to mete out justice. Soon after dark, a group of men estimated at 50 to 80 in number rode into Blanco, led by Lackey's two stepsons, James and Charles, a nephew, Frances Lackey, and Sheriff Pruitt of Johnson City. Lackey had attempted to kill his stepsons' mother, Aley Lackey, and had killed Charles' wife and her parents. The men had intended to get to Blanco in the afternoon and hang Lackey on the courthouse square. That plan did not work out, and when they gathered at the jail after dark, a Blanco man named Phil C. Cage who knew some of the leaders of the mob asked that they not create a commotion because "a very sick woman was in a home near the jail." Some believed that Cage was simply trying to stop the lynching, but one of the leaders knew Cage well and told the men in the mob to keep quiet.[29]

The group of men entered the jail and demanded the cell keys from Sheriff Jackson. Jackson claimed he did not have the keys and could not get them. After Jackson denied having the keys, the mob went to the jailer, who said he had the keys but would not surrender them. A struggle ensued, with the jailer trying to draw his gun without success, and the men finally got the keys. The group went immediately to Lackey's cell, overpowered him, and dragged him from the jail. Honoring Mr. Cage's request, the group of men, supplemented by some local men, quietly rode north out of town.[30]

A mile out of town, they stopped and questioned Lackey about his actions. "When asked whether he had ruined his daughter as was rumored, he replied that he had not. He did not inquire whether his daughter was dead or not," and he thought he had killed more than he actually had. He also expressed regret that he had run out of bullets. When asked why he killed the people, he replied that they were "'fixing to mob me.'" When asked if he remembered his brother telling him the morning of the murders that Albert should leave the area, he said he did. He was also reported to say: "I did the killing, and I intended to kill two more families out there if I had the time, but my gun played out and I went crazy." The mob did not want to hear any more, and they set about to hang Lackey. An argument ensued between Lackey and his accusers about which tree to use for the hanging. Lackey, a big man, judged one potential limb too low and too close to the road. A nearby tree was selected instead, and a noose attached to a suitable limb. Some in the mob suggested shooting Lackey instead of hanging him, revealing their sensitive side regarding Lackey's throat wound, but the rope was slung over the limb anyway. Lackey was placed in the back of a wagon, and his death seemed to suit the brutality of his life.

> As the wagon was started up he was told to jump from the chair in which he had been placed in standing position; he failed to jump and was dragged from the wagon by the rope on the limb. His neck was not broken and strangulation ended the life of one whose only request was to be permitted to return to the scene of the crime to finish his intended work of killing seven others. As the body swung and turned in the night breeze the rope untwisted and stretched until the feet almost touched the ground; another rope was tied in the noose and the body raised quite a distance higher, after which the main body dispersed north, going back to their homes in and about the scene of the tragedy.

Vengeance had been had.[31]

The next morning, a coroner's inquest was held at the scene of the hanging. Lackey's body was still hanging from the tree. "Lackey was a large man with iron gray hair and mustache, and looked a terrible and gruesome giant as he swung in the air, the rope having buried itself in the cut he had inflicted in his throat." The coroner's jury came to the conclusion that Lackey was dead "at the hands of unknown people. The act is universally approved," the reporter noted. The body was cut down and carted into town. There, John R. Robinson was hired to bury Lackey in an unmarked grave "in the southeast corner of the Robinson (now Alvin Wegner) field, one half mile northwest of town." John Robinson was likely related to Esquire Lewellyn Robinson, the coroner. Imagine that.[32]

According to a 1936 story on the murders, "The 'Lackey tree' stands just north of Paradise Hollow, one mile north of Blanco, on highway 66, just west of a topped tree near the highway. The second fork of the oak pointing toward the road is where the rope ended the career of Al Lackey, in a lynching party, for the murder of six of his own family connection; at that time the road was just west of the trees, between them and the old rock fence."[33]

Sadly enough, the Albert Lackey story was not finished yet. At the time of his father's hanging, one of Lackey's boys swore to avenge his father's death. Berry Lackey, who was about 14 when his father was hanged, found himself in the news seven years later. In the evening of April 26, 1892, near where his father had killed at least six people, "a young man named Lackey attempted to kill Tom Bundick by shooting at him. The ball missed Bundick, but killed his horse. Bundick and Lackey were riding along the road together, when Lackey fired without any apparent cause." Just before shooting at Bundick, young Lackey claimed that "he would kill every man that had anything to do with the hanging of his father." The assault on

Bundick, the very same man that Lackey's father had stabbed and crippled seven years before, was the young Lackey's effort to put his threats into action. Alas, as the newspaper reported, "Lackey has been arrested, and failing to give bond languishes in the county jail." Little is known about Berry Lackey after his imprisonment except that he died in 1901. Tom Bundick may have died of old age in Kerr County, Texas, in 1935.[34]

The ghost of Albert Lackey is said still to haunt Blanco County, sometimes at the hanging tree, sometimes at the killing grounds. The ghost is said to appear on horseback, wearing a blood-soaked rag around his neck and carrying a butcher knife.[35] Such notions aside, the murders were a diversion for the people of Austin. Maybe the servant girl killings were the result of jealousy and discord. Maybe the end had come. Unfortunately, after the summer reprieve, just when the citizens of Austin had hoped the violence had moved west, murder returned to the capital city.

Notes

Title: Ramsland, "Servant Girl Annihilator."

1. *Fort Worth Daily Gazette*, 5/13/1885.
2. *Fort Worth Daily Gazette*, 1/30/1884; Gard, *Handbook of Texas Online*.
3. *Fort Worth Daily Gazette*, 5/13/1885.
4. *Fort Worth Daily Gazette*, 12/9/1883; Bicknell and Beck, *Handbook of Texas Online*. 5. qtd. in Bicknell, "The Notorious Ben Thompson Becomes a Peace Officer."
6. *Fort Worth Daily Gazette*, 1/12/1884; *Fort Worth Daily Gazette*, 2/3/1884.
7. *Brenham Weekly Banner*, 1/17/1884; *Fort Worth Daily Gazette*, 1/14/1884.
8. *Fort Worth Daily Gazette*, 1/23/1884.
9. *Fort Worth Daily Gazette*, 2/5/1884; *Fort Worth Daily Gazette*, 2/3/1884.
10. *Fort Worth Daily Gazette*, 2/5/1884; *Fort Worth Daily Gazette*, 2/3/1884.
11. *Fort Worth Daily Gazette*, 2/7/1884; *Brenham Weekly Banner*, 2/29/1884.
12. Alexander and Alexander, *Winchester Warriors: Texas Rangers of Company D, 1874-1901*: 39; "The Lost Valley Fight"; Haley, *Handbook of Texas Online*; *Mercantile and General City Directory of Austin, Texas—1872-1873*; *Mooney & Morrison's General Directory of the City of Austin, 1877-1878*; *Morrison & Fourmy's General Directory of the City of Austin, 1881-1882*.
13. *Biographical Encyclopedia of Texas*: 226-227; Cutrer, "Lee, Joseph," *Handbook of Texas Online*; 1870 Federal Census; Oakwood Cemetery Database.
14. Cutrer, "Robertson, Joseph William," *Handbook of Texas Online*.
15. "Robertson-L Archives"; "Robertson Genealogy Exchange."
16. Daniell, *Successful Men of Texas*: 421-428; Johnson, *A History of Texas and Texans*: 1867; Mayor Robertson qtd. in Daniell, *Successful Men of Texas*: 427; Oakwood Cemetery Database.
17. Connor, *Handbook of Texas Online*; Johnson, *A History of Texas and Texans*: 1719; Brown, *Indian Wars and Pioneers of Texas*: 286-287.
18. *Austin Daily Statesman*, 6/6/1885.
19. *Fort Worth Daily Gazette*, 6/12/1885; *Fort Worth Daily Gazette*, 6/15/1885; *Fort Worth Daily Gazette*, 7/1/1885.

20. O. Henry, *Rolling Stones*: 265; *Morrison & Fourmy's General Directory of the City of Austin, 1885-1886* (William S. Porter, better known as O. Henry, lived for a while in the boarding house owned by Harrell's father at 1008 Lavaca.)

21. "Mostly Blanco County Families" <http://wc.rootsweb.ancestry.com/cgibin/igm.cgi?op=GET&db=nanaj&id=I10814>,<http://wc.rootsweb.ancestry.com/cgi-bin/igm.cgi?op=GET&db=nanaj&id=I10755>, <http://wc.rootsweb.ancestry.com/cgi-bin/igm.cgi?op=GET&db=nanaj&id=I10766>; "Texas Marriages, 1837-1973"; 1880 Federal Census; Brown, "The Lackey Tragedy In Blanco County." (Contrary to the 1880 census transcription that suggested he was born ten years later and identified him as Allen I. Lackey. Lackey was also called Lockie in some reports.)

22. *The National Tribune*, 9/3/1885; "Mostly Blanco County Families" <http://wc.rootsweb.ancestry.com/cgi-bin/igm.cgi?op=GET&db=nanaj&id=I10766>;<http://wc.rootsweb.ancestry.com/cgi-bin/igm.cgi?op=GET&db=nanaj&id=I10814>.

23. *Omaha Daily Bee*, 8/28/1885; *Decatur Saturday Herald*, 8/29/1885; "The Lackey Murders"; "Mostly Blanco County Families" <http://wc.rootsweb.ancestry.com/cgi-bin/igm.cgi?op=GET&db=nanaj&id=I10851>; 1880 Federal Census (Nathaniel Greenberry Lackey was also known as Berry Lackey, and he was called G.B. Lackey in the 1880 census.)

24. *Omaha Daily Bee*, 8/28/1885; "The Lackey Murders"; "Mostly Blanco County Families" <http://wc.rootsweb.ancestry.com/cgi-bin/igm.cgi?op=GET&db=nanaj&id=I18483>.

25. *Omaha Daily Bee*, 8/28/1885; Brown, "The Lackey Tragedy In Blanco County"; "The Lackey Murders"; *The National Tribune*, 9/3/1885; *Decatur Saturday Herald*, 8/29/1885; "Mostly Blanco County Families" <http://wc.rootsweb.ancestry.com/cgi-bin/igm.cgi?op=GET&db=nanaj&id=I18483>; <http://wc.rootsweb.ancestry.com/cgi-bin/igm.cgi? op=GET&db=nanaj&id=I10770>.

26. *Omaha Daily Bee*, 8/28/1885; Brown, "The Lackey Tragedy In Blanco County"; *Dallas Morning News*, 5/8/1892 (Bundick was variously called Al Bundick, Tom Bundick, and Thomas Brunswick. The second name was likely correct because it showed up in a news report several years later regarding one of Lackey's sons.)

27. Brown, "The Lackey Tragedy In Blanco County"; "The Lackey Murders."

28. Brown, "The Lackey Tragedy In Blanco County"; *Omaha Daily Bee*, 8/28/1885.

29. Brown, "The Lackey Tragedy In Blanco County"; "The Lackey Murders."

30. *Deseret News*, 9/1/1885; *Dodge City Times*, 9/3/1885; Brown, "The Lackey Tragedy In Blanco County."

31. *New York Times*, 8/29/1885; *Dodge City Times*, 9/3/1885; *Humeston New Era*, 9/3/1885; Brown, "The Lackey Tragedy In Blanco County."

32. Brown, "The Lackey Tragedy In Blanco County"; *Omaha Daily Bee*, 8/29/1885; *Dodge City Times*, 9/3/1885

33. Brown, "The Lackey Tragedy In Blanco County."

34. *Dallas Morning News*, 5/8/1892.

35. "Al Lackey Still Rides the Night."

Chapter 6

"The Fiend in Human Shape"

The Murders Resume

Albert Lackey was barely stiff in his grave when murder returned to the capital city. The bloody violence that had waned through the long, hot summer months once more reared its hoary head. The thirst for blood, for revenge was too strong. Worse, the murders began to take on a more perverse nature. The "clew" detectives had uncovered at the beginning of July had not yielded a viable suspect, so the investigation was no closer to solving the murders than it was at the beginning of the year.

Saturday, August 29, 1885, was one of the hottest days of the year, hitting 99 degrees. The nights cooled to only the upper 70s. A bit of rain had fallen on August 27, but the heat had quickly dried up that precipitation. Sunday, though, saw about half an inch of rain. The sun set at 6:55 P.M. Saturday night, and the moon rose around 9:30 that night, a waning gibbous, the full moon five days earlier.[1]

In the early morning hours of Sunday, August 30, 1885, around 5 o'clock, Mr. Valentine O. Weed, of 300 East Cedar Street, heard a noise in his backyard. The two-story house, on the northeast corner of Cedar and San Jacinto, had a one-story kitchen attached to the back, with a separate wash house in the yard. Weed asked his wife what the noise was, and she opined it was a dog howling, but he thought the noise sounded unnatural and decided to investigate. The morning sky was still dark, sunrise another hour away, so armed with a lamp, Weed went out behind the house. He then heard a noise coming from the kitchen, a groaning noise that grew louder. Weed alerted his wife and grabbed his gun. Together, they went on the back gallery and discovered that the kitchen door was locked. They called to their servant, Rebecca Ramey, but got no answer. Weed then heard a noise in the kitchen, and, ordering his wife to hold the lamp, pushed the kitchen door open. He called in to Rebecca, asking what the matter was. She replied unsteadily, "I don't know. I'm sick." Weed sensed that something was terribly wrong, so he yelled at his neighbor, Stephen Jaqua, who owned a feed and hay store on Congress Avenue. Weed told Jaqua that he thought his two servants had been murdered, informing the neighbor that one servant was in the kitchen and the other was missing. Weed was convinced the noise he had heard in the kitchen was made by a person, perhaps someone escaping.[2]

When Jaqua arrived at the house, Weed grabbed his jacket and the lamp and went into the kitchen. There he found Rebecca Ramey in critical condition, dying, he thought. Weed told Jaqua to watch the back gate, making sure no one came or went. Then Weed went to fetch Sergeant John Chenneville. Chenneville and another officer, Deputy Sheriff Harry White, arrived in about 15 minutes, followed soon thereafter by Mr. Wilson and his bloodhounds. By that time, Dr. Richard Swearingen, a local physician and the state health officer, had also arrived. Weed, Jaqua, and Swearingen went into the kitchen. They found Rebecca Ramey "in a dying condition," her head bloody. "She had been sand-bagged into insensibility. There were two cuts over her eye." She had possibly been struck by an ax or pierced with an iron spike. Weed noted that when he first saw her, she had only a small amount of blood under her head. By the time he returned with help, that blood had swelled to ten times its original amount. Weed estimated that when he first saw her, she must have been attacked no more than an hour before.[3]

"Killed, but Not Butchered"

Rebecca's Ramey's daughter, 11-year-old Mary, was missing from the kitchen. She was soon found in an adjoining wash house in the backyard. She also had been sand-bagged, or knocked unconscious by a blow to the head, and dragged from the kitchen. In the wash house, she had been brutally outraged, and then an iron spike had been driven into both ears, the same sort of sharp instrument that was likely used to injure her mother. One report claimed "the girl had been assaulted and struck in the head with an ax. She had been killed, but not butchered." Dr. Lucien Johnson had also been summoned by Weed. Johnson lived a block south of Weed at 302 E. Cypress, where the murder of Eliza Shelly had occurred on May 7. With Swearingen, Johnson examined both mother and daughter. He later testified at the coroner's inquest, overseen by Justice Thomas F. Purnell, on Sunday.

> The mother was in the kitchen and the daughter was in the wash house. We examined the girl first as she was still alive.

> The girl was evidently struck by some sharp instrument in both ears, and we probed the ears and found that the wounds were deep, cutting a portion of her ears. . . . She had evidently been struck with a sand bag or something of the kind after which she had been ravished and killed. We then examined the mother. She had not been ravished, but had been struck . . . the same way as the girl, and had two cuts on the left side of her head. I think that the skull is fractured. The girl lived about one hour after I arrived.

Dr. Swearingen also testified that Mary died as a result of the iron spikes driven into her brain. He stayed with the girl for about an hour, at which time she died. He noted that the fresh appearance of the blood suggested that the attack had occurred no more than one or two hours before his arrival a little after five that morning.[4]

As the doctors were tending to the victims, the police were looking for clues. Mr. Jaqua testified that when the bloodhounds arrived, he and the police officers began looking for tracks. They found some that looked as if they had been made by bare feet. He continued: "The dogs went into the alley, and went to my alley gate, and found there the same tracks, leading into my yard, and then out again. Owing to the dampness of the ground, the tracks were very plain. The man with the hounds told me he followed the tracks to Mr. Evan's stables. I then went with him, and saw the same tracks in Mr. Evan's yard, and traced them from the gate towards the house." The Mr. Evan that Jaqua named was apparently William Ervine, who ran a feed stable and wagon yard at 712 East Avenue at the corner of Hickory, about a half mile from Weed's house. Ervine was also a city alderman representing the ninth ward.[5]

At the stable, the officers and dogs went in and found a black man hidden in the hay loft. The man, Tom Allen, drove one of the city water carts. Allen was taken back to the scene of the crime. There, "Allen's feet were measured with the tracks in the sand and they fitted to a hair." Allen also could not give a credible account of his actions after 2 A.M. Sunday morning. Allen was about 23 years old at the time. He lived in the general area of the Weed house with his brother Edmond, his mother, Rose, and two children, Jerry and Mary. Based on the slim evidence, Allen was taken to the city jail, though talk of lynching swirled through the streets. Late Sunday night, Allen was examined by Dr. W.J. Burt, the city physician. On Monday, Dr. Burt told a *Statesman* reporter that "the examination proved very conclusively to his mind that Allen was not the man who raped the girl," based on "certain physical incapabilities."[6]

Another black man, Alexander Mack, was also implicated in the murder, though the police did not consider him a suspect. Mack was about 28 years old and lived with his stepfather, Barney Cook, his mother, Sallie Mack Cook, and his sister, Lucinda Mack, in the third ward. Mack was a laborer, his stepfather a servant, and his mother a washwoman. Mack was arrested late Monday night. "Mack was chased by the dogs for several miles, and he was found in Masontown where he had secreted himself." Masontown was an area of black residents in east Austin. When Mack was arrested, he had a "foetidic tied around his feet. The officers asked him what that was for. He said 'to throw dem hounds offen de scent.' He was locked up under an old charge," but he was not charged with Mary Ramey's murder or the assault of her mother. In a seemingly interesting twist, the 1881-1882 city directory listed Mack as a porter at the Club House Saloon at the corner of Congress and Ash. In that same directory, Valentine Weed was listed as a partner with Fritz Hartkopf in a livery business. By 1885, Hartkopf was no longer Weed's partner, but he was the proprietor of the Club House Saloon.[7]

A report in a New Jersey newspaper about six months after the murder added new details or misinformation to the case. According to the report, "Bloodhounds were put on the scent. They followed the trail for ten miles through the streets, out into the country and back into the city. The murderer knew he was pursued by the animals, for all the old slave methods had been used to baffle the hounds' instinct. One suspected man was traced from the stable across the city to where he took a hack. The wheel marks led up to an alley back of the cabin. There hack and man disappeared." This report seems to disagree with local reports, so parts of it may be fantasy. The Galveston newspaper also gave a slightly different account of the events after the murder. According to the Galveston report, bloodhounds followed a trail about two blocks from the Weed home to a stable, where police found a young black man named Henry Taylor, also called River Bottom Tom. This suspect also drove a water cart. The dogs would not strike a trail away from the stable, so Taylor was arrested and taken to the Weed home, and his footprints fit the ones in the yard, "even to a peculiarly shaped toe."[8]

Rebecca Ramey, also known as Becky, was about 40 years old at the time of the assault. She was described as "a fine looking, bright mulatto woman," weighing about 200 pounds. She apparently had three children: Edward, born in 1869; Miami (or Minnie), born in 1871; and Mary, born in 1875. Rebecca was the older sister of Edward H. Carrington, a local grocer. Edward Carrington was Austin's first black property owner and a successful businessman on East Pecan Street. Rebecca was also the older sister of Albert Carrington, a blacksmith who served on the Austin City Council from 1882 through 1885, representing the seventh ward. Rebecca had apparently been working for Mr. Weed for only a short while, for the 1885 city directory listed her as working for the Austin Steam Laundry in east Austin and living at the corner of Chincapin and Comal in east Austin. According to Weed, Rebecca "had no men going to see her, and I think her a good and virtuous woman." Weed also indicated that "the woman had led an orderly life and he had full confidence in her. He knew of no one whom suspicion might rest with positive weight." When a reporter spoke to her on Monday, she was in much pain, though her doctor thought she was improving. She stated that "she went to bed Saturday night at 9 o'clock, and heard the clock strike 10 and 11, and after this she remembered nothing more, until aroused by the physicians. She says that she didn't recognize the person who committed the awful deed, in fact, that she was asleep when the attack was made, and didn't know what had happened, until the doctors came to examine her wounds." Young Mary Ramey was buried in Oakwood Cemetery in Austin on Monday, August 31—the cause of death: "murdered." In

1900, Rebecca was living with her daughter Minnie (Miami), who had married Lee Green. Rebecca lived in Austin until her death in 1909 from Bright's disease. She too was buried in Oakwood Cemetery.[9]

At the time of the murder, Valentine Osborn Weed was a prosperous young businessman, proprietor of the Globe Livery Stable located at the northwest corner of Colorado and Pine. He was born in 1849 in Tennessee. His wife was the former Isabelle Brush, often called Bella, born around 1854 in New Jersey. Together they had at least eight children, six of them born before the murder in 1885. They also lost a baby to dysentery in 1886. Weed did not seem to have much involvement in politics, though his wife's brother, William B. Brush, was a current city alderman representing the tenth ward. Weed was said to be "the intimate confidant of many Texas pioneers who gained renown for their feuds." Weed called them "'the best of fellows [who] would stand by their friends through thick and thin, and they were not bad men at all." Weed would later open a mortuary service with his son, Thurlow, that would become the well-known Weed-Corley-Fish funeral home. Weed himself died in 1935 and was buried in Oakwood Cemetery.[10]

Research turned up a curious link that was detoured by poor publishing. The 1881-1882 Austin city directory listed a black woman named Sarah Ramey as living with Cynthia Spencer, the mother of Walter Spencer, the injured lover of Mollie Smith in the first murder. Could there have been a link between the two families that might explain the motives behind the murders? The 1880 census pretty much dispelled that link. In the 1880 census, a black woman named Sarah Ramie resided next door to Cynthia Spencer. This Sarah Ramie was 28 years old in 1880. She was born in Missouri to parents from Missouri and Kentucky, whereas Rebecca Ramey was born in Virginia to parents from Virginia. So no direct family link seems evident. Another Ramey family did live in Austin in 1885, but it was a family of white people. William Neal Ramey was the publisher and editor of the monthly *Texian* magazine and also the secretary of the Texas State Senate. He had been a captain in Company K of the 28th Texas Cavalry during the Civil War and a schoolteacher in Shelby County in 1870. The directory also listed Miss Sarah Ramey, who worked for R.M. Thomson, a partner in Thomson and Donnan, land agents, but nothing could be found about her.[11]

"A Criminal of No Mean Ability"

Obviously, the important clue that the officers supposedly had discovered in July had not produced a solid lead, contrary to the assertions of the police department. And the two suspects in the murder and rape of Mary Ramey also did not appear linked to the crime. Tom Allen had been cleared by Dr. Burt, the city physician, and Alex Mack was arrested on an unrelated charge. The Fort Worth newspaper noted that "Cool headed citizens fail to see anything to connect the above individuals with the terrible crime but hot headed tempestuous ones are hot for lynching them. It may be if the first, against whom the evidence appears the strongest, is connected with the case at all it was simply as a guide and decoy for others who got in their hellish work. He was carefully examined by officers and by a physician after his arrest and no indications whatever were found that he had had anything to do with the murder." If Allen did serve as a "guide and decoy," then surely more than one person was involved in the planning and execution of the assault. Was Valentine Weed the target of the attack, that is, intimidation through fright? Were Rebecca Ramey and her daughter simply the unfortunate victims of a random attack? Or were the mother and daughter the intended targets for some unknown reason?[12]

And just who were the culprits in these murders? Surely the murder and rape of Mary Ramey could be linked to some of the earlier murders and outrages. The weapons were similar, especially the use of an ax to wound and the use of iron spikes to discombobulate the victim. The phase of the moon was similar, and the modus operandi was also similar. Galloway noted that the "Ramey murder was carried out in much the same manner as the murders of Eliza Shelley, Mollie Smith and Irene Cross: entry by stealth, the victim stunned while sleeping, taken from the room, sexually assaulted and then murdered. As with the Shelley and Cross murders, bare footprints were left behind by the perpetrator."[13]

Despite these obvious links, Austinites, both officials and citizens, were clueless as to the perpetrators. The *Austin Daily Statesman* opined that

> the fact that the victims are almost exclusively confined to servant girls of the colored race is adduced as proof that the outrager and murderer belongs to the lower ledge of society. Probably a negro, say all, certainly a man of unorganized intellect and debased nature say others. But the fact that this series of crimes is composed of some of the boldest, most startling flagrations in criminal annals, that it has extended over a period of many months and that the perpetrator has, so far, not only accomplished his ends, but successfully escaped and blinded the police, would seem to indicate that he is a criminal of no mean ability, one to be feared and one who will require the best detective skill of the state to ferret out.

The general attitude was still that the murders were the work of black men, though now the contention became that they were smart black men, a conclusion almost totally contrary to the common perception of black people at the time. The notion that the murders were the result of marital discord also seemed to be discarded, and "now the people of Austin were reaching a level of concern about these killings that verged on panic. . . . At least the victims were servants. That was somehow comforting to the white middle and upper classes."[14]

A day after the *Austin Daily Statesman* concluded that the culprit must have been a black person of the lowest level of society, it changed its tune somewhat, stating,

> All the surroundings connected with these murders indicate that they have been cunningly planned, carefully directed and

> intelligently consummated. No ignorant negro, such as is now under arrest committed the crime. They were conceived, and especially the one Sunday, with a superior intelligence, and brain work of a high order will have to be invoked to discover the perpetrators. The crime of Sunday can hardly be laid at the door of an ignorant negro. History of outrages upon women by negroes proves this. They rarely ever deliberately murder their victims, and experience shows that nine times out of ten they invariably leave some clue which leads to their identification and arrest.

This new assessment was reflected in the later report in the New Jersey newspaper, which indicated that "Every citizen now joined in the cry for a searching investigation of every clew at any expense. . . . The whites became somewhat alarmed. The negroes said the strange crimes were the work of white men, and the success in eluding pursuit made everybody believe the story."[15]

Were Tom Allen and Alex Mack the dreaded servant girl annihilators? The police did not seem to think so, the city physician had ruled out Allen as a suspect, and the general citizenry, though they were eager to lynch anyone to ease their own panic, did not think so either. Were black men involved in the murders? The answer seems to be yes. Was a white man controlling the actions of the black men? The answer seems to be probably. What white man in Austin had the influence or connections to command the actions of a few or a legion of black men? The police and city officials, if they knew, certainly were not telling, and the rest of the people in town remained in a state of panic and anger.

"Powerless to Render Good"

The failure of the police again to apprehend a viable suspect brought on a new onslaught of criticism. Marshal Grooms Lee was the first to be the butt of such criticism when it was announced that he did not arrive at the scene of the Ramey murder until 11 o'clock Sunday morning, six or seven hours after Mr. Weed first sounded the alarm. Whereas before the newspapers had groused about the inefficiency of the investigations, now the press was insinuating crimes within the police department and calling for heads to roll. On September 2, 1885, the *Austin Daily Statesman* took the marshal to task.

> The inefficiency of the police management of the city for the past year or two, has been apparent to the casual observer, and ugly rumors of robbery and defalcations within the police circle here have been circulated, and certain it is that more diabolical, cruel, bloody murders have been committed than ever before within the same period of time. The rumors of crookedness reached such a pitch that the clerk of the police station skipped out. The city council ordered an investigation, and it was found that the city marshal, through his trusted agent, was defaulter to the tune of one hundred and fifty

> dollars. The committee of investigation exonerated the marshal from any criminal intimacy in the matter, and said that he was not at fault, but the above shows he has not the capacity to intelligently direct the police affairs of the city. The ineffectual attempts to ferret out those who have committed the horrible, mysterious murders in this city in the recent past enforces this assertion.

The article did not stop by simply chastising the police force once again. It called for a change in leadership in the police department.

> The present marshal is a good, honest, well-meaning man, but is deficient in that ability which should characterize a man occupying the important position he does. If the chief of a police force is inefficient, the force is so too, no matter how capable the men comprising it may be. This fact is recognized in all well regulated cities, and only men of known ability are put at the head of their police machinery. Crimes, intelligently directed, must be met by intelligent effort, or society must be disrupted and go down under the accumulated weight of the bloody crimes and heart rendering outrages. It is high time a change was made in Austin. As it is the police force of the city, except for arresting drunken men, is powerless to render good. Before crime that would delight experienced capable officers to successfully ferret out, the force is helpless.

Grooms Lee's tenure as city marshal certainly seemed to be in danger.[16]

The fault of the failure of the police department was not placed at the feet of Grooms Lee alone. He had help in the various offices of city government. The good-old-boy, Confederate colonel brand of municipal government was showing its threadbare nature. In a city on the verge of leaping into the future, the old guard seemed determined not to let go of its flimsy hold on the local government. But that determination did not stop the newspaper from calling for change. The *Statesman* continued its harangue the next day.

> An inefficient city government seems to be the sad fate of Austin, for all will join with us, we think, in admitting that it has long failed to efficiently meet and handle public exigencies. . . . Comparatively, our crime record is second to no place in the civilized world; even the most savage communities of the most savage peoples can not lay bare to the world more damnable horrors than are today related of Austin. . . . Austin is lawless because it is badly governed; its municipal government is discreditable, because it becomes a part, it seems, of our public policy not to place it in the hands of the most trusted and reputable of its citizens. . . . Wretched administration flows out of our municipal offices as naturally as water finds its way down hill. It is apparently everywhere; it permeates everything; is seen in all our public affairs, in our wretched streets, in the

> green scum that floats on fetid pools even along Congress Avenue, in the deadly smells that ascend from alleys and backyards in every part of the city, in the disregard paid to ordinances, in the grand total of failure attaching to everything emanating from, or permitted by the power of evil which shrouds our city.

Either the local government was unable to find the murderers, or else it was covering up the identity. In either case, a disservice was being perpetrated upon the people of Austin, and those people had finally had enough.[17]

Unfortunately, the end was not in sight. Within a few weeks, the good citizens of Austin would witness the most heinous murders yet in the awful cavalcade.

Notes

Title: *Austin Daily Statesman*, 9/1/1885.

1. "Monthly Record of Observations Taken at Stations in the Cotton Region," Austin, August 1885; "Lunar calendar."
2. *Austin Daily Statesman*, 9/1/1885; *Morrison & Fourmy's General Directory of the City of Austin, 1885-1886*; 1880 Federal Census (The news report called the neighbor William Jacqua, but the city directory listed him as Stephen E. Jaqua, co-owner of Jaqua and Martin at 316 Congress. The 1880 census listed him as Steph. Jaqwa.)
3. *Austin Daily Statesman*, 9/1/1885; *San Antonio Daily Express*, 9/1/1885; *Trenton Times*, 2/1/1886.
4. *Austin Daily Statesman*, 9/1/1885; *Trenton Times*, 2/1/1886; *Fort Worth Daily Gazette*, 8/31/1885; *Morrison & Fourmy's General Directory of the City of Austin, 1885-1886* (Purnell's son, Thomas L. Purnell, was the city clerk.)
5. *Austin Daily Statesman*, 9/1/1885; *Fort Worth Daily Gazette*, 8/31/1885; *Morrison & Fourmy's General Directory of the City of Austin, 1885-1886*.
6. *Austin Daily Statesman*, 9/1/1885; *San Antonio Daily Express*, 9/1/1885; *Fort Worth Daily Gazette*, 8/31/1885; *Fort Worth Daily Gazette*, 11/15/1885; 1880 Federal Census.
7. *Austin Daily Statesman*, 9/1/1885; *Fort Worth Daily Gazette*, 9/1/1885; 1880 Federal Census; *Morrison & Fourmy's General Directory of the City of Austin, 1881-1882*.
8. *Trenton Times*, 2/1/1886; *Galveston Daily News*, 8/31/1885.
9. *Austin Daily Statesman*, 9/1/1885; *San Antonio Daily Express*, 9/1/1885; *Fort Worth Daily Gazette*, 8/31/1885; *San Antonio Daily Light*, 8/31/1885; *Galveston Daily News*, 8/31/1885; Childs, *Images of America: Sixth Street*: 40; *Morrison & Fourmy's General Directory of the City of Austin, 1885-1886*; Oakwood Cemetery Database; 1880 Federal Census (The 1885 city directory listed two black servants working and residing at Weed's home, Lizzie Jefferson and Sallie Scroggins. Rebecca Ramey was not listed as a servant there.)
10. *Morrison & Fourmy's General Directory of the City of Austin, 1885-1886*; 1900 Federal Census; "History of Weed-Corley-Fish"; "Frontier Feudists Were True to Friends"; Oakwood Cemetery Database.

11. *Morrison & Fourmy's General Directory of the City of Austin, 1881-1882*; *Morrison & Fourmy's General Directory of the City of Austin, 1885-1886*; 1880 Federal Census; "United States, Civil War Soldiers Index"; 1870 Federal Census.
12. *Fort Worth Daily Gazette*, 9/1/1885.
13. Galloway, *The Servant Girl Murders*: 268.
14. *Austin Daily Statesman*, 9/1/1885; Ramsland, "Servant Girl Annihilator."
15. *Austin Daily Statesman*, 9/2/1885; *Trenton Times*, 2/1/1886.
16. *Austin Daily Statesman*, 9/2/1885.
17. *Austin Daily Statesman*, 9/3/1885.

Chapter 7

"Deeds of Dreadful Depravity"

A Massacre Near the University

The long, hot summer had come to an end, and the fall brought with it the chill of more murder. The concern about the Ramey incident was still palpable, but that concern was replaced by panic over a double murder near the state university. The culprits did not wait so long for their next atrocity. The new murders followed hard on the heels of the Ramey murder, occurring a scant month later.

An epidemic of dengue fever struck Austin in September, with over 1000 cases reported, including Governor John Ireland. The church bells rang every hour to remind people to take their medicine. By the end of September, the hot temperatures of a month prior had given way to daytime highs in the low to middle 80s, with temperatures at night dipping into the low to middle 60s. True to form, the moon was just a few days past full when the new set of assaults took place. The moon rose at 8:50 P.M. Sunday night, September 27, 1885, and was said to be as bright as day. It did not set until 10:28 Monday morning.[1]

Just a few hours after moonrise, the violence in Austin reached a new high. These new murders differed in at least two ways from the earlier assaults. This time, a man was killed along with a servant woman. And this time, one of the victims that survived apparently got a clear look at the murderers, or at least one of them.

In the early morning hours of Monday, September 28, 1885, sometime around 1 o'clock, Major William B. Dunham was awakened by a noise in his servants' shack only a dozen feet from the main house. Dunham, who lived at 2408 Guadalupe, just west of the state university, got up to investigate. In the shack lived Gracie Vance and her common-law husband, Orange Washington. Dunham believed the noise "to be Orange whipping Gracie—an act that he had been frequently guilty of." Dunham went to the back door and looked out. Satisfied that all was quiet, he locked the door and went back to bed. Little did he know what was really occurring only a few feet from where he rested.[2]

A few hours earlier, on Sunday evening, Major Dunham had gone to the door of the shack to ask if Orange was there. Lucinda Boddy answered the door, saying that Orange and Gracie had gone to church. Dunham asked who else was in the shack then, and Lucinda said that Gracie's cousin was there. Dunham did not know the boy's name but thought he was around 18 years old. Dunham told the boy to leave and not come back unless Orange was at home, though he allowed Lucinda to stay. The boy left the yard, but Dunham turned in for the night and did not know if he returned or not.[3]

A short while after retiring for the night, Major Dunham was awakened by people passing his window. They were heading toward the shack. He supposed them to be Gracie and Orange, returning from church. They were laughing and talking, and he heard them enter the shack. Gracie Vance was about 20 years old at the time, born in 1865 in Texas. She was a servant for Mr. Dunham. Orange Washington was about 25 years old, born around 1860 in Texas. He worked for Michael Butler at a brickyard on the south side of the river. That night, two other people were staying in the shack with Gracie and Orange. One was Lucinda Boddy, whom Dunham had spoken to earlier in the evening. She worked for John B. Taylor, a vegetable dealer who lived nearby at 2400 Guadalupe. The other was Patsy Gibson, who was about 17 years old at the time. She worked as a cook for Dr. Richard Graves, who lived a few blocks away at 2405 Whitis Avenue. Sensing no further commotion, Major Dunham dozed off again.[4]

Sometime after midnight, Dunham was awakened again, as noted earlier. He "heard a noise as if someone had jumped through a window in the cabin, followed by a scream like that of a woman." He would later testify at an inquest held by Justice William Von Rosenberg, Jr.

> I took my gun and went to my back door, which is about twelve feet from their door; I heard two blows and a voice saying 'don't beat me,' or 'don't hurt me,' I can't say which; I said

> 'stop that noise or I will come in,' the noise ceased; I then heard a gasping voice as if the mouth of the speaker was muffled; I waited a little while, and hearing no further noise I locked my door and went to bed again; I think I was asleep, or nearly so, when I heard the breaking of a glass, as though a whole window had been shattered, and a woman screaming and running past my window. I took my gun and went to my front door, and heard the sounds of blows outside my yard; I think they were from six to ten feet from the northwest corner of my fence, on the outside; I could not see them immediately, when I opened the door; I said 'stop that, or I will shoot,' or words to that effect; the struggling ceased immediate; the girl Lucinda ran through the gate, direct to me; I heard the steps of someone, running north on San Marcos street, as well as I could judge; as the girl came to me, she said: 'My God, Mr. Dunham, we are all dead!'

Dunham stopped Lucinda at the door and asked her if she was hurt. She said she was not, but that "my folks are all dead, Orange, Gracie, and all." She was wearing night clothes, and after checking her body for wounds, Dunham told her to lie down on the steps but not to go in the house. Dunham went back to the shack, and, he later testified, "except a gasping sound, as if someone was strangling, I heard nothing."[5]

Major Dunham called to his neighbor, Harry H. Duff, who lived across the street at 2407 Guadalupe. Duff was the proprietor of the popular Iron Front Saloon at 605 Congress Avenue. According to Dunham's testimony, "We took a lantern and went into the negroes' house; the window in the east end of the house was open, the lower sash being on the ground; Orange was lying upon his face between his bed and the open window, and a woman whose name I did not know was resting on her hips and hands about the middle of the floor; her head was bloody; she said she was Dr. Grave's cook; Mr. Duff and I went to the window in the west end." Gracie was noticed missing, so a search was made for her. Dunham's testimony continued:

> Blood was on the floor under the window and on the outside wall of the house; the north fence seems about two feet from the house; about six feet from the corner of the house, on the west side of the fence was blood. We thought we heard groans, and went through the back yard; it was some time before anyone else arrived; a lady at Colonel Hotchkiss's place spoke from her window and said, 'they are behind the stable.' By this time others and officers arrived; then some one came and reported there was another woman lying behind the stable. This point designated was about sixty yards from the negro house; I and others went over to where the woman was said to be lying, and we found Gracie Vance lying on her back, her head was bloody and she was unconscious; near her there was a bloody brick. Around her arm was wound a watch chain to which was attached a small, open-faced, silver watch; someone gave

> notice that some person was running across the vacant lot, and the officers and others gave chase.

At some point in her plight, Gracie must have regained consciousness, as signs of a struggle behind the stable were evident. The killer, "however, overpowered her, and battered her head with a brick to a jelly," then, "while she was struggling between life and death, outraged her." She did not speak before she died.[6]

Mr. Duff had called the police, and soon officers began to arrive. Meanwhile, nearby

> neighbors of Major Dunham had been aroused, and . . . Mrs. W. H. Hotchkiss hallooed from her second story window, that some one was in the rear of her stable. Just at this time, Major Dunham was in his yard; with him Mr. Duff. . . . John Chenneville and Officer Conner, mounted, and Mr. Hotchkiss, were outside. Mr. Duff at once jumped over the fence, pistol in hand, and just about that time the wakeful, watchful eye of Mrs. Hotchkiss saw a person running westward from her stable and she again exclaimed, to the men, "There he runs, toward Nigger Town."

Mr. Duff and Officer Conner fired several shots at the fleeing murderer, but without effect. The killer kept running toward a mesquite grove and disappeared into the night. In the mesquite thicket, "a horse, saddled and bridled, was found hitched to a tree near the scene of the murder. They probably belonged or were stolen by the assassin, or possibly assassins. As in the Ramey case some weeks ago, the fiend of lust may have inspired the murderer."[7]

"The Midnight Lust-Fiend Again at Work"

Over the next few days, the case unfolded in much greater detail. Apparently "the assassins entered the room of the sleeping occupants through a window, and before any of them awoke succeeded in striking all four of them on the head with an ax." Major Dunham testified that he found an ax in the center of the room under bed clothes where Patsy Gibson was lying wounded. He said, "There was blood on the handle. The ax did not belong to me. Neither myself nor the negroes owned an ax; there was none on the place. I don't know to whom the ax belongs." The wounds were severe, knocking all the sleeping negroes insensible. According to the *San Antonio Express*,

> Washington was found lying on the floor of the cabin with a terrible gash on the top of his head which produced death, though he was still breathing when discovered, and was, of course, still insensible. The two girls were both struck violent blows which gashed their foreheads. Gracie Vance was dragged out of a window, thrown over a fence and dragged away fully

> seventy-five yards from the cabin, where she was found dead
> in the weeds, with a bloody brick with which she had been
> beaten, near her body. She was found lying on her face and her
> head was frightfully gashed.

In her later testimony, Patsy Gibson believed that chloroform had been used on all the people in the cabin, just as it likely was used in the Shelly murder and in the attack on Dr. Stoddard in May. Lucinda Boddy said "she was first struck with what she thinks was a sand bag, as it bounced from her when she was struck. Words passed between them while the man was striking her several times, and she took him to be Doc [Woods] from his voice." Though she would claim she saw the man, perhaps she did not.[8]

At this point, the story became somewhat disconnected. Lucinda Boddy had been sleeping on a pallet on the floor with Patsy Gibson. After being struck, Lucinda Boddy came to and got up. She "lit a lamp and she spoke to him, saying, 'Oh, Dock, Don't do it!' His reply was: 'G-d d--n you, don't you look at me.' Looking around the room, Lucinda saw what had been done, viewed the bloody scene, and again said 'Oh, Dock, don't do it. His reply was 'G-d d--n you, don't look at me. Blow out that light.' Soon after she jumped out of the window and rushed toward Major Dunham, who, by this time had come out of his house armed with a gun. The girl threw her arms around Major Dunham saying, 'We are all killed and Dock Woods did it!'" If this account was correct, the killer was in the room when Lucinda lit the lamp.[9]

In another widespread account, the killers dragged Gracie Vance from the cabin and threw her over the wooden fence like a log. According to this report,

> While the fiends were committing this horror Lucinda Bodery,
> recovering somewhat from the blows she had received,
> regained sufficient strength to get up and light a lamp in the
> shanty. One of the assassins, seeing the light, returned and
> sticking his head in the window cursed the woman and ordered
> her to put out the light. At seeing him, she screamed and ran
> from the building. He leaped through the window, put the light
> out and followed and overtook the fleeing woman; just as she
> got to the front gate, there was another desperate struggle,
> during which Bunham, who was awakened by the woman's
> screams, threw open his front door; not knowing a murder had
> been committed, and thinking the disturbance was a simple
> row, leveled his gun at them, without the intention of shooting,
> and ordered them to cease their noise. The woman, by
> desperate struggles, freed herself from the assassin and
> running to Bunham, threw her arms around him and emplored
> his protection, saying the man had murdered everyone in the
> shanty. The murderer ran away as soon as the woman
> appeared to Bunham.

This account, of course, had several names incorrect, which was not unusual.

However, Lucinda Boddy's own testimony before Justice Thomas F. Purnell somewhat corroborated this version. "Lucinda Boddy testified that on the night of the murder Doc Woods came to the window. She had been having dengue fever and was aroused at night by an intolerable thirst; she got up and struck a light, she said that she saw Doc Woods standing at the window on the outside; Doc shouted to her: 'Put down that light g-d d-mn you, or I'll kill you.' She threw the light to the floor and ran out of the house. Before she ran out, however, she saw Orange Washington and Patsy and they were bloody; she said that Doc had on dark brown duck pantaloons, she swore positively that Doc was there, she saw him plainly; was well acquainted with him and could not be mistaken." There is no mention of the cabin catching on fire from the lamp dashed to the floor, but this incident seemed to mark the first time an eyewitness could identify one of the culprits.[10]

As Lucinda fled the cabin, Major Dunham and most of the neighborhood had been awakened by the ruckus. The moon shone bright as day. As Dunham exited his house, "the first thing that met his eyes was the girl, Lucinda Boddy, just outside the gate, engaged in what seemed to be a death grapple with a negro ruffian. The latter raised his hand and as the moonlight fell upon the dusky faces, he struck the girl a fearful blow in the forehead with a brick. She tore herself loose and running to Dunham threw her arms around him in such a way as to prevent him from shooting the scoundrel, who fled." Though Mr. Duff and Officer James Conner "emptied their revolvers" at the fleeing man, no traces of blood were found along the escape route. The killer, or killers, had escaped again.[11]

The minor differing details do not diminish the awful gravity of the crime. The basic facts are clear. One or more men invaded the small cabin. Before any of the inhabitants roused from sleep, they were apparently struck in the head with an ax or a sandbag and knocked insensible. Gracie Vance was dragged from the room through a window, tossed over a fence, and dragged behind a stable. There, as she struggled as much as possible in her condition, she was outraged, and then her head was bashed in with a brick. A watch was found twisted around her arm, and a saddled horse was found nearby, as though ready for an escape. One of the inhabitants of the cabin, upon reviving, encountered one of the killers face to face and swore to his identity. Two of the inhabitants, Gracie Vance and Orange Washington, died soon after the attack, and the other two in the cabin, Lucinda Boddy and Patsy Gibson, were seriously wounded and were given little chance of survival. At last the police had solid clues to go on, or did they?

"Getting a Very Firm Grip on the Outrage Fiends"

A series of arrests quickly followed. Again, the sequence of events grew a bit disconnected. Late Monday afternoon, the man identified by Lucinda Boddy, "Doc Woods, a colored man, was [apparently] arrested by City Marshal Lee and deputy sheriff W. W. Hornsby, at his home across the river, about six miles west of the city. They thought he owned a horse found tied in the brush near the scene of the murder. He was subsequently released, and later, another negro named Beverley Overton, who had just come to claim the discovered animal, was arrested and jailed by order of Judge Rosenburg." Also arrested early the next morning was Oliver Townsend, a notorious chicken thief. Townsend was charged with attempted burglary at the home of Dr. Wade A. Morris at 100 W. Peach Street. Morris's home was also attacked on March 13. As noted in the report of that earlier attack, Mayor Robertson's law partner was one resident at the Morris home.[12]

An inquest jury was impaneled by Justice William Von Rosenberg, Jr., on Monday evening. During the inquest, Justice Von Rosenberg and Major Dunham went to the county jail. When they returned, Dunham said, "I have been to the county jail and identify the prisoner just brought in to be Doc Woods, who has been on my premises frequently, and who is mentioned by Lucinda Boddy as the man who committed the outrages." Soon thereafter, a bunch of clothes, including "a very bloody shirt," were presented to the jury. They had been taken from Dock Woods after his arrest. The jury wasted little time to reach its verdict: "We, the jury of inquest over the remains of Gracie Vance (sometimes called Washington) believe that the deceased came to her death by injuries inflicted upon her person, by some instrument in the hands of Doc Woods, on the 28th day of September, A.D. 1885, between the hours of 1 and 2 o'clock a.m. in Travis county, state of Texas."[13]

At the inquest, Dr. Cyrus O. Weller, a physician and druggist who lived at 2300 Guadalupe, testified about his examination of the four victims in the assault. Gracie Vance had suffered numerous lacerated wounds and incised wounds in her face and frontal bones, though "no fracture of the skull was discovered." Orange Washington had suffered "an incised wound, on top of the head, dividing the scalp to the bone," along with a fractured skull and a cut to the third finger of his right hand. Patsy Gibson had endured an "incised wound, about three and a half or four inches long, diagonally across the right frontal bone, the wound extending to the bone," as well as a fractured skull. Lucinda Boddy had experienced "one lacerated wound over superior lateral portion of right frontal bone, with fracture of the skull." Dr. Richard S. Graves, Jr., who had also examined the victims, agreed with Dr. Weller's findings.[14]

The arrest of Dock Woods was reported in a quite confusing manner. The *Austin Daily Statesman* indicated that the bloody clothes of Dock Woods were presented at the coroner's inquest, which suggests that Woods had already been arrested. Based on the bloody clothes, Woods was indicted for the murder of Gracie Vance. The same report said that "soon after the officers were possessed of the forgoing facts," Oliver Townsend was arrested. The same report then noted that Woods was arrested by Marshal Lee and Deputy Sheriff Hornsby but subsequently released. But the report later stated that Woods was arrested at a different location. According to the report,

> Acting upon all the information developed in the case, Sheriff Hornsby spotted the guilty man, and located him. Summoning two of his deputies, W. W. Hornsby and James Davis, and City Marshal Lee, the party quietly left the city, and proceeded to Mr. Baird's farm, about eight miles south, found and arrested Doc Woods in the cotton patch. He stoutly denied his guilt and

> said he could prove his innocence. Mr. Baird says Doc was on the place at 10 o'clock, Sunday night, and again at 4 o'clock Sunday morning. But it's only eight miles to where he was caught, and his bloody garments tell a horrible tale. He claims that is the result of an old venereal disease. This remains to be proven. He was taken before Lucinda Boddy, who identified him as the perpetrator of the hellish outrage.

Why would Woods be arrested, his bloody clothes taken and presented to the coroner's inquest, and then be indicted for murder, only to be subsequently released and then arrested again later? Either the news report contained factual errors, or the police once again dropped the ball in the case. Other reports suggested that Woods was arrested Monday afternoon by Sheriff Hornsby; Woods was wearing the bloody shirt when he was arrested in the cotton field. Another report indicated that Douglas Woods, the brother of Dock Woods, had also "been arrested on suspicion of being an accessory, if not principal, in the murder." The chronology and details of the events were certainly confused, but the end result was the same: Dock Woods was in custody for the murder of Gracie Vance. (But such reporting does make one wonder what history is based on.)[15]

Further, according to the Fort Worth newspaper, Woods was "without doubt the right man . . . . the author of all the long series of outrages since last fall. This makes seven colored servant girls and women slain and foully murdered in Austin since last Christmas. All were ravished. The only white girls assaulted were two Swedish girls last spring, one of whom still bears the bullet of the scoundrel in her back." Many favored lynching Woods. On Monday night, a large group of blacks gathered on Robertson Hill in east Austin. The Fort Worth reporter felt that "Possibly an attempt may be made before morning. The whites would join the negroes in lynching Woods if they could get to him."[16]

Gracie Vance and Orange Washington were buried in Oakwood Cemetery in Austin on Tuesday, September 29, 1885. According to burial information, Gracie Vance was 22 years old, Orange Washington 21 years old. The cause of death for both was murder. Lucinda Boddy and Patsy Gibson were hospitalized. Various reports indicated that both would die, both had died, Lucinda would probably die, or Patsy would certainly die. Even in their misery, the two survivors were hounded by the press. By Tuesday, Lucinda was "much worse and was very flighty in her statements to Dr. Graves, who questioned her about the matter." Patsy was "in a worse condition and insensible." By Wednesday, the two women were still in "very critical condition." According to an Austin reporter, "Lucinda Boddy is somewhat improved, but there appears to be little, if any, change in Patsy Gibson. Neither are in condition to talk intelligently. Their minds seem to wander and no wonder— Patsy's brain is oozing from the wounds in her skull every few moments. Lucinda's skull is crushed in by the blow she received and the skull bone presses against the brain. If Lucinda recovers there appears to be a chance for the loss of her mind."[17]

Somehow, despite their dire condition, the two injured women gave testimony late Wednesday afternoon. Justice Thomas F. Purnell, District Attorney James

Robertson, and Detectives Mike Hennessy and Hanna, of the Noble Detective Agency of Houston, went to the hospital to interview the women. According to the *Austin Daily Statesman*,

> Patsy Gibson testified that a few nights before the murder Doc Woods came to the house where the murder was committed last Monday morning. He came to the window. No one was there but she and Gracie, and Doc wanted to come in. He was refused admittance. Gracie told Patsy to get the pistol and she would see who it was at the window. The man outside said, it is Doc Woods, and I want to come in and stay all night. Gracie said that she had too many people in the house and that he could not come in. He then ran off. Patsy does not remember much of what happened on the night of the murder; she believes chloroform was used upon all the inmates of the house.

Lucinda Boddy reiterated her earlier claims that Dock Woods was positively the man, or one of the men, who committed the murders.[18]

Beverley Overton, the owner of the horse that was found near the murder scene, had also been arrested. He, however, had a good alibi. Overton lived on E. College Avenue in east Austin. Overton claimed "that on Saturday evening, just before dark, his stepson rode his horse off on an errand. He went to Mr. R.H. Smith's place and hitched the horse to a rack at Wash Craig's. He then went into the store to see Mr. Dunham." Robert H. Smith ran a dry goods and grocery store at 323-325 E. Pecan Street. Washington Craig ran a fruit stand nearby. Mr. Dunham was the same man whose residence was attacked on Monday morning. When the boy left the store, the horse was missing. Overton ventured into town on Monday to see about recovering his horse, and at that time he first heard about the murders. "He told Sergeant Chenneville about his horse and described the property. Sergeant Chenneville told him he knew where the horse was and to go to the station house until he heard from him. He went to the station house and was arrested and lodged in jail." Overton was released a few days later after police accepted his explanation.[19]

Meanwhile, the case against Dock Woods seemed to be strong, and Oliver Townsend had also been implicated. As indicated, a detective agency from Houston had been hired by the Austin City Council to aid in the investigation. For several weeks, two or three of the best men from the Noble Detective Agency had been in Austin working on the various murders and assaults that had plagued Austin for the last nine months. Captain Mike Hennessey of the agency informed the *Austin Daily Statesman* on Wednesday, September 30, that the detectives "had succeeded in getting positive evidence against Dock Woods and Oliver Townsend, the parties charged with the commission of the terrible crime of Sunday night. The evidence is conclusive and leaves no doubt as to the guilt of these parties," according to the detective. Would the police officials for once be correct in their prognostications? Both men were being held without bail.[20]

Two other crimes occurred in the same early morning hours as the murders that had important implications in the Vance case. Twenty minutes before he received the call about the murders at the Dunham residence, Sergeant John Chenneville got a call about an attempted burglary at the home of Dr. Wade A. Morris at 100 W. Peach Street, just west of the capitol. The Morris residence was about a mile south of the Dunham home. Oliver Townsend was arrested for the attempted burglary of the Morris home. Could Townsend have tried to burglarize the Morris home and then traveled a mile north in time to participate in the Vance murders in 15 minutes time? Certainly the distance could be covered in that time, but apparently the Vance murders were already well underway before Major Dunham told Harry Duff to call the police. Could Townsend have been two places at once?[21]

The second crime occurred at the home of James H. Robertson, the district attorney for Travis County and the brother of the mayor of Austin. He lived with his family at 2004 San Antonio, about a half mile from the Dunham residence and halfway between the Morris home and the Dunham residence. Robertson employed a Swedish servant girl to help around the house. At the insistence of Robertson's wife, the girl had moved from the servant's quarters and had "recently commenced sleeping in a room that was deemed safer and less easy of access." At some point late Sunday night, the servant's quarters were entered "by a party, or parties, then unknown. The window was pried up, and through it the intruder gained ingress." The girl was not in the servant's quarters, and she likely had "a narrow escape from the fate that overtook Gracie Vance. The girl's watch, a present from her father in the old country, and inscribed with her name was stolen."[22] This same watch was later found twisted around the arm of Gracie Vance. Was Oliver Townsend the culprit in this burglary? Did he commit the burglary at the Morris home, run north a half mile and burglarize the Robertson home, and then run north another half mile to participate in the Vance killings, all in 15 or 20 minutes time? After all, his initial arrest was for the attempted burglary at the Morris home. Likely the reported times of the crimes were inaccurate. Certainly, though, one of the killers had broken into the room at the Robertson house, unless one wants to believe that Gracie Vance or one of the other victims had committed the crime.

For their part, Woods and Townsend both claimed innocence, as would be expected. Woods said that "he was at Mr. Baird's about eight miles from the town during Sunday and Sunday night; he didn't leave the place until he was at the house at 10 p.m. on Sunday night, and at 4 a.m. Monday; that at 4 a.m. Mr. Baird awakened him from a sound slumber, and he got up, and after eating his breakfast he went to work in the cotton patch; that there are other witnesses to prove this." When the reporter asked Woods if he could prove where he was between 10 P.M. and 4 A.M., Woods admitted only that he could prove he went to bed. Woods claimed the blood on his shirt was from an old venereal disease. When asked if he knew the women who were assaulted, he replied: "I did not. I have seen Gracie a few times; was not much acquainted with her. The other woman I did not know by sight. My first acquaintance with Orange and Gracie was about six months ago." Oliver Townsend claimed he left church about 9 P.M. Sunday night and met his neighbor, Mr. Graham, by his gate. He had no other witness besides his mother to say where he was Sunday night. He also said he did not know the victims and knew Gracie Vance "by sight only."[23]

"Testimony of Johnson Trigg"

But the Noble detectives claimed to have "conclusive" proof of the guilt of Woods and Townsend. That damning proof was in the form of a story by Johnson Trigg, a young black man about 19 years old. In the 1880 census, Trigg was listed as living in Bastrop County in a household of 11 people. He was the sixth of seven children of Wilson and Peggy Trigg. Census notes indicated that the young Trigg was so sick or disabled that he was unable to perform ordinary work. At some point between 1880 and 1882, Trigg moved to Austin. In 1885, he was working as a waiter at the Carrollton House, a hotel at 204-208 West Pecan Street; Trigg resided at the hotel, as well. He was just a young black man trying to earn a living, that is, until he came forward with a story that seemed to confirm the guilt of Woods and Townsend.[24]

Following is the sworn testimony of Johnson Trigg against Woods and Townsend, given before Justice Thomas F. Purnell, in its entirety as published in the *Austin Daily Statesman*. It makes for intriguing reading and seems to seal the fate of the two suspects. The circuitous route taken by Townsend took him "down to that portion of the city known as Mexico," or Guy Town, and then to a couple of other places before heading to Gracie Vance's place. However, no mention is made of Townsend trying to burglarize the Morris residence. The man meeting with Townsend at the post office and later at Vance's house, though suggested by Trigg to be two different men, was reported by the *Statesman* to be Dock Woods.

> I know Oliver Townsend; I saw him on the night of the 27th of September, 1885; I saw him on the corner of Colorado and Pecan streets in Austin; he was talking to some man; I did not know the man Oliver was talking with, but I would know him again if I saw him; Oliver and the man was on the corner and I was on the post office step; they were talking; I heard what they said; I heard Oliver Townsend say to the man with him, that he, Oliver Townsend, was going up to kill Gracie Vance; the other man then said to Oliver Townsend, "you will be caught up with," and Oliver Townsend answered, "I have been killing them and I have not been caught up with yet." They remained on the corner of Colorado and Pecan streets about an hour; when I first saw them on the corner of said streets it was about 9 o'clock p.m.; I saw them when they went away from there. They separated—one going west on Pecan street, and the other going north on Colorado street as far as the next street north of Pecan, and then came back to Pecan street; he then went by the Carrolton house, and from there went towards the Baptist church; he then went from there to the house where Gracie Vance and Orange Washington were murdered. When he got to this house another man met Oliver Townsend near the west corner of the house. They were talking. I heard

the man who met Oliver Townsend say to him: "You had better not go in there tonight." Oliver Townsend said: "Yes I will. I am going to kill Gracie Vance tonight." They then went into the house together—Oliver and the other man. As near as I can measure the time, in about ten minutes after Oliver Townsend and the other man went into the house I heard a woman cry out: "Oh! please don't kill me" and a man's voice answered and said "Shut up, G-d d--n you! Don't look at me;" as near as I can tell this happened about 1 o'clock or a little after; I did not see how they (Oliver and the other man) got in the house; I saw them disappear and the next thing I knew I heard them in the house; I was in about fifteen steps of the house; when I heard the woman cry out I left and went home; Gracie Vance and Orange Washington were murdered that night, which was the 27th of September, 1885; they were killed in the house where I saw Oliver Townsend and the other man; the house where this was done was near the residence of Mr. Duff, who owns the Iron Front Saloon, the house is in this county; I never lost sight of Oliver Townsend, from the time I first saw him and the other man talking on the corner of Colorado and Pecan streets, about 9 o'clock p.m. until he went into the house where Gracie Vance and Orange Washington were murdered; the moon was shining brightly.

I am certain Oliver Townsend is the man I saw on Pecan and Colorado streets, and whom I followed to the house where the murder was done; the reason I followed Oliver Townsend was because I heard him say he was going to kill Gracie Vance, and wanted to see if he would do what he said he would; previous to this, and before Becky Ramey was killed I heard Oliver Townsend say, one night, at the Black Elephant saloon, during the early part of the night, that Ramey was murdered, that he was going to kill her; I saw him go to Mr. Weed's house, on the night Becky Ramey was killed; he went there about 2 o'clock, or perhaps later in the night; another reason why I followed Oliver Townsend on the night of the 27th of September, was because on the night Becky Ramey was killed, I heard Oliver say he was going to kill her, and when I heard him say he was going to kill Gracie Vance I thought I would follow and see what he would do.

The reason I did not tell that I saw Oliver Townsend go to Mr. Weed's on the night Becky Ramey was killed was I did not know for certain that he killed her, but I thought I would wait and see; so when I heard the other threats made by him and followed him and learned what he did, I told what I knew.

An eyewitness account that seemed to solve at least two in the series of murders certainly would be welcome news for the beleaguered police department and all the citizens of Austin, but was Trigg's testimony reliable? Only time would tell. But he did have at least one inaccuracy in his testimony, claiming that Becky Ramey was killed. And one wonders how he could get so close to hear the planning and the voices in the shack without being detected himself. Was he an accomplice in the murders?[25]

In an interesting related note, an unidentified black man told the *Statesman* reporter that on the Sunday night just before her murder, "he heard Gracie Vance say that she was afraid to go home because there were some men in Austin who were mad with her and she feared they might do her harm." Could those men have been Dock Woods and Oliver Townsend? And if so, why did they want to harm Gracie Vance?[26]

Notes

Title: *Fort Worth Daily Gazette*, 9/29/1885.
Map credit: Vance murder scene excerpted from Koch's *Austin Bird's-Eye Map, 1887*.

1. *San Antonio Daily Light*, 9/8/1885; *Bartholomew Diary* 20:186, 9/14/1885; "Monthly Record of Observations Taken at Stations in the Cotton Region," Austin, October 1885; "Lunar calendar."
2. *San Antonio Daily Express*, 9/28/1885; *Austin Daily Statesman*, 9/29/1885; *Morrison & Fourmy's General Directory of the City of Austin, 1885-1886*. (Dunham's address was sometimes listed as 2310 San Marcos. At the time, Guadalupe Street and a section of San Marcos Street ran side by side near the university. The 1887 Koch map clearly shows "W. San Marcos Street" running side by side with Guadalupe Street just above the dogleg turn at 19th Street (MLK Blvd). Some say this placement of San Marcos Street was an error, but the San Marcos River is geographically next to the Guadalupe River.)
3. *Austin Daily Statesman*, 10/1/1885; 1880 Federal Census; Oakwood Cemetery Database (Perhaps the boy was Tom Vance, son of Charles Vance, who was apparently the brother of Gracie's mother, Eliza. Tom would have been about 19 at the time, a year younger than Gracie. The only problem with that supposition was that Tom seemed to have died in 1882 of brain fever. Gracie had another cousin named James, the same as her brother's name, but the cousin would have been about 23 at the time of the murder.)
4. *Austin Daily Statesman*, 10/1/1885; 1880 Federal Census; 1870 Federal Census; *Morrison & Fourmy's General Directory of the City of Austin, 1885-1886*.
5. *San Antonio Daily Express*, 9/28/1885; *Austin Daily Statesman*, 10/1/1885; *Fort Worth Daily Gazette*, 9/29/1885.
6. *Austin Daily Statesman*, 10/1/1885; *New York Sun*, 9/30/1885; *Richmond Dispatch*, 9/30/1885; *Morrison & Fourmy's General Directory of the City of Austin, 1885-1886*.
7. *Austin Daily Statesman*, 10/1/1885; *San Antonio Daily Express*, 9/28/1885; *Fort Worth Daily Gazette*, 9/29/1885.
8. *Salt Lake Daily Herald*, 9/30/1885; *Austin Daily Statesman*, 10/1/1885; *San Antonio Daily Express*, 9/28/1885.
9. *Austin Daily Statesman*, 9/29/1885.
10. *Fort Worth Daily Gazette*, 9/29/1885; *Salt Lake Daily Herald*, 9/30/1885; *New York Sun*, 9/30/1885; *Richmond Dispatch*, 9/30/1885; *Austin Daily Statesman*, 10/1/1885.
11. *Fort Worth Daily Gazette*, 9/29/1885; *San Antonio Daily Express*, 9/28/1885.
12. *Austin Daily Statesman*, 9/29/1885; *San Antonio Daily Express*, 9/28/1885.
13. *Austin Daily Statesman*, 9/29/1885; *San Antonio Daily Express*, 9/28/1885.

14. *Austin Daily Statesman*, 9/29/1885; *San Antonio Daily Express*, 9/28/1885; *Morrison & Fourmy's General Directory of the City of Austin, 1885-1886*.
15. *Austin Daily Statesman*, 9/29/1885; *Fort Worth Daily Gazette*, 9/29/1885; *Atchison Daily Globe*, 9/30/1885; *Galveston Daily News*, 9/29/1885; 1880 Federal Census (The 1880 census listed a Douglas Woods and a D. Woods, one aged 21, the other 22; both were born in Texas to parents born in Virginia, and both were married to a 17-year-old girl named Jennie who was born in Texas. Also, the cotton field in which Woods may have been arrested was owned by a Mr. Baird, either F. J. Baird or M.C. Baird, apparently brothers, located eight miles south of Austin.)
16. *Fort Worth Daily Gazette*, 9/29/1885.
17. *Austin Daily Statesman*, 10/1/1885; *Fort Worth Daily Gazette*, 9/29/1885; *New York Sun*, 9/30/1885; *McCook Weekly Tribune*, 10/8/1885; *Maysville Daily Evening Bulletin*, 9/30/1885; Oakwood Cemetery Database.
18. *San Antonio Daily Express*, 9/30/1885; *Austin Daily Statesman*, 10/1/1885.
19. *Austin Daily Statesman*, 10/1/1885; *Morrison & Fourmy's General Directory of the City of Austin, 1885-1886*; Galloway, *The Servant Girl Murders*: 275.
20. *San Antonio Daily Express*, 9/30/1885; *Austin Daily Statesman*, 10/1/1885; *Fort Worth Daily Gazette*, 9/30/1885.
21. *Austin Daily Statesman*, 9/29/1885.
22. *San Antonio Daily Express*, 9/30/1885; *Austin Daily Statesman*, 10/1/1885; *Fort Worth Daily Gazette*, 9/30/1885.
23. *Austin Daily Statesman*, 10/1/1885; *Austin Daily Statesman*, 9/29/1885.
24. *Morrison & Fourmy's General Directory of the City of Austin, 1885-1886*; 1880 Federal Census.
25. *Austin Daily Statesman*, 10/1/1885.
26. *Austin Daily Statesman*, 10/1/1885.

Chapter 8

"Every Effort to Ferret Out the Fiends"

The Evidence Begins to Unravel

Through October, the local buzz over the Vance case still resonated in the public voice. Had the police and detectives really cracked the case of the servant girl murders? Though Johnson Trigg's testimony might have been considered proof positive by the police and detectives, the young man's story was met with a certain amount of incredulity by the people of Austin. The story seemed too pat, too contrived. How could he have been so close as to hear the conversations without being detected himself? Was he a part of the plot to kill Gracie Vance? Or was he a young country boy from a large family who arrived in the big city and wanted to be the center of attention?

Other questions remained unanswered. If Woods and Townsend did kill Gracie Vance, why? And if Woods and Townsend did kill Gracie Vance, did they also kill all the other women and stage all the home assaults in the spring? Did they act alone, or were they part of a larger scheme? Was Major Dunham, the editor of the *Texas Court Reporter*, the target of intimidation, or was Gracie Vance the target and the other three only hapless victims?

As a lawyer and editor of the *Texas Court Reporter*, William B. Dunham certainly could have generated some enemies in his few years in Austin. Born in Tennessee in 1848, he arrived in Austin sometime in the 1870s. In 1876, he was the chief clerk in the attorney general's office. By the late 1870s, he was an assistant attorney general, arguing cases before the Texas Court of Appeals. He then worked as a clerk in the State Comptroller's Office and resided at Margaret Andrews' boarding house on Congress Avenue. At that time, William M. Brown was the state comptroller. Dunham was married and with a daughter by August 1881. By 1885, he was editor of the *Texas Court Reporter* published by Eugene Von Boeckmann Company. How he gained the title of major is unclear, since he would have been too young to be an officer in the Civil War. Through the remainder of the 1880s, he continued as a lawyer, though he moved from the dreaded Guadalupe address to 303 East 14th Street. By the late 1890s, he was a pardon adviser for the state and working at the capitol. By 1905, he had become a judge and still lived at the East 14th address. His daughter was working as an assistant librarian at the state university. Dunham died in December 1912 at the age of 64. Could his position as an attorney and legal editor make a target for vengeance?[1]

Gracie Vance may have been married before she took up with Orange Washington. On February 22, 1881, in Travis County, Texas, a Gracy Vance married Albert Hall, a mulatto man born around 1861. In 1880, Hall was working as a drayman and residing with his brother William Hall, William's wife, and several siblings. By 1881, Albert Hall was residing with Mary Hall, apparently another sister who was indicated in the 1880 census as having a general debility. By 1885, Hall was living at 304 Onion Street, still in town. Could jealousy and marital discord actually have been the cause of this latest murder, proving the summer prognostications correct?[2]

And though Dock Woods denied knowing Gracie Vance, he may have known her very well. According to the *San Antonio Express*, Woods "had been the friend and supposed keeper of Gracie Vance before Washington possessed her, whether as a wife or mistress whichever was the true relation between the parties, and it may be the murder was the result of a contention for her between the two men without any peculiar violence being contemplated by Woods against Gracie." The fact that Gracie Vance was hacked with an ax, outraged, and then beaten with a brick tends to discredit this supposition.[3]

Just as the summer had its theory that all the murders were the result of jealousy and romantic discord, new theories began to arise. The Fort Worth newspaper reported that "there is feeling now that these outrages will stop unless there is an organized gang." Regarding the Vance murder, a report in the *Salt Lake Daily Herald*, which obviously had a few facts wrong, noted that "the details of the crime resemble closely that of the murder of Mary Rainey and daughter a few weeks ago, and it is generally believed the same fiends committed both crimes." Prosecutor E. Taylor Moore of Austin believed that all the murders had been "committed by a single perpetrator who hated women, but his ideas were mocked by his colleagues." The *Atchison Daily Globe* imagined that the watch found on Gracie Vance "may have been tied to the arm as a device to fasten suspicion on the owner." Was the *Daily Globe's* suggestion that a Swedish servant girl was the murderer?[4]

The *Austin Daily Statesman* was the most spirited in its theorizing. It presented numerous theories about the murders and who might be committing them. But most of the theories had already been sounded before, and nothing had been done to confirm or deny their validity. According to the *Statesman*:

> There are many theories about the frequent murders, and attempts at murder, of negro servant girls during the past summer. One theory is, that it is the work of a secret organization, whose object is to stamp out negro prostitution and compel the race, if they live together, to live in the bonds of matrimony. This theory is confirmed to some extent by two significant facts; one is that the girl Gracie was living with Orange Washington without resorting to the formality of legal marriage, and that the negro population differ in their opinions on the subject of the murders. Intelligent negroes represent that some of their people condemn the murders while others

> think that those who have been killed, or attempted to be killed deserved it. There is one other significant fact connected with the investigation that has been going on; where there were any left alive to tell of the circumstances of the murder, they have several times said they identified the man, but shortly afterwards denied that they did. This seems as if they had been instructed by some secret power that held them under terror.

This theory reiterated the notion of a secret league of negroes committing the murders, but its contention that the goal was to wipe out negro prostitution and cohabitation had limited validity. It might have been potentially true in the cases of Mollie Smith and Gracie Vance, but it did not seem to have any bearing whatsoever on the cases of Eliza Shelly, Irene Cross, and Becky and Mary Ramey.[5]

The *Statesman* continued with its theories, giving voice to a common perception at the time.

> Another theory is that the murders have been perpetrated by a band of negro men out of a spirit of pure cussedness and reckless wickedness. It is hard to believe that negroes who have lived and been raised in a Christian community should at once plunge into such desperate wickedness. But idleness and drink will lead off these ignorant creatures and there is no telling if they are permitted to idle about a town of this size what they will do finally; there is no doubt but they will resort to theft and then it is but a small step to murder.

The article then called on the black population of Austin to rise up against the transgressors, noting that "As a general thing Austin has a very respectable negro population and they ought to do all they can to bring to punishment those of their race who are disgracing their good character. They can do this by giving information of the idle and worthless of their number." The article concluded with a statement of profound irony: "It seems to be very generally understood that there is no danger of attempts of this kind being made on the white population." The article noted that Austin had become the "best armed city in the United States" and that likely each home in town had "at least fourteen rounds of ammunition."[6] Unfortunately, all the ammunition in the world had done little to end the string of murders.

The Fort Worth newspaper chimed in with a ridiculous notion: "The theory has been advanced that the murderer of Austin cooks is some fellow whose spirit thirsted for revenge after having sojourned at the Austin hotels." With such a silly comment, the article only made light of a serious situation, reinforcing the idea that the victims were only negro servant girls, so the crimes were somehow less heinous. And the Waco newspaper added its own sarcastic remark that "No Austin cook climbed the golden stairs last night."[7]

The Noble (Pinkerton) detectives had theories of their own, and those theories coincided with the unraveling of the evidence against Woods and Townsend.

Despite the arrest of the two men and the threats of lynching them, calmer minds prevailed, and with that calm came doubt. The *San Antonio Express* surmised that Woods and Townsend

> may after all not be the guilty parties. Indeed it is now stated that the Pinkerton detectives, who have been here for some time trying to work up the previous Ramey outrage, have by taking all the recent outrages into connection with that of Sunday night evolved a theory of their own, indicating that the men arrested for the crime are not the proper parties and pointing more decidedly, as they think, to others they have in view, who they conclude are the authors of all the recent outrages in Austin, one of whom was lately arrested for some minor offense. It is stated that they have the story of a negro, who planned the Sunday night murder based on the statement of another negro who professed to have heard the planning, if not himself a party to it. This may serve well enough for the usual airy fabric of theorizing in such matters, but any one familiar with the character of such statements by negroes will not take much stock in them, as negroes are proverbial for saying and doing things merely to gratify grudges of their own, or further the grudges of their friends against other parties.

One of those other suspects was Alex Mack. A second may have been Glenn Drummer.[8]

The San Antonio report went on to reveal that the blood on Dock Woods' shirt was not the blood of the Vance victims, but proved "to be the result of an old Syphilitic infection, and fully accounted for from that cause" by Dr. Richard Graves. The newspaper opined that Woods "would have hardly had it on when arrested while picking cotton Monday evening, if it had been befouled with the blood of a murdered victim," which makes perfect sense. An *Austin Daily Statesman* report verified that the blood on the shirt was from a "chronic disease." Based on this evidence, according to Dr. Graves, an outrage of Gracie Vance could not have been the primary motive in the case. Graves believed that "murder only seems to have been their object."[9]

The San Antonio article also added an interesting twist to the watch evidence and the eyewitness account of Lucinda Boddy. The article noted that the watch found on Gracie's body "may have been the cause of a general quarrel among all the parties, including the girls Lucinda and Patsy, who were so badly wounded that they are not expected to recover." This comment does not make much sense unless one believes that one of the four victims in the Vance case had also been the person who burglarized District Attorney Robertson's home and stole the watch. The article further speculated that

> Doc Woods may not have been the murderer, despite the fact that Lucinda says he was the man, as she has not since professed to recognize him and is in such a condition of mind that her statements are not fully reliable, even if not based on

> some grudge against him. Her testimony if she recovers, will be of great importance, in view of her statement, previously made in a rational moment, that Doc Woods was the man who struck her several times with a sand bag, and if so was the assailant, or one of them. If there were others, who did the killing?

That final question was on everyone's mind as the positive proof began to unravel.[10]

The sworn testimony of Johnson Trigg was also being called into question. According to the *Dallas Herald*, "The evidence . . . that he heard Oliver Townsend and Doc Woods plotting the murder and saw them enter the house where parties were murdered and left without giving some alarm is not generally credited." Many thought Trigg should be arrested for lying. One does have to wonder about the motives of Johnson Trigg. His ability to overhear the conversation and follow the men without being detected stretches the imagination. Was he trying to cover his own involvement by incriminating Woods and Townsend? Did he have some grudge against the men? Could Trigg have been the young man in the cabin with Lucinda Boddy on Sunday evening that Major Dunham told to leave? Trigg would have been about 19 at the time of the murder. Another curious fact can be found in the 1880 census. As mentioned earlier, in 1880 Trigg lived in nearby Bastrop in a very large household. One member of that household was an 80-year-old black man by the name of Lewis Washington. Lewis Washington was born in Virginia in 1800. Orange Washington's father, Leo Washington, was born in Virginia around 1831. Could Lewis Washington have been Orange Washington's grandfather, giving Trigg a motive for revenge against Townsend and Woods, if indeed they were the murderers?[11]

Whatever his motive, Johnson Trigg soon revealed that his sworn testimony against Woods and Townsend was pure fabrication. By the middle of October, he was in the county jail. According to the *Austin Daily Statesman*, "Johnson Trigg is the brave youth who put up that big yarn and then acknowledged afterwards that he lied. He is charged with perjury and will probably be slinging hash around Huntsville," the location of the state penitentiary. Later, he "was convicted and sentenced to the penitentiary for 5 years for perjury in swearing that Townsend and Woods committed the Ramey murder." So, the conclusive evidence that left no doubt as to the guilt of Woods and Townsend was no longer so conclusive. Nonetheless, in mid-October, Woods and Townsend remained in jail on charges of murder.[12]

"A Narrow Escape"

A series of other arrests only muddied the circumstances surrounding the Vance murders. On September 25, 1885, the Friday night before Gracie Vance was murdered, a recalcitrant ne'er-do-well named Glenn Drummer tried to shoot two other black men. Drummer, who apparently was only about 15 years old, worked as a cook and boarded at the Capital Hotel, located at 1005 Congress Avenue and managed by Thomas A. Burdett. Drummer had spent considerable time in jail during the summer for carrying a pistol. He was released from jail after failing to pay off his fine on the condition that he leave the city. He did leave temporarily but kept returning and dodging the police. This time, though, he was apprehended, and after a default on a $1000 bond, he was sent to prison to await grand jury action on his charge of assault with intent to murder. Also retained was Alex Mack, "a supposed confederate of Drummer," who was arrested for being a suspicious character. Mack had a long arrest record, possibly the longest in Austin. He was a laborer and gambler in his mid-thirties. Both Mack and Drummer were "suspected of being concerned in other outrages."[13]

On the following Friday night, October 2, a shooting occurred at a house on Nursery Street. In the house resided Anderson Murray and his wife, and also Jim Glover, all black. According to Murray, who was about 23 at the time, he and his wife and Glover had left the house and returned about 9 P.M. on Friday night. They went inside and lit a lamp. Soon after, someone approached the gate, and Murray went to see who it was. As Murray opened the door, the man at the gate started shooting at him. "Glover then ran out of the room he occupied, with a pistol in his hand, and as he did so the would-be assassin opened fire upon him. Glover returned the fire, and discharged five chambers of his revolver at the man near the gate. One of the balls from the attacking party's pistol struck Glover on the forehead, but beyond knocking the skin off, did no harm." The man then fled. Anderson and his wife were not injured. Police arrived shortly thereafter and began an earnest search for the culprit.[14]

Jim Glover in 1885 was working for Harry Duff, the proprietor of the Iron Front Saloon who was involved in the recent Gracie Vance murders a few days earlier, and living at his residence. Duff lived across the street from Major Dunham, at whose home the murders occurred. Anderson Murray worked as a porter at Frand and Frisch's Saloon at 1011 Congress Avenue, about five blocks north of the Iron Front Saloon run by Duff. In the early 1880s, Murray worked for Edward Creary, the county sheriff at the time, and resided at his home.[15]

Though a news report on October 1 suggested that Glenn Drummer had been sent to prison for defaulting on a bond, a report on October 4 indicated that Drummer was arrested by Sheriff Malcolm Hornsby for shooting at Jim Glover in the Nursery Street incident. Drummer was arrested on a Mr. Smith's farm about six miles from Austin. Drummer surrendered without resistance. The report noted that "Drummer favors Doc Woods so much it is possible he may have been the man Lucinda Boddy took for Woods." In any case, Glenn Drummer was in custody again. Alex Mack was also implicated in the shooting. According to Galloway, Jim Glover "accused Drummer of trying to kill him. While no reason was given for the attack on Glover in the newspaper, Glover had been arrested 15 May 1885 on a complaint made by Drummer. This was possibly part of an ongoing feud between the two men."[16]

In the middle of October, at least six black men were in county jail on suspicion of involvement in the murders throughout the year. The charge against

Glenn Drummer was "assault and attempt to kill." The grand jury was expected to indict Drummer on a charge of murder of at least one of the servant girls. Dock Woods and Oliver Townsend were locked up together. Both these men maintained their innocence, and little evidence seemed to implicate them in any of the murders, especially since Johnson Trigg's testimony had been discredited. "Lucinda Boddy, when confronted by Doc, swore positively that he was the man and that Drummer is not. This appears bad for Doc." Johnson Trigg had been charged with perjury and was awaiting trial. Finally, Ike Plummer and some man named Dave Woods were in jail with a charge of murder. Plummer had been implicated in the Shelly murder, but no information could be found about Dave Woods. This was the first appearance of his name in relation to any of the crimes. Perhaps this person was really Dock Woods or perhaps Douglas Woods, the man mentioned in relation to the Vance murders in Chapter 7. Meanwhile, one of the chief suspects, Alex Mack, was apparently running around free.[17]

Despite the fact that several men had been arrested, the evidence against them in relation to the servant girl murders was slim. Lucinda Boddy, with her addled mind, still accused Dock Woods. The damning evidence given by Johnson Trigg was just a fabrication. Galloway suggested that Trigg may have been involved in a frame-up. Galloway too wondered why Trigg would concoct such a story and then offered a possible answer. According to Galloway, "Trigg worked as a waiter at the Carrolton Hotel, which was coincidentally the Austin headquarters of detectives Hennessey and Hanna. Whether he was coaxed into the fabricating the story by the detectives or if he did it on his own initiative is unknown. It seems unlikely that he would testify against Townsend without some sort of compensation, considering that retribution from Townsend was a distinct possibility." Ultimately, the grand jury did not indict any of the suspects on charges of murder. Drummer was indicted for the assault and attempted murder of Jim Glover, but in November Drummer went to trial, provided a suitable alibi, and was acquitted. So all the strong leads and conclusive evidence produced naught.[18]

"To Your Tents, Oh Israel"

The failure of the police and detectives to obtain any solid evidence reignited criticism of the local government. The local *Austin Daily Statesman* again took the lead in calling for change and more decisive action. In recapping the murders, the *Statesman* mirrored the frustration that had seized the Austin populace.

> On a brilliant moonlight night, on one of the principal avenues of the city, and a hundred yards from the university grounds, open and almost public wholesale murder has been done. . . . We make the record with shame that it is possible that such a thing could occur without the perpetrators of the horrible deed being at once apprehended and punished to the full penalty of the law. This last wholesale butchery is in keeping with the several others of the same kind that have been perpetrated in this city during the summer. In every instance the attack has been made on servant girls living in outhouses in the yards of

> residences, and in every instance the murders have been in such conspicuous places and at such times of the night that it would seem even impossible for the guilty parties to escape, but in every instance they have gone scot free, the officer of law not being able to even obtain a clue to be guided in arrest of the murderers. This thing has gone far enough. It must be stopped at any and all cost.

The newspaper then predicted a chilling and ironic scenario that would occur if the crimes were not brought to an end.

> Heretofore, these attacks have been made on negro servant girls, with one exception, and as far as could be found out, by negro men. These people are just as much entitled to protection as anybody else, but we have no assurances if these murderers are permitted to go unpunished, that it will not extend to other victims. If impunity is longer allowed, we will be startled some morning by the announcement that some gentleman's family have been murdered in their beds and it is time now that it should be considered the business of every citizen to become a guardian of life and property. The officers of law have failed to give us protection or any assurances that they can suppress these murders, although we have reason to believe the city authorities have done everything they could to meet the anomalous condition, in regard to these murders. Let us remember that the assassin with the hatchet and revolver, walks with impunity upon our streets, and that there are but frail panes of glass between them and our smooth and fair-skinned wives and daughters, sleeping in fancied security in our homes.

What could be done to stop the wave of murders? How could a man protect his family if the police were unable to do so? The newspaper had a simple solution. The citizenry should rise up and form vigilante committees.

> No man has any assurances that his own family will not fall the victims of these ravishers and murderers. We have trusted to the protection of the officers of the law long enough. Let us organize at once, into a vigilance committee, if necessary, and let us select some man of discretion and shrewdness as the president of the committee to take absolute charge and organize the citizens of every ward into detectives and patrols to keep watch day and night in every part of the city. This is a public duty, just as imperative as if a band of Comanche Indians were encamped near the city, a duty we owe to each other, to our families. Then to your tents, Oh Israel. Meet together in town meeting and organize. You are men capable of protecting your families.

The call to action delved to the heart of civil society. If government cannot protect a person, that person has the right to protect himself. If a group of people are not protected, then they have the right to protect themselves, and vigilante committees, as anarchic as that proposition might be, seemed to be the best solution. "When the most efficient officers are at a loss to detect crime," then the citizenry must take it upon themselves to fight such affronts to civil society.[19]

As if motivated by, or fearful of, the *Statesman's* call for vigilante action, the Austin city council took action of its own. The council met on Monday, October 7, a week after the Vance murders. The meeting began with an address by Mayor John W. Robertson, in which he detailed the actions he had taken to end the crime spree. He noted that he had hired "skillful and trustworthy" detectives as directed by the council, but that he would need additional funds to keep them on the job. He boasted that the detectives had "collected much valuable information concerning the perpetration of the crimes" and had arrested several suspects. He noted that the grand jury was in session, so he could not divulge much pertinent information, but he "confidently believed that some of the authors of these outrages are now in custody, with facts and circumstances that give promise of an early conviction." As noted earlier, though, the evidence collected had been largely discredited and the men arrested were soon released.[20]

Mayor Robertson also commented about the crimes themselves and the criticism of the police force.

> Much has been said about the inefficiency of the police force in preventing and suppressing these crimes. But we should look at all the facts and surroundings before joining in wholesale condemnation of these officers. These crimes are abnormal in their character. They occur when and where least expected. They are shadowed in mystery. A motive is wanting. They have baffled the power of the most skillful experts in the detection of crime. I believe I can safely assert that the police force of the city have discharged their duties to the best of their abilities under the circumstances and that they have been faithful and vigilant.

The mayor went on to make several recommendations to strengthen the police force. He called for the addition of five more officers to the night police force at a cost of $300 a month. He also called for an ordinance that basically considered a person out after midnight guilty until proven innocent. Robertson said that "a person who is unknown to the officer, or who cannot give a reasonable account of himself, or who is found under suspicious circumstances, after midnight, should be arrested, and detained until his conduct and purposes are explained." This ordinance, of course, assumed that the murderers would be someone unknown to the police.[21]

The council then began to deliberate reasonable actions to thwart the continued crimes. The council decided that a reward would help to bring the culprits to justice, but the particulars of the reward generated a goodly amount of ire. Alderman Radcliff Platt, owner of a livery stable, opposed any reward at all. The mayor thought the reward should be offered to nonresidents only, as the local police "should do their duty without moneyed rewards." Aldermen Robert J. Hill, an attorney, and Royal B. Underhill, who ran a marble works, favored a $500 reward. After Alderman Platt railed against the lackadaisical attitude of some police officers, Alderman Hill moved to offer a $250 reward. "Alderman Underhill moved to amend by making the amount $500, and Alderman Platt moved to make it $100." Alderman Hill's motion was finally accepted, and the reward amount was set at $250. Alderman Platt continued his dissent, saying a large "reward would result in convicting innocent men. The story told by Trigg, the darkey, was foxed up for him by somebody. Big rewards would be an incentive to commit perjury."[22]

After the ordinance was passed, Alderman Hill then offered a proviso to the ordinance that excluded local officers from collecting the reward. Alderman Underhill "moved to amend the proviso by including the very ones it sought to exclude." Alderman Platt continued his opposition to the reward. "Alderman Platt thought this looked like fixing up a fat thing for some secret detective force to be imported here to the ignorance and detriment of our own police force. He thought it too late now, to catch up with the perpetrators of the late outrages. The only chance is for the perpetrators to 'blow' on each other. 'It is hardly possible that the one in jail will blow on himself.' He was strongly opposed to the proviso." Alderman Hill's proviso, without Alderman Underhill's amendment, was finally accepted. The council ultimately voted to offer

> a reward of not more than two hundred and fifty dollars for the arrest and conviction of any and every person who has heretofore been, or who may hereafter be guilty of murder, rape, robbery, burglary or arson, or of an assault committed in the night time with intent to commit murder, rape, robbery, within the limits of the city of Austin. Such reward shall be paid to the person or persons securing the arrest and conviction of such offenders, upon the approval and recommendation of the police committee of the city council; provided, that no peace officer or detective of the city, county or state shall participate in any such reward.

The council also empowered the mayor to employ detectives for as long as necessary, and that services provided by the detectives would be kept secret. The council had finally taken some decisive action, but would it be enough?[23]

The next day, the *Austin Daily Statesman* reported that a local author was going to release soon "a thrilling story with the scene laid in Austin." The book was to be entitled *Buckeye Bill; or, the Servant Girl's Terror*. Whether this book was ever published in questionable. If so, it was as ineffective as the police force and the detectives in solving the series of murders.[24]

The Vance murders would be on the minds of Austinites for months. Though eerily similar to the earlier killings, there were some marked differences in this set of murders. As before, the servant girl of a prominent white citizen was attacked. An ax was used against the victims, as in several of the earlier murders, and rape was also a factor. But for the first time, a man was killed, though Walter Spencer had been bludgeoned in the first murder back in December 1884. And the news media began to report on the crime differently, providing many more details than for the earlier attacks. The press also began to intimate that the murders might be committed by more than one person. And though the police and now hired detectives collected mounds of evidence, most of it proved unreliable, and the men arrested were later released for lack of evidence. The string of murders had gone on for nine months, and a solution was no nearer than it had been at the very beginning.

"Enough to Frighten Any Lady"

Just as the mayor and the city council were trying their best to assure Austin citizens that they and the police were managing the crisis, the marshal and several cohorts were doing their best to belie those assurances. After the fabricated testimony of Johnson Trigg failed to stick and all the conclusive evidence seemed much less conclusive, Marshal Lee and the detectives decided to try a new approach. The new approach, abduction and intimidation, failed to produce the desired results and ultimately led to the replacement of Grooms Lee as city marshal.

After Dock Woods and Oliver Townsend lost their luster as potential suspects in the Vance case, Marshal Lee decided to go after Alex Mack again. As noted in earlier chapters, Mack was implicated in the murders of Mary Ramey and Gracie Vance, and he was also suspected in the shooting of Jim Glover. Though Mack had a voluminous arrest record, he managed to be released shortly after each arrest regarding these cases. But Marshal Lee was convinced that Mack was a viable suspect, so he did not give up in his pursuit of Mack. On the night of October 3, Lee and several of his cohorts decided to try to coax a confession from Mack by assaulting him and threatening to lynch him. The assault of Mack would probably have gone unnoticed if he had not contacted the notorious W.Y. Leader of the *Austin Daily Dispatch* to tell his story. Though Leader was involved in several libel and forgery cases, as noted in earlier chapters, he had the support of some of the richest men in Austin. An excerpt from Mack's account, which appeared on October 15 in Leader's newspaper, follows.

> On Saturday night, October 3 . . . Marshal Lee went to the door of Hugh Hancock's saloon, on east Pecan street, the Black Elephant, and called to a colored man named Alex Mack, to come to the door. Mack says he told him he wanted him to go down the street to identify two colored men. He went with the marshal to Red River street, where he found Officer Johnson and three other men, whom he was afterwards told were detectives. One of the men had a rope. Mack asked what they wanted. They told him to go on, and they would show him. He commenced to follow, when they choked him, and finally put the rope around his neck and led him to the vicinity of the colored Methodist church. Here they asked him what he knew about the murder. He told them he knew nothing. He says they knocked him down, stamped and kicked him. They told him

they would make him tell about the murder. He repeated he knew nothing of it and they took him to the city jail, where they kept him chained for nine days, and then discharged him. When brought to our office yesterday, he was covered with bruises and scars.

The route that Mack narrated would have taken the group from the Black Elephant Saloon at 424 East Pecan, east to Red River Street, north to Hickory or Ash, west to near the Wesley Chapel Methodist-Episcopal Church at the southwest corner of East Ash and Neches, and then west to the city jail at the northwest corner of West Hickory and Colorado.[25]

The *Austin Daily Statesman*, upon learning of the article in the *Dispatch*, sent a reporter to get Marshal Lee's side of the story. Marshal Lee, of course, denied any such allegations made by Alex Mack and said that any injuries he had suffered were from his own failure to submit peacefully to arrest. According to Lee's statement in the *Statesman*:

> I emphatically pronounce the publication a malicious falsehood, concocted in the most damnable spirit, and I know the animus which prompted it and is now giving it newspaper prominence. For a long time past I have had sufficient grounds for believing that Alex Mack was connected with the murder of Becky Ramey. . . . About 2 o'clock on Sunday morning, October 4, calling Officers Johnson and Conners, and Detectives Hennessy and Hanna to my aid, I proceeded to the Black Elephant saloon, where I expected to find Alex Mack. Upon reaching the saloon I halted in front, while those with me proceeded some distance beyond. Seeing Alex inside, I called him to come to the door and asked him to go with me. I saw he was very drunk and expected to have trouble with him, knowing his vicious disposition when under the influence of liquor. Passing from the front of the saloon, beyond the light, I said to Mack that I had to arrest him, and it was done on the (pretended) charge that he had struck someone in the face with a beer glass. Mack said "all right, I'll go to jail for that." Upon arriving at the place where my aides were standing, I being behind Alex, he turned on me and said, "but I am not guilty of that charge, so be careful."

The aides referred to were Isaiah W. Johnson and J.R. Conner of the Austin police force, and Detectives Mike Hennessey and Hanna from the Noble Detective Agency in Houston. And contrary to Marshal Lee's statement, Becky Ramey did not die in the attack of August 30; her daughter Mary was murdered.[26]

Marshal Lee continued his defense of his actions, seeking to explain the rationale of his movements through the city streets.

> Anxious to conduct all my movements as quietly as possible, in order not to excite suspicion, I directed that we proceed to the city jail through as many unfrequented streets as possible.

> Sensible people will understand my purpose. While on our way to jail, and particularly while passing Mr. Press Hopkin's residence, Mack was very boisterous, at times violent, struggling with all his might to get away from us. His screams and yelling were enough to frighten any lady. . . . We had several severe tussles with him. But one pair of nippers were used on him. He was not maltreated in any way, and only such force used as was absolutely necessary to conquer him.

The apparent route taken by Marshal Lee and his group is detailed above. One does have to wonder, though, how frequented any of these streets would have been at 2 or 3 o'clock in the morning. The man named in Marshal Lee's account, Press Hopkins, was Preston Hopkins, a carpenter who lived at 908 Trinity near the Wesley Chapel church.[27]

Marshal Lee further denied that anything unusual or untoward occurred to Mack when he was lodged in the city jail. He detailed the actions of his officers regarding Mack's unruly behavior.

> Upon reaching the calaboose, we found the night clerk, Henry Brown, on duty. I think, as well as I remember, that Officers Johnson and Conners held Mack, each by one arm; I was in their rear and the detectives in my rear. Mack at once became furious, and at sight of the two detectives grew more so. He said, "I am not going to jail," and at once commenced to fight vigorously, viciously and well nigh successfully, I was about to say. I never saw such resistance by any prisoner before. We finally got him into the corridor and a cell was opened in which to place him. At the sight of this Mack renewed his desperate struggle. An old rope, which had been used to draw water from the cistern, with a pair of shackles tied to it for a sinker, was hanging on the wall. Someone said, "Rope him, and pull him in." The rope was quickly snatched by someone, I don't remember who, and thrown over Alex's head. It was quickly grasped at each end by Johnson and Conner, who jumped into the cell, and with their pulling, aided by my own and others pushing, we succeeded in putting him into the cell. He was shackled and chained to a ring in the floor, and the key turned on him.

Marshal Lee then continued in defense of his actions and those of his officers, claiming that Mack was in no way abused or overly mistreated.

> If Mack has any bruises or scars on his person, they are the result of his own desperate efforts to resist arrest and incarceration. I never struck him, nor saw any one else strike him. He was, at the time I speak of, one of the most desperate and vicious men I ever saw, and rough handling was necessary. He remained in confinement nine days, and after the third day he was unshackled. During his entire imprisonment he received the same fare as the other prisoners. After consulting with

> District Attorney Robertson, I released him. I have given you
> the facts in the case.

The reporter then contacted several police officers, including Isaiah Johnson, William Henderson, and Richard Boyce, the day clerk, who all corroborated Marshal Lee's account. Officer Henderson also noted that he had presented the marshal's account to the editor of the *Dispatch*, chastising him for publishing "Mack's untruthful story."[28]

Apparently the whole affair was unnecessary because, despite Marshal Lee's claim of evidence against Mack in regard to the Ramey murder, that evidence was not sufficient to keep Alex Mack jailed. The reporter ended with a final skewering of Mack, saying "It is known that Mack has threatened to take the life of certain police officers, and it is also known that he made up a plot to release Glen Drummer from the city jail. He will do to watch." Though Mack was ultimately released from jail, he threatened to file a complaint for the arrest of the officers involved.[29]

That complaint came within a week of the publication of Mack's story. In a meeting on October 19, 1885, the Austin city council passed a resolution "having for its ostensible object the investigation of the alleged assaults and outrages claimed to have been perpetrated upon one Alex Mack, by the special detectives and city officers." A special committee was formed to investigate Alex Mack's charges against Marshal Lee. The committee members were Aldermen Radcliff Platt, Jacob Schneider, and John Driskill. As mentioned earlier, Alderman Platt, who ran a livery stable, was totally against offering a reward, stating that the police should do their duty without the notion of a reward. Alderman Schneider ran a grocery store and wagon yard at 400 West Live Oak at the corner of Guadalupe Street. He represented the first ward along with Calhoun Metz. Schneider also served on the city council's standing committee on the police department. The third member was John Driskill, a stock raiser who lived on Whitis Avenue. He was related, a brother perhaps, to the famous cattle baron, Jesse L. Driskill, who was building the opulent Driskill Hotel as all the murders were taking place. Driskill represented the sixth ward. The committee itself had no power to take any action against Marshal Lee or his officers or the special detectives. They could, however, make recommendations to the mayor and city council, and then they could take any actions they considered necessary. The committee would not meet until the following month.[30]

"A Debased Ruffian Kills His Black Paramour"

As if to take the citizens' minds off the problems with the police force, another murder occurred in Austin in late October. Unlike in the other murders, though, the perpetrators of this new killing were identified and apprehended. This latest in the string of murders occurred just after midnight in the early morning of October 26, 1885, a Monday. The moon was bright, a couple of days after full moon. At that time, as the Fort Worth newspaper reported, "the crack of the assassin's pistol again rang out on the slumbering city. This time it was in the first ward, near Metz's saloon, and the victim one of the colored demi-monde, Alice Davis. It seems she had for some time been the mistress of a white man named Jack Coombs, heretofore employed in a restaurant as cook on East Pecan street." Alice Davis lived in an alley on the east side of Lavaca Street between West Live Oak and West Water Street in Guy Town. Davis was a prostitute or a kept woman. She was about 19 years old and had likely recently moved to Austin from Matagorda County along the Gulf Coast. Jack Coombs worked as a cook for Peter G. Roach, who ran a grocery store at 221 East Pecan. Metz Brothers Saloon was located in Guy Town at 301 West Live Oak at the corner of Lavaca. The saloon was run by Calhoun and Napoleon Metz. Calhoun Metz also served as an alderman on the city council representing the first ward.[31]

The report noted that Davis and Coombs had a stormy relationship, engaging in "several quarrels." Apparently the tension between the two reached a boiling point on October 26. According to the article:

> Last night Coombs came to her house, and charging her with infidelity drew a forty-five caliber revolver, and as the woman was attempting to escape deliberately shot her down. The ball entered the back, injuring the spinal column and paralyzing the lower limbs and lodged under the skin of the left breast. It was extracted by Dr. Bennett. The woman is thought to be mortally wounded. The shooting is generally deemed the act of a cowardly scoundrel. Coombs was arrested and jailed.

An accomplice to Coombs was also apprehended. The article says a "white man named William Luckie was arrested as an accessory, Luckie having received the pistol from Coombs after the shooting." No information about a white man named Luckie living in Austin could be found, though the 1880 census listed a J. Luckey as an inmate at the State Lunatic Asylum. The 1885 city directory did list a black man named William Luckey who lived near Davis. Luckey's residence was on the west side of Lavaca Street between West Cypress and West Live Oak, also in Guy Town. The 1880 census included a young black man named William Luckey living in Fayette County, about 75 miles east of Austin. This Luckey was born in 1866, making him about 19 years old in 1885. Perhaps this young man was the one named in the article. Could he also have been the boy at the Vance shack before the murders? Like Johnson Trigg, he might have made the trek from the farm to the big city and found himself in trouble.[32]

Alice Davis survived the initial shooting but had "little hopes of recovery." The report noted that she was one of "about seven colored women slaughtered in this city since Christmas." The probable cause of the shooting was listed as jealousy. Coombs was placed under arrest. In the first part of November, Coombs was allowed bail in the amount of $1000, and Alice Davis supposedly would recover. A week later, though, she died and was buried in Austin's Oakwood Cemetery on November 18, 1885. She was 19 years old. Her cause of death was a "wound inflicted by pistol shot." On December 4, 1885, Jack Coombs was convicted of murder and sentenced to five years in prison.[33]

Some reports tried to link the Davis murder to the other servant girl murders, but it seemed to have few links to those other outrages. The *Trenton Times*, notorious for incorrect information on the case, reported that "Alice Davis was found dead in the usual way. She was of the same class at the other victims, and the negroes became wild with terror and talked of nothing but the voudoo's fearful work among the people of their race." [34] Several of these details were clearly incorrect. Davis was a prostitute, not a servant girl. She was shot, not hacked by an ax or sandbagged. She was not raped during the assault. Her attacker was quickly identified, apprehended, convicted, and imprisoned. The blacks had already been talking of voodoo and the evil eye as the cause of the murders. Alice Davis's only link to the other murdered victims was that she was black. Her murder was solved, but the cases of the other murder victims continued to languish as the police and city government became increasingly hostile toward one another.

Notes

Title: *Richmond Dispatch*, 9/30/1885.

1. Bentley and Pilgrim, *Texas Legal Directory for 1876-1877*; *Morrison & Fourmy's General Directory of the City of Austin, 1881-1882*; *Morrison & Fourmy's General Directory of the City of Austin, 1885-1886*; *Morrison & Fourmy's General Directory of the City of Austin, 1889-1890*; *Morrison & Fourmy's General Directory of the City of Austin, 1897-1898*; *City Directory of Austin With Street Directory of Residents, 1906-7*; 1900 Federal Census; Oakwood Cemetery Database (See, for example, *Reports of Cases Argued and Adjudged in the Court of Appeals of Texas*, Volume 5: 359.)
2. "Texas Marriages, 1837-1973"; 1880 Federal Census; *Morrison & Fourmy's General Directory of the City of Austin, 1881-1882*; *Morrison & Fourmy's General Directory of the City of Austin, 1885-1886* (The William Hall mentioned here was not the same as the William Hall at whose home Mollie Smith was murdered in December 1884. But the Hall name was certainly common in many of the assaults. Sarah Hall was raped in an assault in March 1885, and Charlotte Hall was the victim of an attempted rape in March. In May, Lucy Hall was the victim of an attempted rape.)
3. *San Antonio Daily Express*, 9/30/1885.
4. *Fort Worth Daily Gazette*, 9/30/1885; *Salt Lake Daily Herald*, 9/30/1885; Ramsland, "Servant Girl Annihilator"; *Atchison Daily Globe*, 9/30/1885.
5. *Austin Daily Statesman*, 9/30/1885.
6. *Austin Daily Statesman*, 9/30/1885.
7. *Fort Worth Daily Gazette*, 10/6/1885; *Waco Daily Examiner*, 10/7/1885.
8. *San Antonio Daily Express*, 9/30/1885.
9. *San Antonio Daily Express*, 9/30/1885; *Austin Daily Statesman*, 10/1/1885.
10. *San Antonio Daily Express*, 9/30/1885.
11. *Dallas Daily Herald*, 10/2/1885; 1880 Federal Census; 1870 Federal Census.
12. *Austin Daily Statesman*, 10/14/1885; *San Antonio Daily Express*, 11/15/1885.
13. *San Antonio Daily Express*, 10/1/1885; Galloway, *The Servant Girl Murders*: 276-277; 1880 Federal Census; *Morrison & Fourmy's General Directory of the City of Austin, 1885-1886*.
14. *Austin Daily Statesman*, 10/3/1885 (Just where Nursery Street was is unclear. None of the city directories listed it as a street in Austin. The 1885 city directory listed Anderson Murray as living on the west side of West Avenue between Bois d' Arc and Hickory, which

was on the west side of town. Perhaps Nursery Street was the road where William Radam, inventor of the notorious Microbe Killer tonic that supposedly could cure all diseases, had his Pleasant Valley Nursery. The nursery was located two and a half miles east of the city, and the road is now apparently Pleasant Valley Road on the far east side of Austin.)

15. *Morrison & Fourmy's General Directory of the City of Austin, 1885-1886*; *Morrison & Fourmy's General Directory of the City of Austin, 1881-1882*; 1880 Federal Census
16. *Dallas Daily Herald*, 10/4/1885; Galloway, *The Servant Girl Murders*: 277.
17. *Austin Daily Statesman*, 10/14/1885.
18. Galloway, *The Servant Girl Murders*: 280-281. (The Carrolton Hotel that Galloway referred to was most likely the Carrollton House at 204-208 West Pecan, where Trigg did indeed work as a waiter.)
19. *Austin Daily Statesman*, 9/29/1885.
20. *Austin Daily Statesman*, 10/7/1885.
21. *Austin Daily Statesman*, 10/7/1885.
22. *Austin Daily Statesman*, 10/7/1885.
23. *Austin Daily Statesman*, 10/7/1885.
24. *Austin Daily Statesman*, 10/8/1885.
25. *Austin Daily Dispatch*, 10/14/1885; *San Antonio Daily Express*, 10/16/1885; *Morrison & Fourmy's General Directory of the City of Austin, 1885-1886*.
26. *Austin Daily Statesman*, 10/16/1885; *Morrison & Fourmy's General Directory of the City of Austin, 1885-1886* (As noted earlier, this officer's name was spelled several different ways in the sources of information: Conner, Conners, Connor, and Connors. For consistency, Conner will be used, except where variant forms were used in news reports.)
27. *Austin Daily Statesman*, 10/16/1885; *Morrison & Fourmy's General Directory of the City of Austin, 1885-1886*.
28. *Austin Daily Statesman*, 10/16/1885.
29. *Austin Daily Statesman*, 10/16/1885; *San Antonio Daily Express*, 10/16/1885.
30. *Austin Daily Statesman*, 11/12/1885; *Morrison & Fourmy's General Directory of the City of Austin, 1885-1886*; Galloway, *The Servant Girl Murders*: 281.
31. *Fort Worth Daily Gazette*, 10/27/1885; *Morrison & Fourmy's General Directory of the City of Austin, 1885-1886*; 1880 Federal Census; "Lunar calendar."
32. *Fort Worth Daily Gazette*, 10/27/1885; *Morrison & Fourmy's General Directory of the City of Austin, 1885-1886*; 1880 Federal Census.
33. *Fort Worth Daily Gazette*, 10/27/1885; *San Antonio Daily Light*, 11/10, 1885; *Fort Worth Daily Gazette*, 12/5/1885; Oakwood Cemetery Database.
34. *Trenton Times*, 2/1/1886.

Chapter 9

"An Impenetrable and Fearful Mystery"

City Politics Reach the Boiling Point

As the autumn deepened, so did the tension between Marshal Grooms Lee and the city fathers. Lee contended that the city council had failed to provide him enough officers to do the necessary work to solve the murders. Some on the city council questioned the attitude of the police force. The failure of the police and detectives to produce reliable evidence caused Austin citizens to question the efficacy of both the police force and the city government. A stalemate was inevitable. But with city elections coming in only a few weeks, a panic began to set in among city officials. At long last they became eager to solve the murders, or perhaps, to save their own jobs.

The inability of the police force to solve the murders continued to draw flak from around the state. The Fort Worth newspaper noted that "influential papers throughout the North had been for years representing Texas to the world as the paradise of murderers," hardly a slogan for tourism. The continued unsolved murders certainly gave the claim some credence. The Fort Worth newspaper also reported that "they keep on arresting 'barefooted negroes' in Austin, who are supposed to have been concerned in the series of brutal murders that have given the capital an unenviable name. The colored servant girls, however, seem to have lost faith in the lynx-eyed police, and continue to emigrate." If the police force could not protect the citizens, then what good was it?[1]

The police force in Austin was said to be "the worst abused set of men in Texas" for its inefficacy. Much of the pressure for the failure of the police to solve the murders fell on Grooms Lee. As noted in an earlier chapter, Lee's credentials for the position were questionable, and the continued inability of the police to arrest viable suspects simply revealed all the chinks in Lee's armor. Now he had resorted to strong-arm tactics to try to wrest a confession from one of his favorite suspects, an approach that seemed to blow up in his face. Lee's position as city marshal was in peril, and reports had already circulated that he had considered resigning in September because of the "inadequate number of policemen furnished him for the protection of the city." Lee's complaint was not unfounded. Austin's population at the time was around 13,000 people, and Lee had only three officers for night duty. And as if to add injury to insult, the city council in September had summoned outside help in the form of a "competent detective."[2]

As indicated in the preceding chapter, the city council had formed a special committee to investigate Alex Mack's claim about being abused by Marshal Lee and some of his officers. That committee held meetings on November 9 and November 10. The committee took statements from Alex Mack, his mother, Sallie Mack (Cook), Hugh Hancock, proprietor of the Black Elephant Saloon, and Preston Hopkins, near whose house the threatened lynching was to take place. The evidence collected seemed less important than the squabbling between Marshal Lee and the committee.[3]

As the committee was meeting, Marshal Lee tried to reinforce the performance of the police force by releasing information about the expenses and arrests of the police department. According to Lee's release, published November 12, 1885:

> The police force has consisted of a marshal, a sergeant and twelve policemen. The expenses of this department, including salaries, has been $16,210.65; number of complaints made, 2,502; number of arrests 2,112. This covers a period from June 13, 1884, to October 31, 1885, and the fines and costs collected and paid in to the assessor and collector, amount to $9,062.90. From December 10, 1883, to October 31, 1885, the number of complaints filed in the recorder's court have been 3,028; convictions, 2,070; acquittals, 295; dismissals, 622; failed to arrest, 41.

The marshal also took the opportunity to chastise the city council regarding police department operations. Lee was not pleased that the city council had such dominant control over the police.

> I must add my dissent to the present method of selecting the marshal and police force. The marshal is elected by the city council, and then, under the provisions of the charter, the council also elects his policemen. The marshal should be left to select his own policemen, and then he should be held to the very strictest responsibility for their conduct. A want of personal responsibility for the appointment and deportment of the police force, and a denial to the marshal of the power of summary removal, defeats all efforts at good discipline, and destroys the usefulness of the force.

Marshal Lee also felt that the police department needed to be reorganized. His feelings had some merit, because for all practical purposes, the marshal and police officers served at the whimsy of the city council.

> The people of this city are dissatisfied with the present police management, and this department needs a thorough reorganization. If there are good and true men on the force, and I know there are such, they should be retained in service. If there are bad or incompetent men, they should be removed, and their places supplied with competent and worthy men. The people demand, and the good name and welfare of the city

demands that there should be a thorough reorganization of the police department, and I earnestly trust that it will be made.

Lee seemed to be making a last-ditch effort to retain his position, an effort that would yield little success. Lee would fall victim to the same thing he was protesting.[4]

"Crime in the City"

Marshal Lee may have scheduled his release of information to coincide with, or perhaps undermine, Mayor Robertson's State of the City address delivered that same day. In his speech, Mayor Robertson recapped the murders and sounded hollow assurances that the city government, the police, the hired detectives, and the grand juries had done all they could to solve the crimes.

> During the last year a number of the most dastardly crimes known to the law have been committed in this city. In some instances murder, and in others murder and rape, and in others murderous assaults with knife, hatchet or pistol. These crimes have been of the most revolting character, attended with evidences of the grossest brutality, and perpetrated at the dead hours of night, in nearly every instance upon colored females. They have occurred in the most unexpected quarters and have always been involved in mystery. The community has been outraged and shocked by these crimes, and the blood of the victims has appealed for vengeance.
>
> Much has been said and written about these crimes, and the city government has been subjected to severe criticisms, sometimes unfriendly and sometimes bordering on the malicious. I undertake to say that the city authorities, ably aided by the state and county officers, have faithfully and earnestly labored to detect the perpetrators of these crimes and bring them to punishment, but they have failed of success. The council directed me to employ detectives and to use all available means to discover and arrest the guilty criminals. I employed detectives who came with the highest endorsement as honest and skillful men. They, too, have failed to detect the guilty parties. At your direction, having been baffled at every point, I offered rewards for their detection, sufficient in amount to anyone having information to come forward and make it known. No one has come forward. Great vigilance and energy has been displayed by private citizens, who have devoted much time and labor to bring to light the real criminals. They have accomplished nothing. On the first Monday in October, the grand jury of Travis county, composed of the most intelligent citizens, white and colored, was organized in the district court, and have been making the most energetic investigation of these crimes calling to their aid the whole power of the state of

> Texas. They too have failed to find evidence that would warrant them in presenting an indictment against a single person.
>
> To say that an honest and faithful effort, by all the means at our command, has not been made to bring these murderers and assassins to justice, is to misstate and falsify the facts. No effort has been spared, no means promising success have been withheld. The crimes still remain a mystery and their guilty authors retain the secret. It was impossible to prevent these crimes. They are abnormal and unnatural, as compared with ordinary crimes among men. No one, not even the expert, skilled in the detection of crime, can find a possible motive. It is all speculation. The mutilated bodies of the victims were found, always in parts of the city where crime was not expected or anticipated, and beyond the fact of the murder we have never been able to penetrate.

Like most politicians, Robertson was adept at stating the obvious. The city seemed to be in a bad state.[5]

Marshal Lee's release may also have been meant to downplay the report of the special committee investigating the Alex Mack affair. The *Austin Daily Statesman* noted, in fact, that the Wednesday paper was so crowded that the publication of the report had to be delayed a day. When the news of the committee's report was published, the newspaper seemed more concerned with the quarrel between Marshal Lee and the committee than it did in publishing the statements of the witnesses. Alderman Driskill reported that the committee's meeting on November 9th was interrupted "by the city marshal and subordinates, demanding that they be heard. We consented to grant them a hearing . . . and authorized them to make their statements in their own way and manner fully." Such a concession by the committee satisfied the marshal and his cohorts temporarily. The next day, though, when they were scheduled to make their statements,

> they demanded that an attorney be admitted, also dictating to the committee as to how the committee should proceed in the manner of investigation. The committee not desiring to be dictated to by the city marshal, or his attorney, informed him that said committee had permission to occupy the room in which they had assembled, and would not be dictated to by anyone. The city marshal was informed that when witnesses were desired by the committee, they would be sent for, whereupon the city marshal and his attorney left the room.

Obviously, the marshal did not like the way the committee was doing its business.[6]

A short while later, Officer R. W. Johnson, one of the policemen being investigated, arrived to summon the committee to a special meeting of the council. The committee, though, decided that since Officer Johnson was present at that time, they would take his statement. He sat down to write his statement, and as he was writing, the committee report noted,

> the city marshal came in and said something to him about not making a statement, and ordered him to come with him. He arose and started, and remarked, "Well, you see how it is," and as it had passed the hour, and no witnesses returned, we concluded that as every obstacle had been thrown in our way by the officers to whom we looked for assistance in our investigation, we had but to adjourn and report the facts as far as we were able to obtain them.

The report also noted that the committee was not aware of any law that required them to allow an attorney's presence during the investigation, suggesting that the marshal apparently believed the committee had some power to act against him. According to the report, the committee members had been "willing to give any and all parties a chance to make a statement. We therefore ask that the city council take such action as they may see proper, from the evidence submitted, and the committee be discharged."[7]

"The Officer's Protest"

The marshal's protest also drew substantial coverage. The marshal first complained that he and his cohorts had not received any notice or subpoena regarding the committee's meeting, and that, in fact, they "were first informed of the meeting of said committee on the afternoon of the 9th day of November, 1885, and then only by hearsay and not by any formal or legal notice or summons." Upon learning of the meeting, Marshal Lee presented himself "to be confronted with the witnesses and charges against him and against those who might be charged or implicated with him, which request was refused." Marshal Lee seemed to think he was going to trial, when in fact the committee was performing only a fact-finding mission. Marshal Lee and his cohorts then hired an attorney, Mr. Dudley Wooten, and demanded that they be allowed to question their accusers and the charges, which also was not granted.[8]

The next morning, November 10, Marshal Lee, his companions, and their attorney returned to the committee meeting. According to Lee's protest, he and his fellow accused

> were present in person and by counsel, and in writing and verbally, requested the right to be heard and represented by counsel, which was emphatically and insultingly refused by the members of the committee present, Mr. Platt stating, in very positive and offensive terms, that the committee proposed to conduct the investigation their own way, and would not be bulldozed by lawyers or anybody else; and demanded that the said Lee and his counsel vacate the room, as the same was sacred to the deliberations of the committee. The written request of the undersigned was submitted to said Platt and Driskill, but they both declared their opinion to be that neither the undersigned or their attorney should be present. Thereupon, the undersigned, Lee, and his counsel withdrew, and afterwards

> communicated to the said committee their intention not to
> enter into nor be subjected to any sort of investigation without
> being allowed their legal right and privilege to be present in
> person and by counsel, and to be notified to be confronted with
> the witnesses against them and permitted to cross-examine
> them. It is the impression of the undersigned that this
> committee was appointed to conduct a full, fair and searching
> investigation into the matters in controversy, and to deny no
> person implicated a chance to be heard, and to throw light on
> the proceedings and to report to the council a complete and
> satisfactory report of the whole matter. On the contrary it
> seems to have been the deliberate purpose and persistent
> design of this committee or at least to a majority of it to
> conduct a purely partisan and secret inquisition, contrary to
> every principle and precedent of American jurisprudence, and
> to the established and immemorial doctrines of English justice.
> If it has come to pass that men can be tried and condemned, or
> even by implication reported as guilty, by an ex pare
> investigation, without being notified; without being confronted
> by the witnesses against them, or allowed to cross-examine
> them, or to be informed of the specific charges against them,
> and are further denied the right to be present in person or by
> attorney, for the purpose of properly guarding and protecting
> their rights and developing their defense, then indeed have the
> bulwarks of reputation and personal liberty been broken down,
> and every man is at the mercy of an irresponsible slanderer.

The protest was signed by H.G. Lee, R. W. Johnson, and J.R. Conner. Marshal Lee seemed to have learned quite a bit about the law and justice now that the shoe was on the other foot. He was being investigated for trying to coax a confession from Alex Mack through cruelty and intimidation. Surely Alex Mack was not presented the opportunity to face his accuser or to have an attorney present.[9]

The attorney retained by Marshal Lee and his colleagues, Dudley G. Wooten, repeated the idle claim that the officers' legal rights were being denied. He insisted that "both sides of the case be heard" so that the city council could render a fair decision regarding his clients.

> To that end and by virtue of his just and legal rights, Mr. Lee
> and those by implication accused with him, offer and demand
> the opportunity to be present and to be heard in person and by
> counsel in vindication of themselves against any and all charges
> or suspicions which may be raised by the testimony of said Alex
> Mack, or any one else. Mr. Lee and the other city officers acting
> with him in the arrest and incarceration of said Mack, deny that
> they, or any one of them, ever used any other violence than
> was absolutely necessary to effect the purpose of placing him
> inside the walls of the city calaboose, and say that they were
> never guilty of any such acts of personal violence and physical
> torture as have been charged by said Mack. In order to have
> the matter thoroughly understood and judged fairly by the
> council, and by the people at large, these gentlemen demand

> the right to be present in person and by their attorney, and to have the witnesses against them confronted with them, and to have an opportunity to cross-examine the said opposing witnesses; and also to have their own witnesses summoned and properly examined, with a view to elicit the truth, and the whole truth. This is supposed to be the mode of procedure of all legal and just tribunals in a free and constitutional government, and we ask nothing more.

Mr. Wooten also seemed to be under the impression that his clients were being tried. Wooten was involved in one of the home invasions back on March 18. He boarded at the home of Miss Ella Rust. At the time of the assault on the house, he had emerged, pistol in hand, ready to blast the intruder, but the culprit had escaped into the night before he could get off a shot. Now he was defending the very men who had failed to solve that attack.[10]

Marshal Lee, not yet finished, fired a parting shot at the committee. He first noted that the committee members had "peremptorily and rather insultingly refused" his demand to be heard in the presence of his attorney. He then sought to defend himself in public if he could not gain his way before the investigating committee.

> I have now to say that this investigation was actively begun without any notice to me of the same; I am informed that several witnesses have been examined who accused me and officers under me of outrageous and cruel treatment toward said Alex Mack. I was never confronted by said witness, nor given an opportunity to cross-examine them. Their story is I well know wholly and utterly false, and their testimony, as could be absolutely proven, entirely untrustworthy, I am now requesting the privilege of being present in person, and by attorney, during the remainder of the so-called investigation; notwithstanding there has never been, so far as I am informed, any character of tribunal, even a Mexican drum-head court martial, where a man was denied the right to be represented, either in person or by attorney, and usually by both. Certainly such a procedure is entirely unknown to the free institutions of this state and union.

Lee seemed to have softened his rhetoric, now "requesting the privilege" instead of "demanding" the right to be heard. He continued to profess his innocence.

> I denounce as false any and all charges against myself, or Officers Johnson and Conner, in the premises; but we insist that if our statements are to be taken, it must be in accordance with the established forms of law, and we must be allowed the protection and counsel of our attorney at the time, and also we must know and be confronted with the witnesses and charges against us. There are several witnesses now in the city who are fully conversant with the facts of this affair, and if it is the

> purpose of your committee to reach the very truth, you will seek to obtain their testimony.

Bless his heart, Grooms Lee did not like to be bullied. Bully he might, but be bullied? Nay! Marshal Lee seemed to realize his official days were numbered, but he would not go down without a fight. He concluded by stating, "I must say now, once for all, that unless I am allowed by legal rights of representation before your committee, in person and by attorney, I cannot in justice to myself, submit to compromise myself and subordinates by appearing before an ex parte, secret, star chamber committee, without a hearing or an opportunity to know what is charged against us, or of being confronted with the witnesses and cross-examining them as I have a right to do."[11]

According to Galloway, the failure of Marshal Lee and his colleagues to testify "resulted in something of a stalemate between the parties involved. Ultimately no action was taken by the city council. With elections less than a month away, they probably felt the easiest solution would be to wait, and if they desired, they could replace Marshal Lee at that time." And, indeed, within the month, Grooms Lee was out of a job. What happened to Officer Johnson is unclear, but Officer Conner was still on the force four years later.[12]

"Suspicion"

As the month of November wound down, a slew of new arrests were made in the servant girl cases. These arrests seemed to be the classic case of grabbing at straws. Many new names were added to the long list of black men arrested for the crimes. First, one article reported that "a negro named James Thompson, has been arrested at this late day on suspicion of having murdered the Ramey girl. The arrest is based on Thompson's 'giving away himself' while under the influence of liquor," though a witness said Thompson made the same boasts before he was drunk. The young man, son of Moses and Matilda Thompson, was about 25 years old at the time and worked as a farmhand. A relation to Walter Thompson, mentioned as a suspect in the Mollie Smith murder, could not be established. Also in the article, an old name resurfaced, Johnson Trigg, though he was mistakenly identified as John Grigg. Trigg was "convicted and sentenced to the penitentiary for 5 years for perjury in swearing that Townsend and Woods committed the Ramey murder."[13]

Then, Cullen Crockett and Richard Bacon, who were arrested in neighboring Bastrop County, were likely to be indicted for the murder of Mary Ramey. Crockett, apparently in his 20s, lived on the west side of Sabine between East Cedar and Cypress streets. He resided with his apparent brother, Joseph Cullen, who was a farmer about 40 years old, and his sister, Josephene, who was about 26 at the time. Richard Bacon was the stepson of Felix Brooks and son of Mollie Brooks. Bacon was about 19 years old at the time of his arrest. It is unclear whether Bacon's stepfather was related to the William Brooks that was a suspect in the Mollie Smith murder back in December 1884. In addition, a black man named Henry Thomas was "arrested on suspicion of 'knowing more than he will tell' about the Ramey killing," whatever crime that might be. The only Henry Thomas located in Austin at the time was a mulatto, aged 46, who lived with his wife, Cassy, at 1310 East Cypress at the corner of Navasota, not far from where Crockett lived.[14]

Finally, as if to heap further infamy on the fire, District Attorney James Robertson, using evidence gathered by the Noble detectives shortly before they were dismissed by the city, got the grand jury to indict Walter Spencer for the murder of Mollie Smith about 11 months prior. The theory of the detectives was that Smith and Spencer were in the room together when they had a quarrel. Spencer struck her "with an ax he had been using as a woodcutter." The blow was fatal, so Spencer then supposedly dragged Smith into the yard and hacked her to bits. The evidence presented by detectives Hennessey and Hanna was apparently as flimsy as all the other evidence they had gathered, for when Spencer was tried early in December, the jury quickly acquitted him of the charge.[15]

"A Doctor Sends a Leaden Pill to the Back of a Cullud Gem'man"

The month of November ended with a bang, literally. A shooting on November 25 reinforced the pervasiveness of violence in Austin and also reflected the racial tensions of the times. In an article headlined "Shot a Coon," a report noted that a white doctor had shot a black man in the Gold Room Saloon, run by David H.L. Hunter, at 611 Congress Avenue.

> This morning about 3 o'clock the crack of the murderer's pistol was heard. After the excitement was over it was found that Dr. G.S. Filder of Weberville had shot a negro named Sam Percer, the ball entering his back and injuring his spinal column, producing paralysis. After putting a ball into Percer the man of pills turned and fired at Mattison, a colored policeman, and turned to run from the avenue across through the Iron Front saloon. Here he met a private watchman, who attempted to stop the fugitive. The latter snapped his pistol in his face, but the watchman captured the doctor, who is now in jail. The wounded negro will probably die. The chief interest centers in the fact that Filder is the nephew of State Health Officer Swearingen. Filder had no provocation and told your reporter at the jail that he did not know why he did it.

The doctor who did the shooting was referred to variously as Filder, Fielder, and Felder; according to court records, the correct name was G. S. Felder. No solid information could be found about him other than the stated relation to Dr. Richard M. Swearingen, a local physician involved in several of the servant girl murder cases. The victim was called both Percer and Pearson, though court records identified him as Sam Persons. The officer that Felder shot at was Henry G. Madison, who served on the Austin police force.[16]

Surprisingly, about a week later Felder was indicted by the grand jury for "assault with intent to murder." The victim was not expected to live. According to the report, "There was no provocation, and the only defence is whisky crazy." Even more surprisingly, when Felder's case finally went to trial a year later, the jury, after a 48-hour deliberation, "brought in a verdict of guilty in the second degree, and assessed the punishment at twenty-five years in the penitentiary. The verdict was a surprise." The article went on to recount the events of the night of the shooting, noting that "Fielder is a young doctor, practicing ten miles down the Colorado river. He came to Austin on a visit last year, got drunk in a billiard room, got into a quarrel with a negro named Pearson and shot and mortally wounded him while he was getting out of the way." Felder's connections in Austin were noted, and an appeal of the verdict was expected. Felder was not tried for murder for a year, but Walter Spencer was tried for murder within days of his indictment on that charge. Such a contrast only reinforced the prevailing attitude toward blacks that persisted in Austin. [17]

Felder's Austin connections served him well. The case was appealed, and on June 8, 1887, a verdict was reached. According to evidence presented in the appeal, Felder had entered the Gold Room Saloon with Jim Glover, who at the time of the shooting had seven weeks earlier been shot at himself, supposedly by Glenn Drummer, but Drummer was acquitted on that charge. After entering the saloon, Felder and several blacks began a game of dice. At some point, Persons walked by Felder and brushed his elbow. Felder then drew a pistol from his overcoat and said, "I'll just shoot that negro for fun." Felder fired, hitting Persons in the back as he was leaving the saloon. Felder then walked calmly out of the saloon, over Persons' bleeding body, and down the street toward the Iron Front Saloon at 605 Congress Avenue. Someone in the crowd shouted, "That is the man who did the shooting." Two black policemen ran after Felder to detain him. As they neared, Felder turned and shot at one of them, Officer Madison. Felder was then arrested and tried. After being shot, Persons claimed he did not know who shot him. Persons did not die immediately, but lingered until April 26, 1886. As he neared inevitable death, he told his sister, Lee Ann Persons, a schoolteacher at the Central Grammar School for black students, that Felder had shot him.[18]

The appeal court's ruling was based on two convoluted technicalities. First, because the person who said, "That is the man who did the shooting," did not appear as a witness in the original trial, the statement was regarded as hearsay and inadmissible. Second, because Persons had initially said he did not know who shot him but contradicted that initial statement in his deathbed confession, and because the defendant did not have the opportunity to cross-examine Persons' contradictory deathbed confession, the deathbed statement was not allowed. Though several people had seen Felder shoot Persons and then shoot at Officer Madison, Felder's guilty verdict was reversed and his case remanded to the lower court, where it apparently was never reheard. Felder got off the hook.[19]

"The New Municipal Administration"

The beginning of December brought with it a local campaign season and heightened discord between the races. The Knights of Labor first organized a boycott urging "the people to withdraw their patronage from all Chinamen in Austin, except Wa Haing, the merchant who is a naturalized citizen and has an American wife." Haing, who was born in 1849, ran a grocery store at 409 Congress Avenue. He had married Caroline Ivey in November 1881. The Knights contended that "the Chinese do not make good citizens; they are generally obnoxious to the people and only hoard their money to take back to China." Members of the Knights were also told to visit hat dealers and tell them not to buy hats made by John B. Stetson & Company of Philadelphia because their hats were "manufactured by 'scab labor,'" apparently Chinese workers. The Knights wanted the people of Austin "to support their action to boycott the Chinese and take their custom among their own people where it is deserved." Cultural diversity did not seem to be popular at the time. The arguments were not unlike the ones used against undocumented Mexicans now.[20]

The city government elections were to be held on December 7. In advance of the elections, white citizens in the seventh ward of Austin formed an "Anti-Colored Movement" to keep Albert Carrington from being re-elected. Carrington had been elected in 1883 and was the fourth black man to serve on the Austin city council since the Civil War. He was also the brother of Rebecca Ramey, who had been assaulted back in August, and the uncle of murdered Mary Ramey. Apparently the string of murders had generated little sympathy for the blacks among white citizens of Austin. When the elections were held, six of the sitting aldermen were replaced. Among the defeated council members was Albert Carrington. He would be the last black man to serve on an Austin city council until 1971.[21]

The police were also criticized for their role in the election. According to a San Antonio paper, "The police of Austin are charged with taking too much 'dish' in the recent city election. The police in this city have often and very recently been used for electioneering purposes. That they can be made a potent factor in elections is undeniable, but their employment for such purposes is undemocratic in principle and only fit for despotic government." The article noted that an alderman was considering an ordinance that would disallow policemen from taking part in an election. They could only participate by alerting the marshal 15 days in advance and then not wearing their uniform during the election.[22]

Mayor John W. Robertson was re-elected, and on December 12, the new city council replaced Grooms Lee as city marshal. The new marshal was James E. Lucy, a former Texas Ranger who was born in Missouri in 1854. Ironically, Lucy had served in the same unit of the Rangers as Grooms Lee did, Company D of the Frontier Battalion. He had also tangled with Ben Thompson, the former Austin city marshal who had caused trouble for Grooms Lee at the beginning of his tenure as Austin's city marshal. According to Lucy, he had defused the situation in January 1884 when Ben Thompson tried to shoot up the stockmen's banquet in Simon's Restaurant in Austin. Lucy married Jennie Platt in Austin in 1882, but she died just a month after he became the new marshal. She may have been related to Alderman Radcliff Platt, but solid evidence could not be located.[23]

The new city council immediately began work on a reorganization of the police department, using several of the recommendations Grooms Lee had made in one of his complaints in November. In its meeting on December 19, 1885, Alderman Anderson, one of the newly elected members, presented an ordinance regulating police hiring, police hierarchy, salaries, moral turpitude, and appearance. The ordinance called for one city marshal, one sergeant of police, and twenty policemen. Twelve of those policemen would work the night shift, a marked increase from the three men that had night patrol before the reorganization. The city marshal would now be permitted to select the police sergeant and the officers, with city council confirmation. Any officer caught leaving his post, neglecting his duty, or drinking liquor on duty, or who was found guilty of insubordination or crime, would be removed immediately. The officers also had to be "neatly uniformed," prompt, and polite while on duty. Whether these changes would help to fight the reign of crime, only time would tell. And the wait would be a short one.[24]

The investigation of Marshal Lee for his alleged actions against Alex Mack seemed based more on politics than on upholding a black man's rights. Besides driving the white citizens of Austin to concern and the black citizens to panic, the spate of servant girl murders had also left the city government in turmoil. In a sweeping sense of frustration, voters ousted six aldermen. The new council swiftly disposed of Grooms Lee as marshal. Though generally inept, Lee had made some good recommendations that the city council saw fit to implement. And poor James Lucy had stepped into a bad situation. But for a city filled with new hope, the worst was yet to come.

Notes

Title: *Fort Worth Daily Gazette*, 11/15/1885.

1. *Fort Worth Daily Gazette*, 11/2/1885; *Fort Worth Daily Gazette*, 11/18/1885.
2. *San Antonio Daily Light*, 9/7/1885; *The Austin Almanac* 46.
3. *Austin Daily Statesman*, 11/12/1885.
4. *Austin Daily Statesman*, 11/11/1885.
5. *Austin Daily Statesman*, 11/11/1885.
6. *Austin Daily Statesman*, 11/12/1885.
7. *Austin Daily Statesman*, 11/12/1885.
8. *Austin Daily Statesman*, 11/12/1885.
9. *Austin Daily Statesman*, 11/12/1885.
10. *Austin Daily Statesman*, 11/12/1885.
11. *Austin Daily Statesman*, 11/12/1885.
12. Galloway, *The Servant Girl Murders*: 281-282; *Morrison & Fourmy's General Directory of the City of Austin, 1889-1890*.
13. *San Antonio Daily Express*, 11/15/1885; *Galveston Daily News*, 11/15/1885; 1880 Federal Census.
14. *San Antonio Daily Express*, 11/19/1885; 1880 Federal Census; *Morrison & Fourmy's General Directory of the City of Austin, 1885-1886*.
15. *San Antonio Daily Express*, 11/22/1885; *San Antonio Daily Express*, 12/11/1885; *Galveston Daily News*, 11/22/1885; Galloway, *The Servant Girl Murders*: 282.

16. *Fort Worth Daily Gazette*, 11/26/1885; *Morrison & Fourmy's General Directory of the City of Austin, 1885-1886*; *Reports of Cases Argued and Adjudged in the Court of Appeals of Texas, Volume 23*: 477-490.

17. *San Antonio Daily Light*, 12/1/1885; *Fort Worth Daily Gazette*, 11/12/1886

18. *Reports of Cases Argued and Adjudged in the Court of Appeals of Texas, Volume 23*: 477-490; *Morrison & Fourmy's General Directory of the City of Austin, 1885-1886*.

19. *Reports of Cases Argued and Adjudged in the Court of Appeals of Texas, Volume 23*: 477-490.

20. *Waco Daily Examiner*, 12/4/1885; *Morrison & Fourmy's General Directory of the City of Austin, 1885-1886*; 1880 Federal Census; "Texas Marriages, 1837-1973."

21. Humphrey, David C. *Austin: A History of the Capital City*: 35; Galloway, *The Servant Girl Murders*: 282.

22. *San Antonio Daily Light*, 12/14/1885.

23. *San Antonio Daily Light*, 12/26/1885; Stephens, *Texas Ranger Indian War Pensions*: 65; Williamson, *The Texas Pistoleers: Ben Thompson and King Fisher*: Chapter 15.

24. *Austin Daily Statesman*, 12/20/1885.

Chapter 10

"A Perfect Carnival of Gore"

The Christmas Eve Murders

James Lucy no doubt found himself in an unenviable position. He had inherited a string of unsolved murders. He had become the head of a mostly inept, highly criticized police force that didn't seem to know what solid evidence was. And his young wife was dying down in Saltillo, Mexico.[1]

One must almost conclude that the killers had worked in virtual obscurity during the year of murders. They came and went stealthily, almost at will, not even alerting neighboring dogs as they worked their evil wiles. They left no clues to their identities. The few eyewitness accounts were unreliable. What happened on Christmas Eve, though, seemed almost a taunt. The killers had kept Austinites, especially black Austinites, in a dither since the murders began. If the intent was something more than pure savage brutality, then the killers likely meant to bring chaos to the city, to bring the city government and police to their knees. And in those regards, the murders had served their purpose. The events of Christmas Eve 1885 seemed almost a thumb-to-the-nose snub of Austin crime fighters.

The white citizens of Austin entered the Christmas season with a relative sense of security. The murders so far had targeted only black servant girls. And the city had a new marshal, and twenty more men had been added to the police force, with most of those men working the night shift. But the murders of Christmas Eve 1885 wiped away any sense of security and left the city in total panic.

The weather that Thursday was mild, not uncommon for Christmas in Central Texas. The moon was bright, just three days past full. The silvery orb rose at a little after 9 o'clock that night, bathing the city with a false sense of joy and calm. Christmas concerts and parties were held, and the world seemed at peace. Alderman Anderson threw a large party, as did Dr. John Tobin. Tobin's party even included fireworks. A time of gaiety and goodwill seemed at hand. By midnight, though, that sense of joy and peace came crashing down.[2]

The first indication that things were going terribly wrong came between 11 and midnight on Christmas Eve. An *Austin Daily Statesman* reporter and Marshal Lucy were conversing in front of Martin's shoe store at the corner of Congress Avenue and Bois d'Arc. Up ran a private watchman named Alexander Wilkie, who worked for Neff and Duff, proprietors of the Iron Front Saloon. Wilkie hallooed to the marshal: "'A woman has been chopped all to pieces down on East Water street, go down there.'"

Marshal Lucy and the reporter hailed a nearby carriage and quickly headed to 203 East Water Street, the home of Moses H. Hancock, a carpenter in his mid-50s. According to the *Statesman*, "the victim of this murderous, diabolical, hellish attack" was a "white lady," Sue C. Hancock, the wife of Moses, about 40 years old. She was described as "still handsome," "beautiful," "one of the most refined ladies of Austin," having been "educated in the Eastern States," and possessing "much literary ability." They lived in the small house with two daughters, Lena, aged 15, and Ida, aged 10. A boarder named David Hagy also lived with the Hancocks.[3]

Moses Hancock could muster only a "distracted, disconnected narration" of what had happened. He noted that his two daughters "had gone out to a Christmas eve party, somewhere in the neighborhood; and as they were not expected to be out late the doors were left unlocked." At some point before their return, "something woke him up." In his sleepy stupor, he suddenly realized his house had been robbed. He reached for his clothes and "discovered that his pants were gone." Because he slept in a room separate from his wife, he went into her room, "in the east end of his humble cottage, which was lighted by the full glare of the moon, when he was almost paralyzed by the sight of clots of blood on the bed, and his wife nowhere to be seen." Her skirts lay on a chair, spotted with blood. Her room too had the telltale markings of a robbery.[4]

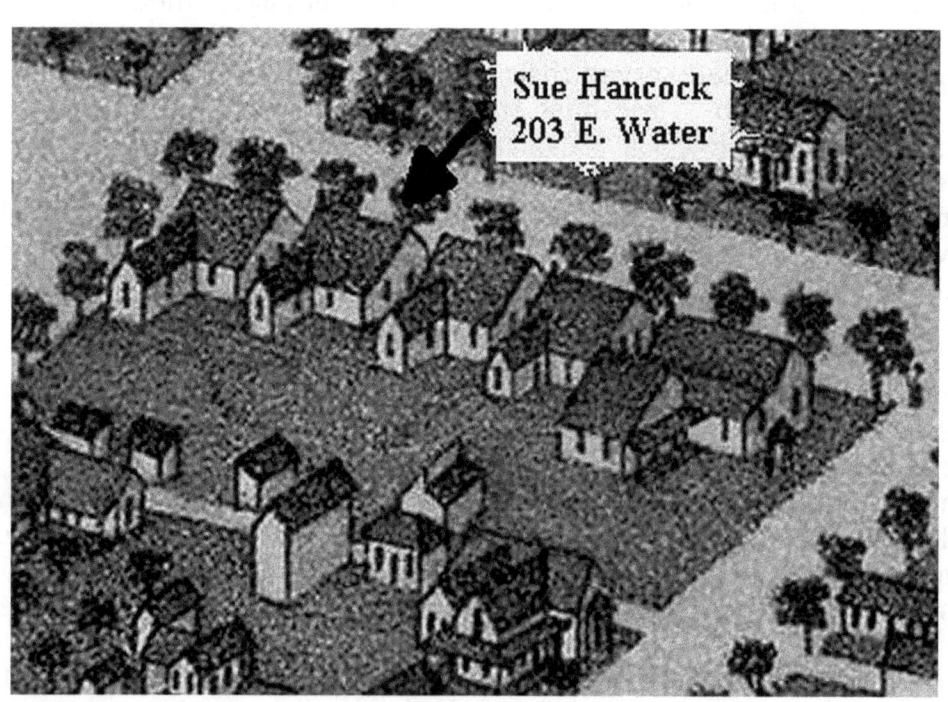

He then heard moans coming from the backyard. Going out a rear door, "he saw his wife, lying prone upon the ground, weltering in a pool of blood." She was bleeding from the head, having been struck two savage blows with an ax. Hancock picked up his badly injured wife and started back to the house, calling for his neighbor, Atlas M. Persinger, a brickmason about the same age as Hancock, for help. Persinger heard the cries, got up quickly and dressed himself. Crossing into Hancock's yard, Persinger "saw the old man lying across a wooden walk, with his bleeding and mangled wife in his arms. Mr. Persinger assisted Mr. Hancock to carry the butchered wife and mother into the parlor, or sitting room." The city physician, Dr. William J. Burt, arrived within minutes, followed by Dr. Richard Graves. Their examination confirmed that Mrs. Hancock "had been struck twice with an ax. Both blows had been dealt on the left side of the head, one directly across the ear, cutting it in two, the other between the ear and eye which fractured the skull." She was not expected to live, and indeed, she died a few days later without recovering her senses. She was buried in Oakwood Cemetery in Austin on December 29, 1885. Curiously, her tombstone lists her year of death as 1884, not 1885.[5]

At the scene of the assault, Marshal Lucy found it hard to locate evidence or clues because of the large number of people that had gathered at the Hancock residence. Lucy coolly and calmly gave orders, and soon the bloodhounds were brought to the house and started off "in the direction in which Hancock said he saw two men jump the fence." The dogs worked well for a while but lost the trail, and they were soon brought back to the house for another try, "and when the reporter left the premises, they were apparently working well, taking a trail which led in a westerly direction, or up the river."[6]

At the scene of the assault, Marshal Lucy found it hard to locate evidence or clues because of the large number of people that had gathered at the Hancock residence. Lucy coolly and calmly gave orders, and soon the bloodhounds were brought to the house and started off "in the direction in which Hancock said he saw two men jump the fence." The dogs worked well for a while but lost the trail, and they were soon brought back to the house for another try, "and when the reporter left the premises, they were apparently working well, taking a trail which led in a westerly direction, or up the river."[6]

Apparently "the murderer entered Mrs. Hancock's room, broke open a trunk and then assaulted her, afterwards dragging her out into the yard," through the sleeping Mr. Hancock's room. The Austin reporter concluded that "the purpose was robbery, there can be little doubt, judging by the appearance of Mrs. Hancock's room," though others doubted that robbery was the sole motive. But the reporter also wondered "why she should have been dragged nearly a hundred feet from her chamber, where the assault was committed." The reporter reaffirmed that the weapon used was an old ax that had been retrieved by the police and taken to the police station. As usual, no other evidence to identify the murderer was found at the scene, and Mr. Hancock knew "of no cause for the attack, as they had no enemies."[7]

"A Crime Worthy of the Imps of Hell"

As the reporter was still taking notes as he knelt by the brutalized lady, a "shrill voice from the street" called out that another murder had taken place about a half mile away, in the second ward near the center of the city, at the home of James Phillips, a respected builder and architect living at 302 West Hickory Street. Phillips lived there with his wife, his son and his wife and their 18-month-old child, and several others. The *Austin Daily Statesman* gave a detailed description of the structure:

> The residence is a one story frame, with an L extending to the south and towards Hickory street. Between this L and the main building, which contains several rooms, there is a sort of platform or covered veranda connecting the two wings. A small room in the L was occupied by Mr. Phillips' son, James Phillips Jr., and his wife, Mrs. Eula Phillips. Last night Mr. Phillips and his wife and little child retired to bed as usual. Sometime past midnight the household were awakened, and their attention attracted by Mr. Phillips Jr., calling for some one. The door of the room, which opened out on the covered veranda, was found open. On entering Phillips was found weltering in blood.

Eula and her husband, Jimmy, lived across the gallery from the main house. The inside of their room presented a most "horrid spectacle." The bed clothes were "literally saturated with blood, and the sheets reddened with gore." Jimmy lay senseless in the bed on his right side, his head sporting "a deep wound just above the ear made with an ax which lay beside the bed." The wound extended "from the back of the head to the throat." His young wife, Eula, was not in the room, but their child was in the bed, "besmeared with blood," holding an apple, but unharmed.[8]

A search began immediately for the missing woman. "A trail of blood, still fresh on the floor of the outside of the veranda, was followed out into the yard, and in the northern part of the enclosure, a few feet from the fence, and at the door of the water closet, Mrs. Phillips was found dead." Her body was in "a perfectly nude condition," lying in a pool of still liquid blood. "A stick of heavy wood lay across each arm and lengthwise the corpse for a hellish purpose, which the assassins must have accomplished before fleeing from the scene of their crime." On her forehead was a terrible wound, made by the butt end of an axe, the skull "entirely mashed." There was ample evidence of a desperate struggle between the woman and her assailants before her demise. When discovered, she had been dead for only half an hour. Her "face, surrounded by hair dishevelled during a struggle, desperate but powerless was turned upward in the dim moonlight with an expression of agony that death itself had not erased from the features."[9]

The assault on Eula also seemed to suggest the presence of more than one attackers. According to the *Austin Daily Statesman*,

> It is believed . . . the assassins stifled her voice, and that she was still alive when dragged into the yard where she was

outraged and then the last and fatal blow delivered. The position of the body indicated that the devilish act was perpetrated by the assistance of a second party, as both hands were held down by pieces of wood, in which position the fiends left their victim and in which she must have died.

The Fort Worth paper agreed with this assessment, reporting that

The theory is that the inhuman fiends (there are believed to have been more than one) first struck Phillips senseless, then his wife, who, perhaps not yet dead, they dragged out and after accomplishing their devilish purpose gave their victim the fatal blow. A bare foot track was found on the premises similar to the track found near the scene of two other murders during the year past and of a similar character to this. The fiends probably took off their shoes to prevent noise.

Many reports also seemed to believe both the Hancock and Phillips murders were committed by the same assassins.[10]

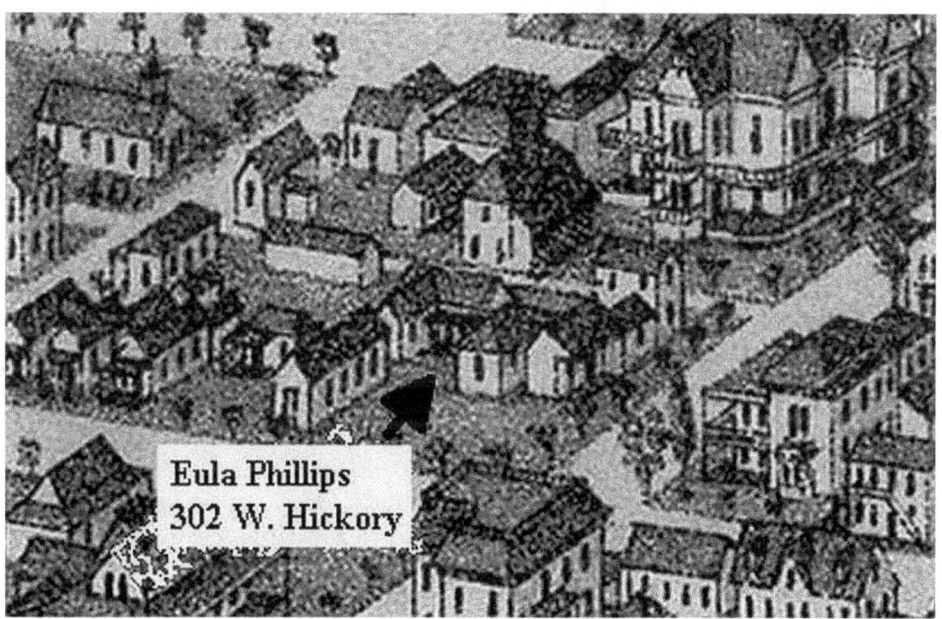

As for Eula's husband, Jimmy, he was not expected to live. He did not know who had attacked him. When he regained consciousness, he "repeatedly called for her—'Eula! Eula! Where is Eula?' and was kept ignorant of her fate." As in the Hancock murder, the assault on Jimmy and Eula had been conducted in silence. As in the earlier murder, an ax that belonged on the premises was used in the attack. But unlike the earlier murder, robbery did not seem to be a motive of any kind. In addition, this murder had one valuable piece of evidence, a bloody bare footprint left on the wood planks of the gallery between the Phillips' main house and the room where Jimmy and Eula slept.[11]

Eula Phillips was a mere teenager when she was murdered, only 17 years old. She had been born in 1868 to Thomas Burditt and Alice Missouri Eanes Burditt. Eula had an older sister, Alma Mayo Burditt. According to Skip Hollandsworth, the girls' mother "died when Eula and Alma were little. Their father, hotelier Thomas Burditt, essentially gave them up, asking one of their aunts, a member of the Slaughter family (for whom Slaughter Creek, south of Austin, is named), to raise them." The 1880 census and other genealogical documents suggested otherwise, however. According to the 1880 census, Eula was 12 years old and living in Austin with her mother, A.M. Burditt, aged 30, and her sister, Alma, aged 13. However, the census also indicated that Alice Burditt, the mother, was widowed. Several sources indicated that Eula's father was Thomas Parker Burditt, not the hotel operator Thomas A. Burdett. Alice Burditt died in the early 1880s, and the two girls did go live with an aunt. Thomas Parker Burditt, however, was not dead. He remarried in around 1890 and died in Dallas in 1901 at the age of 58. In any case, Eula Phillips, nicknamed Luly, was quite young when she died. She was buried in Oakwood Cemetery in Austin on December 26, 1885.[12]

According to Hollandsworth, Eula was "one of the loveliest young women in Austin. Her skin was pale, her eyes soft and contemplative, her dark, curling hair swept back from her temples. She wore billowy white dresses. One enchanted newspaper reporter described her as 'beautiful, frail.'" Hollandsworth even went so far as to dub her "the perfect symbol of the new Texas that was finally emerging after the long, painful years of Reconstruction." More likely, her murder was the sign of the new Texas that was replacing the rough and tumble days of outlaws and bad men. Her murder prophesied the lack of civility and the dehumanization that lay ahead. In January 1883, when she was only about 15 years old, she married James O. Phillips, about seven years her senior. Jimmy was reported to be a playboy and a talented violinist, though he earned his living as a carpenter when he was sober. Soon after they married, they were the parents of a baby boy named Thomas. Not long after that birth, Hollandsworth claimed, Eula was pregnant again. "When she became pregnant with their second child, she asked a family friend to go to a drug store on Congress Avenue and purchase chamomile flowers, extract of cottonwood, and ergot—which, if mixed properly, could induce an abortion." Eula clearly was not happy in her marriage to Jimmy Phillips, and the evidence uncovered in the coming weeks would blow the top off Austin's polite society.[13]

In a bit of literary indulgence, a Fort Worth reporter summarized the Christmas morning to which Austin citizens arose:

> This Christmas morning the capital city awoke, not to the tender chimes of Christmas bells, but to the startling and agonizing cry of murder. As the sun rose, and even before the fiery car of the orb of day ascended above the beautiful eastern hills, tremendous excitement reigned on the streets of Austin and in all the houses of the city, to which consternation had again been carried by the terrible and bloody work of the secret and unknown assassin. Two women, both matrons, each young and beautiful, the ornaments of highly respectable homes, lay prostrate, stricken down without warning and amid the deep

> stillness of the midnight hour they had received the death-blow from some hell-born harpy, utterly unknown except by the horrible and bloody butchery he or they left behind to tell of their horrible presence, not their identity.

The worst of the situation, though, was that Austinites had not heard the last of murder on this yuletide.[14]

"More Blood for Austin"

Austinites learned the day after Christmas that another murder had been discovered in Clarksville, on the west side of town. This murder was as ghastly, if not moreso, as the two murders that had occurred on Christmas Eve. To a city already quaking under the burden of unbridled horrors, the latest news erased any sense of peace on Earth, good will to men. Worse, this time the suspect was "a female fiend," "an artiste in atrocity."[15]

A headline in a San Antonio newspaper told the story: "A Woman Brains Her Two Children With an Axe, and the Hogs Make a Meal of One of Them." The Fort Worth newspaper provided the salient details:

> Investigation revealed the fact that a foul murder of a little boy had been committed. A white woman named Mrs. Eanes had been living in a cabin in Clarksville some time with her two children, one a mulatto boy aged seven, the other a pretty and interesting young girl of twelve. Both children were born out of wedlock. Mrs. Eanes left the place Thursday, the day before Christmas. Her children had previously disappeared, and she explained their absence by telling neighbors she had sent them to friends at Lampasas to be cared for. Nothing more was thought of it until this morning, when hogs rooting out among the cedars unearthed the body of the mulatto boy, which had been buried merely under a covering of cedar brush and leaves. The boy had apparently been dead several days. The head had been entirely severed from the trunk by an ax, and lay out some distance from the body, presenting a horrible sight. In the cabin was found the ax with blood on it, and a bundle of bloody clothes that had been worn by the boy.

Though the daughter was assumed killed as well, she turned up a few days later "safe and under the protection of a citizen named Isaacs, who vouched for her safety, and so the girl has not been murdered as at first supposed." The citizen was apparently Monty Isaacs, who ran a grocery on Mount Bonnell Road southwest of the Lunatic Asylum.[16]

As if often the case in such reports, the names and ages in this event varied greatly. The woman was identified variously as Mrs. Mollie A. Eanes, Mrs. Mollie Eans, Mrs. Eaves, Mrs. Eames, and Mary E. Eanes. The boy was consistently reported as being named Claude, though he was identified as both mulatto and white, and he was said to be five years old, seven years old, eight years old, nine years old, and twelve years old. His sister was identified as Maud and Dollie, and she was generally said to be a white child of eleven or twelve years old. As noted, both children were regarded as illegitimate, and the father of the boy was reputed to be Tom Brown, a black man about 30 years old who worked as a coachman for Mrs. Celest Loomis and lived with her at 900 Lavaca at the corner of Ash, not far from Clarksville.[17]

With so many variations, the story proved a bit complicated to untangle. Mrs. Eanes was married to Hugh Lawson Eanes. One report indicated that Mrs. Eanes was "rather a handsome woman of thirty-five and . . . a niece of Mrs. Eula Phillips, who was mysteriously murdered Thursday night, and hence some connection between the two murders have been thought to be established." Mrs. Eanes, who was apparently the second wife of Hugh Eanes, was indeed related to Eula Phillips, but she certainly did not seem to be Eula's niece. Hugh Eanes, born in 1839, and Alice Missouri Eanes, Eula's mother, born about ten years later, shared a common lineage stretching back to Virginia. The Eanes family is still well-known in the Austin area, "for whom the school district in West Austin is named." At best, Mrs. Eanes and Eula Phillips were distant cousins, and only by marriage.[18]

Hugh Eanes was a painter by trade, perhaps working with his brother, Clay Eanes, who was a painter living on East Avenue in Austin. Hugh apparently served in the Confederate Army in the Civil War, riding as a private with either Wood's Texas Cavalry or McCulloch's Texas Cavalry, or both. In June 1869, he married Barbara A. Green, and they had three or four children: Frank (born 1871), Alice Lenora (born 1875), Lattie, and Lottie. The last two might have been the same person, or they might have been twins, as they were both born in 1878. What happened to these children after the death of their mother is unknown. Barbara Eanes apparently died in 1878, perhaps in childbirth, because in July 1878, Hugh married M.A. Vess. Her first name may have been Mollie or Mary. For consistency's sake, she will hereafter be referred to as Mollie Eanes. This second wife was the one that committed the horrid crime in Clarksville. But the murder of her son may not have been her first heinous act.[19]

If Mollie Vess had an illegitimate daughter who was 11 or 12 in 1885, then the child had already been born when she married Hugh Eanes in 1878. Claude must have been born, also illegitimately, soon after the marriage. The marriage did not seem to be a strong one, and on August 30, 1885, Hugh Eanes died mysteriously "with symptoms of poison, but the doctors attributed it to lead colic or congestion. It is believed now she poisoned him to get rid of him." At the inquest into the death of Hugh Eanes, Mollie Eanes gave the following testimony:

> Last night my husband came home and acted very queerly. After talking awhile he complained of his stomach hurting. He did not sleep any, and was restless all night. This morning he began crying, and when I asked him what was the matter, he said he was thinking of his former wife, that was dead. He came and laid by me and commenced praying. He pinched me, and I told him if he pinched me again I would pinch him. He

> jumped up and fell on my breast, saying, "Oh, Mollie, I am
> dying." I said, "Oh, I think not." He said "Yes." I then went
> after Minnie Thompson, and when we came back he was lying
> on his stomach. He said he was cramping to death. After
> praying he called a doctor and said, "I am dying. Good-bye to
> all; good-bye father, mother, brothers and sisters. I am going
> to heaven where my wife is. I see God."

Hugh Eanes then drew his last breath. Later, "Prof. Everhart of the university made an analysis of the contents of his stomach after death. The coroner's jury gave a verdict of death by poison, but by whom unknown. Dr. Burt, city physician, pronounced it a case of congestion, but the whole truth has now flashed upon the public, and the death of Hugh Eanes now appears in the light of a diabolical murder, equal only to the fearful crime of murder and decapitation of the woman's mulatto son." Mollie Eanes was indeed a "female fiend."[20]

Soon after Hugh Eanes died, "a young white man named Chas. Courtney, said to be a lover of Mrs. Eanes," moved into the cabin. After the death of her husband and the arrival of Courtney, Mollie Eanes began several furtive activities.

> The unnatural mother tried to give the children away, pleading
> poverty, and a couple of weeks ago she told her neighbors that
> she had given Dollie to a school-teacher down the river. On
> Monday night Mrs. Eaves visited a neighboring family and asked
> the privilege of spending the night. She said she had also given
> Claude away to a family in Lampasas, and that Courtney being
> absent she was afraid to sleep in the house alone. Next
> morning the woman departed for Austin, saying that she had
> received a telegram from Illinois, asking her to attend the
> funeral of a relative who had just died there, leaving a legacy.

She also claimed she was going to Tennessee but went to San Antonio instead. Charles Courtney returned the day after Christmas and found the cabin deserted. He reported that the two children were missing.[21]

Soon the boy's body was discovered. Mollie Eanes had made little attempt to conceal the murdered child. "The body was only buried a foot deep," and covered with brush, "but some hogs had found it and devoured the heart and part of the limbs," as well as most of the flesh on the bones. A search of the cabin revealed more clues. "The pick-ax with which the little grave was dug was left in the cabin, with the handle besmeared with tell-tale blood. The bed on which the woman slept and the pillow were all bloody, showing that the boy was killed probably while asleep, the right side of the skull being mashed in with the ax, as in the other murders" on Christmas Eve.[22]

Charles Courtney was arrested on suspicion, and a letter was found that seemed to implicate him in the murder of the boy. Mollie Eanes had traveled to San Antonio but was arrested the day after Christmas at an inn near the San Pedro creek. "Mrs. Eanes denied the deed most positively, telling the officers that she had given her son away to a family at Lampasas, but could not tell the name of the people whom she made the custodians of her children." She denied any knowledge of the boy's death and claimed again that "she was very poor and unable to make a living for both herself and little ones, and, rather than see them perish slowly for want of food, she resolved to leave them with some one who could and would care for them properly." She was soon returned to Austin and placed in jail.[23]

"Austin's Revolting Tragedies"

Though the suspect in the murder of the Eanes boy was somewhat clear, the police again had little evidence to go on in the Hancock and Phillips murders. They had only two bloody axes and a bloody footprint to lead them to the assassins who had again shaken the foundation of Austin. In what should have been a celebration of the Christ and the silent night of the nativity, Austinites instead must have felt they had fallen into Dante's Inferno and ended at the ring reserved for those who promote violence against other people and their property: the first ring of the seventh circle, a river of blood.

Notes

Title: *Fort Worth Daily Gazette*, 12/25/1885.
Map credit: Hancock and Phillips murder scenes excerpted from Koch's *Austin Bird's-Eye Map, 1887*.

1. *San Antonio Daily Light*, 12/26/1885; *Fort Worth Daily Gazette*, 1/16/1886.
2. "Lunar calendar"; Galloway, *The Servant Girl Murders*: 285.
3. *Austin Daily Statesman*, 12/25/1885; *New York Times*, 12/26/1885; *Fort Worth Daily Gazette*, 12/25/1885; *Reno Evening Gazette*, 12/26/1885; *Morrison & Fourmy's General Directory of the City of Austin, 1885-1886*; 1880 Federal Census; Galloway, *The Servant Girl Murders*: 285. (The ages of the Hancocks given in different documents varied. The 1870 and 1880 censuses suggested that Sue Hancock was born in 1844, but her tombstone listed her year of birth as 1840. The 1870 census noted Moses Hancock was born in 1826, but the 1880 census indicated he was born in 1830. His death certificate noted his birth as 1833.)
4. *Austin Daily Statesman*, 12/25/1885; *New York Times*, 12/26/1885.
5. *Austin Daily Statesman*, 12/25/1885; *Fort Worth Daily Gazette*, 12/25/1885; *Galveston Daily News*, 12/26/1885; *San Antonio Daily Express*, 12/26/1885; *Morrison & Fourmy's General Directory of the City of Austin, 1885-1886*; 1900 Federal Census; Oakwood Cemetery Database (Hancock's neighbor's name was misspelled in the newspaper report. The author's personal visit to Mrs. Hancock's grave revealed the error on the headstone.)
6. *Austin Daily Statesman*, 12/25/1885.
7. *Austin Daily Statesman*, 12/25/1885; *San Antonio Daily Express*, 12/26/1885.
8. *Austin Daily Statesman*, 12/25/1885; *Galveston Daily News*, 12/26/1885; Hollandsworth, "Capital Murders."
9. *Austin Daily Statesman*, 12/25/1885; *St. Paul Daily Globe*, 12/26/1885; *Waco Daily Examiner*, 12/27/1885; *New York Times*, 12/26/1885; *Galveston Daily News*, 12/26/1885; *Fort Worth Daily Gazette*, 12/26/1885.
10. *Austin Daily Statesman*, 12/25/1885; *Fort Worth Daily Gazette*, 12/26/1885.

11. *Austin Daily Statesman*, 12/25/1885; *Fort Worth Daily Gazette*, 12/26/1885; *Waco Daily Examiner*, 12/27/1885; *San Antonio Daily Express*, 12/26/1885.

12. Hollandsworth, "Capital Murders"; 1880 Federal Census; <www.records.ancestry.com>;Tarpy, "Burditt family"; *Morrison & Fourmy's General Directory of the City of Austin, 1885-1886*; *Morrison & Fourmy's General Directory of the City of Austin, 1889-1890*; *Waco Daily Examiner*, 12/27/1885 (Eula's maiden name is a matter of some controversy. Ancestry.com indicated her last name was Burditt, the same name given on her marriage certificate to J.O. Phillips. The 1880 census indicated her last name was Burdett. The correct last name was Burditt. Her father was Thomas Parker Burditt. The Burditts were early settlers of Travis County and had sizable land holdings.)

13. Hollandsworth, "Capital Murders"; 1880 Federal Census; "Texas Marriages, 1837-1973"; Bree, "Austin's Bloody Murder Spree, 1884-1885": 117-118.

14. *Fort Worth Daily Gazette*, 12/26/1885.

15. *Fort Worth Daily Gazette*, 12/27/1885.

16. *San Antonio Daily Light*, 12/26/1885; *Fort Worth Daily Gazette*, 12/27/1885; *Fort Worth Daily Gazette*, 12/28/1885; *Morrison & Fourmy's General Directory of the City of Austin, 1885-1886*.

17. *San Antonio Daily Light*, 12/26/1885; *Fort Worth Daily Gazette*, 12/27/1885; *Waco Daily Examiner*, 12/27/1885; *Fort Worth Daily Gazette*, 12/28/1885; *Sacramento Daily Record-Union*, 12/28/1885; *Omaha Daily Bee*, 12/28/1885; *New York Times*, 12/29/1885; 1880 Federal Census; *Morrison & Fourmy's General Directory of the City of Austin, 1885-1886*.

18. *Fort Worth Daily Gazette*, 12/27/1885; "Texas Marriages, 1837-1973"; <www.records.ancestry.com>; Hollandsworth, "Capital Murders"; 1880 Federal Census (Hugh Eanes' great-grandfather was William Eanes (1720-1783), the brother to Alice Eanes' great-great-grandfather, Josiah Eanes (1733-1778). Hugh Eanes' father was Alexandria Eanes (1806-1888), and his grandfather was Daniel Eanes (1775-1830). Alice Eanes' father was Watkins Eanes (1800-?), her grandfather was Herbert Eanes (1770-1852), and her great-grandfather was Henry Eanes (1757-1828).)

19. *Morrison & Fourmy's General Directory of the City of Austin, 1885-1886*; "United States, Civil War Soldiers Index"; <www.records.ancestry.com>; "Texas Marriages, 1837-1973."

20. *Fort Worth Daily Gazette*, 12/27/1885.

21. *Fort Worth Daily Gazette*, 12/27/1885; *Sacramento Daily Record-Union*, 12/28/1885; *Waco Daily Examiner*, 12/27/1885.

22. *Fort Worth Daily Gazette*, 12/27/1885; *Waco Daily Examiner*, 12/27/1885; *Sacramento Daily Record-Union*, 12/28/1885.

23. *Omaha Daily Bee*, 12/28/1885; *Fort Worth Daily Gazette*, 12/28/1885; *Fort Worth Daily Gazette*, 12/27/1885; *New York Times*, 12/29/1885.

24. Dante's *Inferno*, Canto XII.

Chapter 11

"A Saturnalia of Crime"

Fury Erupts Among the Citizenry

After the Hancock and Phillips murders, excitement in Austin was at a fever pitch. The Eanes boy's murder only fanned the fires, though that case seemed to be an isolated event, with a clear idea of who had done the killing. But the killers of Sue Hancock and Eula Phillips continued to walk the streets of Austin unhindered, and likely unsuspected. That ghastly unknown was much more frightening than the fear caused by the depravity of a known killer.

Christmas morning 1885 was like no other in the history of Austin. The news of the Hancock and Phillips murders spread like wildfire, and by 2 A.M. Christmas morning, the streets were thronged with people. The Fort Worth reporter captured the tension in his late-night report:

> No words can portray the excitement. If the fiend or fiends could be found they would be torn limb from limb or burned alive. The indignation is something fearful to behold. Groups of excited men parade Congress avenue and ask each other, with white lips, When will this damnable work end? Whose wife is safe as long as these blood-thirsty hellhounds can commit such crimes in the heart of the city? At this hour (1:45) the crowds are increasing, and but little more sleep will be done in Austin to-night.

And the *New York Times* noted that "If the fiends are apprehended, the citizens are determined that they shall be hanged in the sight of the Capitol." After repeated failures by the city government and the police to protect the residents of the city, the citizens of Austin had had enough, and they were ready to take matters into their own hands.[1]

At 11 A.M. Christmas morning, Mayor John W. Robertson called to order a hastily-organized meeting in the statehouse. An estimated 500 to 1000 infuriated citizens, including many prominent Austinites, were in attendance. Mayor Robertson admitted that the authorities had tried everything to arrest the murderers, but every attempt had proved a failure. So now he was calling upon the people of Austin to suggest measures that could bring the assassins to justice. He insisted that "Every man's hand must be against these men till they are hunted down and brought to justice. White and colored must unite in bringing them to punishment." Then Thomas S. Maxey, a local attorney, was appointed to preside over the meeting, and Will Lambert, a printer and journalist, was chosen as secretary.[2]

Various citizens then addressed the crowd. The first speakers were temperate in their remarks, trying not to incite the listeners to rash action. Mr. Maxey spoke first, saying:

> In the excited state of public sentiment, resulting from these vile assassinations, we may be prompted to take some hasty measure which organized committees might not deem wise, as mob or lynch law. That is worse than no law, and should be the last resort of a law governed people. With the mayor, backed by the city council, with the cooperation of a governor as a man who loves peace and order, I say, with them and with your sheriff and assistants, these things can be stopped, and it must be stopped. I throw out this suggestion that you may not take any hasty and illegal action. Call upon the officers, and with powers of the law, this reign of terror I believe will cease, and the good name of Austin be reinstated throughout the state.

General Nathan G. Shelley, the elderly law partner of John Hancock and a former state senator, spoke next. Hearkening back to his days as a brigadier general in the Confederate army, he suggested placing "a cordon of sentinels around the city" to prevent the guilty from leaving town, in case they had not already done so.[3]

Judge Alexander W. Terrell then delivered some remarks. He too favored a reasonable approach to the crisis, but he doubted that the crowd wanted to hear reason.

> This is a hall of law and justice and yet you propose, in blind frenzy, to tear down the social conditions of law and order, and organize a vigilance committee. It would be fruitless of results, and bring about calamities you would deplore. The mob, you should remember, will have blood. When it rules, reason is dethroned and ceases to act. A vigilance committee means blood, and is likely to victimize the innocent. Any stranger who might get blood upon him without being able to account for it, though innocent, might be the victim of suspicion. I prefer we should assist our officers with the reinforcements of the law, and am not willing to join in a vigilance committee.

Ira Evans, a local land agent, also spoke against a vigilance committee. He proposed that the city hire more detectives, even though the ones already employed had done little to solve the crimes. He also called for a heightened enforcement of moral codes, suggesting that the saloons and gambling houses be shuttered. "Gambling, bawdy houses, and other means of dissipation which lead to greater crimes should be suppressed, and can be as they were in Dallas. Why, Mr. Mayor, do we have such a saturnalia of crime in this city? . . . Why are not the black elephant and white elephant suppressed?" Another land agent, Frank M.

Maddox, suggested that the saloons "and other places of dissipation" be forced to close at 10 P.M. each night. He also called for the use of a hundred secret agents known only to the marshal and the mayor to bring the assassins to justice.[4]

The slate of speakers seemed largely tipped in favor of local authorities, for indeed, most of the speakers gained their livelihood through the government. A few spoke out in favor of a vigilance committee, among them Major Joe Stewart and Colonel Joel Miller. Stewart was a banker whose home had been attacked back in March. Miller was the editor of the *Austin Daily Statesman*. "Col. Miller's speech roused the vast crowd to the highest pitch of fury," and the feeling among many was that the majority of the citizens favored a vigilance committee. As a compromise, Colonel William M. Brown, a local attorney, proposed that "a committee of three citizens from each ward be appointed by the chair to devise such means as may be deemed best to be taken in cooperation with the city, county and state authorities to ferret out and punish the murderers who have outraged this community, and that we as citizens, invest them with full authority, and will back them with full moral and material support." To show support, banker Alexander P. Wooldridge offered $250. Land agent Phineas DeCordova proposed that the meeting set a funding amount of $5000, and he said he was willing to subscribe $50 and called on others to do the same. He said that money would let the city get "good detectives. Those we had were amateurs." Though the crowd seemed more in favor of direct vigilante action, Judge Terrell's plea for reason prevailed, and in the end a so-called committee of public safety was established "to assist city officers." According to several sources, the committee would consist of three white men and one black man from each of the city's ten wards.[5]

Despite Mayor Robertson's claim that "good will result" from the meeting, most left the gathering without relief. The Fort Worth newspaper best summed up the mood in Austin that day:

> The feeling in the city is one of terror. The white women as well as colored are frightened and troubled. Doors and windows have been fastened and barred and a feeling of UTTER INSECURITY is felt. No confidence is felt in the laws, as the police say they recently had the parties who murdered the servant girls, but the grand jury turned them loose even after a colored woman swore to the identity of one of them. . . . Gloom overspreads the city. It has been a terrible Christmas day for Austin.

All the speeches in the world could not alleviate the fear that lay over Austin like a blanket. Only the capture of the assassins could restore even a semblance of security to the shaken city.[6]

"Important Action"

The Austin city council held a special session Christmas evening to discuss actions to take against the continuing crime spree. Two ordinances were quickly passed. One ordinance temporarily added another 30 officers to the police force, giving Marshal Lucy 50 more officers than Marshal Lee had to deal with the problem. A second ordinance sought to regulate the operating hours of saloons and liquor stores. The initial proposal for the second ordinance called for places where liquor was sold to close from 11 P.M. to 5 A.M. The closing hour was later amended to midnight, and the ordinance passed on a vote of 11 to 6. According to Galloway, "At that time, saloons operated under a state license and were state-regulated. They were allowed to remain open twenty-four hours a day. Many felt that the saloons were a breeding ground for the criminal element and that greater regulation of them was necessary. . . . The city council's ordinance overrode state law. While they had no legal authority to enforce the ordinance if the saloons did not comply, many private citizens were ready to take it upon themselves to see that the proprietors did comply."[7]

The Citizens' Committee for Public Safety that was formed in the meeting Christmas morning also underwent further organization. With the feeling that 40 members were too unwieldy for most committee business, an executive committee was formed, and A.P. Wooldridge was elected chairman of the committee. Wooldridge was an unlikely choice for chairman if any hope of solving all the murders was to be had. Wooldridge was not especially sympathetic to blacks, suggesting in a 1919 comment that "whites 'will tolerate no idea of social equality.'" The executive committee included one man from each ward. Most of the members of the executive committee had some association with the government. Elected from the first ward was Ira H. Evans, a land agent. Representing the second ward was Numa O. Lauve, an insurance agent. A.P. Wooldridge, a banker, represented the third ward. A farmer, C.G. Caldwell, served for the fourth ward. The fifth ward's representative was Phineas DeCordova, a land agent. Druggist J.W. Graham was elected from the sixth ward. In the seventh ward, a clerk in the Comptroller's Office, Alfred O. Evans, was chosen. Another land agent, F.M. Maddox, represented the eight ward. For the ninth ward, Stephen K. Morley, another druggist, was elected. For some reason, the tenth ward had two representatives: John R. Blocker, a stock dealer; and William H. Holland, a school teacher who had spoken at the meeting and who was the only black member of the executive committee.[8]

The group issued a statement, indicating that "It is not the purpose of this executive committee to act independently of the civil authorities, but rather to aid and support them by every means in its power." One way the executive committee hoped to help the civil authority was by raising money to support the effort to find the murderers. The committee also noted that "For effective work, some men must be trusted implicitly, and no questions be asked them, as secrecy is essential to success." The executive committee seemed to be establishing the very kind of star chamber that Grooms Lee complained had led to his dismissal a few weeks earlier.[9]

"Sores on the Body Politic"

Though most civic leaders expressed their satisfaction with the Christmas day meeting, others were not so thrilled by the outcome. The editor of the *Austin Daily*

Statesman had preached vigilantism at the meeting, but his views were generally not shared by the other speakers. He continued his call for a vigilance committee in the next day's newspaper, playing upon the fear that every citizen felt.

> Murders were committed in this city night before last when the moon and stars were most effulgent and shot their mellow light over all the earth and in nearly every crevice of our houses and garden fence. Residences stood out boldly in full glare of moonlight and two gentle women and one man were assaulted with a virulency and infernal accomplishment that struck with terror the bravest men. Now every stick that the foot cracks and breaks, every latch that is innocently lifted by members of a household, sends alarm and fright to its sleeping inmates.
> In a word, there is a state of affairs in the city of Austin that is unendurable, not another day or night can we, its citizens, whose wives and children are at the mercy of this demon of murder and worse than that, outrage, not another night can we submit. Gentlemen may talk of law and order under constituted and legal authority, but when the constituted and legal authority is unequal to the occasion, when they have demonstrated that they are as powerless as infants to avert the impending fate of our wives and children under this riot of murder, when they admit that they cannot assign a cause or impede the stroke of the ax in a single instance, then what is our duty? What then, is the duty of the people to themselves and to their families? It is plainly their duty to protect themselves.

The newspaper tried to downplay the notion that such vigilance committees might lead to chaos and injustice. The idea was to organize "a sufficient number of citizens of each ward into a watch to keep constant guard throughout the night over every part of the city." But the main idea was to organize into citizen groups because the government could no longer protect the citizenry.

> It is not proposed, and it has never been contemplated, that such a vigilance committee should assume the power to arrest and hang men on its mere "ipse dixit." That was the construction forced upon the meeting yesterday, of its object by those interested in protecting the constituted authorities from what they considered a reflection of their efficiency, when none was contemplated. We all know that the mayor and police have done all they can do as men to discover the perpetrators of these crimes, but to them, as it is to us, these crimes are singularly mysteries and it is folly for any city administration to be so sensitive about its authority as to object to private effort to protect our families from outrage and murder. Go to work, fellow citizens, and form your patrol and let it be so constituted that a man cannot go into his back yard without being discovered, and that all tramps and unauthorized persons will for the time be forbid the liberty of the city.

The newspaper also noted that the general tone of the meeting favored the city government, but the people by and large were in favor of vigilante action.

> The people seem fully determined to take the authority in their own hands. It was frequently remarked that we have long enough trusted to constituted authority of our police system to find out and punish the villains who are disgracing our city, and we now intend to organize ourselves in our respective wards and protect ourselves. The gentlemen advocating that idea in the public meeting yesterday did not press it, because, while it was apparent that they were sustained by two-thirds of the people of Austin there assembled, they thought best to let the meeting do what it pleased and to secretly and quietly organize for that purpose.

The newspaper stressed that a vigilance committee was not illegal and that it might be the only means to end the reign of terror that had seized Austin for the last year. The vigilance committee would include "the very best people in this city" who "will do nothing illegal but, what is actually necessary for the protection of life."[10]

The article also contained specific recommendations to help curb the wave of crime. One recommendation was for the citizens to band together to close the saloons and gambling houses where the criminals gathered to plan their dastardly deeds, not by law but by force and intimidation. The newspaper obviously felt that the recent ordinance regulating saloons and liquor stores did not go far enough.

> Law and order may be efficient to a certain extent, but there are places in this town, licensed by the law and order men, places that they cannot shut up by law, that are . . . the haunts where the midnight conclave of assassins assemble and plan their deeds of murder. These are the sores on the body politic that need the knife of the surgeon. The law officers cannot close them; the committees of citizens who act in connection, and advised by the mayor, cannot close them, but a committee, self-constituted and endorsed by the people for solid respectability and the highest judgment of prudence; a committee consisting of ten in each ward, and supported by every good citizen in that ward can say to the proprietors of these hell holes: "We want you to close your establishments. We are aware of the fact that you have a license to do business, but we do not care for this authority given you by the law. We, the good and respectable citizens of this ward, demand that under the present circumstances you close your place, and if you do not obey the will of the people of this ward, then take and suffer the consequences." This is what a committee of that nature could say to these people who keep the places where every crime is plotted and from which orders are issued to be carried out. The mayor with the city council at his back, has no authority to do this, for these places are kept under a license; but such a committee, with that as its primal duty, . . . could use the surgeon's knife in cutting out the great sore that breeds a condition of rape and murder.

The newspaper seemed to be advocating the very thing it sought to curb: lawlessness.[11]

"The Dark and Bloody Ground"

Marshal Lucy began to enact some of the recommendations. He instructed the police that "after a certain hour at night, to critically examine every man they met, and if he could not give a good account of himself, to give him just twenty-four hours within which to leave the city." The *Austin Daily Statesman* applauded Lucy's initiative, noting, though, that "It ought to have been done months ago and perhaps the list of appalling murders would not have been so long." Try as he might, though, driving out the vagrants was no guarantee the murderers would be caught. And the *San Antonio Times* wondered "where the thugs are going when they are run off from their chosen haunt. . . . Is it just for any city, when it fails to manage its own lawless elements, to shove them off to deprecate on other cities?" The *Times* article, reprinted in the *Austin Daily Statesman*, also wondered "If the city police of Austin had been doing their whole duty during the last year, would that city have gained the reputation it now has as 'the dark and bloody ground?'"[12]

Other Austin citizens had ideas on how to catch the culprits, or certainly how to prevent a recurrence of their vile deeds. A woman identified only as Mrs. F. offered the following tip: "Let me tell you how, in a measure, we can protect ourselves. One good dog and a revolver will do it; the dog in your house and the revolver under your pillow. Does any sane person think that those women could have been murdered if there had been a dog in the house? It would have been utterly impossible for any one to have entered the house without the dog arousing the inmates." Another citizen, identified as B., suggested that "the city be at once lighted with gas." This fellow also suggested the city be outfitted with Gamewell's fire alarm boxes. According to him, the city should also provide weapons for several citizens in every block of the city.

> Then when a murder has been committed, let the first one who has knowledge of it, turn in the alarm, which can readily be designated or arranged to indicate differences between murder and fire. Then when the alarm goes out from the central station, murder can be signaled to the public. Then let those citizens living on the street corners at once go to the alley corner and those living in the middle of the square go to the corner, with their arms. Let them go in shirt sleeves, as a distinguishing mark, and let them keep their positions until the signal for their retirement is given from the central station. While on duty, let them stop every man, who shall attempt to pass near them, or go at once to the assistance of any watchman who he may see needs his aid. This plan ought to thoroughly police the entire city in three minutes after a murder has become known, and certainly should secure the arrest of the criminal in the case, and will also secure midnight prowlers, who should properly account for themselves or be made to leave the city in an hour.

The plan, though thorough, would likely prove quite expensive to implement.[13]

A wag calling himself Walkabout had several ideas on how to solve the crisis. His first proposal was based on finances. He believed that "If this killing and robbing business is kept up property will be depreciated to an incalculable extent. . . . For less than one-half of this depreciation property owners can back up the common council to the required extent." Walkabout also proposed that the police force be expanded to "an unlimited extent" and that the city undergo a thorough cleansing of its criminal element.

> Until this city is purified and cleansed of its vagrants, thieves, robbers, murderers, and others of like ilk, let there be placed at sundown and kept there until sunrise, two policemen at the junction of every two streets in the city. If we have not inhabitants enough to do this let us import some. Let these corner policemen, on the corners, arrest every person who cannot give a satisfactory account of himself, and one of the two take him to the jail while the other remains on duty, and having deposited his prisoner hurry back. As soon as the hoodlums find out that every corner is guarded they will lie low and not circulate. They will remain in their holes.

Walkabout expanded on his plan for a police state in Austin.

> Hence 100 extra day policemen for each ward should be appointed, whose duty should be to search every nook and corner in each ward and drag out every person who could not give a satisfactory account of himself and imprison him. For this latter duty volunteers could be found. This might take several days and several large rooms. Then let all these be tried, and if any are found guilty of crime let them be sent to jail to await the action of the grand jury, and if any innocent and deserving persons have been arrested let them be set free, and then let all the vagrants be given twenty-four hours to leave town, with the understanding that if they did not do so they must take their chances, and then let these 100 people in each ward and these extra policemen on the street corners be empowered and instructed to see that they do take their chances, and let all of these law-abiding citizens assist these special policemen in dealing out these chances. In less than two weeks all the chances would be taken.

Walkabout also proposed an increase in the number of mounted policemen. Their job would be to "scour the country for at least six miles from Austin, in search of tramps, and order them to leave or take their chances." It's amazing how those who preach the loudest for law and order are usually the first to dispense with the law to attain their notion of order.[14]

Walkabout ended his catalog of suggestions by impugning the manliness of Austin's male population, saying, "If Austin cannot protect the women and children within its borders, its able-bodied men had better doff their breeches and don petticoats, and call on their mothers, wives, sisters, and daughters to go to the front and defy the enemy." Walkabout, of course, was not brave enough to attach his real name to his recommendations.[15]

"Monumental Stupidity"

As should be expected, the new crop of murders in Austin brought criticism of Austin's civil authorities from around the state and the nation. The Fort Worth newspaper was one of the more vocal, stating that "As a rule capitol cities are dull places. Austin is a bright exception. She drives a brisker business than any five towns in the state—in the slaughter of servant girls." It also sniped that "Austin is peacably disposed—all lazy people are. They haven't the energy to run a murderer more than a block." The Fort Worth newspaper also attacked the local police, suggesting that the Texas Rangers be called in to solve the problem: "Don't they need rangers at Austin? Martial law might protect human life at Austin. Civil law seems to be powerless." A poke was also taken at the state government: "If Gov. Ireland should call an extra session of the legislature, does anybody suppose he could get a quorum of members to go to Austin? None of them want to figure in the newspaper headlines as another victim of the Austin ghoul." Other Texas newspapers were a bit more subdued in their criticism. The Waco newspaper posed the question on everyone's lips: "Another awful murder in Austin—This series of crimes is altogether without parallel in the criminal history of the country. Why is it no discoveries have ever been made?"[16]

A St. Paul newspaper offered a likely answer, noting that "the story that no clue can be discovered to the perpetrators of seven murders which have occurred in Austin, Tex., within the last eight months, either indicates that the Austin authorities possess monumental stupidity or that a talented sensationalist is at present residing in Austin." Not to be outdone, the Fort Worth newspaper offered a candid explanation of why so little had been done to solve the crimes in an article titled "Better Late Than Never."

> On the night of the 30th of December 1884, a mulatto woman named Mollie Smith was foully murdered while asleep in her room on one of the principal residence streets of Austin. All the circumstances attending the taking off of the poor victim were of the most atrocious character. She was knocked in the head with an ax, and her nude and gory corpse was discovered early the next morning in the back yard, where the fiend who killed her had dragged her, perhaps while still in the agonies of death. To this day the perpetrator is unknown. Not many weeks had gone by before another woman was slain; she too, a poor negro serving girl. The second murder was a repetition of all the diabolical features of the first. Another and another followed until the whole country stood aghast in horror at the bloody deeds enacted at the Texas capital. Before the expiration of the year just ended eight women were butchered in this same city—all after the same inhuman fashion that marked the first.

Scores of arrests were made, but in no instance were there any direct proofs of guilt to fasten the crime on any of the parties accused.

Besides the murders a number of women were assaulted and several badly hurt. The methods of the villain or villains were marked by monotony and mystery—monotonous because always done at the dead of night, always in the same way, and always directed against females; mysterious because it seemed impossible to find out, or catch the demons in their awful crimes. Of the eight women thus made way with, the first six were of African blood; the other two were white women, whose recent assassinations are still fresh in the memories of THE GAZETTE's readers. Their fate seemed to add horrors upon horrors, until the situation reached a point which language could scarcely portray. Could the guilty wretch have been found, not all the sheriffs in the state could have kept an infuriated people from rending him limb from limb, or burning him at the stake. The devilish ingenuity or luck that had so long baffled all efforts at detection, stood like an impassable gulf between the populace and the revenge they so eagerly thirsted to take. What could be done? How was the reign of terror ever to be terminated? Would the wretches ever be caught?

Public gatherings were quickly held, and thither flocked all Austin, all animated with one idea, all moved by a common impulse. Thousands of dollars were freely subscribed and a reward of $1000 for the arrest of any of the murderers was offered. Money was no object. The wives and daughters of the citizens must be protested at any cost.

There was a break in the monotony at last. The color line had been overleaped. No longer were ignorant and lowly black women the only victims. Impunity had lent boldness and the dwellings of the whites were no longer safe. Indeed, it was time to do something. To speak truth, while the people of Austin were horrified at the killing of the servants, they did not realize how bad the state of affairs was until two unfortunates of the superior race were added to the list. They seemed to forget that murder is no less heinous because of race or condition. "It's all among the niggers" was heard far too frequently. Of course all were not thus indifferent. But it can not be doubted that if the same determined and repressive measures had been adopted at the outset, fewer of these disgraceful occurrences would have stained the fair fame of Austin and the state. Had this been done both Mrs. Hancock and Mrs. Phillips might now be living. There was a most culpable and inexcusable delay of the right sort of action, which none can see half so clearly now as the very people whose seeming negligence and indifference had no little to do in the continuation of a carnival of crime almost unprecedented in modern times.[17]

Was the Fort Worth article correct? Had racial indifference been the main cause of the delay? As long as the murders involved only black servant girls, little action was taken by the local government, certainly not to the magnitude that was seen following the murders of Sue Hancock and Eula Phillips. Maybe the reason the crimes had not been solved was not due to "monumental stupidity," but to monumental indifference. The feeble efforts to solve the crimes had finally spawned the very thing so many had feared. The color line had been crossed, and now no household in Austin was safe.

Notes

Title: *Austin Daily Statesman*, 12/26/1885.

1. *Fort Worth Daily Gazette*, 12/25/1885; *New York Times*, 12/26/1885.
2. *Fort Worth Daily Gazette*, 12/26/1885; *Galveston Daily News*, 12/26/1885; *Reno Evening Gazette*, 12/26/1885; *Austin Daily Statesman*, 12/26/1885.
3. *Austin Daily Statesman*, 12/26/1885; "United States, Civil War Soldiers Index"; 1860 Federal Census.
4. *Austin Daily Statesman*, 12/26/1885; *Morrison & Fourmy's General Directory of the City of Austin, 1885-1886* (The Black Elephant and the White Elephant were saloons.)
5. *Fort Worth Daily Gazette*, 12/26/1885; *Austin Daily Statesman*, 12/26/1885; *Galveston Daily News*, 12/26/1885; *St. Paul Daily Globe*, 12/26/1885; *Waco Daily Examiner*, 12/27/1885; *Morrison & Fourmy's General Directory of the City of Austin, 1885-1886*.
6. *Austin Daily Statesman*, 12/26/1885; *Fort Worth Daily Gazette*, 12/26/1885.
7. *Austin Daily Statesman*, 12/29/1885; Galloway, *The Servant Girl Murders*: 285.
8. *Austin Daily Statesman*, 12/29/1885; *Morrison & Fourmy's General Directory of the City of Austin, 1885-1886*; Humphrey, *Austin: A History of the Capital City*: 35.
9. *Austin Daily Statesman*, 12/29/1885.
10. *Austin Daily Statesman*, 12/26/1885.
11. *Austin Daily Statesman*, 12/26/1885.
12. *Austin Daily Statesman*, 12/29/1885; *Austin Daily Statesman*, 12/30/1885.
13. *Austin Daily Statesman*, 12/29/1885.
14. *Austin Daily Statesman*, 12/29/1885.
15. *Austin Daily Statesman*, 12/29/1885.
16. *Fort Worth Daily Gazette*, 2/17/1886; *Fort Worth Daily Gazette*, 1/24/1886; *Fort Worth Daily Gazette*, 12/26/1885; *Fort Worth Daily Gazette*, 1/6/1886; *Waco Daily Examiner*, 12/27/1885.
17. *St. Paul Daily Globe*, 1/5/1886; *Fort Worth Daily Gazette*, 1/6/1886.

Chapter 12

"Worse Than Babel"

More Mischief, Theories, and Arrests

The murders of Sue Hancock and Eula Phillips had put the city of Austin in a state of general alarm. But not even the heightened sense of awareness of the citizenry could stop the mischief and mayhem that continued to plague the capital. And as usual, no identification of the perpetrators could be made. Could anything this side of heaven stop the crime spree?

On the same night as the Hancock and Phillips murders, Christmas Eve, Alexander Thornton, "a hard working respectable colored man," was enjoying a yuletide party with his family and friends. Thornton was about 40 years old and lived at 410 Willow Street at the corner of Neches, near the Colorado River, with his wife and five children. After the party, late Thursday night, he escorted some friends home. About six blocks from his house, one of the friends suddenly realized she had forgotten something at Thornton's place. Thornton went back to fetch the forgotten item. "When he reached his gate he saw a man inside his yard, who he at once hailed and asked who he was, and what his business was at that time of night. The fellow ran and jumped over the fence before Thornton could get close enough to him to tell whether he was a white or black man. Thornton pursued him some distance, but finally lost him in Waller creek bottom." No damage had been done, and no one was injured, but Thornton was alarmed. Why was this bit of information important? Willow Street was one street south of Water Street where Sue Hancock was murdered. Thornton lived only a couple of blocks from the Hancock house.[1]

That same night, John Leonard, Jr., a pressman for the *Austin Daily Statesman*, attended a party on West Pine Street near West Avenue. Around midnight, Leonard and a young lady left the party to head back into town. At the intersection of Pine and West, they saw two men coming toward them. "One of them was a short, thick set man, bareheaded, and with him was a tall man, who carried a small bundle wrapped up in an oilcloth. The two walked aside in a sort of half-circle, and stopped in the shadow of some trees near by. They acted as if they were afraid to be seen." The two men did not cause any trouble, but the next night, three men were seen in the yard at Leonard's father's home, where Leonard lived, at 909 San Jacinto near the intersection with Mulberry. Two of the men fit the description given. Again, no damage had been done, and no one was injured, but why the men should show up in Leonard's yard was a mystery.[2]

Late Saturday night, December 26, a man was seen inside the yard of the house next to the Hancock home on Water Street. The house belonged to Atlas Persinger, who had aided Moses Hancock the night his wife was attacked. The man "was discovered by a party in the house, who threw a rock at him as he jumped the fence." Travis County Sheriff Malcolm Hornsby was called, and he arrived with a bloodhound. The dog, though, would not track the intruder, and no suspect could be found.[3]

Early Sunday morning, December 27, Officer Henry Brown was called to the east side to investigate a disturbance near the Austin and Northwestern Railroad depot on East Cedar Street between Medina and San Marcos streets. An old black woman told Officer Brown that "a man trying to break in her door woke her up, and that her screams for help had the effect of running him off." Brown searched the neighborhood but did not discover any clues or suspects.[4]

Even in the dives of Guy Town, unrest was felt. Late Saturday night, "two men met a man in Tin Cup, one of the disgraceful localities of Guy Town, and ordered him to hold up his hands, which he did, and lifted up his feet in a very lively manner also, judging by the order in which he left the alley." Though shaken by the episode, the man did not lose anything to the assailants, and of course they were not found. These incidents were sometimes no more than petty crimes and overreactions, but they served to keep the city on edge.[5]

"Demon in Human Flesh"

The latest murders spawned a new wave of theories, as might be expected. The *Austin Daily Statesman* reasonably surmised that the yearlong series of murders were "all seemingly done by one, two or three and perhaps four persons." The newspaper continued in its theory, noting that

> The murderers have so completely concealed their trail that the very bloodhounds are at fault in tracking and establishing their identity. In fact so mysterious has been the accomplishment of these horrible murders that the superstitious are beginning to attribute them to supernatural agencies. Of course this is an error of excited fancy. They are undoubtedly perpetrated with great shrewdness, and accident has largely favored the concealment of the perpetrators.

The Fort Worth newspaper seemed to concur, stating that "It is believed to be certain that all these horrible killings have been the work of the same demon in human flesh, but whoever or whatever he may be, is still utterly unknown, dark and inscrutable." The *Austin Daily Statesman* also reported that the city leaders and the executive citizens committee believed that "all the murders for the last year in this city can be traced to a special cause and to a certain class of persons." The city leaders also claimed that they "will be enabled in ten days, to give the public such a solution of the seemingly mysterious murders, that will free all good citizens from apprehensions of danger. The city authorities and the citizen's executive committee are in possession of facts that will convict the murderers and demonstrate the fact to the whole world that there is no danger to a good citizen in this city." Of course, no such solution was presented, and the guarantee that good citizens were not in danger was preposterous, considering that Sue Hancock and Eula Phillips were relatively good citizens who had been murdered. One San Antonio newspaper reasonably suggested that "there must be a gang of these lust fiends at work here, their object being rape or robbery, or both, and murder being resorted to to prevent the possibility of detection." The theory was also advanced that the Hancock and Phillips murders were connected—"that one resulted from the other."[6]

Detective Mike Hennessey of Houston's Noble Detective Agency, who was dismissed by the city in December, was convinced that Glenn Drummer, Oliver Townsend, and Dock Woods were "the perpetrators of these series of awful crimes." Hennessey based his theory on the fact "that the murders would stop while they were in jail, but would start again as soon as they were out, all of which has been verified." He was interviewed by a reporter for the *Houston Age* and gave the following response about the so-called Thug Gang.

> The gang of scoundrels are well known. Soon after the outrage upon Gracy Vance and Patsy Bottom, I went to Austin to see what I could do in the matter, and soon got Doc Woods and Glenn Drummer, Oliver Townsend and Alleck Mack, all negroes, in jail. I took Doc Woods before Gracie Vance, in the presence of the district attorney, the sheriff, and the hospital physician of Travis county, and she identified him instantly. She said: "I know you, Dock. What did you try to kill me for? I never did anything to you." The grand jury of Travis county, for some reason, satisfactory I suppose to itself, failed to indict either Dock Woods or the balance of his gang; but they were kept locked up for three months, and during that three months the women of the capitol of Texas slept secure from the ravishing murderous attacks of the thugs.

One can likely see why Hennessey was dismissed by the city. His response was filled with incorrect names, and Gracie Vance died the night she was attacked, so she hardly could have identified Woods later. One assumes he meant Lucinda Boddy.[7]

The theory that a lunatic was responsible gained widespread support. The Waco newspaper reported that "The theory is becoming general that the Austin murders so mysteriously carried on are the work of some lunatic confined in the asylum. There is no doubt but there is some truth in this. And yet let no new theory carry off the attention of the authorities in any doubtful direction. Austin is in a bad box in this thing and the general sentiment is one of pity for its misfortune." A Reno, Nevada, newspaper indicated that "the crimes were perpetrated by some insane individual, who cunningly devised how he could shed the women's blood without apprehension." The *Galveston Daily News* published a letter from Laredo that considered the lunatic theory at length. The Galveston news report was reprinted in the *Austin Daily Statesman*.

> The long series of horrible butcheries of people in Austin during the past year, it is stated, creates a profound sensation in this section of the state. The News reporter, claiming some experience as a detective, ventures to suggest that these brutal murders are the work of a lunatic, who escapes, at stated periods, from the lunatic asylum near Austin, at night, and after his hellish work is accomplished returns within the asylum walls without detection, where he is safe from the search of the detectives. The history of those crimes from their first commencement, one year ago, sustains, in a high degree, this theory. Briefly mentioned, the facts surrounding each instance of these murders are similar to a startling degree. They all occur about the same time of night, and about the usual period of time apart. The victims in every instance but one have been women, and the same instrument—an ax—is always used. Nearly always the victim's skull is crushed in the same place, and as a rule the bodies are dragged some distance from where the death blow was struck. The absence of a motive commensurate with the atrocity of the crime, and lastly, the entire failure to find any clue by detection, confirms the theory that these acts of the murderer after the crime is committed are different from those of a sane man, who would certainly commit some act that would lead to his detection. Whenever this fiend is found, the assertion is ventured that he will prove to be the same person who, twelve years ago, at New Braunfels, crushed the skulls of Mrs. Faust and the little daughter of Dr. Voelober, and for which the husband of Mrs. Faust was killed in the court house at New Braunfels while held by the sheriff for trial for the crime.

The letter had several incorrect assumptions, one that the murders took place at a "usual period of time apart." Some of the murders were months apart, others a few weeks apart. And an ax was not used in all the murders, notably the murder of Irene Cross. Finally, why would an insane person be more careful and calculating than a sane person? The opposite conclusion seems true.[8]

The marshal in Waco, though, disputed the lunatic theory. He placed faith in the jealousy or lust theory.

> We read a great deal of theorizing about the series of murders in Austin, that all the assassinations were the work of a cunning lunatic—a monomaniac on the subject of murder. From what I can learn, I don't believe anything of the kind, and it is my deliberate opinion that these murders can not only be unearthed, but when probed to the bottom, it will be found that they were committed by different individuals and that in each case they were prompted by lust, jealousy, or hatred. The same state of affairs given the same motive might exist in Waco, or any other large town.

The *New York Times* presented the notion that "Many people believe the murders were committed by some cunning madman, who is insane on the subject of killing women. Following out this theory, nearly every man in the city, black and white, known to have idiosyncrasies of any kind have been watched by the detectives, but without avail." Everyone seemed to have a theory, but no one seemed to have a viable suspect.[9]

Not to be outdone, the Fort Worth newspaper, displaying a decidedly literary bent, published a series of speculations on the matter. The first article alluded to Mary Shelley's famous monster.

> People who have read "Frank Einstein" [*Frankenstein*] will be reminded of that nondescript monster's career of murder by reading the news from Austin. The addition of three more victims to the number of those who have fallen beneath the assassin's ax brings the number up to ten, if we have kept correct count. "Frank Einstein" was literally a man without a soul. A German student discovered the primal element of vital existence and he built up in his laboratory a human form of perfect proportions and wonderful strength, which he then endowed with life. But the being had no soul and lacked utterly the sense of responsibility that springs from conscience. It delighted only in the destruction of life and was so stealthy that it always evaded detection. Like the Austin horror, its victims were principally women who were slain in their sleep by being struck in the head by some heavy instrument. Possibly it may turn out that some supernatural being infests Austin.

Perhaps the killers were supernatural beings, as some in the black population of Austin seemed to think.[10]

A day later, in an article titled "The Austin Saturnalia," the Fort Worth newspaper waxed eloquently about the plight of women in Austin.

> The people of Austin are living in a state of terror that appeals to the sympathy of every citizen of Texas. No man can conceive what must be the mental torture of the women of Austin or the glad feeling with which each new morn is greeted. So many and so merciless have been the brutal murders and attempts at murder, that no woman, white or black, in the capital city retires for the night without a terror at her heart which robs even the safety of the daylight of all pleasure, for again the night must come with, perhaps, the pitiless assassin, the horrible bludgeon, the fearful outrage, the fatal blow, and death. No more horrible story was ever told or heard than that which could be written of female life in the proud capital of Texas for the past year, and it is a story which should be ended at once. Not alone Austin, but all Texas, all the Union, is interested in the *detection* of the midnight assassin and his prompt *legal* punishment. He should be *detected*, that encouragement may not grow from this assassin's immunity. He should be *legally* punished, that the law may be strengthened and made more fearful to the criminally inclined.

> It is past belief that in a city so large as Austin, and no larger than Austin, the perpetrators of such deeds could go undetected so long. Who is the bloody demon, and what is his object? The object is, beyond all doubt, WOMAN.
> The purpose of the beastly murderer is plain to all who have read the record of these hellish crimes. Who is the assassin? A negro. The evidence points to the murderer as a negro. White men have assaulted colored women vary rarely, but white women are the objects of assault by men of every color, and negro men more frequently assail white than black women. The assaults recorded in Austin were made first on colored women, then on foreign servant girls, now on wives and mothers. The murderer is a negro, and, possibly, an ex-convict, who has served a penitentiary term for similar crimes to those now being committed. Having once suffered because he permitted his victim to escape to testify to his identity, he now secures himself by murdering her.
>
> The people of Austin owe it to their women, to their fair name, to their city's welfare and prosperity, and to the people of every other town in this state and country, to catch the inhuman perpetrator of these diabolical crimes. And no expense should be considered too great to effect his detection, capture and punishment.

The newspaper's assertion that the culprit was a black man was neither bold nor unusual, though its rationale was certainly worthy of thought.[11]

A couple of weeks later, the Fort Worth newspaper summoned the ghost of Ben Thompson to solve the crimes.

> One expects to find Austin a very volcano of excitement over the brutal and persistent slaughter of its women; instead, Austin discusses the matter very quietly, and leaves it to its neighbors to get excited. In many respects, this is a peculiar town. When it was held up to the world as a shining example of virtue—the Athens of the South—where crime was an almost unknown quantity, the capital complacently accepted the compliment as a matter of course. Now that its name is becoming a by-word for lawlessness of the most repulsive type wherever electricity has flashed the horrors of its many crimes, the capital again accepts the situation, certainly not without regret but as a matter of course. I should say that there is too much belief in destiny here for the general good. Without it the hum of a dozen factories might now be heard from the state-house, and half as many railroads would make this the supply depot of the Southwest. Still one often hears the expression: "If Ben Thompson were only marshal."
>
> Innumerable theories have been spun out of the thread of imagination to account for a series of murders that in truth admit of no reasonable explanation. It is recognition of this

which has led so many to the conclusion that a madman is responsible for the whole bloody work. And yet nothing could be more unreasonable than such a suggestion. A madman whose thirst for blood renders him a model of prudence and discreetness for fourteen months, and gives him such cunning that no one discovers his insanity would, indeed, be a novelty. To the devil with all such insanity. My own opinion is that whatever of mystery attaches to the long chain of assassinations arises from ignorance of the history of each of the victims. Crime is not stopped by mere enjoinder of law, but through fear of the law. There are thousands of people in the world who have murder in their hearts, but who have not the courage, on account of a dread of the penalties, to take it in their hands. Once demonstrate to them that the danger in crime is past and no deed is too damnable for them to conceive or too brutal for them to execute. The earlier murders in this horrible record were perpetrated, as was generally conceded at the time, on account of jealousies among the negroes. The escape of the murderers undetected was a signal to those of equal mind of the deplorable imbecility of the agencies of the law. Since then the record of Austin's crimes has simply been one of the gratification of private and long-pent-up revenges. The similarity that may be traced between the various murders is simply a mark of that cunning sagacity which would naturally cause the assassin to mystify his crime. Never an admirer of the dead desperado, I am tempted to echo the remark: "If Ben Thompson were only marshal."

The reporter's comment that the history of the victim might be more informative than the history of the killer warrants reflection. The reporter is also convinced that the early murders were the result of jealousy, and the later murders were just copycat events spurred by revenge. The later killers were supposedly emboldened by the failure of the Austin police to solve the earlier crimes. If any of these theories were valid, only time would tell.[12]

"Mere Suspicion"

After the Hancock and Phillips murders, a raft of arrests followed. By Christmas evening, less than 24 hours after the murders, at least six black men were arrested on suspicion. One was Dock Woods, who was suspected in the Gracie Vance murders. Oliver Townsend was also arrested, but only on suspicion, as there was "absolutely no clew to the hell-hounds who committed these infernal deeds." The police did have something of a clue, though no more than in the other murders. "Two men were seen jumping into an alley near Hancock's residence just after the deed, and the big tracks found near the scene of the Phillips' murder seemingly identifies the murderer with the Ramey assassin. A short, thick-set negro with rolled-up trousers was seen by one of the murdered servant girls last summer, and he is believed to be the perpetrator of all these horrible crimes. He is thought to have a pal." But the police had little more than mere suspicion to arrest suspects.[13]

The list of usual suspects did take an unusual turn when two white men were detained in Belton, about 60 miles northeast of Austin, for wearing bloody clothes. The men, J.T. and J.P. Norwood, claiming to be brothers, were arrested the day after Christmas while riding the train from Temple. The smaller of the two weighed about 145 pounds and had a fresh cut over one eye. The second man weighed 150 pounds and had gray eyes, dark hair, and a "little dark mustache." Both men had blood on their coats and vests. The marshal of Belton also thought they had blood on their shoes, and they still had blood on their hands. According to the *Austin Daily Statesman*, the brothers "came through Austin today and were farming at San Marcos. Subsequently they claimed to be from Hunter, in Hays county. Their clothes are bloody, but they say this was the result of a difficulty they had at San Marcos. The authorities there say they have no knowledge of such a thing. Their tickets show they got on the train at San Marcos. They seem restless and uneasy." One would expect persons charged with murder to be a bit unsettled, especially if their only crime was wearing clothes with blood on them. Would they really have left the blood of their victims on their hands for two days?[14]

The Norwoods were expected to be brought back to Austin by train, but Sheriff Hornsby was probably reluctant to expose the men to a lynch mob. When the train arrived on the evening of December 27, the prisoners were not on it. "A rumor soon spread over the city that the sheriff had gotten off with them north of the city and was bringing them in around another way to elude the crowd." At the time of the train's arrival, "an immense crowd" swarmed up Congress Avenue toward the county jail out of "mere curiosity," according to the reporter. An hour later, "vast and dense crowds" hovered around the entrance to the county jail. Another rumor began to circulate, "that the sheriff and prisoners had got off the train at the water tank north of the city and that the two men were actually in jail," but a deputy, who said he had no reason to lie, claimed the Norwoods had never left Belton. "The deputy stated to the Gazette man that Sheriff Hornsby had thoroughly investigated the Norwoods, and believing them innocent he did not propose to bring them into Austin to be mobbed. It seems the Norwoods are known in Austin. The deputy also said it was his opinion and that of nearly all other officers here that the authors of the Thursday night murders are still in Austin and never left it."[15]

Another white man, identified as J.Q. Echols, was also arrested as a suspect. A telephone call was made from a lime kiln near Mount Bonnell, about seven miles from the city, saying that a man had been "seen washing bloody clothes." Sheriff Hornsby and Officer Conner were soon on their way, and an arrest was made. Echols was brought back to the city and placed in the county jail. The man, who was about 35 years old, claimed to be a wood hauler. He claimed that "his clothes were colored by pecan stains and washing them with red socks. A piece of paper in a memorandum book, however, has an unmistakable stain of blood upon it, and altogether the circumstances are very suspicious against him. His shirt is considerably stained on the bosom, and his drawers are slightly red colored at the lower extremities." Those who saw him washing the clothes insisted that they were bloody, not stained by wood. An examination of the clothes remained to be made. The man was expected to prove where he had been on Christmas Eve when the recent murders were taking place.[16]

Detective Mike Hennessey claimed that a black man named John Gray, sometimes called Gray Jo, was another member of the Thug Gang, but he had so far escaped arrest. Gray was a dishwasher at Peter Roach's restaurant on East Cedar Street. On the night before the Hancock and Phillips murders, for some unknown reason Gray had tried to "chop his way into a colored woman's house" in Austin. He was later arrested in San Antonio after making a boast while drunk that "he and Doc Woods, and others that he named, had done the work of blood and rape in Austin." He was returned to Austin, charged with murder and lodged away in jail on the supposition that he knew something about the Austin servant murders. According to Hennessey, he had been "informed that on the way from San Antonio to Austin John Gray made a full confession, giving the full particulars of the commission of the horrible crimes and the parties who committed them. I am satisfied that I had the right scoundrels. I think the grand jury will yet indict them, and that proof ample to convict them will be produced on the trial. After conviction, I need hardly say that they will all be hung very speedily. They are the bloodiest brutes that I was ever called to work up in the course of my career as a detective." Other reports suggested, though, that Gray apparently did not make any such confession.[17]

"A Solution of the Bloody Mystery"

Another interesting twist came with the arrest of a Mexican man, Anastacio Martinez, at a house at the corner of Live Oak and San Antonio streets in Guy Town on December 30. With the arrest, it was "authoritatively announced that the committee of safety and city authorities have reached a solution of the bloody mystery and traced the murders to a reliable source, and that the perpetrators will all be in jail inside of ten days. Startling developments are expected to-night." Obviously, those startling developments never came, but the arrest of Martinez was indeed intriguing. Martinez was described as cranky, about 40 to 45 years old, and of stout build and good size. He claimed "he had been two years in jail at Brownsville, Texas, for assaulting women, and afterwards laid in a hospital for several months." He said he had been in Austin for five or six years, and that he was "told and ordered by the Almighty to go out at night and draw blood." Most of the servant girl murders occurred between 11 P.M. and 1 A.M. when the moon was shining, and people who knew Martinez said "he was frequently out at that time of night, and on moonlight nights."[18]

Martinez was believed to be one of the "outrage-fiends." In one of the many attempted home invasions during the year, "a man entered the room of Mrs. Blake and awakened her; she saw his purpose and sprung up out of bed, and as she did so the intruder laid his hand on a long sheath-knife at his waist. A terrific struggle for possession of the knife ensued, but Mrs. Blake finally seized the handle and the ruffian the blade, and as it was drawn through his hands made a gash across all four fingers. The Mexican arrested to-night shows that identical gash, and, moreover, claimed the knife when the officer showed it to him." As the man fled, he tore the dress off the woman. An examination of the Mexican's foot showed it was similar to the big footprints left at several of the murder scenes, and his stout, squat physical form seemed to match a description given by one of the servant girls before she died. Underneath his shirt he carried a roll of 32 silver dollars, "there being a piece of cardboard, cut to fit the coin, placed between each dollar, the whole being rolled so compactly that when it struck the floor the sound was more like that made by a piece of iron." Such a roll of dollars could be used for inflicting damage on a person.[19]

After Martinez was arrested, his residence was searched. Several incriminating items were found, among them two hatchets and a hammer, a woman's bloody dress, some ladies' gloves and stockings. "In addition to a large number of articles of female wearing apparel, many of which were stained with blood, the officers found a Colt's cap and ball six-shooter; a variety of butcher and other knives, seven in number, some of them bearing blood stains; a razor, a small ice pick or blunt bodkin, and a long iron spike," such as one that might have been driven into the ears of Mary Ramey and Mrs. Hancock. The spike had blood on the point. Also in his possession was a small prayer book with the name Ella R. Rooney or Ella R. Ramy written inside. He also had a pair of white handkerchiefs with the initials J.R. or A.R. on one and a red A on the other. "Quite a number of dresses were found in his possession, one of which is expected to be identified to-day by a German woman, whom it is now thought this Mexican attempted to outrage last summer, and in his flight tore the dress off her." Many of the items in his house had "old blood stains and blood marks." Things did not look good for Martinez, who spoke little English.[20]

The city authorities likely thought they had captured the servant girl annihilator at long last, but on the morning of December 31, Martinez was conveyed from his jail cell to the city marshal's office. There he was confronted by the woman he was suspected of trying to outrage early in the summer of 1885. The woman, though nervous at first, surveyed the Mexican head to foot so that she could satisfy herself that he was the man. She could not do so. She could not identify Martinez positively, but she also would not say he was not the man who had broken into her home. She was shown a butcher knife that had been in Martinez's possession, and she said it was identical to the one the man had carried and that she had cut his hand with in the struggle. Martinez's hand showed evidence of a scar in the same place she had cut the man. The woman did not say she had lost her dress, but that it had been torn, and that perhaps the assailant carried away a piece of it when he fled. She did mention that a lady living nearby had lost some dresses about the same time she was assaulted. When shown two dresses in the Mexican's possession, she could identify neither. She then left. Afterwards, Martinez had to wet one of his feet and make an impression on the floor. This impression was compared to the footprint found on the gallery of the Phillips' home. The two footprints did not match.[21]

Though the authorities had no solid evidence to hold Martinez, he was kept in jail. After a week or so, he muttered only short monosyllabic responses when asked a question. According to the reporter, he seemed "indifferent to his situation, unconscious, perhaps, of the terrible suspicion resting over him." Finally, in the middle of January, he was tried in county court and found to be inflicted with lunacy. He was committed to the lunatic asylum.[22]

"Reward"

Perhaps sensing that the real assassins had not yet been caught, on December 30 Governor John Ireland offered a reward of $300 "for the arrest and conviction of each of the murderers of Mrs. Hancock and Mrs. Phillips." The reward did not, however, apply to any of those men already arrested for suspicion of the murders, nor did it apply to the murderers of any of the numerous servant girls killed throughout the year. The *Austin Daily Statesman* seemed to feel the reward was not big enough. In making its complaint, the newspaper made the confident statement that the string of murders had positively ended.

> Day has broken and the light of the sun fully and clearly illuminates the dark deeds of the past year. There will be no more murders, for before the investigation ceases every culprit will be revealed. We do not pretend to assert that every one of the murderers is known, so fully as to insure a legal conviction, and, therefore, elsewhere we advocate a large reward for any and all information that will guide investigations now in progress.

The newspaper faulted the governor's reward for two reasons. First, the newspaper believed the reward should be "general, including all parties to the crime," including those already under arrest. The suggestion was that the governor assumed the arrests already made were valid and that conviction would follow, but the facts showed that convictions did not follow arrests. Second, the newspaper believed the reward offered by the governor was "too small to induce anyone to give the information." If a citizen gave information to gain the reward, he might find himself at risk, and for such a paltry sum. The newspaper suggested that a larger reward, such as $1000 or even $2500, would "spur the zeal and excite the detective qualities of the very kind of men who are most apt to have opportunities to know of the perpetrators of the crime or the habits of men, which would dovetail into such crimes." Even further, the newspaper suggested that a person who provided valid evidence that ended the wave of murders should receive any amount he or she requested, just so the city could be freed from the terror.[23]

As if on cue, on January 2, 1886, A.P. Wooldridge, chairman of the Citizen's Committee, officially announced "a reward of $1,000 for the arrest and conviction of the persons guilty of the murders in this city of the following persons: Mrs. Eula Phillips and Mrs. M. H. Hancock, both white, and Mollie Smith, Eliza Shelley, Irene Cross, Mary Ramsey, Orange Washington, and Gracie Vance, all colored." Would $1000 be enough to draw the kind of information needed for a conviction? As in all other aspects of the case, only time would tell.[24]

"The Mysterious Axman"

Fully a year had passed since Mollie Smith was murdered on December 30, 1884. Since that gruesome night, the list of murders had only grown longer: Eliza Shelly and Irene Cross in May, Mary Ramey in August, Gracie Vance and Orange

Washington in September, Susan Hancock and Eula Phillips in December, among others. After a year, there were still no viable suspects, no valid evidence worthy of a conviction, no assurance that the murders had ended. The year had seen ineptitude on a grand scale by the Austin city government and police force. Racial indifference had played a large role in the failure to solve the crimes, and only with the murders of two white women did any serious action to end the crimes take place. The string of murders had been an ongoing embarrassment for the capital city, a stain upon what was supposed to be the Athens of the West. Instead, Austin found itself little better than a Wild West town where anarchy reigned and murder was commonplace.

Just as no truly viable suspects had been tagged, no reasonable motive had been identified, either. Were all the murders, despite their similarities, simply the acts of jealousy between lovers? Were some of the murders copycat killings staged to appear like the earlier murders? Were all the murders totally random with no connection between them? Or were the murders orchestrated to attain some end, to gain revenge perhaps? Were the members of the Thug Gang ultimately responsible for the murders? And if so, did they act independently, or was someone pulling their strings? The following months would uncover mounds of information, some of it startling and embarrassing, but none of it ultimately convincing enough to warrant a lasting conviction.

Notes

Title: *Fort Worth Daily Gazette*, 1/6/1886.

1. *Austin Daily Statesman*, 12/27/1885; *Morrison & Fourmy's General Directory of the City of Austin, 1885-1886*; 1880 Federal Census.
2. *Austin Daily Statesman*, 12/27/1885; *Morrison & Fourmy's General Directory of the City of Austin, 1885-1886*.
3. *Austin Daily Statesman*, 12/27/1885; *Morrison & Fourmy's General Directory of the City of Austin, 1885-1886*.
4. *Austin Daily Statesman*, 12/27/1885; *Morrison & Fourmy's General Directory of the City of Austin, 1885-1886*.
5. *Austin Daily Statesman*, 12/27/1885.
6. *Austin Daily Statesman*, 12/26/1885; *Fort Worth Daily Gazette*, 12/26/1885; *Austin Daily Statesman*, 12/31/1885; *San Antonio Daily Express*, 12/26/1885; *San Antonio Daily Express*, 1/2/1886.
7. *Fort Worth Daily Gazette*, 12/27/1885; *Austin Daily Statesman*, 12/30/1885.
8. *Waco Daily Examiner*, 12/31/1885; *Reno Evening Gazette*, 12/26/1885; *Austin Daily Statesman*, 12/30/1885.
9. *Austin Daily Statesman*, 1/30/1886; *New York Times*, 12/26/1885.
10. *Fort Worth Daily Gazette*, 12/26/1885.
11. *Fort Worth Daily Gazette*, 12/27/1885.
12. *Fort Worth Daily Gazette*, 1/17/1886.
13. *New York Times*, 12/26/1885; *San Antonio Daily Express*, 12/26/1885; *Fort Worth Daily Gazette*, 12/26/1885.

14. *Austin Daily Statesman*, 12/27/1885; *Fort Worth Daily Gazette*, 12/28/1885.
15. *Fort Worth Daily Gazette*, 12/28/1885.
16. *Austin Daily Statesman*, 12/30/1885; 1880 Federal Census.
17. *Austin Daily Statesman*, 12/30/1885; *San Antonio Daily Light*, 12/26/1885; *Fort Worth Daily Gazette*, 12/31/1885; *Morrison & Fourmy's General Directory of the City of Austin, 1885-1886*.
18. *Austin Daily Statesman*, 12/31/1885; *Fort Worth Daily Gazette*, 12/31/1885.
19. *Austin Daily Statesman*, 12/31/1885; *Fort Worth Daily Gazette*, 12/31/1885.
20. *Austin Daily Statesman*, 12/31/1885; *Fort Worth Daily Gazette*, 12/31/1885.
21. *Austin Daily Statesman*, 1/1/1886.
22. *Austin Daily Statesman*, 1/6/1886; *Austin Daily Statesman*, 1/16/1886.
23. *Fort Worth Daily Gazette*, 12/31/1885; *Austin Daily Statesman*, 12/31/1885.
24. *New York Times*, 1/3/1886; *Fort Worth Daily Gazette*, 1/3/1886; *St. Paul Daily Globe*, 1/3/1886.

Chapter 13

"The Bloody Enigma"

Unrest, Inquests, Surprising Arrests, and a Lynching

The year of savagery had ended. The death toll was staggering. At least seven women, including the Ramey girl, and one man were linked to the so-called servant girl murders. Numerous others had been killed or assaulted in and around Austin, and attempted home invasions had become commonplace throughout the year. The city was in a panic, and the killers apparently roamed the city at will, seemingly unafraid of detection or capture. Would the new year bring more of the same?

The approach of each new full moon brought heightened fears. A full moon was due on January 20, 1886. Would that full moon bring new murders? The newspapers worked to stoke the fires of fear, reporting, for example, that "a great many people here are tremulous till the moonlight nights are over because the history of the servant-girl murders shows the fiend generally selects nights about the full of the moon for his horrid and bloody deviltries." Another report considered the nature of the killer and catalogued the year's murders.

> Do sane men calmly plot and carry into effect horrible murders under the glare of the light of the moon? Does the moon, as some assert, affect certain maniacs and intensify their disease? These are questions left for The Statesman readers to ponder over this morning. One thing is certain: all the terrible and cruel assassinations which occurred in this city during last year, with but one exception, were committed in the light of the moon, and below will be found the time, which elapsed after the full moon when the horrible crimes were perpetrated. The first victim to fall in the series of bloody mysteries was Mollie Smith, on the night of December 30, 1884, and the night of the full moon. Just four months and seven days after, or on May 7, or exactly seven days after the full of the moon, Eliza Shelly met her death. Irene Cross was assassinated about three weeks after and five days past full moon; on August 30, the insatiable fiend cruelly murdered and outraged little Mary Ramey. On September 28, nearly one month after Mary's death, Gracie Vance and Orange Washington were killed, just four days after the full of the moon. On December 24 Mrs. Phillips and Mrs. Hancock met their horrible fate, and it was exactly three days past the full moon.

> The moon will soon be full again, and then will wane. Will it be
> on a scene of blood and cruel and ghastly death?

All the assurances that the killing spree was over disappeared when panic and fear again reared their monstrous heads.[1]

The new year began with a report that seemed to echo the Eanes case: "To-day another case of child murder was discovered. The body of a negro boy, aged five, was found under the pasture fence of C. M. Rogers, two miles out of town. He had probably been dead one month and he is thought to have been stabbed or shot." The unidentified child was buried in Stranger Ground in Oakwood Cemetery in Austin on January 2, 1886. Perhaps due to decomposition, the boy was identified as white in burial records. An inquest was held, and the results were quickly announced, "a verdict that the child came to its death by the hands of its mother, who said her name was Mary Taylor, but whose real name is Fannie Owens." The news that a mother could kill her own child was as troubling as any of the servant girl murders. What was in the air or water in Austin that could cause such cruelty?[2]

"Parties Unknown"

Eula Phillips died on the night she was assaulted, just after midnight on December 25, 1885. She was buried in Oakwood Cemetery in Austin on December 26. Two days later, the coroner's jury held an inquiry regarding her death. The decision of the jury merely stated the obvious. She was "thought to have been assaulted before being killed." The final verdict was "that death had resulted from wounds inflicted with an axe in the hands of parties unknown." As usual, no suspect was identified.[3]

Meanwhile, Sue Hancock was in a "dying condition." She finally died from her wounds in the evening of December 28. She was buried in Oakwood Cemetery in Austin on December 29. Her husband, Moses Hancock, was being held as a witness at the inquest regarding her death and was not allowed to attend her burial. After her death, Dr. William Burt and Dr. Richard Graves had performed an autopsy on the body. The examination centered on three wounds on her head.

> One cutting through the upper part of the left ear, through the
> soft tissues and fracturing the squamous portion of the left
> temporal bone, for about one inch.
> One wound about one inch above and to the left of the left eye,
> making an external wound about one and one half inches long,
> in a horizontal direction. This wound penetrated the soft tissues
> and the instrument used fractured the left parietal, the frontal,
> the sphenoid and aquamous portion of the left temporal bones,
> at the point of their articulations one with the other. This
> fracture and the first one described made one fracture, both
> running together, the bones being broken and comminuted for
> a space of three by one and one-half inches, between the left
> ear and left eye. These broken pieces were forced into the brain

substance, tearing the membranes and brain and involving mostly the middle lobe of the left side of the brain. The brain for two or more inches around the fracture was filled with clotted blood in a state of partial decomposition. The other wound was in the right ear and done by a sharp pointed instrument, piercing through the auditory canal and through the bones, fracturing them and penetrating the brain for two or more inches. The wounds on the left side were made by an ax, a hatchet, a smoothing iron or some such instrument. No other wounds were the cause of her death.

An unusual disturbance took place at the Hancock home "while Mrs. Hancock lay a corpse." A newly married couple were "misbehaving in the presence of death." Whoever the young revelers were, they were not invited to the Hancock home, and they had no relation to the family. The moral code seemed to be breaking down even more.[4]

Meanwhile, the inquests in the Hancock, Phillips, and Eanes cases were ongoing. "The jury of inquest investigating the murder of Mrs. Hancock were in session the principal part of yesterday, and conducted their examination with closed doors. . . . The coroner's verdict in the case of Mrs. Phillips and the Eanes boy are still withheld from the public." Secrecy had become the standard operating procedure for these cases. Just what information was being withheld from the public? On the first day of the new year, a San Antonio newspaper reviewed the state of affairs in Austin.

> This being New Year's day, the public offices and places of business are generally closed. The city is quiet. Even the outrage fiends, who for the past year have played such havoc with human life in this capital city as to rank them with the devotees of Bowahnie, have so far failed to inaugurate the new year with a fresh sensation, and there are no new developments in the old ones. Arrests and coroner's verdicts are kept within the knowledge of the officers, and, according to some mysterious authority, the monsters in human shape who have been doing the devil's bidding, or are suspects of the horrid crimes so recently committed, have either been jailed or are "spotted" and watched so that they cannot escape. The minions of Old Nick, however, are used to espionage, and it may be that the spotting and watching are a mere matter of assumption, based as heretofore upon some vague theory. At all events, the public mind seems to have settled into a conviction, for some reason, that the guilty men have already been caught and that their conviction is assured.

A letter found on the streets of Austin by an officer and turned over to the *Austin Daily Statesman* provided a similarly dim view of the ongoings.

> Dear Joe—In reply to your inquiries about the murders here, I would say that developments, so far as known to the public, are quite meager. Almost as many opinions as there are

> individuals are advanced on the streets. Insanity, robbery, revenge, and other theories have been discussed and exhausted, without result. The desire of amateur detectives to establish favorite notions, as you know, often confuses the trail and misleads investigation.
>
> One class contents itself with a tirade against the saloons and gambling houses, and another class goes for the tramps; while the moral lepers, in disguise and in closed carriages, who ply their avocations at midnight in houses they would not dare to visit in the day time pass unnoticed.
> Blighted homes and broken hearts are too often the effect of causes that may be traced through the dawning influence of the night drives and the assignation houses. The expert dude or the professional lothario, who deliberately plans the debauchery of his victim, and assures the ruin of her family, he contributes as much to a tragedy as the ax-man who, either for pay or for vengeance, closes the scene.
>
> There might be a cause and responsibility behind these assassins, which, if understood, would make crooked things straight.

Perhaps to calm themselves, the citizens wanted to believe that the killers had been captured. The events of the next few days threw all those beliefs into chaos.[5]

"Slanderous Cowards"

Perhaps the delay in releasing the details of the inquests became apparent. On New Years Day 1886, in a startling development, James Phillips, Jr., who was so seriously wounded in the Christmas Eve attack that for days he was believed incapable of surviving and who remained in critical condition, was "placed in the custody of an officer, by virtue of a warrant from Justice Von Rosenberg, on the charge of the murder of his wife." Apparently no one outside the inquest jury believed Phillips was guilty, because he was believed "to have been too drunk to have accomplished such a thing, and would hardly have dragged her out of the house. In any event, his own injuries seem to preclude his guilt, unless they were inflicted by his wife, which is exceedingly improbable. He is said, however, to have made threats to kill her." To compound the startling verdict even more, the inquest jury refused to release the testimony to the press. Perhaps the inquest jury wanted to sweep the sensational case under the rug. After all, even as the warrant was issued for his arrest, Phillips was not expected to recover from his injuries.[6]

After young Phillips, also known as Jimmy, was charged with his wife's murder, various details about the case began to emerge. When asked about the arrest of his son, James Phillips, Sr., the father, said "the death of his daughter was horrible and the arrest of my son a grievous outrage perpetrated by the officers without the shadow of evidence." The elder Phillips also believed the shocking development might kill Jimmy's mother.

> The senior Phillips was asked if it was true that Mrs. Etta Phillips was out riding the night she was assassinated and her husband was drunk and quarreled with her on her return home. "No, sir," replied Mr. Phillips, "there is not a word of truth in it. They were as happy as any young couple I know of, and always got along smoothly." This year they farmed near Hutto, Williamson county, but failed to make anything, and two weeks before Christmas they came home and lived with me until they could fix up, and furnished the rooms they occupied the night of the murder. A few days after their return my son got on a spree and, with my advice, his wife went off to the country and stayed with an aunt until three or four days before Christmas. In the meantime my son sobered up and promised me never to drink again. He faithfully kept that promise and gave his wages to his wife on her return home. On the night of the murder he and she were at home all the time except a few minutes when James went down town to buy toys for his child. They were in the parlor till after 10 o'clock talking, and both were in the best of humor and spirits. I retired at 10 o'clock and my wife shortly after. They went to their room and carried their nuts, apples and refreshments. The talk that daughter was out in a hack that night is absolutely false. Phillips denied that his son drank a drop on that night.

The reporter gauged the old man as an honest sort, and his statement would likely "refute the slanderous stories put out probably in the interest of the parties connecting the name of Mrs. Phillips with two young bloods of the city; in fact an unworthy attempt has been made to slander Mrs. Phillips in her grave." The rumor was that Eula had been unfaithful in her marriage to Jimmy, and on the night of her murder she had visited an assignation house at the foot of Congress Avenue and was seen riding with a man other than her husband in a carriage. Eula Phillips' father, Thomas Burditt, was expected to arrive the next day from Bell County, and the "slanderous cowards" that had prompted the arrest and the stories had better watch out then. The Norwood brothers were arrested as they were traveling from San Marcos to Belton in Bell County. Could they possibly have been on their way to meet Eula's father?[7]

Jimmy Phillips was arrested on the insistence of a detective, who turned out to be Thomas Bailes, a fired Austin policeman. Justice William Von Rosenberg, Jr., though, saw no real evidence against the young man. One wonders, then, why the justice would bow to the wishes of the detective. Was an arrest more important than justice? The detective's evidence was certainly questionable. According to the detective, "Phillips, after killing his wife in the room, dragged her out." The questionable part of the evidence was that "when first discovered his clothes were free from blood, except what came from his head. The bloody imprints of the murderer still remain on the gallery, and the bloody marks of his hands on the fence." To suggest the severity of Jimmy Phillips' injuries and cast further doubt on his guilt, Dr. James M. Litten believed that "a sharp instrument was driven into young Phillips' brain, which shows signs of derangement; if so, it was just like Mrs. Hancock and Mary Ramy." Though the physical condition of Jimmy Phillips strongly suggested his inability to commit the murder of his wife, still he was charged with that murder, though most people in Austin did not believe he had committed the act. Galloway summarized the possible reason for the murder charge against Jimmy Phillips.

> Initially, Phillips was beyond suspicion because the severity of the injuries he sustained the night his wife was murdered seemed to preclude his guilt. However, evidence presented to the jury of inquest brought to light details of the tumultuous relationship between the young couple, and Phillips became suspect. Phillips was a heavy drinker and was prone to making violent outbursts and threats. It was reported that he had been drinking on Christmas Eve and it was also asserted he had on previous occasions made threats to kill his wife.

Of course, Phillips' father had denied that Jimmy was drunk on Christmas Eve, but such a denial should be expected. The preliminary hearing for Phillips was set for February 11, 1886. Just as the inquest was kept secret, the press was denied the evidence on which the arrest warrant was based. "The only imaginable theory is the rather strained one, that the parties themselves did the work which ended in such mysterious results. Young Phillips himself is astounded at such a charge as has been made against him. He says he has no idea how the murderous assaults happened to him and his wife." Of course, the city officials may also have been looking for a fall guy.[8]

The rumor continued to swirl around town about Eula Phillips and a mystery man in a carriage on Christmas Eve. Hack drivers were being interviewed and accused of driving Eula home. One hack driver, William Red, flatly denied that he had transported Eula Phillips home that fateful night. He believed that he was suspected because "he drove three ladies home from a Knights and Ladies of Honor lodge meeting the night of the murder, one of whom resides on the Phillip's block, and his hack was seen going to that locality." Red felt that the accusation against him was costing him business, and he also feared that the women he drove home, the wives of respectable citizens all, would be humiliated and upset if their names were made public.[9]

By the second week of January, Jimmy Phillips was no longer at death's door. In fact, he "had recovered sufficiently to be able to walk about in his room, and even out into the yard." A month later, he would find himself in court, charged with murdering his young wife.[10]

"Dreadful Tidings"

Around the middle of January 1886, Marshal James Lucy received a telegram that his wife was very ill in Mexico. He departed to be by her side. Marshal Lucy had left Austin a few days after the Christmas Eve murders to be with his ailing wife. She had gone to Saltillo, Mexico, hoping the mountain air and water would help restore her health. Lucy had returned to Austin around the first of the new year after his wife seemed to be in better condition. But she took a turn for the worse and died on January 15. Lucy's private woes could only worsen the public problems he faced in Austin.[11]

"The Rockdale Lynching"

The anxiety and panic felt in Austin began to reach into the outlying areas. In Rockdale, about 60 miles northeast of Austin, a white man named Sam Ford was "robbed and left for dead" a few miles outside the city along the railroad tracks. A black man named Sydney Brown "did the deed and afterwards came back to town, stayed all night and started off early this morning, walking down the railroad" toward the east. Brown was soon caught near a neighboring town, carrying with him several of Ford's possessions.

> The attack was made about dark, the negro striking Ford with some iron weight and shooting at him three times. Supposing his victim dead, the culprit dragged the body across the railroad track, covered up the body in sand, and left, expecting a train to come by and mangle the corpse so as to conceal the murder. Ford came to consciousness and after being left, he managed to get off the tracks and spent the remainder of the night trying to get home, a distance of two miles, which he reached about daylight, being terribly bruised . . . and having one eye entirely knocked out. After being arrested and placed in jail the negro made a full confession, saying he took Ford's clothes and things because he made him mad.

Brown was raised in neighboring Burleson County, having been born around 1862. When captured, Brown said he was from Austin, and immediately he fell under deeper suspicion. Some people believed he must have known something about the servant girl murders in the capital city. Brown was said to have a "very bad countenance." The report spread around town that Sam Ford had died, and many believed that Brown should be given "his just dues" through hanging.[12]

Later that day, "an infuriated mob attacked the calaboose and demanded the negro who so brutally beat and left for dead the man Sam Ford." The mob overwhelmed the constable and his assistants and then "took the negro a distance of about one mile from town, where they hanged him to a hickory tree. The negro acknowledged all and tried to make peace with his God." A later report noted that "Sam Ford, the white man reported to have been murdered by the negro Sidney Brown at Rockdale Wednesday night, is not dead as reported but is alive and is thought to be in a fair way to recover, but the negro was hanged all the same."[13]

Despite the fact that Sam Ford was not murdered by Brown and would likely recover, the *Austin Daily Statesman*, which had preached vigilantism throughout the autumn of 1885, published an incendiary article supporting the lynching in Rockdale. The newspaper made the lynchers out to be noble citizens who had been forced to take the law into their own hands.

> There is something more in the Rockdale affair than the mere stringing up of a wretched and brutal negro assassin. The Rockdale mob—if mob it can be called—was a body representative in its character, and, paradoxical as it may seem in intention, at least, the conservators instead of the breakers of the public peace. The Rockdale lynchers were the type of a large and growing element in this state, composed of . . . good citizens, who, worn out and disgusted with the failure of the court machinery to put down crimes of the class perpetrated by the negro, Brown, in pure self-defense are forced to become, themselves, the dispensers of justice and the executors of laws not enforced by their agents. Everywhere throughout the state the people, as a general rule, are growing tired of the everlasting dilly-dallying, the continuances, . . . the running off of dangerous witnesses, or else buying them off, the appeals, the reversals of the higher courts, the pardons, and the numerous other avenues of escape whereby desperate criminals steer clear of the penalties due their crimes. Good people everywhere throughout this country, long suffering and enduring, loath to commit violence to prevent violence, raping and murder, like the Rockdale people, nevertheless find a limit to forbearance in the face of such crimes as that which led to the suspension of Sydney Brown to a hickory limb.

Despite the fact that Brown had not killed anyone and that he had not had the advantage of a court trial at all, the newspaper praised the "good citizens" who had taken the law into their hands. Perhaps such good citizens of the Rockdale type were needed in Austin.[14]

"Suit for a Reward"

In an ironic twist, a young man sued the city of Austin for the payment of a reward associated with an October murder. On October 26, 1885, a white man named Jack Coombs murdered his black mistress, Alice Davis, and was sentenced to five years in prison. At the time, a young man named William Luckie was arrested as an accessory for receiving the pistol after Coombs had shot Davis. Luckie was not tried for his part in the murder. Three months later, though, Luckie tried to collect a reward authorized under an ordinance passed by the city council on October 5, 1885. Under the ordinance, the "Mayor was empowered and directed to offer a reward of not over $250 for the arrest and conviction of any and every person guilty of the crime of rape, robbery, murder, burglary, or arson, or of an assault committed in the night time with the intent to commit murder, rape, or robbery within the city limits, to be paid to the person or persons securing the arrest and conviction of such offenders." Though Luckie was implicated in the murder, he somehow felt he had helped to secure the arrest and conviction of Coombs. Whether Luckie received the reward is not known.[15]

"Very Grave Suspicions"

After the arrest of the debilitated Jimmy Phillips for the murder of his wife, the arrest of Moses Hancock for murdering his spouse was no big surprise. As Galloway pointed out, "As in previous inquests, the effort to ascribe a motive to the imagined perpetrator was of considerable importance. In these cases, testimony presented by the immediate families of the victims brought to light certain details of the victims' personal lives and suspicion was soon cast on the husbands of the murdered women. Without tangible evidence of other suspects, Moses Hancock and James Phillips, Jr., became the prime suspects." On January 27, 1886, Moses Hancock was arrested and charged with the murder of Susan Hancock. The warrant was issued by Justice William Von Rosenberg, Jr., but the supporting evidence was kept secret. The damning facts must have become available between the inquest and the end of January.

> At the inquest they evidently were not sufficient on which to base an arrest, or it would have occurred right there and then, as Justice Von Rosenberg is not exactly the man to turn any person loose who is charged with a fiendish, demoniacal crime. Then, other sad more potent facts have been obtained, and to a question proposed last night, the reporter was informed that such certainly was the case, but no further would the officer venture to lift the veil of mystery, which on the horrible night of blood, fell over the appalling, ghastly crime. The *Statesman* can only refer to certain facts, obtained some three weeks ago, from a reliable source, to tell whence the evidence has probably been in the hands of the detectives for some three or four weeks, that he and his wife did not live peaceably together. It is also further asserted that on more than one occasion he threatened to take her life, and, rumor has it, that on one occasion he attempted to do so, but she saved herself by fleeing from the premises and taking refuge with a neighbor. It is also asserted that, before leaving San Antonio, she expressed to the minister of the church to which she belonged, that she felt that at some time her husband would kill her. It is possible the officers have fully corroborated the foregoing, and with these, and probably other evidence, they determined to make the arrest. So far as Mr. Hancock's neighbors in this city have expressed themselves to the *Statesman's* representative, they believed that he and his wife lived peaceably.

As usual, no direct evidence supported the arrest warrant, only circumstance. Would the police ever find a suspect based on viable evidence?[16]

Soon after Hancock was arrested, a reporter visited him in jail cell 13. When the reporter identified himself, Hancock complained that the newspapers had treated him unfairly and that he had nothing to say. Hancock then proceeded to answer all the reporter's questions. He said he had come to Texas in 1856, that Sue Hancock was his second wife, and that she was the mother of his two daughters. They had moved to Austin after living in San Antonio for a couple of years. When the reporter asked if Hancock and his wife had lived peacefully in San Antonio, Hancock provided a reference that could validate that they were a harmonious couple. The reporter then shared some recent developments in the case. One of Hancock's hatchets, covered in blood, was found concealed in one of the walls of his house. Hancock denied any knowledge of the hatchet. The reporter asked about a letter written by Sue Hancock to her sister, saying she feared Hancock would kill her some night, and that she had taken up sleeping in the girls' room. The letter had bloody fingerprints on it. Hancock denied seeing the letter but suggested that the house had been ransacked and that someone could have picked up the letter off the bloody floor. When asked if he had gone on drinking binges in San Antonio, Hancock admitted that he "sometimes got on a spree, but couldn't stand it more than two days." Hancock could not recall ever abusing his wife.[17]

The reporter then asked a pointed question: "Mr. Hancock, can you prove by anyone that at one time, while drunk, you did not abuse your wife and threaten to kill her and she went to a neighbor's house for fear you would?" Hancock admitted that he could not, but he again gave references who could vouch that the couple lived peaceably together. When asked if he had hired a lawyer, Hancock said that he was a poor man and could not employ anybody. "The reporter then thanked the gentleman who would have nothing to do with the newspapers, and had nothing to say, and left." Hancock did not know who had sworn out the warrant against him, and the police and judges would not say. The reporter wondered about the quality of the evidence, but believed that "the evidence of the best trained blood hounds, as those are in this city, is sufficient for that. Why would they not follow trails any distance from the scene of the crimes? There were none to follow, in the opinion of some who are familiar with sagacious nigger dogs. They do not state this as a positive fact, but the keepers of such dogs would feel themselves justified in holding any man on just such evidence alone, and of itself." Phillips and Hancock were under arrest, it seemed, because the bloodhounds could not find a trail.[18]

As it turned out, the warrant against Hancock was initiated by Detective Thomas O. Bailes, who was listed as the assistant chief of the Capital Detective Association, an agency that apparently existed for only a few months in 1885, most likely to try to gain business regarding the servant girl murders. Bailes had been an Austin policeman but had been "relieved from service on the city police on account of some misunderstanding about the Hancock and Phillips cases." Whatever evidence Bailes had against Hancock, he would not divulge it. Bailes was aided in his investigation by the Waco marshal, Luke Moore. Moore believed that Hancock had murdered his wife, but he too refused to give any solid evidence. Some of his evidence might have been a letter found in Sue Hancock's possessions after her death. The letter was rumored to indicate that Sue Hancock feared that her husband might kill her. This letter was apparently forwarded to Marshal Moore by Sue Hancock's sister, Mrs. Fallwell, with whom the two Hancock daughters went to live after the murder. Moore also intimated that important information about Hancock could be secured in San Antonio, and he noted that Hancock and his family had lived in Waco around 1880. Moore went further to claim that all the servant girl murders "were committed by different individuals and that in each case they were prompted by lust, jealousy, or hatred." Moore's theory was "directly opposed to that put forth by the Houston detectives, who claim that the whole series of crimes, at least up to and including the murder of Gracie Vance and Orange Washington, were the work of two or three persons of the colored persuasion," the so-called Thug Gang.[19]

As the month of January ended, the Hancock case began to take on increased notoriety after "one of the very best citizens in Austin, and one of the ablest intellects in the country, a man of national reputation, an ex-congressman, Hon. John Hancock, . . . voluntarily offered his professional services to defend the prisoner, with no money to employ counsel to defend himself, in what is going to be a rough and tumble tussle for his life." John Hancock had been a district judge and now was one of the richest men in Austin. His nephew, Lewis Hancock, served on the Austin city council but was ousted in December 1885. John Hancock was not related to Moses Hancock, but curiously, their wives had the same first name. The newspaper also suggested that if Moses Hancock was innocent, all the amateur detectives who had made his life a living hell

> should be promptly shoved into a nine-hole. What is wanted is to get at the bottom of this horrible business, which has damaged our city in more ways than one. We desire the assassin, or assassins, unearthed, whoever or whatever they are, and when discovered to be made to suffer the full penalty of their crimes. But in the attempt let no innocent man suffer; no guilty man escape the terrible reckoning that should await the author or authors of a series of crimes unparalleled in this or any other country.

As if to encourage the dubious investigations of the amateur detectives, though, the Citizens Committee increased the amount of the reward offered for the arrest and conviction of the murderers. A reward of $1000 was offered for "the arrest and conviction of the party or parties who upon the night of December 24, A.D. 1885, in this city, murdered Mrs. Eula Phillips." An identical $1000 reward was offered for the arrest and conviction of those who murdered Sue Hancock. Finally, a reward of $1000 would be paid "upon the arrest and conviction of the perpetrator or perpetrators first convicted" for the murders of Mollie Smith, Eliza Shelly, Irene Cross, Mary Ramey, Orange Washington, and Gracie Vance. The rewards would be paid even if the guilty parties were already in custody, and were largely for the solid evidence that would result in a conviction.[20]

"Are the Mists Clearing Away?"

The arrests of Jimmy Phillips and Moses Hancock shocked most citizens of Austin. The police had made hundreds of arrests in the other servant girl murder cases, but all had proved unreliable in one way or another. Were the arrests of Phillips and Hancock any different? Both men had occasionally tumultuous marriages, and both were given to drink, sometimes excessively. Both had been rumored to have threatened their wives. Certainly the men might have a motive to murder their wives, but did they really kill them? Could Phillips have killed his wife and then inflicted a near fatal wound upon himself? Could Hancock have murdered his wife, dragged her silently outside, and then gone back to sleep, never knowing when his daughters might be returning from a night of revelry? Perhaps, but the circumstances just did not seem to brand the two men as wife murderers.

After the arrests of Phillips and Hancock, the other victims and their murder cases were largely forgotten. Though a substantial reward was offered for evidence that could solve the earlier murders, no real effort was made to solve them. True, Oliver Townsend and other members of the Thug Gang had been implicated in the earlier murders, but they were never charged with murder. Certainly Phillips and Hancock were not the servant girl annihilators, were they?

Notes

Title: *Austin Daily Statesman*, 1/29/1886.

1. *Fort Worth Daily Gazette*, 2/18/1886; *Austin Daily Statesman*, 1/14/1886.
2. *Fort Worth Daily Gazette*, 1/2/1886; *Galveston Daily News*, 1/3/1886; Oakwood Cemetery Database.
3. *Waco Daily Examiner*, 12/27/1885; Hollandsworth, "Capital Murders"; *New York Times*, 12/29/1885.
4. *New York Times*, 12/29/1885; *Austin Daily Statesman*, 12/30/1885; Oakwood Cemetery Database.
5. *Austin Daily Statesman*, 12/31/1885; *San Antonio Daily Express* 1/2/1886; *Austin Daily Statesman*, 1/6/1886 (Old Nick was a common term for the devil. Information regarding Bowahnie could not be found. Perhaps the reference is to the Bhuwani faith. The Guardian form of that faith was known to be aggressive and offensive.)
6. *Austin Daily Statesman*, 1/2/1886; *Fort Worth Daily Gazette*, 1/3/1886; *New York Times*, 1/3/1886.
7. *Fort Worth Daily Gazette*, 1/3/1886.
8. *Fort Worth Daily Gazette*, 1/3/1886; Galloway, *The Servant Girl Murders*: 294; *San Antonio Daily Express*, 1/20/1886; *Morrison & Fourmy's General Directory of the City of Austin, 1885-1886*.
9. *Austin Daily Statesman*, 1/7/1886.
10. *Austin Daily Statesman*, 1/7/1886.
11. *Austin Daily Statesman*, 1/16/1886.
12. *Austin Daily Statesman*, 1/22/1886; 1880 Federal Census.
13. *Austin Daily Statesman*, 1/22/1886; *Fort Worth Daily Gazette*, 1/25/1886.
14. *Austin Daily Statesman*, 1/23/1886.
15. *Austin Daily Statesman*, 1/23/1886.
16. *Austin Daily Statesman*, 1/28/1886.
17. *Austin Daily Statesman*, 1/29/1886.
18. *Austin Daily Statesman*, 1/29/1886.
19. *Austin Daily Statesman*, 1/29/1886; *San Antonio Daily Express*, 1/30/1886; *Austin Daily Statesman*, 1/30/1886; *Austin Daily Statesman*, 1/31/1886; Galloway, *The Servant Girl Murders*: 295; *Morrison & Fourmy's General Directory of the City of Austin, 1885-1886*.
20. *Austin Daily Statesman*, 1/31/1886; 1880 Federal Census; *Morrison & Fourmy's General Directory of the City of Austin, 1885-1886*.

Chapter 14

"Insane Passion for Blood"

Theories and Motives

During the year of murders, over 400 black men were arrested on suspicion, along with a sprinkling of white men. Almost all were quickly released for lack of evidence, and only three were tried. The trial of Walter Spencer for the murder of Mollie Smith has already been discussed. The trials of Jimmy Phillips and Moses Hancock will be discussed in later chapters. Along with these arrests came a raft of theories regarding the motive for the murders. A recap of the theories is in order to give a better idea of the reasons for the arrests and trials.

One of the earliest and most durable of the theories was the belief that jealousy or marital discord played a part in the murders. This theory began with the murder of Mollie Smith. And in fact, in most of the murders, this theory had some validity. Jealous or irate lovers or former lovers or husbands were implicated in most of the murders. However, if this theory was truly valid, then certainly some convictions would have resulted. One also has to wonder why a lover or husband would drag the beloved victim outside, brutally outrage her, and then mutilate her with an ax or hatchet. True, anger and jealous rage can provoke severe emotional reactions, but this theory seems too farfetched to be valid in all the cases. And if all the murderers were different men, why did they all adopt essentially the same method of murder, and how could all of them have evaded detection at the crime scene or conviction by the courts? And in several of the cases, the suspected men had been critically injured in the event. Could men with such serious wounds have carried out the outrage and murder?

When the home invasions began in March 1885, the popular theory was that an organized gang of black men was responsible. The supposed motives varied but included rape and robbery. Many of the homes that were attacked were the residences of men associated with the state and local governments, as well as men involved in banking and land transactions. Were the home assaults aimed at the servants in those homes or at the white residents? Since no convictions were ever attained for the assaults on all the homes, no particular motive was ever established.

In late spring, murder again took the forefront when Eliza Shelly was murdered. In this case, two possible motives were advanced, jealousy and robbery.

One of Shelly's sons stated that when a man entered their small shack, he asked where his mother kept her money. The boy replied that he did not know. From the boy's statement, the theory was proposed that the killer was a man belonging to one of the gang of northern robbers that had plagued Austin and Dallas in 1884, especially since the man told the boy he was headed to St. Louis. A train track also ran very close to the scene of the murder. But a man named Ike Plummer was also accused of quarreling with Shelly and demanding money from her. Plummer was supposedly romantically involved with Shelly, though Shelly was reportedly devoted to her imprisoned husband. Her murder was similar in execution to the murder of Mollie Smith, suggesting the robbery motive was weak. And Shelly also was not likely involved with Plummer, suggesting the jealousy motive was also weak.

About two weeks after the Shelly murder, another murder occurred, along with another home invasion. The home invasion occurred on Water Street, where a ruffian tried to break into the home of a white woman, apparently with the intent of rape. And then another servant woman was killed, this time with a knife or razor instead of an ax or hatchet. Irene Cross lived in a small two-room building with her son and nephew. The son was gone on the night of the attack, but the nephew saw the attacker and gave a description of a barefooted, stocky black man with rolled-up pants. Cross was severely gashed and later died of her wounds. This murder seemed to have no motive at all, since no money was taken and rape did not occur.

More home invasions occurred in the next two weeks, and violence accompanied most of them. A woman was shot, another had rocks thrown against her room, and a third room was entered and burglarized, though no violence was visited upon the servant girl living there. These attacks served only to muddy the search for a motive, though many still believed that an organized gang was responsible.

As the summer came on and criticism of the Austin government and police force escalated, the theories continued to swirl. The marital discord-jealousy theory was still popular, though that theory certainly did not explain the rash of home invasions. With a healthy dose of xenophobia, some believed all the crimes were committed by foreigners working on the capitol. The black citizens of Austin began to voice the notion that the crimes were somehow linked to supernatural beings or to a black man cursed by voodoo or the evil eye.

At the end of the summer, a new murder occurred, one more brutal than the earlier ones. This time, an 11-year-old black girl was savagely raped and murdered. This crime was similar to the earlier murders, with bare footprints found at the murder scene. The girl was hacked with an ax and had an iron spike pounded in her ear. A day after proclaiming that such brutality could only be performed by someone on the lower rung of society, that is, a black man, the local newspaper reversed course and suggested that an ignorant black man could not have planned and carried out the murder without being caught. Because the killer was able to escape capture, people began to believe he must have been a white man. Robbery did not seem to be a motive, and marital discord or jealousy also did not seem a likely motive since the victim was a child. Rape and murder could certainly have been the driving force for the offense, but why?

A month later, a double murder occurred near the newly opened University of Texas. In this case, four people sleeping in a small cabin were bludgeoned, and one woman was carried out and raped, and then her head was smashed with a brick. A man in the cabin also died of his wounds. This time, the belief began to spread that more than one killer was involved in the rampage, simply because a single assailant likely could not have quelled all the occupants of the cabin simultaneously without an alarm being sounded. And though the belief had recently emerged that white men might be the culprits, only black men were arrested as suspects. The motive of romantic jealousy was again advanced for this set of murders, for one of the suspects had supposedly at one time been the lover of the murdered woman. One of the victims that survived claimed to have recognized one of the killers. The case was further complicated by the story of a young man who claimed to have overheard one of the suspects plotting the murder and claiming responsibility for another of the murders. That story was later admitted to be a fabrication.

As the autumn deepened and the murders near the university continued to resonate in the public consciousness, new theories and motives began to arise. The notion that an organized gang was committing the murders gained renewed strength. A variation of this theory was that a secret organization was at work to stamp out negro prostitution and force the race to live within the bonds of conventional matrimony. A secret organization of Baptists, perhaps? Another variation was that a gang of black men were committing the atrocities due to pure cantankerousness and general spite. The Houston detectives working the cases believed that the murders were the work of a group of black men known as the Thug Gang, a bunch of local ne'er-do-wells and miscreants. But a local prosecutor involved in the later Hancock and Phillips trials, E.Taylor Moore, believed that the murders were done by a single man who hated women, though his idea was roundly mocked. One wonders how he could reconcile his theory with his prosecution of two men, Hancock and Phillips.

The last murders directly associated with this string of incidents occurred on Christmas Eve, 1885. A shift in victim type occurred, and two white women were murdered and outraged. Along with the shift in victim type came a shift in theories regarding the motive. Though the belief that the same killer or killers were responsible for the murders remained strong, with the Houston detectives clinging to their belief that the Thug Gang was culpable, many people began to believe that a lunatic had committed the murders. After all, who but a lunatic would outrage and murder white women? The notion was that a lunatic escaped from the asylum just outside Austin to commit the crimes, and then returned to the safety of the asylum. Many thought that some insane man had somehow cleverly planned the murders, carried out the plan, and then retreated to the refuge of the asylum, all without detection. How an insane person could be so clever was not explained, but who but a madman could commit such grievous offenses?

Others clung tenaciously to the jealousy or lust theory, and some began to spout new theories. One reporter suggested that a Frankenstein type monster, a man without a soul, roamed the streets of Austin committing crimes at will and without remorse. Some believed the earlier murders were caused by jealousy or marital discord and that the later murders were simply copycat crimes spurred by revenge. A later theory proposed the rather novel idea that the killer was "another Dr. Jekyll who transforms himself into a murderous Mr. Hyde when the passion for crime overcomes him." The notion further theorized that "perhaps his propensity for murder was first developed by reading Mr. Stevenson's powerful romance." This theory surmised that the murders were likely committed by a single hand and that "the lack of any apparent motive in any instance and the ease with which the assassin conceals his identity" logically led to the existence of some Jekyll-Hyde type character. The basis of this theory is quite interesting, but the killer was not likely motivated by reading Stevenson's novella, which was first published early in 1886.[1] Could the driving force behind the murders have been an upstanding citizen whose stature protected him or perhaps caused others to cover up his involvement?

Could the murders have been random, each committed by a different, unassociated person? The lurid details of the murders were printed in the newspapers, so anyone could have copied the modus operandi. The crime scenes were open, with many spectators stomping around, so clues could have been lost in the shuffle. Most of the murders were relatively nearby one another in the city, though the city proper was only about two miles square at the time. Axes and hatchets were readily available, with one in most every household. Some of the murders did differ slightly, such as the Irene Cross murder, in which a knife or razor was used instead of an ax or hatchet. And the spike in the ear was used on only two or three of the victims. If the goal of the murders was the rape of a black woman, why didn't the killer or killers seek out readily available prostitutes instead of risking detection by attacking the servants of prominent Austinites, and then the families of prominent Austinites? And how could numerous killers have enjoyed the relative impunity that accompanied the murders? Certainly, if many men were involved, at least one would have left some significant clue or revealed himself by boasting or some other stupidity. In fact, the murders seemed to have no apparent motive.

Perhaps numerologists can make something of the addresses at which the murders occurred. Three of the seven murders took place at locations with 302 in the address: 302 E. Cypress, 302 Linden, and 302 W. Hickory. One murder occurred at 300 E. Cedar, and one took place at 203 E. Water. The murders near the university took place at a residence listed variously as 2408 Guadalupe or 2310 San Marcos. The first murder occurred at 901 W. Pecan. Many of the addresses had the same digits. Could some motive be derived from these interesting address coincidences?

Though revenge as a motive is mentioned only in connection with copycat murders, revenge might in fact have been the primary motive behind the murders. Whether the murders were focused on the victims themselves or as intimidation against their employers is not certain. Because of the ferocity and brutality of the mutilations, some personal vendetta might be likely. In any case, the string of murders seemed to be related, not random events with totally different assassins.

But the murders may have been totally random. According to Carolyn Simpson, humans "'are pattern-finding creatures. . . . Randomness makes us nervous, so sometimes we find patterns where none exist.'" These murders, though, seemed to have too much of a pattern to disregard. If the murders were related, then a serial killer or killers were loose in Austin.[2]

What Is a Serial Killer?

In 2005, the FBI, in order to gain a better understanding of serial murder, held a symposium in San Antonio at which hundreds of experts gathered to share their views. From that conference came some standards for defining and characterizing serial murder. The attendees agreed that serial murder included one or more assailants, two or more victims killed in separate incidents at different times, with the time period between the incidents separating serial murder from mass murder. Albert Lackey, for example, a man who killed eight people on one summer day in 1885, was a mass murderer, whereas the servant girl annihilator was likely a serial killer. From these agreements emerged the FBI definition of serial murder: "the unlawful killing of two or more victims by the same offender(s), in separate events."[3]

The conference also served to dispel numerous myths about serial killers. One myth dispelled was the belief that serial killers are reclusive social misfits. Most serial killers "are not monsters and may not appear strange. Many serial killers hide in plain sight within their communities. Serial murderers often have families and homes, are gainfully employed, and appear to be normal members of the community. Because many serial murderers can blend in so effortlessly, they are oftentimes overlooked by law enforcement and the public." The conferees also agreed that serial killers come from all racial and demographic groups. Another agreement was that serial murders are not all sexually-based. Other motives include "anger, thrill, financial gain, and attention seeking." The conference also dispelled the belief that "serial killers have either a debilitating mental condition, or they are extremely clever and intelligent." Though serial killers often suffer from personality disorders such as psychopathy or anti-social behavior, few are considered insane under the law. And like the general population, "serial killers range in intelligence from borderline to above average levels."[4]

The conferees also agreed that "serial killers are driven by their own unique motives or reasons." Indeed, a motive may be hard to determine for a serial killer. The serial killer may have more than one motive for the murders, and the "motives may evolve both within a single murder as well as throughout the murder series." Even if a motive is established, the motive alone may not help to identify the murderer because "regardless of the motive, serial murderers commit their crimes because they want to." General motivations can be assigned, though. Many serial killers feel anger toward a certain subgroup or society at large. Some serial killers are motivated by some criminal enterprise wherein the killer stands to gain in money or status, such as in a gang or organized crime. Financial gain through insurance or welfare fraud is another general motivation. Ideology is another motivation, with the murders being committed to advance the goals or ideas of a particular person or group. Power or thrill is another motivation that drives some serial killers, with the murder providing empowerment or excitement for the killer. The sexual needs or desires of the killer may also serve as a motivation. And some serial killers suffer from psychosis and commit murder because of that disease.[5]

Many serial killers also share common traits with psychopaths. Among these common traits are "sensation seeking, a lack of remorse or guilt, impulsivity, the need for control, and predatory behavior." Psychopathy is considered "a personality disorder manifested in people who use a mixture of charm, manipulation, intimidation, and occasionally violence to control others, in order to satisfy their own selfish needs." The degree of psychopathy a person suffers can be measured using four factors: interpersonal, affective, lifestyle, and anti-social.

> The interpersonal traits include glibness, superficial charm, a grandiose sense of self-worth, pathological lying, and the manipulation of others. The affective traits include a lack of remorse and/or guilt, shallow affect, a lack of empathy, and failure to accept responsibility. The lifestyle behaviors include stimulation-seeking behavior, impulsivity, irresponsibility, parasitic orientation, and a lack of realistic life goals. The anti-social behaviors include poor behavioral controls, early childhood behavior problems, juvenile delinquency, revocation of conditional release, and criminal versatility. The combination of these individual personality traits, interpersonal styles, and socially deviant lifestyles are the framework of psychopathy and can manifest themselves differently in individual psychopaths.

However, not all psychopaths are serial killers, and not all serial killers are psychopaths. If serial killers are psychopathic, "they are able to assault, rape, and murder without concern for legal, moral, or social consequences. This allows them to do what they want, whenever they want." As a result, psychopathic serial killers place little value in human life and display extreme callousness in their treatment of their victims.[6]

Katherine Ramsland elaborated on these serial killer characteristics in her book *Inside the Minds of Serial Killers*. Ramsland attributed similar motives to serial killers, including lust, omnipotence, intellectual exercise, glory, delusions, rage, profit, sexual deviance related to blood or dead bodies, and no particular purpose. She believed that many serial killers begin their antisocial behavior when they are young, applying the "bad seed" theory. She also contended that some serial killers truly have Jekyll and Hyde personalities and that "their 'potion' of transformation is psychological."[7]

The sexual serial killer is "generally motivated by aggression, sex, or power, and the fantasies through which these urges are expressed." Ramsland noted that sexual serial killers are either "impulsive or ritualistic." She suggested that "impulsive offenders are opportunistic and generally of lower intelligence and economic means, and their sexual behavior often serves power or anger needs.

Ritualistic offenders, on the other hand, indulge in paraphilias (abnormal sexual behavior) and compulsive behaviors that satisfy some psychological need." Part of the pleasure of the murder, then, is in the sexual assault, as the stronger male overwhelms the "weaker sex." Such sexual serial killers often "live double lives, going through the motions of normalcy as much as possible to prevent others from detecting their darker activities, but also seeking opportunities to engage in that which has become most pleasurable to them. And that pleasure can take many different forms." Though rape was involved in most of the murders, the motive of the servant girl annihilator did not seem to have been strictly sexual. And, if someone had ordered the murders, then the one ordering the murders and the ones doing the killings were likely operating under two different motivations.[8]

A second motivation Ramsland developed is omnipotence. This motivation satisfies the killer's "need for outright control, and it's girded with the killer's belief that he is special in some superior way." Such killers exhibit a "a pattern of grandiosity and excessive need for admiration," such as a politician might do. This type of killer has "a high level of self-regard, but they treat others as inferior beings," suggesting the ability to mutilate the victims. Such killers are arrogant and without humility, believing they are important and that others envy them, even if such suppositions are false. In fact, "their belief in their superiority is particularly strong in relation to law enforcement," which was highlighted in the relative ease with which the servant girl killers could evade the police. Such killers also "lack empathy or a sense of responsibility, and they manipulate, lie, and con others with no regard for anyone's feelings." Such a person could easily kill and mutilate without qualms.[9]

Ramsland also suggested that some serial killers are motivated by an intellectual exercise, that they properly exhibit the "will to power." Such killers believe that "life is based in overpowering the weak." They may, however, be suffering from delusions caused by a mental disorder such as schizophrenia or bipolar affective disorder. Such persons may have a chemical or structural brain abnormality that causes psychotic episodes. Bipolar affective disorder, also known as manic-depressive disorder, can also produce psychotic episodes. This disorder is "a cyclical disturbance characterized by dramatic mood swings between mania and depression, and people suffering from it may have intense periods of high energy in which they seem superhuman. They go without rest for long periods of time, have grandiose ideas, and accomplish an astonishing amount. However, they may then swing into serious depression, sometimes accompanied by delusions and thoughts of suicide. They may hear voices during either phase, but between phases, they may feel normal." This disorder fits the Jekyll-Hyde condition mentioned earlier.[10]

A serial killer may also act from rage or anger, though Ramsland distinguished between a serial killer and a spree killer, noting that "a spree killer's rampage is generally related to a single precipitating incident." Such spree killing, then, could be associated with revenge. Such rage or revenge killers have the feeling that someone must pay for some assumed slight, and the murders help to "reinforce a sense of entitlement." The murders also help to prepare the way for other murders, because such killers don't want to lose their rage. They seem to relish in the rage and the resultant murders, which allow them to perfect the modus operandi in anticipation of more murders. Such killers often maltreat the victims way beyond what is necessary to kill them, suggesting that the rage itself is pleasurable.[11]

A more disturbing motivation is a fascination with blood and dead bodies, promoting sexual stimulation and necrophilia. Such motivations are usually caused by paraphilias, or "patterns of behavior based in a preoccupation for sexual arousal on objects, unusual activities, or deviant situations." These paraphilias include various fetishes, such as necrophilia, sadism, or piquerism, which is sexual arousal provided by stabbing with a sharp instrument. One can see some of this type of motivation in the servant girl murders, in which dying or dead females were raped, and sharp instruments such as an ax, a spike, or a knife were used to injure the victim. And perhaps the most distressing reason for serial murders is no particular purpose, no reason at all. This last motivation echoes the theory that black men were committing the murders out of pure "cussedness."[12]

Ramsland also pointed out that serial killers have the ability to mask their murderous behavior and operate normally in society. This Jekyll-Hyde scenario allows such serial killers to remain undetected even by their immediate families.

> Many serial killers blend in because they're the type of person who can go through the motions of ordinary living while acting out against others without giving themselves away. In other words, they're not obviously deranged, and while they're morally deviant they can hide it in their bland everyday manner. Among their most dangerous features are a callous disregard for the rights of others and a propensity for violating norms. They can charm and manipulate others for their own gain, conning with no regard for anyone's feelings. In fact, they fail to think of other people as human.

According to Ramsland, most serial killers are psychopaths that are "narcissistic, impulsive, and pitiless, with a tendency to divert blame from themselves to others so that they come out looking like the victim." Such killers have no fear of consequences. They exhibit a public persona that is good and upstanding while "nurturing a darker side that allows their murderous fantasies free reign." Each subsequent murder actually strengthens the dual personality.

> As the killers get away with their acts, they learn the best ways to deflect others from discovering their secrets and then enjoy the lack of accountability. They devise different sets of values for different life frames, so that they can speak convincingly about socially approved venues of right and wrong, yet have no qualms about their socially condemned behavior. Their secret lives grow darker and more perverse, because the morality that justifies them is entirely of the killers' making, separate from the social morality in which they were raised and by which they get along with others. They can feel satisfied about their murder while condemning the same thing in someone else, or denouncing divorce, teenage promiscuity, or prostitution . . . .

> They can also carry on a high level of functioning even while they seek another victim, because the murder helps them to achieve something they believe they need.

Such a Jekyll-Hyde personality could easily explain why an upstanding Austin citizen could actually be the master pulling the strings of his negro puppets.[13]

In *Cold Case Homicides*, Richard H. Walton provided some techniques for uncovering serial killers. Walton asserts that "many unsolved rapes and murders are stranger crimes. Most homicides are cleared for the simple reason that people are typically killed by someone they know. If there is no relationship between the offender and the victim, the crime is usually much more difficult to solve. Stranger crimes, however, may be part of a larger series." The establishment of guilt in a crime can be accomplished in three ways: a confession, a witness, or physical evidence. The servant girl murders did not have the first way, and the second and third ways were sparse and often unreliable. Walton also noted that the information leading to the solution of a crime typically comes first from the public, then from patrol officers, and finally from detectives. In the servant girl murders, the public and patrol officers provided little evidence, and most of the detectives' evidence was shown to be inconclusive or total fabrication.[14]

Two techniques pertinent to the servant girl murders are linkage analysis and geographic profiling. Linkage analysis, or comparative case analysis, examines key components of the investigation, such as physical evidence, description of the assailant, the assailant's behavior at the crime scene, proximity in time and place of the murders, a common modus operandi, and a signature. The murders attributed to the servant girl annihilator had numerous commonalities. Though physical evidence was limited, the same bare footprint was found at the scene of several of the murders. A few witnesses gave a physical description of the assailant as a stocky black man. Behavior at the crime scene was similar in most of the murders. The murders typically included the bludgeoning and rape of the victim. In many of the murders, the victim was dragged outside after being knocked unconscious. The murders were also committed in the early morning hours on days near a full moon. The modus operandi was another similarity. The killers would enter the room of the victim, knock her unconscious, usually with an ax or hatchet, perhaps drive a spike into her ear to discombobulate her, drag her outside to outrage her, and then escape unnoticed by even neighborhood dogs, all without leaving much physical evidence. The signature of the servant girl annihilators would have to be the repeated use of an ax to savage the victim.[15]

The second pertinent technique would be geographic profiling. Such profiling might not be very effective in the servant girl murder cases because the city of Austin was so small at the time, scarcely more than two miles square. Several of the components of this technique are also irrelevant, such as a directional trend or physical boundaries such as rivers or highways. The killers also did not seem to be deterred by psychological boundaries, as the murders did their evil deeds in the white neighborhoods where black men are supposedly loath to strike. The pattern of the crime scenes also lends little useful information, as the murders ranged from the west side to the north side to the central core of the city. The only curious aspect to the grid of the murder lay in the similar digits found in many of the addresses, as noted earlier. The most useful geographic profiling technique might lie in the so-called anchor point. Walton listed several possible anchor points in and around Guy Town and the railroad depot. Many researchers of the servant girl murders consider the Pearl House an anchor point because a supposed suspect, a cook named Maurice, lived there. They also contend that the Pearl House, located at 223 Congress Avenue, was close to all the murders. As noted earlier, because the city was only about two miles square, basically every location in Austin was close to all the murders. A more likely anchor point was the Black Elephant Saloon at 423 E. Pecan Street. Run by Hugh Hancock, this saloon was more centrally located than the Pearl House. The Black Elephant was also a significant gathering point for many of the black suspects in the servant girl case. Lem Brooks, a suspect in the first murder, supposedly worked at the Black Elephant. Alex Mack was lured from the Black Elephant when Marshal Grooms Lee tried to intimidate him into making a confession. One can assume that other members of the Thug Gang also spent time in the Black Elephant.[16]

The servant girl annihilator would certainly seem to be a serial or spree killer, though many of the modern techniques for identifying a serial killer are not really applicable. A frontier town like Austin in 1885 was not like modern day Los Angeles or even modern day Austin. Now, investigators have DNA sampling and a host of other techniques available to identify and track serial killers. At the time, the police and even the detectives had little but seat-of-the-pants analysis for detecting the culprit. Perhaps the true servant girl annihilator is lost to time, but several likely suspects are still debatable.

Notes

Title: *Fort Worth Daily Gazette*, 7/30/1887.

1. *Fort Worth Daily Gazette*, 7/30/1887 (reprinted from *Philadelphia Press*).
2. Pennebaker personal interview, 12/24/2011; Carolyn Simpson, qtd. in O'Connor, *Palm Beach Post*, 1/27/2011.
3. "FBI—Serial Murder."
4. "FBI—Serial Murder."
5. "FBI—Serial Murder."
6. "FBI—Serial Murder."
7. Ramsland, *Inside the Minds of Serial Killers*: 9-118, 177.
8. Ramsland, *Inside the Minds of Serial Killers*: 12, 19.
9. Ramsland, *Inside the Minds of Serial Killers*: 22, 24, 26.
10. Ramsland, *Inside the Minds of Serial Killers*: 33, 34, 58, 59-60.
11. Ramsland, *Inside the Minds of Serial Killers*: 65, 68, 70.
12. Ramsland, *Inside the Minds of Serial Killers*: 85-87, 109-111.
13. Ramsland, *Inside the Minds of Serial Killers*: 178, 180.
14. Walton, *Cold Case Homicides*: 538, 539.
15. Walton, *Cold Case Homicides*: 544.
16. Walton, *Cold Case Homicides*: 544-547, 549-551, 557.

Chapter 15

"Mysterious Barefoot League of Assassins"

The Usual Suspects

Moses Hancock and Jimmy Phillips had been arrested for the murders of their wives. Were they also involved in the other servant girl murders? That prospect seems highly unlikely. Certainly, their names had never come up in any of the earlier investigations. Many other names had been bandied about, though. A review of the usual suspects seems in order. According to some reports, over 400 black men were arrested or questioned in relation to the murders.

In the early months of 1885, a general sentiment emerged that the many attempted home invasions and perhaps the murders themselves were the work of an organized group. In February, the Fort Worth newspaper wondered editorially: "Have the negroes at Austin formed a secret association, pledged to run out the Swedish and other servant girls? It looks like it." In March, the *Austin Daily Statesman* echoed this notion, saying that the crime wave was the "diabolical doings of what appears to be a regular band of organized ruffians." The newspaper supported its belief by stating, "From the similarity of the offenses, and the identical methods employed in nearly every case, it is evident that the foul work has been perpetrated by the same set of lawless libertines." Though this belief wavered over the year, occasionally replaced by the practical conclusion that the murders were all the result of romantic jealousy, the argument that an orchestrated group effort was behind the murders and assaults remained at the forefront of most theorizing. Was a murderous cabal, a "mysterious barefoot league of assassins," if you will, responsible for the year of murder and mayhem? Or were the murders totally unrelated, random, or truly just the result of domestic upheaval?[1]

Walter Spencer

Walter Spencer was one of the first suspects in the murders and one of the very few who were actually tried. Spencer was the boyfriend or common-law husband of Mollie Smith, the first servant girl murdered. Spencer was a laborer and about 30 years old at the time Mollie Smith was murdered. Spencer was in the room with Smith on the night of the murder, and he received five facial injuries in the assault. The injuries, though, were not caused by an ax, according to the city physician, Dr. William J. Burt, but by some sharp pointed object, such as a piece of metal or a rock. Spencer was so severely injured that he was left in a daze, unaware of anything that transpired after he was hit in the head. Spencer had been courting Smith for several months, and they were living together as man and wife. Their relationship was said to be harmonious, and Smith was reported to have a great influence over Spencer, so much so that he would do whatever she requested. Though seriously injured in the attack, Spencer was nevertheless regarded as a suspect. The theory was that he and Smith had been involved in some sort of spat and that Spencer had killed her in his rage. Smith was killed with an ax, but there was no ax on the property where she was killed. However, Spencer had recently borrowed an ax for some temporary work. The belief was that Smith had first attacked Spencer with the ax, causing his wounds, and that in retaliation he had killed her, dragged her outside in the snow, outraged her, and then hacked her body to bits. Such a scenario is of course possible, but the facts in the case don't support the supposition very well.[2]

Despite the improbability of his having committed the murder, Spencer was taken to trial in December 1885. In late November, District Attorney James H. Robertson, the brother of the mayor, using flimsy evidence collected by two private Houston detectives, Hanna and Hennessey, decided to charge Walter Spencer with murder. The grand jury issued a murder indictment against Spencer, and a two-day trial was held in early December. After a very brief discussion, the jury acquitted Spencer, and he was released. The two detectives who had provided the flimsy evidence were soon dismissed by the city.[3]

Was Walter Spencer a viable suspect in the servant girl murders? Not really. He was not a suspect in any of the other murders, and his trial for the murder of Mollie Smith ended quickly with his acquittal. Walter Spencer just happened to be in the room when Mollie Smith was murdered, and he suffered as a result.

William "Lem" Brooks

William Brooks, also known as Lem, was another suspect in the Mollie Smith murder. Brooks was in his mid-twenties at the time and perhaps worked as a bartender in a saloon on East Pecan Street. He was supposed to have been Mollie Smith's lover when she lived in Waco, so his motive was regarded as jealousy. He freely admitted that he knew both Mollie Smith and Walter Spencer but that he had no trouble with them and had nothing to do with Mollie Smith in Austin. Spencer claimed that Brooks had wanted to fight him in the early fall of 1884, but that charge may have been caused by Spencer's jealousy over Brooks' former relationship with Smith. Brooks was able to produce a reasonable and verifiable alibi, that he had been a prompter at a dance on the east side of Austin until about 2 in the morning, about the same time Smith was murdered. Though Brooks produced witnesses who agreed with his alibi, others differed on the time he claimed he left the dance and the time he arrived home. With sufficient speed, Brooks could have run from the east side to the far west side of Austin, murdered and raped Mollie Smith, and then run back to his residence at 705 Lavaca before the time he was said to arrive home, a total of about three miles.[4]

When the inquest regarding the murder of Mollie Smith was held on January 1, 1885, the secret proceedings ended with the declaration that Mollie Smith had died from ax wounds inflicted by William Brooks. Most people in Austin found the conclusion unacceptable. Brooks was arrested and jailed, but after an examining trial on January 26, 1885, he was released due to lack of evidence. Like Walter Spencer, Brooks was not a suspect in any of the other servant girl murders, and he was never convicted of any crime in relation to the murders. Brooks' major wrongdoing seemed to be that he had known Mollie Smith intimately several years before she was murdered.[5]

"A Regular Gang of Brutes"

During the late winter and early spring of 1885, Austin suffered through a slew of attempted home invasions and several successful assaults. Through these numerous incidents of mischief and some serious injury, no specific suspect was ever identified publicly. At first these attempted assaults were aimed at black servants, but they soon spread to include white servant girls, mainly German and Swedish girls. Because the servant girls often lived in an outbuilding detached from the main house, they were easy targets. In March, a white man attacked a German girl in her bedroom in a well-to-do area on East Hickory Street, demanding her money. She screamed, and he knocked her in the head several times with a rock. Others in the house came running, and the man escaped, though later a rock was launched at one of his pursuers. At this time, the stone-cutters association, mostly white men, was in a labor dispute over the construction of the capitol. No positive identification was made in the case.[6]

The early morning of March 13 pulsed with criminal activity. Just after midnight, a black cook awoke to the sound of her door being violently shaken. She screamed, and others in the main house were roused. The attackers ran into the street and pelted the building with rocks. As the people in the main house came out to investigate, the attackers disappeared into the moonless night. Later that night, two black servants awoke to a pounding on the door, with someone outside demanding entrance. They refused and the attacker tried to open a window. The girls then fled, and the attacker caught one and threw her to the ground. Soon people from the main house came out, and the attacker ran away. Another incident near City Hall had similar results. One attack, though, turned violent and ended in the rape of a black servant, Sarah Hall. In this incident, Hall's bedroom was entered by two attackers, both black men, but one was supposedly painted yellow. Despite the paint job, Hall recognized one of her attackers as Abe Pearson, a mulatto barber. Pearson was apprehended, quickly tried and convicted, and sent to the penitentiary for two years. The other attacker was not apprehended. But Pearson was not identified as a suspect in the servant girl murders.[7]

All these incidents occurred within a mile of each other, and most of the attacks were on the homes of prominent, respectable Austinites. The culprits could be generally described as black men throwing rocks. But the onslaught caused the *Austin Daily Statesman* to revive the organized gang theory, calling the attackers "a regular gang of . . . brutes who perambulate the city at the small hours of night to do their unholy work." The attacks were annoying but not deadly, yet they continued without relief. The newspaper advised citizens to keep a loaded shotgun by the bed and promoted a gold medal for the first person to shoot one of the assailants.[8]

A slew of attempted home invasions also took place before dawn on March 18. At least five homes of prominent Austinites were targeted, with German and Swedish servant girls working at most of them. At the home of Colonel John Pope, black attackers tried to break into the servant quarters with the intent of robbery and rape. The two Swedish girls tried to flee, though one was caught and dragged to the ground by her hair, but the attack was thwarted when Colonel John Templeton, a boarder at the house and also the attorney general of Texas, appeared on the scene. The other girl made her way into the main house but was shot in the back by one of the invaders. At another house, "unknown parties" tried to rape a black servant, but this outrage was too thwarted by a neighbor. In at least two other homes, black assailants tried to break in and rape the servants, some black, some Swedish.[9]

These assaults differed from the murders because they were usually not committed around the full moon, and they were noisy and careless, unlike the stealthy silence that marked the murders. Though on a few occasions the race and number of the assailants were determined, in most cases they were not. A gang of "organized ruffians" was blamed for the crime spree. Whether these ruffians were directly or indirectly related to the servant girl murders is not clear.[10]

The home attacks ceased for a few week but began anew at the end of April. On April 29, a black intruder attacked a white woman in her home, but through great strength, the woman was able to wrest a knife from the assailant's hand, and he fled without much injury to the woman. A strange episode occurred that same morning. A black cook was attacked by a black man who had inexplicably taken a dress from the clothesline and donned it before entering the cook's outbuilding. Wielding a razor, he grabbed the cook's throat and threatened to kill her. Hearing voices outside, though, he fled, still in the dress. A neighbor later saw the black man trying to cut the dress off, apparently cutting himself in the process. This attack was later credited to "Old John," an insane black man who had recently been discharged from the lunatic asylum.[11]

The assaults reached their height in the early morning hours of May 1. The story line was much the same: black men trying to break into outbuildings, apparently to rape the occupants. All the home attacks occurred within a stone's throw of one another, and not far from the capitol. Some of these assailants were seen and fired upon, but to no effect. One was described as a "big black fellow," another as a "burly negro." The intent in all the attacks seemed to be robbery and rape. During one attack, the assailant dropped a coat and hat. The coat and hat were traced to Doc Tobin, a black bartender working in Guy Town. Tobin, though, claimed the items had been stolen. Later, two black men named Andrew Jackson and Henry Wallace were arrested on suspicion of participating in the assaults. These two men were believed to have something to do with the assaults, but they were not thought to be the "main perpetrator."[12]

Andrew Williams

Then, on May 7, the attacks turned deadly again. Eliza Shelly, living in an outbuilding on the property of Dr. Lucien Johnson on East Cypress Street, was brutally murdered with an ax. Shelly shared the small house with her three sons, the oldest about 8 years old. That son awoke when a man entered the room and asked where the money was kept. The boy was not sure if the man was black or white, but he apparently told Mrs. Johnson that the man was white, though the Fort Worth newspaper reported that the boy said the murderer was a black man. The man apparently wore a white cloth over his face. He hacked Shelly several times with an ax and dragged her from the bed onto a pallet he had made on the floor, but he apparently did not rape her. He left without harming the children. Bare footprints, a major clue in the series of murders, were found leading to the house and away from it.[13]

Later that day, Andrew Williams, "said to be a half-witted colored boy, about 19 years old," was arrested about a half-mile from the murder scene. His great crime? He was barefooted at the time of his arrest. Of course, the footprint at the murder scene had been measured, and those dimensions would absolve or condemn the young man. Apparently, he barely escaped the noose because he was not tried for the crime. He was, however, arrested later in June for the brutal rape of a black girl in east Austin. For that crime in June, Williams was sentenced to life in prison.[14]

Ike Plummer

Ike Plummer was another black man whose crime seemed to be the lack of shoes. A few days after the murder of Eliza Shelly, Ike Plummer was charged with that murder. But Plummer, who was regarded to be as simple as Andrew Williams, did not even grasp that he was being charged with murder. He thought he was being arrested for an earlier vagrancy charge. Plummer was described by an Austin reporter as "a tall, ungainly, ill kempt negro, with a countenance suggestive more of idiocy than brutality, and about thirty years of age." A preliminary hearing for Plummer was held before Justice William Von Rosenberg, Jr., and Colonel John Pope testified in his behalf, saying Plummer did not have a "violent disposition." The reporter also noted that Plummer was not uneasy during the hearing, but that an occasional "half imbecile grin played over his black face."[15]

The most damaging witness against the simple-minded Plummer was Andrew Rogers, who had lived with Shelly earlier. The situation between Plummer and Rogers seemed similar to the situation between Walter Spencer and Lem Brooks in the Mollie Smith murder. Rogers said he had known both Plummer and Shelly for about a year, and that he knew of a quarrel between Plummer and Shelly that took place around the first of April. Soon after the quarrel, Shelly moved and became a cook for Dr. Lucien Johnson. Rogers claimed he saw Plummer and Shelly together in the early evening of May 6, and that he overheard their conversation. According to Rogers, Plummer demanded money from Shelly, but she refused him any. She told him not to come around anymore. So Plummer left, but he said he would see Shelly again. Rogers claimed he saw the handle of a hammer or hatchet in Plummer's pocket. Rogers concluded his testimony by saying he lived near Plummer and that he heard Plummer coming home late on the night of the murder. Plummer, of course, strongly denied any involvement in the murder.[16]

Could Rogers' testimony against Plummer have resulted from jealousy, as in the case of Spencer and Brooks? Did Plummer kill Eliza Shelly for a few dollars? And if Plummer had a history with Shelly, wouldn't Shelly's son have recognized Plummer or his voice? In any case, Plummer was not charged with the murder of Eliza Shelly, nor was he implicated in any of the following murders. Plummer seems to have disappeared from Austin, though he might have ended up in Fayette County, about 80 miles from Austin, where a man named Ike Plummer married Eliza Johnson in 1892. The first name of the bride is indeed curious.[17]

Tom Allen

After the murder of Mary Ramey in August, the bloodhounds led the police to a stable near the murder scene. There, they found a black man hidden in the hay loft. The man, Tom Allen, was about 23 years old and drove one of the city water carts. He lived in the general area of the Weed house where the murder was committed. Allen was taken back to the murder scene and had his feet measured against the footprints left in the sand. His feet fit the tracks "to a hair," and he could give no good account of his whereabouts during the early morning hours of that Sunday. Based on those two bits of evidence, Allen was taken to jail, though the people of Austin would likely have lynched him in a moment. However, the city physician, Dr. Burt, examined Allen and concluded that Allen could not have raped the Ramey girl because of "certain physical incapabilities." Allen had not been implicated in any of the earlier murders, and he was not named in the later murders. In fact, he was not believed to have anything to do with the murder, though he might have served as a "guide and decoy for others who got in their hellish work." In another report, this suspect was called Henry Taylor, a young black man who also drove a water cart. Taylor's footprint was said to fit exactly the footprints in the Weed yard, even to a toe with an unusual shape.[18]

Alexander Mack

Alex Mack's name first arose in connection with the murder of Mary Ramey, though the police did not consider him a suspect. Mack was arrested the Monday night after the Ramey murder after being chased by the bloodhounds. He was found hiding in East Austin. Mack, a laborer, was not charged in the Ramey case, but he was jailed under an old charge. Mack was a well-known criminal with one of the longest arrest records in Austin. If he was not involved in the murders, he probably knew pertinent information about them. After the Vance murders, Mack was arrested for being a "suspicious character." He was also suspected in the shooting of Jim Glover by Glenn Drummer early in October 1885. He was considered a "confederate of Drummer." Both Mack and Drummer were "suspected of being concerned in other outrages."[19]

Mack became a more important figure when the case against Dock Woods and Oliver Townsend began to unravel. On the night of October 3, 1885, Mack was at the Black Elephant Saloon on East Pecan Street. Marshal Grooms Lee called to Mack from the door of the saloon. According to Mack, Lee wanted Mack to go with him to identify two black men. Instead, he was led to Red River Street, where two other police officers and two detectives were waiting. One of them had a rope. Mack said that the men choked him and put the rope around his neck. They asked what he knew about the Vance murder, and he said he knew nothing. Then they knocked him down to the ground, stomped and kicked him, and finally took him to jail, where he was held chained for nine days before finally being released. Mack then told his story to the *Austin Daily Dispatch*, a story that Lee vigorously denied. Lee claimed he had long suspected Mack of the Ramey murder. As Lee passed the Black Elephant, he saw that Mack was very drunk. He coaxed Mack out of the saloon and told him that he was under arrest for some false charge of hitting someone with a beer glass. Mack agreed to go along, though he vigorously denied the charge. Lee then contended that any injuries that Mack suffered were a result of his rowdiness and failure to submit peacefully to his arrest. The rope, Lee claimed, was used only to drag Mack into the cell, where he remained for nine days, but was chained only for three days.[20]

Whatever evidence Lee had against Mack, it must not have been much, for Mack was released from custody, though he was also suspected of threatening several officers and plotting to release Glenn Drummer from jail. Mack also filed a complaint with the city council against Lee, the other officers, and the detectives. A special committee was formed to investigate Mack's allegations against the police and detectives. The committee met on November 9 and 10, hearing testimony from Mack, his mother, the proprietor of the Black Elephant, and a man near whose home the hanging was threatened. Lee refused to attend the meeting without counsel present, thinking he was being tried for some crime, and he prevented other officers from testifying. Because the committee had no real power and, more importantly, because city elections were only a month away, no action was taken by the city council. Within a month, Marshal Grooms Lee was out of a job. In an ironic twist, when Eula Phillips was murdered, Sallie Mack, Alex's mother, who lived near the Phillips home, was called to wash and dress Eula's body before it was laid out in the parlor.[21]

Mack was an unsavory character with a long criminal record. He likely was involved in some, if not all, of the murders, assaults, and attempted home invasions.

Beverley Overton

Beverley Overton was more a victim of circumstances than a suspect. At the Vance murders, a horse was found tied in a nearby grove, as if placed there for the murderer's escape. The horse belonged to Overton, and when he went to the police station to claim the horse, he was arrested for the murder of Gracie Vance and Orange Washington. Overton, however, had a solid alibi. His stepson had ridden the horse to a store, and when he left the store, the horse was missing. Overton was soon released.[22]

Dock Woods

Dock Woods was named by an eyewitness to the Vance murders, and he became the first serious suspect in the murders. Woods was an acquaintance of Gracie Vance and Lucinda Boddy, the woman who identified him, though he denied knowing them. In fact, Woods may have been the "keeper of Gracie Vance" before she became involved with Orange Washington, suggesting the jealousy motive so often advanced. Whether Boddy actually saw Woods clearly is debatable, but she claimed to recognize his voice. After Boddy was struck in the head in the attack, she got up and lit a lamp. At that point, she apparently recognized Woods and said, "Oh, Doc, don't do it," to which he supposedly replied, "God damn you, don't look at me." And then the assault continued. The events surrounding the arrest of Woods were confused, but apparently he was arrested late Monday where he lived about six miles west of the city. At the time of his arrest, he was wearing a bloody shirt, which he attributed to an old venereal disease. Once the bloody shirt was presented to the inquest jury looking into the Vance murders, the jury quickly issued a verdict: Gracie Vance was killed by Dock Woods. The Houston detectives working the case also claimed to have conclusive evidence against Woods, and he was jailed without bail.[23]

But the watertight case against Woods began to leak. Dr. Richard Graves confirmed that Woods had a syphilitic condition that might account for the bloody shirt, and the likelihood that Woods would continue to wear a shirt soaked with a murder victim's blood was a bit thin. And the Houston detectives who had been working on the murder cases also later seemed to discount their own conclusive evidence, believing that Woods was not the murderer. The witness who named Woods, Lucinda Boddy, was suffering from an addled mind and at times professed an inability to recognize Woods at all. At other times she swore that Woods was positively one of the attackers. However, Woods was said to look very much like another suspect in the murders, Glenn Drummer, so that Boddy may have mistaken one for the other. And the testimony that had conclusively implicated Woods, given by a young man named Johnson Trigg, was soon revealed to be a fabrication. Nevertheless, Woods remained in jail through October. Later, he was arrested in connection with the Hancock and Phillips murders, but again, he was not charged with the murders.[24]

Was Woods possibly one of the murderers or a member of the so-called Thug

Gang? Though evidence against him came and went, he more than likely was involved in the series of murders. He seemed to have the physical build of the murderer seen by several witnesses: a short, stocky black man. But as noted, he apparently was very similar in appearance to Glenn Drummer, so his involvement might have been a case of mistaken identity.

Oliver Townsend

Before his implication in the servant girl murderers, Oliver Townsend had the reputation of being a notorious chicken thief. He was in his mid-20s, a mulatto with blue eyes, standing at 5'7" and weighing about 150 pounds. Townsend was not initially suspected in the Vance murders, but he was arrested on a charge of attempted burglary of the home of Dr. Wade Morris only a short while before the Vance murders. Then, based on the same conclusive evidence against Woods, Townsend was implicated in the murders of Gracie Vance and Orange Washington. For his part, Townsend claimed he was in church until 9 P.M. Sunday night, and then he visited with a neighbor by his gate. His only witness for his whereabouts during the murders was his mother. Townsend also denied knowing the victims that night, though he did claim to know Gracie Vance by sight.[25]

Somehow Townsend had raised the ire of Johnson Trigg, the young man who concocted the story about Townsend's involvement in the Vance murders. Even though Trigg's account proved false, Townsend remained a suspect in several of the murders. Like Dock Woods, he was arrested in connection with the Hancock and Phillips murders but was not charged. Was Townsend a viable suspect in the murders? As a probable member of the Thug Gang, he likely was involved to some degree in one or more of the murders.[26]

Johnson Trigg

Johnson Trigg was a key player in the servant girl murders for a while, though he wasn't really a suspect. Trigg's testimony was the conclusive evidence used to implicate Dock Woods and Oliver Townsend in the murders of Gracie Vance and Orange Washington, and perhaps Mary Ramey and the others. Trigg was a young black man about 19 years old who had recently moved to Austin. He worked and lived at the Carrollton Hotel on West Pecan Street. He claimed to know Oliver Townsend and said that on the night of September 27, 1885, he overheard Townsend speaking to another man. Trigg claimed that Townsend told the other man that he was going to kill Gracie Vance, but that the other man tried to dissuade Townsend from his goal. Trigg testified that Townsend also said, "I have been killing them and I have not been caught up with yet." Trigg said that he followed Townsend to the house where Gracie Vance was killed, and there Townsend met another man, who also tried to talk Townsend out of his mission. Townsend persisted, and the two went into the house. Trigg reported hearing the same conversation that Lucinda Boddy had mentioned. Then he heard a woman scream and he left.[27]

Trigg gave more damning evidence against Townsend. Trigg said that one night, he overheard Townsend in the Black Elephant Saloon saying that he was going to kill Becky Ramey. Trigg again claimed to have followed Townsend to V.O. Weed's home, but he did not know if Townsend actually killed Becky Ramey. Trigg said he did not tell about Townsend's involvement with the Ramey murder because he was not certain Townsend had killed her, so he waited, and when he heard other threats by Townsend, he came forward and told what he knew. Of course, Becky Ramey was not killed, but her daughter, Mary Ramey, was murdered.[28]

Whatever his reasons for accusing Townsend, Trigg soon admitted that his testimony against Townsend was fabricated. One speculation is that Trigg was involved in a frame-up of Woods and Townsend. Trigg worked at the hotel where the Houston detectives investigating the murders lived during their time in Austin. By the middle of October, Trigg was in the county jail. He was later convicted of perjury for swearing that Woods and Townsend had committed the Ramey and Vance murders, and he was sentenced to five years in the penitentiary.[29]

Glenn Drummer

From all reports, Glenn Drummer was a bad apple, a kid gone wrong. Drummer apparently was only about 15 years old at the time of the murders. He worked as a cook and boarded at the Capital Hotel on Congress Avenue. During the summer of 1885, Drummer was sent to jail for brandishing a pistol. Because he could not pay his fine, Drummer was released from jail on the condition that he leave the city. He did leave temporarily, but he returned and dodged the police. A few days before the Vance murders, Drummer tried to shoot two black men in East Austin. He was captured and charged with attempted murder. He was also a suspect in several of the servant girl murders. In November, Drummer went to trial on the attempted murder charge but was acquitted.[30]

As noted earlier, Drummer was said to look much like Dock Woods, likely possessing the short, stocky build described by the few witnesses who saw the assailants. At his young age, Drummer was also likely very impressionable and easy to manipulate, which would have made him a prime candidate to carry out the wishes of another. Though Drummer entered the conversation late in the string of murders, he seems a probable suspect.

Jack Coombs

Jack Coombs was one of the few white men suspected in the murders, but he was not a likely suspect. His murderous rage seemed focused on one woman only, Alice Davis, who was a prostitute or kept woman and apparently Coombs' young black mistress. In late October, Coombs went to the home of Davis and ironically charged her with infidelity. As she tried to escape, he shot her in the back with a .45-caliber revolver. Coombs was quickly arrested. Another young man named William Luckie was also arrested as an accomplice. Davis died in the middle of

November, and Coombs was convicted of murder and sent to prison for five years. Ironically, the other young man later filed a claim for a reward from the city. The city council had established a reward on October 5 to be paid to the person or persons who aided in capturing a murderer, rapist, or other like criminal. Though Luckie was implicated in the murder of Davis, he felt he had helped to apprehend Coombs. Whether he got the reward is unknown but doubtful.[31]

Though the Davis case is sometimes linked to the servant girl murders, it does not really qualify. The only real link was her skin color. She was a prostitute, not a servant girl. She was shot, not hacked or cut, and she was not raped at the time of her shooting. Her assailant was known, captured, convicted, and sent to prison.

Assorted Arrests

At the end of November, several new arrests were made in the servant girl murders. New names arose, and most did not seem remotely linked to the murders. One such name was James Thompson, a young black farmhand about 25 years old. Thompson was arrested as a suspect in the Mary Ramey murder. Apparently the only evidence against Thompson was his "giving himself away" while drunk. A witness said Thompson made the same claims before he got drunk. Two more names added to the long list of arrested black men were Cullen Crockett and Richard Bacon. Crockett was in his twenties, and Bacon was about 19 years old at the time of his arrest. They were arrested in neighboring Bastrop County on suspicion of murdering Mary Ramey. Finally, a black man named Henry Thomas was arrested for "knowing more than he will tell" about the Ramey murder, an inventive charge if nothing else. All these arrests led nowhere.[32]

The Norwood Brothers

After the Christmas Eve murders, the arrests took an interesting twist. Though the same broad, bare footprints that appeared at several of the earlier murders also appeared at the Phillips murder scene, white men were suddenly being arrested, along with a crazed Mexican. Two white men, J.T. and J.P. Norwood, were arrested at Belton, about 60 miles northeast of Austin, while riding the train. The two men had blood on their coats and vests, as well as blood on their shoes and even on their hands. The two men had come from San Marcos, about 40 miles south of Austin, where they claimed to have had a difficulty that resulted in their bloody apparel. Officials in San Marcos knew nothing of the difficulty. Travis County Sheriff Malcolm Hornsby had gone to Belton to pick up the men, and as the train that was to carry them back neared Austin, a large crowd gathered around the county jail. When the train arrived, the prisoners and sheriff were not on it. In fact, Sheriff Hornsby had investigated the two men and believed them innocent, so he saw no good reason to return them to Austin where they might be mobbed or lynched. The father of Eula Phillips was in the Belton area when Eula was killed. Could the Norwood brothers have been traveling to meet him? Could they have been involved in the murder of Eula Phillips or others? That prospect is unlikely.[33]

J.Q. Echols

Echols was another white man arrested on suspicion of the murder of Hancock and Phillips. The evidence against Echols was that he was seen washing red-stained clothes about seven miles west of Austin. Those who saw him washing the clothes were certain that the clothes were covered in blood, but Echols, who was a wood hauler about 35 years old, said the clothes were colored by pecan stains and from washing them with red socks. His shirt was stained at the bosom, and his pants had stains around the cuffs. A memo book he carried also had an unmistakable blood stain on one page. Echols was arrested and taken to the county jail, but the evidence against him did not hold up. He was not a likely suspect.[34]

David Hagy

David Hagy was a suspect in the Hancock murder. Hagy was a boarder at the Hancock house and had taken the two Hancock daughters to a Christmas party. He mysteriously disappeared for a couple of hours during the party. Hagy will be discussed more thoroughly in the chapters on the Hancock trial.

Anastacio Martinez

Anastacio Martinez was an interesting suspect that was believed to be one of the "outrage-fiends." Martinez was about 40 to 45 years old, and was described as cranky, with a stout build. With the arrest of Martinez in Guy Town on December 30, it was "authoritatively announced that the committee of safety and city authorities have reached a solution of the bloody mystery and traced the murders to a reliable source, and that the perpetrators will all be in jail inside of ten days." Of course, this bold claim proved false. Martinez had been in Austin for five or six years. Prior to arriving in Austin, he had spent a couple of years in a Brownsville, Texas, jail for assaulting women, and then he had been in a hospital for a while. Those who knew Martinez said he frequently went out late at night when the moon was shining, and that habit made him a likely suspect.[35]

But Martinez had other evidence against him. In one of the home invasions earlier in the year, a man had entered the house of a Mrs. Blake with the intent of assault or outrage. Mrs. Blake jumped out of bed, and a struggle over a knife ensued. Mrs. Blake was able to grab the handle of the knife and draw the blade across the hand of the assailant, making a gash across the four fingers. Martinez had a similar scar at the same location and even claimed the knife when an officer showed it to him after he was arrested. His foot was similar to the big footprints found at several of the murder scenes. His squat physical form also matched the description given by one of the murdered servant girls before she died. Martinez's residence was searched after his arrest, and it revealed a variety of interesting items. Found in the house were two hatchets, a woman's bloody dress and several other pieces of women's apparel, including several other dresses. Also found were a Colt six-shooter, seven knives, some with blood on them, a razor, an ice pick, and a long iron spike with blood on the tip. He also had a prayer book with the name Ella Ramey or Rooney in it, along with white handkerchiefs with J.R. or A.R. on them.[36]

The city authorities thought for sure they had captured the servant girl annihilator. But when Martinez, who spoke little English, was confronted by Mrs. Blake, she could not positively identify him or any of the dresses in his possession. She did say a knife in his possession was similar to the one used in the attack. Failing to provide a positive identification, Mrs. Blake left. Martinez was then made to wet his foot and make a footprint on the floor, but his footprint did not match the ones found at the murder scenes. Though the police had no solid evidence against Martinez, he was kept in jail anyway. In the middle of January, he was tried in county court and was determined to be insane, after which he was confined in the lunatic asylum.[37]

John Gray

John Gray, sometimes called Gray Jo, was another reputed member of the Thug Gang. Like other members of the gang, he was a suspect, but he had not yet been arrested. On the night before the Christmas Eve murders, for some unknown reason Gray tried to hack his way into a woman's house in Austin. He escaped to San Antonio, where he was arrested after drunkenly boasting that he and Dock Woods and others had done the murders and rapes in Austin. Gray was returned to Austin, charged with murder, and put in jail. According to Houston detective Mike Hennessey, Gray made a full confession, giving details and perpetrators of the murders. Other reports say Gray made no such confession. As a member of the Thug Gang, Gray was a likely suspect but never indicted for any of the murders.[38]

A Rich Cattleman

Another rumor that spread through Austin was that "a rich cattleman was likely to be implicated as the guilty party." That rich cattleman would have to be Jesse L. Driskill, who was building the grandiose Driskill Hotel while the murders were taking place. After making and losing fortunes in merchandising and cattle, Driskill and his family moved to Austin in 1871. Driskill continued in the cattle trade, building ranches in South Texas, Kansas, and the Dakota territory. In 1885, he purchased a whole city block in Austin for $7,500, and there his famous hotel was built. The Driskill Hotel opened in December 1886. Driskill lost another fortune in 1888 when a spring freeze on the northern plains killed many of his cattle. He was forced to sell the hotel to S. E. McIlhenny. Driskill died of a stroke in 1890. His involvement in the murders was considered no more than a rumor.[39]

Emile Francois

In 1879, Emile Francois married a woman three generations removed from a black ancestor. The woman, Lottie Stotts, was said to be lighter in complexion than

Francois was. However, Francois was arrested and tried for violating the Texas anti-miscegenation law. He was convicted and sentenced to five years in prison. Francois contended that the law was unconstitutional and that his civil rights were violated because only the white male in such marriages was penalized, not the black female, an obvious violation of the Fourteenth Amendment. In 1884, Francois applied for a writ for his release. The governor at the time, John Ireland, declared that the Fourteenth Amendment "was passed for the benefit of the negro race, and not the white." When the case was called in court, the state announced that Ireland had pardoned Francois. Francois refused the pardon because it did not restore his voting rights, and instead he had a subpoena issued for Ireland on the basis that the governor and others had conspired to deprive him of his civil rights. In a strange twist, a warrant was issued for the governor to testify. Francois was eventually released in late 1884. Stotts continued to live in Austin. In the early 1880s, she lived on Cypress Street, not far from the scene of several of the murders. Whether Francois moved back with Stotts after his release is unknown. Francois could be said to have a motive to murder the mulatto women, and also to taunt the governor and the courts of Austin. He was never named as a suspect in any of the murders, and he is an unlikely suspect.[40]

The Thug Gang

Collectively, the so-called Thug Gang was made up of some of the most unsavory characters in Austin. Reputed members included Dock Woods, Oliver Townsend, Glenn Drummer, Alex Mack, John Gray, and perhaps Nathan Elgin. Most of these black men were suspects in one or more of the servant girl murders. Mike Hennessey, one of the Houston detectives hired to investigate the string of servant girl murders, said that the Thug Gang consisted of "the bloodiest brutes that I was ever called to work up in the course of my career as a detective." Hennessey was convinced that Glenn Drummer, Oliver Townsend, and Dock Woods were the servant girl assassins. He based his belief on the fact that while these men were in jail, the murders stopped, but as soon as the men were released from jail, the murders started again. He noted that "they were kept locked up for three months, and during that three months the women of the capitol of Texas slept secure from the ravishing murderous attacks of the thugs."[41]

Though Hennessey was eventually dismissed by the city of Austin for his overstated evidence and his participation in the threatened lynching of Alex Mack, he may have been correct in his assessment of the murderers. Likely the murderers were a part of this gang. The question that remained, though, was whether they acted on their own volition or whether they were manipulated by someone else, a white man perhaps.

O. Henry's Contribution

William Sidney Porter, better known as O. Henry, was a resident of Austin during the servant girl murders. He did not really write much about the murders, except to note in a letter to a friend on May 10, 1885, that "Town is fearfully dull, except for the frequent raids of the Servant Girl Annihilators, who make things lively during the dead hours of the night." Before residing in Austin, Porter worked on a ranch in south Texas. That experience gave rise to a story titled "Law and Order." In the story, Porter ended the tale with a statement hauntingly reminiscent of the attitude toward the murders in Austin prior to the Christmas Eve killings. The story concerns a sheriff in Mojada County, Texas, who goes to New York City to bring back a young man who shot "Pedro Johnson, the proprietor of the Crystal Palace *chili-con-carne* stand" in the Texas town where the sheriff holds office. Turns out, in typical O. Henry fashion, the young man is really the long-lost son of the sheriff. The sheriff forgives his son's transgressions. When told that law and order need to be upheld in the town, the sheriff replies about the victim, "'Oh, hell! . . . That fellow was half Mexican, anyhow.'" Could O. Henry be subtly suggesting that the son of some important figure in Austin was the servant girl annihilator and the police investigation was stymied by a cover-up?[42]

Saylor's Suspects

In 2000, Steven Saylor published a novel about the Austin servant girl murders. In the novel, titled *A Twist at the End*, O. Henry serves as the protagonist trying to solve the murders. O. Henry was also supposed to be in love with Eula Phillips. William Sydney Porter, better known as O. Henry, did indeed live in Austin during the time of the murders, but he had no real involvement with them. In the novel, Saylor pins the murders on two white doctors. Dr. Kringel is the editor of *The Monist* and pretends to be Dr. Fry, a blind phrenologist. Dr. Terry develops a liver tonic and a ginger laxative. Together, Kringel and Terry rape and kill all the women for the pure pleasure of the brutal acts. In 1900, Terry drowns himself in the Colorado River. About that same time, Kringel is sent to the lunatic asylum for pretending to be Dr. Fry, but he escapes. After his escape, he sends O. Henry a satchel containing news clippings and a confession. At the book's end, O. Henry and Kringel meet on Mount Bonnell, a hill west of Austin. O. Henry shoots Kringel, who then tumbles off Mount Bonnell into the river below. Both Kringel and Fry are purely fictional characters and have no relation to the crimes. Though Saylor's novel is steeped in historical research, it does little to suggest a reasonable solution to the murders and perhaps distracts from such a solution.[43]

Other than Walter Spencer, none of these suspects was ever tried for the murder of any of the servant girls or Sue Hancock and Eula Phillips. Spencer was tried but was quickly acquitted for lack of evidence. Though the men discussed in this chapter were not tried and convicted of murder, at least some of them, notably the members of the Thug Gang, were likely participants in the murders. Two white men, Moses Hancock and James Phillips, were tried for the murder of their wives. And one black suspect matched the most compelling evidence found at some of the murder scenes, the bare footprint. Those three men are discussed in the next chapter.

Notes

Title: *Fort Worth Daily Gazette*, 11/15/1885.

1. *Fort Worth Daily Gazette*, 2/22/1885; *Austin Daily Statesman*, 3/20/1885; *Fort Worth Daily Gazette*, 11/15/1885.
2. 1880 Federal Census; *Austin Daily Statesman*, 1/1/1885; *Austin Daily Statesman*, 1/2/1885; *Austin Daily Statesman*, 1/3/1885.
3. *San Antonio Daily Express*, 11/22/1885; *San Antonio Daily Express*, 12/11/1885; Hollandsworth, "Capital Murders"; Galloway, *The Servant Girl Murders*: 282.
4. *Austin Daily Statesman*, 1/1/1885.
5. *Austin Daily Statesman*, 1/2/1885; *Austin Daily Statesman*, 1/6/1885; *Austin Daily Statesman*, 1/25/1885.
6. *Austin Daily Statesman*, 3/10/1885.
7. *Austin Daily Statesman*, 3/14/1885.
8. *Austin Daily Statesman*, 3/14/1885.
9. *Austin Daily Statesman*, 3/19/1885; *Austin Daily Statesman*, 3/20/1885; *Fort Worth Daily Gazette*, 11/15/1885.
10. *Austin Daily Statesman*, 3/20/1885.
11. *Austin Daily Statesman*, 4/30/1885; *Fort Worth Daily Gazette*, 4/30/1885; *Austin Daily Statesman*, 5/1/1885.
12. *Austin Daily Statesman*, 5/2/1885.
13. *Austin Daily Statesman*, 5/8/1885; *Waco Daily Examiner*, 5/9/1885; *Fort Worth Daily Gazette*, 11/15/1885.
14. *Austin Daily Statesman*, 6/24/1885.
15. *Austin Daily Statesman*, 5/14/1885.
16. *Austin Daily Statesman*, 5/14/1885.
17. "Texas Marriages, 1837-1973."
18. *Austin Daily Statesman*, 9/1/1885; *San Antonio Daily Express*, 9/1/1885; *Fort Worth Daily Gazette*, 8/31/1885; *Fort Worth Daily Gazette*, 11/15/1885; *Fort Worth Daily Gazette*, 9/1/1885; *Galveston Daily News*, 8/31/1885.
19. *Austin Daily Statesman*, 9/1/1885; *Fort Worth Daily Gazette*, 9/1/1885; *San Antonio Daily Express*, 10/1/1885; Galloway, *The Servant Girl Murders*: 277.
20. *Austin Daily Dispatch*, 10/14/1885; *San Antonio Daily Express*, 10/16/1885.
21. *Austin Daily Statesman*, 11/12/1885; Galloway, *The Servant Girl Murders*: 281-282; *The Texas court of Appeals reports: cases argued and adjudged in the Court of Appeals of the State of Texas, 1886*: Case no. 2271, James O. Phillips v. the State.
22. *Austin Daily Statesman*, 9/29/1885; *Austin Daily Statesman*, 10/1/1885; Galloway, *The Servant Girl Murders*: 275.
23. *Austin Daily Statesman*, 9/29/1885; *San Antonio Daily Express*, 9/28/1885; *San Antonio Daily Express*, 9/30/1885; *Austin Daily Statesman*, 10/1/1885; *Fort Worth Daily Gazette*, 9/30/1885.
24. *Austin Daily Statesman*, 10/1/1885; *San Antonio Daily Express*, 9/30/1885; *Austin Daily Statesman*, 10/14/1885; *San Antonio Daily Express*, 11/15/1885; Galloway, *The Servant Girl Murders*: 277; *San Antonio Daily Express*, 12/26/1885; *Fort Worth Daily Gazette*, 12/26/1885.
25. *Austin Daily Statesman*, 9/29/1885; *San Antonio Daily Express*, 9/28/1885; *Austin Daily Statesman*, 10/1/1885; "Convict Record, Texas State Penitentiary," 1886.
26. *San Antonio Daily Express*, 12/26/1885; *Fort Worth Daily Gazette*, 12/26/1885.
27. *Austin Daily Statesman*, 10/1/1885.
28. *Austin Daily Statesman*, 10/1/1885.
29. *Austin Daily Statesman*, 10/14/1885; *San Antonio Daily Express*, 11/15/1885; Galloway, *The Servant Girl Murders*: 280-281.

30. *San Antonio Daily Express*, 10/1/1885; Galloway, *The Servant Girl Murders*: 280-281.
31. *Fort Worth Daily Gazette*, 10/27/1885; *San Antonio Daily Light*, 11/10/1885; *Austin Daily Statesman*, 1/23/1886.
32. *San Antonio Daily Express*, 11/15/1885; *San Antonio Daily Express*, 11/19/1885; *Galveston Daily News* 11/15/1885.
33. *Austin Daily Statesman*, 12/27/1885; *Fort Worth Daily Gazette*, 12/28/1885 (Some reports placed Burditt in Bell County on the night of the murder. Other reports placed him at a Christmas party with George McCutcheon in Williamson County.)
34. *Austin Daily Statesman*, 12/30/1885.
35. *Austin Daily Statesman*, 12/31/1885; *Fort Worth Daily Gazette*, 12/31/1885.
36. *Austin Daily Statesman*, 12/31/1885; *Fort Worth Daily Gazette*, 12/31/1885.
37. *Austin Daily Statesman*, 1/1/1886; *Austin Daily Statesman*, 1/6/1886; *Austin Daily Statesman*, 1/16/1886.
38. *Austin Daily Statesman*, 12/30/1885; *San Antonio Daily Light*, 12/26/1885; *Fort Worth Daily Gazette*, 12/31/1885.
39. *Galveston Daily News*, 5/26/1886; Walsh, *Handbook of Texas Online*.
40. *Fort Worth Daily Gazette*, 5/3/1884; *Salt Lake Daily Herald* 8/16/1884; *Morrison & Fourmy's General Directory of the City of Austin, 1881-1882*.
41. *Fort Worth Daily Gazette*, 12/27/1885; *Austin Daily Statesman*, 12/30/1885.
42. O. Henry, *Rolling Stones*; O. Henry, "Law and Order."
43. Saylor, *A Twist at the End*.

Chapter 16

"Probable Cause for Murder"?

A Tale of Three Suspects

Jimmy Phillips and Moses Hancock had been arrested for murder on evidence supposedly held by private detectives. Neither the detectives nor the courts that issued the warrants would divulge the evidence. In such a climate of secrecy, the public was forced to trust the courts to administer justice, though many in town had already made up their mind that Phillips and Hancock were innocent of the charges.

Though Moses Hancock was arrested after Jimmy Phillips, his preliminary trial was held before Phillips', perhaps because the Phillips case was much more sensational. Hancock was just a reputed old drunk who had finally acted out his threats against his wife, or so the story went. Hancock's legal chances improved dramatically when Judge John Hancock volunteered to represent him for free.

The preliminary trial of Moses Hancock was scheduled for the morning of February 4, 1886. A large crowd of people had gathered in the office of Justice William Von Rosenberg, Jr., about 30 of them witnesses from San Antonio and Waco, many just curiosity seekers. The trial was supposed to start at 10 A.M., but nothing happened at that time. The trial was not called to order. Many in the crowd grew impatient, wondering what was the cause of the delay. As the minutes passed, many in the crowd began to leave. By 11 A.M., few people remained in the office, and still the trial did not begin. The attorneys were in an adjoining room, questioning the witnesses. Moses Hancock was finally "brought in from the jail and quietly took his seat. He looked anything but guilty, and, as one gazed upon his face, the impression was at once fixed that he was a man in whom the milk of human kindness predominated, rather than the bitter of cruelty and evil passion."[1]

As noon passed, the attorneys finally made their appearance. District Attorney James H. Robertson and E.T. Moore represented the prosecution, and Bethel Coopwood served as the defense attorney. John Hancock was not present at the trial. Robertson and Moore had been interviewing the prosecution witnesses and "discovered that they knew absolutely nothing to warrant the proceedings against the prisoner." At that point, Robertson and Moore read a written statement to that effect and requested that the case be dismissed and the prisoner released.

> The defendant listened to the reading with breathless attention, and at its conclusion drew a sigh of relief while he endeavored to force back tears which filled his eyes. Guilty men don't often shed tears, and when the judge said, "This case is dismissed and the defendant released from custody," there was not a man in the room but who recognized the justice of the act, and declared that the defendant had been the victim of overzealous amateur and decidedly veally detectives.

Hancock said the murder of his wife was as big a mystery to him as to anyone else, and he offered his services to the officers to help them capture the real murderer.[2]

Meanwhile, the detectives who had procured the warrant against Moses Hancock, primarily Thomas Bailes, "who possibly imagined and really did believe in the guilt of Mr. Hancock, for they told outsiders so, just as if it was a part of the duty of detectives to gad about and let the world know what they had been and what they were doing, were sorely disgusted and put out by the action of the attorneys for the state." Bailes complained loudly before leaving the courtroom. Some, though, were not through with Bailes. Public opinion turned heavily against him, and some said he should be arrested for perjury. The local paper noted that "thus has the work of inexperienced detectives come to an inglorious end." Unfortunately, the amateur detectives would not give up so easily, especially with thousands of dollars of rewards at stake.[3]

"The Shooting of the Negro Nathan Elgin"

The preliminary trial of Jimmy Phillips was set for a week later, on February 12, 1886. In the interim, though, a potentially pivotal event in the servant girl murders case occurred. In the early morning hours of February 9, just after midnight, a disturbance took place at Dick Rogers' saloon in Masontown on the east side of Austin. A large group of black people had gathered near the saloon after a night of drinking. They were in an uproar because of the actions of Nathan Elgin, a young black restaurant cook. Elgin had

> knocked down and beat a colored girl named Julia, whom he dragged away two blocks to a house where he continued to beat her, and was beating her when [Officer John] Bracken, Claibe Hawkins and Rogers came to the house. Here Elgin was heard to threaten to kill the girl. Bracken remained outside while Hawkins and Rogers went in and tried to stop Elgin, who had commenced kicking the girl furiously. The two men pulled him off, despite his cutting at them with a knife, and when Bracken tried to put the nippers upon him a crowd of negroes surrounded Bracken, and Elgin struck him a violent and almost stunning blow on the head. When Bracken renewed his efforts to nipper Elgin someone in the crowd fired a pistol, which Bracken naturally supposed was aimed at him, and which caused him in fear of his own life to fire back. Bracken's bullet

> struck Elgin, inflicting what Dr. Cummings thinks, will prove a
> fatal wound, the ball having lodged in Elgin's spine.

Elgin had supposedly pulled a knife and tried to slash Bracken. A crowd of about fifty black people then tried to shield Elgin, at which point had Bracken fired the fatal shot. The girl that Elgin assaulted was "quite young," and Elgin's intent seemed to be "the purpose of outrage, and perhaps murder." Because of Elgin's violent behavior and because Elgin was quite drunk, Officer Bracken was held blameless in the shooting.[4]

Elgin's wound was serious. Dr. Josephus Cummings and Dr. Richard Graves examined Elgin and concluded that "the ball had entered the spinal column, and was in such a position as to make it impossible to extract it." Elgin was paralyzed below the waist. He lingered a few days but died on Thursday night, February 11, 1886. An autopsy by Dr. William Burt confirmed the earlier diagnosis by Cummings and Graves. The bullet was embedded in the spinal column.

> It penetrated to the center of it, and by some means turned
> and adjusted itself to the hollow, channel, or whatever the
> blessed doctors call it, through which the spinal cord passes. It
> was a perfect fit, and so out of the usual order of such things
> that Dr. Burt, who has an inquiring turn of mind, took out the
> section of the bone in which it was embedded, and sawing and
> opening it so as to disclose the bullet, had it photographed.

Prior to the autopsy, there was some doubt if the bullet that killed Elgin was actually fired by Bracken because another shot had been fired, and it might have struck Elgin. The autopsy, though, revealed that the bullet was .45 caliber, which matched Bracken's gun.[5]

Bracken was a young policeman, about 27 years old at the time he shot Elgin. He had been an Austin police officer only a year or two. In the 1880 census, his occupation was listed as huckster. According to burial records, Elgin was about 24 years old at the time of his death in 1886, though the census listed his age as 14 in 1880. In 1885, he worked as a cook at Simon's Restaurant at 609 Congress and boarded there, though he had a wife and two children. His wife, Sallie Elgin, worked for Fritz Hartkopf, who owned the Club House Saloon where Alex Mack had worked. They had been married in December 1882.[6]

Nathan Elgin had a criminal record in Austin, though he had not been implicated in any of the servant girl murders. In 1881, when he apparently was only about 15 years old, he had a shouting spat with another black boy near the governor's mansion. After lengthy yelling and disturbing the neighborhood, the other black boy, Green Alexander, pulled out a pistol and shot at Elgin three times without effect. By the time officers arrived, the youths had fled. Elgin was arrested the next day for carrying a pistol. A year later, Elgin wrote a note threatening to kill John Rainey, a black deputy sheriff, and was arrested. The newspaper article about the incident called Elgin "a kind of bad citizen." His violent behavior would continue and ultimately end in his death at the hands of a police officer.[7]

Justice William Von Rosenberg, Jr., was informed of the death of Elgin, but because he had the Phillips preliminary trial beginning the next day, he turned over the inquest into Elgin's death to Justice Thomas Purnell. The inquest began immediately, and "Justice Purnell adopted the singular course of excluding the reporters. This seems to be the favorite way in Austin for doing everything. Even to committing murders, which, so far, with all the investigations, remain as mysterious as ever." Though "nominally under arrest" for the shooting, Bracken had continued to work his beat as an officer. What was so important or compelling about the Elgin shooting that the inquest required secrecy? What information was being withheld? Who was being protected?[8]

The inquest ended quickly, and the verdict was announced on February 13. Nathan Elgin "came to his death from the wound of a pistol shot fired by some party unknown to the jury." Though the bullet extracted from Elgin's spine matched the caliber of Officer Bracken's pistol, two shots were fired simultaneously at the disturbance the night Elgin was shot. The jury gave Bracken the benefit of the doubt, and ultimately no one was held responsible for Elgin's death.[9]

Why was the shooting of Elgin a pivotal event? One of the few clues found at the scene of some of the murders was a broad, bare footprint. Upon his death, Elgin's foot was examined. "In Elgin's case it is stated that he had the little toe gone from one of his feet, the foot corresponding in this respect to the track of the murderer of the Ramey girl. It may be, if this is correct, that he made a confession that will throw some light upon the Austin outrages." Though the information about the bare footprints at some of the murder scenes had been published frequently, no mention had been made about the missing toe until this information was revealed in relation to Elgin's death, though a peculiarly shaped toe on the footprint was mentioned in relation to the Ramey murder. And the information about the missing toe was not published in the Austin newspaper, but in a San Antonio newspaper. Why had this vital detail been withheld from publication? Had the Austin city authorities deliberately concealed the clue? If so, why? Galloway suggested the authorities might have withheld the clue to keep from putting the murderer on guard. They might have believed that he would be careless if the clue was not known publicly, making his arrest easier. Obviously, if those notions were the reason the clue was concealed, they certainly didn't work. And if Elgin's foot matched the footprint left on the Phillips' gallery, why did the prosecution of Jimmy Phillips continue? And if Elgin did kill Eula Phillips and Mary Ramey, did he also kill all the other victims? What was his motive? The death of Elgin unleashed more questions than it answered.[10]

Meanwhile, the crooks kept up their mischief in Austin. Late in the night of February 11, the day before the Phillips preliminary trial would begin, two burglaries were committed. One of the burglaries occurred at the store of Joel P. Pearl, who sold groceries and produce on the east side of Austin. The burglars "blew his safe to atoms and got $130." The battle against crime requires eternal vigilance.[11]

"The Phillips Case"

The preliminary trial of James Oliver Phillips began on February 12, 1886, and lasted a couple of days. Before the trial began, the assumption was that Phillips would be "discharged as Hancock was, for want of evidence." Phillips was represented by Major William M. Walton, and the prosecution team was made up of District Attorney James H. Robertson and ex-District Attorney E. Taylor Moore. Justice William Von Rosenberg, Jr., presided. "The witnesses were all put under the rule of secrecy and the reporters under the ban of not publishing the testimony, which precludes giving the evidence, for fear one witness may read what another said." A more likely reason for the secrecy was the explosive nature of the case and the possibility that one of the sixty scheduled witnesses might give embarrassing testimony about some of the city and state leaders. A headline writer summarized the trial: "It progresses slowly, with but little, if anything, being unearthed."[12]

Jimmy Phillips had not yet recovered from his wounds received in the Christmas Eve assault. His condition was one thing the reporters could discuss. "Young Phillips was brought from jail into court, looking quite feeble and tottering in his walk. His nerves showed great weakness, and his hand trembled in holding a glass of water. He is evidently still suffering greatly from the severe wound which he received on his head the night his wife was killed. He is a good looking young man, and his general health does not seem worsted," though he was said to look "much wasted."[13]

One of the first to give testimony was Jimmy's mother, Mrs. Sophia Phillips, who was almost sixty years old at the time. Her testimony "developed nothing sensational," though she was asked about "the relations which existed between defendant and his deceased wife." Most people thought the state's lawyers would try to discredit her testimony. During her questioning, Major Walton made a motion for a change of venue from Justice Von Rosenberg's court. Von Rosenberg agreed to hear the motion, and court was adjourned until the next morning.[14]

The next morning, Major Walton did not press for a change of venue, so Jimmy Phillips' trial continued under Justice Von Rosenberg. Three witnesses were examined during the day. Mrs. Sophia Phillips continued her testimony. She said that Jimmy and Eula occasionally quarreled, and

> that on coming into the room where her son lay in the bloody bed immediately after his wife's body was found in the yard, her son having come to and seeing his wife gone, asked: "Is Eula dead?" His mother's reply was: "Yes, my child." "Then I will go to hell," said her son, meaning not remorse but that he, too, might as well be dead if she was gone.

She also stated that Eula did not go out on Christmas Eve. Mrs. Phillips was followed by George McCutcheon, who had rented a farm to the young couple in 1885. The last witness of the day was George Allen, the brother-in-law of Jimmy Phillips. Publishing the testimony was still banned, but the *Statesman* "reporter, at the risk of being thrown into prison and sat down by Mr. Moore and Mr. Robertson," reported some of the testimony anyway.

> Mr. George Allen was on the stand, and stated in a clear, truthful tone of voice, that on the morning of December the 25th, he saw bloody tracks leading from the premises where the crime was committed to the alley in the rear of the same. The bloodhounds were put on this trail and the dogs started on a run, followed by Justice Von Rosenberg, who, in turn, was followed by Mr. Allen, with a procession of less important persons, stringing out far behind. The dogs passed out of the alley, followed by the justice, Mr. Allen and the procession, and taking down a street, scurried along in the direction of west Austin. All at once the dogs stopped; the justice reached them and stopped, then Mr. Allen and then the procession. The justice went down on his knees, then Mr. Allen, then the procession. "Here's where the villain put on his shoes," said the justice as he made a critical examination of the ground. "Here's where the villain put on his shoes," repeated Mr. Allen. "Here's where the villain put on his shoes," echoed the procession while old George, the blood hound, growled his concurrence and he and his assistant refused to go any further. Then the justice refused, Mr. Allen refused and the procession refused, and all, headed by old George, returned to the house.

This information was the most important evidence that the trial had revealed, and it did not do much to point the finger of guilt at any party, especially Jimmy Phillips, who was found badly wounded in his bed that night.[15]

The trial continued through the weekend. Next to testify were James Phillips, Jimmy's father, and Adelia (Delia) Phillips Campbell, Jimmy's sister. Also called were Dr. James Litten, Fannie Whipple, and May Tobin. All the witnesses testified that the young couple had a tumultuous relationship and that they did not get along well. Fannie Whipple was a black woman who ran an assignation house on Red River Street. She stated that Eula Phillips came to her house in late November or early December. "She came to my house with another woman, and asked me to let them stay here. Eula stayed from 10 o'clock and all night, and the next night till about 2 o'clock. A gentleman came after her, and the other woman was with her when they left. They left about 2 o'clock at night." She also testified that Mrs. Sophia Phillips knew that Eula was at her house because Fannie Whipple had to go to the Phillips' home to get clothes for Eula and that she and Mrs. Phillips had conversed about Eula's whereabouts.[16]

Adelia Phillips Campbell, Jimmy's sister, gave some of the most sensational testimony in the preliminary trial. She stated that she hired a carriage and along with Eula went to Fannie Whipple's house on Red River Street.

> Mrs. Campbell, rather a handsome young woman, a sister of the prisoner, and whose husband is said to be in Mexico, was put on the stand and testified that Mrs. Eula Phillips, the

> murdered woman, left her husband toward the latter part of November or the first of December. That on one occasion the witness and Mrs. Phillips together visited the house of Fannie Whipple (colored) on Red River street in this city, thence they went in a carriage to Sabine street and then to the well-known house of Mrs. Tobin at the foot of the avenue. Mrs. Campbell testified that Mrs. Phillips remained at Fannie Whipple's some two weeks and two or three days at Mrs. Tobin's; that she was not true to her husband; that she held intercourse with other men; that she (Mrs. Campbell) had seen her in bed with other men on two occasions; that about the last of November, a few weeks before the murder, she went down to Elgin and her husband went and brought her back to Austin. After her return she had engagements to meet other men here before she was killed.

Mrs. Campbell said that Eula's last appointment at May Tobin's house, as far as she knew, was on December 23, but she did not know who the man was. She stated that she had seen Eula in bed with other men on at least two occasions since she married Jimmy. She also said she knew nothing about the murder of Eula, as she was not at the Phillips' home at the time. Though Mrs. Campbell's testimony threw doubt on Eula's virtue, it also gave credence to the theory that Jimmy might have killed Eula out of jealousy.[17]

May Tobin, a white woman who ran an assignation house at 103 Congress Avenue, also testified about Eula's activities. Some of her testimony contradicted the testimony of Jimmy's mother. May Tobin stated that "Mrs. Eula Phillips, the murdered woman, came to her house, at the foot of the avenue, in a hack between 11 and 12 o'clock, on the night of the murder. This was an hour before her dead body was discovered. She did not get out, but called witness out and talked with her. She was alone." Though May Tobin said that Eula was alone, rumors flew that Eula was supposed to meet some man at May Tobin's house on Christmas Eve. The rumors connected "that last visit of the murdered woman with a prominent and well-to-do citizen of Austin, who is said to have ridden back with her in the hack." Was Eula alone, or was a man with her in the carriage? If the latter, who was that man? None of the lawyers asked that question.[18]

Other testimony was not so sensational. It was more technical, focusing on bloody footprints in Eula and Jimmy's room.

> It was proven that bloody tracks led from the room out of the east door, through which Mrs. Phillips was carried. That the toe of these tracks pointed from the bed on which she had lain. It was also shown that bloody tracks were on the floor, pointing in the direction of the bed. It was shown that there was very little, if any, blood on the side of the bed which it is alleged, Mrs. Phillips occupied. It was proven that blood was on the floor near a stove in the room, almost back of the west door, and some distance from the bed. It was shown that blood was scattered pretty freely over the floor.

The location and direction of the footprints might be used to suggest that Jimmy Phillips had killed Eula, dragged her out of the room, and then returned. The reporter concluded by providing a concise summary of the testimony in the trial.

> It was clearly set forth that young Phillips and his wife did not live harmoniously together. That she was unfaithful to her marriage vows. That she feared him when he was drinking. That they quarreled when he was sober. That at one time he was violent and she left home, it is supposed through fear.

Would this slim amount of evidence be enough to put Jimmy Phillips on trial for the murder of his wife?[19]

District Attorney Robertson believed it was, for he made a brief argument suggesting that the prosecution had shown probable cause for murder. Major Walton then made a brief closing argument for the defense, and Mr. Moore spoke briefly for the prosecution. The testimony and arguments then concluded, and a decision would be made by Justice Von Rosenberg on Monday, the following day.[20]

Justice Von Rosenberg's decision no doubt surprised many. The justice decided that the evidence was sufficient to order a murder trial for Jimmy Phillips, and the young man was remanded to jail without bail. The supposed theory behind the decision seemed based more on fantasy than fact.

> The theory provoked and given currency by the evidence deduced on the trial is that young Phillips was extremely jealous of his wife, and it seems from the testimony, he had ample reason to be. On Christmas eve night she left home about 11 o'clock and visited an assignation house at the foot of the Avenue, where she conversed with the mistress of the establishment for about five minutes. She then got into a hack and was conveyed home, where, as the theory has it, she expected a war of words, if not something worse, from her husband. Anticipating this and to intimidate, if not to protect herself from a violent assault she herself secured the ax and carried it into the room, not even dreaming for a moment that it was to be the instrument of a tragedy, and she the victim, which was to send a thrill of horror, not only through the city, but the entire state and the entire country. Entering the room, her husband who perhaps with his and her prattling child by his side had been brooding over her conduct, was infuriated at her appearance, and assaulting her, received the blow which wounded him at her hands. This made him more furious than ever and in a moment of frenzy he wrenched the ax from her hand, and with a blow nerved by anger, pain, and harrowing wrongs, he struck her down. Appalled at his terrible deed he conveys her from the room and arranging matters to cast suspicion from himself, he alarms the family.

How could the badly injured young man have lifted the heavy timbers that were used to pin Eula down? Would Jimmy have raped his dying wife as part of his scheme to cast suspicion away from himself? The theory seemed too far-fetched, but the string of murders had certainly been unusual.[21]

Phillips' lawyer, Major Walton, immediately filed an application for habeas corpus, claiming that jail without bail would illegally deprive Phillips of his liberty and that confinement would be dangerous to the young man because of his wound. The application was heard the next day by District Judge Alexander S. Walker, who granted Phillips bail in the amount of $2500. Most believed bail would be made, as Phillips' father was "a man of considerable means in city property." And indeed, bail was made that evening for the young man, though Galloway claimed Phillips was released on his own recognizance. Local reactions were mixed.

> Public opinion is very much divided, about as many believing Phillips guilty as those who think him innocent. The evidence being circumstantial, though pointing to guilt, a jury will probably give the prisoner the benefit of any doubt. The testimony is quite conflicting, and the action of Judge Walker in admitting Phillips to bail would seem to indicate some measure of doubt as to the guilt of the accused. As for a motive, his wife's conduct was certainly such as was calculated to provoke him to desperation. It is believed that all the evidence in the case has not yet been developed.

Though his lawyer argued that jail would endanger Phillips' health, within ten days, Jimmy Phillips had recovered enough to be out on the streets of Austin.[22]

"Insane"

On the same day Jimmy Phillips was sent to jail without bail, another interesting case appeared in the Austin courts. Dr. Joseph G. Green was an assistant physician at the lunatic asylum. He was also the son-in-law of the superintendent of the asylum, Dr. Ashley N. Denton. On February 15, 1886, Dr. Green was judged to be insane by the county court. He was ordered sent to "the branch asylum at Terrell to remove him from the effects of his present association." Acquaintances said he was "a genial and accomplished gentleman" and knew of no cause for his going insane. The development was regarded with surprise and sorrow by his friends. Many people ascribed to the lunatic theory to explain the servant girl murders. They believed that a lunatic regularly escaped from the asylum to commit the murders and then returned to the safety of confinement. Dr. Green could have come and gone from the asylum at will. Could Dr. Green have been that lunatic?[23]

Though Dr. Green was never regarded as a suspect in the murders, Moses Hancock, Jimmy Phillips, and Nathan Elgin were considered suspects. Elgin escaped prosecution by being killed. Hancock was promptly released after his preliminary trial found the evidence to be insufficient. Though Phillips' case did not provide much more evidence than Hancock's trial, Jimmy Phillips was found to have probable cause for murdering his wife and was sent to jail to await a full trial. No one believed that Jimmy Phillips was the servant girl annihilator. Though some resolution might yet be found for the murder of Eula Phillips, the other murders were left to languish. But Moses Hancock was not yet out of the woods, either.

Notes

Title: *San Antonio Daily Express*, 2/14/1886.

1. *Austin Daily Statesman*, 2/5/1886; *Fort Worth Daily Gazette*, 2/5/1886.
2. *Austin Daily Statesman*, 2/5/1886; *Fort Worth Daily Gazette*, 2/5/1886.
3. *Austin Daily Statesman*, 2/5/1886; *Fort Worth Daily Gazette*, 2/5/1886; Galloway, *The Servant Girl Murders*: 296.
4. *Fort Worth Daily Gazette*, 2/5/1886; *San Antonio Daily Express*, 2/10/1886; *Austin Daily Statesman*, 2/10/1886; *Fort Worth Daily Gazette*, 2/9/1886.
5. *Austin Daily Statesman*, 2/10/1886; *San Antonio Daily Express*, 2/12/1886; *Austin Daily Statesman*, 2/12/1886.
6. *Morrison & Fourmy's General Directory of the City of Austin, 1885-1886*; 1880 Federal Census; *San Antonio Daily Express*, 2/10/1886; Oakwood Cemetery Database; "Texas Marriages, 1837-1973"; 1880 Federal Census (In the marriage records, Elgin was listed as Nathion Elgain. His wife's maiden name was Sallie Wheat. In the 1880 census, Elgin was listed as Nathan Elligan.)
7. *Austin Daily Statesman*, 7/29/1881; *Austin Daily Statesman*, 7/30/1881; *Austin Daily Statesman*, 6/16/1882; Galloway, *The Servant Girl Murders*: 316-317.
8. *Austin Daily Statesman*, 2/10/1886; *San Antonio Daily Express*, 2/12/1886; *Austin Daily Statesman*, 2/12/1886; *Galveston Daily News*, 2/12/1886.
9. *San Antonio Daily Express*, 2/14/1886.
10. *San Antonio Daily Express*, 2/12/1886; Galloway, *The Servant Girl Murders*: 313-315.
11. *Galveston Daily News*, 2/12/1886; *Fort Worth Daily Gazette*, 2/12/1886.
12. *San Antonio Daily Express*, 2/12/1886; *Austin Daily Statesman*, 2/13/1886.
13. *San Antonio Daily Express*, 2/12/1886; *Galveston Daily News*, 2/12/1886.
14. *San Antonio Daily Express*, 2/12/1886; *Galveston Daily News*, 2/12/1886; 1880 Federal Census.
15. *Austin Daily Statesman*, 2/14/1886; *Fort Worth Daily Gazette*, 2/14/1886; *Austin Daily Statesman*, 2/13/1886; *San Antonio Daily Express*, 2/14/1886.
16. *Austin Daily Statesman*, 2/14/1886; *Fort Worth Daily Gazette*, 2/14/1886; *San Antonio Daily Express*, 2/14/1886.
17. *Fort Worth Daily Gazette*, 2/14/1886; *Austin Daily Statesman*, 2/14/1886; *San Antonio Daily Express*, 2/14/1886.
18. *Fort Worth Daily Gazette*, 2/14/1886; *Austin Daily Statesman*, 2/14/1886; *San Antonio Daily Express*, 2/14/1886.
19. *Austin Daily Statesman*, 2/14/1886.
20. *Austin Daily Statesman*, 2/14/1886; *San Antonio Daily Express*, 2/14/1886.
21. *Austin Daily Statesman*, 2/16/1886; *San Antonio Daily Express*, 2/16/1886; *Fort Worth Daily Gazette*, 2/16/1886.
22. *San Antonio Daily Express*, 2/16/1886; *San Antonio Daily Express*, 2/17/1886; *Galveston Daily News*, 2/17/1886; *San Antonio Daily Express*, 2/26/1886; Galloway, *The Servant Girl Murders*: 297.
23. *San Antonio Daily Express*, 2/16/1886; "Texas Marriages, 1837-1973" (Green married Denton's daughter, Ella T. Denton, on February 12, 1885. In the marriage records, Green was listed as J.G. Gwen.)

Chapter 17

"Base Libel"

The Swain Affair

After Jimmy Phillips was charged with the murder of his wife, the rumor mill began to turn swiftly in Austin. Jimmy's mother had testified that Eula did not leave the house on Christmas Eve. May Tobin had testified that Eula came to her house on Congress Avenue at about 11 P.M. on Christmas Eve. Jimmy's sister had testified that she had seen Eula in bed with other men during her marriage to Jimmy. All these were salacious allegations, but the biggest question that drove the rumor mill was: Who was in the carriage with Eula?

Eula Phillips had been seen in a carriage with a man shortly before her murder. Who was the mystery man in the carriage drawn by two white horses? Was it a suitor of Eula? Or was it just a good Samaritan giving her a ride home? Most important, was the man in the carriage, or the driver, the murderer of Eula Phillips? Could the man in the carriage have been some rich politician, as one rumor hinted? If so, just as some banks are deemed too big to fail, are some people too influential to indict?

The rumor that gained the most traction was that the man in the carriage was a high official in state government. Even more damning, the man was said to be a candidate for governor of Texas. There was only one state official running for governor, and he was the state comptroller, William J. Swain. Like most politicians, Swain had accumulated his share of political supporters and enemies. The rumor that he had been intimate with Eula Phillips was blamed on one of those enemies. Smear campaigns are certainly not a new phenomenon.

William Jesse Swain was born in Kentucky in 1839. In 1859, he moved to Clarksville in north Texas, where he attended McKenzie College while working in a store. In December 1861 he married Mary Frances Bohannan, and immediately thereafter enlisted in Company F of Whitfield's Legion. He rose to the rank of first lieutenant in the Confederate army and fought at Carter's Creek. Swain was captured but escaped when a group of prisoners overpowered their guards while being transported to Fort Delaware. Swain rejoined his regiment at Richmond. He returned to Clarksville in 1864 and became a farmer. He and his wife had four children. Swain soon began to study law and was admitted to the Texas State Bar in 1872, the same year he began publishing the *Clarksville Times*. With his military record, Swain was poised for a rapid political rise following Reconstruction. In 1873, he was elected to the Texas House of Representatives in the Fourteenth Legislature. He was later elected to the Texas Senate in the Sixteenth and Seventeenth legislatures in 1879 and 1881. In 1882 he was elected as Texas state comptroller, a position he held until January 1887. In 1885, though, he tried a run at the governorship, a move that put him ever more in the public eye and led to the slander campaign against him in the case of Eula Phillips.[1]

Swain's involvement in the Phillips case, though, was not the first accusation of political misconduct against him. One such set of accusations came from W.M. Brown, who had been comptroller prior to Swain. Brown charged Swain with nepotism for hiring his two sons to do temporary work in his department during December 1884 and January 1885. Nepotism, though widely practiced, was not allowed in Texas government. Swain stated that "nearly all state officials are equally guilty," and therefore "he deemed there was no wrong in it." Nepotism is a fairly minor charge, but Swain apparently tried to hide the fact that he had employed his two sons. "In response to a legislative resolution requiring a list of his clerks Colonel Swain furnished one which did not contain the names of his sons. In this list were the names of two persons who were not employees of his office, and the inference seems to follow that they were given to avoid the necessity of naming his sons. A clear case of nepotism seems to be made out." Brown also charged that one of Swain's sons was paid $5 more than he earned.[2]

Brown further charged that "public money was paid to an unknown person representing a young lady, who was not an employee, but only a guest of the comptroller. This is a scoop to which there is objection. Lady clerks of some of the departments may be permitted to work at home, but there is a limit somewhere to the privileges of the sex. When any person not serving the State in any office, or at home, is able to draw through some unknown friend a regular salary out of the public crib, the limit has been passed." In response, Swain said that the lady in question was the daughter of an old friend. According to Swain,

> Her name is Lula Cockrell, daughter of Judge Cockrell, of Jones county. Her father, an old friend of Colonel Swain, wrote him asking if his daughter could obtain employment. Colonel Swain was able to answer favorably, and Judge Cockrell sent her down with the understanding she should board at Colonel Swain's house. When the work for which she was employed, recording mainly, had been completed, her employment was discontinued. An examination of the warrants in the treasurer's office shows no discrepancy between the comptroller's report of monthly payment and the amount actually paid.

Brown's charges against Swain were fairly minor, almost a tiff between two political adversaries. But then a rumor spread that Swain "was in collusion with the building syndicate of the state capitol for the purpose of swindling the people." Either Swain was full of political hanky-panky, or else his higher public profile during the gubernatorial campaign simply made him an easier target. And one wonders how a lieutenant in the army came to be called colonel.[3]

"Vilely Slandered"

But the charge that Swain was intimate with Eula Phillips was a major accusation, one that was almost universally greeted with disbelief. In this case, the accuser was unknown, and just how the rumor started was also not certain. As the newspapers lined up behind Swain and the other candidates in the race, the blame was widely spread. The *San Antonio Daily Light* charged the *Houston Post* with being "the organ of Comptroller Swain," saying:

> Its antics in trying to revive the Swain boom causes no little merriment in political circles. It has been broadly hinted that in the event of Swain's election to succeed Governor Ireland, that the editor of the Post, as a reward for his fidelity to the present Comptroller, will be made Secretary of State. Therefore it is not difficult to see why the Post sets up its agonizing howl on seeing its favorite gubernatorial candidate gradually being retired from the race as a prominent candidate. The Swain boom has now got the death-rattle, and inside of three months it will be too utterly dead to kick.

And this charge was made before the rumor about Swain and Eula Phillips. The *Waco Examiner* was another opponent of Swain, so much so that some speculated the rumor about Swain had originated in Waco. The *Fort Worth Daily Gazette* challenged the Waco newspaper, opining that "if the Waco Examiner is a fair paper, let it assert that Mr. Swain was vilely slandered in the Phillips matter." In fact, though, no one really knew who started the rumor or where. Some said the dispatch originated in Austin and was sent to the *Denison News*. Some said it originated in the Waco Western Union office. The Waco telegraph office was "satisfied it never originated here, but is the work of some irresponsible Bohemian in South Texas who had no special object in view except to create a sensation."[4]

The scandalous rumor supposedly first appeared in the *Texas Figaro*, a San Antonio society newspaper. The *Figaro* said that one of the Pinkerton detectives had discovered that Eula Phillips

> was in the habit of meeting secretly a distinguished state politician at a secluded house, and that she was accompanied sometimes by another woman who consorted with another prominent politician and state official. He discovered further that on the night Mrs. Phillips was murdered she met this politician, who escorted her home in a closed carriage. These facts were divulged to the city police authorities, who sent an emissary to the woman friend of Mrs. Phillips and gave her $3,000 to leave Texas and not appear at the preliminary examination against Phillips. The woman consented, but the detectives prevented her going. In her guarded testimony the woman corroborated the fact related, but she was not asked to name the politician who must have witnessed the murder of Mrs. Phillips. This man, says The Figaro, is a prominent state official and an active candidate for the governorship of Texas.

> The other man is assistant to a chief of department. Both are married.

The other woman mentioned in the article must have been Delia Campbell, Eula's sister-in law, Jimmy's sister.[5]

The report in the *Figaro* was then supposedly telegraphed from Austin to the Denison newspaper.

> The telegram purported to quote a statement in the Texas Figaro, a San Antonio society paper, to the effect that a high state official and head of a department and a prominent candidate for governor, had been the paramour of the late Mrs. Eula Phillips, and rode in a carriage with her on the night of her murder, and that said official was cognizant of all the horrible details of that awful murder on Christmas eve night. Of course the inference was that none other than the Hon. William J. Swain, state comptroller, was meant, and the indignant friends of that gentleman today prosecuted a thorough investigation and search for the sender of the dispatch. It was ascertained that no such telegram was sent from the Western Union office [in Austin] and evidence went to show that it went from San Antonio. The United Press seems to have distributed it to Northern papers, no names, however, having been called.

No names were necessary, as Swain was the only high-ranking state official running for governor. As the story leaked out, though, it grew in accusations and viciousness. The Fort Worth newspaper added fuel to the fire with the following report.

> A telegram was sent from San Antonio to outside newspapers to the effect that two gentlemen, both heads of departments of the Texas state government, and both married men, were seen in a hack with Mrs. Phillips the night she was so foully murdered. The telegram stated further that one of these gentlemen was a prominent candidate for governor. There is but one prominent candidate for governor in Austin, and he is W. J. Swain. At San Antonio is a newspaper violently opposed to Mr. Swain. Did any one connected with the San Antonio Times send that vile telegram?

Now two high-ranking state officials were supposedly in the carriage with Eula Phillips the night she died.[6]

That second state official was likely Benjamin M. Baker, the state superintendent of public instruction. Baker was born in 1850, making him 35 years old at the time. He also had no formal schooling, so his ascension to the head of education in Texas was somewhat ironic. Baker served in the Fifteenth, Sixteenth, and Seventeenth legislatures in Texas. In 1883, he became secretary of the State Board of Education, which appointed him to his position as state superintendent, an office he held until 1887. Baker quickly denied the claim, saying that "I had no acquaintance with Mrs. Phillips and never met her anywhere and never spoke to her in my life." Baker's name would surface again in the upcoming trial of Jimmy Phillips.[7]

After the rumor about Swain spread across Texas and then the nation, his allies rallied to deny the allegation. Editorials appeared in newspapers friendly to Swain. The *Greeneville Banner* called the rumor "the vilest attempt to ruin a public man's reputation ever known in Texas. If the villain who started the report can be found he should be prosecuted to the last extremity." The *Temple Times* opined that "Lying on Swain seems to be the chief object of a few papers and people." The *Big Springs Pantagraph* was more bold, saying that the rumor "was prompted purely by political hostility to that gentleman. It was a scurvy trick, and deserves exposure and universal condemnation." The *Willis Index* felt the rumor would backfire, saying, "That cruel slander on Swain was started by some one evidently very much opposed to seeing our present comptroller governor of Texas, but it has done decidedly more good than harm for the man against whom the cowardly shafts were directed." The *Hillsboro Mirror* concurred, stating, "The attempt to connect Comptroller Swain's name by innuendo as being intimate with the Mrs. Eula Phillips who was murdered in Austin on Christmas eve night, let it originate where it may, has been nipped in the bud and shown up as a base fabrication of the Hon. Mr. Swain's enemies."[8]

The *Fort Worth Daily Gazette* likewise defended Swain, commenting that "The people of Texas know the purity of the life of Mr. Swain, and this attempt to blacken his fame can only rebound to his advantage. The people of Texas do not condone such vile political practices as this, and their resentment will add to the already overpowering strength of Mr. Swain as a gubernatorial candidate." After the rumor became national news, Colonel Miller, editor of the *Austin Daily Statesman*, chastised the papers for printing a rumor that suggested that Swain had met Eula Phillips at an assignation house on Christmas Eve and that "he probably witnessed her murder." Miller sent a telegram to the *New York Tribune*, trying to correct the falsehoods being spread by the press.

> In your edition of the 22nd inst. you published a dispatch purporting to be an extract from the Figaro, a society paper of San Antonio, in which appears the following: "This politician," the Figaro says, "is an active state officer and is a candidate for the governorship of Texas." As Col. Swain is the only state officer who is a candidate for governor, it is evident the above was intended to refer to him. The Figaro contained no such charges, nor any charge that would point to Col. Swain. It is a foul slander that an honored life in the community positively negates, and as it did not appear in the Figaro, it can only be attributed to the opponents of Col. Swain for governor, especially as the detective alluded to, and the attorney prosecuting the case, whose names for verification are hereto appended, deny utterly Col. Swain's connection with the case. The whole community in which Col. Swain resides are indignant

> that his enemies would resort to such a device, and declare
> that in all the close investigation, Col. Swain's name has never
> been thought of or alluded to by intimation or otherwise.

To support his claim, Miller included two sworn affidavits exonerating Swain of any suspicion. One affidavit came from E. Taylor Moore, an attorney who was "employed by the citizens' executive committee to aid in the investigation and prosecution of the case of the State of Texas vs. James Phillips." Moore claimed familiarity with the case and its details and swore that the name of William J. Swain had never come up as a suspect or in any other context. The second affidavit came from Thomas O. Bailes, the amateur detective who had worked up cases against Moses Hancock and Jimmy Phillips and drawn the scorn of many Austinites. Bailes also swore "the name of Wm. J. Swain has not in the remotest way been mentioned in this connection," as if Bailes would know.[9]

"The Infamous and Lying Dispatch"

An investigation was begun to try to determine who had started the vicious rumor. Some believed the rumor originated in San Antonio, some said Austin, and others said Waco. Many people still did not trust Detective Bailes. The *Kerrville Eye* chastised Bailes, saying that "Swain is down off the fence. He is on solid ground, and don't you forget it, you anti-Swain trumpets. . . . . That amateur detective who charged and had arraigned James Phillips, the husband of the woman who was so foully murdered in Austin, for committing the deed, ought to be kicked out of the city, and the authorities who listened to his cold-hearted charge should be severely condemned." Despite the criticism, Bailes continued to dog witnesses. Bailes arranged for H.L. Henderson, the manager of the Waco Western Union telegraph office, to be attached as a witness to appear before the Travis County grand jury. Henderson was to search the telegraph office diligently and bring to Austin all telegrams and documents "relating to a telegram sent about February 22, 1886, connecting W. J. Swain with the Phillips scandal, at Austin." Bailes was apparently aware that no such documents or telegrams existed in the Waco office.

> The detective is a good chin musician, and persuasive to such
> an extent as to have induced Colonel Swain to mail the
> attachment to Sheriff Harris, of this county, accompanied with
> a personal letter, saying that as this case is one in which the
> State makes no provision for the payment of attached
> witnesses fees he (Swain) will individually pay all the expenses
> of the attached witness if the manager of the Western Union
> offices will obey the summons. If payment has been made to
> the detective, it is a case of obtaining money under false
> pretenses, for he has been assured by correspondence with the
> manager that no papers or telegrams connecting Mr. Swain
> with the scandal had ever been sent through the Waco office,
> or any matter that could be construed as having reference to
> the Christmas eve tragedy in Austin had ever been wired from
> this point.

In an interview, Henderson was told that the telegram in question supposedly "reached Denison over the Baltimore and Ohio wires." Henderson responded that Western Union "would not accept a message for transmission over its wires for delivery over the Baltimore and Ohio at any point where the Western Union had an office. The message would have had to go the entire distance over the Western Union wires to Denison, if sent from Waco or any point having a Western Union office." Did the libelous telegram originate in Waco? That possibility was rather remote.[10]

The Swain scandal did not do much to advance the investigation of the servant girl murders or, more specifically, the murder of Eula Phillips. It did, however, reveal the adversarial nature of Texas politics. The alleged connection of Swain to the Phillips murder did reinforce the fact that certain prominent citizens of Austin were in the hot seat in connection with Eula Phillips.

> One of these citizens, a man of some distinction, is said, and positively asserted, to have ridden in the hack with Mrs. Phillips from the assignation house, at the foot of the avenue, back to her husband's residence, it being the woman's last fatal ride on the night of the murder. During all this time, and when the names of young and middle-aged men were bandied about the streets of Austin, the name of Col. Swain was never heard of in this connection till the infamous and lying dispatch alluded to.

Certainly some prominent Austinites had consorted with Eula Phillips, but William J. Swain did not seem to be one of them. The scandal was regarded as "one of the most damnable and infamous libels ever attempted in Texas."[11]

Was William Swain a viable suspect in the murder of Eula Phillips? Did he see her murder? The possibility is highly unlikely. Even most of his enemies regarded Swain as a moral man who kept regular hours. "In fact, no man stands higher with the honest and moral portion of the community here than the comptroller. Col. Swain's friends believe the dispatch was sent by a newspaper man formerly a resident of Austin but not now. All evidence here now points to a foul and infamous conspiracy to injure Col. Swain in his canvass, a conspiracy thought to be abetted by opposing political forces and the partisans of political rivals; but Col. Swain's fair name cannot be thus easily besmirched." Swain's name was not besmirched, perhaps, but it was certainly on many people's lips, and not in a good way.[12]

Many newspapers prophesied that the scandal would have little effect on Swain's gubernatorial aspirations. Hollandsworth noted that Swain

> was considered a shoo-in for governor. His biggest rival for the Governor's Mansion was Sul Ross, an Indian fighter with the U.S. Army and a Texas Ranger whose major claim to fame was that he had recovered the captive Cynthia Ann Parker while pursuing a Comanche raiding party. Ross was an ineffective orator—no match for the charismatic Swain. Yet suddenly the front-runner was backpedaling. He angrily claimed he was the

> victim of a whisper campaign, perhaps started by Ross's "cohorts," and vowed he would expose the identity of the author of a telegram sent to newspapers saying he "knew something about the murder of Eula."

But by the time the trial began, Swain was strangely silent. Perhaps, like other men in Austin, he was holding his breath to see what would happen. The *Breckenridge Texan* seemed to predict the campaign more correctly, opining that "it is highly probable that he will retire from the race long before the convention meets."[13]

Swain did not become governor of Texas in 1886. In fact, he was not even his party's nominee for governor. That honor went to Sul Ross, who won the 1886 gubernatorial election handily, defeating the Republican candidate, A.M. Cochran, by over 160,000 votes. Ross took over 70% of the votes cast. As for Swain, he held the office of comptroller until 1887. After that, he somewhat disappeared from the public eye, dying in Houston in 1904.[14]

Despite Swain's apparent innocence in the Phillips murder, the scandal had achieved its goal, to thwart Swain's run for the governorship. Did Swain have intimate relations with Eula Phillips? Though the possibility always exists, the reality is that any such relationship was unlikely. Did Swain ride in the carriage with Eula Phillips the fateful night of her murder? Did he witness her murder or even participate in it? Again, the possibility exists, but the possibility is highly unlikely. Swain seemed to be an unfortunate man maligned at the hands of his political enemies, and no more.

Notes

Title: *Fort Worth Daily Gazette*, 2/26/1886.

1. Hazlewood, *Handbook of Texas Online*.
2. *Galveston Daily News*, 5/30/1886; *Galveston Daily News*, 6/1/1886.
3. *Galveston Daily News*, 5/30/1886; *Galveston Daily News*, 6/1/1886; *Fort Worth Daily Gazette*, 3/16/1886.
4. *San Antonio Daily Light*, 12/26/1885; *Fort Worth Daily Gazette*, 3/25/1886; *Fort Worth Daily Gazette*, 2/25/1886; *Fort Worth Daily Gazette*, 4/24/1886.
5. *Chester Times*, 2/23/1886.
6. *Fort Worth Daily Gazette*, 2/26/1886; *Fort Worth Daily Gazette*, 2/27/1886.
7. Anderson, *Handbook of Texas Online*; *Galveston Daily News*, 5/28/1886.
8. *Fort Worth Daily Gazette*, 3/3/1886; *Fort Worth Daily Gazette*, 3/21/1886.
9. *Fort Worth Daily Gazette*, 2/27/1886; *San Antonio Daily Express*, 2/26/1886; *Fort Worth Daily Gazette*, 2/26/1886.
10. *Galveston Daily News*, 2/25/1886; *Galveston Daily News*, 5/23/1886.
11. *Fort Worth Daily Gazette*, 2/26/1886.
12. *Fort Worth Daily Gazette*, 2/26/1886.
13. Hollandsworth, "Capital Murders"; *Galveston Daily News*, 2/25/1886.
14. "Our Campaigns."

Chapter 18

"The Notorious Whitechapel"

The Links to Jack the Ripper

In the Whitechapel section of London, England, a serial killer went on the rampage in 1888. During a killing spree that lasted only about ten weeks, from August 31, 1888, to November 9, 1888, the killer, known as Red Jack or Jack the Ripper, murdered five prostitutes. The women—Mary Nichols, Annie Chapman, Elizabeth Stride, Catherine Eddowes, and Mary Kelly—had been surgically mutilated, and most had body parts taken from them. Other murders in a similar fashion continued into the 1890s, some of them known as the "embankment murders." Whether these later murders were done by the same hand or whether they were copycat murders is unknown, though most people at the time thought that two or more murderers were involved.[1]

Contemporary sources and modern researchers have tried to link the Austin servant girl murders to the Whitechapel murders, but no real link seems to exist. Could an unskilled killer who mutilated women with an ax in 1885 in Austin have refined his method in three years so that he was able to dissect with surgical precision the victims in Whitechapel? Such a supposition seems quite unlikely. Most of the Austin victims were raped, whereas the Whitechapel victims apparently were not. Other differences in the modus operandi also suggest that the two sets of murders were not connected.

Many people believe that Jack the Ripper was the first serial killer. Others think that the Austin servant girl annihilator was the first serial killer. Both groups are incorrect in their beliefs. History has known numerous serial killers: Locusta, a female poisoner in the Roman era of Nero; Gilles de Rais, a wealthy Frenchman in the 15th century; Erzebet Bathory, a 16th-century Hungarian countess who thought bathing in the blood of virgins would keep her young; Peter Stubbe in 16th century Germany; Marle de Brinvilliers and Catherine La Voison in 17th century France; and the list goes on. Victims of these few numbered in the thousands.[2]

In America, several serial killers predated the Austin murderer. In the late 18th century, Micajah and Wiley Harpe, who were either brothers or cousins, wreaked havoc in the Kentucky and Tennessee territories and Mississippi. After being jailed for murdering a man, they escaped and began a nine-month series of murders. They were finally captured, tried, and hanged. Then their heads were placed on poles near Greenville, Mississippi. They were credited with killing between twenty and forty people, some relatives and their own children.[3]

In Boston, Jesse Pomeroy, the "Boy Fiend," tortured and killed several children in the early 1870s. Only 14 at the time, Pomeroy would slash and maim his victims, which included a four-year-old boy and a ten-year-old girl. Pomeroy was tried and sentenced to 56 years in prison for his murders. Pomeroy, when asked why he did the murders, said, "I couldn't help it." A couple of years later, Thomas Piper, known as the "Boston Belfry Murderer," confessed to four sex murders in Boston, including a five-year-old child. Piper blamed his use of opium for the murders, but he was hanged anyway. Also, in the late 1870s, Stephen Richards, known as the "Nebraska Fiend," killed nine people before being arrested in 1879. And then the Austin murders garnered national attention.[4]

Those who claim Jack the Ripper was the first serial killer contend that the murders took place in a major urban setting and attracted international attention, so those qualities alone made the Whitechapel murders more important. Indeed, Jack the Ripper is credited with murdering only five women, and his reign of terror lasted only a few weeks. His death total is overshadowed by many of the earlier and later serial killers, but his case remains well-known over a century later. With many people still trying to solve the Ripper murders, just as many are still trying to solve the Austin servant girl murders. But the Austin murders have somewhat been lost to history, whereas the Whitechapel murders are still amazingly fresh in the public psyche.

Who Was Jack the Ripper?

The answer depends on whom you ask. There are many more possible Ripper suspects than there were murders in the series. Among the long list of suspects were Prince Albert Victor, Joseph Barnett, Alfred Napier Blanchard, W.H. Bury, Lewis Carroll, David Cohen, Dr. T. Neill Cream, Frederick Deeming, Montague John Druitt, Carl Feigenbaum, James Kelly, George Chapman, Aaron Kosminski, Jacob Levy, James Maybrick, Walter Sickert, Francis Thompson, Francis Tumblety, and Dr. John Williams. Some of these names are unusual suspects. Prince Albert Victor was born in 1864, the grandson of Queen Victoria. The theory goes that the prince was mildly retarded and suffered from syphilis. The disease drove the prince insane and compelled him to commit the murders. Supposedly the royal family was aware of his involvement but did nothing to stop it. However, the prince was apparently not even in London when most of the murders occurred.[5]

The suspicion of the famous author Lewis Carroll, whose real name was Charles Lutwidge Dodgson, is based solely on anagrams that Richard Wallace concocted from Dodgson's work. Dr. Thomas Neill Cream was in prison in Illinois during the murders, but when he was hanged for murder, he uttered the three words, "I am Jack." Those words alone, and the farfetched theory that Cream had a double who actually served his time in prison, form the basis for his supposed involvement in the murders. Walter Sickert was linked to the murders because of similarities between the paper he used for correspondence and the letters supposedly sent by Jack the Ripper. Francis Thompson had a checkered career. He was a poet who became a vagrant living south of Whitechapel. Early accounts of the Ripper said he had a leather apron, which Thompson claimed to have. He studied surgery and worked in a medical factory. He was an opium addict who had a mental breakdown. He was shunned by his family. Some of his poems dealt with the murder of young women. And he had a passing resemblance to the description of the man who was supposedly the Ripper.[6]

W.H. Bury was an interesting case with an appropriate name. He first came under suspicion when he was arrested in Dundee, Scotland, for the murder of his wife in early 1889. Bury lived in Whitechapel and left there in January 1889, only a few months after the five murders occurred, refusing to say why he left Whitechapel. Relatives said Bury was subject to "fits of an unconscious murder mania." The mutilated remains of his wife were found in a chest in Dundee.

> A post mortem examination held on the body of the Dundee victim proved the woman had first been strangled and her body had been mutilated, the abdomen being ripped open and the legs and arms twisted and broken. Bury . . . says he and his wife drank heavily last night before retiring and that he does not know how he got to bed. Upon awakening, he says, he found his wife lying upon the floor with a rope around her neck. Actuated by a sudden impulse for which he cannot account, he seized a knife and slashed the body. Upon reason returning he became alarmed and hastily crushed the body into the chest in which it was found, thinking to make his escape.

However, he claimed he could not leave his wife's remains, so he turned himself in to the police. The theory for Bury's implication in the Whitechapel murders was that his wife knew of his involvement in the murders, and she took him to Dundee to try to stop the atrocities. Unfortunately, her efforts failed, and she fell victim to her husband's mania.[7]

Over the years, other men emerged as Ripper suspects. One was a man named Williams who was arrested in Melbourne for murdering a woman. Williams had formerly lived in Liverpool, where his wife and children had disappeared. An investigation of the house where the family lived uncovered the remains of the wife and children buried in quicklime under the hearthstone. While a resident of Liverpool, Williams made frequent trips to London, and those trips corresponded to the dates on which the Ripper's victims were murdered. A man seen with some of the Ripper victims matched the description of Williams given by residents of Liverpool.[8]

In 1895, Dr. Forbes Winslow of London, who was a specialist in insanity, claimed that Jack the Ripper was an inmate at a county lunatic asylum in England. Winslow said the doctors at the asylum knew about the inmate's involvement in the murders but "hushed up the facts." The inmate was a medical student who suffered from homicidal mania. According to Winslow,

> "Jack the Ripper" was a medical student of good family. He was a young man of slight build, with light hair and blue eyes. He studied very hard, and his mind, being naturally weak, gave way. He became a religious enthusiast, and attended early services every morning at St. Paul's. His religious fervor resulted in homicidal mania toward the women of the street, and impelled him to murder them. He lodged with a man whom I know, and suspicion was first directed toward him by reason of the fact that he returned to his lodgings at unseasonable hours; that he had innumerable coats and hats stained with blood.

While the man was in the asylum, the murders ceased. The inmate may have been John William Smith Sanders.[9]

Another unusual suspect was Buck Taylor, who was sometimes called the King of the Cowboys for his involvement in Buffalo Bill's Wild West Show. Taylor was born in Fredericksburg, Texas, which is about 80 miles west of Austin. Before he became a cowboy, Taylor was an opera singer. The Wild West Show was in London during the time of the murders and sailed to New York on May 11, 1888. Little evidence is available to link Taylor to the murders, and that evidence is strictly circumstantial.[10]

Francis Tumblety was perhaps the most eccentric of the suspects. Born either in Canada or Ireland around 1833, as a youth Tumblety was regarded as "an ignorant, uncared-for, good-for-nothing boy" who sold pornography in Rochester, New York. Around 1850, he left Rochester, likely for Detroit, and began to call himself an Indian herb doctor. He later appeared in Toronto, calling himself a prominent physician. After a couple of scrapes with the law regarding drugs he had prescribed to patients who died, Tumblety moved to Boston, where he would parade around in a military outfit atop a white horse. In Boston, he proudly displayed a collection of uteri. When the Civil War began, he put on that he was a Union army doctor and a friend of President Lincoln. In the late 1860s, Tumblety left the United States and travelled to London, then to Berlin, and then to Liverpool in 1874. There he met and likely had a homosexual relationship with Sir Henry Hall Caine. A couple of years later, Tumblety traveled to New York, returning to Liverpool in June 1888. In November 1888, after the five murders credited to Jack the Ripper had occurred, he was arrested for homosexual activities. He posted bail a few days after his arrest and fled to France and then back to New York. In New York, Tumblety was under police surveillance because of the belief he might be the Whitechapel murderer. But Tumblety disappeared from New York, later surfacing in Rochester in 1893, where he lived with his sister. His last known whereabouts were in St. Louis, where he died in 1903. Because of his supposed medical experience, his collection of uteri, his use of aliases, his repeated flight from the law, his arrest on suspicion during the series of murders, and his apparent hatred of women, Tumblety was considered a likely suspect as Jack the Ripper. Because of his travels, he may have been involved in murders in other cities, notably in the United States. But there is no evidence he was ever in Austin.[11]

"Was It the Man from Texas?"

Soon after the Whitechapel murders in 1888, several reporters began to notice the striking similarities between the Jack the Ripper murders and the murders in Austin three years earlier. Because the victims in the Austin murders were mostly black women, they generated less interest than if the victims had been white. Because the same brutality was evident in both sets of murders, the theory arose that "the perpetrator of the latter may be the Texas criminal, who was never discovered." The *Atlanta Constitution* tried to make a connection between the Austin and Whitechapel murders. The newspaper's conviction was based on the belief that there was no other man capable of committing the Whitechapel murders than the Austin murderer. The newspaper also made the rather specious argument that since the murderer was no longer killing women in Austin, he must be killing women somewhere else:

> The Texas and London murders are precisely alike. There is the same absence of a reasonable motive, the same grotesque brutality in the mutilations, the same mystery, and the same suspicion that the criminal is a monster or a lunatic. . . . In our recent annals of crime there has been no other man capable of committing such deeds. The mysterious crimes in Texas have ceased. They have just commenced in London. Is the man from Texas at the bottom of them all? If he is the monster or lunatic, he may be expected to appear anywhere. The fact that he is no longer at work in Texas argues his presence somewhere else. His peculiar line of work, executed in precisely the same manner, is now going on in London. Why should he not be there? The more one thinks of it, the more irresistible becomes the conviction that it is the man from Texas. In these days of steam and cheap travel, distance is nothing. The man who would kill a dozen women in Texas would not mind the inconvenience of a trip across the water, and once there he would not have any scruples about killing more women. Undoubtedly, it must be the man from Texas.

Though reporters hopped on the supposed link, police officials were more reserved. The superintendent of the New York police, for example, said that the link between the two sets of murders might be possible, but he believed it probable that the two were not related. He stated, "I hardly believe it is the same individual."[12]

The newspapers continued to promote the possible link, contending that "a maniac was at large—a maniac with the cunning of a devil and the cruelty of a hundred of them." The *New York Times* also intimated that the two sets of murders were connected: "On reading of the London Whitechapel murders citizens of Austin recognize a likeness to the servant-girl murders, as they are called, so startling as to lead to the conclusion that the London assassin is the Austin murder fiend of 1885." After the murder of Mary Ann Nichols, the *Austin Daily Statesman* propounded upon the link, noting that "the victim was literally cut to pieces with a knife in the hands of a mysterious being, whose footsteps could not be heard." The report described the Whitechapel murderer as a "short, thickset, half crazy creature, with fiendish black eyes, and known as 'Leather Apron.' He frequented the dark alleys, and like a veritable imp haunted the gloom of the halls and passage ways of Whitechapel. . . . Of powerful muscle, carrying a knife which he brandished over his victims, the London murder fiend was too terrible an assailant for the victim that cowered beneath the glitter of cold steel." Was the Austin newspaper ready to make the leap and suggest that the Austin servant girl annihilator and Jack the Ripper were one and the same? Not really.

> There is a striking similarity which must be a mere coincidence between these murderers across the water and the servant girl murderers in Austin in 1885, which latter remains a mystery as profound and unraveled as that of Whitechapel. All were perpetrated in the same mysterious and impenetrable silence, and what makes the coincidence more singular is that the Austin murder fiend, who was seen on one occasion, was, like "Leather Apron," a short, heavy set personage.

But was the Whitechapel murderer barefoot?[13]

The *Fort Worth Daily Gazette* was more convinced that the London assassin and the Austin murderer were one and the same. In recapping the Austin murders, the report noted the common aspects of the crimes.

> These murders have never been explained, and the assassin is still enveloped in dark and bloody mystery. He left no trace whatever to identify him. There was a fearful similarity among all these murders. Nearly all were killed about midnight and usually within a few days of full moon, the murderer seeming to select moonlight nights for his dreadful work. All of the victims were struck with some sharp instrument about the head and on the same side of the head. The bodies were generally found with clean underclothing. None of them made any noise or outcry, although in more than one instance evidences were left of a terrible struggle, and they were slain in profound silence, even persons in adjoining rooms hearing nothing. The bodies were almost all found in the same position. All were dragged out into the back yards. On reading the accounts of the London White Chapel murders the citizens of Austin recognize a likeness to the servant girl murders, as they are called, so startling as to lead to the conclusion that the London assassin is the Austin murder fiend of 1885. Accounts show that the position of the bodies of the women killed at White Chapel last Sunday when found was identically the same as that of Mrs. Eula Phillips, the last of the victims in this city killed on Christmas of 1885.

Though the Austin and Whitechapel murders took place at night and the bodies were mutilated, the manner in which the mutilation was done differed markedly. The report does make the point that the body position of the victims in Whitechapel was similar to the position of Eula Phillips, but one can assume that the body position of most sexual murder victims would be similar.[14]

Most of the newspaper reports trying to link the two series of murders focused on the nature of the murders and the manner of killing. One newspaper interviewed a gentleman from Austin who was visiting London during the Jack the Ripper murders. When asked how many women had been killed in Austin, the gentleman replied: "Twelve; all women, and all, or nearly all, of questionable character. Ten of them were negresses and two white women. They mostly belonged to the servant class, who were of loose reputation. The two white women moved in fairly good circles; but they were also women who had not the highest character." When asked if the modus operandi of the two sets of murders was similar, the gentleman replied: "No, except that both selected women and women of a certain class." When asked if the method of murder was similar, if the women's throats were cut, the gentleman stated: "No; not one. They were all killed with a blunt instrument; their skulls in most cases were battered in. They were also very much bruised and slashed about the body; but again with a blunt instrument." When asked if the Austin murders were committed with a periodical frequency, the gentleman said: "Yes; but the intervals were longer. They took place usually at a month's interval, though sometimes a couple of months intervened. It was curious, too, that they always took place when the moon was full. The idea was that they were the work of a madman who became more intensely insane under the influence of the full moon." Based on the gentleman's knowledge of the two sets of murders, the assailants were not the same.[15]

The newspapers were not the only ones trying to make the connection between the two sets of murders. Noted neurologist E.C. Spitzka, writing in the *Journal of Nervous and Mental Disease* in 1888, added his expertise to the attempt. Spitzka first discussed some of the more notoriously brutal rulers in history, suggesting that the horrible nature of a crime does not necessarily mean its perpetrator is insane. His attention turned to the Whitechapel murderer, and he compared Red Jack to Andrew Bichel and Sergeant Bertrand, two men whose sexual perversion involved their reveling among the intestines of living and dead persons. Bichel, known as the Maiden-Killer, attracted young girls to his home under the pretense of reading their fortunes. Then, he would kill and mutilate them for sexual release before burying them on his property. Bichel was tried in 1808 and admitted he had killed the girls for their clothes. Sergeant Bertrand was born in 1828 to normal parents, but he began masturbating at a young age. In his developing perversion, he began to kill animals and mutilate them before masturbating among their intestines. His perversion then turned to human corpses, which he would dig up and use for his masturbatory purposes. Though he was fired upon repeatedly by cemetery guards, he continued his perversion until caught. At trial, he claimed he was cured and received a one year imprisonment.[16]

Spitzka emphasized the relative singularity of the Whitechapel murders, noting that few in history had achieved such heights of horror.

> None are exactly like it. Long series of murders on women, done in the same manner and committed from evidently similar motives are on record, but they were all committed in comparatively deserted localities. Only one was continued after

> the murderer knew that the hue and cry had been raised and skilled measures adopted for his capture. But while he mutilated his victims in the same way as the Whitechapel unknown, Bertrand selected bodies of the dead and not the living. . . . The cases of Andrew Bichel and Bertrand resemble the Whitechapel one in the fact that both revelled among the intestines, the former of living, the latter of dead subjects. Both describe their penchant as irresistible and the delight they experienced as indescribable, and probably the Whitechapel fiend experiences the same.

Spitzka felt that the dissection performed by the Whitechapel murderer necessitated some amount of skill, especially in the removal of the uterus. Spitzka believed that the murderer had "served an apprenticeship on the dead body, be he butcher, medical man, or amateur."[17]

Spitzka also believed that the letters and inscription on a window shutter saying that Jack the Ripper would kill twenty women and then surrender meant that the murderer had a literary bent. Spitkza claimed if the letters and inscriptions were

> really the writing and signature of the Whitechapel assassin, it may put an entirely different aspect on the case. If it be a genuine expression of intention it is impossible to account for it on the theory of impulsive periodical or of epileptic insanity. It is not inconsistent with sexual perversion, that he might have written this to mislead. Indeed, it would not surprise me if this person were an acquaintance of an author of eminence, unbosomed himself to him, and thus utilized in a sensational tale.

This comment makes the suspicion of Lewis Carroll a bit more understandable. Of course, the Austin murderer had no such notes or inscription, in fact, no evidence left behind at all besides the bare footprints.[18]

Spitzka then mentioned the Austin murders and subsequent murders that took place in Gainesville, Texas. Some believe the murders in Gainesville were committed by the Austin servant girl annihilators. These Gainesville murders will be discussed in a later chapter.

> At Gainesville, and near Austin, Texas, ten murders, terribly similar in every detail, were committed in 1887. The first blow was with an ax, and afterwards the bodies so mutilated that they fell apart on being lifted up. The killing was uniformly done in bed, the victim was, as a rule, dragged into the yard and there hacked to pieces. Most of those destroyed were colored servants. In his tenth case he failed to complete his task, the victim escaping with her life. The perpetrator has not been discovered.

As can be seen, Spitzka had an incorrect date for the Austin murders, though the Gainesville murders did occur in 1887. Spitzka also delineated similarities between the Whitechapel and Austin murderers.

> I am prepared to learn that, like the Texas and Westphalian assassins, he may discontinue his work and remain forever unknown. Such a mind is not immune to the influence of fear and the necessity of caution, and as regards the last phase in the history of the Texas and Westphalian assassins it may remain an unsolved alternative between latency of the impulse and suicide of the assassin. Strange motives crop out among impulsive lunatics. Singular antipathies, romantic notions of revenge, pseudo-philanthropic ideas, mysterious associations of certain numbers, may all bear a part in the horrible scheme to which the Whitechapel fiend appears to have devoted himself, if paranoia be one of his mental loads. If so, we may look for peculiarities in dress, peculiarities of writing, and peculiarities of countenance in him.

Were notions of revenge or mysterious links between numbers pertinent in the Austin murders? As noted in an earlier chapter, address numbers where the Austin murders were committed showed a curious trend.[19]

Spitzka seemed increasingly convinced that the Austin servant girl annihilator and Jack the Ripper were the same person.

> I would suggest that not the least probable theory is that the same hand that committed the Whitechapel murders committed the Texas murders. We can well picture the man to ourselves: of Herculean strength, of great bodily agility, a brutal jaw, a strange, weird expression of the eyes, a man who has contracted no healthy friendships, who is in his own heart as isolated from the rest of the World as the rest of mankind are repelled by him. . . . The English medical and secular journals have been strongly censured for attributing the Whitechapel murders to an American. Undoubtedly they did this on absurd grounds and in a cockney spirit; but to any one familiar with the Texas homicides of a year ago, the theory that both acts were committed by one and the same person does not seem unreasonable.

Spitzka concluded with the statement that among animals, the murderous impulse is often associated with the sexual life of the individual. Insanity is not needed to stir the impulse to kill. According to Spitzka, "The wild beast . . . is slumbering in us all. It is not necessary always to invoke insanity to explain its awakening."[20]

Spitzka was quite clear in suggesting that insanity or lunacy was likely not the motive of the Whitechapel murderer or the Austin servant girl annihilator. Certainly some mental imbalance was at play, for no reasonable person commits such heinous crimes without perversion. Were the two sets of murders committed by the same person? Spitzka seemed to think so, and so do other current researchers.

James Maybrick

Shirley Harrison has made a career promoting the belief that James Maybrick was both the Austin murderer and Jack the Ripper. She has published at least two books on the subject: *The Diary of Jack the Ripper—The Chilling Confessions of James Maybrick* and *Jack the Ripper—The American Connection*. James Maybrick was born in Liverpool in 1838 to a well-established family there. Around 1873, Maybrick started a cotton business in Liverpool. In 1874, he moved to Norfolk, Virginia, where he contracted malaria. To fight the ailment, he took quinine, which proved unsuccessful. He then tried a mixture of arsenic and strychnine, which apparently cured his malaria but left him addicted to arsenic. In 1880, he sailed from America back to Liverpool. On the voyage, he met 18-year-old Florence Chandler, who would become his wife. The Maybricks spent their time between Liverpool and America during the next few years, but an economic downturn made his business suffer. He continued to use arsenic and other addictive powders. In 1887, his wife discovered he was having an affair, and she engaged in the same activities herself. The marriage deteriorated, and domestic violence broke out in March 1889. Maybrick's drug use increased, and he died in May 1889. Ironically, his wife was tried for poisoning him; she was found guilty and spent 15 years in prison.[21]

Maybrick was not really considered a suspect in the Whitechapel murders until 1992, when his diary was discovered. Harrison's book on the diary was published in 1995. Whether the diary is authentic is certainly debatable, though many believe it is a hoax. Harrison suggested that James Maybrick was descended from a Liverpool convict exiled to America in 1775. During his time in America, Maybrick reportedly took trips south conducting cotton business. He also had friends in the south, including John Aunspagh in Dallas, whose young daughter had stayed with the Maybricks in England in 1888. Maybrick also was supposed to maintain a previously unknown office in Galveston, about the same distance from Austin as Dallas is. Harrison's most incriminating bit of evidence revolved around the International Cotton Exposition held in New Orleans beginning on December 23, 1884, a week before Mollie Smith was murdered. Though Maybrick had resigned as a director of the Norfolk Cotton Exchange in 1884, he had asked to remain in the exchange as a foreign member, "obviously intending to return from time to time." Harrison contemplated:

> Did James use the opportunity to mix business and pleasure? It seems unlikely that he was not in New Orleans, enjoying the illuminated fountains and the bands set among 249 acres of gardens along the banks of the Mississippi. He had left Florie over Christmas on a previous occasion. But so far, I have found no sighting of him on the crucial dates.

Harrison pressed on with the link between Maybrick and the Austin murders, noting that Maybrick attended the funeral of his wife's brother alone, presumably in Alabama, where Florence Maybrick was born. There were no murders in Austin in April. Harrison indicated out that Eliza Shelly was murdered on May 23, during the closing ceremonies of the cotton exposition. Shelly was actually murdered on May 7, and the cotton exposition closed on June 2, 1885, closer to the murder of Irene Cross, who was killed in the early morning hours of May 22. Harrison concluded her campaign for Maybrick by equating the eerie similarity of two women being murdered on the same night both in Austin and in Whitechapel as proof that the two series of murders were connected.[22]

Maurice, the Malay Cook

Many researchers who believe a link exists between the Austin murders and the Whitechapel murders hang their hopes on a Malay cook named Maurice, sometimes referred to as Alask or Alaska. The story of the Malay cook began with a seaman named George M. Dodge. Dodge claimed that in August of 1888 "he met a Malay cook named Alask, with whom he had previously been acquainted on shipboard, in a music hall in London, and that Alask told him he had been robbed of all he had by a woman of the town and threatened that unless he found the woman and recovered his money he would kill and mutilate every Whitechapel woman he met." The Malay supposedly showed Dodge a double-edged knife. According to Dodge, the Malay was "about five feet seven inches in height, one hundred and twenty pounds in weight, and apparently thirty-five years of age. He was very dark." Dodge would not tell where the Malay lived until he knew if a reward was being offered, but another seaman said he thought the Malay had already taken to sea again on a vessel in the North Sea.[23]

Unfortunately, seaman Dodge's story did not hold much water. When police officials in London heard the report about Dodge's claim, detectives were dispatched to the steamship company, the Home for Asiatics, and other locations in the East End where information about the Malay might be found.

> Mr. Freeman, manager . . . of the Asiatic Home, said he had been at the home for thirty years and had never known a Malay of the name Alaska. Malays, he said, are Mohammedans and do not use European names, but the word "lascar" is the Mohammedan name for seaman, and Dodge might have been misled. . . . The Queen's Music-Hall, where Dodge says he met Alaska, is most luxuriously fitted up, in a style equal to many of the West End music-halls. Mr. Wood, the manager, says that he had heard nothing of the alleged robbery of the Malay, and referred his inquirer to two attendants, Alexander Nowland and Henry Pierce, who look after the boxes in which sailors just returned from a voyage usually disport themselves. Both men declared that no such robbery could have taken place on the premises without their hearing of it, and as far as they were aware no such thing had happened. . . . Messrs. Magregor's Son & Co., owners of the Glen Line of steamers trading to Singapore, China, etc., stated that the Glenartney sailed in April from London for China and returned Aug. 14. After taking in a cargo at Antwerp she again sailed for China Sept. 8 and was last reported Sept. 23 at Suez. They have no one named

> Alaska on board. The chief cook of the Glenartney is a thoroughly respectable Chinaman, who has been in the service of the firm for many years, and they have had no Malays on the ship.

Based on the detectives' findings, Dodge's story about the Malay cook and his threat was considered to be just a sailor's yarn.[24]

A strange twist existed in the story of the Malay cook, one that some researchers claim proved a link between the Whitechapel killer and the Austin servant girl annihilator. When the report about Dodge's story about the Malay was published in the *Austin Daily Statesman*, it spawned a letter to the editor. The letter claimed that "a Malay cook had been employed at a small hotel in Austin in 1885, the date of the Austin assassinations." The small hotel, the Pearl House, located at 223 Congress Avenue across from the Union railroad depot, was a restaurant, saloon, and lodging house. It was run by Hermann Schmidt. An Austin reporter visited the Pearl House and talked to Mrs. Schmidt. "It was ascertained that a Malay cook calling himself Maurice had been employed at the house in 1885 and that he left some time in January 1886." The report noted that the last of the Austin murders occurred on Christmas Eve 1885 and that the Malay cook left shortly thereafter. The Christmas Eve murders were considered the last of the Austin servant girl murders. "A strong presumption that the Malay was the murderer of the Austin women was created by the fact that all of them except two or three resided in the immediate neighborhood of the Pearl House." This last statement is only partially true. The Shelly, Ramey, and Hancock murders occurred a short distance from the Pearl House. The Phillips murder was more distant, and the other murders were quite distant from the Pearl House. As noted in an earlier chapter, because Austin at the time was relatively small in size, any point in the city was relatively close to at least one of the murders, so the location of the Pearl House in relation to the murders seems relatively inconsequential.[25]

Were the Whitechapel and Austin murders committed by the same person? That prospect seems highly unlikely. The fact that the string of murders ended in Austin does not necessarily mean that the murderer had to resume his activities elsewhere. The method of murder, from brutal mutilation to skilled dissection, is too great a leap to accept easily. The idea that a person would travel thousands of miles several times in a year to commit a murder in Austin is somewhat preposterous. Finally, the descriptions of the Malay cook and the Austin murderer don't really match. The Malay in Dodge's story was short, but at 120 pounds he was rather slight in build. The description of the Austin murderer suggested that he was short and stocky, not short and slight. All these differences make the theory that Jack the Ripper and the Austin servant girl annihilator were the same somewhat hard to swallow. A better suspect was closer to home, not thousands of miles overseas.

Notes

Title: *Fort Worth Daily Gazette*, 8/8/1891.

1. "Jack the Ripper 1888"; *St. Paul Daily Globe*, 9/11/1889.
2. Ramsland, *Inside the Minds of Serial Killers*: 1-3.
3. Ramsland, *Inside the Minds of Serial Killers*: 3; "Frontier serial killers: The Harpes."
4. Ramsland, *Inside the Minds of Serial Killers*: 4; "Jesse Pomeroy, The Boy Fiend."
5. "Jack the Ripper—Suspects": <http://www.casebook.org/suspects/eddy.html>.
6. "Jack the Ripper—Suspects": <http://www.casebook.org/suspects/carroll.html>; <http://www.casebook.org/suspects/cream.html>; <http://www.casebook.org/dissertations/dst-pamandsickert.html>; <http://www.casebook.org/suspects/ft.html>.
7. *Fort Worth Daily Gazette*, 2/12/1889.
8. *Sacramento Daily Record-Union*, 3/17/1892.
9. *Brownsville Daily Herald*, 9/5/1895; "Jack the Ripper—Suspects": <http://www.casebook.org/dissertations/rip-thirdman.html>.
10. Begg, et al. *The Complete Jack the Ripper A-Z*; *The Medical News*, volume 50: 718; Csida and Csida, *American entertainment: a unique history of popular show business*: 25, 58; Warren, *Buffalo Bill's America*: 318.
11. "Jack the Ripper—Suspects": <http://www.casebook.org/suspects/tumblety.html>; *Frederick News*, 11/20/1888.
12. *Atlanta Constitution*, reprinted in *Fort Worth Daily Gazette*, 10/1/1888; *Woodford Times*, 10/12/1888.
13. *Frederick News*, 11/20/1888; *New York Times* 10/7/1888; *Austin Daily Statesman*, 9/5/1888.
14. *Fort Worth Daily Gazette*, 10/5/1888.
15. *London Star*, 10/12/1888.
16. Spitzka, "The Whitechapel Murders: Their Medico-Legal and Historical Aspects": 765-778; *The Eclectic Magazine of Foreign Literature, Science and Art*: 714; *The Medico-Legal Journal*: 164-165.
17. Spitzka, "The Whitechapel Murders: Their Medico-Legal . . .": 765-778.
18. Spitzka, "The Whitechapel Murders: Their Medico-Legal . . .": 765-778.
19. Spitzka, "The Whitechapel Murders: Their Medico-Legal . . .": 765-778. (The "Westphalian assassins" that Spitzka refers to may have been the Femgerichte, discussed in an earlier chapter.)
20. Spitzka, "The Whitechapel Murders: Their Medico-Legal . . .": 765-778.
21. "Jack the Ripper—Suspects": <http://www.casebook.org/suspects/james_maybrick/maybrick.html>.
22. "Jack the Ripper—Suspects": <http://www.casebook.org/suspects/james_maybrick/maybrick.html>;<http://www.casebook.org/dissertations/maybrick_diary/deardiary2004.html>.
23. *Atchison Daily Globe*, 10/6/1888; *Freeman's Journal and Daily Commercial Advertiser*, 10/6/1888; *The Daily Telegraph* 10/6/1888.
24. *Chicago Tribune*, 10/6/1888.
25. *Atchison Daily Globe*, 11/19/1888; *Morrison & Fourmy's General Directory of the City of Austin, 1885-1886*.

Chapter 19

"Austin Agog"

The Trial of Jimmy Phillips

When the murder trial of Jimmy Phillips began in May 1886, the citizens of Austin were divided over the young man's guilt. Some felt his drunken binges and violent behavior might have caused him to murder his wife. Others believed that a person so badly injured in the assault was not a likely candidate to murder anyone, especially his wife. The trial, most thought, would settle the matter once and for all.

Though a full trial was ordered for Phillips at his preliminary trial in February, subsequently he was indicted for murder by the grand jury in April. That indictment brought a fiery condemnation of the grand jury system by the *San Antonio Daily Light*.

> There is no institution in America so un-American as that of the grand jury. The system is wrong in conception, iniquitous in practice and damaging if not damning in its results. It is a chamber of inquisition without the presence of the suspect; a star court, which presupposes the guilt of an absent and unheard party; the engine of malice, the tool of injustice and the official defamer of society. It opens the door to every meanness of which the human mind is capable, pays premiums upon hate and revenge, makes the State the responsible prosecutor in all manner and matters of personal spite, and shelters the devil of defamation behind the impenetrable wall of a secret tribunal. It brands men, innocent men, and untainted with crime, brands them as suspect and turns them over to the wagging jaws of earth's character-scavengers without a possibility of being heard in their own behalf. Its doors and ears are open to the presence and voice of accusation and crimination, but practically closed to all else. It breeds mischief, is the legal instrument of personal enmity, answers no good purpose that might not otherwise be achieved and should be forever abolished as a part of our system of criminal procedure.

After the grand jury indictment, Judge Alexander Walker reset the trial date from May 25 to May 24, 1886. At the end of April, a rumor spread that Phillips had left Austin and was being sought by officers, but that rumor proved to be false.[1]

When the full trial began in May, the courtroom was packed with spectators, as one might expect from such a sensational affair. The morning was spent selecting a jury. The telegraph operator from Waco also was called, when the jury was out, to present evidence about the scandalous telegram linking Comptroller William Swain to the murder. The operator declared that no such telegram had passed over his wires. As the trial developed, much of the evidence and testimony presented at Phillips' preliminary trial in February was repeated. The prosecution was represented by District Attorney James H. Robertson, brother of the mayor, and E. Taylor Moore, a former county attorney and legislator in the 1885 session. The defense was represented by William Walton, John Hancock, and J.E. Hamilton. Walton was an ardent secessionist during the war, and he successfully represented Ben Thompson, the gunfighter who was the Austin city marshal in the early 1880s, on a murder charge. Walton also wrote the first biography of Thompson, published in 1884. Ironically, John Hancock was an ardent Unionist during the war, so his presence on the defense team with Walton was somewhat unusual. Hancock had also been a judge, state legislator, and U.S. Congressman. The presiding judge was Alexander S. Walker.[2]

As in the preliminary trial, the first witness in the full trial was Mrs. Sophia Phillips, Jimmy's mother. Her testimony was essentially the same as she gave at the preliminary trial. Mrs. Phillips was only partially questioned on the first day, but her

> testimony was substantially that she was in the house on the night of the murder; that a little after 11 o'clock she had occasion to go into the room occupied by her son and his wife, Mrs. Eula Phillips; that they were lying on the bed sleeping. Her son's arm was stretched across the bed and his wife's head was resting on it; that their child was quietly sleeping between the two; that being broken of her sleep by having to attend a sick child, she had occasion again to go into the room at half past midnight, when she found Mrs. Eula Phillips gone from her place in the bed and her son, the defendant, in a wounded condition.

Because the newspapers were under somewhat of a gag rule concerning evidence presented in the trial, the testimony reported in the newspapers was somewhat limited. The appeal trial report, however, provided a much more thorough discussion of the testimony. Mrs. Phillips' testimony in the appeal trial report included a layout of the house and many more details. According to the appeal trial report,

> Witness last saw the deceased alive about eleven o'clock, on the night of December 24. She was then in bed with her husband and child in her room in the witness's house. The bed stood north and south against the wall, in the southwest corner of the room. Deceased lay behind, next to the wall, and was then laughing and talking with defendant and their child. The child lay between the two on the defendant's arm, the hand of which was resting on the deceased's head. The defendant and

> the deceased lay facing each other. The purpose of the witness's visit to the room was to take in some candies and nuts, and to get the defendant to show her how to manipulate a toy she designed as a Christmas present to a grand child.

Mrs. Phillips then gave a layout of the room in which Eula and Jimmy stayed and its relation to the main house.

> In order to reach the room occupied by the defendant and the deceased, the witness, going from her room, had to cross an intervening gallery. The door to defendant's room opening on the gallery was secured by a bolt—not a lock—which could be sprung from either the inside or the outside. A bureau stood on the east side of the room, against the wall, and immediately opposite the foot of the bed. A lamp was burning on the left hand side of the bureau. There was a window about opposite the right hand corner of the bureau, another in the northwest corner of the room, and a door and window opened to the ground on the west side of the room. There was a lock to the door but no key. The door was closed, and there was a warming stove so near it that it would open far enough only to admit a person passing in sideways. A small table stood near the head of the bed. The room was small, not exceeding twelve by fourteen feet in size.

Mrs. Phillips also gave testimony concerning her return to the room just after midnight and the horrifying scene she encountered there.

> An hour and a half later, or at about half past twelve o'clock, the witness again visited the defendant's room. His wife, Eula, the deceased, was then gone; his child was sitting up in the bed, crying, and the defendant was lying down in the middle of the bed, wounded, and waving his hands frantically over his head. An axe lay in the bed, in front, and alongside the defendant, the blade resting near his hips and the handle pointing towards his feet. The axe lay on the sheet and the handle was somewhat bloody. The bed cover was drawn up to the defendant's waist, and was rolled around him. His pillow was saturated with blood. The pillow on which Eula's head had reposed had a very little blood on it on that end next to the defendant. Blood had run lengthwise of the defendant on the bed, and thence to the floor. The blood ran to a point not quite but nearly in the middle of the bed, or about where the hips of the defendant lay, and thence through or off the bed to the floor. The end of the axe handle rested about one foot from the foot board of the bed. There was but little blood on Eula's pillow, and none on the bed on the side occupied by her. There was some blood on the axe handle. It did not run on to the axe handle, but was put on it by some one, perhaps by the witness when she removed it from the bed. That axe belonged to the witness's husband, and was usually kept at the wood house, about thirty feet from the defendant's back door, and not far

> from the point where the body of the deceased was found. The
> witness did not know whether or not the defendant knew where
> that axe was usually kept. He did not keep his wood with that
> of the witness. The pillow used by the defendant on that night,
> being rendered by the blood unfit for further use, was burned.
> If any thing else was burned witness did not know it.

After this traumatic testimony, the court was adjourned for the day.[3]

When the trial resumed the next day, Mrs. Phillips was again called to the stand to testify. Her testimony at first dealt with the location of bloody tracks but moved to a discussion of the nature of the marriage relationship between Jimmy and Eula. Mrs. Phillips noted her distraught emotional state on the night of the murder that caused her not to remember clearly all the details she saw. Though she had testified in the preliminary trial that she had seen two foot tracks in the room, one pointing toward the door and the other toward the head of the bed, her recollection at the full trial was that there were no clear foot tracks in the room, which was carpeted. Examined further, she said she was not certain one way or the other. There were bloody tracks on the gallery, and all the other tracks she saw on the premises were made by bare feet. She also noted that only two outside parties knew where Jimmy and Eula slept, and both of those parties lived in Williamson County. According to court records, those two parties were George Beauregard and John McCutcheon. (The court records may have confused the names of the men from Williamson County. They were more likely John Beauregard and George McCutcheon, the man on whose farm Jimmy and Eula lived. George McCutcheon also had a brother named Beauregard McCutcheon.) Mrs. Phillips also mentioned that after discovering the murder scene, no one in the family searched for Eula's body.[4]

Mrs. Phillips also detailed what happened earlier in the evening of the murder. Most of the household had gone out that evening, many to "an entertainment at the Presbyterian church." Eula did not go out, Mrs. Phillips said, but had been in the house all day on Christmas Eve. When Mrs. Phillips made her second visit to the room, a little after midnight, the lamp had been turned down low, but she knew something was wrong. She went to get her own lamp, and on returning, saw the blood.

> She could not explain why she did not turn up the defendant's
> lamp at once, except that she was too much frightened and
> excited to control her thoughts. She could not say whether she
> removed the axe from the bed when she first went in, or
> whether she did it when she returned with her own light. The
> witness was well satisfied that the axe was left that night at the
> wood house, and not, originally, in defendant's room. She had
> never before seen it in defendant's room. After he was
> wounded, but not on the night of December 24, the defendant
> asked witness where Eula was. Witness told him that his wife
> was dead, and he replied: "I'll go to hell."

Mrs. Phillips' testimony then turned to the ongoing marital troubles between Jimmy and Eula. January 1886 would have marked the third anniversary of the couple's wedding. After marrying, the couple lived in the Phillips' home in Austin until January 1885. At that time, they moved to Williamson County to live on the farm of George McCutcheon. They returned to the Phillips' home in October 1885. They did not separate during that time, but they also did not set up housekeeping on their own because they were not prepared to do so. "The defendant was acting very badly—that is, drinking heavily—and witness suggested to Eula that if she would visit her relatives under the pretense to the defendant that she had left him, he would probably 'straighten up' and prepare to keep house."[5]

After this suggestion, tension mounted in the Phillips home. The night before Eula left, about six to eight weeks before her murder,

> the defendant came home late, drinking heavily. He passed through the witness's room into that of his sister Delia, having offended Delia in some way. Delia struck him across the face with a shovel and fled into her room, locking her door. Refusing to open for him, the defendant kicked in one of the panels. Eula and Delia ran into the yard and called for the police. Eula passed the balance of the night in witness's parlor, and next morning started to Manschac on a visit to her relatives.

Jimmy was not told where Eula had gone in the hope that he would stop drinking and prepare himself to set up house with Eula. Instead of going to her relatives, Eula instead apparently went to Fannie Whipple's house on Red River Street. Fannie Whipple went to the Phillips home to get Eula's clothes. Eula then went on to her relatives in Manchaca, returning to Austin after a couple of weeks because Mrs. Phillips wrote her and told her to come back. Eula stayed with Mrs. Kate Creary, Jimmy's sister, for a couple of days, and then went to Elgin with her baby to visit relatives. About two weeks later, Jimmy and Kate Creary went to Elgin and brought Eula and the child back to Austin. Eula was murdered a few weeks later.[6]

Mrs. Phillips was also asked about a rumored plot to pay Delia Campbell, one of Jimmy's sisters, to leave town so she could not be used as a witness against Jimmy. Supposedly Mr. Phillips, Delia, Jimmy, Eugene Maguire, and John Penn had a conversation on the gallery of the Phillips home a few nights after Eula was murdered. At that meeting, Delia was supposedly offered a thousand dollars to leave town so she could not tell what she knew. Mrs. Phillips answered that some men were at her home on Saturday night following the murder, but that no such agreement was made and that any offer of money to Delia was absolutely not true. Mrs. Phillips did reveal, however, that on the same night Delia went to her sister Kate Creary's home alone. The next day, Delia did leave the city for three weeks, but she returned to testify at Jimmy's preliminary trial.[7]

Upon cross-examination, the witness added little relevant information. Mrs Phillips noted that when Eula had gone to Elgin, Jimmy had "bought a set of bed room furniture, on the installment plan, from Booth & Son, and had not completed paying for it at the time of the killing." She also clarified Jimmy's response when told that Eula was dead. He said, "'Then I'll go to hell,'" but added, "'For I can't live without her.'" She said that Jimmy had not been drinking for about a month prior to the murder and that he had recently finished working on the Fireman's Hall, leaving his carpenter's tools within a few feet of his bed. When Jimmy kicked in Delia's door, the problem, she stated, was between Jimmy and Delia, not Jimmy and Eula. She was then asked to recount the sequence of events on the evening of December 24, 1885.

> About five o'clock on the fatal evening, she overheard the defendant and Eula in the house, reading and talking, she lying partly in the defendant's lap. After a while defendant proposed to go down town and pay Booth & Son an installment on the furniture. The witness objected that, it being Christmas eve night, he would meet his friends and take a drink. He promised to return speedily, and witness wagered him some trifle that he would not get back within fifteen minutes by the clock. He and Eula then came into witness's room, and the conversation became general, the defendant speaking of his prospects for getting work. Eula sat down on the floor and let her hair down, and proceeded to arrange her front hair in curl papers. She and defendant had perfected their arrangements to take the early train next morning to spend Christmas day and night. Between ten and eleven o'clock, witness went out of the room, and found them as stated on her examination in chief. Witness then returned to her room, but did not undress entirely, as she had to be up and down with her sick grand child. She took off her skirt and some under garments, but kept on her basque, stocking and a light shawl, thrown around her shoulders and breast, laid down and soon dropped into a light sleep. After a time, she was awakened by a voice from the direction of defendant's room. The voice called twice: "Oh, Mama—Eula, darling." Witness made her way to defendant's room, and found the situation as detailed in her examination in chief. As soon as she reached the room, she took up the crying child, returned to her room, awaked her husband, and then called Mr. Allen, stating that some one had murdered defendant, and that she could not find Eula. She then returned to defendant's room, and could not recollect with particularity what afterwards occurred. Witness's husband and Mr. Allen went for physicians, and Drs. Litten and Fisher soon arrived. Witness, then, being completely prostrated, lay down. A large concourse of citizens soon arrived.

Mrs. Phillips also noted that most things in the room were in their usual place. She recalled that both doors to Jimmy and Eula's room were closed on her visit around 11 o'clock. The doors were not locked, and the couple did not have keys. She could not recall if the gallery door to the room was open when she made her second visit after midnight, after hearing Jimmy's call for help. She stated that she discovered the stains on the floor after several people had arrived, and if the stains were footprints, they were made by a barefoot person or persons. She concluded her testimony by saying she knew nothing about the discovery of Eula's body.[8]

Most of the remaining witnesses on the second day of the trial were fairly unimportant. John Abrahams, who lived in the neighborhood near the Phillips, testified for the State, saying that he and two other Swedes by the names of Lundell and Westbrooks were walking on the south side of West Hickory Street near the Phillips house between midnight and 1 A.M. on the night of the murder. They reported hearing a child crying and a man's voice soothing it. "Suddenly a light appeared in the house, and a woman's voice rang out: 'Mercy me—murder!'" The three men were about 100 feet from the house when they heard the cries. They then ran to the police station, about 200 yards away, to fetch Henry Brown, the night clerk at the station. Abrahams returned with Brown but did not search the premises and went only to the door of the room in which Jimmy lay wounded. He did not stay until Eula's body was found.[9]

The next witness was Henry Brown, the night clerk summoned by Abrahams and his friends. Brown went to the Phillips house and "found the defendant, quite bloody, lying in bed." Mrs. Phillips was also present. Brown asked Jimmy who had done the deed and got no reply. Upon identifying himself as a police officer, Brown was told by Jimmy to leave. He saw an ax in the room and took it to the police station for evidence. Brown then left Grooms Lee at the station, placing him in charge of the Phillips premises, and went to find Marshal Lucy. Lucy was at the Hancock house on Water Street, about three-quarters of a mile away, investigating the murder there. Brown found Lucy and was ordered back to the station. When he got back and apparently went on to the Phillips house, Eula's body had not yet been found. Brown estimated his travel time from the station to the Phillips house and then to the Hancock house and back to the Phillips took twenty to twenty-five minutes. When Brown returned to the Phillips house, Jimmy was lying on the bed, apparently unconscious, a serious wound to the left side of his head apparent. Brown noted that no one in the Phillips family had reported the murder to the police station.[10]

The following witness for the State was Fannie Whipple, a black woman who had a house on Red River Street. Her testimony was essentially the same as she gave in Jimmy's preliminary trial. She said that Eula Phillips and her sister-in-law, Delia Campbell, came to her house five or six weeks before Eula's murder. Eula and Delia arrived in the morning and stayed all day and all night and all the following day until two o'clock in the morning, when an unknown man arrived and the two young women left with him. Whipple stated that she went to the Phillips house to get Eula's clothes, informed Mrs. Phillips where Eula was, and received Eula's clothes from Mrs. Phillips. Whipple claimed her house on Red River was not an assignation house. She had been tried by Justice Thomas F. Purnell shortly after Eula's death for running an assignation house but was acquitted. Whipple did not receive immunity from prosecution for testifying at the trial.[11]

"The Scarlet Woman, the Procuress, the Shameless Cyprian"

The most sensational witness of the day and perhaps the whole trial was May Tobin, who ran an assignation house at 103 Congress Avenue. Testifying for the

State, Tobin said that she had lived in Austin for two years and knew Eula Phillips. She stated that Eula had come to her house several times with different men, the "gay gallants of the town. The object of the prosecution in Mrs. Tobin's testimony was to show that Mrs. Phillips, young and handsome as she was, had been guilty of continuous infidelity to her husband, the defendant, and that in this lay the motive for taking her life."

> Taylor, for the prosecution, put the question to Mrs. Tobin if Mrs. Phillips had been in the habit of visiting her house, and if she came alone. The courtroom was crowded to suffocation, and the multitude, including the long-visaged, sharp-eyed judge on the bench and the gaunt attorneys at the bar, panting and blowing with the heat, listened with breathless attention. The crowd and court hung upon her words like a man listening to his own death-sentence. In reply to the questions as to what persons were with Mrs. Phillips, Mrs. Tobin mentioned the names of one or two young men of the town, including a young gentleman connected with the building of the new capitol. Mrs. Tobin also mentioned the name of the superintendent of public instruction of the state of Texas.
>
> This created a profound sensation, and the audience, with suppressed excitement, waited in breathless suspense, expecting the witness to name some luckless officer still higher up in the state government, but those who listened for the name of the comptroller, whom an infamous slanderer some time ago charged with being connected with the scandal, listened in vain. Col. Swain's name was not mentioned, and stands clean of all imputation and unbesmirched. This is one of the most extensive and profound scandals ever known in Austin, and it is understood the superintendent of public instruction denies all knowledge of Mrs. Phillips. It is freely charged that many leading citizens were blackmailed by Mrs. Tobin, and they planked down the spot cash, and others, who refuse, were brought into the scandal. It is charged by friends of some of the young men implicated that Mrs. Tobin is the tool of parties behind the scenes who have concocted a scheme for their ruin.

Tobin testified "under the promise of immunity from prosecution for keeping a disorderly house," and many considered her testimony unreliable, most likely those implicated and their supporters. She named three members of the state government who had visited Eula—"one of them the head of a state department, one of them a secretary, and the other a clerk in the state government"—and of course they all denied her allegation. The head of the state department was Benjamin M. Baker, the state superintendent of public instruction. The "young gentleman connected with the building of the new capitol" was likely John T. Dickinson, the secretary of the State Capitol Building Commission. The clerk was likely William D. Shelley, a clerk in the comptroller's office.[12]

Tobin further testified that Eula came to her assignation house in November

1885 around midnight, accompanied by a Mr. Dickerson. Eula stayed that night and the next two days and nights, and Mr. Dickerson shared a bed with her each of those nights. From Tobin's house, Eula went to Manchaca. According to Tobin, "no man other than Dickerson visited Eula" during the period mentioned. Eula returned to Tobin's house between ten and eleven o'clock on the night of December 24, the night Eula was murdered. Eula tapped on Tobin's window, and Tobin asked who was knocking. Eula replied, "Eula. Don't you know me?" Tobin went to the door and spoke briefly with Eula but did not see the man with her. The man remained in the carriage at the gate. Tobin did not have room for Eula that night, so Eula left with the man. About three o'clock the next morning, Tobin heard of Eula's death.[13]

When cross-examined, Tobin stated that Eula had visited her house prior to the three nights in November 1885. Eula came early one night accompanied by Mr. Dickerson, but Tobin was not certain how long they stayed. Eula

> visited witness's house during the day on one occasion in company with a young man who was introduced to witness as Jones, which the witness did not believe to be his right name. She was at witness's house on another occasion during the day with one Shelly, and at another with one Baker. Witness then kept an assignation house, and was testifying now under promise of exemption from prosecution extended to her by city marshal Lucy and district attorney Robertson.

As noted, the Dickerson man was more likely John T. Dickinson. The Shelly man named by Tobin was likely William D. Shelley, a clerk in the comptroller's office. William D. Shelley was about 28 years old and apparently the son of Nathan G. Shelley, the law partner of John Hancock, who was serving as a defense attorney for Jimmy Phillips. The Baker man would have been Benjamin M. Baker, the state superintendent of public instruction.[14]

More Witnesses

The next witness for the State was R.B. Eanes, an uncle of Eula Phillips. Eanes stated that Jimmy Phillips had come to his house in November 1885, the afternoon after Eula had left home. Jimmy asked if Eanes had seen Eula; he had not. Jimmy said he and Eula had separated, which the witness had not yet heard. Jimmy then took an open pen knife from his coat pocket and announced that he would kill any person who sheltered Eula. Jimmy had been drinking, and he asked Eanes what he should do. Eanes told him to go home and get sober.[15]

Following Eanes was Albert Highsmith. Highsmith, testifying for the State, noted that in late October 1885, on George McCutcheon's farm in Williamson County, he heard Jimmy Phillips say, in a casual conversation and in the presence of others, that "if he knew his wife to be unfaithful to him, he would destroy her, and then destroy himself." Highsmith also stated that he had known George McCutcheon for twenty years. Highsmith was asked about McCutcheon's feet, to which he replied that he "knew of nothing peculiar about McCutcheon's feet, but had never taken any particular notice of them." This question likely came from the defense, which hoped to deflect attention to McCutcheon as a possible suspect in the murder of Eula Phillips.[16]

Next to the stand was Delia Campbell, Jimmy's sister, as a witness for the State. Campbell said that in December 1885, she was living with her mother at the Phillips home. She left Austin on the morning of December 24 and went to Rosenberg Junction, so she was not in town when the murder occurred. She said that Jimmy and Eula had planned to go to Manchaca for Christmas. Campbell also stated that Eula was unfaithful to her husband. She had seen Eula in bed with John Dickerson in November 1885, but she had never seen Eula in bed with any other man other than her husband. Delia, who was about 21 in the end of 1885, was much like Eula. Delia had married Lum Campbell in 1881, when she was only 17. Lum was about ten years older than Delia, just as Jimmy was about ten years older than Eula.[17]

Cross-examined, Campbell said that she had seen Eula and Dickerson in bed together at May Tobin's house. Dickerson was also the man who accompanied Eula and Campbell from Fannie Whipple's house to May Tobin's house. Delia Campbell returned from Rosenberg Junction on December 26. She stated that she had paid her own expenses on that trip. But she soon left Austin again, this time for two or three weeks. For this trip, she was furnished money by a Mr. Kirk, likely John P. Kirk, who was at the time the acting city marshal because Marshal Lucy had gone to Mexico to tend to his ailing wife. Kirk was also a deputy sheriff along with Grooms Lee under Travis County Sheriff Dennis Corwin in the late 1870s and likely was a deputy under Sheriff Edward Creary in the early 1880s. And Edward Creary was married to Jimmy's sister, Kate Phillips Deats Creary. According to Campbell, she did not see Kirk in person or even know him. "The object in getting the witness away, as the witness understood it, was to shield the married men of Austin. Witness's parents had nothing to do with the sending away of the witness, and were opposed to it."[18]

On re-examination by the prosecution, Campbell stated that Kirk had given her only twenty dollars. Two weeks after she left Austin, she was told by Eugene Maguire, a mail agent for the Houston and Texas Central railway who had conveyed the money from Kirk to Campbell, that Kirk provided the money to pay for Campbell's board while she was in Houston. She admitted that she "did not positively know the object in sending her away from Austin" was the reason she had stated, but she assumed it was. She also thought she was sent away to prevent an "easy interview" of her in Austin. Again questioned by the defense, Campbell denied that on the Saturday night following Eula's murder, she had a "conference with officers or other persons at which her mother and father were present." She did admit to a meeting with Eugene Maguire and John Penn at her house, but her parents were not present. Her parents did know that she was leaving town, but she did not think that Jimmy was aware of her intent to leave.[19]

The next witness for the State was Alma Burditt, Eula's older sister. She claimed that Jimmy Phillips' "jealousy of his wife extended to every man who merely spoke to her." She recounted an event at George McCutcheon's farm in Williamson County in the summer of 1885. Jimmy, in his anger, threw a cup of milk at Eula while they were all sitting at the dining table. Jimmy also threatened to kill Eula. Alma Burditt ran from the table into the yard and then came back to get Eula. Together, they both ran into the yard. The cup was shattered to bits against the pie safe. McCutcheon then called on Alma and Eula to come back inside, and they did. When questioned by the defense, the witness admitted that Jimmy and Eula continued to live together after the cup event, and that she saw only that one quarrel between the couple. In late November or early December of 1885, Eula visited Alma in Manchaca and stayed with her for several days. Alma confessed that she did not have very good feelings toward Jimmy. She explained that her "reason for saying that defendant was jealous of Eula was that every time Eula would mention a man's name he would ask her: 'What in the devil do you know about that man?'" Alma Burditt's testimony then concluded.[20]

Following Alma Burditt as a witness for the State was Sallie Mack. She testified that she lived near the Phillips home and that she was summoned by George Allen about two o'clock on the morning of the murder. She was asked to "attend and assist the Phillips family." By the time she arrived, a large crowd had gathered on the premises. Eula's body was brought in, and Sallie Mack washed and dressed the body before it was laid out in the parlor. She later fetched a bowl of water for someone, but she did not know for what purpose. Later that morning, she "saw the bowl, with bloody water in it, in the room then occupied by the defendant. She emptied the bowl, and then rinsed it, to clean it of adhering dirt." Mack said she heard no conversation between Jimmy and his mother until later in the morning. She helped Mrs. Phillips into Jimmy's room, at which time Jimmy asked, "'Ma, where is Eula?' Mrs. Phillips said: 'She is dead;' and defendant replied: 'Then I'll go to hell.' Doctor Litten thereupon ordered witness to take Mrs. Phillips away, and witness did so." As noted earlier, Sallie Mack was the mother of Alex Mack, who was an alleged member of the Thug Gang and a suspect in several of the servant girl murders.[21]

"Powerless to Do Anything"

Doctor J.M. Litten was the last witness of the day. Testifying for the State, he said that about one o'clock on Christmas morning 1885, he was summoned to attend to the defendant.

> He found the defendant lying in bed, in considerable blood, and badly wounded about the upper portion of the left ear. The wound extended in a curved line, and passed down in front of and below the lobe of the ear. It was deepest at the point above the ear, and was punctured in part, and in part contused. It went to the bone in the upper part. Witness found the periosteum abraded and bruised—roughed by the stroke of some instrument. The witness could not say that the bone was injured. Defendant lay on the front side of the bed in a great

accumulation of blood. This blood, though in larger quantity on the front side of the bed, extended to the middle.

While Dr. Litten and Dr. Josephus Cummings were dressing Jimmy's wounds, Eula's body was discovered. Dr. Litten went to the body and provided a graphic report on its condition.

> Witness went to the body, and found it lying prone on the back, the head and shoulders being in rather depressed ground. One arm lay under and the other at right angles to the body, and the legs were distended. The body was nude up to the waist. The forehead had been broken in by the stroke of some instrument, the wound running from the root of the nose upwards across the forehead. The upper portion of the wound was sunken, say an inch and a half, and shallowed gradually to the lower edge. The wound was about an inch and a quarter wide throughout its length, and was such a wound as could be inflicted with an ordinary axe. It was necessarily a fatal wound, and was unquestionably the cause of Eula's death. A small wound, a cut or bruise, was also found on the right ear. One side of her face showed indications of a slight wound. Witness found no bones in the body broken, other than the skull. Deceased was a small woman and would hardly exceed a hundred pounds in weight.

The prosecution ended its questioning of Dr. Litten for the time being.[22]

Dr. Litten was then cross-examined by the defense. He described the wound to Jimmy's head and its effects. Dr. Litten

> testified that the wound on the defendant's head was such as was calculated to produce a great nervous shock and much physical disability for at least two months. It had such effect upon the defendant, who was under witness's professional care for that length of time. It produced upon his system, for the period mentioned, nervousness, feverishness, sleeplessness, poverty of circulation, and it impaired the action of his heart. The wound near the ear was of a contused character and divided the parts down to the bone about a half inch, but was greater when seen by the witness, because of the swelling. The direction of the wound in depth was towards the cavity of the ear. It went directly to the bone, and was evidently stopped by the bone. Finding the surroundings as he did, the witness never thought of the wound on defendant as having been self inflicted. Whether or not it could have been a self inflicted wound had been subsequently discussed. In the opinion of the witness, there was no probability that the defendant's wound was self inflicted.

Dr. Litten was then questioned about Eula's body. He believed that

> the effect of the wound upon Eula must inevitably have been instant death and immediate suspension of all functionary power. The position of the dead woman's body indicated to the witness, when he saw it, that it had been dropped there. Witness saw no indications of dragging. The private parts of the woman were neither closed nor widely distended. The vagina contained about a tea spoonful of fluid resembling the male semen, but a little darker in color. Witness did not think that any muscular act of Eula had anything to do with the position of her legs. She was powerless to do anything, and the legs must have been placed in the position in which the witness saw them.

The defense had no further questions at the moment.[23]

Dr. Litten was then re-examined by the prosecution. He said he did not attach any special importance to the fluid in Eula's vagina, and he did not examine it with a microscope. The fluid was given to Dr. Cummings. Dr. Litten said that "the passage of the fluid may have been natural, or it may have been retained from previous sexual intercourse on that night." Turning to Jimmy's wound, Dr. Litten considered "the ability of the defendant to have inflicted the wound on himself as improbable. He could not say that it was impossible for him to have inflicted it." Dr. Litten also noted that he found a redness, accompanied by soreness, on the right side of Jimmy's chest. He believed the redness and soreness could be caused "by the pressure of a sufficient weight." After Dr. Litten concluded his testimony, the trial was adjourned for the day and set to resume at 9 o'clock the following morning. All through the day's proceedings, the courtroom was filled with spectators eager to hear the scandalous details of the case. In addition, "the extreme heat in the afternoon was almost insupportable," but order was maintained nonetheless.[24]

After two days of testimony and about a dozen witnesses, little new evidence had been provided in the trial. Eula was alleged to be promiscuous and unfaithful to her husband. Jimmy was alleged to be drunken, jealous, and abusive. Names of some prominent Austinites who allegedly visited May Tobin's assignation house were revealed. Details of an alleged plot to get a major witness out of town were provided. All in all, though, no direct evidence linked Jimmy Phillips to the murder of his wife. Perhaps the coming days of testimony might supply some solid evidence. One of the key points yet to be uncovered was who rode in "the hack with the white horses in which Mrs. Phillips rode on the terrible night of the murder." Apparently it was not William J. Swain.[25]

Notes

Title: *Fort Worth Daily Gazette*, 5/26/1886.

1. *San Antonio Daily Light*, 4/24/1886; *Fort Worth Daily Gazette*, 4/24/1886; *Fort Worth Daily Gazette*, 4/28/1886; *New York Times*, 4/24/1886 .
2. *Fort Worth Daily Gazette*, 5/25/1886; *Galveston Daily News*, 5/25/1886; *Austin Record*, 5/29/1886; *Reports of Cases . . . in the Court of Appeals of Texas, 1886*. Case 2271, James O. Phillips v. the State; *Morrison & Fourmy's General Directory of the City of Austin, 1885-1886* (The newspaper report identified Attorney Hamilton as J.S. Hamilton. The Court of Appeals records identified him as J.E. Hamilton. He might actually have been James R. Hamilton, an attorney who was a law student in 1885.)
3. *Fort Worth Daily Gazette*, 5/25/1886; *Reports of Cases . . . in the Court of Appeals of Texas, 1886*. Case 2271, James O. Phillips v. the State.
4. *Austin Daily Statesman*, 5/26/1886; *Reports of Cases . . . in the Court of Appeals of Texas, 1886*. Case 2271, James O. Phillips v. the State.
5. *Reports of Cases . . . in the Court of Appeals of Texas, 1886*. Case 2271, James O. Phillips v. the State (The court records may have confused the names of the men from Williamson County. They were more likely John Beauregard and George McCutcheon, the man on whose farm Jimmy and Eula lived. George McCutcheon also had a brother named Beauregard McCutcheon.)
6. *Austin Daily Statesman*, 5/26/1886; *Reports of Cases . . . in the Court of Appeals of Texas, 1886*. Case 2271, James O. Phillips v. the State; Bree, "Austin's Bloody Murder Spree, 1884-1885" (Manschac, currently spelled Manchaca, was a small town south of Austin. Elgin is a small town east of Austin. The Mrs. Creary mentioned was Katherine Frances "Kate" Phillips Deats Creary. Her first husband, Eugene Thompson Deats, died in 1878. She later married Edward Creary, who was the sheriff of Travis County from 1880 to 1882.)
7. *Austin Daily Statesman*, 5/26/1886; *Reports of Cases . . . in the Court of Appeals of Texas, 1886*. Case 2271, James O. Phillips v. the State.
8. *Reports of Cases . . . in the Court of Appeals of Texas, 1886*. Case 2271, James O. Phillips v. the State.
9. *Austin Daily Statesman*, 5/26/1886; *Reports of Cases . . . in the Court of Appeals of Texas, 1886*. Case 2271, James O. Phillips v. the State; *Morrison & Fourmy's General Directory of the City of Austin, 1885-1886* (The name of this witness is uncertain. The newspaper identified him as John Abrahams. The appeal court records identified him as John Abrahamson. Neither name could be found in listings of Austin residents at the time, though a Phil Abrahams ran a grocery store in the 100 block of East Pecan Street and lived at 310 East Live Oak.)
10. *Austin Daily Statesman*, 5/26/1886; *Reports of Cases . . . in the Court of Appeals of Texas, 1886*. Case 2271, James O. Phillips v. the State.
11. *Austin Daily Statesman*, 5/26/1886; *Reports of Cases . . . in the Court of Appeals of Texas, 1886*. Case 2271, James O. Phillips v. the State (The newspaper report said Eula went to Fanny Whipple's five or six days before she was murdered, but the appeals court records and the preliminary trial report indicated five to six weeks was correct. In her testimony at the preliminary trial, Delia Campbell said that Eula stayed at Fannie Whipple's house for about two weeks and then went on to May Tobin's house for two days.)
12. *Austin Daily Statesman*, 5/26/1886; *Reports of Cases . . . in the Court of Appeals of Texas, 1886*. Case 2271, James O. Phillips v. the State; *Fort Worth Daily Gazette*, 5/26/1886; *Morrison & Fourmy's General Directory of the City of Austin, 1885-1886* (The appeals court records mentioned a Mr. Dickerson, but John Dickinson was more likely the person named by May Tobin.)

13. *Austin Daily Statesman*, 5/26/1886; *Reports of Cases . . . in the Court of Appeals of Texas, 1886*. Case 2271, James O. Phillips v. the State (As mentioned in the preceding note, the man named by Tobin was likely John T. Dickinson, not Dickerson.)
14. *Reports of Cases . . . in the Court of Appeals of Texas, 1886*. Case 2271, James O. Phillips v. the State; *Morrison & Fourmy's General Directory of the City of Austin, 1885-1886*; 1880 Federal Census.
15. *Austin Daily Statesman*, 5/26/1886; *Reports of Cases . . . in the Court of Appeals of Texas, 1886*. Case 2271, James O. Phillips v. the State.
16. *Reports of Cases . . . in the Court of Appeals of Texas, 1886*. Case 2271, James O. Phillips v. the State.
17. *Austin Daily Statesman*, 5/26/1886; *Reports of Cases . . . in the Court of Appeals of Texas, 1886*. Case 2271, James O. Phillips v. the State; 1880 Federal Census; "Texas Marriages, 1837-1973" (As mentioned in preceding notes, the man named by Campbell was likely John T. Dickinson, not Dickerson.)
18. *Austin Daily Statesman*, 5/26/1886; *Reports of Cases . . . in the Court of Appeals of Texas, 1886*. Case 2271, James O. Phillips v. the State; *Austin Daily Statesman*, 5/27/1886; "Past Sheriffs"; *Mooney & Morrison's General Directory of the City of Austin, 1877-1878*: *Morrison & Fourmy's General Directory of the City of Austin, 1881-1882*; 1880 Federal Census (As mentioned in preceding notes, the man named by Campbell was likely John T. Dickinson, not Dickerson. The 1880 Federal Census listed Kirk's occupation as deputy sheriff.)
19. *Reports of Cases . . . in the Court of Appeals of Texas, 1886*. Case 2271, James O. Phillips v. the State.
20. *Austin Daily Statesman*, 5/26/1886; *Reports of Cases . . . in the Court of Appeals of Texas, 1886*. Case 2271, James O. Phillips v. the State.
21. *Reports of Cases . . . in the Court of Appeals of Texas, 1886*. Case 2271, James O. Phillips v. the State.
22. *Reports of Cases . . . in the Court of Appeals of Texas, 1886*. Case 2271, James O. Phillips v. the State; *Austin Daily Statesman*, 5/26/1886.
23. *Reports of Cases . . . in the Court of Appeals of Texas, 1886*. Case 2271, James O. Phillips v. the State; *Austin Daily Statesman*, 5/26/1886.
24. *Reports of Cases . . . in the Court of Appeals of Texas, 1886*. Case 2271, James O. Phillips v. the State; *Austin Daily Statesman*, 5/26/1886.
25. *Fort Worth Daily Gazette*, 5/26/1886.

Chapter 20

"Blood and Bob"

The Trial of Jimmy Phillips Continues

Before the third day of the trial of Jimmy Phillips resumed, the city of Austin was all abuzz with the scandal created by May Tobin's testimony. "When the people read the newspapers this morning and the names of high public functionaries implicated in the gaiters of the young and handsome, but frail, Mrs. Phillips, now in the ground, the scandal grew in magnitude." A Fort Worth reporter visited Benjamin Baker, the superintendent of public instruction who was said by May Tobin to be a paramour of Eula Phillips. A friend of Baker said that Mr. Baker denied any knowledge of Eula Phillips, that he did not know Eula Phillips, and that he had an alibi that would disprove Tobin's testimony. When told of a rumor that the governor might ask Baker to resign, the friend said that Baker would never resign.[1]

When the trial resumed on the morning of May 26, Jimmy's mother and his two sisters were present in court. Jimmy "looked pale, care-worn and haggard, and as if he had not yet recovered from the terrible wounds in the side of the head received on Christmas eve night, when his young wife's head was split open with the ax of the assassin." The crowds in the courtroom were also not as large, as most people assumed the "most sensational part of the testimony was over." However, a sizeable crowd filled the courtroom.[2]

"Criminal Intimacy"

The first witness of the day was George McCutcheon, testifying for the State. McCutcheon was considered a well-known resident of Williamson County. He owned the farm where Eula and Jimmy lived shortly after they were married. The prosecution's questions to him sought to develop the nature of the relationship between Jimmy and Eula. McCutcheon repeated the episode about the cup that Alma Burditt had described. He told what precipitated the episode. Jimmy had come home from Taylor somewhat drunk and sat down at the supper table with the others. Someone made up a drink of cream, sugar, and whisky. Then, Eula told Jimmy, "'Jim, you look like a fool; your eyes are that big,'" and she made a circle with her thumb and forefinger. Jimmy dared Eula to repeat her comment, and when she did, he threw the cup at her. Then Alma and Eula ran out into the yard. As he rose to throw the cup, Jimmy grabbed a case knife and started after Alma and Eula.

McCutcheon told him to stop. Jimmy asked belligerently, "'Do you interfere in my family affairs?'" McCutcheon replied, "'No, but you must stop. You are making a fool of yourself.'" McCutcheon told Jimmy to wash his face and lie down, which he did. Then Alma and Eula came back inside.[3]

After returning to Austin, Jimmy drank a lot, according to McCutcheon. The two went to the Austin train depot together around the first of December 1885. Along the way, the witness said he told Jimmy to quit drinking, "as he was making everybody about him miserable and unhappy." Jimmy replied that it was not natural for him to act the way he was, that he used to be "cheerful and contented" but was now full of the blues and alcohol. Jimmy then asked McCutcheon if he thought Eula was "too fast." McCutcheon replied, "'I think she is a good and virtuous woman, but may be she talks a little too much.'" Jimmy said he thought so too, but Mrs. Phillips thought Eula was too fast, and Jimmy said if he thought Eula was not "nice and virtuous," he would kill her and then himself. McCutcheon then testified that he was at home on December 24. He traveled to Austin on December 25 with Eula's father, Tom Burditt, reaching there in the afternoon. McCutcheon went directly to Jimmy's room, and Jimmy told him, "'George, Eula is gone and I am d----d near killed, and ought to be dead.'"[4]

The defense then cross-examined McCutcheon, and the intent of the defense team became clear. The line of questioning sought "to fasten upon him the guilt of the murder with which Phillips had been charged." At the time of the murder, McCutcheon was about 36 years old, almost 20 years senior to Eula. His wife, Lovey, had died in March 1885, a week after giving birth to their fifth child, Ardry, who died five months after its mother. So, with his wife's death, McCutcheon was burdened with four children aged 11 to 6 and a dying infant. Still, he apparently had time to make numerous trips to Austin to see Eula. The defense lawyer asked about Jimmy's conversation with McCutcheon on the way to the train depot. McCutcheon said that Jimmy's statement "to the effect that if he had an unfaithful wife he would kill both her and himself, was made in casual conversation. . . . Defendant's wife was not then the subject of conversation." McCutcheon said the only other person he remembered as being present was Albert Highsmith. According to McCutcheon, Jimmy had been drinking at the time.[5]

The defense continued with a rather incriminating line of questioning, clearly trying to cast McCutcheon as the one having a good reason to kill Eula.

> *Question.* "Is it not true that you were in the habit of having carnal intercourse with Eula Phillips while she lived at your house, in Williamson county? You need not answer the question unless you please to do so."
> *Answer.* "I decline to answer the question."
> *Question.* "Were you not in the habit, after she moved to Austin, of coming to Austin and seeking her for that purpose—carnal intercourse?"
> *Answer.* "I did not; not once."
> *Question*. "When were you openly in Austin last before December 25?"

Answer. "I don't know; I can't tell; but I am satisfied it was after the conversation on the street. I was not in Austin on the night of December 24, 1885."

As the questioning continued, McCutcheon "manifested a disposition of resentment that singularly imparted a high degree of excitement to the large audience that thronged the court room." He was clearly not pleased being made the object of suspicion, especially when he was compelled by the defense lawyer to remove "the shoe and sock from his right foot in order to prove that the peculiarity of that member corresponded with the bloody imprint of a foot, preserved upon a wooden panel that had been sawed out of the gallery of Phillip's house." His foot did not fit the bloody footprint from the Phillips gallery, nor did he have a missing toe on his right foot. The man with the missing toe, Nathan Elgin, had been killed over three months prior.[6]

Trying to build an alibi, McCutcheon testified that on Christmas Eve he had been in Williamson County at the place of Captain Fred Mitchell, over 20 miles from Austin. Others in attendance were Tom Mitchell, Jack McCutcheon, "one of the Frame boys and others." McCutcheon said he got to the Mitchell place about 9 o'clock, and the party broke up around midnight, all the men "pretty drunk." McCutcheon then went home and heard about the murder of Eula the next day. He had been summoned to Austin, and he went in with Tom Burditt, Eula's father.[7]

The blistering cross-examination continued. McCutcheon was asked about his acquaintance with Delia Campbell. He said that Delia had once visited Eula when she lived at his place, but that he had been sick for part of that visit.

> Witness had never talked to Delia Campbell about his relations to Eula, or about a criminal intimacy between himself and Eula, either in Williamson county or elsewhere. Witness never, at any time or place, either at home, in Austin, or elsewhere, told Delia Campbell that if Eula threw him off or discontinued her criminal relations with him, he would kill her. Witness never, at any time, at his home in Williamson county, in the presence of Delia Campbell and Albert Highsmith, or any body else, made an attempt upon the life of the defendant with a knife or any other weapon.

He was also asked if he had ever threatened to kill Mrs. Campbell if she told of his carnal relations with Eula, and he denied the charge. Then he was "asked if he had not, upon one occasion bought medicine from Tobin's drug store and delivered it to Mrs. Campbell for the purpose of being used by Eula Phillips to produce abortion." This charge he also emphatically denied.[8]

McCutcheon stated that he did not attend the funeral of Eula Phillips. At the insistence of Edwin J. Ledbetter, a painter who lived about three blocks from the Phillips home, McCutcheon stayed at the Phillips home with Jimmy, "for the purpose of seeing or hearing anything that would throw light upon this tragedy." The defense continued trying to implicate McCutcheon.

> *Question.* "Is it not true that, at about night after Eula's funeral, you were in the parlor at the Phillips house, and did not a child come in and tell old Mrs. Phillips that two officers were at the door; and did you not get up at once and ask to be concealed, saying that the officers were after you? Did not something of this substance occur?"
>
> *Answer.* "Nothing of the sort occurred."
>
> *Question.* "After Eula's death, did you not meet Delia Campbell at Mrs. Creary's, and, during a talk with her, did you not say to her that, if she ever told on you, and what she knew about you and Eula that you would kill her; and did not Delia say that if called upon, she would tell the truth; and did you not then start towards her angrily, and did not she, Delia, then step towards a bureau, in which she had a pistol; and did you not then say to her: 'Would you shoot me?' and did she not reply: 'I will if you lay your hand on me;' and did you not then resume your seat?"
>
> *Answer.* "I remember meeting Delia at Mrs. Creary's, but nothing of which you ask took place."
>
> Question. "Did you not, at another time, on the train, meet Delia Campbell, and again threaten her—threaten to kill her if she told what she knew about you and Eula?"
>
> *Answer.* "I remember meeting her on the train, but I did not threaten her."
>
> *Question.* "Did you not, on two occasions, at Doctor Tobin's drug store, buy chamomile flowers, extract of cotton wood and argot for Eula, to aid her in producing an abortion upon herself, and did you not deliver the said drugs to Eula, in the presence of Delia Campbell, after tearing the labels off the phials?"
>
> *Answer.* "I bought drugs at the instance of Delia Campbell, and gave them to her, but did not remove the labels."

McCutcheon then claimed that he did not know how often he came to Austin after Eula and Jimmy moved back to Austin from Williamson County, but he guessed five or six times. He stated that he came to Austin each time to collect fifteen dollars that Jimmy owed him. He admitted that he gave Eula ten dollars for expenses when she went to Elgin in late November or early December. McCutcheon also said there was "nothing peculiar" about the little toe on his right foot.[9]

McCutcheon then faced another round of questions from the prosecution. He stated that three men in attendance at the trial—Jack McCutcheon, Bob Mitchell, and A.D. Wooldridge—were with him at Captain Fred Mitchell's place on Christmas Eve 1885. He again said that he got home from the Mitchell place about midnight. He denied any involvement with Eula's murder.

> Witness had never threatened to kill Eula; he did not kill her; he did not know that she was going to be killed, though he had feared for some time that the defendant would ultimately kill her. Mr. Creary and witness's brother, Beauregard, were present when witness gave Eula the money to defray her expenses to Elgin. Eula and Mrs. Creary went together that evening to the Phillips house to get Eula's trunk. There was no

concealment about Eula going to Elgin, but she appeared to be afraid to go after her trunk. Eula got her trunk, returned to Mrs. Creary's, and said that defendant met her kindly and put his arms about her neck. Witness saw Eula about a week before her death. She and Delia Campbell invited witness to spend Christmas day with them in Austin.

McCutcheon also noted that he had been a widower for about a year.[10]

The defense then had another go at McCutcheon. McCutcheon said that he awoke Tom Burditt, Eula's father, upon his return from the Mitchell place, and he gave his drinking as the reason for that act. Burditt apparently was staying with McCutcheon at the time and occupied a bedroom across the hall from McCutcheon's room. McCutcheon also stated that he did not tell Jimmy Phillips about giving money to Eula to go to Elgin. When he was in the defendant's room after he was wounded, McCutcheon said someone else was there, but he could not remember who, though he thought it was either Mrs. Phillips or Mrs. Creary. McCutcheon claimed that Jimmy appeared rational on that occasion. McCutcheon ended his long occupancy of the witness chair by swearing that if he had killed Eula, he would now confess it under oath. He did not offer any such confession.[11]

More Witnesses

The next witness for the State was Annie Dyer, who lived on the same block as the Phillips home. She stated that she was called by Mr. Phillips sometime between midnight and one o'clock on Christmas morning. She dressed quickly and went to the house, where she saw Mr. Phillips, Mrs. Phillips, and George Allen dressed in the clothes she had seen them wearing the evening before. Mrs. Dyer said

> that she herself cut the garments from Eula Phillips, which had been tightly twisted into a rope on her shoulders as if having been caused from dragging. That the skin was all dragged off on each side of her spine from the waist to her shoulders, and the back of her hair filled with dirt and chips and saturated with blood, showing, evidently, that she had been dragged along the ground.

Mrs. Dyer also testified that about six weeks before Eula's murder, she had heard a quarrel at the Phillips house. A man, not Mr. Phillips, said loudly, "God d--n you I'll kill you.'" Then she heard a woman's voice calling for the police. This quarrel occurred on the night of the argument between Jimmy and Delia Campbell. Cross-examined, Mrs. Dyer said that when she went to bed just before midnight on Christmas Eve, everything was quiet at the Phillips house.[12]

Justice William Von Rosenberg, Jr., testified for the State that he arrived at the murder scene after a crowd had gathered but before Eula's body was discovered. He said he saw splotches of blood on the gallery from the door of

Jimmy and Eula's room to the steps and into the yard. He followed the blood with some dogs to Eula's body. Under cross-examination, Justice Von Rosenberg identified several planks in evidence that he had instructed to be cut from the gallery floor along the line of blood. He also stated that he had examined the fence between the Phillips' yard and the alley near where Eula's body was found.

> On the side of a plank near the top of the fence the witness saw a blood spot, between three-fourths and an inch wide, and one and a half or two inches long. A piece of scantling, two by four inches, lay across the breast of the body. Witness thought he was the first to find the body. It lay from one hundred and fifteen to one hundred and forty feet distant from the defendant's room. The night was a bright moonlight night. The blood spot on the fence was not a splotch, but such a spot as would be made by the ball of the thumb or a finger. Witness saw no blood on the fence post.

Justice Von Rosenberg noted that Eula's body "lay on the back, face up and legs apart, the knees crooked or a little raised. There was but one garment on the body, and it was unevenly drawn up about the upper part, partially covering the bust." He could not say if the garment had any blood on it, but he did indicate that Eula's head rested in a considerable pool of blood.[13]

Justice Von Rosenberg continued the cross-examination by stating that bloodhounds were brought in to follow tracks found in an adjoining yard by George Allen.

> The dogs led thence into the Phillips yard, across it into the alley, thence down the alley, westward, down the street by the colored church, through a ravine that ran from a branch, thence to the bridge on the bank, thence back, thence to the house on the Burlage place, thence across Shoal creek, thence to the hills near the old military academy, in a northwest direction, in the neighborhood of General Shelley's place, and thence into the post oaks. The young dog now led in leash, and the witness and his party followed the old dog through Clarksville, when the old dog was placed in leash. The party followed the dogs to Clarksville, one and a half miles from town, and went on to Cook's place, a mile farther.

Justice Von Rosenberg admitted he had little experience with bloodhounds, so he could not say if the dogs were actually trailing anything on that trip. He was also shown a blood of spot in the alley, and the dogs were taken there. He could not say for certain the spot was blood, and he could not say for certain that an impression near the spot was made by a human foot. The impression was in the middle of the alley, directly opposite where the body and the blood on the fence were found.[14]

The prosecution then asked Justice Von Rosenberg a few more questions. He confessed that "the pursuit with the dogs occurred on the evening of December 25," or at least 14 hours after the murder. The justice had no idea how many people had been in the alley in the intervening hours. He concluded his testimony by saying he had noticed several scratches on Eula's body, which led him to believe that her body had been dragged along the ground.[15]

The next witness for the State was Sergeant G.R. Thompson, in charge of the group of penitentiary bloodhounds. He and two dogs, one of them his favorite, Old Bob, reached the Phillips home around four o'clock on Christmas afternoon.

> The dogs were started at about the place where the dead body of the woman was said to have been found. Thence the dogs went towards the Phillips house, creating considerable excitement among the on lookers. Witness stopped the dogs and circled them around the spot where the body was found, to see if they could strike a trail. They were then put on a track in an adjoining yard. They led to the alley fence, were lifted over, and went thence down the alley into a street and out into the country. Justice Von Rosenberg was with the party. The dogs were followed until the old dog appeared to want to go through a wire fence, some two miles from town. Witness then leashed the dogs and led them on about a mile further. Witness could see no evidence that the dogs were following tracks.

Ironically, the sergeant could not cut the wire fence to continue the search because the legislature had passed a statute against fence-cutting earlier in the year in an attempt to settle problems on the range.[16]

Thompson and the dogs returned to the city. After supper, Thompson requested to make another search, and police officers present consented.

> Starting from the spot at which the body of Eula Phillips had been found in the yard, "Bob" followed directly the course leading into the room in which Phillips lay wounded, and, although there were several persons in the room, he passed by them all, and approaching the bed, reared up on it and smelt Jim Phillips. Witness then called the dog off, and the hound led the way into an adjoining room, which was lighted by the reflection from another room, and began smelling a bundle, which witness opened and found to contain bloody white garments and a bloody pillow. From there the dog trailed into the parlor to the corpse of Eula Phillips, but was quickly called away by witness because of his frightening the ladies in the room. Next the dog led the way around the house to a tub containing bloody water, and here witness discontinued his investigation.

When cross-examined, Thompson said that Old Bob was a cold trailer, but he could not say for certain how cold a trail the dog could follow. He did know that Bob could follow a trail six or eight hours old, but his ability to follow a colder trail depended on the climatic conditions, dew, brush, and other factors. Because Bob would howl when he struck a trail, and because he did not howl during the two searches, Thompson concluded that Bob had failed to find a trail to follow.[17]

The string of witnesses for the State continued. Next was E.J. Ledbetter, who lived a few blocks from the Phillips home. He said that he was present at the Phillips home on Saturday night, December 26, 1885. Sometime between two and four o'clock on Sunday morning, Mrs. Phillips took a bowl of water into Jimmy's room, took off his red socks, and washed his feet. When she finished, she took the bowl of water out of the room, but Ledbetter did not know what she did with it. He said that she did not appear to be acting secretly.[18]

R.B. Mitchell, Jack McCutcheon, and A.D. Wooldridge were the next three witnesses. Mitchell said that he was present at the trial at the insistence of Jack McCutcheon. Mitchell said he saw George McCutcheon at Captain Fred Mitchell's place on the evening of December 24, 1885. Mitchell stated that George McCutcheon left there about midnight to go home. Mitchell saw George McCutcheon the next day, Christmas, waiting for a train in Hutto to go to Austin with Tom Burditt, Eula's father. Jack McCutcheon testified that he went to Captain Mitchell's ranch with his brother, George, about nine o'clock on Christmas Eve. They left about midnight. Jack McCutcheon stated that he "got Wooldridge and R. B. Mitchell to attend this trial, to prove the thereabouts of his brother on that night, because he had been informed that an effort would be made to implicate him in this trouble." A.D. Wooldridge claimed that he attended a "stag dance" at Captain Mitchell's place, about 24 miles from Austin, on Christmas Eve, with George McCutcheon and several others. He said about "ten old stags were in attendance," and that George McCutcheon left about midnight. A.D. Wooldridge was the father of A.P. Wooldridge, the head of the Citizens' Committee for Public Safety, the group that was formed after the Christmas Eve murders.[19]

Tom Burditt, the father of Eula Phillips, testified for the State that he saw George McCutcheon on McCutcheon's place in Williamson County between midnight and one o'clock on Christmas morning 1885. He also rode the train to Austin with McCutcheon on Christmas day, arriving in the evening. Burditt said that George McCutcheon had told him about a month before Eula's murder that McCutcheon had loaned Eula $10 to pay for her expenses when she went to Elgin. Burditt told McCutcheon he considered the loan "a great favor," and that he would repay McCutcheon the money.[20]

Finally, Mrs. Sophia Phillips was recalled by the prosecution to refresh her memory about when she first discovered the bloody tracks near the bed in Jimmy and Eula's room. She stated that she "had but an imperfect idea of the lapse of time after she discovered the murder, but thought that not more than fifteen or twenty minutes elapsed from the time she discovered the murder until she discovered the stains she took to be bloody foot tracks by the bedside." She said that she herself got blood on the heels and balls of her feet when she went in Jimmy's room. She affirmed that she did not wash Jimmy's feet until early Sunday morning, and at that time there was no blood on them. Mrs. Phillips admitted that she was exhausted on the night of the murder and left others to care for things, so she really knew nothing of many things that occurred that night. When Mrs. Phillips ended her testimony, the State rested.[21]

After the parade of State witnesses gave their testimony, the prosecution had produced little direct evidence to show that Jimmy Phillips was guilty of the murder of his wife. The strategy of the prosecution was clearly to show that young Eula Phillips was an unfaithful wife who had fueled Jimmy's violent jealousy, thus providing a motive for the murder. The prosecution also placed great weight on the fact that Old Bob, the bloodhound, had failed to strike a trail leading away from the house but instead went to Jimmy's room and, bypassing others present, went to Jimmy in the bed, as if the dog had sniffed out the guilty party. But more effort seemed expended to show that George McCutcheon was not guilty than to show that Jimmy Phillips was guilty. At this point, most people believed that Jimmy Phillips would be acquitted.

Notes

Title: *Fort Worth Daily Gazette*, 5/27/1886.

1. *Fort Worth Daily Gazette*, 5/27/1886.
2. *Fort Worth Daily Gazette*, 5/27/1886.
3. *Reports of Cases . . . in the Court of Appeals of Texas, 1886*. Case 2271, James O. Phillips v. the State; *Austin Daily Statesman*, 5/27/1886; *Fort Worth Daily Gazette*, 5/27/1886.
4. *Reports of Cases . . . in the Court of Appeals of Texas, 1886*. Case 2271, James O. Phillips v. the State; *Austin Daily Statesman*, 5/27/1886.
5. *Austin Daily Statesman*, 5/27/1886; *Reports of Cases . . . in the Court of Appeals of Texas, 1886*. Case 2271, James O. Phillips v. the State; "Lovey S. McCutcheon"; "Ardry 'Aubry' McCutcheon."
6. *Reports of Cases . . . in the Court of Appeals of Texas, 1886*. Case 2271, James O. Phillips v. the State; *Austin Daily Statesman*, 5/27/1886; *Fort Worth Daily Gazette*, 5/27/1886.
7. *Reports of Cases . . . in the Court of Appeals of Texas, 1886*. Case 2271, James O. Phillips v. the State; *Austin Daily Statesman*, 5/27/1886 (As noted earlier, some reports placed Burditt in Bell County on the night of the murder. Other reports placed him at a Christmas party with George McCutcheon in Williamson County.)
8. *Reports of Cases . . . in the Court of Appeals of Texas, 1886*. Case 2271, James O. Phillips v. the State; *Austin Daily Statesman*, 5/27/1886.
9. *Reports of Cases . . . in the Court of Appeals of Texas, 1886*. Case 2271, James O. Phillips v. the State; *Austin Daily Statesman*, 5/27/1886; *Morrison & Fourmy's General Directory of the City of Austin, 1885-1886*.
10. *Reports of Cases . . . in the Court of Appeals of Texas, 1886*. Case 2271, James O. Phillips v. the State.
11. *Reports of Cases . . . in the Court of Appeals of Texas, 1886*. Case 2271, James O. Phillips v. the State.
12. *Austin Daily Statesman*, 5/27/1886; *Reports of Cases . . . in the Court of Appeals of Texas, 1886*. Case 2271, James O. Phillips v. the State; *Fort Worth Daily Gazette*, 5/27/1886 (Some newspaper reports said Annie Dyer lived in part of the Phillips house or in the Phillips yard.)
13. *Reports of Cases . . . in the Court of Appeals of Texas, 1886*. Case 2271, James O. Phillips v. the State.

14. *Reports of Cases . . . in the Court of Appeals of Texas, 1886*. Case 2271, James O. Phillips v. the State.
15. *Reports of Cases . . . in the Court of Appeals of Texas, 1886*. Case 2271, James O. Phillips v. the State.
16. *Austin Daily Statesman*, 5/27/1886; *Reports of Cases . . . in the Court of Appeals of Texas, 1886*. Case 2271, James O. Phillips v. the State.
17. *Austin Daily Statesman*, 5/27/1886; *Reports of Cases . . . in the Court of Appeals of Texas, 1886*. Case 2271, James O. Phillips v. the State; *Fort Worth Daily Gazette*, 5/27/1886.
18. *Reports of Cases . . . in the Court of Appeals of Texas, 1886*. Case 2271, James O. Phillips v. the State; *Austin Daily Statesman*, 5/27/1886.
19. *Reports of Cases . . . in the Court of Appeals of Texas, 1886*. Case 2271, James O. Phillips v. the State; *Austin Daily Statesman*, 5/27/1886; 1880 Federal Census.
20. *Reports of Cases . . . in the Court of Appeals of Texas, 1886*. Case 2271, James O. Phillips v. the State; *Austin Daily Statesman*, 5/27/1886.
21. *Reports of Cases . . . in the Court of Appeals of Texas, 1886*. Case 2271, James O. Phillips v. the State; *Austin Daily Statesman*, 5/27/1886.

Chapter 21

"Almost Impossible and Entirely Improbable"

The Defense Presents Its Case

The prosecution in the Jimmy Phillips case rested after over a dozen witnesses and three days of testimony. The defense began its case late on the third day of the Jimmy Phillips trial. The only defense witness called on May 26 was John P. Kirk. He was questioned in an attempt to impeach the statement made by Mrs. Sophia Phillips that Kirk had sent Delia Campbell twenty dollars through Eugene Maguire, an employee of the Houston and Texas Central railway, "for the purpose of keeping her away, that the married men of Austin might be shielded from shame; but the court, upon objection of the state's attorney, declined to admit the evidence, on the ground of immateriality." At that point, court was adjourned until 9 o'clock the following morning.[1]

When the trial resumed on the morning of May 27, 1886, the defense first recalled Justice William Von Rosenberg, Jr. Von Rosenberg's testimony was meant to identify two pieces of plank taken from the floor of the Phillips house. One plank contained the bloody track of a right foot, the other the bloody track of a left foot. The planks were "identified and exhibited to the jury as ghastly relics of the presence of the author or authors of the mysterious murder of Eula Phillips." Upon his identification of the two planks, Von Rosenberg was released as a witness.[2]

The next witness called by the defense was George D. Allen, the brother-in-law of Jimmy Phillips. George Allen was about 27 years old at the time of the murder. He worked as a clerk at the dry goods store of Frank E. Jones at 203 East Pecan. He had married Jimmy's sister Dora in May 1879 and lived in part of the Phillips house at 304 West Hickory. Allen testified that he arrived home about 10 o'clock on Christmas Eve 1885. As he passed Jimmy and Eula's room, a light was burning in the room, and he heard them playing with the baby. He then went to bed around 11 o'clock and fell asleep in about 15 minutes. Later, he was aroused by Mrs. Phillips, "calling to him that 'Buddie is knocked in the head, and Eula is gone.'" Allen and his wife awoke instantly. He put on his pants and boots and quickly left his room.

> As he opened the door onto the gallery he discovered, by the moonlight, a path of blood along the gallery, but did not stop to examine whence it had come or where it ended. Upon entering the room of defendant, he found him rolling in bed and his little

child sitting in bed surrounded by blood. After glancing around, but without asking any questions as to who committed the deed, he went in great haste to notify the officers of what had occurred and to procure the services of a physician, Dr. Litten.

When Allen got back to the house, he met Mr. Phillips, who had gone to get Dr. McLaughlin. Allen next went to the police station and told Grooms Lee what had happened. Allen then headed toward Congress Avenue, but he met Justice Von Rosenberg and some other men in a hack, so he told them where to go and returned to the house himself. Allen pointed out the blood trail to Justice Von Rosenberg, and at that time he learned of the earlier murder of Sue Hancock in another part of town. Von Rosenberg followed the blood trail "to where the body of Eula Phillips lay stretched upon its back in an almost nude condition, and with the forehead mashed in to the depth of an inch and a half."[3]

Allen continued by testifying that later on Christmas Day he found blood on the fence and on a fence post near where Eula's body was discovered.

> The blood on the fence was on the top plank and had apparently been put there by the ball of the hand. The blood on the post was in spots which seemed to have been dropped. Witness also saw blood on the lower plank of the fence, which was put there by contact with some bloody substance. Witness saw, in the second yard from Phillips' place, several bare foot tracks, made evidently by some person leaping from the fence. Those tracks, three in number, pointed diagonally toward the alley fence, and were distinctly marked by the toes. Witness pointed them out to Von Rosenberg.

In the alley about a hundred feet from where Eula's body was found, Allen discovered a spot of blood about the size of a quarter and near it an impression of a foot. Allen surmised that the blood clot came from the foot that made the impression. "Some feathers adhered to that clot of blood, and witness observed chicken feathers in the alley near the point where the body was found, and where the blood was found on the fence and post." Allen also observed a small quantity of blood specks on the privy near the alley and not far from where the blood clot and foot impression were located. The blood appeared to have been thrown against the privy. Allen did not recall if the elder Mr. Phillips was in Jimmy's room when he arrived, but he knew not more than two minutes elapsed between the time he was alerted by Mrs. Phillips and the time he reached Jimmy's room. Allen credited his fast response to his experience as a fireman. He entered Jimmy's room through the west door, which he pushed open, it being closed at the time.[4]

Cross-examined by the prosecution, Allen stated that he did not recall testifying in the preliminary trial that the back door of Jimmy's room was open when he reached it, which would contradict his statement moments earlier. Allen reiterated that he saw blood on the gallery floor as soon as he opened the door to his own room, and he also saw blood on the ground. Allen clarified that when he reached Jimmy's room, Jimmy was lying in bed, on the front side, and the baby was sitting up in the bed, crying. The cover was pulled up around Jimmy's waist, but Allen could not say if Jimmy had on pants. The lamp was burning in the room, so there was enough light to see well. Allen stated that he looked around the room, noticing blood on the front part of the bed but none on the back part. He said he did not pay any special attention to Jimmy or speak to him, but left immediately to get Dr. Litten.[5]

The prosecution continued to question Allen, pressing him on the matter of whether Jimmy was wearing pants at the time Allen first saw him on the night of the murder.

> *Question.* "Did you not find him with his pants on, and did you not say to him: "Jim, why Jim, haven't you been to bed?" And didn't he answer: 'No, by G-d, I am not going to'?"
> *Answer.* "No; not one word of it."
> *Question.* "Did you not, at Jones's store in Austin, in last January, say to John P. Kirk that, when you went into defendant's room on the night of the tragedy, he was lying on the bed with his pants on, and that you said to him, defendant: 'Have you not gone to bed yet?' and he replied: 'No, nor do I think I can'?"
> *Answer.* "No, I said no such thing, and Kirk knows I did not."

Allen restated that when he first went to Jimmy's room, he saw only Jimmy and the baby, not Jimmy's parents. He then went immediately to get the doctor and to notify the police. Allen said that he "saw Eula's body where it was found, and soon after it was found. Three pieces of scantling lay across the body; two across the breast and one across the abdomen." At that point, Allen was allowed to leave the witness chair.[6]

The next witness for the defense was Albert S. Burleson, a lawyer who boarded with his partner, Thomas Sneed, at 310 East Hickory. Burleson testified that he was at the Phillips house early on Christmas morning 1885. He stated that he saw blood on the top plank of the alley fence near where Eula's body was found. The blood was in the form of four bloody fingerprints, on the alley side of the fence. Burleson concluded that the bloody imprint "appeared to have been made by the palm of a hand and clinching of fingers." Burleson also searched for tracks or footprints in the alley but found none. Cross-examined by the prosecution, Burleson did admit that the bloody imprint on the fence could have been made "just by a man putting his hand on the fence without getting over it."[7]

"Profound Temporary Insensibility"

Dr. Josephus Cummings followed as the next witness for the defense. He was considered a very important witness for Jimmy's side. Cummings testified that he was called to the Phillips house about one o'clock on Christmas morning 1885. He found Jimmy in "an unconscious condition, wounded about in the manner described by Doctor Litten" in his earlier testimony. Cummings believed that two or more blows were necessary to make the wound, and that the wound "was of a most serious and dangerous character, and was sufficient to produce profound temporary insensibility." The doctor did not find any fracture of the skull. Cummings stated that he cared for Jimmy for two weeks before he was placed in jail, and then after his release, in conjunction with Dr. Litten, for about two months. He could not say that Jimmy had recovered or would recover entirely from the effects of the wound. But his "positive opinion" was that Jimmy's wound could not have been self-inflicted. Cummings also examined the dead body of Eula Phillips.

> It was nude from the bust down. The legs were apart and the privates were distended. Witness removed a white opaque fluid from the vagina, which resembled the male semen, and at the time thought it likely the woman had been outraged after death. He saw no blood on the legs. The wound on her forehead was the cause of her death.

Cummings also said that Eula had a slight wound on one ear, but that wound was inconsequential. He stated that "the probabilities were that she had been ravished," and he believed she had been.[8]

The prosecution then cross-examined Dr. Cummings about the fluid found in Eula's vagina. Cummings said that he had examined the fluid under a microscope

> but found it to contain no vital or life imparting germs, such as usually inhabit the male semen. Such germs, however, are not always present in the male semen. As a rule the male semen always contains the germs, but certain conditions of the body destroy them, sometimes before and sometimes after deposit. The fluid was thinner, and of a shade lighter color than the male semen usually is.

Cummings ended his testimony by emphasizing that he "thought it almost impossible and entirely improbable, that defendant could have inflicted the wound upon himself. Upon the whole, he thought it impossible." To emphasize his point fully to the jury, Dr. Cummings had Jimmy Phillips come before the witness stand. The ax used in the attack was produced, and Dr. Cummings illustrated to the jury just where and how Jimmy had received his wounds.[9]

Dr. C.E. Fisher also testified for the defense. Fisher described Jimmy's wound in much the same way that Dr. Litten and Dr. Cummings did. Fisher, however, said that "in his opinion, the blow that caused the wound was struck by some one from behind the defendant. The blow, to have made that wound, must have been struck with great force." If Jimmy was struck from behind, certainly he could not have been lying face-up in bed when attacked. After carefully studying the wound, Fisher was satisfied that "it was next to impossible for the defendant to have inflicted that wound upon himself." When cross-examined, though, Fisher "stated that he could not swear that it was impossible for defendant to have inflicted the wound himself, but he did not believe it possible, and it was entirely improbable." He described the wound as very serious, inflicted on one of the hardest bones in the human skeleton.

Fisher also believed that Jimmy's skull was fractured, and "this view was strengthened by the fact that the fluid injected into the wound ran through into the orifice of the ear." The intent of the testimony of Dr. Fisher and, earlier, Dr. Cummings, was to show that Jimmy had received two blows to the head, and the first would have stunned him so much that he could not have inflicted the second blow. As a result, they had to be struck by someone else, and "if his wife had struck him such a blow on the head he could not have killed her afterward, much less drag her away to the back of the premises. If he struck her first, it seems equally impossible for her to have struck back with the violence necessary to inflict such injuries as he received."[10]

Another important witness for the defense was United States Deputy Marshal Harry M. White. He testified that he was at the Phillips house soon after the murder and again later. White found "tracks in the defendant's room, on the gallery of the Phillips house, and on the Allen gallery, and blood marks on the fence dividing the yard from the alley." White measured the tracks using paper, and later applied a ruler to the paper to gain dimensions. All of the tracks were similar in size, leading White to conclude that they were all made by the same person. The width across the ball of the foot of all the tracks measured from "from four to four and a quarter inches, the length in each case being ten and a half inches." White made no mention of a missing toe on the tracks. White also observed the track in the alley with the blood clot near it, and walled off the area with sticks to

> prevent obliteration by curious searchers. That track showed a blood spot as though impressed by a small quantity of blood adhering to the middle of the foot, and a clot of blood rested on the side as though cut from the foot by the sand or gravel. Witness measured this track as well as he could, and found the width to correspond with the other measurements, but, the impression of the heel and toes being indistinct, it was impossible for witness to get the length accurately. Some small feathers were adhering to the blood spot near this track.

White also saw the blood on the fence and on the privy. He described the bloody imprint on the fence much as Albert Burleson had. White believed the blood on the fence post had dripped from the foot of a person climbing over the fence.[11]

Upon cross-examination, White stated that the bloody mark on the fence showed a palm print on the yard side and finger marks on the alley side. He had made the observation of the bloody mark on the fence during the daytime, and he did not know how many people had been in the alley between the time of the murder and the time of his investigation. He did say that several people were in attendance when he measured the footprint in the alley. George Allen had told him about that track, and that Mrs. Creary and other people saw the track, too. The track was about twenty feet up the alley from where Eula's body was found, and the ground near the track was composed of earth and ashes, making it softer than the ground where the body was discovered. White saw no other tracks between the point where the body had lain and the track in the alley, but he did see a bloody track in the Phillips yard near where the body was found, though he did not know if anyone else had seen the track in the yard. White noted that he worked alone, but that "considerable rivalry arose between the different policemen and detectives working on the case." He was not employed by the Phillips family to develop a case for the defense. He did, however, live on the Phillips premises in the house of Mrs. Annie Dyer, his sister, who had earlier testified for the prosecution. Because of his law enforcement background, "the thoroughness of his investigation, and his experience in ferreting out crime," White's evidence was considered vital for the defense.[12]

Frank E. Jones, George Allen's employer, testified next for the defense. He was present at the Phillips house on Christmas morning. He observed the bloody imprint on the fence, which he believed was made "by the pressure of a human hand." He thought the blood on the privy had been thrown off from something. He also saw the clot of blood in the alley near what seemed to be a footprint. Cross-examined, Jones said that the blood clot was about five inches from the apparent footprint in the alley. He noted that there were many other tracks in the alley because people were going up and down the alley. Jones had no idea how the track came to be there or who made it. He said that none of the tracks he saw in the alley were bloody. He also saw no indications of a person having climbed the fence at the point of the bloody imprint on the fence.[13]

Charles E. Booth was the next witness for the defense. Booth was a clerk at his father's furniture store at 408 East Pecan. He testified that on Christmas Eve 1885, between 5:30 and 6:00 in the evening, Jimmy Phillips came to the store to pay $5.00 for furniture he had recently purchased on the installment plan. At that time, Jimmy was sober. Cross-examined by the prosecution, Booth said that the furniture store was three blocks east of Congress Avenue, or about eight and a half blocks from the Phillips house. "Austin city blocks were two hundred and seventy-six feet long," making the distance between the two points under half a mile. Booth's testimony attempted to show that early on Christmas Eve, a few hours before the murder, Jimmy "had no murderous intention toward his wife, or he would not have concerned himself to pay for the furniture."[14]

Next to testify for the defense was M.C. Miller. Miller said he lived next door to the Phillips house and about sixty or seventy feet from the point where Eula's body was discovered. Miller said he arrived home around 10 o'clock on Christmas Eve and retired about an hour later. Before he fell asleep, he heard a noise in his yard. Investigating the noise, Miller found several cows in his yard, which he drove away. He was not certain what time he drove the cows away, thinking it was around midnight, but he said at the time there was no disturbance at the Phillips house to draw his attention. He went back to bed, but before he got to sleep he was called by Mr. Phillips, who told him of the murder and asked him to go to the house. However, because his wife was greatly alarmed, Miller did not go to the Phillips house that night.[15]

Charles Raymond, a printer who lived at 304 San Gabriel, next took the witness stand for the defense. Raymond gave additional testimony about the various blood splotches observed around the Phillips property, corroborating the testimony of other witnesses. He stated that he nursed Jimmy in his room on Christmas day and left there about 5:30 that evening. He returned about 8:00 that night and sat up with Jimmy until about midnight. Raymond testified that during all the time he was nursing Jimmy in Jimmy's room, George McCutcheon did not come to the room. When cross-examined by the prosecution, Raymond noted that Eula Phillips was buried at about 4 o'clock on the afternoon of December 26, 1885. Raymond attended the funeral at Oakwood Cemetery on the east side of Austin, so he did not know what happened at the Phillips house during that time. Raymond sat with Jimmy on alternating days, but he did not enter Jimmy's room on December 26. He also did not see or hear E.J. Ledbetter invite George McCutcheon into Jimmy's room on Christmas night. Raymond said he thought that the southbound International and Great Northern train reached Austin after 5:00 on Christmas evening. He said that he knew Tom Burditt by sight, but he did not see Burditt in Jimmy's room before he left at midnight. He did see Tom Burditt at the Phillips house later. Raymond reiterated that if anyone had come into Jimmy's room while he was nursing Jimmy, he would have noticed that person. George McCutcheon did not come in the room while Raymond was there.[16]

Ham Riley also served as a nurse for Jimmy on the Wednesday and Thursday following Christmas, or about a week after the murder. Testifying for the defense, Riley said that Jimmy was unconscious during most of his time there, but Jimmy did awaken on occasion before he would again "go off into foolishness." During one of those lucid moments, after recognizing Riley, Jimmy said, "'Them fellows hit me a h-ll of a lick.'" Riley asked Jimmy whom he meant, but before giving an answer, Jimmy drifted off into unconsciousness again. Riley noted that Jimmy's "intervals of reason were very brief." Cross-examined, Riley said that in his lucid moments, Jimmy would ask for water or medicine, or call out the name of a friend. Raymond could not get Jimmy to tell him who "'them fellows'" were, nor did he succeed in getting Jimmy into a "connected conversation."[17]

Monroe Miller, who ran an undertaking business next to his Eclipse Livery Stable on East Bois d'Arc, was the next witness for the defense. Miller had immediate supervision of the body of Eula Phillips and the preparation of it for burial. Miller testified that the wound on Eula's forehead "was almost horizontal across the forehead—not perpendicular, as stated by Dr. Litten" the day before. According to Miller, "the wound ran from the center of the forehead, to the left and a little downward, inclining to the left temple. It did not range up and down the forehead. . . . The wound was deepest in the center, and shallowed as it ran downward towards the left temple." Miller filled the indentation with cotton and used court plaster to secure the lips of the wound.[18]

"Bloody Impressions"

In the evening session of the trial on May 27, the defense staged a dramatic demonstration to show that Jimmy's footprints did not match the footprints left on the gallery at the Phillips house. "The tracks had been sawed out of the flooring and preserved in all their hideous distinctness." Jimmy, with the jury present, took off his shoes and socks and stepped in a platter of ink. He then stepped on a pine board, making two tracks.

> The crowd in the court room got on tiptoe as the prisoner stood and Maj. Walton fitted his client's foot to the terrible track left by the bloody fiend as he bore the bleeding body of Mrs. Phillips out into the back yard, where it was found nude, with the knees drawn up and pieces of wood across the arms. The audience drew a long breath when it was found young Phillips' foot did not fit the murderer's track, which was both longer and broader than his. Still further to illustrate, the prisoner was made to take up Walton, who is a large man, in his arms and again stand in the assassin's tracks. Still his foot failed to fill it.

Major Walton was said to weigh about 175 pounds, and Eula weighed only about 100 pounds.[19]

Then Thomas H. Wheeless, a notary public in Austin, was introduced as a witness for the defense. Wheeless stated that he had made accurate measurements of the footprints on the gallery boards procured by Justice Von Rosenberg, as well as the ink tracks made by Jimmy on the deal board in the courtroom. Wheeless gave his findings.

> "The defendant's track made with ink on the ironing board, with Major Walton in his arms, measures across the ball of the foot three and three-eighths inches. Another like test measures three and seven-sixteenths inches. The defendant's track, made with his own but without other weight, is three and three-eighths inches across the ball of the foot. Another like test three and three-eighths inches across the ball of the foot. Defendant's toe and ball of foot track made with Major Walton in his arms, measures across the ball of the foot three and five eighths inches. The panel with bloody imprint upon it is placed before me. The track across the ball of the foot measures four and one-eighth inches. From the end of the big toe to the hollow of the foot measures five and a quarter inches. The ink track made by defendant with Major Walton in his arms measures four and three-eighths inches from the end of the toe to the hollow of the foot."

In other words, Jimmy's footprint did not match the footprint found on the gallery at the Phillips house. When cross-examined by the prosecution, Wheeless did admit that "'the tracks here made by the defendant in ink have enlarged since they were made—spread—but they evaporate quite quickly; much quicker than blood will dry." Wheeless concluded his testimony by pointing out the blood track would enlarge more than the ink track.[20]

The discussion of footprints was advanced by the next witness for the defense, Evan Campbell, who owned a furniture store on East Pecan with his brother. Campbell was at the Phillips house on Christmas morning at around seven or eight o'clock. He saw the place where Eula's body was said to have been found, as well as "blood on the fence, foot prints on the outside and drops of blood on the fence post, on the inside of the fence, at the place where he saw the spot." He also "saw a foot track and a blood spot with feathers adhering to it further up the alley, and still further up he saw blood on an out house." Cross-examined by the prosecution, Campbell said he thought the feathers in the alley were chicken feathers. He said the clot of blood in the alley appeared to have been dropped from a shoe, but he could not tell if the track near the blood clot was made by a shoe or boot. "It was a track, and near it was the clot of blood and feathers." Campbell looked for other tracks in the alley but gave up the search as futile because of the great number of people who had been walking in the alley since the murder. Campbell also noted that there was little blood on the top of the fence but enough to make him think that the bloody imprint was left by someone scaling the fence. He said that he noticed tracks along the trail of blood from the house and also where the body had lain, but he could not identify them. "'They were simply blood impressions made by the foot, but not defined tracks. The route of blood and of the dragging of the body, part of the way, were clearly defined, and tracks, or what I took to be tracks, of blood accompanied it. . . . I saw no bare foot tracks that could be identified as such in the yard. There were bloody impressions that I took to be tracks.'"[21]

Campbell was then re-examined by the defense. He said that after he saw the feathers by the blood clot in the alley, he returned to the point on the fence where the bloody imprint was. He wanted to see if there were feathers by the fence, suggesting that the feathers might have been carried into the alley from that point. Campbell did see feathers by the fence. Campbell was adamant in saying that he could not tell how the tracks were made.

> "I saw the impression of a foot track in the alley by the clot of blood, but I do not undertake to say that the track was made by a boot, shoe or bare foot, although counsel for the State have tried hard to make me say it was a boot or shoe track. I don't know what it was made with. The ball of the foot was plainest. I can't swear it was a foot print at all. I thought it was then and think so yet, but it was not distinct enough for me to swear it was a foot track."

With that confession, Campbell's testimony ended.[22]

Delia Campbell was recalled to the stand, this time as a witness for the defense. The purpose of her testimony was to provide "an impeachment of the denial of George McCutcheon that his relations with Eula Phillips had not been criminal." On the day before, the defense had attempted to throw the shadow of guilt on George McCutcheon, and Delia Campbell's recall to the stand was meant to reinforce that attempt. Mrs. Campbell testified that

> she was at George McCutcheon's house, off and on, for about twelve weeks. She never heard George McCutcheon threaten Eula or utter threats against her. He tried once, while witness was on a visit to his house, to kill the defendant with a rock and

> a knife, but was held and restrained by the witness and Eula.
> He had been drinking and had one of his "spells."

In fact, Mrs. Campbell said that McCutcheon's "threats and confessions all, with the exception of one were made while McCutcheon was in one of his 'spells' of raving unconsciousness." When McCutcheon threatened to kill Jimmy, he was in "a state of delirium." Mrs. Campbell said that McCutcheon made the threat because he believed Jimmy had stolen money from him. "Part of the money was afterwards found hidden away in a crib and the balance secreted beneath the flooring in McCutcheon's room."[23]

According to Mrs. Campbell, the "relations between George McCutcheon and Eula appeared to be and were intimate." McCutcheon himself had told her about their intimate relationship at the Phillips house several weeks before Eula was murdered. McCutcheon also "bought extract of cottonwood, chamomile flowers, ergot and another medicine at Doctor Tobin's drug store, in Austin, for the purpose of producing an abortion on Eula." McCutcheon ripped the labels off the bottles and gave the bottles to Eula while in Mrs. Campbell's presence. The witness also testified that McCutcheon twice threatened to kill her if she told of his intimate relationship with Eula. One threat occurred at the home of Mrs. Creary, Delia's sister, on the day that Jimmy made bail and was released from jail.

> George McCutcheon asked the witness what she had testified
> on the habeas corpus proceeding. Witness replied that she did
> not know. McCutcheon then said: "If you give me away I will
> kill you." Witness laughed in a manner to anger him, and he
> strode towards her. Witness stepped towards a bureau in which
> she had a pistol, when McCutcheon stepped up and asked:
> "Would you shoot me?" Witness replied: "Yes, if you put your
> hands on me." McCutcheon then turned the matter off.

The second threat occurred when Mrs. Campbell and McCutcheon met on a train. McCutcheon again threatened to kill her if she told about his relations with Eula.[24]

Mrs. Campbell also testified about an event involving George McCutcheon on the evening of Eula's funeral. McCutcheon was present in the parlor of the Phillips house that evening.

> A little child came to Mrs. Phillips and said: "Two officers at the
> door want to see you." McCutcheon sprung from his seat
> excitedly and said: "They are after me about the murder!"
> Beauregard McCutcheon, George's brother, was present, and
> witness told him to take his brother off as he was going to have
> one of his "spells." When in his "spells" George generally
> becomes unconscious, and appears to suffer.

With the conclusion of Delia Campbell's testimony, the defense closed its case.[25]

"State's Rebuttal"

After the defense rested, the prosecution offered several rebuttal witnesses. Dr. Thomas H. Bragg was the first rebuttal witness. Dr. Bragg testified that he went to the Phillips house with Dr. Fisher sometime between three and four o'clock on Christmas morning. At that time, Jimmy "replied rationally" to Bragg's questions. Dr. Bragg also examined the wound on Jimmy's head. The doctor

> thought it both possible and probable that defendant could have inflicted that wound upon himself. The witness directed attention to the fact that a part of the front cuticle of the ear was knocked off as by a glancing blow. The most serious wound was above the ear, and in the rear of the front angle. It went inward and downward, and was deepest at the top, shallowing as it went down. The edges of the wound were irregular, lacerated. The witness could see no reason why a person could not inflict such a wound upon himself.

The only thing that might make such a wound impossible to self-inflict "was that it was so unnatural that a man should inflict such a wound unless maddened by some desperate circumstances." Cross-examined by the defense, Dr. Bragg admitted that he did not probe the wound. He did, however, wash it out using a syringe. He found no fracture of the bone, and Dr. Fisher did not tell Dr. Bragg that he saw a fracture. Dr. Bragg also noted that the water injected into the wound did not come out through the ear orifice, which contradicted the testimony given earlier in the day by Dr. C.E. Fisher, a witness for the defense. Re-examined by the prosecution, Dr. Bragg said that he conducted "a reasonably careful examination of the wound," but not as careful as he would have examined it had Jimmy Phillips been his case. He noted that Dr. Litten and Dr. Cummings were in charge of the case. Still, Dr. Bragg "did not find, nor did he believe there was, a fracture of the bone."[26]

The State next called Richard A. Boyce, the day clerk at the police station who boarded at 106 West Hickory. Boyce testified that he saw Eula's body before it was moved, and that he threw a blanket over the body to "cover its nudity." He stated that three pieces of scantling were on the body, "two across the breast and one across the pit of the stomach."[27]

The trial ended with a bit of controversy. The State called to the stand Jerry Brown, a well-known black hack driver. Brown's testimony was meant to prove that "Mrs. Campbell had on last Monday (May 24) stated in the presence of three persons that she had been offered a large amount of money if she would not divulge what she knew about the murder of Eula Phillips." The defense objected to the testimony on the ground that Mrs. Campbell "could not be impeached on a collateral matter." The judge accepted the objection but stipulated that if District Attorney Robertson had obtained information pertinent to the questioning of Brown after Mrs. Campbell had left the stand, then he would allow the testimony. Robertson said he had heard some information about the matter before Mrs. Campbell took the stand, but he had not received the details until after court adjourned on May 26. As a result of that admission, "the court excluded the testimony, and thus eliminated from consideration of the jury the most important branch of the state's case, and with these facts and this grave omission, the whole testimony closed." The attempt by the prosecution to introduce the evidence was considered a blunder.[28]

"As Profound a Mystery as Ever"

After three days of testimony, little direct evidence had been presented to connect Jimmy Phillips to the murder of his wife. Most people in Austin thought Jimmy would be acquitted. In addition, several key questions remained unanswered. The main question was who was the man who rode in the hack with Eula Phillips on Christmas Eve. Many believed that May Tobin knew the answer to that question, but that she had successfully blackmailed the man to keep his name out of the trial.

> Reports are circulated that the prosecution did not put upon the stand parties known to them to be connected with the murder, people whose influence has screened them so far. The man who left Mrs. Tobin's assignation house on the night of the murder in a hack with Mrs. Phillips is suspected to be known to Mrs. Tobin, also to the prosecution, whether he was the murderer or not.

Other rumors began to fly as the trial drew near its end. One juicy rumor was that "a rich cattleman was likely to be implicated as the guilty party," but that rumor "had previously been thoroughly sifted by detectives and found to be without foundation." Another rumor was that "a clerk of one of the state boards had been asked to resign on account of being a visitor at the Tobin assignation house," but that rumor was also untrue.[29]

The notion that pertinent witnesses had not been called by the prosecution was not limited to scalawags or malcontents.

> Three of the wealthiest and most influential citizens of Austin have addressed letters to papers demanding to know why E.T. Moore and District Attorney Robertson, lawyers for the prosecution, did not question the witnesses on the stand who knew all about the murder, and why they did not question persons who washed the bloody clothes.

Such an omission only reinforced the idea that a cover-up was underway. As it turned out, the mystery man in the hack with Eula might not have been such a mystery after all. "The mysterious man who rode with Mrs. Phillips on the night of the murder, and was probably cognizant of it, is supposed to be a man of high position and wealth in this city. They may force him from his lair notwithstanding his money, which made way with the hackman," suggesting that the wealthy person had bribed the hack driver to keep his name out of the public discussion. But who was that "man of high position and wealth"?[30]

Benjamin M. Baker, the superintendent of public instruction who had been implicated by May Tobin, published a card denying his involvement.

> Pending the trial of the Phillips case May Tobin testified that I went to her house one afternoon and met the unfortunate Mrs. Phillips. The statement was not true. I had no acquaintance with Mrs. Phillips and never met her anywhere, and never spoke to her in my life. Friends advise that my position as an official demands that I dignify the statement with a public denial, otherwise I would not feel called on to publicly notice the cruel slander.

Though Baker's name had been mentioned in the trial, he was never really considered a suspect.[31]

The trial would resume the next morning with the closing arguments. Many wondered why the closing arguments were even necessary. Certainly Jimmy Phillips could not be convicted on the flimsy evidence presented by the State, could he?

Notes

Title: *Reports of Cases Argued and Adjudged in the Court of Appeals of Texas*, 1886. Case 2271, James O. Phillips v. the State.

1. *Reports of Cases Argued and Adjudged in the Court of Appeals of Texas, 1886.* Case 2271, James O. Phillips v. the State; *Austin Daily Statesman*, 5/27/1886.
2. *Reports of Cases . . . in the Court of Appeals of Texas, 1886.* Case 2271, James O. Phillips v. the State; *Austin Daily Statesman*, 5/28/1886.
3. *Austin Daily Statesman*, 5/28/1886; *Reports of Cases . . . in the Court of Appeals . . . 1886.* Case 2271, James O. Phillips v. the State; *Morrison & Fourmy's General Directory of the City of Austin, 1885-1886*; "Texas Marriages, 1837-1973"; 1880 Federal Census.
4. *Reports of Cases . . . in the Court of Appeals of Texas, 1886.* Case 2271, James O. Phillips v. the State; *Austin Daily Statesman*, 5/28/1886.
5. *Reports of Cases . . . in the Court of Appeals of Texas, 1886.* Case 2271, James O. Phillips v. the State.
6. *Reports of Cases . . . in the Court of Appeals of Texas, 1886.* Case 2271, James O. Phillips v. the State.
7. *Austin Daily Statesman*, 5/28/1886; *Reports of Cases . . . in the Court of Appeals of Texas, 1886.* Case 2271, James O. Phillips v. the State; *San Antonio Daily Express*, 5/28/1886.
8. *Reports of Cases . . . in the Court of Appeals of Texas, 1886.* Case 2271, James O. Phillips v. the State; *Austin Daily Statesman*, 5/28/1886; *San Antonio Daily Express*, 5/28/1886.
9. *Reports of Cases . . . in the Court of Appeals of Texas, 1886.* Case 2271, James O. Phillips v. the State; *Fort Worth Daily Gazette*, 5/28/1886.
10. *Reports of Cases . . . in the Court of Appeals of Texas, 1886.* Case 2271, James O. Phillips v. the State; *Austin Daily Statesman*, 5/28/1886; *San Antonio Daily Express*, 5/28/1886.

11. *Reports of Cases . . . in the Court of Appeals of Texas, 1886*. Case 2271, James O. Phillips v. the State; *Austin Daily Statesman*, 5/28/1886.
12. *Reports of Cases . . . in the Court of Appeals of Texas, 1886*. Case 2271, James O. Phillips v. the State; *Austin Daily Statesman*, 5/28/1886.
13. *Reports of Cases . . . in the Court of Appeals of Texas, 1886*. Case 2271, James O. Phillips v. the State; *Austin Daily Statesman*, 5/28/1886.
14. *Reports of Cases . . . in the Court of Appeals of Texas, 1886*. Case 2271, James O. Phillips v. the State; *Austin Daily Statesman*, 5/28/1886; *San Antonio Daily Express*, 5/28/1886.
15. *Reports of Cases . . . in the Court of Appeals of Texas, 1886*. Case 2271, James O. Phillips v. the State; *Austin Daily Statesman*, 5/28/1886; *Morrison & Fourmy's General Directory of the City of Austin, 1885-1886* (The newspaper report identified this witness as M.C. Millen, but the appeals court report called him Mr. Miller. Likely the witness was Mason C. Miller, a cashier at the City Bank.)
16. *Reports of Cases . . . in the Court of Appeals of Texas, 1886*. Case 2271, James O. Phillips v. the State; *Austin Daily Statesman*, 5/28/1886; *Morrison & Fourmy's General Directory of the City of Austin, 1885-1886*.
17. *Reports of Cases . . . in the Court of Appeals of Texas, 1886*. Case 2271, James O. Phillips v. the State; *Austin Daily Statesman*, 5/28/1886.
18. *Reports of Cases . . . in Appeals of Texas, 1886*. Case 2271, James O. Phillips v. the State; *Austin Daily Statesman*, 5/28/1886; *Morrison & Fourmy's General Directory of the City of Austin, 1885-1886*.
19. *Reports of Cases . . . in the Court of Appeals of Texas, 1886*. Case 2271, James O. Phillips v. the State; *Fort Worth Daily Gazette*, 5/28/1886; *Austin Daily Statesman*, 5/28/1886.
20. *Reports of Cases . . . in the Court of Appeals of Texas, 1886*. Case 2271, James O. Phillips v. the State; *Austin Daily Statesman*, 5/28/1886; *Morrison & Fourmy's General Directory of the City of Austin, 1885-1886*.
21. *Reports of Cases . . . in the Court of Appeals of Texas, 1886*. Case 2271, James O. Phillips v. the State; *Austin Daily Statesman*, 5/28/1886; *Morrison & Fourmy's General Directory of the City of Austin, 1885-1886*.
22. *Reports of Cases . . . in the Court of Appeals of Texas, 1886*. Case 2271, James O. Phillips v. the State.
23. *Reports of Cases . . . in the Court of Appeals of Texas, 1886*. Case 2271, James O. Phillips v. the State; *Austin Daily Statesman*, 5/28/1886.
24. *Reports of Cases . . . in the Court of Appeals of Texas, 1886*. Case 2271, James O. Phillips v. the State; "Texas Marriages, 1837-1973" (Delia Campbell apparently was not related to Evan Campbell. Adelia Phillips married Lummie F. Campbell on September 24, 1881, when she was about 17 years old.)
25. *Reports of Cases . . . in the Court of Appeals of Texas, 1886*. Case 2271, James O. Phillips v. the State.
26. *Reports of Cases . . . in the Court of Appeals of Texas, 1886*. Case 2271, James O. Phillips v. the State; *Austin Daily Statesman*, 5/28/1886.
27. *Reports of Cases . . . in the Court of Appeals of Texas, 1886*. Case 2271, James O. Phillips v. the State; *Austin Daily Statesman*, 5/28/1886; *Morrison & Fourmy's General Directory of the City of Austin, 1885-1886*.
28. *Austin Daily Statesman*, 5/28/1886.
29. *San Antonio Daily Express*, 5/28/1886; *Fort Worth Daily Gazette*, 5/28/1886; *Galveston Daily News*, 5/28/1886.
30. *Fort Worth Daily Gazette*, 5/28/1886; *Fort Worth Daily Gazette*, 5/29/1886.
31. *Fort Worth Daily Gazette*, 5/28/1886; *Galveston Daily News*, 5/28/1886.

Chapter 22

"A Victim to Peculiar Circumstances"

The Outcome of the Phillips Trial

Testimony in the Phillips trial ended on the evening of May 27, 1886. Closing arguments began promptly on the morning of May 28, 1886, a Friday. District Attorney James H. Robertson spoke first, carefully outlining the case and demonstrating the "probabilities of the murder." The nature of his argument was clear. Jimmy Phillips was a violent, jealous man given to drink, and his wife's numerous infidelities gave him ample motive to kill her. The ax present on the Phillips premises gave him the means. All he then had to do was carry out the murder and then injure himself, thereby fooling the police and detectives and making himself appear an unfortunate victim of the attack. The dramatic act of the bloodhound Bob ignoring all others and going immediately to the bedside of Jimmy Phillips was a clear indicator of his complicity. His lamentation to his mother that he would go to hell had to be the remorse of a guilty man. And the fact that Jimmy's feet did not match the bloody footprints on the Phillips gallery meant little. The defense may even have rehearsed the footprint demonstration to skew the results. Robertson spoke for about two hours, ending his forceful argument around noon.[1]

Robertson was followed by the venerable Judge Hancock for the defense, speaking in "his usual logical and forcible style." Hancock ridiculed the State's theories, especially the evidence associated with the bloodhound. Hancock pronounced that he "'would not hang a dog upon such testimony of a dog.'" Jimmy Phillips was an unwitting victim of the same fiend that murdered his wife. He was a responsible and caring husband who was making every effort to reform himself. Jimmy did not even know of his wife's infidelities, so how could those infidelities be his motive to murder her? And if his wife's infidelities were indeed true, then several men in Austin might have a reason to kill her. Further, three out of four doctors testified that he could not have inflicted his injuries upon himself, and he could not have carried out his wife's murder if she had first struck him with the ax. His footprints did not match the bloody footprints found on the Phillips gallery, so how could he be the murderer? The State clearly had not proved beyond a reasonable doubt that Jimmy Phillips was the one person who murdered Eula Phillips.

> These are some of the reasonable probabilities which the circumstances of the case seem naturally to suggest in the prisoner's behalf, independent of the strangeness of the

> coincidence of two murders the same night, the mysteries of
> which are in keeping with so many similar outrages, of which
> the Hancock and Phillips murders may have been the sequel on
> the part of the same gang of villains.

Judge Hancock spoke for more than an hour, ending "with an eloquent appeal to the jury in behalf of the innocence of the prisoner." After Hancock finished his argument, the court adjourned for lunch.[2]

In the afternoon session, defense attorney J.E. Hamilton spoke first, again stressing that the prosecution had failed to prove its case against Jimmy Phillips beyond a reasonable doubt. William Walton then provided the last closing argument for the defense, carefully controverting District Attorney Robertson's "sixteen points" that Robertson had used to build his closing argument. With the ease of an experienced advocate, Walton dismissed the theories promoted by Robertson. After a two-hour speech, Walton ended his analysis of the case. The final speaker was prosecutor E. Taylor Moore, who reiterated many of the points made by Mr. Robertson. Moore too spoke for about two hours, ending around 7 o'clock in the evening. When the closing arguments ended, the case was given to the jury.[3]

Even as the jury deliberated, many in Austin still believed Jimmy Phillips would be acquitted. The feeling was that not enough direct evidence had been given to prove that Jimmy had committed the murder. The trial certainly had been sensational, "but few more sensational murders were ever committed" than the one for which Jimmy had been tried. But sensation and evidence are two different things, and the prosecution had provided little evidence to show beyond a reasonable doubt that Jimmy Phillips was guilty of murdering his wife.[4]

After deliberating into the night of May 28, the jury continued its consideration on May 29. On the afternoon of May 29, the verdict was returned. Jimmy Phillips was found guilty of the second-degree murder of Eula Phillips and was sentenced to seven years in the state penitentiary![5]

"An Austin Jury's Blunder"

The return of the verdict unleashed a raft of rationalizations and reactions. Most newspapers and people expressed great surprise or even shock because of the perception that the prosecution had not really presented a solid case. For example, the *Galveston Daily News* offered the following explanation of the verdict:

> There was a general expectation that Phillips, the husband of
> the murdered woman, would be acquitted. It doesn't seem as if
> there was sufficient evidence submitted to convict him of the
> crime. Probably the jury acted on this theory: Phillips
> discovered that his wife was away from home and supposed
> that she was dishonoring him. He got an ax and awaited her
> return. When Mrs. Phillips and her paramour alighted from the
> carriage, Phillips in a rage hacked her with the ax and killed

> her. He also tried to kill her companion, but in a scuffle the ax
> was taken away from him, and in a life-and-death struggle
> Phillips was wounded. It will be remembered that Phillips was
> discovered dangerously wounded at the time his wife was found
> dead. Unless there is some inside history to the business that
> was made known to the jury privately, it is difficult to account
> for the verdict.

This interpretation is interesting, but it overlooks the fact that Eula was dragged out in the yard, ravished, and left mostly nude in the yard. Who did all those things to Eula, the paramour?[6]

Many believed that May Tobin knew more than she had revealed. "Austin in particular, and Texas in general, have a very considerable curiosity to know just how much Mrs. Tobin knows, but won't tell, about certain certain and uncertain gentlemen of Mrs. Eula Phillips' acquaintance." At the same time, she was vilified for naming some of the prominent Austinites who had allegedly visited her assignation house with Eula. Some thought she was an outright liar and should be charged with perjury. Her testimony, though, certainly had Austin talking. And most said the verdict was incorrect.

> Public opinion acquits Phillips of the crime, and the feeling is
> general that important evidence has been suppressed. Phillips
> was found in his bed the night of the murder with a fearful
> wound above the ear extending downward. Physicians testified
> he could not possibly have walked from the backyard, where
> the victim was found, to his bed with this wound, which
> rendered him unconscious.

Some of the journalistic reactions were much more shrill. The *Austin Optic* made the outrageous claim that "May Tobin and Della Campbell were responsible for the murder of Eula Phillips." The editor of the *Austin Dispatch*, William Y. Leader, took exception to the claim and criticized the editor of the *Optic*, L.E. Daniels. "That gentleman undertook to chastise Mr. Leader, and a bloody encounter was only prevented by the interference of bystanders." Leader had been involved in run-ins with other editors as well.[7]

The *Fort Worth Gazette*, seldom a fan of Austin, as usual did not mince words in condemning the verdict. The newspaper did not put much stock in juries in general, and certainly not in the jury that convicted Jimmy Phillips.

> The Texas jury is a queer contrivance. In this respect, however,
> it does not seem to differ from the juries of other states. . . . At
> some time, now unknown to man, some rare jury may have
> given a verdict in accordance with the evidence put before it;
> but that was long ago. If the jury of to-day ever found a just
> verdict, it was by chance. A chance enters largely into the
> decisions of that body, it might be inferred that its decisions
> would be correct as often as incorrect, for the chances are
> even, for and against a just verdict; but as there are twelve

> men who must unanimously agree, the chances that each one of them will view the evidence in its true light and arrive at a correct conclusion, are so improbable that a just verdict is, as we have said, almost an unknown thing. Indeed, by a strict computation of the doctrine of probabilities, the chances that twelve men will agree as one, correctly, are as 1 to 479,001,600. That is, out of 479,001,600 cases there will be one that can be depended upon as just and in accordance with the facts. Perhaps this will serve to explain why it is that so many murderers escape the gallows. In Texas, while occasionally a poor fellow is caught up and made to suffer, it is all the work of chance.

The newspaper turned its attention specifically to the Phillips trial verdict.

> The young man Phillips, who was found guilty by an Austin jury of the murder of his wife, seems to be a victim to peculiar circumstances as much as to chance. There have been half a score of women murdered in Austin within little more than a year, and the assassin or assassins remained undiscovered. The people were wrought up to a supreme pitch of fury and dread. At last the wife of this man Phillips was murdered under the same peculiar circumstances that attended the others. He himself was wounded in the head with an ax. Some astute detective advanced the theory that he was the murderer. Upon that charge he was arrested and tried. No evidence was produced showing his hand in the murder. Physicians testified that he could not have inflicted the wound upon himself. The bloody foot-prints left by the murderer did not fit his feet. Nevertheless he was found guilty, not of murder, but of manslaughter. The chance fell the wrong way that time. Men, some of whom have probably sat on juries that turned loose confessed murderers, unanimously resolved that this man was guilty. There was, however, something more than mere chance in this case. It was the thirst for a victim. Austin was excited and in terror, and demanded that an example be made of somebody. Who, it was immaterial. Phillips was accused, and because nobody else was offered he was made the victim. Unless a new trial is given, or the decision reversed on appeal, he is likely to suffer for an odious crime, which nobody but the jury believes him guilty of, while there is not a county in the state that does not hold from one to a dozen men more guilty of murder than he, who were turned loose by the verdict of petit juries.

Was the newspaper's contention correct? Was Jimmy Phillips really just the fall guy for the whole string of servant girl murders?[8]

The *Austin Daily Statesman* adopted a more tempered approach to the verdict, but it too felt the results were somewhat inconclusive. If Jimmy Phillips did indeed murder Eula Phillips, then who killed all the other victims in the servant girl murders? And was all the evidence really presented to the jury?

> Like every other decision of a jury, the verdict in the Phillips case, which was not unexpected, may not meet with universal commendation. But it is the deliberate judgment of twelve citizens of sound mind and discretion, who had before them all the evidence attainable, and therefore can claim popular acquiescence. Thus has one, at least, of the long list of murders in this city been fastened by a jury upon its alleged perpetrator. But what of the others? No clue has been found to the murders of Mollie Smith, Eliza Shelly, Irene Cross, Mary Ramey, Grace Vance, or Mrs. Hancock. These crimes yet remain a dark and profound mystery.

The newspaper then ventured to explain the effects of the verdict. Did the conviction of Jimmy Phillips really shed any light on who might have committed the other murders? Or were those murders now to be forgotten totally since a sacrificial lamb had been chosen to perish on the altar of justice?

> Much of the evidence developed in the Phillips trial apparently tended to strengthen the theory of a large number of our citizens that these fearful assassinations were the work of different personages, and had their motive in jealously, and the worst and most debased passions of our nature. Yesterday's verdict detaches so far as a jury could detach the murder of Mrs. Phillips from the others as a continuous chain of crime. But it does not destroy the theory of the identity of all the assassinations of women from Mollie Smith to Mrs. Hancock, nor the belief in a sole and solitary fiend, still unknown.

And even if the conviction of Jimmy Phillips provided an unsatisfactory resolution to one of the murders, certainly Jimmy Phillips could not be construed as the servant girl annihilator. What mysterious killer still roamed the streets of Austin?

> Mollie Smith, Eliza Shelly, Irene Cross, Mary Ramey, Grace Vance and Mrs. Hancock, were all dragged out into the yard or back premises. All these murders occurred about midnight, in a majority of instances on moonlight nights, and the same mysterious and utterly impenetrable silence, unbroken by sound or cry, reigned while the assassin was at his terrible work. In a majority of the murders—notably Eliza Shelly, Mary Ramey and Mrs. Hancock—a large, broad, naked track was left on the scene of the crime. Were these the footprints of the murderer ghoul, who is yet utterly inscrutable and wrapped in mystery?

The conviction of Jimmy Phillips seemed to prompt more questions than the ones it answered. Worse, it seemed to have some profound effects on the Phillips family. On July 23, Delia Campbell attempted to commit suicide by taking morphine. She failed and was recovering.[9]

"A Travesty on Law"

The defense attorneys for Jimmy Phillips certainly did not agree with the verdict. They quickly filed a motion for a new trial, calling the verdict "a travesty on law, logic, justice and common sense." The motion for a new trial was based on four grounds:

> 1. That the court erred in admitting the testimony of Delia Campbell, Fannie Whipple, May Tobin, and George McCutcheon for reasons set out in the bill of exceptions.
> 2. Because said evidence as stated in the bill was admitted by the court on the assurance on the part of the state, that the state would throw around the defendant such a state of facts that his knowledge of the irregularity of his wife's conduct was so inferable that the jury would be justified and warranted in easily and naturally drawing the deduction, that he was advised of and knew of her irregularities, when in truth and in fact no such evidence was produced of the character named, or pretended to be introduced by the state, that authorized or warranted the jury to draw said deductions and inferences named.
> 3. The court erred in failing to stop attorney for the state (in his closing address) in his argument on matters of fact that were not in the evidence before the jury: viz., on the alleged fact that counsel for defendant had experimented with defendant's feet prior to making the demonstration before the jury, and that they, the attorneys, refused to permit the state to experiment further before the jury.
> 4. Because the evidence in this case, even as admitted to the jury does not support the verdict, returned for various reasons stated in the motion.

Judge Alexander S. Walker, who had presided over the trial of Jimmy Phillips, heard the motion on Saturday, June 5, 1886. He took the matter under advisement and declared that he would issue a judgment on the following Monday. On Monday, June 7, 1886, Judge Walker overruled the motion for a new trial for Jimmy Phillips. The defense attorneys then filed an appeal and "were granted an order for the panels marked with murderer's bloody tracks and the ironing board on which Phillips' tracks are impressed in ink to accompany the papers."[10]

"Reversed and Remanded"

The Phillips case was submitted to the Texas Court of Appeals in October 1886. William Walton, one of the original defense lawyers for Phillips, provided the oral argument. The main thrust of Walton's argument was that the prosecution simply did not provide evidence sufficient to warrant the guilty verdict.

> The evidence for the state did not show guilt. The testimony for the defense shows that some one else than the defendant did

> the killing. There is no chain of circumstances connecting the defendant with the murder which leads the mind to believe he did the deed beyond a reasonable doubt. The physical facts on the ground, singly and together, break the chain of circumstances. The preponderance of evidence is in favor of the defendant's innocence and somebody else's guilt. It is not necessary for defendant to show who committed the murder, but only that he did not. It is the duty of the state to show that defendant and no one else did the killing. The evidence in the case does not account for the verdict. . . . The verdict is a travesty on law, logic, justice, right and common sense, and we claim that appellant is the victim of oppression, wrong and violated law.

In his closing remarks, Mr. Walton not only called for a reversal of the verdict but also took a final rather scathing parting shot at District Attorney James Robertson, who had been the chief prosecutor in the case.

> "This wrong has gone to such an extent that it is considered to be an outrage, and it is said that the average prosecuting officer forgets that in him repose, to a less extent, judicial functions; forgets that it is his duty, either as a man or as an official, to convict the individual whom he prosecutes; that it is also his duty only to see in each instance that a trial of the accused is had in the interest of law and order, to the end that strict justice be done in all quarters, and to all men, whether he wins the case or not. For ambition to be successful in the criminal matters entrusted to his care, the uncanny itch to win the case at all hazards, irrespective of the guilt or innocence of the accused, has made the average prosecutor a veritable thug who runs amuck every chance he gets among the miserable human beings who have the misfortune to be arraigned in court on a charge of violating the law. . . . He leaves no human contrivance, no trick of the trade, no art untried to secure a conviction. Hence it comes about that innocent men are sometimes convicted. I do not envy the man, no matter how prominent he may rise in fame as a prosecutor, if that eminence cost his hands steeped in the blood of his victims, or his soul burdened with the wail of dying curses from the pale lips of him who has been robbed by unfair means of his life or his liberty."

With those biting remarks, Mr. Walton left the fate of Jimmy Phillips to the Texas Court of Appeals.[11]

The court's decision was delivered about three weeks later. On November 10, 1886, the court announced its decision on the case: "Reversed and remanded." Judge Samuel A. Willson wrote the opinion. The reversal was based on two errors in the proceedings, both centering on inadmissible evidence. The court did not rule on the sufficiency of evidence to convict. as the case was remanded to the lower court for retrial. In brief, the court reversed the verdict for two reasons.

> First, that the court erred in permitting the state to prove the unchastity of the defendant's wife as a motive for the killing, without having shown that this unchastity was brought to defendant's knowledge.
>
> Second, that the court erred in permitting the state to prove conditional and insignificant threats made by the defendant, which threats, under the circumstances when they were made, showed no intention of the defendant's carrying them out.

In the first reason, Judge Walker erred by allowing evidence regarding Eula's infidelities. The prosecution had assured the judge that it would show that Jimmy Phillips knew of his wife's infidelities, so Walker allowed the evidence to provide a motive for the murder. The defense objected on several grounds, claiming that the evidence was foreign and immaterial, and that it introduced new issues in the case that were scandalous and emotional. The result, according to the defense, was that the evidence drew the minds of the jury from the true issues in the case, that it confused the jury, and that it prejudiced the jury against the defendant. The prosecution had told the judge that upcoming evidence would "prove that defendant was informed of and did know of his wife's infidelity at the time of her murder." As a result, the objection of the defense was overruled, and the evidence was admitted. Judge Walker at no point instructed the jury that the evidence was not admissible. However, the court of appeals, upon review of the testimony, did not agree that the prosecution had definitely shown the defendant knew of his wife's infidelities, so the evidence should not have been admitted.

> At least, considering the very meager and unsatisfactory evidence tending to show such knowledge or belief, the jury should have been instructed that, unless they were satisfied from the evidence that defendant did know or believe, at the time of the murder, that his wife was unfaithful to him, they should wholly disregard all the evidence in relation to the improper conduct and infidelity of deceased.

In the second reason, the testimony of Albert Highsmith and George McCutcheon regarding the speculative threats made by Jimmy Phillips against his wife should not have been allowed. According to the Court of Appeals:

> These threats were conditional. They were that if he knew his wife was not virtuous, he would kill her and himself too. They were of but little significance when viewed in the light of the circumstances under which they were made, and were not pertinent evidence to prove motive, unless accompanied by proof that defendant knew that his wife was not virtuous. They were inadmissible for the same reason that the evidence relating to the wife's conduct has been held to be inadmissible, and should have been excluded from the consideration of the jury.

Because of these two errors by the presiding judge in the Phillips trial, the guilty verdict was reversed and the case was returned to the lower court.[12]

On March 28, 1887, "the case of the State vs. Philips, charged with the murder of his wife, Eula Philips, in Austin, Christmas Eve of 1885, was called in the District court . . . and dismissed. The murder is now as great a mystery as the servant girl murders of a year ago." Jimmy Phillips was a free man, and only Moses Hancock remained under the cloud of suspicion. His trial would be held in the upcoming months.[13]

In a case eerily similar to the other servant girl murders, Jimmy Phillips was convicted of killing his wife, but he was not even considered a suspect in those other cases. His foot did not match the bloody footprint left on the Phillips gallery, though Nathan Elgin's foot apparently did, but still Jimmy Phillips was tried and convicted after Elgin was dead. The actions of District Attorney James Robertson to try Jimmy Phillips for murder seemed almost vengeful, as if Robertson needed to put someone on trial to save face. He had done the same thing with Walter Spencer, but that attempt fell flat on its face. In the Phillips case, Robertson had more success, convincing or at least cajoling a group of Austin citizens to convict a young man who himself had been severely injured in the assault. Robertson seemed intent on dragging Moses Hancock through the same ordeal. As William Walton labeled him, Robertson seemed to be acting like a "veritable thug" who was no better than the men he was trying.

Did Jimmy Phillips murder his wife, Eula? Of course, the possibility always exists, but the likelihood is small. The prosecution in the case certainly provided no evidence to prove he had committed the murder, only that he might have had a reason to kill her, if in fact he knew she was being unfaithful to him. But in his almost constant drunken state, Jimmy probably did not even realize Eula was being unfaithful, only that his mother had suggested that Eula was "too fast." Yes, he was a drunk. Yes, he was jealous. Yes, he was at times violent. But was he a murderer? Probably not.

Though the case eventually turned out in favor of the Phillips family, the effects of the trial on the family were numerous. As mentioned earlier, Delia Campbell tried to commit suicide in the summer of 1886, no doubt as a result of her involvement in the events that resulted in her brother's prosecution. However, as late as 1930 she was still married to Lum Campbell and living in Orange, Texas. Mrs. Sophia Phillips died a year after Jimmy's case was finally dismissed. She was said to die of a serious case of diarrhea and was buried in Oakwood Cemetery in Austin. Jimmy and Eula's son, Thomas, lived with old Mr. Phillips instead of with Jimmy. Old Mr. Phillips died of the exhaustion of age at 88 years old in 1909. What became of Thomas is unclear, though he might have died in 1928 and been buried in the Cedar Knob Cemetery in Salado, Bell County, Texas.[14]

Jimmy himself left Austin and moved to Georgetown, Texas, about 30 miles north of Austin. There he remarried, taking Ida Mae Hart as his wife in 1890. Ida Mae was the daughter of Archie and Sophronia Hart. Archie Hart was a deputy sheriff for Williamson County. Together, Jimmy and Ida Mae had four children—Nida, James Oliver, Annie, and Archie—born from 1892 to 1900. Jimmy taught music, and his family performed as the Phillips Family Band at local events. Jimmy continued to suffer from ileus, a blockage of the intestines, that limited the kind of work he could do. Perhaps this medical condition, noted as early as the 1880 census, played a role in his troublesome marriage to Eula. Ida Mae died in May 1910 at the age of 41. She was buried in Odd Fellows Cemetery in Georgetown. Jimmy died on January 2, 1929, and was also buried at Odd Fellows Cemetery in Georgetown.[15]

After the trial, conviction, and subsequent release of Jimmy Phillips, the murder of Eula Phillips remained as much a mystery as the other murders in 1885. The Hancock trial would begin soon, but if it was anything like the Phillips trial, it would shed no new light on the mysterious servant girl murders.

Notes

Title: *Fort Worth Daily Gazette*, 6/4/1886.

1. *Austin Daily Statesman*, 5/29/1886; Saylor, *A Twist at the End*: 417.
2. *Austin Daily Statesman*, 5/29/1886; *Austin Daily Statesman*, 6/5/1886; Saylor, *A Twist at the End*: 417; *San Antonio Daily Express*, 5/28/1886.
3. *Austin Daily Statesman*, 5/29/1886; *Galveston Daily News*, 5/29/1886.
4. *San Antonio Daily Light*, 5/29/1886; *San Antonio Daily Express*, 5/29/1886.
5. *Galveston Daily News*, 5/30/1886; *San Antonio Daily Light*, 5/31/1886.
6. *Galveston Daily News*, 5/30/1886.
7. *San Antonio Daily Express*, 5/30/1886; *San Antonio Daily Light*, 5/29/1886; *New York Times*, 5/30/1886; *Galveston Daily News*, 5/27/1886; *San Antonio Daily Light*, 5/31/1886.
8. *Fort Worth Daily Gazette*, 6/4/1886.
9. *Austin Daily Statesman*, 5/30/1886; *Fort Worth Daily Gazette*, 7/25/1886.
10. *San Antonio Daily Express*, 6/1/1886; *Fort Worth Daily Gazette*, 6/6/1886; *San Antonio Daily Express*, 6/8/1886.
11. *Austin Daily Statesman*, 10/22/1886.
12. *Austin Daily Statesman*, 11/11/1886; *Reports of Cases . . . in the Court of Appeals of Texas, 1886*. Case 2271, James O. Phillips v. the State; *Fort Worth Daily Gazette*, 11/12/1886.
13. *Fort Worth Daily Gazette*, 3/29/1887.
14. Bree, "Austin's Bloody Murder Spree, 1884-1885"; Oakwood Cemetery Database; 1930 Federal Census; "Thomas Phillips."
15. Bree, "Austin's Bloody Murder Spree, 1884-1885"; "Ida M. Phillips"; "James O. Phillips"; "Ida Mae Hart"; 1880 Federal Census; 1900 Federal Census.

Chapter 23

"A Whirling Mass of Confused Rubbish"

The Preliminary Trial of Moses Hancock Begins

Moses Hancock had been scheduled for a preliminary trial in February 1886, but even before the trial began, District Attorney James Robertson and prosecutor E. Taylor Moore moved to dismiss the case. However, after his temporarily successful prosecution of Jimmy Phillips, District Attorney Robertson, described as a "veritable thug" by Phillips' defense attorney William Walton, decided to try Hancock again, using supposed evidence from the miscreant detective Thomas Bailes. Robertson seemed to be grabbing at straws, hoping to pin at least one of the murders on somebody.

The swirl of activities in the Hancock case began anew with the re-arrest of Moses Hancock on June 4, 1886, about a week after the conclusion of the Phillips trial. At the same time, David C. Hagy was arrested in San Antonio. Hagy was a young man about 30 years old who boarded at the Hancock house and took the Hancock girls to a party on the night Sue Hancock was injured. Hagy was considered an accomplice in the murder and was returned to Austin by Detective Thomas Bailes. Though Hagy had been in San Antonio for a while, his arrest was delayed because "the detective had a good deal of trouble in finding him for the reason that he changed his location so often."[1]

The new arrest of Moses Hancock was prompted by William T. Scaggs, a brother of Sue Hancock. Scaggs did not think at first that Hancock had killed his wife, but he changed his mind and decided that Hancock was indeed guilty. Scaggs had arranged for former U.S. District Attorney Jack Evans to aid in the prosecution, though what new evidence Scaggs might have obtained was unknown. Jack Evans had served as a U.S. district judge. He was born in 1837 and was a long-time attorney in Waco.[2]

Moses H. Hancock was a carpenter who was about 55 years old at the time of his wife's murder. He appeared in the federal censuses variously as Moses Hancock and H. Hancock. He was born in North Carolina around 1830. By 1860, he had arrived in Texas, living in Bonham, Texas, along the border with Oklahoma. During the Civil War, he served in the Confederate Army, with the rank of private. He may have been a farrier during his service. By 1870, he was living in Burton in Washington County, Texas, about 100 miles east of Austin. He had married Sue, his second wife, and had his first daughter, Lena, who was one year old at the time. By 1880, he was living in Waco, Texas, about 100 miles north of Austin. He had a second daughter, Ida, who was about five years old at the time. After living in Waco, he and his family moved to San Antonio for a couple of years. The family arrived in Austin in late 1884. At the time of the attack, they lived at 203 East Water Street. Moses Hancock died at the age of 86 in March 1919 and was buried in Waco.[3]

The second preliminary trial of Moses Hancock began on June 17, 1886, a Thursday. Hancock was charged with murdering his wife, Sue Hancock. The presiding judge was William Von Rosenberg, Jr. The prosecuting attorneys were District Attorney James Robertson and Dudley G. Wooten. Attorneys for the defense were John Hancock and Judge Bethel Coopwood. Aiding in the defense was C.F. Robinson, a lawyer from San Antonio who was representing David Hagy. John Hancock was no relation to Moses Hancock.[4]

The first witness was Mrs. Emma M. McDowell, who lived with her husband, Henry, a carpenter, at 609 East Water Street, about four blocks east of the Hancock house. Mrs. McDowell was about 32 years old at the time of the murder. She testified that she had known Moses Hancock and his wife for about three years. She had known them first in San Antonio. She claimed to know little of their marital situation, but she did say she had only a short acquaintance with David Hagy. Mrs. McDowell related one incident when she was at the Hancock house in Austin. Mrs. Hancock was quite ill, but Mr. Hancock did not seem to care about her sickness and paid no attention to her. Instead, he sat under a tree in the front yard reading. Mrs. McDowell also spoke of an incident in San Antonio. Mrs. Hancock told her husband that she wished to send something to one of the neighbors, but Mr. Hancock walked by without speaking to his wife. Other than those two incidents, Mrs. McDowell had no insight to their relations. Cross-examined by Colonel Coopwood, Mrs. McDowell said she had never seen Hagy at the Hancock house. She did spend two or three hours at the house the time Mrs. Hancock was sick. Hagy was not there, but several ladies were present, among them Mrs. Persinger. During that time, Mr. Hancock did not attend to his ailing wife.[5]

The next witness was 12-year-old Maud Houston, who was apparently a playmate of the Hancock girls. She stated that she had seen Mr. Hancock on one occasion, in July or August of 1885. Mrs. Hancock was there, but David Hagy was not. The girl told of how Mr. Hancock treated his wife on the day she visited. Mr. Hancock

> was drunk and very cross; he only said a few words to her [his wife]; he called her a son of a bitch; his manner was very harsh; he was so drunk that he could not walk straight; he sat upon a chair in the parlor and fell asleep; Mrs. Hancock seemed to be very uneasy and afraid of waking him and sent us to the back yard to play.

Cross-examined, the young witness said that they did not awaken Mr. Hancock but left him to sleep.[6]

Samuel H. Dixon was the next witness. Dixon was a clerk in the city and about 27 years old; he had formerly been a schoolteacher. Dixon stated that he saw Moses Hancock on the night of the attack, but he had not known him before that time. He had known David Hagy for about ten years. On Christmas Eve, Dixon was at the Rust's dwelling house until about midnight, playing cards with the Rust family. At midnight, Mrs. Rust said it was time to quit, as the next day was Christmas. Dixon went outside with Mr. Rust and conversed for about ten minutes. Just then, Officer John Chenneville rode up, looking for Marshal Lucy. Mr. Rust went inside the house and checked a room, but Marshal Lucy was not in. Dixon asked Chenneville what the matter was, and Chenneville replied that a woman had been killed. Dixon thought the time then was about 12:15. He left the Rust house and went to the Hancock house on Water Street.[7]

Under cross-examination, Dixon continued his narrative. He arrived at the Hancock gate and saw one or two people inside the Hancock house, with several more moving about the house outside. He went up on the gallery and looked in. Inside, he saw someone "wounded or killed." He went in to offer assistance and saw Mrs. Hancock "bleeding very profusely." People were trying to make her comfortable by placing pillows under her head. Dixon admitted, "I am a poor hand for blood and I grew sick and came out." Outside, he went around to the back of the house. There he saw two or three people talking, one of them Mr. Hancock. Dixon asked Mr. Hancock what had happened.

> He replied that he was sleeping, and something awoke him; he (Hancock) did not know what noise it was, and he seemed to feel the presence of some one about the place. He went to his wife's room and looked for her and heard her groaning from the outside; he ran to the door and saw a man on her, or about her; he (Hancock) spoke and the party ran; he (Hancock) was not sure whether there were one or two men there; he threw a rock at the man as he jumped over the fence.

About that time, Dr. William Burt, the city physician, arrived. Dixon noted that other people asked Hancock what had happened, and he told the same story. Hancock said "he felt the presence of persons and looked for his pants and found that they were gone." At that time, Dixon went around the front of the house, and Dr. Richard Graves arrived.[8]

Continuing under cross-examination, Dixon said he left then and went home by horseback. He heard later that Hancock's pants had been found, and he said that Hancock seemed to him "a very sober man." Dixon aroused several people around his house, among them Evan Campbell. Then Dixon went back to the Hancock house. On the way, he met a man on horseback.

> I halted him and asked him where he was going; he replied to Mrs. Skaggs' and he told me that Mrs. Phillips had been killed and Mr. Phillips almost killed; do not know who the person was, but he was young, no more than 20; thought perhaps he was Hancock's son; I made inquiries the same night and found out

he was not the man who went to Skaggs'; I have met the man who went to Skaggs, and he is not the man whom I met upon the bridge; the man who went to Skaggs was fully six feet in height and about forty years of age; I have heard his name but have forgotten it; the man is now on the police force (a lawyer suggested the name of Gassaway, and witness said that was the name). I am not able to state whether the man I met was armed or not; I went up to the Phillips' house as fast as I could get there; I saw several parties there, and saw Mr. P. lying badly wounded, and I thought he was dying.

Dixon then said that "they had not found Mrs. Phillips when I went there; they found her when I was there the first time; I felt her arm and found that it was warm." He said that he did not make an examination and that he did not know who found Eula's body.[9]

Dixon was then cross-examined about his knowledge of David Hagy. Dixon said he first met Hagy in September 1875 in Independence, Texas, in Washington County. During the three years Dixon lived in Independence, he met Hagy at several parties and also knew his family. At that time, Hagy was a carpenter. Dixon then said he had lost contact with Hagy for about seven years until the incident at the Hancock place. Dixon testified that when he went back to the Hancock house, several people were on the gallery, and one was crying bitterly. He thought that person might be one of Hancock's daughters. Under re-examination by Mr. Robertson, Dixon said that he did not see any blood on the man on the bridge, and that the man did not seem excited or nervous. He answered Dixon's questions clearly and promptly. With that statement, Dixon was released as a witness, and the court was adjourned until 3 o'clock that afternoon.[10]

"Somebody Has Killed My Wife"

The first witness of the afternoon session on June 17 was Thomas Glass, a next-door neighbor. Glass was about 31 years old and had married Alena Steiner in 1884. He worked as a driver for the Capital Ice Company. Glass said he was at home most of the night Mrs. Hancock was wounded. Around 8 o'clock that evening, Mrs. Hancock came to the fence to speak to him. She said she would come over and stay with Mrs. Glass if he would take Mr. Hancock to town with him. Mrs. Hancock said she was afraid to stay there with Mr. Hancock, fearing he would beat her. Glass went to Mr. Hancock and asked him to go along to town, but Hancock refused. Mrs. Hancock then returned and asked if her husband had agreed to go to town. Glass said he had not, and then Glass thought Mrs. Hancock went to his house to visit Mrs. Glass. Glass then went to town and did not return until 11 o'clock or midnight. According to Glass,

> When I did get back I found Mrs. Hancock all butchered up. Mr. Hancock, Mr. Persinger and Mr. Heanel were in the room where she was. I was told of the murder in the Iron Front saloon before I went back. When I was talking to Mr. Hancock, at

> about 8 o'clock, he was pretty drunk, but when I got back, after
> the murder, he was sober.

Glass also testified that he saw David Hagy at the Hancock place after he returned from town. Hagy had arrived with the two Hancock daughters. The girls were understandably upset, and Hagy expressed surprise at the attack.[11]

Cross-examined, Glass said that he heard the Hancock girls ask Hagy to take them to a party. He saw Hagy at the Hancock place around 7:30 on Christmas Eve. He had frequently seen Hagy at the Hancock house, and he knew that Hagy and the Hancocks were on good terms. Mrs. Hancock particularly liked Hagy, having said that "she thought more of him than any young man in town." Glass had never seen Hagy drunk, and on the night of the attack, Hagy "was not excited, nor did he try to run away from the place." Glass said that he asked Hancock to go to town about a half hour after Hagy left for the party with the Hancock girls. He saw no one go to the Hancock place after Hagy left. When Glass left to go uptown, lights were burning in the Hancock house, and Hancock was seated on his front gallery. Glass did express some concern for Mrs. Hancock's safety that evening.

> I thought from what Mrs. Hancock said that night that she was
> in danger of being hurt and I had the impression when I left to
> go up town. I made no effort to have her protected, nor did I
> tell anyone that I expected she would be hurt before I got back.

Glass said he had never seen anything to believe that Hancock was jealous of his wife, and he had no reason to believe that Mrs. Hancock was in any danger of being injured by Hagy. When Glass went to the Hancock house after the attack, he stayed about two hours. Then he went down to the river with William Davis to search for the assailants, with no luck, of course.[12]

The next witness was Rosa King, a black servant who was about 40 years old at the time of the attack. She lived in Thomas Glass's house next door to the Hancock place. She had seen Mrs. Hancock shortly before dark on Christmas Eve, and she also saw Mr. Hancock about 7 o'clock, but she did not know if he was drunk but that he was very quiet. Between 11 o'clock and midnight, King heard groaning coming from outside, but she had heard no disturbance before the groaning started. Mrs. Glass also heard the groan and thought that her husband was coming home drunk. King pulled aside a curtain and looked out to the front street but saw no one. The groan was repeated, and Mrs. Glass again thought the groaning was caused by her drunk husband. King and Mrs. Glass conversed a short while, and then they heard a man shouting in the alley. Mrs. Glass started to the door, but King told her not to open it. King feared there were drunken men in the alley who were celebrating Christmas a bit too enthusiastically.

> Shortly after we heard someone cry out: "Help, help, help,
> somebody has killed my wife!" Myself and Mrs. Glass both run
> to the window, and looking out saw Mr. Hancock standing up
> over his wife hollowing. He cried out: "Run, run, you murdering
> s-ns b-t-hes, I see you!" but we could not see anyone running.

> Mr. Heanel, who was in Mr. Glass's house, then went out and
> helped Mr. Hancock to carry Mrs. Hancock in the house. I saw
> no one running, nor did I hear any one.

Before Haenelt got to the Hancock place, King saw Mrs. Hancock lying beside the kitchen with her feet toward the house and her head toward the alley. Mr. Hancock was standing by her feet. From the time King heard the groans until she saw Hancock standing over his wife, no more than five minutes had elapsed. "The groans and the cries for help were almost together." King saw no one in the alley, and she did not hear anyone about the Hancock premises except Mr. Hancock until Haenelt arrived. She had heard no quarrel or fighting that evening, and she did not know how Mr. and Mrs. Hancock got along.[13]

Under cross-examination, King revealed that Mr. Hancock came to the Glass house early in the evening. He sat in the front room but did not stay long. He talked briefly to Mrs. Glass and the baby, but was generally very quiet. Hancock then left, and King supposed he went home but was not sure. Mr. Glass had gone uptown and did not return until after Mrs. Hancock was injured. When the yelling started, Mrs. Haenelt awoke her husband, who went to the Hancock house in his night-shirt. King was not sure how Mr. Hancock was dressed because she was so excited. She could not tell if he had on pants and a shirt, but she did know that he was wearing light or white clothes when she saw him in the back yard yelling. The defendant's wearing of pants seemed to be a key emphasis of the prosecution, just as it had been in the Phillips trial. The assumption apparently was that if the defendant was wearing pants, he had likely committed the murder. After Haenelt arrived at the Hancock place, he and Mr. Hancock picked up Mrs. Hancock and carried her into the back part of the house. Then,

> Mr. Heanel got his horse and went after the doctor. Just as he
> passed out of the gate, which I opened up for him, four men
> passed up and went into Mr. Hancock's and at once came out,
> two going in a different direction. I saw no one else hollow to
> the men to halt.

King did not recall seeing Mr. Hancock after Haenelt left for the doctor. She also did not see Mr. Persinger arrive. She did, however, have contact later with Thomas Bailes. He had come to talk with her about a week before the trial began, but he did not offer King any money or any other inducement for her "to tell anything but the truth."[14]

"Knocked My Wife in the Head"

The last witnesses in the afternoon session were Henry McDowell and Dora McDowell. Henry McDowell, the husband of earlier witness Emma McDowell, was about 50 years old at the time of the attack. He was a carpenter who lived at 609 East Water Street, a few blocks from the Hancock house. McDowell testified that he had known the Hancocks for about three or four years. He had been to their house several times but had never heard them quarreling. Their relationship was, though, somewhat cool toward each other. About three months before the attack, McDowell had heard Hancock curse his wife on a Sunday morning after he had been on a drinking spree. Mrs. Hancock had been badgering her husband, not furiously but in a "very reasonable way," about spending his money on drinking. Dora McDowell testified that she knew nothing of the relationship between Mr. and Mrs. Hancock. The court then adjourned until 8:30 that night.[15]

The only two witnesses in the night session were Mr. and Mrs. Persinger, who lived next door to the Hancock house at 201 East Water Street. Mrs. Mary Persinger testified first. She stated that she thought the Hancocks had lived peacefully as man and wife, and she heard no disturbance on Christmas Eve until Mr. Hancock started yelling for help around 11:30.

> At first I thought it was some one pretty full, as it was Christmas night. I heard the hollow out again and got up and looking out saw Mr. Hancock standing at the alley gate. He was saying "yonder he goes catch him, for he has murdered my wife." I looked out but could see no one except Mr. Hancock. I could see distinctly in the yard, but could not see all the alley, the stable being in the way. I looked but could see no one.

Mrs. Persinger said that Hancock had been renting the house from her for about nine months. She also revealed that she had a conversation with Jack Ramsey while Mr. Hancock was present. She told Ramsey that a man had come by, and she thought he was a detective. Ramsey told her not to speak to any detective or to tell anyone what she knew. Mr. Hancock heard her comments but said nothing.[16]

Mrs. Persinger was then cross-examined about the events of the evening. She said that her husband helped carry Mrs. Hancock into the house. Hancock then called Mrs. Persinger to come attend to his wife. When she first saw Hancock, he was in a shirt and drawers. She found his clothes the next day near a rear gate in her yard. She had seen Mr. Hancock twice earlier in the evening, around 5 o'clock and again around 6 o'clock, and both times he was sober. She went uptown with Mrs. Hancock that evening to have some shoes mended, and they returned around 6:30. When they left to go to town to have the shoes fixed, the Hancock girls had not yet left for the party with David Hagy. Mrs. Persinger had known Hagy about two months at the time of the attack, and he had been "a perfect gentleman." He seemed to have a pleasant and cordial relationship with the Hancocks, as well.[17]

Mr. Atlas M. Persinger followed his wife to the witness stand. He noted that he was awakened by his wife sometime between 11 o'clock and midnight on Christmas Eve. He did not immediately get up, but his wife got up and looked out. Then she called to him,

> saying she knew there was trouble over at Mr. Hancock's. I then got up and put on my pants and as I did so, I heard Mr. Hancock's call "come here Persinger, for God's sake. Somebody has knocked my wife in the head and dragged her off." I went out to the side gate opening into Mr. Hancock's yard, and went

> to the platform leading from Mr. Hancock's house to the
> kitchen. I saw Mr. Hancock with his arms around his wife and
> her head resting on his breast or shoulder. I spoke to Mrs.
> Hancock and got no reply. Mr. Hancock said "for God's sake,
> take hold of her and let's get her into the house."

At that time, Joseph Brunet, the owner of the Austin Ice Factory, arrived. Brunet, who was about the same age as Hancock, lived nearby on the east side of Brazos Street between Water Street and the river. The doors of the Hancock house were wide open, and a lamp on the piano was burning brightly. Brunet, Hancock, and Persinger carried the wounded woman into the front room and there made her a pallet of quilts. Persinger then left to fetch a doctor, but along the way, he met a Mr. Leonard and his son, and the Leonard boy went after the doctor. Persinger said he had been with Hancock about 5 o'clock that evening, and at that time Hancock was sober. During the remainder of the evening, he saw no one on the Hancock premises except Mr. Hancock. After the attack,

> Hancock told me that he saw a tall man, dressed in black jump
> the fence, and that he threw a brickbat at him. He said he did
> not know whether he was black or white. . . . The next morning
> Mr. Hancock's clothes were found in my yard near the gate on
> the alley. I did not move them, and the officers, I think
> Constable Thorpe and Fred Peck, took them in charge. Dr. Burt
> was the first doctor there.

Persinger pointed out that when he first saw Hancock after the attack, Hancock was wearing shorts, not pants. Persinger also noted that he owned a dog, but it was not on the place on Christmas Eve. His child found the dog on the street the next morning. After Mr. Persinger finished his testimony, the long first day of the trial was completed, and court was adjourned until the next morning.[18]

The Fort Worth newspaper regarded the first day of the trial as ridiculous and political grandstanding. "The whole testimony . . . was migratory and utterly incompetent to connect Hancock with the crime. The opinion here is the whole thing is an outrage, after the prisoner had once before turned loose, and that it is a political move to help out certain candidates for office." What would the next day hold?[19]

Notes

Title: *Austin Daily Statesman*, 6/18/1886.

1. *Austin Daily Statesman*, 6/5/1886; *San Antonio Daily Express*, 6/5/1886; *Fort Worth Daily Gazette*, 6/5/1886; "Texas Deaths, 1890-1976" (Hagy was identified at least five different ways in news reports: Hagy, Hagga, Haggi, Hegga, Heggi. Hagy was apparently the correct spelling.)

2. *Austin Daily Statesman*, 6/5/1886; 1880 Federal Census; Oakwood Cemetery Database (Scaggs was identified variously as Scaggs or Skaggs or Scraggs. Scaggs apparently was the correct name. W.T. Scaggs was incorrectly listed in the 1885-1886 city directory as William T. Scraggs; Scaggs was operating a grocery store at 907 East Cedar Street and residing at the same address.)

3. 1860 Federal Census; "United States Civil War Soldiers Index"; 1870 Federal Census; 1880 Federal Census; *Austin Daily Statesman*, 6/19/1886; "Texas Deaths, 1890-1976."

4. *Austin Daily Statesman*, 6/18/1886.

5. *Austin Daily Statesman*, 6/18/1886; *Morrison & Fourmy's General Directory of the City of Austin, 1885-1886*; Oakwood Cemetery Database.

6. *Austin Daily Statesman*, 6/18/1886.

7. *Austin Daily Statesman*, 6/18/1886; *Morrison & Fourmy's General Directory of the City of Austin, 1885-1886*; 1880 Federal Census (The news report referred to Rost, but Rust appeared to be the correct name. Miss Ella Rust ran a boardinghouse at 206 East College Avenue at the corner of San Jacinto. The boardinghouse had been attacked in the rash of home assaults in March of 1885. Miss Rust was about 50 years old at the time and the apparent sister of Edwin Rust, about 62 at the time. Edwin Rust lived with his wife and daughter at 400 West Hickory at the corner of Guadalupe. Dixon must be referring to the Rust boardinghouse in his testimony. However, Dixon did state that "Rost's building is only two or three blocks from Hancock's." Both addresses for the Rust family given here were about ten blocks away from the Hancock place on Water Street.)

8. *Austin Daily Statesman*, 6/18/1886.

9. *Austin Daily Statesman*, 6/18/1886.

10. *Austin Daily Statesman*, 6/18/1886.

11. *Austin Daily Statesman*, 6/18/1886; *Morrison & Fourmy's General Directory of the City of Austin, 1885-1886*; 1880 Federal Census; "Texas Marriages, 1837-1973" (The Mr. Heanel mentioned by Glass was likely Paul Haenelt, a barber about the same age as Glass. The Haenelt family also lived in the Glass house.)

12. *Austin Daily Statesman*, 6/18/1886.

13. *Austin Daily Statesman*, 6/18/1886; 1880 Federal Census (The name of the witness was Rose or Rosa King. As mentioned in an earlier note, the Mr. Heanel named by King was likely Paul Haenelt.)

14. *Austin Daily Statesman*, 6/18/1886.

15. *Austin Daily Statesman*, 6/18/1886; *Morrison & Fourmy's General Directory of the City of Austin, 1885-1886*; 1870 Federal Census (Dora McDowell may have been a niece of the McDowells.)

16. *Austin Daily Statesman*, 6/18/1886; "Texas Marriages, 1837-1973" (A.M. Persinger married Mary Brown on May 18, 1882.)

17. *Austin Daily Statesman*, 6/18/1886.

18. *Austin Daily Statesman*, 6/18/1886.

19. *Fort Worth Daily Gazette*, 6/18/1886.

Chapter 24

"A Great Trial"

The Preliminary Trial of Moses Hancock Concludes

Overnight, the attitude of the *Austin Daily Statesman* toward the Hancock trial changed dramatically. Its headline on June 18 called the trial "A Whirling Mass of Confused Rubbish." On June 19, the article covering the previous day's proceedings was headlined "A Great Trial." The first day of the trial had certainly not produced any solid evidence that might suggest Moses Hancock killed his wife. Would the second day of the trial deliver that damning evidence?

The first witness on June 18 was Mrs. M.A. Scaggs, a sister-in-law of Sue Hancock. She had married W.T. Scaggs in July 1859 in McLennan County, Texas. She stated that she had been at the Hancock house on the night after the attack, but she had no information about the attack itself. About six weeks after the attack, though, Hancock was at her house. He asked Mrs. Scaggs if she had seen his daughters that day, and she said no. Mr. Scaggs had asked Ida to come to their house, but Lena would not let her go there. Hancock then said, "'If any one takes my babies, by God I'll kill them,'" and then repeated the threat. Hancock then asked where Joe Gassaway, a boarder at the Scaggs house, was. Mr. Scaggs said that Gassaway had left, and Hancock said, "'It will be hell if Gassway has gone back on me but it don't make any difference, I'll be in Brazil in three days.'" Gassaway came back and supper was served. Throughout supper, Hancock continued to grumble about the murder of his wife, as if it had been troubling him all day. Hancock then said about the detective Bailes, "'Let him work it up, God damn him, he can't prove it; there was neither man, woman nor child saw it.'" Hancock also threatened to kill Bailes and Justice Von Rosenberg, Jr., for causing him trouble.[1]

Mrs. Scaggs then testified under cross-examination about a trip Moses Hancock made out west with Joe Gassaway. Mr. Scaggs wanted Hancock to leave town because Hancock was being "meddled with" in Austin. Gassaway supplied the money and accompanied Hancock on the trip. Hancock said he was going out west to find a place for all of them to move, but Mrs. Scaggs did not want to move west. Hancock instructed them not to tell anyone where he had gone. Mrs. Scaggs did admit, though, that she knew Gassaway had been hired as a private detective by the police force to keep an eye on Hancock. Defense attorney Coopwood asked Mrs. Scaggs if she and her husband had hired Gassaway "as a detective to decoy Mr. Hancock off." Mrs. Scaggs did not answer the question directly, but said she supposed that Gassaway was a detective. She denied that she and her husband had any understanding with Gassaway about such a job.[2]

Mr. Bethel Coopwood had visited the Scaggs home while Hancock was in jail. According to Mrs. Scaggs, Coopwood "told us that he would find the party who committed the murder, and that some of the party was in Mexico." Mrs. Scaggs could not remember telling Coopwood that Hancock had gone to Fort Concho, though she made no secret about Hancock's having gone out west. She claimed she had never seen detective Bailes until about a month before the trial began. She said she never had a falling-out with Hancock, nor did she talk about his not paying board. She did say she could not afford "to board him for nothing." She also was not promised any part of the reward if Hancock was arrested and convicted. Mrs. Scaggs expressed ignorance about the relations between the Hancocks, though

> Mrs. Hancock and Lena both said it was a perfect disgrace when he was drinking; Mrs. Hancock also said that he threatened to kill her, but Mr. Scaggs laughed at her, but she said: "It is certainly in him, for he makes so many threats." She said she was afraid of him; Lena was present and heard her say this.

Mrs. Scaggs said that Mrs. Hancock made these comments in July of 1885 at the Moore house near the Narrow Gauge depot. Mrs. Scaggs admitted that Mrs. Hancock "was afraid of a drunken person." Mrs. Scaggs knew nothing about David Hagy and first saw him after Mrs. Hancock was wounded.[3]

The next witness was a sister of Mrs. Hancock, Mrs. M.J. Fallwell. She had married E.C. Fallwell in 1857 in Rusk County, Texas. She lived in Waco at the time of the attack. She stated that she had not been around the Hancocks much in the last five or six years. She had gone to their home in San Antonio once when Hancock had been drinking.

> My sister was afraid of him, and other drunken men, and she said she was tired of his drinking so; I never saw him mistreat her in my life; sometime when he was drunk he would curse, and say "Damn you, if you don't get out of my way, I'll kick you out." I have talked to him about the killing, and he said he was in Lena's room, and he was awakened by some kind of a struggling noise. He jumped, he said, and ran into the room where she was lying, and she was gone, and that he turned and ran out, but fell over a chair, and as he ran out into the yard he saw the glimpse of some one jumping the fence, and that he threw a rock at him; he said he did not know who did it. I know nothing about his making threats against his wife, or of his mistreating, except to get drunk.

Under cross-examination, Mrs. Fallwell said she had known Hancock about twenty years, since he had married her sister. The only mistreatment she had seen was his getting drunk, because Mrs. Hancock was "exceedingly nervous and easily excited, and she was afraid of any drunk man." Hancock treated his wife and daughters the same way when drunk as when sober. Mrs. Fallwell identified Mrs. Scaggs as her sister-in-law, but said she knew nothing about any plans the Scaggs might have to get Hancock convicted. She also knew little about David Hagy other than he had been kind to her and Mrs. Hancock's daughters, and he acted like "a perfect gentleman."[4]

J. Alexander Nisbet was the next to testify. He had first met the Hancocks in 1867 and had known them since they moved to Austin "in the latter part of 1884." He had been a regular visitor at their home and had never seen anything wrong other than when Mr. Hancock was drunk; then, Mrs. Hancock would be "uneasy." At one point Mrs. Hancock asked Nisbet to talk to Mr. Hancock about his drinking, which he did to little effect. He had never heard Hancock make any threats and never "saw anything unpleasant between them." Nisbet did not know David Hagy, but he had heard from Mrs. Scaggs a few weeks back that Hagy might be implicated in the murder of Mrs. Hancock.[5]

The next witness created a bit of controversy. Daniel J. Weed, about 50 years old, was a carpenter from San Antonio. He had known the Hancocks before the Civil War and again in San Antonio from about 1881 to the time they moved to Austin. Hancock had worked for Mr. Weed in San Antonio. He did not know much about the marital relations of the Hancocks, but he thought they lived together well. He had never heard of any threats or violence. The controversy came over who had called Weed as a witness. District Attorney Robertson asked who had attached him as a witness. Colonel Coopwood retorted that Weed was a witness for the state, so that Robertson must have had him attached, but Robertson claimed he knew nothing about it. Weed said that he "was attached and brought over, but attachments for other witnesses were not served as they were out of town." Again Robertson claimed he knew nothing about the attachment, and Coopwood demanded that all the evidence about the attachment be put down. Robertson said he would because he wanted to get to the bottom of the mystery, again claiming he knew nothing about the attachment. Regardless, the witness was asked a final question about Hancock. Weed said that Hancock had talked to him in San Antonio about the murder of his wife, "saying he thought he saw three men in his yard the night it was done; one of them being quite small."[6]

Mrs. M.J. Fallwell was then recalled. She stated that after the death of Mrs. Hancock, David Hagy was very poor. Hagy had told her that if she could not take Ida, the younger Hancock daughter, as had been arranged, then "he would take her to live with his mother, who was old and wanted company. He said he would give her a good education and dress her nice, if I and her father would consent to let her go." Mrs. Fallwell would not allow it, because she and her sister "had made an agreement years ago that if one died the other would take her little children and try to raise them right." District Attorney Robertson then asked Mrs. Fallwell whether she had told detective Bailes that Hagy said he would take one girl and a Mr. Sullivan would take the other. She emphatically denied that claim and also said that Hagy had never told her such a thing. In fact, she had never talked to Bailes about the disposition of the girls. Detective Bailes seemed to be making up much of his evidence.[7]

One of the Hancock daughters, 11-year-old Ida, was the next witness. She told her version of the events that occurred the night her mother was attacked. She and her sister had gone to a party at the home of Henry C. Ivey, a carpenter in his forties who lived at 704 West Ash. They were escorted to the party by David Hagy and arrived between 8 and 9 o'clock on Christmas Eve. Soon after they arrived, Hagy left, and Ida did not see him again until around 11 o'clock. At that time, Hagy rapped on the window and told Ida to get her sister so they could leave. When they got near home, they could see the commotion at the house. They knew nothing about their mother being injured before they arrived home, and Hagy had made no mention of it on the way. Under cross-examination, Ida revealed that the reason Hagy wanted them to leave the party was because a man was getting drunk and creating a disturbance. She said that Hagy had always been kind to them and to the family, and that they had asked him to take them to the party. He had also taken them to a dance at the Phillips place the night before. Hagy, however, had "hurt his knee on a nail and could not dance." Ida's parents had consented to their going to the party with Hagy, and they did not leave until Mrs. Persinger and their mother had returned from town after getting shoes mended. They had left a light burning in the parlor. Ida noted that her mother usually slept in the room where she was attacked, and her father slept in a back room. Ida slept with her father, and Lena slept with her mother. Her father was not drunk that night, and he was sober when they left for the party. Ida knew of no quarrel that evening.[8]

"The Letter"

Ida's sister followed her to the stand. Lena Hancock Ramsey, who was about 16 years old at the time of the murder, had married M.H. Ramsey just a few weeks after her mother was killed. Lena also talked about going to the Ivey party, saying that Hagy left after the first set. He later told her he had gone uptown to get some cigars and a handkerchief. They arrived home shortly after her mother was injured. When they arrived, Mrs. Hancock was on a pallet in the front room, being tended to by the doctors. Her testimony then turned to the supposedly incriminating letter written by her mother. Lena said she had seen her mother write the letter "long before she was killed," at a time when her father was building a house near the river bridge.

> The letter was produced and is the one upon which the detective and brilliant array of clue finders were going to convict Mr. Hancock. It was used in the Russian star chamber inquest and with the verdict in the case has been sealed until today. No man's eye was permitted to see it, and the mighty array of brilliant detective genius when alluding to it looked profoundly wise and with bated breath and hushed whispers said just enough to excite curiosity and Madam Rumor with her thousand tongues all agog. This famous letter. This marvelous piece of composition which rumor said was gory with bloody finger marks and which detectives had led one to believe contained a warning to Mrs. Hancock's sister living in Waco that

> she (Mrs. Hancock) was living in hourly dread of being murdered by her husband.

The letter had been recognized the day before by Mrs. Ramsey, a neighbor. The letter contained no date.

> Dear Husband:
> I have lived with you 18 years and have always tried to make you a good wife and help you all I could. I have loved you and followed you day and night. You won't quit whiskey, and I am so nervous I can't stand it, you know, it almost kills me for you to drink, and Lena is almost crazy and will lose her mind. If I was to do anything to disgrace you and our children, you would leave me, you would have quit me long ago. Take good care of yourself. Write to me at Waco, and I will answer every letter.
>
> Your wife until death,
> Sue Hancock

Lena confirmed that the letter was her mother's handwriting. Mrs. Hancock had written it because her husband had been drinking, causing tension in the family, but Mr. Hancock had never seen the letter. "It was put in a box of my artificial flowers, and it stayed there until mama was killed." Lena said she did not know who had removed the letter from the box, but she knew her mother did not write it on the day she was attacked, and she knew her father had never seen the letter.[9]

Lena continued her testimony, saying that her father was at home when Mrs. Hancock and Mrs. Persinger returned from getting the shoes fixed, and he was at home when she and Ida left for the party. He was sober at those times. Lena explained the sleeping arrangement, saying that "My mother, when nervous and sick, always slept with me, so I could attend to her, and not have papa disturbed, so he could sleep and be ready for work the next morning." Lena said that Hagy had not said anything about the attack on their way home from the party. Lena also stated that she knew Mrs. Scaggs, but she added that "I never heard my mama at the Moore house, tell Mrs. Scaggs that she was afraid of papa and that he had threatened to kill her. She never said any such thing." Lena said her father was kind to them and never whipped them, leaving any discipline to Mrs. Hancock. She also knew of no falling-out between Mr. Hancock and the Scaggs. When Lena concluded her testimony, the court recessed until 6 o'clock that evening.[10]

In the evening session, Mrs. M.J. Fallwell was recalled again. She said that she had a conversation in San Antonio with Mr. Hancock. Hancock wanted to get on the police force in Austin, and Marshal Lucy had promised him a position, but Hancock had made the remark in a joking way. Hancock also said if he was on the police force, he could carry a gun and "possibly prevent Tom Bailes and Luke Moore from dogging and dragging him about." This remark, too, was made in a joking way. Mrs. Fallwell told Hancock that the detectives were pretty much able to take care of themselves. Hancock "replied he could pour kerosene oil over their houses and touch a match to it, and it would bring them out. He was speaking about the way they had been treating and dogging him. He laughed when he said it." Apparently a suggestion had been made that Bailes and Moore, the sheriff in Waco, had "fixed up a job to kill him and claim the reward." Under cross-examination, Mrs. Fallwell clarified that she and Hancock were talking about Hancock losing a job because he had been arrested. Hancock had said nothing about Bailes and Moore plotting to kill him. He said that Bailes and Moore had arrested him and made him lose some work.[11]

Mrs. Fallwell was then asked by Justice Von Rosenberg, Jr., if she had ever seen the letter written by Mrs. Hancock. She said she first saw the letter the day Mrs. Hancock was buried. Sallie Ramsey had shown it to her at the Hancock house.

> "I think she said she got it out of a little satchel; we were packing up, and the floor was full of papers. When Miss Ramsey handed me the letter, I said I knew Mrs. Hancock had written it. I asked Mrs. Ramsey when she wrote it, but she did not know. I asked Ida if her mother wrote it, and she said that she did, and that it was written the day before her mother was killed, and that her mother was going off to Waco, and leave it in the trunk. I asked Lena about it, and she said that Ida was mistaken; her mother did no such thing."

Lena had said her mother wrote the letter in San Antonio, not recently.[12]

"A Decoy Detective"

The next witness was Joseph W. Gassaway, a rather spurious participant in the proceedings. Gassaway was about 38 years old at the time. The newspaper headline correctly called him "a decoy detective."

> Unbeknown to Hancock, the police had recruited Gassaway to watch Hancock and gather any information he could about the murder. Under instructions from his superiors, Gassaway suggested to the harried Hancock that it might be a good idea to get out of town for a while and he suggested that Hancock accompany him on a trip out west. Hancock agreed and on 21 February 1886 the two men boarded a train and headed for Fort Worth. From there they went to Colorado City, then to San Angelo. They then camped along the Concho river and eventually returned to Austin about the first of April.

Most of Gassaway's testimony dealt with what he learned on that trip.[13]

Gassaway first noted that he had known both Mr. and Mrs. Hancock before Mrs. Hancock had been killed, but he did not have an intimate acquaintance with either of them. He had first heard of the attack on Mrs. Hancock when he was in the Iron Front saloon on Christmas Eve 1885. At the time, he was boarding with Mr. Scaggs, the brother of Mrs. Hancock. He had gone from the saloon to the Scaggs house, awakened Mr. Scaggs, and together they went to the Hancock house. There,

Gassaway talked to Hancock.

> Hancock told me there that about 10 o'clock he and his wife were up, and he smoked and she dipped snuff. He said after they went to bed he heard a groaning noise, and got up, thinking his wife had a nightmare. He said he went into her room and, not finding anyone there, he went through the dining room and out of the back door, and that when he went through the dining room he made a fuss, and then he heard something drop on the ground, which he believed to be his wife who had been dropped. He then went out of the back door and saw his wife lying on the ground and a man standing close to her. He said that when the man saw him coming he started and ran away, and he (Hancock) picked up a brickbat and threw at him as he ran. He said that the man jumped over a back fence, near a little building that was back there. He said then that he took his wife up and brought her into the house, and when he got there he found he had no pants, somebody having taken all his clothes out of the house. At this time he had on a small pair of pants, which he said belonged to a young man who was boarding there; he told me afterwards that they were Mr. Hegga's; he told me that some one had broken open the trunks and plundered the house and went through the wardrobe that was in his wife's room, but that he hadn't missed anything except his clothing.

About that time, Mayor John Robertson and J.L. McCutcheon arrived. McCutcheon asked Hancock where his wife had been found, and Hancock led them into the backyard and showed them the place. The mayor asked Hancock what had happened, and Hancock started to tell the story but then became distracted and nervous. He pointed out the building by the back fence where he saw a man jump over. Gassaway returned to the Hancock place the next morning to investigate the scene by daylight. He saw someone pick up some clothes in the Persinger yard. He went into the alley to look for tracks, but he could find none that looked as if someone had jumped down from a high fence. He examined the top of the fence to see if there was any dirt there, as if someone might have stepped on the fence, but he found none. Then he went home.[14]

On the first of February, Gassaway was "detailed to watch Mr. Hancock and see that he did not get away. At the time Mr. Hancock was in jail and Mr. Scaggs was trying to get him out." When Hancock was released from jail, Gassaway was informed by Mr. John Kirk that he was no longer on the special police force, or so they would pretend. Gassaway would still collect his pay and was to report to the police any suspicious activities by Hancock. Gassaway, though, had no direct authority to arrest Hancock. Gassaway was instructed to try to convince Hancock to leave town, which was not hard to do since Hancock was tired of being dogged by the police and detectives. On February 21, 1886, the two left for Fort Worth and arrived there the next day. Hancock had a friend in Fort Worth named Frank Fogg. On February 24, they left Fort Worth for Colorado City. On the train ride, Hancock told Gassaway he had arranged with Mr. Fogg to receive his mails so that if an attempt was made to find out or follow him, or that if anything went wrong Frank Fogg would notify him of it, and that if they fooled with Fogg he would kill them or have it done; he went on to say that if he could raise money enough and about ten men, he would come back to Austin and raise more hell than had ever been raised here before; he would kill Von Rosenberg the first one and as for Bailes, he would hang him up by the neck.

After a few days in Colorado City, the two went on to San Angelo and then down to the Concho River around March 14. There, the two talked about the murder of Mrs. Hancock, and Hancock told a different story than he had given in Austin.

> He said that he saw two men with his wife; one of them had her under his arm carrying her off. This man had on either a Mother Hubbard or a slicker. He (Hancock) ran out and caught him by the arm and told him to turn her loose, and he dropped her on the ground. Just at that time, he said, a man poked a pistol around the corner of the kitchen, and told him that if he didn't turn that man loose he would blow the top of his head off; and he turned him loose and he ran off. The man with the pistol then ran, and as he ran, he (Hancock) threw a brick at him.

By March 19, the two had traveled to Coleman City, and there Hancock got drunk. Gassaway did not want to get drunk, and Hancock grew increasingly suspicious of Gassaway. Hancock asked if Gassaway was going back on him, and Gassaway said no, that "I never went back on a friend; not, at least until I had spilled every drop of blood in me." Hancock then made the strange remark that he had "spilled more blood than any one ever dreamed of." Hancock fumed, "Them damn sons of bitches down at Austin are trying to work up something on me, but they have not got anything, nor never will out of me." Gassaway then convinced Hancock to go to bed for the night.[15]

A couple of days later, Hancock said he was afraid something might have gone wrong in Austin because Jack Ramsey had not written to him. Gassaway asked Hancock if he thought his daughters would give him away, and Hancock said no, but he wanted to get them away from Austin as soon as possible. The two arrived back in Austin around the first of April. A couple of weeks later, Hancock got drunk, and Gassaway asked him if Hagy knew anything about the murder. Hancock said that he did not. The next day, at the dinner table at the Scaggs house, Hancock was again drunk. Detective Bailes came up in the conversation, and Hancock and Gassaway both said that Bailes couldn't prove anything because no one had seen the murder. Gassaway seemed to pump Hancock when he was drunk, and most of his incriminating comments came during those drunken sprees.[16]

Cross-examined, Gassaway said that on the morning after the murder, he saw Officer Thorp pick up some clothes in the Persinger yard. He also searched for tracks in the alley.

> I saw some tracks in the alley which I suppose had been made that night; they were going both ways; on Mr. Persinger's gate where the clothes were found, it seemed as if some one had climbed over the gate; there was dirt on it; the dirt indicated that two persons had got over it, or that one had got over it both ways; I did not try to follow a trail. I walked the full length of Mr. Hancock's yard, but I did not examine closely to see if there was blood on the wall of the stable or privy, nor did I examine the inside of the fence, nor did I examine the east end of the alley, but as far as I went I saw tracks going both ways.

With those comments, Gassaway was released as a witness, and court was adjourned for the day.[17]

"Hagy's Case"

The trial of Moses Hancock resumed the following Monday morning, June 21. But "a great deal of testimony was taken without material developments as to Hancock, and without showing anything against Dave Hagy, charged with being accessory to the murder." Most of the day was spent on testimony concerning David Hagy.[18]

The first witness to testify about Hagy was James Deison. James was an 18-year-old boy, the son of C.W. and Eliza Deison. James testified that he was at the party at the Ivey house on Christmas Eve 1885. Hagy and the Hancock girls arrived around 8:30 that evening. James did not have a lengthy conversation with Hagy, but Hagy did ask James if he wanted to go uptown. James said no, that he wished to stay and dance. Then Hagy went off and returned about 11 o'clock. He remained at the party a few minutes and then left for home with the Hancock girls. James affirmed that someone was getting drunk and making a disturbance at the party. However, he did not hear Hagy say "he had 'got back alive' or, 'that the work was done and he was ready to go home with the girls,' or, any thing of the kind." He had "never told Tom Bailes any such thing." Apparently Bailes had made up more evidence.[19]

The next witness, Louis Deison, was the younger brother of James Deison, about 13 years old. Louis gave much the same evidence his brother had. He had been at the Ivey party and had seen Hagy there about 9 o'clock. Then Hagy left and returned about 11 o'clock. Hagy and Louis said only good evening to each other, and Hagy asked Louis to fetch the Hancock girls to leave because a drunken man was creating trouble. Louis too denied that Hagy had made any boasts when he returned.

> He said nothing to me about "getting back alive", etc. nor did I hear him say such a thing to anybody else. I never told Bailes such a thing; I didn't know him; nor did I tell Carrington or

> Chapman such a thing; I told Carrington that I heard brother
> said he heard Hagy say it, but brother said I was mistaken.

The Carrington mentioned was probably Wiley H.D. Carrington, an attorney. Just who the Chapman person was is unclear.[20]

The following witness was another young man, 19-year-old George W. Ivey, the son of Henry Ivey, at whose home the Christmas Eve party took place. Like the Deison brothers, young Ivey stated that Hagy came to the party with the Hancock girls, left for a couple of hours, then returned and escorted the Hancock girls home. Ivey too did not hear Hagy make any boasts or suspicious remarks.[21]

The last witness regarding Hagy was Henry Reepe. He testified that he was with David Hagy at the corner of Congress Avenue and Pecan Street around 9 o'clock on Christmas Eve. He provided a schedule of their activities that evening.

> He stopped and asked me to go to the dance with him; he was alone, and I went with him to Hirshfield's where he bought a handkerchief; we went across to the corner of the bank and stopped there a few minutes talking; then we went up the Avenue and met three gentlemen, one of them Henry Hunt; Hagy introduced me to them; we went on up the Avenue to the Siftings saloon where we stopped a few minutes; we came back down the avenue to the National bank; Hagy asked me to go with him again to the dance; I went with him to West Pecan street to the dance; we stopped there about half an hour and saw them dancing a set or two; we were not inside the house; he came back with me as far as the Texas Siftings saloon; we left there and came back to the bank corner and sat down; Hagy tried to persuade me to go to the dance, to take one of the young ladies home; I told him I would go half way, and started out West Pecan street; I met Henry Hunt a second time; while at the corner of Lavaca going west, the town clock struck 11 o'clock; I went with him to the corner of Guadalupe and Pecan streets, where we talked about ten minutes; he started west and I came east on Pecan street to the corner of San Jacinto, to my room; that was the last I saw of him that night.

District Attorney Robertson asked why they were "running around so that night." Reepe replied that Hagy had a sore knee and didn't care to dance. They were just passing time uptown on Christmas Eve. Apparently Reepe was telling about two different parties, one on West Pecan and the other at the Ivey home.[22]

After hearing a wealth of testimony in Hagy's favor, Justice Von Rosenberg, Jr., decided to allow bail for Hagy. Thereafter, Hagy "was discharged on application for habeas corpus to Judge Walker." More of detective Bailes' evidence had failed to garner any sort of conviction.[23]

The next day, the *Austin Daily Statesman* published a blistering article that condemned Tom Bailes and his insubstantial evidence. The article began with a reprint of an article published in the *San Antonio Express* earlier in June. The article concerned the arrest of David Hagy in San Antonio by Captain Hughes, "the gallant captain of the detective force of the Alamo city, and T.O. Bailes—God knows who he really is—but he appears to be a private detective of the city of Austin." The Austin article then took Hughes and Bailes to task for tarnishing the reputation of Hagy.

> Upon an affidavit made by T. O. Bailes, David C. Hagy, a young man of exceptionable good character, an honest, hard-working man, born in this state, and raised here to manhood, was arrested. Up to the date of that arrest Hagy's character stood without a tarnish; yet, the moment the leprous hand of a hireling detective was laid upon him, its fetid grasp seemed to soil the fair escutcheon of Hagy's name. Yet, not so; for today, after nearly a week's time spent in the examining trial, the state failed to produce a scintilla of evidence against Hagy. Yet, in a few minutes, Hagy, through his attorney, proved by competent evidence, that Hagy not only had nothing to do with the killing, but beyond any reasonable doubt knew nothing about it. The only present solace Hagy can have, is in the relief that the little, shriveled souls of all perjured scoundrels shall crisp in hell throughout eternity. The arrest of young Hagy seemed to be the result of a "coalition," the soul and inspiration is corruption, and the putrid rottenness of which stinks in the nostrils of all people; and even a decent turkey-buzzard would have poised in mid-air before sticking his bill in such a mess of corruption. Yet T. O. Bailes seemed to get mad when C. S. Robinson, attorney for Hagy, pointed to him and said, "that man's oath is all the evidence you have against my client, and between Hagy's record and Bailes' oath let the next grand jury of Travis county decide."

Who was Thomas O. Bailes? He was born in Tennessee in 1847. By 1880, he was married with five children. He was working as a deputy sheriff in Belton, Bell County, Texas, where the Norwood brothers were captured and apparently where Eula Phillips' father lived. By 1885, Bailes was the assistant chief of the Capital Detective Association. He was also responsible for the failed attempts to try several of the suspects in the servant girl murders.[24]

"Judge Hancock's Testimony"

Meanwhile, the preliminary trial of Moses Hancock, interrupted by the persecution of David Hagy, was winding down. The last witness of the day on June 21 was Judge John Hancock, who was also one of the defense attorneys for Moses Hancock. Judge Hancock's testimony focused on his dealings with Mr. W.T. Scaggs, the brother of Sue Hancock.

> He came to my office about three weeks ago for consultation with me. I took him into a private room, when he alluded to the

> murder of his sister, and asked me if I would prosecute the
> person who had murdered her. I asked him who he meant, and
> he said he had changed his mind and now believed that
> Hancock, the defendant, had murdered her. I remarked to him
> that it was absurd, and that if that was what he meant, I would
> not prosecute him. I also told him in the conversation that I did
> not know the defendant, Hancock, but that he bore my name
> and that he was a poor man, and having heard from
> respectable parties that knew him that he was an inoffensive
> man, I had got Mr. Coopwood to join me in looking into the
> case, and the result of the investigation that he (Scaggs), said
> to Coopwood when Coopwood was making the investigation,
> that he (Scaggs) regarded Hancock as innocent of the crime.

Scaggs told Hancock that new facts had arisen that had made him change his mind about his brother-in-law. Judge Hancock asked Scaggs what was the matter with Hancock, and Scaggs replied that Hancock had sent him "a very insulting message" recently. Judge Hancock asked Scaggs if Hancock had been drinking, and Scaggs said yes, that Hancock was drinking and not doing any work because he was drinking. Judge Hancock replied that Hancock's drinking might account for the insulting message, and that he would hear no more from Scaggs. With the end of Judge Hancock's testimony, court adjourned for the day.[25]

"Deeper Mystery"

When court resumed on the morning of June 22, the preliminary trial for Moses Hancock was terminated. "The prisoner was, after a full and searching investigation into all the circumstances, admitted to merely nominal bail. The $500 bond required by the examining court under so grave a charge, is equivalent, almost, to a presumption of innocence." The trial had developed little evidence against Hancock. He drank a lot and often made threats, but he was not unkind to his wife or daughters. His wife, though, was nervous and uneasy around drunk men. Whether Hancock was wearing pants on the night of the attacks was another key point in the trial, and most witnesses agreed he was not. A few bits of evidence regarding the attack were also gathered.

> Among them, the tracks found in the alley after the fatal
> assault on Mrs. Hancock; the four unknown men seen running
> from the house immediately after the alarm was raised;
> Hancock's statement to a witness that he saw a man standing
> over the prostrate form of his wife out in the yard; and the
> connection of the Pinkerton's detectives with the case. Another
> curious fact developed in the testimony was the striking
> similarity of this to all the other assassinations of women in
> Austin during 1885. Mrs. Hancock was cut in the head with an
> axe and dragged into the back yard. So were all the other
> victims.

If the small bond required suggested Hancock's presumed innocence, then the police and detectives had failed again to find the perpetrator of the awful murders. The apparent failure to find the killer of Mrs. Hancock made "that awful crime, along with the other murders, a far deeper, more startling mystery than ever before."[26]

Though Moses Hancock was indicted in the preliminary trial, the flimsy evidence against him and the modest bond required of him might make one assume that the case would simply wither away. One would be mistaken. In October 1886, after the grand jury of Travis County again indicted him, Moses Hancock was arrested by Sheriff Malcolm Hornsby. Hancock was apprehended in Elgin, about 25 miles east of Austin, where he had been working as a carpenter on the Missouri Pacific railroad extension for about three weeks. When arrested, Hancock "appeared embarrassed and nervous. He tried to appear calm and collected, but could not conceal his evident uneasiness." Hornsby did not think the state had a very strong case against Hancock. According to the Fort Worth newspaper, "It is not pretended there is any more evidence against Hancock now than at his preliminary trial, and that was almost nothing." The newspaper was not convinced of Hancock's guilt.

> Even supposing Hancock and Phillips did murder their wives at the same hour of the same night, or very near it, the murderers of the other five women and servant girls have not yet been discovered. It will be remembered they were all committed in the same style, all knocked in the head with a hatchet or ax, and dragged out to a remote part of the yard. Mrs. Hancock was the only one of the victims who was left alive after the assault. She never spoke, and was only partly conscious before her death.

The full trial was set for November 8. However, later in October the Phillips trial was appealed to the Texas Court of Appeals. The Phillips verdict was reversed and remanded to the lower court. With those developments, the Hancock case was apparently delayed until the early summer of 1887.[27]

Notes

Title: *Austin Daily Statesman*, 6/19/1886.

1. *Austin Daily Statesman*, 6/19/1886; "Texas Marriages, 1837-1973"; *Morrison & Fourmy's General Directory of the City of Austin, 1885-1886* (W.T. Scaggs was incorrectly listed in the 1885-1886 city directory as William T. Scraggs; Scaggs operated a grocery store at 907 East Cedar Street and resided at the same address.)
2. *Austin Daily Statesman*, 6/19/1886.
3. *Austin Daily Statesman*, 6/19/1886.
4. *Austin Daily Statesman*, 6/19/1886.
5. *Austin Daily Statesman*, 6/19/1886; 1870 Federal Census; *Morrison & Fourmy's General Directory of the City of Austin, 1885-1886*; "Texas Marriages, 1837-1973"; Morrison &

Fourmy's General Directory of the City of Austin, 1889-1890 (The news report identified this witness as J.A. Nesbit, but it was likely J. Alexander Nisbet, about 25 years old, who grew up in Bell County, Texas. In July 1886, he married Eliza J. Davis, and by 1889 she was running a boarding house on East 6th Street.)

6. *Austin Daily Statesman*, 6/19/1886; 1880 Federal Census.
7. *Austin Daily Statesman*, 6/19/1886.
8. *Austin Daily Statesman*, 6/19/1886; 1880 Federal Census; *Morrison & Fourmy's General Directory of the City of Austin, 1885-1886* (David Hagy could not dance because of an injured knee, but he could wander all over downtown Austin on that same injured knee.)
9. *Austin Daily Statesman*, 6/19/1886.
10. *Austin Daily Statesman*, 6/19/1886.
11. *Austin Daily Statesman*, 6/19/1886.
12. *Austin Daily Statesman*, 6/19/1886.
13. *Austin Daily Statesman*, 6/19/1886; Galloway, *The Servant Girl Murders*: 302-303; Oakwood Cemetery Database.
14. *Austin Daily Statesman*, 6/19/1886; *Morrison & Fourmy's General Directory of the City of Austin, 1885-1886*; "J.L. McCutcheon"; "H.L. McCutcheon" (In the Phillips case, George McCutcheon played a key role in the trial. The McCutcheon mentioned here apparently was not related to George McCutcheon or the McCutcheon clan from Williamson County. Joshua L. McCutcheon was a partner in Thompson & Company, which sold agricultural implements on East Pecan Street. His brother, Henry L. McCutcheon, worked there as a clerk. The two apparently were born in England in the 1840s and were buried in Houston in the early 1900s.)
15. *Austin Daily Statesman*, 6/19/1886.
16. *Austin Daily Statesman*, 6/19/1886.
17. *Austin Daily Statesman*, 6/19/1886.
18. *Austin Daily Statesman*, 6/22/1886.
19. *Austin Daily Statesman*, 6/22/1886; 1880 Federal Census.
20. *Austin Daily Statesman*, 6/22/1886; 1880 Federal Census; *Morrison & Fourmy's General Directory of the City of Austin, 1885-1886* (The Chapman mentioned might have been Charles C. Chapman, the proprietor of the Lodge Saloon, or Frank A. Chapman, the treasurer of the Capital Gaslight Company.)
21. *Austin Daily Statesman*, 6/22/1886; 1880 Federal Census.
22. *Austin Daily Statesman*, 6/22/1886; *Morrison & Fourmy's General Directory of the City of Austin, 1885-1886* (This witness was probably Henry Reef, a carpenter who boarded at the San Jacinto House at 606 San Jacinto.)
23. *Austin Daily Statesman*, 6/22/1886.
24. *Austin Daily Statesman*, 6/22/1886; 1880 Federal Census; *Morrison & Fourmy's General Directory of the City of Austin, 1885-1886*.
25. *Austin Daily Statesman*, 6/22/1886.
26. *Austin Daily Statesman*, 6/23/1886; *Brenham Weekly Banner*, 6/24/1886.
27. *Fort Worth Daily Gazette*, 10/18/1886; *Fort Worth Daily Gazette*, 10/19/1886; *Austin Daily Statesman*, 10/22/1886; *Austin Daily Statesman*, 11/11/1886.

Chapter 25

"Distressingly Conflicting Statements"

The Full Trial of Moses Hancock Begins

The full trial of Moses Hancock began on May 31, 1887, a Tuesday. For the most part, the full trial retraced the testimony in the preliminary trial a year earlier. A few new witnesses were called, but little new evidence surfaced.

One of the new witnesses was Horace Roscoe Burt, the teenaged son of Dr. W.J. Burt, the city physician. Roscoe went with his father to the Hancock house on the night Mrs. Hancock was attacked. When they arrived, a large crowd had already gathered, thirty or forty people. About a half hour after they arrived, Roscoe met a schoolmate named Davis, and the two, in the finest Hardy Boys tradition, decided to examine the premises to see what clues they could find. They first went into the room in which Mrs. Hancock slept. The cover was turned down, and on the bottom sheet they noticed a small quantity of blood. They next went into Mr. Hancock's sleeping chamber, and there on the bedsheet they found a spot of blood about the size of a dollar. On a stand in the room was a bowl of greasy-looking water, but there was no sign of blood in the water, and on the floor near the bowl was spilled water. They next looked through the bureau and under the bed but found nothing. David Hagy soon arrived with the Hancock girls, and Hagy showed the boys his room. They found nothing suspicious in Hagy's room. Then they ventured outside through the front room in which Mrs. Hancock lay wounded. Outside, using a "common globe lantern," they investigated the Hancock yard. Near the front door they found a bloody ax. "It seemed as if the body of Mrs. Hancock had been dragged over it, as it had blood on the top and had made an impression in the ground." They followed a trail of blood back to the house. Where the front porch joined the house, Roscoe found a pearl shirt button that Mr. Hancock later said had been torn off when he picked up his wife to carry her inside. The two young investigators found no blood on the fences or the outbuildings, but they saw lots of tracks, especially since a large crowd of people had gathered and were traipsing around the yard. The two made a brief examination of the Persinger yard but discovered nothing. Roscoe saw Mr. Hancock once in the yard while they were investigating. He believed Mr. Hancock had on pants, but he could not remember the color, but he did notice that Hancock was missing a button from his shirt sleeve.[1]

Under cross-examination, Roscoe Burt could not remember whom he saw there. He did recall Tom Glass coming to fetch his father, Dr. Burt, but he could not recall when Dr. Graves arrived; he did not know if Mrs. Persinger was present, but he did see Mr. Persinger and Paul Haenelt, the barber. Roscoe reiterated that he had investigated Mrs. Hancock's room first.

> I don't remember seeing any blood leading from her room to the room where she was lying wounded; when we went trailing round the axe was still lying on the ground and had not been moved; I picked it up; it left its print on the ground; there was no blood on the ground where it was lying; I put it back; Mr. Davis was with me when I picked it up; I don't remember that Mr. Davis told me that the axe was there before we started out; we passed the axe before we reached the large pool of blood; the blood was on the top of the axe as if it dropped there when the body was dragged over it and I don't remember seeing any blood on the bottom of it.

Roscoe noted that the moon was shining brightly as they investigated using the lantern. Roscoe repeated that they examined the fence and stable carefully but found no blood on either of them.[2]

Rosa King repeated much of her testimony from the earlier trial. She had been living at the home of Mr. and Mrs. Tom Glass for about two weeks, nursing Mrs. Lena Glass, who had given birth to a child a couple of months before the attack. The couple had been married in 1884. The Hancock house stood to the west of the Glass house, separated by a fence about four feet tall. Around 11 o'clock on Christmas Eve, Mrs. Glass heard a groan outside and thought her husband was coming home drunk. The groan repeated, and this time Rosa King heard it, too.

> We jumped up and ran to the window and looked over into Hancock's yard, and saw Mrs. Hancock lying on the ground and her husband standing at her head; he was hollering some one has murdered my wife; run you thieving son of a bitch I see you; we could see no one running; I never heard anyone jump over the fence; I never saw a man standing at the corner of the house; I never saw a man standing with his six shooter drawn on Mr. Hancock; I saw no one but Mr. Hancock who had got up and went to Mrs. Hancock's relief.

King recalled that Mr. Hancock appeared to be dressed in light clothing, and "Mrs. Hancock seemed to be dressed in white, or had a sheet about her." Paul Haenelt, who lived at the Glass house with his wife, quickly went over to the Hancock house, jumping the fence. He helped Hancock carry the injured woman into the house. King saw four men enter the Hancock house and then leave quickly; she assumed they were the police. Two went east down the street, and two went up the street. King heard no one yelling except Hancock, and "no man could have passed across the Hancock yard from where Mrs. Hancock lay" without her seeing him.[3]

Next to testify was Lena Glass, the young wife of Tom Glass. She stated that she lived on East Water Street near the Hancock house. She had been at home sick the night Mrs. Hancock was attacked, and Rosa King was there nursing her. Mr. Hancock had come over to the Glass house earlier that evening to visit Mrs. Glass and her baby. Later, she heard groans and thought they came from the alley, and she suspected her husband was coming home drunk. But the groaning persisted, and then she heard Mr. Hancock yelling. She looked out and saw Hancock standing over his wife in the backyard. She saw Hancock throw rocks in the direction of his stable, but she saw no one running. Before the groans, she had heard no disturbance at the Hancock place. Under cross-examination, Mrs. Glass gave further details on Hancock's visit to her house. Hancock came over about 6:30 that evening. He did not stay long, nor did he sit down, and he left before Mr. Glass departed for town. She thought that Mr. George Brown was in the Hancock's yard shortly after Mrs. Hancock was wounded. Mrs. Glass had not talked to any young men on the evening of the attack, and she did not talk to the two young men who had a lantern, assumedly Roscoe Burt and his friend Davis.[4]

Mrs. Glass was followed to the witness chair by David Hagy. Hagy stated that he was a boarder at the Hancock house and that he left the house with the Hancock girls at about 7 o'clock on Christmas Eve. When they left, only Mr. and Mrs. Hancock were at home. They returned a little after midnight, for they heard the town clock strike 12 as they crossed Congress Avenue, about two blocks from the Hancock house. They first sensed trouble when they reached the Persinger place, for they saw all the carriages and people milling about. Ida Hancock cried out that someone had killed her father, and she tried to break loose and run to the house, but Hagy held her by the hand. Cross-examined, Hagy said when they entered the house, he saw Mrs. Hancock lying on the floor, with three men dressing her wounds. Mr. Hancock was also in the room. Marshal Lucy and Justice Von Rosenberg went with Hagy to his room, where he noticed that his bank checks and other accounts had not been disturbed. Hagy then held the lamp as Lucy and Von Rosenberg searched Mr. Hancock's room. They noted the spot of blood on the sheets and the water on the floor by the washstand. Hagy said that Hancock was sober when they left for the party and sober when they returned.[5]

"A Mass of Testimony"

The next witness was J.W. Gassaway. Gassaway stated that he was a boarder at the Scaggs home, and that Mr. Scaggs was a brother to Mrs. Hancock. Gassaway went to the Hancock house on the night of the attack. There, Hancock told him what had happened.

> He told me that at 10 o'clock he and his wife were up, and that he smoked and his wife dipped snuff; about a quarter to 11 he heard a noise and thought it was his wife having a nightmare. He heard it again and got up and went to her room, but she not being there he passed out. While in the room he said he heard something fall, and supposed afterwards that it was his wife when she fell; he passed out the door and saw a man standing over his wife; he threw a rock at him, and he ran and jumped over the fence.

Gassaway recounted his trip out west with Hancock, noting that on March 14 on the Concho River, Hancock told him a different version of the night's events.

> He told me at this time as we walked down on the Concho river, that when he went into his wife's room and not finding her, that he went into the yard and saw a man with a Mother Hubbard or slicker on, carrying his wife, and that he caught the man by the arm and said, drop her, god damn you, and he dropped her; he said that at this time another man near the house drew a six-shooter on him and said to him, If you ever say anything about this I'll kill you. As he held the pistol on him the one who had his wife ran off and that he (Hancock) threw a brick at him.

On the night of the attack, Hancock had pointed out to Gassaway where the killer had jumped the fence. The next morning, Gassaway examined the ground, which was soft and sandy, but could find no tracks. He believed a man jumping from the top of the fence would have to make tracks. He also could not see any dirt at the top of the fence. He did see Hancock's clothes being picked up in the Persingers' yard. Gassaway then gave "a mass of testimony relating to a conversation he had with Hancock which was ruled out, as it did not bear directly upon the fact of the murder of his wife."[6]

Under cross-examination, Gassaway gave details about his serving as a detective to watch Hancock when he was released from jail. Gassaway had "orders to watch him, talk to him and get his confidence and find out what I could." Gassaway was made a policeman by Marshal Lucy, and then Captain Kirk introduced Gassaway to a man named Roberts, whom Gassaway would work under. Roberts also gave Gassaway money to pay for expenses on his trip out west with Hancock. Gassaway was ordered to lure Hancock out of town, but he could not arrest Hancock even if Hancock tried to leave him. During their trip west, Hancock and Gassaway parted at Coleman City. Gassaway returned to Austin, and later Hancock returned to Austin on his own.[7]

Daniel J. Weed of San Antonio was the next witness. Weed testified that he had known Hancock since the time of the Civil War, first in Bryan, Texas, then later in San Antonio. Weed had never heard Hancock say an "ill word" to his wife, and he believed they got along together well. He stated that after getting out of jail, Hancock came to visit him in San Antonio. At that time, Hancock had told Weed about the murder of his wife.

> He said somebody had knocked her in the head; that on the night of the killing he and his wife ate cake about 9 or 10 o'clock; and that he then smoked and went to bed; he did not sleep well and finally he heard some groans, and, getting up and going into the yard, he saw two men with his wife, one of them having his hand on her breast and the other standing over her. He said one of the men . . . looked as if he had on a Mother Hubbard.

Weed said he thought the Hancocks left San Antonio because of some trouble they had with people named Woods living on Flores Street. Apparently one of the Woods' boys hit Mrs. Hancock in the head, cutting her badly.[8]

Following Weed was Mrs. M.J. Fallwell, the sister of Mrs. Hancock who lived in Waco. She had come to Austin the day after the attack. Mrs. Fallwell had visited the Hancock family in San Antonio and in Austin.

> They had plenty to eat when I visited them, but sister said they were not doing so well in Austin, as Mr. Hancock had been drinking some; in dressing her I found that one of her knees had been badly bruised and was very black; her leg was swollen almost as large as a stove pipe; her throat was also swollen as if she had been choked. I took her children to Waco.

Mrs. Fallwell said she corresponded with Mrs. Hancock regularly and knew her handwriting. When presented a letter, Mrs. Fallwell said it had been written by her sister and that Miss Sallie Ramsey had given her the letter the morning they were packing the girls' trunk after Mrs. Hancock had died. Mrs. Fallwell noted that Miss Ramsey had since died. Though the letter was admissible in the preliminary trial, in this trial the defense objected to admitting the letter because it was "incompetent and irrelevant." The objection was sustained for the time being.[9]

Mrs. Fallwell continued her testimony, focusing on the marital relations between Mr. and Mrs. Hancock.

> From my own knowledge I don't think Mr. Hancock and my sister lived together happily for the last two or three years of her life. My sister made arrangements secretly with me to come to Waco with her children and live with me; she intended to leave Mr. Hancock. I have heard my sister and Mr. Hancock quarrel; I have heard Mr. Hancock when drunk curse her, but I never saw him strike her. He was a drinking man for three or four years.

Mrs. Fallwell then explained that Mr. Hancock was in jail when Sallie Ramsey gave her the letter. Mr. Hancock had told her what had happened the night of the attack, and her version was similar to the one generally told. Under cross-examination, Mrs. Fallwell pointed out that she had known Mr. Hancock for about twenty years, and that he was given to cursing when drunk: "When drunk, he would curse the children, or dog, or anything that was in his way; he would curse my sister and she would cry." With those comments, Mrs. Fallwell was released as a witness.[10]

Marshal James Lucy testified next. Lucy was on Bois 'd Arc Street between 10 and 11 o'clock on Christmas Eve when he heard about the attack on Mrs. Hancock. He got in a hack with Will Lambert and went immediately to the Hancock house. There, Lucy saw Mrs. Hancock lying seriously wounded in the front room. He questioned Mr. Hancock about the attack and received the most common version.

> He told me that he was awakened by hearing groans, and went
> out and found his wife. A man was dragging her; he picked up
> a brick and threw it at him, and he ran and jumped over the
> back fence. He said he thought there were two men; he told me
> the same story the next morning.

Lucy made a brief examination of the room in which Mrs. Hancock had been sleeping and also of the back fence, though Hancock had not given him the exact spot the attacker supposedly jumped the fence. Lucy could find no trails leading away from the scene. Two dogs were summoned, but they too could find no trail. Lucy then noted that a few months later, Hancock gave him a slightly different version of the events.

> Some months afterwards in my office he told me that when he
> came out to where his wife was he grabbed the man who had
> her and just then another man stepped out and drew a pistol
> on him and told him to turn the man loose, and that if he ever
> said anything about it he would kill him.

Cross-examined, Lucy repeated some of the same details. He could find no tracks going across the fence. Hancock thought there were two men but saw only one. The Hancock girls arrived after Lucy was on the scene.[11]

The last witness of the day was O.W. Picker. Picker had talked to Hancock the morning after the attack. Hancock told Picker a similar version of the events, but he also seemed quite interested in showing Picker some blood on the privy. Hancock

> stated that he was in the room separate from his wife, and that
> he was awakened by a noise in his wife's room and that he got
> up to go and see the cause of it. At first, he said, he thought
> his wife had a nightmare as she was subject to them. Going to
> her room, he said, he fell over a chair and just then he heard
> something drop in the yard. He looked out and saw his wife
> lying on the ground and had men near her; they ran and he
> threw a rock at one of them. He showed me where the men had
> jumped the fence, and called my attention to a spot of blood on
> the rear of the privy; it was a small spot and looked to me as if
> it was fresh blood. . . . He told me before I got down off my
> horse that he would show me blood, on the rear of the privy.

Under cross-examination, Picker stated that the sand was on the fence on the west side of the lot, and the blood was on the privy in the Hancock yard. When Picker concluded his testimony, the court adjourned for the day.[12]

The Second Day of the Trial

On the second day of the trial, June 1, the first witness was Thomas Glass, who lived in the house to the east of the Hancock place. Glass's testimony in this trial was much like his testimony in the preliminary trial, but this time he had some trouble keeping his comments consistent. Glass first discussed the living situation at his home. Mr. and Mrs. Paul Haenelt and their family lived there, as did Glass, his wife, his baby, and Rosa King, a black servant. Glass next discussed the events of Christmas Eve 1885.

> I was at home on Christmas eve about 6:30. I saw Mr. Hancock that evening, and also his wife; I saw her on the porch one time, and again standing at the fence, where I talked to her. At this time Mr. Hancock was sitting on the porch about seven feet from her; our conversation was in the ordinary tone of voice, but loud enough to be heard by Hancock, if he listened. Mrs. Hancock called me from the gallery and said, "will you please get Mr. Hancock to go up town with you," and that she would go and stay with my wife; she said she was afraid to stay with him, as he had threatened to kill her. I said "oh, no," but she said, "I wish to gracious you would get him to go, for I'm afraid to stay with him." I promised to try and get him to go, and asked him to go up town with me, but he refused saying that he did not want to go. It was the first time he ever refused to go with me. After supper Mrs. Hancock asked me if Hancock was going with me; I told her no. She again said, "I wish to gracious you would get him to go for I'm afraid of him." I told her I would try him again but he still refused and I went off alone.

Glass noted that he was alone at the Iron Front saloon when he heard the news of the attack from a hack driver named Farrar. He rode Farrar's hack back to the Hancock place.[13]

    Cross-examined, Glass indicated that Mr. Hancock had eaten supper at his house on Christmas Eve, along with Mrs. Glass and Joe Glass, Tom's brother. According to Glass, no one else was at the table. About a half hour after supper, Glass went uptown alone after Hancock had refused to go with him. When he heard of the attack on Mrs. Hancock, he was alone at the Iron Front saloon playing billiards. He was informed by Mr. Farrar and went home alone in Farrar's hack. When he reached home, "only Mr. Haenelt and the home folks were there." He met Haenelt outside; Haenelt was on his way to fetch a doctor. Glass then went to the Hancock house, and he thought the hack driver went, too. He did not recall if Mr. Persinger or Mr. Brunet was present. Mrs. Hancock was lying with her head toward the front door, but Glass could not recall if she was lying on the floor. Glass stayed at the Hancock house only ten or fifteen minutes, then went home. Glass said that a number of people came to his gate, but he did not think anyone came in the house.[14]

    Glass then became confused about some of his answers. Glass said that his conversation with Mrs. Hancock occurred after the Hancock girls left for the party. He said he saw them leave as he stood on his porch, but he did not know which way they went. The defense attorney questioned his memory, noting that he had said in the preliminary trial that the Hancock girls passed by his gate, suggesting he knew which way they were going. Glass said he could not remember making that statement in the preliminary trial. Glass then said that after the Hancock girls left, he went inside his house and told his wife he was going uptown. Glass then said, "My two conversations with Mrs. Hancock and my conversations with Mr. Hancock all occurred after the girls left." He said that after Hancock ate supper, he went home. Glass then said, "I think the girls were in the house when I talked with Mr. Hancock." The defense attorney quickly caught Glass on his conflicting statements: "Then why did you say awhile ago that all these conversations occurred after the girls left?" Glass could not recall having made that statement only minutes earlier. He tried to clarify, but his testimony became more confused:

> The conversation I had with Mr. Hancock was before the girls left, but they had gone when I had the second conversation with Mrs. Hancock. I don't remember meeting Mrs. Hancock and Mrs. Persinger in front of the Raymond house as I went up town. I did not start from my house before it was dark; I left Mrs. Hancock there when I left. I went up the avenue, but don't remember which side. I think I talked with Mrs. Hancock a half an hour; Mr. Hancock was sitting on the porch at the time.

Glass was then questioned about George Brown, the brother of Mrs. Persinger. Glass could not recall if Brown ate supper with him or not, though earlier he stated that Brown was not at the table. Glass said Brown did not go to the Iron Front with him, though Brown later said he did. He did not know how long Brown was at his house or which way Brown went when he left. Glass also could not remember at what time of the evening he talked to Mrs. Hancock. Re-examined, Glass admitted, "My memory is not good about dates or times. I have told everything as I remember it." He did not seem to remember so well.[15]

The next witness for the prosecution was W.T. Scaggs, the brother of Mrs. Hancock. His testimony was much the same as he gave at the preliminary trial, but it did add a few details. He noted that he was living near William B. Walker's grocery store at 907 East Cedar on the night of the attack. He heard about the attack around 11 o'clock and went with Joe Gassaway to the Hancock house.

> When I got there the house and yard were full of people. I saw that my sister was wounded in the head, and that she was restless and that she appeared to be dying. I have visited the house, but never made an examination of the place; my family and Mr. Hancock's visited. I came from Waco here, and they came from San Antonio. My sister had been in bad health, and Dr. Bragg had been treating her. She had two children. I took no steps to have anyone arrested for the murder, but of course I was looking and trying to find out something but nothing was satisfactory. After my sister's death Mr. Hancock stayed at my home several weeks. Once he went off and then came back.

Scaggs noted that after Hancock returned from his trip out west with Gassaway, he was at the Scaggs home on April 14. Conversation turned to the murder case, and Hancock asked Scaggs if he had heard any recent news about it. Hancock stated that some people were still working on the case, but they could get nothing on him because no one saw it happen. He also hoped that Gassaway was not going to betray him, but even if he did he was not worried because he was going to Brazil in about three days. After that night, Hancock never went to the Scaggs house again.[16]

Scaggs also recounted the version of the events Hancock had told him on Christmas morning.

> He told me that he did not know who killed her, but said that my sister appeared lively that night and in good spirits, and that the children had gone to a party. He said that they went to bed, but could not sleep and that they got up and he smoked and she dipped; they also ate some cake. Then they went to bed again, and shortly after he heard a strange noise; he thought my sister had a nightmare and got up to see. She was not in her room, and he said he looked in the yard and saw her lying on the ground and a man running away; he threw a rock at him. He could not tell whether he was white or black. He spoke of the doors and windows, and said anybody could open them; he said a light was burning in the house.

Hancock also told Scaggs about being in jail with a man who had robbed the mail. Hancock was sure the man was not a detective, but even if he was, it didn't matter because "he'd be damned if he told him anything."[17]

The last witnesses for the prosecution were relatively minor. J.M. Casanova testified that he and Hester Johnson went to the Hancock house about 8:30 on Christmas Eve to see if the Hancock girls were at home. The girls had gone to a party, and only Mrs. Hancock seemed to be at home, though Casanova recalled on cross-examination that Mr. Hancock might have been in the next room. They stayed with Mrs. Hancock for about 15 minutes. She was lying across a bed the whole time. Casanova saw no one outside around the place. The front door was open when they arrived and open when they left.[18]

The final prosecution witness called to the stand was Isaiah W. Johnson, a popular policemen. He was on duty on Congress Avenue on Christmas Eve and first heard of the attack on Mrs. Hancock from Joshua McCutcheon. Johnson immediately went to Smith's opera house to find Marshal Lucy. Not finding Lucy there, Johnson went to the Hancock house on Water Street. There were already several people on the scene when Johnson arrived.

> Mr. Hancock was pointed out to me and I called him out and asked him about the murder; he said he did not know how it occurred. He showed me an axe, which he said he supposed was used to kill his wife; it was standing against the shed room when he picked it up and he stated to me that he found it there. It had blood on one side of it and on the handle. He stated that he had gone to bed and was awakened by groans. He thought it was his wife with a nightmare and got up and went to her room, she was not there and he says he turned and

> fell over a chair and got his hand in some blood. This first created a suspicion that something was wrong, and that his wife had been hurt and he looked for her into the yard and saw his wife lying on the ground and a man running away from her. He threw a rock at the man as he ran, but missed him and struck the stable.

The location of the ax in Johnson's account differed greatly from the account given by Roscoe Burt on the first day of the trial. Under cross-examination, Johnson said that when he arrived, Mrs. Hancock's wounds were being washed in the house. Two or three ladies were in the room, but Johnson did not see Dr. Burt. The defense apparently tried to suggest that more than one ax was on the place, or that Johnson had pointed out the ax to Hancock. But Johnson stated: "I only saw one axe. I don't remember calling out Mr. Hancock and showing him the axe and telling him here is the instrument the work was done with."[19]

Before closing, the prosecution presented Mr. Hancock's statement made before the coroner's jury. In it, he told much the same story he had repeated numerous times.

> They ate supper about 7 o'clock on the night of the murder; that after supper his wife and Mrs. Persinger went up town to have buttons fixed on a pair of shoes. They were gone about half an hour or three quarters; he did not know that she had gone to the shoe store until she came back and told him where she had been. He stated that he and his wife ate cake and he smoked after Hagy and the girls left for the party a little after 8 o'clock. He and his wife went to bed about 9 but afterwards got up and ate some cake and he smoked a pipe full of tobacco, they then retired again, his wife went to bed in her room, and he in his room, a light was left in Mr. Hagy's and in the front room. The doors and windows were left open. He then relates the nightmare story, and him going into his wife's room and his not finding her.

He then heard groans outside and, turning to go outside, bumped into a chair. He heard something drop. Getting outside, he saw his wife in the yard and saw a man running away from her. He threw a rock at the running man. Hancock and Mr. Persinger carried the injured Mrs. Hancock into the house. Mr. Haenelt was the first one to show him the bloody ax. Hancock knew of no one who harbored ill will against him or his wife. They visited little but had a good amount of company. Hancock stated that his wife was 40 years old and had been suffering from rheumatism for several years. With Hancock's statement read, the prosecution rested.[20]

Notes

Title: *Austin Daily Statesman*, 6/2/1887.

1. *Fort Worth Daily Gazette*, 6/1/1887; *Austin Daily Statesman*, 6/1/1887 (Many different locations were given for the ax/hatchet, near the front door or "a short distance from it," by the stable, against the fence, near Mrs. Hancock's window. Also curious was Hancock's statement that he tore off the pearl button when he picked up his injured wife to carry her inside. Roscoe Burt said he found the button where the front porch met the house. Various reports indicated that Hancock and either Haenelt or Persinger carried her inside through a back door.)
2. *Fort Worth Daily Gazette*, 6/1/1887; *Austin Daily Statesman*, 6/1/1887.
3. *Austin Daily Statesman*, 6/1/1887.
4. *Austin Daily Statesman*, 6/1/1887.
5. *Austin Daily Statesman*, 6/1/1887.
6. *Austin Daily Statesman*, 6/1/1887.
7. *Austin Daily Statesman*, 6/1/1887.
8. *Austin Daily Statesman*, 6/1/1887.
9. *Austin Daily Statesman*, 6/1/1887.
10. *Austin Daily Statesman*, 6/1/1887.
11. *Austin Daily Statesman*, 6/1/1887.
12. *Austin Daily Statesman*, 6/1/1887 (Who this witness was is unclear. No one named Picker could be found. Perhaps it was James Pickle, a carpenter.)
13. *Austin Daily Statesman*, 6/2/1887 (The hack driver named by Glass was probably Bickham F. Farrow.)
14. *Austin Daily Statesman*, 6/2/1887.
15. *Austin Daily Statesman*, 6/2/1887.
16. *Austin Daily Statesman*, 6/2/1887.
17. *Austin Daily Statesman*, 6/2/1887.
18. *Austin Daily Statesman*, 6/2/1887; 1880 Federal Census; *Morrison & Fourmy's General Directory of the City of Austin, 1885-1886* (This witness was probably Jacob Casanova, the 18-year-old son of Thomas Casanova.)
19. *Austin Daily Statesman*, 6/2/1887; *Morrison & Fourmy's General Directory of the City of Austin, 1885-1886* (The news report may have called the witness J.M. Johnson, but the correct name was almost certainly I.W. Johnson.)
20. *Austin Daily Statesman*, 6/2/1887.

Chapter 26

"Disconnected and Conflicting Circumstantial Evidence"

The Full Trial of Moses Hancock Concludes

The defense began its presentation on the afternoon of June 1, 1887. Several of the defense witnesses were not present at the trial. Instead, their testimony in the preliminary trial a year earlier was read. The first absent witness whose testimony was read was Mrs. Mary Persinger, who lived next door to the Hancock house on the west side. An interesting situation was developing in the trial. The Glass family, who lived on the east side of the Hancock house, had teamed with the Scaggs family to prosecute Moses Hancock. The Persinger family, who lived on the west side of the Hancock house, had come to Hancock's defense. Mrs. Persinger's testimony stated that she was at home the night of the attack and heard no disturbance at the Hancock house until she heard Mr. Hancock yelling about 11 o'clock. Hancock called Mr. Persinger's name three times and said that somebody had murdered his wife and dragged her off. He screamed, "Yonder he is, catch him, for God Almighty's sake!" Mrs. Persinger could see the Hancock yard, but she could not see all of the alley, and she could not see the person Hancock was indicating. Mr. Persinger went to help Hancock carry his wife into the house, and then many people began to arrive. Mrs. Persinger recalled seeing Hancock at least twice during the evening, and both times he was sober. She stated that she and Mrs. Hancock went uptown to get some shoes mended, and on the way they saw Tom Glass and her brother, George Brown, and another man she did not know. The trio were heading uptown as she and Mrs. Hancock were heading home. Mrs. Persinger also noted that she found Hancock's clothes in her yard the next morning. Mrs. Persinger's account contradicted some of the statements made by Tom Glass about his trip uptown on Christmas Eve.[1]

Mr. A.M. Persinger also was not present at the trial, but his testimony from the preliminary trial was read. Persinger also heard Hancock yelling, saying, "Come, Persinger, for God's sake, somebody has knocked my wife in the head." When Persinger arrived, Hancock "had his wife in his arms close to the platform leading from the back door to the kitchen." As Persinger and Hancock carried Mrs. Hancock inside, other men, including Mr. Brunet and Mr. Leonard and his son, arrived. Hancock told Persinger "that he saw a tall man dressed in black run from his wife," and that was all the explanation Hancock gave him.[2]

Lena Hancock Ramsey, one of Moses Hancock's daughters, was present for the trial and testified for the defense. As she did at the preliminary trial, she detailed the events of Christmas Eve 1885 as she knew them. She ate supper at home that evening, and her parents, her sister, and David Hagy were present for supper. Tom Glass had testified that Moses Hancock had eaten supper at his house that evening. During supper they heard Tom Glass and others in the Glass yard. After supper, Mr. Hancock went in the front room to smoke and read the newspaper. Contrary to a statement made by Tom Glass, Lena said that her father was not on the gallery at all. He was in the front room when she, Ida, and David Hagy left for the party around 7:30 that evening. When they returned from the party a little after midnight, Lena first heard of her mother's injury at the front gate of the Hancock place. She was met there by Mrs. Persinger. At that time, the yard and house were full of people. Lena stated that her parents were kind to her and her sister, and her father was never cruel to her mother. Lena detailed the sleeping arrangements: Lena slept with her mother in case she needed any assistance; Ida slept with her father. Lena stated that her father was sober on Christmas Eve.[3]

Under cross-examination, Lena said she was positive her father was in the front room and not on the gallery. Then a letter was produced, and Lena said she recognized her mother's handwriting. The letter was the same one that was read at the preliminary trial and that earlier in the full trial had been objected to by the defense, and that objection was sustained temporarily. Now, the letter was admitted into evidence. Lena said the letter was written in the summer before her mother's death. Moses Hancock had been drinking, and Mrs. Hancock was fed up with his drinking sprees. However, the next day Hancock was sober, and Mrs. Hancock never showed the letter to him. Instead, the letter was placed in Lena's box of artificial flowers, and it was unearthed a few days after Mrs. Hancock died. The letter was read in court, the same letter as read in the preliminary trial. Upon re-examination by the defense, Lena reiterated when the letter was written and the circumstances. Her mother had written the letter hoping to scare Hancock, but when he came home sober, she never gave the letter to him. After that time, "they lived happily together." Mrs. Hancock found fault only with Hancock's drinking sprees, which did not occur often but were sometimes close together.[4]

Sam Dixon was the next witness for the defense. He heard about the murder about midnight and went immediately to the Hancock house. He saw several people in the house, among them Officer Isaiah Johnson. He did not enter the house when he first got there and soon left for home.

> On the way I overtook two or three men and told them of the crime; on my way back I met a young man on the bridge whom I did not know; he was on horseback and was riding fast; I had a pistol in my hand and halted him; I asked him where he was going; he said he was going after Mrs. Scaggs and said that Mrs. Phillips had been killed, and that she lived near the market house; I went to Phillips' and found that she had been killed; the man was a young man and of rather small size.

Dixon said the young man on horseback rode up and down Water Street.[5]

David Hagy was recalled and took the witness stand for the defense. He stated that he had been living with the Hancocks for about two months. "They got along very nicely except when he was drinking; he was very fond of his children, and was a very quiet man." Hagy ate supper at the Hancock house on Christmas Eve, and later he escorted the Hancock girls to the party at the Ivey home. They left between 7 and 8 o'clock, and Mr. and Mrs. Hancock were sitting by the fire in the front room, contrary to a statement made by Tom Glass that Hancock was on the gallery when they left. Hagy said they did not pass the Glass gate, contrary to a statement Tom Glass had made in the preliminary trial and which he testified in the full trial he did not remember making. Hagy also said that he did not see Tom Glass when they left, though Glass had testified he was standing on his front porch and watched Hagy and the girls leave for the party. Cross-examined by the prosecution, Hagy said he could tell when Hancock had been drinking: "On the night of the murder, I think he had a drink or two; I could smell it on his breath." Hagy said that Mrs. Hancock was also uneasy when her husband drank. On the night of the attack, Hagy asked Hancock how it happened, and Hancock replied, "God knows, I don't." The next day Hancock showed Hagy "some blood on the stable and where he said the man had jumped the fence."[6]

The next witness was George Brown, the brother of Mrs. Mary Persinger. Brown testified that he ate supper at the Glass house around 6:30 on Christmas Eve. Tom Glass, Joe Glass, and a stranger ate supper then, too. Moses Hancock was not there, contrary to what Tom Glass testified. Brown did not know if Glass had talked to Mrs. Hancock, as he claimed he did. After supper, Brown, Tom and Joe Glass, and the stranger went uptown. On the way, they met Mrs. Hancock and Mrs. Persinger, who were returning home after having some shoes mended. The men also stopped at Paul Haenelt's barber shop, where Glass paid Brown some money. The group of men then went to the Iron Front saloon, contrary to Tom Glass's statement that he had gone to the Iron Front alone. Brown said they arrived at the saloon about 8 o'clock, and he stayed there until about 11:30, when he heard of the attack at the Hancock house. He claimed he was not drunk. About 10 o'clock, Tom Glass left the Iron Front for about an hour and then returned shortly before they heard of the attack. Then, they both went to the Hancock house and found the place full of people. Curiously, David Hagy's absence from the party had made him a suspect in the attack on Mrs. Hancock, but Glass's absence from the Iron Front and his contradictory testimony apparently raised no suspicions.[7]

The last witness of the day was Paul Haenelt, who lived with the Tom Glass family next door to the Hancock house. Haenelt's testimony was similar to Rosa King's account of how Haenelt went to the assistance of Hancock after the attack.

> As he jumped the fence he found an axe about three feet from the window of Mrs. Hancock's bedroom; it had blood on it; he assisted Mr. Hancock to get his wife to the platform leading to the kitchen, then went and saddled his horse and started for a doctor; as he started to mount he saw four men run out of Hancock's yard; two going east and two west. He did not know them; they were running fast; when he first saw Hancock he

was standing over his wife; near her head; he was in his drawers and shirt and Mrs. Hancock had on a gown.

Haenelt also stated that he saw blood on the stable the next morning. With the end of Haenelt's testimony, court was adjourned for the day.[8]

"It Was Oliver Townsend"

The last day of testimony was June 2, and the testimony ended by noon. The first witness of the day was Alex Thornton, a black man who lived with his wife at 410 Willow Street at the corner of Neches, about two blocks east of the Hancock house. On Christmas Eve, Thornton and his wife were at home doing cooking for Christmas. With them were Mr. and Mrs. Moses McCormick, a black couple who lived at 311 East Water Street, not far east of the Hancock house. After they finished cooking, the McCormicks started home. Thornton went out into the yard to see them off.

> My wife was with us, and she called my attention to a man some distance off, but I said, "Oh, it's Christmas night and it's somebody just walking around." Mr. McCormick and his wife then went out of the yard and I walked with them a short distance, and my wife went back into the house. When we got a distance Mrs. McCormick missed her key and I went back after it. I turned back just 125 steps from my gate, for I afterwards measured it. On my way back I heard my wife call rather excitedly, "Who is that" and looking I saw a man at my gate. I ran him from there down to the creek and when he got into the bottom he hollowed. I followed his trail the next day to near where Mr. Norton lives. He was dressed in dark clothes, and wore a soft hat; his coat, I thought, struck him below the knee, I knew him that night. It was Oliver Townsend. I was close enough to him to recognize him. This was between 11 and 12 o'clock.

Under cross-examination by the prosecution, Thornton said he was satisfied in his own mind that the man he followed was Oliver Townsend, though when he spoke to a reporter just after the incident, he said he had not been close enough to the man to tell if he was black or white. Thornton said he told his story to a crowd the next day at the Hancock house, and he also told the mayor. Thornton believed the motive in the attack "was robbery and murder."[9]

Moses McCormick also testified, but he was mostly confused in his statements. He first said that he and his wife were at home on the night of the attack: "My wife was at home that night; we were both at home and we were met at Thornton's helping to fix up a Christmas dinner." Upon cross-examination, he said he did not remember being at the Thornton house on Christmas Eve, and that Thornton's wife did not call his attention to a man nearby that night. The defense attorney then asked McCormick which Christmas night he referred to, and he replied, "the one past gone." The attorney clarified that he was asking about Christmas Eve 1885.

McCormick responded that he didn't remember much about the Christmas night that year: "I have a bad memory. I suffer a great deal with neuralgia in the head, and my memory is not good at times." Since McCormick was little help as a witness, he was released.[10]

Mrs. Mary Snyder was not present at the trial, but her testimony from the preliminary trial was read. She lived with her husband, John, at 301 East Water Street, not far from the Hancock house. She testified in the earlier trial that on the night of the attack,

> she heard some one in the alley by the rear of her house, and thinking they were after her chickens, she got up and slipped out in the yard. As she did so she saw two men running. They were coming from the direction of Hancock's and joined another who was standing in the alley, and then all three ran off in the direction of the river.

Mrs. Snyder said she remained in her yard for about 30 minutes, and when she went back inside, her clock read 12:20.[11]

In an obvious attempt to connect the Hancock murder to the other servant girl murders, the defense then called two doctors to testify. Dr. Lucien Johnson testified about the wounds received by Eliza Shelly, who was murdered at his home at 302 East Cypress Street. Johnson stated that he had heard of no other murders like those of Eliza Shelly or Sue Hancock since Mrs. Hancock had died. Dr. Josephus Cummings then testified about the wounds received by Eula Phillips.[12]

The final witness in the trial was Travis County Sheriff Malcolm Hornsby. Hornsby stated that "since the death of the colored man, Elgin, and the sending to the penitentiary of Oliver Townsend, there had been no mysterious murders in the city." Hornsby said that he made a plaster cast of Elgin's foot after his death, and that one toe was missing from one of Elgin's feet. Elgin's foot matched the bloody footprint that Hornsby had examined on the Phillips gallery the morning after Eula Phillips was murdered. Hornsby's testimony was another attempt by the defense to link the Hancock murder to the earlier murders in the city because in official circles the general belief had been that all the servant girl murders committed in Austin in 1885 had been the work of half a dozen negro desperadoes, of whom Oliver Townsend was one.[13]

"Full of Conflicting Accounts"

After testimony ended on June 2, the attorneys began to deliver their closing arguments. District Attorney James Robertson went first, outlining the state's case. The intent of the prosecution had been to show there was no evidence of anyone else having been at the crime scene other than Moses Hancock. The belief was that if someone other than Hancock had committed the attack, then the attacker would have been heard and likely seen by the neighbors, though the attackers in the previous servant girl murders had seldom been heard or seen. The prosecution had called the Glass family and members of its household to bolster the claim that only Hancock was at the scene of the crime. The prosecution had also shown that Moses Hancock liked to drink and that sometimes he went on drinking sprees that frightened his wife. But it presented no evidence directly linking Hancock to the crime.[14]

Judge John Hancock made the first closing argument for the defense. The defense had tried to show that other people had been present at the scene of the crime. Both Rosa King, a prosecution witness, and Paul Haenelt, a defense witness, claimed they saw four men running from the Hancock place. Mary Snyder had also seen two men running from the direction of the Hancock place, and those two men joined a third in the alley before heading toward the river. Alex Thornton also testified to seeing Oliver Townsend in the vicinity, though in an earlier interview with a reporter he claimed he could not tell if the man was black or white. The defense also tried to show that Hancock had been sober the night of the attack, and that he was not wearing pants when he found his wife in the yard. The absence of pants would suggest he had been in bed when the attack occurred. The defense was also able to contradict much of the testimony of neighbor Tom Glass, whose reports of Hancock's activities and a conversation with Mrs. Hancock on the night of the attack had put Hancock in a bad light. Finally, the supposedly condemning letter found after Sue Hancock's death, and which was instrumental in getting Hancock indicted in the first place, was little more than a claim that Sue Hancock was going to leave her husband if he didn't quit drinking. She had not written the letter on the day of the attack, but during the summer before, and Hancock had never seen the letter. Two doctors and the Travis County sheriff also testified that the murder of Sue Hancock was similar to the earlier servant girl murders and that the murders had ceased after Nathan Elgin was killed and Oliver Townsend was sent to prison.[15]

On Friday morning, June 3, Colonel Bethel Coopwood presented a closing argument for the defense, and the Honorable Jack Evans presented a closing argument for the prosecution. Then the case went to the jury. The jury deliberated for several days. By late Saturday night, the jury "was still out agreeing with all their might to disagree." By Sunday evening, no progress had been made. The Fort Worth newspaper reported that "the general belief is it will be a hung jury and mistrial. A majority of the community believe in the innocence of Hancock because the testimony seems to point to the fact that the murder of Mrs. Hancock evidently belonged to the series of notorious assassinations of women in Austin in 1885." By Monday, all hope was lost for a verdict. "The jury in the Hancock case failed to agree after a two day's tussle with knotty problems of disconnected and conflicting circumstantial evidence." Late Monday afternoon, the jury was discharged by Judge Walker. The final tally of the jury was, much like the trial, full of conflicting accounts. On June 7, the *Austin Daily Statesman* reported that "the jury stood six for acquittal and six for conviction." The next day, the same newspaper reported that on the first ballot, the count stood at "eight for acquittal, three for murder in the first degree and one doubtful." The Fort Worth newspaper reported on June 7 that "seven were for conviction of murder in the first degree, four in the second, and one . . . for acquittal." In any case, the jury could not reach a verdict, and a mistrial was declared.[16]

In reviewing the trial, the *Austin Daily Statesman* praised the conduct of the attorneys, especially those for the prosecution.

> The case from its opening until its close was conducted by both sides with consummate skill and ability. Especially did the attorneys for the prosecution display marvelous legal power and skill as prosecutors. They brought out all the evidence possible and used it with all the force and adroitness their astuteness and ability were capable of, and yet a most intelligent jury failed to be impressed with the guilt of the defendant.

After the failure of the jury to reach a verdict, the rumor circulated that the case against Moses Hancock would be dismissed because further prosecution would likely be useless.[17]

In fact, the trials of Moses Hancock and Jimmy Phillips seemed to be useless to begin with. Both Marshal Lucy and Sheriff Hornsby seemed to believe that other men had committed the murders, and the only solid evidence in the case, the bare footprints with a missing toe, had been shown to match the foot of Nathan Elgin, who was killed months before either Phillips or Hancock stood trial. One such footprint was found on the gallery of the Phillips home. Why the prosecution of Phillips and Hancock continued is as big a mystery as the murders themselves. As in the Phillips case, no direct evidence tied Moses Hancock to the crime other than he was at home when the attack occurred. In the Phillips case, the prosecutors promoted the motive that Phillips was enraged by his wife's unfaithfulness, but no evidence was ever presented that Jimmy Phillips knew about Eula's lack of virtue. In the Hancock case, the supposed smoking gun was the letter written by Sue Hancock that allegedly expressed her fear that her husband would kill her. The letter contained no such fear, and Hancock never saw the letter anyway. The prosecution had no viable motive in the Hancock case other than his drunkenness, and the prosecutors presented no solid evidence linking him to the crime. According to witnesses, Hancock wasn't even wearing pants when first seen by neighbors, a fashion detail that seemed important to the prosecutors in both cases.

Walter Spencer had been tried in December 1885 and quickly acquitted. Jimmy Phillips had been tried in May 1886 and found guilty of second-degree murder, but his verdict was reversed on appeal five months later, and his case was remanded to the lower court, where it was dismissed. Moses Hancock was tried in June 1887, and his case ended with a hung jury and a mistrial. No further prosecution of Hancock occurred. Thus, after three prosecutions and months of investigations, the infamous servant girl murders were no closer to being solved than they were the day after Mollie Smith was murdered. Perhaps District Attorney James Robertson, brother of Austin's mayor, was trying to save face for the city by aggressively prosecuting Spencer, Phillips, and Hancock, but his actions were almost as criminal as the murders he was trying. Perhaps District Attorney

Robertson *was* a "veritable thug," as charged by Jimmy Phillips' defense attorney William Walton, and his actions were part of a cover-up at the highest levels of government.

Notes

Title: *Austin Daily Statesman*, 6/7/1887.

1. *Austin Daily Statesman*, 6/2/1887.
2. *Austin Daily Statesman*, 6/2/1887.
3. *Austin Daily Statesman*, 6/2/1887.
4. *Austin Daily Statesman*, 6/2/1887.
5. *Austin Daily Statesman*, 6/2/1887.
6. *Austin Daily Statesman*, 6/2/1887.
7. *Austin Daily Statesman*, 6/2/1887.
8. *Austin Daily Statesman*, 6/2/1887.
9. *Austin Daily Statesman*, 6/3/1887; *Fort Worth Daily Gazette*, 6/3/1887; *Morrison & Fourmy's General Directory of the City of Austin, 1885-1886* (The Mr. Norton mentioned by Thornton was likely Nimrod L. Norton, who lived at 401 Willow Street.)
10. *Austin Daily Statesman*, 6/3/1887.
11. *Fort Worth Daily Gazette*, 6/3/1887; *Austin Daily Statesman*, 6/3/1887; *Morrison & Fourmy's General Directory of the City of Austin, 1885-1886* (One news report identified this witness as Mary Saider, but Mary Snyder was the correct name.)
12. *Austin Daily Statesman*, 6/3/1887; *Fort Worth Daily Gazette*, 6/3/1887.
13. *Fort Worth Daily Gazette*, 6/3/1887; *Austin Daily Statesman*, 6/3/1887.
14. *Austin Daily Statesman*, 6/3/1887; Galloway, *The Servant Girl Murders*: 308.
15. *Austin Daily Statesman*, 6/3/1887; Galloway, *The Servant Girl Murders*: 309.
16. *Austin Daily Statesman*, 6/3/1887; *Austin Daily Statesman*, 6/5/1887; *Fort Worth Daily Gazette*, 6/6/1887; *Austin Daily Statesman*, 6/7/1887; *Austin Daily Statesman*, 6/8/1887; *Fort Worth Daily Gazette*, 6/7/1887.
17. *Austin Daily Statesman*, 6/8/1887.

Chapter 27

"Revenge in Texas"

The Kenward Philp Solution

Kenward Philp was born around 1844 in England. He moved to the United States and became a journalist writing for such publications as the *Brooklyn Eagle* and *The Truth*, rising to the post of assistant editor of *The Truth*. Philp was regarded as a "brilliant but erratic journalist." He was small in stature, just a little over five feet tall, "with a high forehead and a restless eye." His reputation as a practical joker was well known, but he was also "gifted with the power of penetrating the weaknesses of people, and was . . . uniformly successful in hitting the mark." He was considered "a man of the most prodigal liberality, a welcome guest wherever he presents himself and is a pretty fair sample of the once famous but now almost extinct race of metropolitan Bohemians."[1]

Philp was famous for writing one of the first detective dime novels, *The Bowery Detective*, published in 1873. Another of his novels was *Texas Tom: or the Savage of the Prairie*, also published in the 1870s. Philp was sometimes known to make up news stories. One such incident concerned a story Philp presented to A.C. Cazauran, editor of the *Brooklyn Sunday Sun*, about a ferry wreck. Philp rushed into the newsroom, claiming he had just been on a ferry on which the pilot had died at the wheel and the ferry had crashed into its slip, killing several people. Philp offered his completed manuscript on an exclusive basis for $10 cash. Philp was paid and left. The story was rushed into production. Soon, another reporter appeared and asked about the sensation in the office. The editor told the reporter about the ferry crash, and the reporter asked who had presented the story. When told that Philp had written the story, the reporter snorted and said the story was a fake. He had just taken the ferry half an hour earlier, and no such ferry accident had occurred. The editor was forced to write a short paragraph explaining that the story was fiction and was meant to show what could happen in such a situation. Almost ironically, within a year two ferry pilots in the New York area fell dead at the wheel, though no great damage resulted.[2]

"The Morey Letter"

Philp was perhaps more famous, or infamous, for his alleged involvement in the notorious Morey letter that almost derailed the presidential election of 1880.

> No forgery ever occurred more famous than the Morey letter, which was published in facsimile in Truth during the presidential campaign of 1880. No other forgery probably had such far-reaching consequences. Others have wrecked commercial companies and wiped out the fortunes of private individuals, but this Morey forgery nearly changed the result of a presidential election. . . . The letter purported to have been written by James A. Garfield, the Republican candidate, to a Mr. Morey, a manufacturer in Massachusetts, and dealt with the Chinese question in such a way as would undoubtedly lose the Pacific States to the Republican party had the genuineness of the letter not been doubted. Mr. Garfield himself wrote a prompt denial, but the denial scarcely reached as many persons as the letter itself, for a facsimile of the letter in electrotype was published in every Democratic newspaper in the land.

The letter suggested that Garfield was in favor of Chinese immigration without restrictions, though in fact he was opposed to such immigration. As in modern times, immigration was a key issue in the 1880 presidential campaign, and the letter prompted outrage among the electorate. Morey himself could not be found, but many Democrats familiar with Garfield's signature swore the letter was genuine. Garfield won the election, defeating the Democrat Winfield Scott Hancock, but not as easily as had first been expected, winning by only 2000 votes out of nine million votes cast.[3]

Because the facsimile of the letter was first published in *The Truth*, Philp came under suspicion and was arrested on two charges, forgery of the letter and criminal libel for publishing it. The hope was that the case could be resolved before the election, but it was not. The letter itself was ruled to be a forgery, with a doctored envelope and changes to the date stamp on the envelope. The stamp used on the envelope was not even available in Washington, where Garfield allegedly mailed it, until a month after the letter was supposedly posted. Philp was believed to be the forger. The trial was held in November 1880 and Philp was finally acquitted, but not before several of the witnesses had been indicted on charges of perjury. The authorship of the letter was never established conclusively.[4]

"More Frightful Than Poe"

In early 1886, though, Philp may have traveled to Austin in an attempt to solve the servant girl murders. His report on his solution to the murders appeared in the *Omaha Daily Bee* (and perhaps other newspapers) on January 30, 1886. Whether Philp really visited Austin is unknown, but his theory is rather compelling. Sharp readers will notice a few discrepancies in his report. The newspaper article is included in its entirety below. The coroner mentioned in the article would be Justice William Von Rosenberg, Jr. The chief of police would be Marshal James Lucy. Mysteriously, Kenward Philp died of blood poisoning at the age of 42 in Brooklyn on February 21, 1886, just three weeks after the article was published.

A STORY OF REVENGE IN TEXAS

Two Assassins Hanged in 1878 the Cause of Nine Frightful Murders.

Every Victim Proved to Have Been Related to Some One of the Jurors in the Old Trial.

[Note—The following sketch is founded on fact. The author, Kenward Philp, a well known New York newspaper man, says he has altered the names of persons and localities for obvious reasons. For the enlightenment of the readers of the BEE, however, we supply most of the real names. The scene is laid in Austin, Texas, where a series of horrible and mysterious murders has been committed during the past year, the last one being committed only a few weeks ago, since which time arrests have been made which, it is believed, will result in the conviction of the guilty party. In Philp's story, the name of Mollie Smith stands for Mollie Brown, colored; Lizzie Bryon for Lizzie Shelley, colored; Jane Crescent for Irene Cross, colored; Mary Cullen for Mary Rainey; Mrs. Gracie Lee and Orange Jefferson, for Grace Vance and Orange Washington respectively, colored; Jennie Page for Alice Davis, colored. The names of the two white married women murdered on Christmas eve, 1885, were Mrs. Phillips and Mrs. Hancock. Philp's theory is that the murders were the result of revenge on the part of the relatives of the assassins, who were hanged in 1878, having been convicted by a mixed jury of white and blacks, the murdered persons being mostly the relatives of the jurors.]

THE FACTS.

1. On Christmas day of 1884, a little over twelve months ago, the body of Mollie Brown, a colored servant in the city of B—, in Texas, was found hacked to pieces in the yard about a hundred feet from her house. Her murder, which had been committed on a bright moon-light night, had been accompanied by terrible outrage.

2. On May 7, 1885, Lizzie Byron, another colored domestic, was murdered under precisely similar circumstances.

3. In the following month Jane Crescent, still another colored servant, was found hacked and mutilated and dead in her own room.

4. On August 30 little Mary Cullen's body, mutilated in the same way, was found in a stable half a mile from her mother's house, whither she had been dragged, bleeding all the way. The child was but 12 years of age. Her mother, who lay in bed with her on that fatal night, was horribly wounded in the head with an axe but recovered.

5. On September 29 came the next. Mrs. Gracie and Orange Jefferson, colored, lived as man and wife in a cabin. Lucinda Wilson and Patsy Dobbins, mulatto girls, boarded with them. The man and woman slept in one apartment, the girls in another. On the date mentioned, at night, Jefferson was hammered into insensibility and died the next morning; Gracie Lee was taken from his side, pulled out of the window, and had her brains beaten out with a stone; the two girls were beaten presumably with a sand-bag, and when they recovered consciousness could tell nothing about the affair.

6. In October Jennie Page, another colored domestic, was found dead in the usual way and after having suffered similar horrors.

7. On Christmas eve, 1885, just one year from the first murder, two white married women were assassinated and dragged from their beds to the grounds outside their houses. The body of one was found with a heavy log across it. Both had been killed with an ax. The husband of one of them was found weltering in blood from the blow of an ax over the ear. He recovered.

More than four hundred persons have been arrested in B— for these crimes, but none of them has been held. Northern and southern detectives, the local police, bloodhounds, and all the paraphernalia ingenuity could devise have been used in the endeavor to discover the murderers, but to no purpose.

THE THEORY.

Sitting in my room at midnight, reading the details of this mess of horrors, more frightful than Poe or Hugo or Dumas ever conjured up from romantic brain—sitting there with nothing else in my room alive save my lamp—I tried to think this matter out. Three days after I alighted to the railway station of B—the scene of this remarkable series of murders.

I, Gerald Shanly, a New York newspaper man, had a theory concerning them. So strongly had the conviction that it was the correct one grown upon me that I felt it to be my bounden duty to test it.

My steps were first bent to the office of the principal newspaper in the town, where I asked to see the editor. I found him accessible and ready to grant an interview to a northern confrere at a moment's notice. A young lady, however, sat at a desk in another part of the room, and, glancing at her, I suggested that our interview must be private. The editor looked inquiringly at me, but gracefully got rid of the young lady, nevertheless.

"I have come, Mr. Blank," I said to the editor, "to try and solve the mystery of these terrible murders."

It was plain at once that he took me for a crank.

"Well," he answered, "everybody in B— has been trying to do that for a year past."

"I know it; but don't be discouraged because they have failed."

"Well, have you any clue?"

"I think I have—but let me ask you one question. If the answer is negative my theory fails at the outset, and I take the next train for New York."

"Well!"

"Do you have mixed juries in your town?"

"Well, some of them are very mixed occasionally," he answered, laughing. "But you mean juries composed of both white and colored citizens?"

"Yes."

"Certainly we do."

"For how long have you had them?"

"Why, ever since the principle of the civil-rights bill was imbedded in the constitution of the state."

"For more than five years?"

"Yes."

"Now, Mr. Blank," I said, "I am thoroughly in earnest in belief that these dreadful mysteries can be solved. You can help me if you will, by pretending to employ me as an outside reporter on your paper, so that I shall have some apparent reason for being here, and also can gain access to officials, documents, etc."

The editor thought the matter over.

"Why do you not go to the chief of police?" he said, "or to the detectives?"

For answer I asked him whether the police had not announced their belief that these murders were the work of one man.

"Yes, they have," he replied, and upon the grounds of similarity of facts in all the cases, and that every suspicious or suspected person in the town is under close watch. Had there been more than one, discovery must have been brought about before this."

"Is that your theory, too?"

"Yes."

"I shall have the honor of disproving it."

An hour later I had taken a neat room near the office, and had made the acquaintance of the reporters for the paper, who were very jolly and hospitable to their new colleague, as they thought me.

Of course we could not talk long without getting upon the subject of the murders. Vigilance committees had been formed, ward associations patrolled the streets at night, no woman ventured out after sundown, and every man in B— slept with a loaded revolver ready to his hand. The negroes were in an agony of terror, every one of them wearing a voudou charm.

That night a paper said: "So there is no theory left but that one inhuman monster has sacrificed a life every time he wished to gratify a ghastly passion."

Thinking over the sentence in my new quarters that night, I said to myself, "Bosh! Those murders are not committed for the sake of theft, for no property has ever been disturbed in the victim's homes. Lust, strong as it is as a motive to crime, is not powerful enough in these cases as an incentive. There is but one human passion devilish enough to furnish the motive for this horrible series of crimes—revenge.

"But can it be possible that one man can entertain equal feelings of revenge against nine persons, living apart, some white and some colored? And is it not still more incredible that two persons (if my theory be correct, that more than one was engaged in these murders) should have precisely the same feelings of vengeance against precisely the same persons and should take precisely the same means of wreaking them?"

We shall see.

I put my revolver on the table by my side, turned down the lamp and went to sleep.

The editor had promised to assist me in any way he could. I was not slow to ask his assistance on the next morning. The first favor I asked of him was a note of introduction to the coroner. From what I had learned of him from the reporters I had determined to make him my only confidant as to the real mission I had come on. After telling him, therefore, I asked whether I might be allowed to see the records of the office for some few years back. He willingly complied, giving me a private room in which to investigate them. When we were alone I said: "Doctor, did you conduct the inquest in the case of all these murders?"

"I did."

"Eight victims out of the nine were killed by the blow of an axe, were they not?"

"Yes."

"Was the frontal bone crushed in each case?"

"Yes."

"Then the blow, no matter how sharp the axe, must have been a very heavy one?"

"Decidedly."

"Now, doctor, please try and think whether the incision made by the ax was deeper at one point than at another in any or in all cases?"

The doctor reflected. "Yes, it was," he replied.

"Was it not deeper toward the lower part of the face than toward the other?"

"Yes, in all cases, if I remember aright. But what does that prove?" he asked.

"It proves that the theory of the police that these murders are the work of one man is wrong. You have doubtless noticed that in striking a log of wood with an ax the incision is deepest at the point where the ax strikes first. While the heel of the weapon comes away easily, the striker has often to wriggle the other end of it two or three times before it is released. Supposing a man to be standing up to wield the ax (as he must necessarily be to strike a blow of such force as to crush the frontal bone), the incision would be deepest at the point farthest from him. If the deepest incision in these cases had been at the lower part of the face, therefore, the man who wielded the ax must have struck while standing behind the head of his victim. This proves that two persons at least were engaged in the murders; the one holding the body while the other struck."

"That seems to be so," said the doctor, reflectively.

"I say nothing," continued I, "about the impossibility of one man wielding a sandbag upon two girls in one room and murdering two full-grown persons in the next room at the same time without creating sufficient noise to alarm the neighbors. That is a circumstance for your police to reconcile with their one-man theory. No; there were two men engaged in this crusade of blood and outrage. In my belief, one was a white man, the other colored. Perhaps these records will lead us to determine who they are."

An hour or so passed in searching and the coroner again came into the little room.

"Doctor," I said, suspending the investigation of the records for a moment, "the newspapers declare that immediately after one of these murders a suspected man was traced (these are the very words) from the stable across the city, to where he took a hack. The wheel marks led us to an alley back of the cabin in which the murder was committed. There hack and man disappeared. Is that so?"

"Yes."

"Then there must have been somebody to drive the hack. This was the fourth or fifth murder, and of course was made public the next day?"

"Yes."

"Were the hackmen investigated, or any friend of his, or any other hackman, was the person hired?"

"The hackmen were investigated. All proved it impossible that they could have been implicated. Nobody came forward to say a word as to his being hired."

"Precisely. Do you know why? Simply because this hack the suspected man took was not a regular hack but his own. The hack of a white man, driven by a negro; each having his revenge to wreak. Further, the newspapers again say, and the police corroborate it, that on another occasion a carriage was used; that its tracks were followed for some miles from the scene of the murder, and were found to lead back precisely to the scene of the crime. Is that so?"

"Yes."

"And that when bloodhounds were put on the track they followed the trail for some distance, but suddenly were at fault."

"Does not that prove to your mind that the old slave methods of confusing the scent had been adopted, and that in all probability a colored man drove that hack."

The doctor admitted that it looked like it.

Turning to the records, I said: "I see here that about six years ago the body of a well-known hackman, John Smith, was found in the suburbs of your town with a bullet in his head. Do you remember the case?"

"Oh, yes, perfectly; although I was not coroner at that time."

"Had he ever been engaged in litigation?"

"No; but he was an important witness for the prosecution in a murder trial a year or so before."

"Who was the lawyer on his side?"

"Mr. White Johnson, a well known member of the bar."

"Your records here show that this lawyer, after the hackman's murder, was found on a suburban highway with his head crushed in by a stone as in the case of Gracie Lee, last year. Is that so?"

"Yes."

"And that shortly afterward his father was found murdered?"

"Yes."

"And then that his brother was found murdered?"

"Yes."

"In this murder trial, in which the murdered hackman appeared as an important witness, and in which the murdered lawyer was also a figure, what was the verdict?"

"Guilty."

"Was the sentence carried out?"

"Yes."

"Now, doctor, can you tell me by your jury lists, so far back, what was the composition of that jury?"

"Not by the lists—they are not accessible easily. But I perfectly remember the case. It was a mixed jury—some white, some black."

"What was the criminal?"

"There were two—a white man and a colored man, equally concerned in the crime—the double crime of outrage and murder."

I shut the book and the coroner and I walked out together.

"Now, doctor," I said, after a pause, "you have lived all your life in this town. You know everybody in it. Will you, without saying a word to anybody, get the names of the persons who composed that jury about six years ago?"

"Of what use, my dear sir?"

"I want to see whether any person, white or black, who has been a victim of these fiends during the last year was in any way related to any of those jurors."

The amiable doctor was thoroughly startled.

"I see now exactly what you are driving at," he said, "if there should have been upon the jury relatives of both colored and white victims of the recent murders the motive is established."

"Precisely."

Two days passed and I did not see the coroner. In the meantime I visited the scenes of the different murders, but gained nothing new from my inquiries. On the third day I again went to the coroner's office. I found him there, pale and almost trembling.

He took me silently into the inner room and we sat down.

"You were right," he said, almost breathlessly. "In five cases, at all events, the persons who were murdered were related in some degree to those who served on that jury. I have not had time to investigate the others, but will do so at once."

"Among those five cases there is one of a white man?"

"Yes."

I confess that the revelation startled me, even though I had expected it.

"The next question is," I said, "who are likely to find interest enough in this vendetta to be the instigators of it? Naturally the relatives or friends of the men who were hanged."

The doctor nodded assent.

"Do you know if any such exist?"

No, he did not. The trial had occurred a long time ago, and he could not say as to that.

"Then we must find out," said I. "And depend upon it, when you have located them you are not far from the assassins of the past terrible year."

Two days were spent in investigation, which had to be conducted with the utmost caution, not only to prevent suspicion on the part of those whom we were in search, but to baffle the police, who with their usual fatuity chose to consider me a suspicious person, and dogged my footsteps until I managed to elude them, which was a comparatively easy matter.

On the third day the doctor triumphed.

This second discovery seemed to paralyze him.

"If what you suspect is true, my dear sir," he said, breathlessly, "it is awful—terrible."

"You have found them."

"No. Only one."

"White or black?"

"White"

"Precisely. He is the man who wielded the ax. The white man dominated all through. The colored man's cunning baffled the bloodhounds, the white man's intelligence befogged the police. What is his name?"

"John Doe."

"Is he in good circumstances?"

"Yes, a sort of gentleman farmer."

"What relation was he to the man who was hanged?"

"Brother."

"And where is his place?"

The doctor told me it was at a distance of some three miles. I buttoned my coat and prepared to leave.

"You will not whisper a word of this," I asked, "until all is ready?"

"Not a word—but where are you going?"

"To the residence of Mr. John Doe."

"Man alive!" cried the good doctor; "you must not! You will be slaughtered! Just think a moment! You cannot be so rash!"

"My good doctor," I replied, "I am not going there to tell Mr. Doe he is discovered. We are to be even now on the wrong scent unless two things are cleared up: First, does Mr. Doe keep a private hack? Second, has he in his employ a confidential colored man? I am going to just casually find out those two things. I shall see you in the morning."

I was well aware, however, that the mission was a dangerous one, for I had now been in B— long enough to be spotted by any one who took an interest in the arrival of a stranger. But my old reporting instincts came to my aid, and I set out to interview the farming people within the radius of a mile on the prospects of the spring crop, etc. I went to three houses, made copious notes, was kindly treated, and in all of them was asked eagerly, the first thing, whether there was anything new in town about the murders.

Armed with my notes, I unlatched the front gate of John Doe's and walked up the stoop.

The house stood fully half a mile from the next in either direction and some distance from the road. It was neither tidy nor dirty—evidently the home of a bachelor.

The man who opened the door I knew for John Doe instantly. A steely-gray-eyed man of powerful build, sallow complexion, six feet in height, slow-spoken, with bushy, standing-out black eye-brows.

"Is this Mr. Doe?" I asked.

"It is."

I told him my alleged errand and showed him the notes I had taken at other houses.

Somewhat ungraciously he pulled the door aside and bade me come in.

I confess I felt a tremor as I passed the threshhold. Not another soul was about, and I was helpless in the presence of a man whom I believed the murderer of nine persons in one year.

Now and then, as I was taking my notes, I caught his cold, glittering eye fixed in a very uncomforting way on me. But I got through all right. He did not ask me to drink. He said nothing about anything but what I asked him and precious little about that.

And not a word about the murders.

I bade him good-day, neither of us proffering his hand, and got out as nonchalantly as I could, but inexpressibly relieved.

But so far I had done nothing to further the investigation. Come what might, I determined to find out what I wanted to know, one way or the other, before I left. So I sauntered down the side lane by the house, lighted a cigar, and kept a watchful eye over the fence.

I had gone but thirty or forty paces when my heart stood still, as it seemed to me.

Right before me was a gigantic negro washing the wheels of a private carriage with a mop and talking to himself and to the wheel alternately.

In his own way he was as villainous looking as his master. Silently I turned—now thoroughly frightened at the confirmation of all my suspicions—to the high road, and was soon back in B—.

No sleep that night. The next morning, all being in readiness, the coroner and I laid the whole matter before the chief of police.

"But there is no direct evidence," said that official.

"No," I said, "there is not. But here is a paragraph concerning one of the murders, clipped from your own local papers, which will give you direct evidence if you choose to seek it."

I read the following (which was printed also in the *New York World*): "The criminals did not try to remove evidence against themselves, for Gracie Lee's lifeless fingers had a death-clutch on a chain attached to a watch with a broken crystal, the fragments of which were found near her body."

The coroner, the editor, and I succeeded at last in convincing the chief of police, that the proper thing to do was to make a raid on the estate of Mr. John Doe, and to secure the persons of him and his colored servant.

It was done. Much to his surprise, Mr. Doe was arrested, at the same time that his coachman was overpowered in the garden before he could utter a cry. A long and patient search resulted in the finding of the mutilated watch in the barn where the negro had hidden it. Upon this he—the colored man, the brother of the man who was hanged in company with Doe's relative, confessed all; and the secret of the B— murders which had paralyzed an entire state was out.[5]

As suggested, several discrepancies existed in Philp's story. First, Alice Davis was not considered one of the servant girl murders. Her killer, Jack Coombs, was captured, tried, and sent to prison. Second, Philp seemed to contradict himself regarding the watch. He repeated the news article that said that Gracie Vance's "lifeless fingers had a death-clutch on a chain attached to a watch with a broken crystal, the fragments of which were found near her body." However, he then said that the direct evidence, the "mutilated watch," was found in the barn at the Doe place. How could the watch have been attached to the chain in Gracie Vance's fingers if it was also in John Doe's barn? Or was only the watch chain in Vance's grasp, with glass fragments nearby, and the watch itself was missing? The news reports indicated that the watch was attached to the chain at the murder scene. Third, Philp mentioned that the white man and his negro accomplice were arrested, though no such arrest was reported or apparently even made. Curiously, though, a large, stocky black man, Nathan Elgin, whose footprint matched the ones found at several murder scenes, even to the missing toe, was killed in a scuffle with police in east Austin within ten days after the publication of Philp's article. Could Elgin have been killed purposefully to protect the identity of the white man?

Was Philp's report accurate or fabrication? Did it actually solve the case of the servant girl murders? Certainly it offered a unique theory that gave some sense to the series of murders. And the fact that Philp died mysteriously of blood poisoning at the age of 42 just three weeks after the article was published makes his theory even more intriguing. If his account was accurate, then the trials of Jimmy Phillips and Moses Hancock continued after the coroner already knew the truth about the murders. Whether Philp's theory was plausible will be discussed in a later chapter.

Notes

Title: *Omaha Daily Bee*, 1/30/1886.

1. Walling, *Recollections of a New York Chief of Police*: 344; *Los Angeles Herald*, 11/18/1880.
2. *Rochester Democrat and Chronicle*, 2/28/1886; "A Plot For A Million: Or, the Minister and the Penny Paper."
3. Walling, *Recollections of a New York Chief of Police*: 343-344; *Cumberland Times-News*, 7/31/2011; "A Plot For A Million: Or, the Minister and the Penny Paper."
4. *New York Times*, 10/28/1880; *New York Times*, 11/15/1880; Walling, *Recollections of a New York Chief of Police*: 344; "A Plot For A Million: Or, the Minister and the Penny Paper."
5. *Omaha Daily Bee*, 1/30/1886, page 7 <retrieved at http://chroniclingamerica.loc.gov>; *New York Times*, 2/22/1886.

Chapter 28

"A Dark and Profound Mystery"

Who Was the Servant Girl Annihilator?

Suppose that Kenward Philp's theory was correct—that the servant girl murders were committed by a white man and a black man, and that the white man was a "a sort of gentleman farmer" who lived a "distance of some three miles" out of town. The 1885 city directory included numerous men who lived two or three miles outside of town and who had business, legal, or government connections that would allow them to be gentleman farmers. Could one of these men really have been the servant girl annihilator? Who done it?[1]

John Andrewartha was an architect and civil engineer who lived about three miles northeast of the city. He was born in England in 1839 and moved to Austin in 1881, hoping to be chosen to design the new capitol. He did not win the commission, but he remained in Austin and designed numerous other buildings and homes. In 1883 he won a commission to design a building for the *Austin Daily Statesman*, but that project fell through because of financial problems. The next year he designed the Austin City-County Hospital, located at 1405 Sabine Street, the first public hospital in Texas. That building was razed in 1929. He also designed the Montopolis bridge across the Colorado River, but that bridge was destroyed by a flood in 1935. Andrewartha died in November 1916 and was buried in Oakwood Cemetery in Austin.[2]

John T. Brackenridge was a bank president who lived about three miles south of the city. He was born in Indiana in 1828 and became a lawyer there in 1851. He moved to Texas in 1861 and joined the Confederate army the next year, rising to the rank of major. In 1866 Brackenridge worked as a cashier at a San Antonio bank and later became president of the First National Bank of Austin in 1877. In the mid-1880s, he was considered to be one of the three richest men in Austin. He died in San Antonio in 1906 and was buried in Oakwood Cemetery in Austin.[3]

Austin McGary was a minister and publisher who lived three miles east of the city. He was born in Huntsville, Texas, in 1846. He served with the Huntsville Grays in the Civil War and then became sheriff of Madison County, Texas, in 1872, serving two terms. While sheriff, he never carried a gun. In 1883 he moved to Austin and in 1884 established the religious *Firm Foundation* periodical. McGary was an influential member of the Church of Christ. He died in 1928 and was buried in Huntsville.[4]

Joseph Spence was a lawyer and land commissioner who lived about three miles east of the city. He was born in Philadelphia in 1826 and became a lawyer in Tennessee in 1853. In 1859 Spence and his family and slaves moved to a cotton plantation at Montopolis near Austin. Though he was a slave owner and a Republican, he opposed the Civil War. Because he was not involved in politics before the war, he became a likely candidate for involvement in the Reconstruction government in Texas. He served as chief clerk for the Texas secretary of state in 1866 and was appointed land commissioner in 1867, an office he held until 1870, when he was defeated in the first general election since the war. He then went into the real estate business and became a collecting agent for the Austin Water Works and Electric Light and Power Company. He died in Austin in 1894.[5]

John D. McCall was a politician who lived about 2 miles west of the city. He was born in Tennessee in 1846 and moved with his family in 1853 to Travis County, Texas. McCall served briefly in the Confederate army and then held positions in the Texas state government, mainly in the comptroller's office. In the early 1880s, he was a clerk under Comptroller William M. Brown and then became chief clerk under Comptroller William J. Swain. Swain, of course, was implicated in the Eula Phillips murder case. McCall himself was elected comptroller in 1885 and served four terms. He was elected mayor of Austin in 1897 and served two terms, after which he unsuccessfully ran for governor. He never married and died in Austin in 1909.[6]

Dr. Ashley N. Denton was a physician who lived two miles north of the city at the State Lunatic Asylum. He was born in Indian Territory in 1836, and his family moved to Texas the following year. Denton County in north Texas was named for his father. Young Denton studied medicine and then joined the Confederate army when war broke out. Denton returned to San Antonio, Texas, and was elected state representative in 1872 as a Democrat. In 1883 Denton was appointed superintendent of the State Lunatic Asylum and served in that capacity until 1888. One will remember the several theories about the servant girl annihilator being an inmate at the asylum. Also, Denton's son-in-law, Joseph Green, who worked at the asylum as an assistant physician, was suddenly declared insane by a Travis county court in February 1886. Denton died in San Marcos, Texas, in 1901.[7]

William C. Walsh was a politician and businessman who lived three miles west of the city. He was born in Ohio in 1836 and moved to Austin in 1840. He became a clerk in the General Land Office in 1857 and then joined the Confederate army, suffering a serious injury that made him use a cane the rest of his life. After the war, Walsh, a Democrat, refused a position in the Republican Reconstruction government in Texas. He bought a farm on Barton Springs in 1866, owning it until 1905. In 1873, Walsh became chief clerk of the Texas House of Representatives, a position he held until 1878, when he was appointed commissioner of the General Land Office, which he held until 1887. Walsh was instrumental in managing lands for the funding of higher education in Texas and also in choosing materials for the new state capitol being built in the 1880s. Walsh later served on the board overseeing the construction of the Austin dam in the 1890s. Walsh never married. He died in 1924 and was buried in Oakwood Cemetery.[8]

John Hancock was another lawyer and politician who lived three miles north of the city. Hancock was born in Alabama in 1824. He studied law in Tennessee and moved to Austin in 1847, where he began a successful law practice. In 1851 he was elected as a district judge, but he resigned after four years to return to his law practice and also to farm and raise stock. He acquired large tracts of land north of Austin stretching from Hancock Drive to Parmer Lane. During the war, Hancock, though a Democrat and slave owner, was a staunch Unionist and anti-secessionist. In 1871 he was elected to Congress, where he served as a representative until 1877. He was re-elected to Congress in 1883 and served until 1885. His law practice and his other dealings allowed him to become one of the three richest men in Austin. He died in Austin in 1893 and was buried in Oakwood Cemetery.[9]

Several other men lived on the outskirts of Austin. Charles Thiele ran a meat market two miles north of town. J.A. Beck ran a meat market four miles east of the city. William Stiles, a dentist, lived two to three miles east of the city. And John T. Dickinson lived two miles east of the city. As noted earlier, Dickinson was the secretary of the State Capitol Building Commission. He was implicated as a paramour of Eula Phillips in the Jimmy Phillips murder trial.[10]

Could any of these men have been the servant girl annihilator or the man pulling the strings of the negro puppets who committed the murders? The men who ran meat markets would be adept at the use of tools such as knives, hatchets, and axes. The unmarried men might have some incentive to commit rape. The men in business, law, and government surely would have accumulated enemies. But would any of these men be driven to murder, and serial murder at that?

"A Man of High Position and Wealth"

Shortly after the Jimmy Phillips trial ended, the people of Austin still did not believe that Phillips was guilty. They also wondered why no questions had been asked in the trial about the mysterious man allegedly in the coach with Eula Phillips the evening she was murdered. According to news reports, the mysterious person was supposed to be "a man of high position and wealth in this city." And in Katherine Ramsland's *Inside the Minds of Serial Killers*, she made the rather cryptic comment, without support, that "While the murders were never solved, evidence in retrospect points to a wealthy politician as 'the Servant Girl Annihilator.'" If these statements are valid, then several of the men discussed above would have to be eliminated quickly from consideration: Andrewartha, Brackenridge, McGary, Beck, Thiele, Stiles, and Denton, certainly.[11]

Philp's article, however, made the offhand comment that the home of the apparent white perpetrator was "neither tidy nor dirty—evidently the home of a bachelor." But then Philp's article provided a vivid description of the man: "A steely-gray-eyed man of powerful build, sallow complexion, six feet in height, slow-spoken, with bushy, standing-out black eye-brows." More men can be eliminated based on this description. Dickinson, though implicated in the Phillips murder, did not match the description, nor did Spence. And McCall was apparently not a wealthy man, even though he was a bachelor, so he was an unlikely candidate.[12]

William Walsh made many enemies during his tenure as Texas land commissioner from 1878 to 1887. When he took office, land frauds and bogus land certificates were rampant in the state. "The wholesale issue of bogus land certificates, together with numerous other irregularities in the land business," offered many opportunities for lawyers. One of the most famous of the land lawyers was William H. Jack, also known as Bill Jack. Other players in the land litigation game were Judge Joseph Lee (Grooms Lee's father), former Florida governor William Duval, and John Hancock. Walsh said that the land frauds were "'dragging their slimy forms about the State and enmeshing many people and land titles,'" and he worked to correct the problem. As a result, "numerous threats were made on Walsh's life. . . . Bodyguards were forced to guard the land office and armed sentinels protected Walsh's home at night." Walsh seemed more the target than the aggressor in the turbulent situation. Walsh also did not match the description, and though a bachelor, he was not mentioned among the wealthy men of Austin.[13]

Which leaves John Hancock, who was a longtime lawyer, judge, and politician, and who was considered one of the three richest men in Austin. John Hancock was born near Bellefonte, Alabama, on October 24, 1824. He was the seventh child of John Allen Hancock and Sarah Ryan Hancock. Many of his siblings eventually moved to Texas, notably George Duncan Hancock, a prominent merchant, legislator, and civic leader in Austin. George's son, Lewis, served on the Austin city council during the servant girl murders and later was elected mayor of Austin. John Hancock was the closest match for the description given by Philp. At the time of the murders, John Hancock was 60 or 61 years old. He had a lean build and was about six feet tall. A news article about him in 1886 mentioned "his lithe form—which he says, by way of pleasantry, 'is greatly admired by the ladies.'" Philp also mentioned the man's slow speech. Hancock was an able speaker, but a contemporary said that "he possesses no superior natural gifts as an orator and has never cultivated the artificial embellishments of speech or the mere flowers of oratory." He was also said to speak in a "logical and forcible style." Finally, Philp mentioned the man's bushy eyebrows, and Hancock's photo taken during his time in the House of Representatives in the mid-1880s showed some pronounced eyebrows. Of course, any number of other men could have fit the description, as well.[14]

John Hancock worked on his father's farm in Alabama before studying law in Tennessee. He joined the Alabama bar in 1846 and soon after moved to Austin, where he began his law practice. He was elected as a judge of the Second Judicial District in his mid-twenties, the youngest man elected a judge in Texas. He was a no-nonsense kind of judge. "He opened court one beautiful May morning in 1852 at La Grange, and announced that no lawyer, witness or juror would be called from the court house; they must be on hand or pay a fine. This was the first time this time-saving rule, now so commonly in vogue in District Courts, was announced." He was a conscientious and able judge, and was perhaps "the ablest lawyer in the state. He was not an orator in the common acceptation of that term; he was not a brilliant man, but he worked constantly at whatever there was to do. His mind was a powerful one. It is said that he was never known to spend an idle moment upon the streets during his over forty years' residence in Austin." Hancock resigned from the bench after four years to return to his law practice and also to farm and raise livestock. As a farmer, Hancock was not much of a success. He himself admitted that "considered in a financial sense his farming was a flat failure."[15]

"Moping on My Own Condition"

Hancock had a checkered political career. In 1855, he ran for Congress as the American Party candidate but lost the election to former Texas governor Peter H. Bell. In 1860, he was elected to the Texas House of Representatives as a Unionist. "He had always been a firm and consistent Democrat of the Jackson school, and was in consequence opposed to the secession and nullification doctrines of the Southern extremists." As a result of these beliefs, in March 1861 he refused to take an oath of allegiance to the Confederacy, despite the fact that he was a slave owner, and was expelled from the Texas legislature. During the Civil War, his activities in Austin and elsewhere could not have won him many friends among the supporters of the Southern cause. He claimed to be neutral, but he refused to practice law in Confederate courts and would not recognize their authority. Hancock's brother George owned a store at the corner of Congress Avenue and Pecan Street. George Hancock kept a U.S. flag flying there until the attack on Fort Sumter. In the second story of that building, "a company of 'Union men' called 'home guards' drilled there in the manual of arms until a short time after Fort Sumter was assaulted." Among these Union men were Thomas H. Duval, John Hancock, James H. Bell, E.B. Turner, and A.J. Hamilton. Many of these men were elected judges. Soon after the fall of Fort Sumter, many left Austin for Mexico to avoid conscription in the Confederate army.[16]

In Mexico, Hancock engaged in actions intended to free Texas from the Confederacy. The Unionist sentiment was strong along the Rio Grande. Many of the Union sympathizers from the state government had gathered in Brownsville. "Provisional governor Andrew J. Hamilton established a provisional government, and Col. Edmund J. Davis and Lt. Col. John L. Haynes recruited Unionists, Confederate deserters, and Hispanics into the First and Second Texas Cavalry regiments." John Hancock and Thomas Duval also helped to recruit troops for the Union cause, and "attempted to convince Union authorities to invade the interior of the state." Major-General F.J. Herron, head of the volunteers, even sent a letter to President Lincoln requesting the appointment of "Judge John Hancock as a brigadier-general of volunteers, with authority to take special charge of recruiting in this State and at once form a brigade." Herron believed that Hancock "could fill up a brigade within a few months." In this insurgency, known as the Rio Grande Campaign, as many as 2,000 volunteers filled the ranks of this Unionist army in Mexico, though they saw limited action against the Confederates. In March 1864, Colonel Davis and about 200 American and Mexican troops attacked Laredo. The Confederate forces in Laredo, led by Colonel Santos Benavides, numbered only about 100, but they were able to repel the Unionist attack all day long, and as night fell, the Unionist forces retreated, and no further attempt was made to take Laredo.

A few other skirmishes took place, but none had any effect on the outcome of the war. One can see why Hancock's Unionist activities might have rankled those loyal to the Confederacy. And if one accepts the sovereignty of the Confederate States, then his activities were close to treason.[17]

After a few months in Mexico, Hancock went to New York and then to Kentucky. He was in New Orleans when Robert E. Lee surrendered at Appomattox. In New Orleans, Hancock kept a diary from the end of November 1864 until the middle of April 1865. His diary revealed a man of grandiose schemes and deep depression. His first journal entry detailed a scheme to "bring a large amount of stock cattle . . . within the Federal lines and sell such as might be suitable to the Government." A few days later, he discussed a plan "to terminate the war, and . . . to make plenty of money besides." This second scheme involved going to Mexico and wiping out Maximillian, then receiving a pardon from the President. A third scheme dealt with "making shingles on an intensive scale" to help Hancock make some money. A more ambitious scheme dealt with a canal. Hancock wrote a bill hoping to gain funding for the Louisiana and Texas Canal Company, apparently to build a steamboat canal through the swamps of Louisiana from Vermilion Bay to the Sabine River. Hancock quickly learned that his bill conflicted with the new state constitution in Louisiana. In addition, a report by the Louisiana State Land Office called the whole idea "simply preposterous."[18]

Hancock's writings also displayed his sadness in being in exile. He wrote of Christmas Day 1864 as "one of heavy, painful gloom" because he did not really know the fate of his family back in Texas. His depression worsened in a few weeks:

> Today has been a dreary day. Misting rain and cool and wind. My feelings have been in strong sympathy with the weather, a heavy pall-like gloom weighed heavily on my spirits. I can not throw it off. I know not what to ascribe it to. It may be in part the weather and in part the constant thought of my dear wife and child. . . . I must bear all for their sake, and if it be God's will I shall meet them again and strive, in some measure, to secure their happiness in the future. What can I do? What can anyone, a mere private citizen, like myself, do? Literally nothing. I must stand with folded arms and see the inevitable ruin roll over me in common with all the South. It is painful to think that I have not averted this, as to my family at least, for I saw it plainly and predicted it from the first. Yet I somehow clung to a delusive hope that this ruin would not come. While my reason told me it would, I let the delusion control. I suffer the penalty, were I alone the sufferer it would be less intolerable, but those whom God has blessed me with must be victims too. And what is to be the final destiny of us all is veiled in imperishable gloom. Utter poverty and want may come.

In a later entry, he confessed that he had "devoted most of the day to unprofitably moping on my own condition and the probable situation of my family. How horrible this life is." His life seemed to bounce between highs and lows.[19]

John Hancock, ca. 1875

"A Mass of Incongruities and Contradictions"

When the war finally ended, Hancock returned to Texas and helped to organize the Reconstruction government of the state. He served as a delegate to the state constitutional convention of 1866 and promoted "the restoration of the seceding States to their original status in the Union." In 1870, the Democratic party offered Hancock the nomination for a seat in Congress, but he declined, wishing to rebuild his law practice instead of seeking "the empty honors of political office." In 1872, he yielded and accepted the nomination, winning the election and serving in the House of Representatives until 1877, at which time he lost a bid for re-election to George "Wash" Jones by fewer than 1400 votes. In that spirited campaign, Jones accused Hancock of not being a Democrat at all. He "charged both Hancock and [John] Ireland of being Know-Nothings—fossilized Know-Nothings." In the mid-1870s, Hancock was to be the Texas leader of a new Southern party that would weaken the Democratic party in the state. That new party apparently was not formed, for Hancock was again elected to Congress as a Democrat from 1883-1885. He chose at that time not to seek another term. During those terms he favored placing the Indians on reservations, prohibiting hunting on the plains unless accompanied by U.S. troops, and establishing a military telegraph system on the Texas frontier. He favored limiting the distribution of rations to the Indians to once a week so that the Indians would remain dependent on the government and could not stray from the reservations. His concern seemed not so much for the Indians as for the government he so often ennobled. Though he gave up his seat in Congress, in 1884 he was considered an attractive candidate for vice-president of the U.S.[20]

Though Hancock was generally praised for his legislative service, he was also ridiculed and scorned. As a Congressman, he saw to it that "the requests of the humblest citizen were as promptly and faithfully attended to as the highest in the land." He did not ignore the interests of the state, and he was known as "a tried patriot and statesman." Hancock's campaign against Wash Jones, though, unleashed a torrent of vitriol. In 1873, Hancock supported the so-called "Salary Grab Act" that increased national legislators' salary by 50% and also made the pay raise retroactive for the preceding two years. His support of that act, which was later killed, came back to haunt him a decade later. One newspaper, the *Clarksville Standard*, called him "a man who could not afford to avoid digging into the treasury of the United States for money that was not due him. How much did that vary from highway robbery?" The same newspaper said that Governor John Ireland "is not the statesman that Hancock is; at least not that sort of a statesman—Ireland would never have gone in for the salary-grab, had he been in congress; his moral perceptions and his constitutional organization would have shrunk from that sort of statesmanship." Hancock was also involved in shady dealings concerning a default on funds due to the State of Texas by Stillwell Russell when he was a tax collector for Harrison County. Hancock arranged a loan with a soon-deceased doctor through a private bank in Austin to help Stillwell settle his account. Hancock refused to tell anything about the loan. Later, Russell became the U.S. Marshal for the western district of Texas. Another marshal caught in a similar scandal was James E. Lucy, later the city marshal of Austin during the latter part of 1885. The private bank was run by James H. Raymond, later in the dam syndicate with Hancock.[21]

In 1884, Hancock gave interviews on the same day to reporters for two different newspapers. The interviews suggested that Hancock was either two-faced or mentally unbalanced. "The man who reads both papers must either conclude there are two John Hancocks in Austin, or that if there is only one he is a wonderfully inconsistent man. It is suggestive of 'Phillip drunk and Phillip sober.'"

The two reporters asked similar questions about the topics of the day: fence-cutting, free grass, Governor Ireland's policies. The result of the two interviews "was a mass of incongruities and contradictions that are absurd enough to be laughable." In one interview, Hancock had good words for Ireland and thought he should get nominated again; Hancock also disapproved of a bill by A.W. Terrell. In the other interview, Hancock lambasted Ireland and wondered how the state would have fared "if a statesman were occupying the executive chair"; he also said he was sorry the Terrell bill did not pass. A smart man certainly could have sensed how the affair would have played out, but Hancock apparently did not comprehend what he was saying, if his comments were reported accurately. His interviews were ridiculed as "a sort of marching up the hill and down again, or, I did and I didn't, affair." And when he read the reports, he was likely tempted to repeat a notorious comment he had made years earlier: "D—n the newspapers!" Hancock truly seemed to have a Jekyll and Hyde personality; he was at times two-sided and two-faced. He was gracious but vindictive, he had grandiose schemes that led to utter depression, and his sterling ethics clashed with some of his political actions, such as the salary grab. Hancock seemed aware of his foibles, noting that he "sometimes erred in judgment, as I often do, being but a frail, fallible mortal, almost every day looking back to find some error of yesterday I would correct."[22]

In 1886, Hancock was apparently making a run for a U.S. Senate seat against an old friend, Alexander W. Terrell, the man whose bill Hancock disapproved of but hoped had passed. The duplicity apparent in the 1884 interviews had turned into discontent and rage. In 1862, when Hancock's life was in danger in Texas because of his Unionist views, Colonel Wash Jones went to Terrell to ask his aid in saving Hancock. According to Terrell in a speech given in Gatesville in July 1886:

> In twenty minutes I was in the saddle and rode that day fifty miles through a snowstorm and fifty miles each following day for 500 miles until I reached Austin. The first time I ever entered John Hancock's home was the night of my arrival in Austin. I afterwards, through a gentleman then living in Burnet, and whom I saw only yesterday, turned away the wrath of Southern men who sought Hancock's life for what they regarded treason to the South. For months afterwards Hancock remained in Texas.

Later, Terrell defended Hancock for his activities during the war and supported Hancock in his various campaigns. Terrell

> disregarded the charges made by Gov. Davis and others, that Hancock had desired to command the negro troops at Brenham. I worked in the convention as his friend and helped to secure his nomination over Col. Giddings. . . . I afterwards sustained him in the congressional convention where he was nominated, crucifying the young ambition of Seth Shepard, a true and noble man. . . . When he was a candidate against Coke for the United States senate I refused to grow angry like others over his flings at Southern men, and voted for him solitary and alone on the last ballot. . . . When he sought the

> nomination for congress against Col. Upson I went to
> Williamson county to reconcile old Democrats to his support. . .
> . When afterwards Governor Davis began his canvass against
> Hancock, there was no one to answer him, for Hancock was in
> Europe. I took the stump and answered Davis at Georgetown,
> at Round Rock and elsewhere, and Hancock on his return
> circulated thousands of my published speeches before he began
> that canvass. . . . Wash Jones was the bosom friend of my
> early manhood and when time and again at Florence, at Taylor,
> at Liberty Hill and elsewhere . . . I answered Jones in Hancock's
> interest from the stump, I felt that I had struck a brother.

In all that time Terrell never sought or received a favor from Hancock, be it political, financial, or personal. And how did Hancock repay the many favors Terrell had bestowed upon him? With lies and slander. According to Terrell, Hancock "is reported as being courteous to others, but severe on me. . . . [Hancock's] unprovoked malignity has its root in an ingratitude so phenomenal as to require exposure and leaves no room for pity." Terrell implored his listeners to consider Hancock's words and actions and to acknowledge them for what there were— political accusations with no basis in fact or reality.

> I say to you, . . . if ever a dog shall save my life by barking
> when an assassin approaches me, I will feed that dog and not
> strike him. The right of Mr. Hancock to run for the senate I do
> not question, but an assault, an unprovoked and utterly
> groundless accusation, would have come with better grace from
> some other man. And now, gentlemen, the time has passed
> when any man's sympathy with the North in her struggle with
> the South shall constitute his one qualification for office here. It
> should be urged against no man, for we must bury the bloody
> shirt; but we are not yet ready to degrade our Southern
> manhood or Southern soil by making a man's loyalty to the
> North in the late war his own passport to favor in Texas.

As it turned out, neither Terrell nor Hancock won the nomination for U.S. Senator. For all practical purposes, Hancock's political life was over, though he still dabbled in land and local projects.[23]

"All the Important Land Cases"

John Hancock acquired thousands of acres of land north of Austin, stretching from current Hancock Drive in Austin all the way north to Parmer Lane. In 1852, Hancock purchased a large area of land from Rebecca Spear, the widow of George W. Spear. The land was the northern "part of Spear's original 1841 Republic of Texas land grant, which stretched north from the Colorado River to where Anderson Lane is today and between, roughly, Balcones Drive and North Lamar Boulevard." On this land, Hancock built a stately home called "The Oaks," located at what is now 2200 West North Loop. In 1866, Hancock bought over 500 acres in the same area from Elizabeth Moore, the widow of Martin Moore. The cabin on this property, called the Moore-Hancock Farmstead, is located at 4811 Sinclair Avenue and was restored in the 1980s. "Considered the only log dwelling in Austin known to survive on its original site, it is on the National Register of Historic Places and is a Recorded Texas Historic Landmark." The property around Parmer Lane was farmed by Rubin Hancock, a former slave of John Hancock, in a small community called Duval. In 1860, Hancock's land holdings around Austin were valued at $60,000, a tidy sum.[24]

Hancock also took part in a deal in 1880 for the purchase of a million acres in the Cassas Grande river valley in Mexico. The purchase included merchandise, livestock, and 2500 peons, debtors who were essentially slaves for life. Shortly after the purchase, an oral emancipation was given to the peons, because Hancock and his partners suspected that "their peons were about to run away from them, and it would probably cost more . . . to keep them bound in that way, and so they concluded that it would be an excellent stroke of policy" to free them. The oral emancipation was little more than a declaration of freedom, because the peons were still bound to the land. Once again, Hancock displayed a remarkable disregard for minorities, be they Indians, black slaves, or Mexican peons.[25]

As a lawyer, Hancock was involved in "nearly all the important land cases that have come before the courts in his section of the State." Some of Hancock's legal actions were rather audacious. In 1886, as a private lawyer, not a judge, he issued an opinion to several cattlemen "on the action of the state land board in increasing the lease price of the school lands from 4 to 8 cents." Hancock argued that the land board's action was unconstitutional because the legislature had "no authority to delegate legislative powers to inferior agents." He told the cattlemen to pay the 4 cents and they would be exempt from all penalties. The cattlemen were pleased with the opinion, especially since "they paid, so it is said, a good round sum for it." At a time when land dealings were rife with fraud and corruption, Hancock certainly must have engendered a healthy stable of enemies. As noted earlier, many of the men whose homes or servants were attacked were involved in the land office or were land agents. And Hancock's wealth also caused him legal problems. In April 1885, Hancock was involved in a forgery case. His name was "forged to paper upon which a considerable sum of money" was raised. And in May 1887, the newspaper editor W.Y. Leader was arrested for forging the names of A.J. Jernigan and John Hancock on an $80 note. Could some sort of blackmail be behind the forgery?[26]

In 1871, the Texas state legislature passed an act to incorporate the Austin Trust Company, which included Judge John Hancock, E.M. Pease, William Von Rosenberg, and others. The trust was empowered to issue stock certificates amounting to two million dollars to build a dam across the Colorado River. The trust was to organize and conduct business before January 1, 1873, but the charter was allowed to lapse without any progress made on building a dam. In 1888, A.P. Wooldridge wrote a letter to the *Austin Daily Statesman*, stating that "Our community as a whole, is a poor one, and becoming poorer every day." What was Wooldridge's solution to the lamentable situation? Austin should build a dam across the Colorado River to generate power for all the factories that would surely come to the city if the dam were built. A campaign was mounted for the dam, with John McDonald promoted as mayor of Austin. During the campaign, the dam was estimated to cost about $150,000 to build, an amount that could be paid off without raising taxes. McDonald won the election in 1889, and designs for a new dam moved ahead quickly. The end result was a dam that would cost nine times the original amount, over $1.3 million dollars. A bond election was quickly mounted, and the bonds passed by a 27 to 1 ratio. The first bond allotment of $400,000 drew only three bids. One of the bids "was made by an Austin syndicate, who offered par for $400,000 worth of the bonds. The syndicate is composed of John and Lewis Hancock, K. T. Brackinridge, George W. Breckinridge, James H. Raymond and A. P. Wooldridge. The syndicate got the bonds, of course."[27]

The dam was dedicated in May 1893. It was a marvelous structure, 60 feet high and 1200 feet long. It included a powerhouse to generate electricity for the city and to power the new electric trolley lines on Congress Avenue. Two months later, Hancock was dead and buried at Oakwood Cemetery. Unfortunately, the dam collapsed in a torrential rainstorm in April 1900, killing five workers and three boys and washing away homes, barns, and livestock. The dam was somewhat symbolic of John Hancock's life—grandiose schemes and accomplishments that led to deep depression and collapse. If indeed John Hancock was involved in the servant girl affair, perhaps the dam had a deeper psychological meaning: holding back the deadly vengeful urges.[28]

Of course, all this evidence against John Hancock is not worthy even of the indictments handed out during the servant girl murders. Every politician or person in the public arena attracts malcontents and enemies. The higher the position, the greater the attraction. John Hancock was an esteemed lawyer and judge, an able legislator, and one of the wealthiest men in Austin. But he was also a conflicted soul, a slave owner who actively opposed the Southern cause, and one who could backstab with the best of them. He was supposedly responsive to all people, but he supported the Union more for the sense of government than for his sense of compassion for minorities. And he had a dark secret, one he shared with his father, that linked him to the servant girl murders.

Notes

Title: *Austin Daily Statesman*, 5/30/1886.
Photograph credit: Library of Congress Prints and Photographs Division <http://www.loc.gov/pictures/item/brh2003001275/PP>.

1. *Omaha Daily Bee*, 1/30/1886.
2. Long, "Andrewartha, John," *Handbook of Texas Online*;
Morrison & Fourmy's General Directory of the City of Austin, 1885-1886.
3. "Brackenridge, John Thomas," *Handbook of Texas Online*; *Morrison & Fourmy's General Directory of the City of Austin, 1885-1886*; *Fort Worth Daily Gazette*, 6/5/1887.
4. Roberts, *Handbook of Texas Online*; *Morrison & Fourmy's General Directory of the City of Austin, 1885-1886*.
5. Todd and Knape, *Handbook of Texas Online*; *Morrison & Fourmy's General Directory of the City of Austin, 1885-1886*.

6. Cutrer, "McCall, John Dodd," *Handbook of Texas Online*; *Morrison & Fourmy's General Directory of the City of Austin, 1885-1886*.
7. Miller, *Handbook of Texas Online*; *Morrison & Fourmy's General Directory of the City of Austin, 1885-1886*; *San Antonio Daily Express*, 2/16/1886.
8. Gilman, *Handbook of Texas Online*; "Commissioners Historical Bios," Texas General Land Office; *Morrison & Fourmy's General Directory of the City of Austin, 1885-1886*.
9. Hooker, *Handbook of Texas Online*; *Morrison & Fourmy's General Directory of the City of Austin, 1885-1886*; *Fort Worth Daily Gazette*, 6/5/1887.
10. *Morrison & Fourmy's General Directory of the City of Austin, 1885-1886*.
11. *Fort Worth Daily Gazette*, 5/28/1886; Ramsland, *Inside the Minds of Serial Killers*: 4.
12. *Omaha Daily Bee*, 1/30/1886.
13. Smithwick, *The Evolution of a State, or Recollections of Old Texas Days*: 261-262; "Commissioners Historical Bios," Texas General Land Office.
14. "Missouri Project"; Cutrer, "Hancock, George Duncan," *Handbook of Texas Online*; *Fort Worth Daily Gazette*, 7/16/1886; Lynch, *The Bench and Bar of Texas*: 427.; *Austin Record*, 5/29/1886; Photograph of John Hancock: <http://www.loc.gov/pictures/item/brh2003001275/PP/>.
15. Hooker, *Handbook of Texas Online*; Lotto, *Fayette County, Her History and Her People*: 203-204; *Fort Worth Daily Gazette*, 7/16/1886.
16. Guttery, *Representing Texas*: 23; *Biographical Encyclopedia of Texas*: 50-51; Hooker, *Handbook of Texas Online*; "Hancock Creek/Arroyo Seco, Part 1"; Terrell, "The City of Austin from 1839 to 1865": 120-121.
17. Marten, *Handbook of Texas Online*; Johnson, *A History of Texas and Texans*: 549.; *A Twentieth Century History of Southwest Texas*: 204.; *The War of the Rebellion*: 409.
18. Hooker, *Handbook of Texas Online*; *Biographical Encyclopedia of Texas*: 51; *The Twentieth Century Biographical Dictionary of Notable Americans*, vol 5; "The Diary of Judge John Hancock": Entry 1, November 28, 1864; Entry 32, December 29, 1864; Entries 36-40, January 3-7, 1865; Entry 71, February 7, 1865; *Report of the Register of the State Land Office for the Year 1866*: 4.
19. "The Diary of Judge John Hancock": Entry 28, December 25, 1864; Entry 52, January 19, 1865; Entry 84, February 26, 1865.
20. *Biographical Encyclopedia of Texas*: 51; *The Twentieth Century Biographical Dictionary of Notable Americans*, vol 5; Lotto, *Fayette County, Her History and Her People*: 204; Hooker, *Handbook of Texas Online*; *Weekly Colorado Citizen*, 12/26/1878; *San Saba News*, 6/21/1884; *Colorado Citizen*, 8/24/1882; Horton, *Samuel Bell Maxey: A Biography*: 86; *San Saba News*, 6/21/1884; Lynch, *The Bench and Bar of Texas*: 429.
21. *Weekly Colorado Citizen*, 7/18/1878; *Fort Worth Daily Gazette*, 2/13/1884; "Testimony Taken by the Committee on Expenditures in the Department of Justice," 1884: 237-242.
22. *Fort Worth Daily Gazette*, 1/31/1884; Lynch, *The Bench and Bar of Texas*: 430.
23. *Fort Worth Daily Gazette*, 7/16/1886.
24. Hooker, *Handbook of Texas Online*; "Hancock Creek/Arroyo Seco, Part 1"; "Milwood History"; "Rubin Hancock Farmstead"; 1860 Federal Census.
25. *Colorado Citizen*, 7/8/1880.
26. Lynch, *The Bench and Bar of Texas*: 423; *Fort Worth Daily Gazette*, 6/12/1886; *Waco Daily Examiner*, 4/4/1885; Bartholomew Diary 21:133, 5/20/1887.
27. *General Laws of the Twelfth Legislature of the State of Texas, First Session—1871*: 338-339.; Mead, *Report on the Dam and Water Power Development at Austin, Texas*: 40; Humphrey, *Austin: A History of the Capital City*: 25-26; Humphrey, *Austin: An Illustrated History*: 128-133; *Fort Worth Daily Gazette*, 10/16/1890 (The Gazette article was aptly titled "Austin Hilarious." The K. T. Brackinridge mentioned as a member of the syndicate was more likely J.T. Brackenridge.)
28. Barkley, *History of Travis County and Austin 1839-1899*: 132; Humphrey, *Austin: An Illustrated History*: 153-154.

Chapter 29

"One Human Passion Devilish Enough"

Was Revenge the Motive?

Plain and simple, John Hancock and his father were miscegenists. Four slaves of Judge John Hancock who became well known in the Austin area—Rubin, Payton, Orange, and Salem Hancock—were all reputed to be the half-brothers or sons of the judge. In the 1880 census, Rubin was reported to be 45 years old, Payton 39 years old, Orange 42 years old, and Salem (or Solom) 42 years old, though Salem was reported to be 40 in the 1870 census. Because John Hancock was born in 1824, he would have been about 11 years old when Rubin was born, making the notion that Rubin or the others were John Hancock's sons a bit hard to accept. All four of the slaves were said to be mulattos in the 1880 census, and all were born in Alabama, though at least two had different mothers. Likely, then, Rubin, Payton, Orange, and Salem were the illegitimate sons of John Allen Hancock, John's father, who was born in Franklin City, Virginia, in 1779 and died in Alabama in 1855. The four men were more likely the half-brothers of John Hancock than his sons. After the Civil War, they were given their freedom. Most of them worked on John Hancock's property closer to town for a while, and then most bought small farms about ten miles north of Austin in the area of the Upper Georgetown Road, now Burnet Road off Loop 1 in the Milwood neighborhood.[1]

John Hancock's indiscretion was a bit more compelling. In November 1855, John Hancock married Susan E. Richardson, the granddaughter of Asa Brigham, an early settler who signed the Texas Declaration of Independence and served as Austin mayor from 1842-1843. John and Susan had one child together, Edwin B. Hancock, born in October 1856. Edwin later married Marie Fiset in Germany and became a lawyer like his father. Susan Richardson Hancock died in 1911 and was buried in Oakwood Cemetery in Austin. Edwin died in 1917 and was buried in Oakwood Cemetery. Marie died in El Paso in September 1938 and was also buried in Oakwood Cemetery.[2]

There is nothing really remarkable about Hancock's marriage to Susan Richardson. However, to be a viable suspect as the servant girl annihilator, John Hancock would need access to the Thug Gang to do his bidding. What better access than to have a son running the hub of black congregation on East Pecan Street, the Black Elephant saloon? The proprietor of the Black Elephant was Hugh B. Hancock. And sure enough, Hugh B. Hancock was the son of Judge John Hancock.[3]

Thomas Montgomery Gregory was the son of James Monroe Gregory, who wrote a famous biography of Frederick Douglass. The younger Gregory was educated at Harvard and later became an English professor at Howard University. In 1919, he founded the Howard Players, making him instrumental in nurturing the National Negro Theatre Movement. A year earlier, he had married Hugh Ella Hancock, the fourth daughter of Hugh B. Hancock and Susie James Hancock. In a family history featured on "PBS Frontline," it was revealed that several members of the prominent Gregory family were "the descendents of some white person's secret black child. A Supreme Court Judge, a U.S. Congressman, and a Texas state senator had, during the mid-1800s, each harbored a black mistress and child, afforded them shelter, clothing, and education and thus helped this family on its way to prominence." The U.S. Congressman was John Hancock of Texas.[4]

In a family history written by Thomas Montgomery Gregory, he gave pertinent details about his father-in-law.

> Oberlin [College in Ohio] was the center for Negro families who left the south to educate their children. Many children were sent there by their white fathers. One was Hugh Berry Hancock (my wife's father), whose father, John Hancock, of Austin, Texas, moved his common-law wife and child from Austin at the beginning of the Civil War, and established a home for them in Oberlin. He completed his elementary and high school, and possibly college, education. My father told me he remembered "little Hugh Hancock" in Oberlin. He returned to Austin around 1878, marrying Susan James O'Connor in 1879. She had been sent to a Catholic Convent in Baltimore at age 14 by her white father, Major O'Connor, a confederate. . . . Later Susan James was also sent to Oberlin, where she met her future husband, Hugh Hancock.

The statement that Hancock "moved his common-law wife and child from Austin" seems to fly in the face of reason. The 1900 census indicated that Hugh B. Hancock was born in June 1855, five months before John Hancock married Susan Richardson, so Gregory seems clearly to be discussing some woman other than Susan Richardson and some child other than Edwin Hancock. John Hancock's New Orleans diary lamented the sad fate of his family stuck in Confederate territory in Austin and his inability to help them. Did he really move his common-law wife and child to the relative safety of Ohio and leave his legal wife and child to suffer their fate in Austin, where his shenanigans during the Civil War probably brought the family much acrimony? That must have been the case, because Hugh Hancock was living in Oberlin, Ohio, in 1870, in the household of William Henderson, a barber. Though his mother's name is not really known, she might have been Elizabeth House, a mulatto woman aged 60, living in the same household.[5]

Gregory clearly identified John Hancock: "John Hancock returned to Austin after the Civil War and was elected to the U.S. Congress, serving many years. Previously, he had been a member of the Texas legislature. The Hancocks were a prominent family in Austin." Gregory continued with details about Hugh Hancock.

> Hugh Hancock taught school after his marriage, and later, sponsored by a white friend of his father's, opened a saloon, and then entered politics in Austin. He refused his father's offer to send him to the University of Michigan Law School. When my wife was a teenager, he left the family and moved to Pocatello, Idaho, where he died around the turn of the century.

The saloon, of course, was the Black Elephant. John Hancock seemed to be trying to groom Hugh Hancock just like his other son, Edwin, who did become a lawyer.[6]

After the murders, Hugh Hancock did not suddenly leave town, nor did John Hancock. In 1889 and 1890, Hugh Hancock was still running a saloon, but this one was at 302 Colorado, not on Pecan Street. By that time, too, Edwin B. Hancock had joined his father's law firm. As late as 1897 or 1898, Hugh Hancock was running a saloon in Austin, his last one back on East Pecan Street, at 404 East 6th Street. The Black Elephant had been at 424 East Pecan. By 1900, though, Hugh Hancock and his family had moved to Evanston, Illinois, where Hancock lived for about nine years. Then he left his family suddenly, as noted, and moved to Idaho, where he died in January 1910 at the age of 55. Hugh Ella Hancock must have become a teenager around 1909, so his death followed quickly his departure. The death report did not give a cause of death, but Hugh Berry Hancock was identified as Hugh P. Hancock in the records. Black was given as the race of the deceased, married was listed as the marital status, and his father's name was Judge Hancock. His birthplace was not given. By 1920, Hugh Hancock's widow, Susie E. Hancock, was living with her daughter Hugh Ella and her son-in-law in Washington, D.C. Both mother and daughter were described in the census as mulatto.[7]

One wonders why Hugh Hancock would suddenly leave his family in Illinois and move to Idaho to die. Was he the victim of a terminal disease, or did shame and guilt finally drive him from his family? As noted, he remained in Austin for almost 15 years after the murders. Did new evidence arise to cause him to leave Austin and then to leave his family behind in Illinois? Or was he totally innocent of any involvement in the murders? The Black Elephant saloon was a well-known hangout for members of the Thug Gang. Alex Mack was lured from the Black Elephant by Marshal Grooms Lee when Lee was trying to make Mack confess. Obviously, having a direct line of access to the Thug Gang did not make John Hancock necessarily guilty of any involvement in the servant girl murders, but he had the one thing that most other white men in town lacked—and that was the access to the Thug Gang.

"Presumption of a Marriage"

Most of the servants who were murdered were mulattos. Could Hancock have been killing mulattos to soothe his own conflicted soul? Clearly, he and his father practiced miscegenation, and the many mulattos in Austin could have been a daily reminder of his sin. Even by 1885, Texas had a long and strange history of interracial relations. As early as 1841, David L. Wood of Fayette County was charged with the crime of miscegenation. His wife appeared white, but in fact she had been born a slave and was legally still a slave. Wood petitioned Congress to legalize his marriage, but that petition apparently failed, for David L. Wood and his family soon thereafter disappeared from Texas records. In 1858, a statute was passed that outlawed interracial marriage in Texas. A case in 1867, though, did legalize interracial marriage in Texas, for a while, at least. A.H. Foster, a white man, owned several slaves, among them a woman named Leah that he apparently loved and wished to marry. Interracial marriage was not legal in Louisiana, where they lived, so Foster moved Leah and her children to Ohio, emancipated them, and provided them with living expenses. When he visited them in Ohio, he stayed with Leah. In 1851 Foster moved with Leah and her children to Texas. When Foster died in 1867, Leah claimed his property as his widow. The executor said the estate would not cover Foster's debts, but Leah went to court, claiming that the Texas homestead law prevented some family property from being sold to cover debts. The trial judge ruled that Foster and Leah had the "'presumption of a marriage'" in Ohio, where interracial marriage was not prohibited, and that such a presumption was not canceled because of the move to Texas, even though Texas had a law against such marriages. The ruling was appealed, and the Texas Supreme Court concurred with the lower judge. In fact, not only did the Texas anti-miscegenation law not abrogate the presumed Foster marriage, but the Fourteenth Amendment and the Civil Rights Act of 1866 had abrogated the Texas statute. As a result, marriage between races could be contracted in Texas. The judge on the Texas Supreme Court that wrote the majority opinion was Alexander Walker, the same judge that presided over the Jimmy Phillips and Moses Hancock trials.[8]

In 1869, a new Texas constitution was written, and in *Honey v. Clark* in 1872, the Texas Supreme Court ruled that "the state constitution of 1869 had brought legitimacy to the common-law nature of interracial relationships." However, in 1874, a political shift occurred, with most of the Radical Republicans replaced by a more conservative Democratic regime. A new angle on the anti-miscegenation statute emerged. Thomas Duval, an associate of John Hancock, ruled in the Eleventh District Court in Austin in July 1877 that the "Fourteenth and Fifteenth Amendments and the Civil Rights Act of 1875 had in effect invalidated the Texas anti-miscegenation statute." In December 1877, though, the Texas Court of Appeals ruled in *Charles Frasher v. The State* that the amendments and the civil rights act were actually applicable only to blacks, not to whites, and that "the purpose of these federal laws was never to interfere with state efforts to regulate the institution of marriage." For all practical purposes, then, interracial marriage was again illegal in Texas. In 1879, the anti-miscegenation statute caught Emile Francois in its grasp after he married Lottie Stotts. "Emile Francois, white, in 1879 intermarried with a woman three generations remote from a negro ancestor. Such intermarriage was in violation of the Texas penal code (article 386) then in force, and in the state district court at Austin Francois was convicted of miscegenation and sentenced to five years imprisonment in the Texas penitentiary." Ironically, the presiding judge was Thomas Duval, who reversed his ruling on the anti-miscegenation law that he issued two years earlier. The Texas statute punished only the white party in the interracial marriage. "Duval curiously held that the Texas statute did not violate the letter of the Constitution or the Civil Rights Act.

Duval pointed to the greater influence of whites over blacks as justification for punishing whites only," so Francois' prison sentence was upheld.[9]

Francois did not give up without a lengthy legal fight, though. Francois contended that the statute was discriminatory. "Francois is a pure white. He married a colored woman whose complexion was fairer than his own. The State statute under which he was convicted provided only for the punishment of the white person in cases of miscegenation, hence his claim of being discriminated against." As his five-year sentence was nearing its end, Francois's case was finally gaining traction in the federal courts. Fearing "unlawful" federal intervention, Governor John Ireland pardoned Emile Francois, a pardon that Francois refused because it did not fully restore his citizenship. Instead, Francois was able to get warrants issued against the superintendent and various officers at the penitentiary, "charging them with unlawfully restraining him of his liberty." In addition, Francois got the federal court in Galveston to issue an arrest warrant for Governor John Ireland "for violation of section 5510 of the revised statutes of the United States." In essence, Francois claimed that "Ireland, as governor of Texas, with the penitentiary officials, conspired and confederated together for the purpose of depriving him of the right and privileges secured by constitution and laws of the United States." The marshal charged with serving the warrant did not do so after the governor and U.S. District Attorney Jack Evans questioned his authority to serve the warrant in Austin. The federal court in Galveston ruled that section 5510 did not apply to the case, and the case was dismissed. Francois was eventually released and was presumably in Austin during the servant girl murders. Jack Evans would later serve as a prosecution lawyer in the Moses Hancock trial.[10]

Which all means that John Hancock's miscegenation—the common-law marriage mentioned by Thomas M. Gregory, the "presumption of a marriage" in the court case—would have been considered illegal under Texas statute. John Hancock had an illegal relationship with a black woman that yielded a child. The Gregory article noted that John Hancock sent Hugh Hancock and his mother to Ohio to be safe from the ravishes of the Civil War. After the war, John Hancock got a friend to help finance a saloon for Hugh, the Black Elephant, even after Hugh had refused the elder Hancock's offer to send him to law school. John Hancock was never prosecuted for his violation of the anti-miscegenation statute, though his relationship with Hugh Hancock was apparently common knowledge.

"The Motive for This Horrible Series of Crimes"

Kenward Philp indicated in his article that he visited "John Doe's" property three miles out of town. As noted earlier, John Hancock had two properties north of Austin, one a more stately home called "The Oaks," the other a rustic cabin about a half mile closer to town. Philp described the place he visited to interview his John Doe: "The house stood fully half a mile from the next in either direction and some distance from the road. It was neither tidy nor dirty—evidently the home of a bachelor." Could the cabin pictured on the next page, the Moore-Hancock farmstead at 4811 Sinclair Avenue, have been the place that Philp visited?

359

One problem with the solution of the servant girl murders revolves around a motive. Of course, a variety of motives was offered in the newspapers and by local officials as the murders continued. Many believed the murders were the result of jealousy or domestic spats. Others credited rape or robbery or simply the desire to murder. Some blamed voodoo or the evil eye or some supernatural being. All of these motives were justifiable to a degree, but the severity and brutality of the attacks seemed to rule them out. Would a jealous lover or husband hack his beloved to pieces with an ax? Would a robber choose the poorest segment of the population for his plunder, especially when greater riches lay only feet away? Would a rapist seeking carnal delight mutilate the object of his desire? Kenward Philp considered all these motives in his article and offered a reasonable alternative.

> "Those murders are not committed for the sake of theft, for no property has ever been disturbed in the victim's homes. Lust, strong as it is as a motive to crime, is not powerful enough in these cases as an incentive. There is but one human passion devilish enough to furnish the motive for this horrible series of crimes—revenge.
>
> "But can it be possible that one man can entertain equal feelings of revenge against nine persons, living apart, some white and some colored? And is it not still more incredible that two persons (if my theory be correct, that more than one was engaged in these murders) should have precisely the same feelings of vengeance against precisely the same persons and should take precisely the same means of wreaking them?"

Philp's theory of revenge seemed more logical than many of the theories advanced during the year of murders.[11]

Certainly, John Hancock had the means and influence to orchestrate the servant girl murders. He had the wealth, the position, the looks, and the location to meet the qualifications of the Ramsland and Philp contentions. He also had the access to some of the more recalcitrant black men in Austin through the saloon of his son, Hugh Hancock. But, if he was involved in the servant girl murders, what was his motive? What would cause him to seek revenge? Could a motive deal with land or legal transactions? As noted, at least two of the men whose servants were murdered were land agents, and many of the homes that were attacked in the early spring of 1885 also belonged to land agents or officials in the state land office. Philp, however, stressed that the revenge stemmed from a trial in 1878 that was the impetus for the string of servant girl murders. What was that trial, if indeed it took place?[12]

"The Trial"

Philp, during his conversation with the coroner, indicated that two men were tried for the double crime of outrage and murder. One of the men was black, and one was white. The white man was supposedly the brother of the gentleman farmer that Philp contended had orchestrated the servant girl murders. The black man and white man were tried, convicted, and hanged. The jury was made up of both black and white people. Philp further complicated the situation by saying that the prosecution attorney, whom he called White Johnson, had been found murdered shortly after the trial. A short while later, Johnson's father was found murdered, and not long after, Johnson's brother was also found murdered. In addition, a key prosecution witness, a hackman named John Smith, was found murdered just outside of Austin. Philp's basic claim was that the servant girl murders were revenge upon the jurors or relatives of the jurors involved in the case.[13]

This part of Philp's article poses several problems. First, though Hancock had several siblings and other relatives in the area, no evidence could be found that any of them were involved in a rape-murder case or had been hanged as a result. In fact, no legal hanging occurred in 1878 or 1879 that matched the particulars of Philp's claim. Bowen Brown, a 28-year-old white man, was hanged in Austin in May 1878 for the murder of another white man, Tom Halderman. Fred Robinson (or Robertson), a 22-year-old black man, was hanged in Groesbeck, about 135 miles northeast of Austin, in June 1878 for the rape of a white woman. Numerous other legal hangings occurred in 1878 and 1879, but none matched the particulars of Philp's trial. Further, no news reports or death records could be found to suggest that several members in the family of a prominent lawyer had been murdered as noted in Philp's article. A perusal of county trial records and Texas Court of Appeals cases produced no cases matching Philp's trial.[14]

One intriguing part of Philp's story, however, may have some validity. In November 1878, August Wittman, an Austin hackman, was discovered dead in

Horst's pasture northeast of Austin near the reservoir by young boys hunting rabbits. "His skull was fractured with a stone. He was shot or stabbed in several places and his throat cut." He had last been seen in Guy Town on a Thursday night a few days before his body was discovered. In Guy Town, "he was on a spree, and had, it is said, about $100 and a gold watch on his person." His corpse carried no watch or money. The theory was that he had been killed in town and dumped in the pasture where he likely would not be found for a while. Even in 1878, Austin had an unsavory reputation. The Brenham newspaper opined that "Austin is rapidly establishing a very unenviable reputation for murders and lawlessness, a reputation in fact, not at all creditable to the capital of the State, where law and order should reign supreme."[15]

Was August Wittman the hack driver that Philp called John Smith? Could he really be attached to the servant girl murders? On November 16, 1869, 27-year-old August Wittmann married 32-year-old Sophie Schmidt in Fayette County, Texas. Sophie had a two-year-old son, Charles Schmidt, from a previous marriage. Nine years later, August was killed in Guy Town and dumped in a pasture. Seven years after that murder, widow Sophia Wittman and her son, Charles Smith, a barber, lived at 302 East Linden, the same yard in which Irene Cross was murdered. Coincidence? Or could Philp's theory have some credibility?[16]

Almost ironically, by 1880, August Wittman had become a ghost haunting the outskirts of Austin. Wittman's murderer was never found, so his ghost nightly was "seen stalking in the pasture, lantern in hand waiting to go with some one to the house of the murderer. Ghosts," the report noted, "are singular beings and have ways peculiarly of their own." Was the hand that murdered August Wittman the same that struck down Irene Cross in his widow's yard years later?[17]

Philp's notion that jurors or witnesses might be killed for their participation in a trial was not far-fetched. In Bell County in 1879, a black man and woman, Logan and Emily Elliott, were killed by five men for testifying in a rape trial against Walter Canterbury and Albert Dobbins, who belonged to a band of thieves. Later, a couple of men named Smothers were arrested for their part in the murders. Ironically, the two people murdered were not voluntary witnesses in the rape trial.[18]

But did the trial Philp mentioned actually take place? The existing records don't seem to support his claim. But more adept researchers might be able to turn up the evidence. John Hancock, though, was involved in numerous trials, both directly and indirectly. He even served as lawyer for the appeal of a murder case that saw William B. Dunham as the attorney for the state. Dunham, on whose property Gracie Vance and Orange Washington were killed, worked on several cases before the Texas Court of Appeals in the late 1870s. Dunham served as the attorney for the state. In the case involving Hancock, *A. Hernandez v. The State*, Dunham prevailed, with Hancock losing the appeal. In another intriguing case in 1878, Hancock was the lawyer in the appeal of *R.J. Swancoat v. The State*. Swancoat was charged and convicted of adultery. His defense was that he could not be living in adultery because he was married to the woman in question, though the marriage was bigamous, and Swancoat had already been convicted of bigamy.

Hancock argued that since Swancoat had already been convicted of bigamy, he could not also be convicted of adultery with the same woman. The court disagreed, and Hancock lost the appeal. In the case, though, Hancock made a quite interesting argument, one that applied to himself. Hancock claimed that "while a son born of parents living in adultery is illegitimate, a son born in a state of unlawful marriage is no bastard, but a lawful son." Hugh Hancock was born to Hancock in an unlawful marriage, so Hancock considered him a lawful son and treated him as such. Again, though, the illegality of Hancock's "marriage" to Hugh's mother was reinforced.[19]

"A Fiend Incarnate"

A couple of cases might have some bearing on the servant girl murders. One case occurred in 1878, and it involved a young black man who raped a white girl. The case, *Burke Ake, alias Tobe Williams, v. The State*, was tried in Travis County in December 1878. Ake, who was also called Bunk Ake, Taylor Ake, and John Williams, was convicted of raping a thirteen-year-old girl in July 1878 and sentenced to death by hanging. An appeal was mounted by Dudley G. Wooten and N.S. Walton, based on two points. The first point dealt with the ability of the young girl to understand the solemnity of the oath of testimony. The second point dealt with the age of the defendant, who was assessed the death penalty though his lawyers contended he was not yet seventeen years old at the time of the offense. State law stated that a person not yet seventeen years old at the time of the offense could not be given the death penalty. Several witnesses believed that Ake was born late in the fall of 1861, but they were not sure. Ake's conviction and punishment were affirmed by the Texas Court of Appeals. This crime was not Ake's first. In 1875, he was tried for raping a little German girl in the cedar brakes in the hills outside Austin. No witness appeared against him, the German girl and her family having left the county. He was also believed to have attempted the rape of at least two other girls and to have murdered two white men. He was branded "a fiend incarnate" and described as "a black man indeed; of large, heavy features, sensuality and animal propensities marked most palpably upon them. Of little force or capacity mentally, the man seems very capable of any crime." Ake's father was said to be "a thieving runaway slave, and all his children have turned out to be criminals of the deepest dye."[20]

Ake was hanged in the river bottom near Austin on August 22, 1879. His hanging was attended by about 4000 people, most of them black. All day long Austin was thronged with visitors who had come to see the hanging. Before the hanging proceeded, prayers were given and songs were sung. People in the audience asked Ake questions, which he willingly answered as he smoked a cigar, "his hat shoved on the back of his head, and leaning against the railing, presenting a very comfortable appearance and attitude, and with expression of much less concern on his face than any one else on the platform." He continued to deny his guilt, blaming the crime on "'Ed. Williams, and he is in Galveston. It isn't the Ed. Williams that lives here.'" After the black hood was placed on his head, Ake began a peculiar chant. Minutes later, Dr. Robert H.L. Bibb, the city physician, pronounced Ake dead, and the crowd quietly dispersed. But the man that Ake fingered as the true culprit may have been involved in a rape in Gainesville, Texas, in 1886. "The negro outrager, Ed. Williams," was lynched in Gainesville on June 30, 1886, for the rape of a white woman. Marshal Lucy in Austin "had been requested to telegraph to Gainesville for a measurement of Williams' foot, in view of the possibility of its fitting the tracks found on the scene of nearly all the servant girl murders" in Austin. Of course, the lynching of Williams occurred after the death of Nathan Elgin, whose foot did match the prints found at the murder scenes.[21]

What link might this case have to the servant girl murders? The young lawyer who defended Ake, Dudley Wooten, lived in one of the homes assaulted in the spring of 1885. The sheriff who cut down the lifeless Ake was Dennis Corwin. In 1885, Corwin was a partner with Dr. Lucien B. Johnson in Corwin and Johnson, a real estate and land agent business. Eliza Shelly was murdered on the premises of Dr. Johnson. One of Corwin's deputy sheriffs in the late 1870s was Horatio Grooms Lee, the ineffectual city marshal during most of the servant girl murders in 1885.[22]

"Insulting Words or Conduct"

Another case that could be linked to the servant girl murders was *William and Robert Eanes v. The State*. The Eanes brothers were convicted of the murder of C.D. McMillan, whom they contended had caused the ruination of their sister, Annie Eanes. The murder occurred in February 1880, and the trial was held in Travis County in July 1880. Both brothers were convicted of first-degree murder, and William Eanes, who was said to have shot McMillan, received the death penalty, though his brother received a life sentence. The Eanes family first met McMillan and his wife when the McMillans moved onto the John Murch place in Williamson County near the Eanes. Annie Eanes and McMillan's wife, Lizzie, became friends, and Annie often would stay over at the McMillan place. In 1879, the McMillans moved onto John Hancock's place near Austin, and the friendly relationship with Annie Eanes continued. However, during one of Annie's visits to the McMillans' home in Austin, she was allegedly raped by C.D. McMillan, who threatened to kill her if she told. As a result of the attack, Annie Eanes became pregnant. Even though she knew she was pregnant, Annie again visited the McMillans in January 1880. At that time, McMillan gave her $10 to go to Round Rock, about 20 miles north of Austin, until the baby was born.[23]

Annie's brother-in-law, Maurice Moore, eventually traced her to Round Rock and returned the twenty-year-old Annie to her home on February 18, 1880. At that time, she first told her family that McMillan had raped her and that she was pregnant. Later that day, William and Robert Eanes went to Austin to the home of McMillan, who was now living on East Pecan with his wife and children. The Eanes brothers arrived about one in the afternoon, but McMillan was not home, so after polite conversation with McMillan's wife, they left. McMillan arrived about a half-hour later, and the Eanes brothers soon returned. McMillan and William Eanes went into a separate room, where Eanes shot the defenseless McMillan. McMillan staggered back into the room where his wife was, and Eanes continued to shoot him, six times altogether. The Eanes brothers then left the house and ran into the street, where they waited until they voluntarily surrendered to Maurice Moore, their brother-in-law, who apparently was some sort of law officer. As it turned out, Moore knew about the plan to murder McMillan and was charged as an accessory. The brothers and Moore were promptly released on bail by Judge Joseph Lee, which brought criticism from many in Austin because they had killed "an unresisting man in his own house, in the presence of his wife and children." C.D. McMillan was buried on February 20, 1880, in stranger ground in Oakwood Cemetery, dead at 34 years of age. Annie Eanes gave birth to a child in mid-March 1880.[24]

At the trial, McMillan's widow testified that she had never seen her husband display any undue affection toward Annie Eanes, though she had seen Maurice Moore mistreat the girl. "In 1878 and at Maurice Moore's own house she saw him try to pull Annie on his lap." James Hancock, a nephew of John Hancock, testified for the defense that McMillan drove a milk wagon for him but that he argued with McMillan about "not keeping accounts." McMillan said he did not have time to keep accounts and quit the job. Dr. Josephus Cummings, for the defense, said that "impregnation might result from a rape," but that "it was difficult for a man to rape a well-developed woman by mere force," though threats and force could be helpful. He testified that prior to the attack, Annie Eanes was "a chaste, modest and truthful girl," and that the Eanes family in general were "peaceable and law-abiding citizens" before the killing of McMillan.[25]

As the trial neared its end and county attorney E.T. Moore was making his closing remarks, he was interrupted by the protests of Maurice Moore, to whom he was alluding at the time. Maurice Moore stood and gestured as if drawing a gun.

> Immediately a younger brother of the defendants rushed upon and struck the county attorney, whilst both defendants attempted to join in the melee, and one of them grabbed a chair and attempted also to strike with it. Excitement naturally rose instantly to the very highest pitch, and was participated in by the one hundred and fifty or two hundred spectators, who were present in the court room. The proceedings of the trial were stopped, and for a few moments the wildest confusion seems to have prevailed. Moore was ordered to jail by the court, and was taken out by the sheriff. Silence and order were commanded by the officers of the court. After order and quiet were restored, the court ordered the county attorney to proceed with his argument, and he requested the court, before proceeding, to have the prisoners removed from his rear, remarking that he did not wish to be assassinated. Defendants were removed and counsel resumed his argument under much excitement. He said "he might be assassinated before he got through, but before he would be intimidated by Maurice Moore, in the discharge of his duty, he would see him dead and in hell and follow him there."

The comment E.T. Moore had made about Maurice Moore concerned his relationship with Annie Eanes. The attorney stated, "I think from the evidence in this case, the Eanes would be justified as much in suspecting Maurice Moore of committing the rape as in suspecting McMillan of it." Maurice Moore was said to be a dark character. But Maurice Moore had no gun when corralled by the sheriff, and the judge soon released him from jail. The other defendants also apologized for their actions, and the trial proceeded.[26]

The case finally went to the jury, and a verdict of first-degree murder was returned against both William and Robert Eanes. William Eanes was given the death penalty, and Robert Eanes was given a life sentence. The case was soon appealed to the Texas Court of Appeals on the grounds that the Texas penal code "makes insulting words or conduct toward a female relative of the slayer an adequate cause for the passion which reduces voluntary homicide to manslaughter," assuming the killing happened immediately or soon after the slayer was informed of the insults, as was the situation in this case. Several other complaints were also raised. The appeal was successful, the judgment of the lower court was reversed, and the case was remanded to a lower court for a new trial. Whether a new trial was held is unclear, but the two men did not seem to receive any severe punishment. Robert Headen Eanes died in 1918. William Howell Eanes died in 1914 and was buried in Odd Fellows Cemetery in Georgetown, Texas.[27]

Maurice Moore apparently was not convicted in the trial, but he met his doom soon enough. Edgar Maurice Bowie Moore was not a very popular fellow in the Austin area. A biography had few kind comments about him.

> The news that Maurice Moore had been killed was not a surprise to anyone who knew the man. During his residence in Travis County he had been regarded as a man quick to shoot and had more than one serious difficulty, being at one time involved in a murder case which created some excitement and a great deal of comment. He always went armed and prided himself on being a crack shot. He was said to be domineering and of tyrannical disposition and counted but few friends in the section where he lived. Knowing him to be a man quick to quarrel, few persons cared to associate with him. Yet, he knew all the hard characters that infested the hills, and was a friend to none of them.

Because he was familiar with the people and the territory, Moore sometimes helped the sheriff by serving warrants in the area. On one occasion, Moore delivered a subpoena to the home of Wilson McNeil, ordering his two sons to court. McNeil pulled a rifle on Moore and told him to get off the property. Moore said he would get a warrant and return to arrest McNeil. Moore returned with the warrant and another officer a couple of days later, at which time McNeil stepped out of the house with rifle in hand. He told Moore he would kill him if he stepped on the gallery. The two men scuffled over the gun, and suddenly another door opened and someone fired a shotgun. The buckshot killed Moore instantly.[28]

How was the Eanes trial related to the servant girl murders? Many of the principals in the Eanes trial were also involved in the servant girl case. The Eanes brothers were related to Eula Phillips, whose mother was an Eanes. In addition, the

Eanes brothers were related, by marriage, to Mollie Eanes, whose murdered young son was found being eaten by hogs the same day that Eula Phillips was murdered. Ed Creary, the sheriff in the Eanes case, was married to a Phillips daughter, Katherine Frances "Kate" Phillips Deats Creary. C.D. McMillan, the murdered man, lived for a time on the property of Judge John Hancock and worked for Hancock's nephew, James Hancock. The judge who released the Eanes brothers on bail was Joseph Lee, the father of Horatio Grooms Lee, the city marshal during most of the servant girl murders. One of the prosecution attorneys was Col. John W. Robertson, the mayor of Austin during the servant girl murders. The other prosecution attorney was E.T. Moore, who also prosecuted Jimmy Phillips. One of the defense attorneys was William Walton, who served as one of the defense attorneys for Jimmy Phillips. Certainly, all these links could be coincidental, but one has to wonder.

"Hopelessly Impaired"

The last few years of John Hancock's life were rather uneventful. In 1886, he made a failed run for the U.S. Senate. He still dabbled in local projects and land deals, such as the dam, but he was not the force he had been in his younger days, though he was still quite wealthy. His mind began to fail rapidly, suggesting perhaps that he was already afflicted in 1885 when he was 60 or 61 years old. Perhaps his mental condition had something to do with his two-faced nature. By 1891, he had lost the ability to manage his own affairs.

> Owing to the failing condition of his mind, the county court today appointed E.B. Hancock guardian of his father, Judge John Hancock, recently brought home from a watering place in Minnesota, where he had spent the summer. The judge's mind is hopelessly impaired, it seems. The amount of the bond is $460,000, with Frank Hamilton, Maj. J.T. Breckenridge and A.P. Wooldridge as securities.

A.P. Wooldridge might have been called in again to rescue John Hancock from ignominy. Had Wooldridge protected Hancock's reputation during the servant girl investigations? A famous photograph of Hancock taken by Mathew Brady and Levin C. Hardy in the last 15 years of his life has the feature of greatly enlarged pupils, which would be unusual in a photograph employing a flash, as this photograph surely did. Could Hancock have been addicted to morphine or opium, two drugs readily available in Guy Town? John Hancock finally died at his old home on Wednesday afternoon, July 19, 1893, at the age of 69. He was buried the next day in Oakwood Cemetery in Austin. The cause of death according to the attending physician, J. W. McLaughlin, was brain disease.[29]

The information given on John Hancock is not meant to be an indictment, only a report of facts, circumstances, and coincidences. Now, well over a century after the murders, no one knows for sure who committed the crimes. But what if Katherine Ramsland was correct in saying that the evidence in retrospect pointed to a wealthy politician as the servant girl killer? What if the rumor at the Phillips trial was true—that a rich, influential Austinite had been in the carriage with Eula

Phillips? What if Kenward Philp was correct in his theory? What if the servant girl murders were committed by a wealthy white man and a black man, or perhaps a gang of black men under the orders of a prominent white man? If Ramsland, the rumor, and Philp were correct, then John Hancock would seem to be a logical choice for that prominent white man. Certainly, John Hancock had the means and the access to the Thug Gang. Could Hancock's son, Hugh Hancock, a mulatto, be the yellow man reported by some of the witnesses? Could O. Henry have been correct in his story that the son of an influential man committed the murders? If Philp was correct, and one of the black men in question was Nathan Elgin, then Jimmy Phillips was innocent from the beginning, and his trial was a sham. Jimmy Phillips must have been a fall guy, as was Moses Hancock. And if the wealthy white man was John Hancock, the supreme irony would be that one of the lawyers defending Jimmy Phillips and Moses Hancock *gratis* actually had taken part in the murders!

Notes

Title: *Omaha Daily Bee*, 1/30/1886.
Photograph of Moore-Hancock cabin by the author.

1. "Rubin Hancock Farmstead"; 1880 Federal Census; "Missouri Project"; "Rubin Hancock Homestead"; "Historic Resources Survey of East Austin, City of Austin, Texas, September 2000": 117-118 (According to the East Austin survey, "Many of the Hancock descendants and others who lived in the 'Negro Community' near the Waters Park and Duval community eventually moved to East Austin for better schools and greater job opportunities, particularly in the 1930s and 1940s. Among their names are Hancock, Daniels, Wicks, Dickerson and Hansborough.")
2. Hooker, *Handbook of Texas Online*; Guttery, *Representing Texas*: 23; *Biographical Encyclopedia of Texas*: 51.; Kemp, *Handbook of Texas Online*; "Brigham, Benjamin Rice"; 1880 Federal Census; "Susan E. Richardson Hancock"; "Edwin B. Hancock"; "Marie Fiset Hancock"; Oakwood Cemetery Database (The 1880 census called the Hancock son Edward, but the grave marker clearly indicated Edwin. The Oakwood Cemetery records stated Edwin died in April 1916, but the grave marker showed 1917.)
3. *Morrison & Fourmy's General Directory of the City of Austin, 1885-1886*.
4. "Thomas Montgomery Gregory—The Black Renaissance in Washington, D.C."; "The Gregory Family" (In the 1900 census, Hugh Ella Hancock was identified as Huella Hancock. Another daughter of Hugh Hancock, Nettie B. Hancock, apparently married Booker T. Washington, Jr., a real estate broker, in Houston in 1914.)
5. "The Gregory Family"; 1900 Federal Census; 1870 Federal Census.
6. "The Gregory Family" (Saylor's portrayal of Hugh Hancock in *A Twist at the End* as an ignorant, uneducated Negro appears to be grossly inaccurate.)
7. *Morrison & Fourmy's General Directory of the City of Austin, 1889-1890*; *Morrison & Fourmy's General Directory of the City of Austin, 1897-1898*; 1900 Federal Census; "Idaho, Deaths and Burials, 1907-1965"; 1920 Federal Census (The 1900 census listed Huella Hancock's age as 4. The death record for Hugh Hancock suggested he was born in 1858 and was 52 years old when he died. The 1900 census, though, indicated he was born in 1855.)
8. Hardin, *Handbook of Texas Online*; Wallenstein, *Tell the Court I Love My Wife*: 86-88.
9. Robinson, *Dangerous Liaisons: Sex and Love in the Segregated South*: 41, 44-45, 47-48; *Fort Worth Daily Gazette*, 5/3/1884 (Thomas Duval was the son of former Florida governor

William Duval. The elder Duval was involved in the litigation of bogus land certificates, just like John Hancock.)

10. *Fort Worth Daily Gazette*, 8/16/1884; *Salt Lake Daily Herald*, 8/16/1884; *New York Times*, 8/20/1884; *Fort Worth Daily Gazette*, 8/28/1884; *Maysville Daily Evening Bulletin*, 8/28/1884; *Fort Worth Daily Gazette*, 8/29/1884.

11. *Omaha Daily Bee*, 1/30/1886.

12. *Omaha Daily Bee*, 1/30/1886.

13. *Omaha Daily Bee*, 1/30/1886.

14. "Executions in the U.S. 1608-2002"; *Gonzales Daily Inquirer*, 5/18/1878; "Brown Bowen of Florida and Texas"; *Brenham Weekly Banner*, 6/7/1878; "Travis County Court Criminal Minutes 1876-1886"; Hendrix, *Handbook of Texas Online* (A survey of Travis County court minutes for 1876-1886 produced some familiar names as jurors but no significant cases.)(A famous Texan named Francis White Johnson did live in the area in the late 1870s, but he apparently was not a lawyer. In addition, he died in Mexico in April 1884.)

15. *Galveston Daily News*, 11/26/1878; *Brenham Weekly Banner*, 11/29/1878; *Bartholomew Diary*, 17:258, 11/24/1878; *Mooney & Morrison's General Directory of the City of Austin, 1877-1878*; *Morrison & Fourmy's General Directory of the City of Austin, 1885-1886*; Oakwood Cemetery Database (The victim was identified by several names, among them Wittman, Wichtman, Witteman, and Whitman. The 1877 city directory called him August Witteman and gave his address as the north side of Linden Street between Trinity and San Jacinto. His widow was identified as Witman in the 1885 city directory and in Oakwood Cemetery records. Sophie Witman died in September 1918 and was buried in Oakwood Cemetery.)

16. "Marriage Records of St. John Lutheran Church at Ross Prairie & Ellinger 1861–1963," Entry 29 <http://www.fayettecountyhistory.org/st_john_lutheran_marriages.htm>; *Morrison & Fourmy's General Directory of the City of Austin, 1885-1886*; 1870 Federal Census.

17. *Brenham Weekly Banner*, 5/7/1880.

18. *Galveston Daily News*, 4/8/1879; *Galveston Daily News*, 4/15/1879; *Brenham Weekly Banner*, 4/11/1879; *Brenham Weekly Banner*, 5/9/1879.

19. *Reports of cases argued and adjudged in the Court of Appeals of Texas, Volume 4*: 425-427; *Reports of cases argued and adjudged in the Court of Appeals of Texas, Volume 4*: 105-120.

20. *Reports of cases argued and adjudged in the Court of Appeals of Texas, Volume 6*: 398-420; *Galveston Daily News*, 8/23/1879; *Brenham Weekly Banner*, 7/25/1879; *Brenham Weekly Banner*, 8/9/1878.

21. *Galveston Daily News*, 8/23/1879; *Bartholomew Diary* 18:17, 8/22/1879; *Saline County Journal*, 8/29/1879; *Austin Weekly Statesman*, 7/1/1886.

22. *Morrison & Fourmy's General Directory of the City of Austin, 1885-1886*; *Mooney & Morrison's General Directory of the City of Austin, 1877-1878*; *Morrison & Fourmy's General Directory of the City of Austin, 1881-1882*; *Morrison & Fourmy's General Directory of the City of Austin, 1889-1890*.

23. *Reports of cases argued and adjudged in the Court of Appeals of Texas, Volume 10*: 421-455; *Galveston Daily News*, 2/21/1880.

24. *Reports of cases argued and adjudged in the Court of Appeals of Texas, Volume 10*: 421-455; *Galveston Daily News*, 2/26/1880; Oakwood Cemetery Database.

25. *Reports of cases argued and adjudged in the Court of Appeals of Texas, Volume 10*: 421-455 (James Hancock was the son of William Ryan Hancock, John Hancock's brother.)

26. *Reports of cases argued and adjudged in the Court of Appeals of Texas, Volume 10*: 421-455; *Galveston Daily News*, 7/9/1880.

27. *San Saba News*, 7/17/1880; *Brenham Weekly Banner*, 7/15/1880; *Reports of cases argued and adjudged in the Court of Appeals of Texas, Volume 10*: 421-455; "Robert Headen Eanes (1854-1918)"; "William Howell Eanes (1848-1914)"; "William Howell Eanes."

28. "Biographies of Oakwood Cemetery Residents."
29. *Fort Worth Daily Gazette*, 10/31/1891; *Colorado Citizen*, 7/27/1893; Oakwood Cemetery Database (The Maj. J.T. Breckenridge mentioned as securing Hancock's bond was more likely J.T. Brackenridge.)

Chapter 30

"The Approved Capital City Style"

Did the Murders Really End?

Even though Marshal James Lucy and Sheriff Malcolm Hornsby had made the confident statements that the hideous murders that had plagued Austin for a year had ended with the death of Nathan Elgin and the imprisonment of Oliver Townsend, investigators and newspapers around the state were not so certain. Even before Nathan Elgin was killed and Jimmy Phillips and Moses Hancock were put on trial, brutal ax murders began to occur in places not far from Austin.

On January 29, 1886, ninety miles south of Austin in San Antonio, a mulatto servant named Mrs. Patty Scott was killed in a thoroughly familiar fashion. The murder took place late at night at the home of E.B. Chandler, a well-known San Antonio citizen who lived at the corner of Arsenal and South Flores Street. The murder was not discovered until about 7 o'clock the following morning when the butcher boy employed by Mr. C. Spelser called for the servant to come get the meat delivery at the gate on Arsenal Street.

> Receiving no answer to his summons he descended from his cart, opened the gate and looked in the yard and saw the door of the little outbuilding used by the mulatto woman as a sleeping room wide open. The body of the woman lay upon the floor, weltering in its blood. He aroused the family and Mr. Chandler came down, and they together went in and saw the woman lying upon the floor on her back, her knees raised and legs spread out, and her underclothing torn partially away, her arms spread out, and on the top of her head towards the back was a deep wound made apparently with a hatchet, about two or three inches in length, laying open the skull. Another cut an inch long was visible on the top of her chin, extending to the lips, and a black bruise on her cheek showed where a blow had been struck by some blunted instrument. She was lying in the middle of the room between her bed and a rocking chair, which was placed against the wall. The bed had not been used that night. Her upper clothing was on the body, excepting her corset, hoop skirt and bustle, which were found lying on another chair close by. Blood was smeared in a great pool over the floor, and the position of the woman would indicate that she had been struck down and killed instantly and lay motionless

> where she had fallen and afterwards been outraged by the
> fiend while the corpse was yet warm.

Patty Scott was about 28 years old at the time of her death. She was married and had two children, though their whereabouts at the time of the murder was unclear. The Fort Worth newspaper noted that the woman had been killed "after the approved capital city style."[1]

Suspicion immediately fell upon the dead woman's husband, William Scott, as the killer, for the two "had not been living on very agreeable terms for some time." William Scott had been fined in November 1885 for beating his wife severely, and was also placed under a peace bond toward her. She had complained that "her life was in danger and had been threatened by her husband." She had also filed for divorce, and the case was pending in district court. The coroner's inquest began on the morning of January 30, and one witness, Willis Webb, who was related to the dead woman, testified that "Scott abused his wife terribly before they were separated, and afterward had compelled her at the point of a pistol to submit to his brutal desires, and Webb also testified to hearing him threaten her that if she left him and went out to service with Mr. Chandler that he would kill her some night." Patty Scott was said to be "a fine looking mulatto woman" who "was born in San Antonio and raised by Colonel N. O. Green, the well-known attorney. She bore the character of being a hard-working woman, a good servant and the best cook in the city. Mr. Chandler testifies to the fact that while she has been in his service (since January 4) her morals have been beyond reproach, no male visitor ever being seen in her company."[2]

The property on which Patty Scott was murdered had a similar arrangement to the homes in Austin at which the servant girls were killed.

> The building occupied by the woman was a short distance
> removed from the main house, was a low one-roomed affair,
> with one door, fastening with a wooden button, which was
> found to bear the marks of bloody fingers. A bowl of water was
> under the bed and a bucket of water in the room, which was
> impregnated with blood, where the fiend had evidently washed
> his bloody hands and bloody weapons after committing the
> deed. A hatchet and crowbar were also found in the room.

The hatchet and crowbar were bloody. Mr. Chandler said that the crowbar had been on the premises, but it belonged outside in the yard, so the killer must have picked it up and carried it into the room. Also found was a bloody piece of newspaper, as if it had been used to wipe the blood off something. Chandler said he had noticed nothing unusual the night of the murder. Patty Scott had served dinner as usual at 6 o'clock and then cleared away the dishes. The family had retired about 10 o'clock and slept soundly, hearing no noises or commotion during the night. The moon was in the last quarter, nine days past the full moon.[3]

William Scott was about 29 years old and worked at a lime kiln on the San Antonio River. During the day of January 30, he was arrested at the lime kiln, which was located two miles from town. Scott was placed in jail to await the outcome of the investigation. Scott, of course, denied any knowledge of the murder. However, when his room at the Central Hotel was searched, "some clothes were found which were apparently washed during the night. They were quite damp, as though the blood stains had been washed out." As did the murders in Austin, the killing created much excitement in San Antonio, and the public belief was that Scott had committed the foul deed. Within a few days, though, many began to think the murder was associated with the Austin servant girl murders. And less than a month later, a San Antonio judge's house was invaded. The judge, who shot at an escaping black man, thought that two men were involved, and "that one was a white man and that their object was murder." The judge also believed that since the police had not found the murderer of Patty Scott, there would be more bloodshed in San Antonio "on the Austin plan." [4]

"The Blanton Murder"

Then, a little over a year later, murder returned to the outskirts of Austin. On the afternoon of March 7, 1887, Mollie Blanton was killed on a farm on Walnut Creek about seven miles from Austin. She had married Thomas Blanton only four months earlier. The killing was at first believed to be "a case of self-destruction," but on investigation it was found "to be murder, attended with all the sickening evidence of outrage and brute cruelty." The crime scene suggested that Mrs. Blanton had begun the daily task of preparing supper for her husband's return from the fields. "A fire was in the stove, a frying pan with meat in it was on top, a churn with milk in it and a chair by it showed that the busy little housewife had started to give this part of her daily duties attention." The belief of the officers investigating the scene was that the murderer had approached the house by way of the barn in the rear, then entered the kitchen from the back porch.

> What struggle took place then in defense of honor and life may not be known in all time to come. Certain it is that the unfortunate victim passed out of the kitchen through the dining-room and into the family room. In this apartment there was lying on a table in the corner of the room a large Colt's 45-caliber six-shooter. This it is supposed she grasped, her assailant meanwhile struggling to overpower her. A shot from the pistol struck the corner of a bed in the room, passed through the mattress and footboard, setting the bed clothing on fire. How long a struggle ensued is one of the unknown measures of the crime. It must have been a fight of desperation for the left hand of Mrs. Blanton was powder-burned, going to show that her assailant must have wrestled with her for the weapon. Releasing herself she must have run to the front door at this time, as a little sister about nine years of age, who was on her way to visit her, and who was coming up the pathway from the main road, saw her open the door, throw her hands above her head and then disappear within.

The little sister continued to the house, but after a few moments she heard another shot, and then all was quiet. The sister was frightened by the shot and waited for a few minutes on the front porch. She then looked in a side window and "saw her sister lying on the floor with blood all around her." The sister ran to a neighboring house to sound an alarm, and men rushed to the Blanton place.[5]

At first, it appeared that Mrs. Blanton had only been shot, which perhaps led to the belief that she had committed suicide.

> The fatal shot fired struck the lady in the right temple about an inch above and to the front of the ear, ranged upward, passed out the left side below the crown and penetrated the wall of the room in the corner near the ceiling. At the point of penetration the death wound was smooth and round cut, but at the place of exit the ball crushed a place in the skull as large as a silver dollar.

However, a report the next day indicated that "Mrs. Blanton was cut on the side of the head with some sharp instrument, and also was struck on the head with some blunt instrument, in the same way as the other victims" during the series of servant girl murders.[6]

The murder of Mollie Blanton rekindled fears that the servant girl annihilators were still on the rampage. The belief was that Mrs. Blanton's murder "belongs to and is a resumption of the dreadful servant girl and woman murders which, at intervals throughout the year 1885, startled the people of Austin. Where or how the mysterious murder fiend has lain dormant since the murder of Mrs. Hancock and Mrs. Eula Phillips, Christmas Eve, 1885, is a dark and profound mystery." One news report headline positively stated: "The Austin Ravisher and Murderous Demon Again Abroad and Takes the Life of a Farmer's Wife." As noted, Mrs. Blanton was shot, but apparently also was struck in the head several times, as were the others murdered in 1885. Except for the pistol shots heard by Mrs. Blanton's little sister, "the same mysterious silence reigned during the commission of the crime." The sister saw a face through the open door, and her older sister threw up her hands, but she issued no cry. The murderer left no clue, as was common in the 1885 murders, and he escaped in "the same mysterious silent manner" as did the killers in the earlier murders. In addition, "the body was also mysteriously moved after it was first seen by the little girl. It is believed the fiend would have dragged the body out just as those of the dead servant girls were, but the presence of the little girl prevented him." The murderer in all the cases, including the Blanton murder, was believed to be the same "short, heavy, thick set negro" that had killed Irene Cross and was seen by her, and who had been described by Cross the next day before her death. And though the attack occurred during the day, the moon was two days before full. Were the Austin servant girl murderers really on the prowl again?[7]

"The Gainesville Tragedy"

Then, about four months after the Blanton murder and only a month after the Hancock trial ended, another gruesome attack occurred in Gainesville, Texas.

Gainesville is about 250 miles north of Austin and about 75 miles northwest of Dallas. During the early morning hours of July 13, 1887, two young white girls were attacked as they slept in a room in a house with the rest of the family. The house was located at the corner of Hancock and Bird streets on the west side of Gainesville. The victims were Mamie Bostick, who lived in Gainesville, and a friend, Genie Watkins, who lived in Dallas but was visiting her aunt in Gainesville. Both young ladies were about 18 or 19 years old. Miss Watkins was spending the night with Miss Bostick. The attack was uncannily similar to the servant girl murders in Austin, but the moon was in the last quarter, eight days past full moon.

> The room occupied by the young ladies was the east front room of the house with windows opening on the porch, and a window on the east. Mrs. Bostick and the rest of the family slept in rooms immediately back of the one occupied by the young ladies. Captain Bostick, the head of the family, was absent in the Indian Territory looking after his cattle interests there. About 2 o'clock this morning Mrs. Bostick was awakened by the noise of a struggle in the room occupied by the young ladies and immediately arising from her bed she went to the door of the young ladies' room just in time to see the form of a man jump through the east window. Upon entering the room a horrible and pitiful sight presented itself to Mrs. Bostick's gaze. Upon the bed lay her daughter and Miss Watkins weltering in their blood and the bright moonlight which flooded the whole apartment revealed a gaping wound upon the faces of both girls.

Mrs. Bostick screamed immediately, and the neighbors were aroused. They hurried to the house to see what was the matter.

> A light was struck and it was then seen the assassin or assassins had done their work bunglingly but brutally. Miss Watkins slept on the side of the bed next to the wall, and the scoundrel had to reach over Miss Bostick in order to reach her, but Miss Watkins received worse injuries than did Miss Bostick. Miss Watkins was struck over the right eye with some sharp instrument, thought by some to have been a very large and heavy butcher knife, but generally believed to have been a hatchet, and the force of the blow of this instrument, whatever it may have been, was such as to penetrate both frontal bones. The gash made by the instrument extends almost entirely across the forehead, and part of the brains oozed out, a teaspoonful at least being taken up by the doctors. Her right eye was also driven from its socket, and when she was discovered it was lying upon her cheek, hanging only by a slight thread. One of her arms was fearfully lacerated and bruised, and it is supposed from this that she resisted to her utmost capacity the assault of the murderer, and that the blow described above was struck by the villain with one hand while with the other he grappled with her and prevented her stopping his cowardly blow. Miss Bostick was wounded by the same

> instrument in several places. One blow which seems to have
> been inflicted by the corner of the weapon used was just under
> the right eye. Another blow struck the right temple, and the
> third cut the upper lip completely in two.

Doctors were summoned and soon arrived. The wounds received by Miss Watkins were judged to be considerably more severe than those received by Miss Bostick, and Miss Watkins was not expected to live.[8]

The doctors did all they could for Miss Watkins, dressing her wounds and trying to relieve her suffering. Her death was imminent, though she clung "to life with wonderful vitality." But her condition continued to worsen, and she weakened during the night. She drank a little water and ate a little soup, but she could not keep anything on her stomach, and she vomited up the liquids as well as a considerable amount of blood. She tried to talk several times during the day, but her efforts were for naught. She was able to signal recognition of the name of her boyfriend, Abe Norwood of Dallas, but her sad state kept her from further communication. Her parents, Captain J.C. Watkins and his wife of Dallas, and her boyfriend were notified by telegraph, and they arrived in Gainesville on the afternoon of the attack. But all the efforts of the doctors and relatives were unsuccessful, and Miss Watkins died in the early morning hours of July 15.[9]

The wounds of Miss Bostick were also judged to be far worse than originally thought. "The blow struck her on the temple, fractured the skull, and the wound is considered a very bad one. The blow that cut the lip in two knocked out two of her upper teeth and chipped the tips of two more lower ones." The doctors were certain that she would recover. She regained consciousness temporarily in the morning, long enough to ask where she was. When told she was in her mother's room instead of her own, she asked why she was there. Her mother told her that she and Miss Watkins had been badly hurt, to which Miss Bostick mournfully replied, "Why was I not next to the wall?"[10]

Just as in the Austin murders, the police officers could not find any clues that would lead them to the identity or motive of the attacker. By the time the police arrived just before daylight, the ground around the house had been trampled by the many curiosity-seekers who had rushed to the Bostick house. Officers could not tell which tracks might have belonged to the attacker. "Some tracks of enormous size being made by a foot eleven inches long were found in the garden, but on account of the dryness of the weather it was impossible to tell whether the tracks were fresh or not." Bloodhounds were summoned from Fort Worth and arrived on the morning train. However, because of the large crowd, the dogs were unable to strike a trail. The crowd was then told to disperse, which they did, and the dogs were taken away from the scene for a while. The dogs were soon returned and given a scent, and they struck a trail. They followed the trail to a creek bottom, where the trail was lost again. The dogs were taken back to the Bostick house and allowed to stay for a while in the room where the attacks occurred. They were also shown a spot of blood on the windowsill, apparently left by the hand of the fleeing attacker, and then were taken to the large tracks in the garden. Again the dogs struck a trail along the same route toward the creek bottom, where the trail was lost once more.[11]

Only a few hours after the attack, a citizens meeting was held at city hall, and Sheriff Ware of Gainesville deputized all those present to help the police to find the attacker or attackers. Squads of citizens patrolled the city all day and into the night but discovered nothing of consequence. Subscriptions for a reward were started soon after the attack and quickly reached a total of over $2000. The Governor was also being asked to contribute an additional $1000. The whole city was in "a fever of excitement all day," and most businesses were closed. The belief was that if the culprit were found, he would certainly be lynched. But the efforts of the police and the citizen squads had yielded nothing, and by nightfall the whole affair was still a great mystery.[12]

The reason for the attack on the young ladies was unclear. "The man or men who perpetrated the deed from all appearances were not actuated by lust or desire to rob, but the most tangible theory now presented that can be sustained by the facts of the case is that willfull and deliberate murder was the actuating cause." Perhaps outrage was in store for the two young women if Mrs. Bostick had not entered the room when she did. Most believed the motive was "pure murder," though the young women "did not have an enemy in the world that they knew of." The attacks were considered "the most cowardly and atrocious crime ever committed in Cooke county."[13]

An inquest was quickly organized and conducted in secret. Only the justice, the county attorney, and the sheriff were allowed in the room with each witness, of which there were 15 called. On the afternoon of July 15, the inquest issued its verdict that "Miss Genie Watkins came to her death, at 3:35 this morning, from the effects of blows struck with some edged instrument in the hands of some person or persons unknown on the morning of July 13." As in the Austin murders, the inquest simply stated the obvious. Meanwhile, Miss Bostick continued to improve, with her memory growing stronger as time passed, and she remembered "having been awakened by the struggles of Miss Watkins before she was struck herself." The hope was that with her full recovery she could shed some light on the mysterious attack.[14]

"A Whip of Scorpions"

The outpouring of sympathy for the murdered Genie Watkins was unmatched by anything that happened in Austin after the murders of the servant girls or the two white women on Christmas Eve 1885. Her parents, Mr. and Mrs. J.C. Watkins, and her boyfriend, Abe Norwood, had quickly travelled from Dallas to Gainesville and were by her side when she died in the early morning of July 15. Her remains were transported by train from Gainesville to Dallas on July 16, and at each town along the way people turned out to show their sympathy for the fallen young lady. In Denton, a reporter noted that "the sad and unfortunate affair of her death strikes a chord of deep regret, and also of indignation in the hearts of the people here." In

Dallas, her remains were met by a large gathering of people, "many bringing wreaths and garlands to place upon the bier of the beautiful human flower cut down in its first bloom." A procession stretching several blocks followed her casket to the Floyd Street Methodist Church, where her funeral was conducted by Rev. G.W. Briggs. Her body was then taken to the cemetery for burial.[15]

As usual, the newspapers were quick to condemn the culprits. The Fort Worth newspaper was one of the most vociferous, saying that if caught, the killer or killers should be treated "with brutality worse than a fiend's." The newspaper theorized about the cause of such crimes and concluded that idleness was at the root of all crime.

> It may be that the perpetrators of this crime shall be captured and made to pay the penalty with their lives, but this should not satisfy our people. The vicious system that breeds and fosters this class and all other classes of criminals should be sought and removed. . . . In the history of crime there is one strand running through from beginning to end which connects it together, and that is idleness. It is seldom that men who work for a living during the day commit burglaries and murders during the night. Crimes of this character are perpetrated by the loafers and bummers. Officers should be doubly vigilant in watching for these social pests and they should be scourged out of every community they enter, without pity or remorse. . . . A whip of scorpions should be applied to the backs of these worthless animals, and this can not be done until a public sentiment stands firmly behind the officers of the law.

Despite the efforts of the police, though, they had little success. As in the Austin murders, "the villain who committed the deed seems to have had an unusual amount of devilish cunning, for he has completely covered his tracks, leaving no trace behind."[16]

Rumors also began to fly, as would be expected. One rumor quickly began to circulate that "the officers had fastened the guilt upon one of two parties—one a member of the Bostick family, the other upon a prominent young business man of this city. Both of these reports were without a shadow of support, and have caused nothing but injured feelings." Another rumor was that a man had been arrested for the murder "in almost every city in North Texas." The Austin murders of 1885 were not forgotten in the rumor mill, and soon many came to believe that the Gainesville murders were just another in the series of murders started in Austin: "The general opinion now in Austin is that the same man or men perpetrated the Austin, San Antonio and Gainesville murders." This opinion was shared by famed neurologist E.C. Spitzka, who suggested in 1888 that the Austin murders, the Gainesville murder, and the Whitechapel murders were very possibly committed by the same person.[17]

The large footprint found in the Bostick garden following the murder harkened back to the large footprint found at several of the murder scenes in Austin. The newspapers continued to report that the owner of that Austin footprint had not been found, though other reports clearly indicated that the footprint of Nathan Elgin matched the footprints found at the murder scenes in Austin, even down to the missing toe.

> At the scene of nearly all the Austin murders a large, broad, naked foot print was found the morning after the murders. This foot print made in blood was left on the veranda adjoining the room in which Mrs. Phillips was killed. It was carefully measured by the authorities, who still have the dimensions. The murderer of Mrs. Phillips also left the bloody print of his fingers on the yard fence as he jumped over into the alley. This is about the only real clew that was ever discovered. It will be remembered that Phillips, who was tried for the murder of his wife, had his foot measured to the bloody track, and it did not fit.

Another interesting bit of reported news was that on the night of Eula Phillips' murder, the bloodhounds supposedly struck a trail to a house "where a certain man then lived." A watch had supposedly been kept over this man since the murder, though the reporter did acknowledge that he might have been innocent all along. The report concluded with the curious statement that the man under watch "suits the description given by Miss Watkins before her death." An earlier report in the same newspaper noted that Miss Watkins "tried several times during the day to talk, but her efforts were unavailing." If she was unable to talk, how could she have provided a description of her killer? And in fact, a report in the same newspaper a week later dispelled the rumor that Miss Watkins had named her attacker before her death, noting that

> Miss Watkins did not have a lucid interval from the time she was injured, and that she did not speak more than three words at any one time and then only in response to direct questions put to her by her friends around the bedside. She did give a name, but she gave several instead of one, and the names she did give were given when asked: "Was it so and so?" The poor girl was under the influence of opiates during the whole time, and seemed to be impelled by an irresistible desire to answer almost every question asked her in the affirmative.

The general belief continued that the killer of Miss Watkins was "the same who played such havoc with the Austin servant girls, and that he is insane."[18]

"A Lot of Foolish Statements"

As in the Austin murder cases, few clues were left at the scene of the attack. One supposed clue was a piece of iron pipe found in the backyard of the Bostick residence. The pipe was thought to be bloody, but in fact it was only a piece of rusty pipe. Meanwhile, also as in the Austin murders, in Gainesville the report was that "the woods have been full of amateur detectives" hoping to find significant clues or nab the murderer and collect the growing reward money. And in fact, potential suspects were coming out of the woodwork. On July 14, John Shipp, son of the sheriff of Fort Worth, arrived in Gainesville with a second set of bloodhounds. The dogs were taken to the room where the attack occurred, and they struck a trail with no problems. The dogs followed the trail "to a house some 600 yards north of the Bostick residence. They were taken back to the room a second time and again took the same trail, carrying it to the same house. A third time they were taken back with the same result. This was deemed sufficient to warrant the placing of officers to guard the house." And when Shipp arrived back in Fort Worth, he received a telegram from Gainesville stating, "we've got your man." Apparently, though, the man they got was not the killler.[19]

A crazy man was reported ranging through the streets of Gainesville, so he immediately became a suspect, but the police were unable to corral him to question him about his whereabouts on the night of the attack. Another rumor suggested that the police in Gainesville had "the guilty man spotted and that they are only waiting until a few days have passed by in order to effect an arrest." Why they would wait to arrest a guilty man is unclear. One of the most tantalizing bits of information came from Mr. J.C. Watkins, the father of the murdered girl. He stated that his daughter

> was a very important witness in a case several years ago where a man was sent to the penitentiary for robbery, and that the man's sentence was out a few days before the murder was committed. The man was heard to vow vengeance at the time of his conviction, and it is possible he may be the guilty one, having committed the crime at the first opportunity he had to get the vengeance he vowed long ago.

This report, though, seemed to be just another dead end.[20]

Then a slew of arrests followed. A man was arrested in Denison, about 40 miles east of Gainesville, and charged with the murder in Gainesville. Marshal Honeycutt of Gainesville went to collect the man, named Charley Hunter, but returned alone.

> There was no evidence against Hunter at all except a lot of foolish statements made by him that he was glad he was not in Gainesville Wednesday, etc. As this talk was a little suspicious the Denison citizens thought it best to arrest him and detain him until the authorities here could be heard from. There is no evidence that Hunter was here, and it seems that he was in Fort Worth Wednesday night. His too free use of his tongue caused him to get into the clutch of the law.

Hunter was released the same day he was arrested. "The perpetrator of the foul deed at Gainesville" was also supposedly captured at Hawkins, about 160 miles southeast of Gainesville, but that arrest too did not prove fruitful. Another man was arrested in Dallas soon after the attack. The man, C.E. Brazill, had recently arrived in Dallas from Gainesville. Brazill

> acted and talked in such a manner as to excite the suspicion of City Marshal Arnold that he might be the murderer of Miss Watkins, and he was this morning arrested. He claims to be a detective in the employ of a Cincinnati agency. He claims to have gone to Gainesville only yesterday, and to have been previously working at Belcher with a Mr. Seekers. He went to Gainesville, thence to Whitesboro, thence to Denison, thence here, stopping off on his way to Austin, in search of work at his trade, brick masonry. He is heavy, low set, weighs about 160 pounds, is a decided blonde, light moustache, blue eyes, and is apparently about forty years old.

After being identified by a friend who had seen him in Belcher, Brazill was released. Every man who talked or acted a bit queerly was a suspect. "The Gainesville horror" had made everyone nervous. Several people in Gainesville had requested the police to keep an eye on their homes, "as suspicious looking characters were observed lurking in their neighborhoods." With all the uneasiness and suspicion in town, "some unrestrained shooting" was sure to follow.[21]

As the summer heat increased, so did the search for suspects. One such suspect was Allen Ward, a "rather thick-skulled and weak-minded" black man who was arrested on July 25, 1887, in Greenville, Texas, for making contradictory statements about the Gainesville murder. These conflicting comments were attributed to his simple-mindedness. Ward was transported from Greenville to Gainesville, but there was no evidence he had ever been in Gainesville before being lodged in the jail there. Though no evidence had been found to implicate him in the Gainesville crime, Ward was still held in jail in case something "new and unexpected" should turn up. The Greenville sheriff, though, felt he had "the right negro," and Genie Watkins' father went to Pittsburg, Texas, where Ward supposedly worked, trying to find clues to solve the case, but his trip was fruitless. By the end of July, Ward was still in jail in Gainesville, but the contention was that he was being held for the Greenville sheriff, in whose county a criminal charge had been lodged against Ward.[22]

And then political shenanigans entered the investigation. An election for the statewide prohibition of liquor in Texas was held on August 4, 1887. The amendment was soundly defeated, with some estimates suggesting a victory margin of 100,000 votes. On August 3, an article appeared in the *Fort Worth Evening Mail* that had been revamped from an article that appeared in the *Denison News*. According to the article,

> The father of Miss Watkins has written a letter in which he makes certain ex parte statements in regard to a negro in jail at Gainesville, that the proof of guilt was conclusive, and that liquor was the cause of the crime. The Mail says also: "It is also claimed here that the negro has made a full confession."

The *Fort Worth Daily Gazette*, in which the news about the article appeared, expressed the common sentiment that "It is a terrible thing to believe that for campaign purposes such a statement could be made, but such appears to be the fact." In response to the article, a bevy of telegrams were received from Gainesville officials and the father of Miss Bostick, the injured girl. The telegrams clearly challenged the statements in the article, stating: "We most solemnly swear that there is not the slightest evidence of any complicity on the part of said negro in connection with said crime, and that whisky had nothing to do with the same in any manner so far as we know." The telegrams were signed by R.F. Bostick, as well as the United States marshal in Cooke County, the sheriff and deputy sheriffs of the county, the mayor of Gainesville, and the county attorney. The sheriff, H.P. Ware, added that Allen Ward had made no confession.[23]

Nevertheless, Captain J.C. Watkins, the father of the murdered girl, persisted in his belief that Allen Ward was the guilty party, or at least one of them. Watkins credited his belief to a statement Ward made in his presence. Watkins claimed that

> Ward, although apparently very weak minded, is in fact a shrewd negro and only owned up when closely pinned down. Ward states that just before the murder he had been working for a man living near Gainesville, that he came into the city on the eventful night and that he was ACCOSTED BY TWO MEN, who told him they wanted him to assist them in a job. They all three later on in the night went to the Bostick residence and got into the house, the negro going in from the front and the two others at the east window. Then, according to the negro's account, he stood at the foot of the bed while one of the other two men did the murderous work, striking first the smaller of the two young ladies and then striking the other young lady in the mouth. The negro failed to state to Mr. Watkins how he made his escape, but left the impression that he went out through one of the front windows while the other two parties, one of whom he said was a white man and the other a very DARK-SKINNED WHITE MAN, or a negro, jumped out of the east window. As it will be remembered, Mrs. Bostick, when she came into the room, saw the assassin, or one of the assassins, go out of the window on the east side of the house. Captain Watkins further states that the negro gave quite an accurate description of the Bostick premises and his claim that he had been working for some time past on a construction train near Pittsburg was totally unfounded as he, Captain Watkins, had gone to Pittsburg and discovered that neither of the two men the darkey claimed to have worked under was known in railroad circles in Pittsburg at all. The captain said that according to Ward's statements a desire TO COMMIT RAPE seems to have been the impelling cause of the outrageous crime.

Watkins claimed he would present evidence to the grand jury that would lead to Ward's indictment and conviction. However, the general consensus in Gainesville was that "Ward is not the guilty party, and that having learned of the details of the tragedy in some way made the confession at Greenville, that he did on account of a weak and disordered mind." Ward was still being held in the Gainesville jail, with no evidence against him except the statement to Watkins, and the local police put little faith in that statement because of Ward's habit of telling wildly conflicting tales.[24]

Not long after, another arrest was made in the case. Again, the belief was that "the guilty man had been caught at last." This suspect was a Mexican named George Spaniard. He was arrested near Ardmore in the Indian Territory and transported to Gainesville.

> The Mexican when arrested by the officers confessed to having been concerned in the killing of Miss Watkins and the wounding of Miss Bostick. He said he and a negro were the parties concerned in the crime, and that the negro was the one who did THE BLOODY WORK, the Mexican claiming he only stood by and saw the deed done. He further stated that they went together till they reached Red river, seven miles north of here, where they parted company, the negro turning east and the Mexican keeping on into the Territory and working his way as far up as Ardmore, where he was arrested. Among his personal effects was found a shirt with a bloody right sleeve, which was covered with dirt. He had also in his possession a large butcher knife, which had blood around the hilt. The Mexican's tale was zigzag considerably throughout and many of his statements were contradictory, but what he told was sufficient to instill into the minds of his captors the firm belief that they had caught the right man. Spaniard's trail was struck by them ON RED RIVER and they have been camping on his trail for past two weeks until yesterday they ran their game to the ground. But while the facts seem very strong against Spaniard and while those who captured him believe strongly in his guilt, there are circumstances which tend to show the perpetrator of the foulest crime ever committed in Cooke county is yet undiscovered. The Mexican has been traveling the public roads for the past two weeks, stopping at different places to spend the night, and has made no effort to conceal his identity; besides no one has ever seen him in Gainesville, although he stated to the officers he was never in Gainesville except on the night the murder was done. The local officers here have no faith in Spaniard's being the culprit, and Sheriff Ware this afternoon REFUSED TO HOLD HIM in custody on the charge.

Spaniard, though, also confessed to killing a negro in Tarrant County and was being held in Gainesville on that charge. When asked about that murder, Spaniard "began immediately to make conflicting and widely varying statements, apparently proving that but little faith can be put in what he says." The Fort Worth reporter ended the article with a sentiment that echoed the case of the Austin murders: "We have gone through three weeks to-night and it seems that the work of unravelling the great murder mystery is now no nearer completion than it was when the horrible crime was first committed."[25]

The lack of evidence and the lack of credibility in the confessions of the suspects did not stop more arrests being made. The next man in the cavalcade of suspects was Frank McBroom, who was arrested and jailed in Fort Smith, Arkansas, in connection with the Gainesville murder. Deputy Marshal Lum Johnson of Gainesville went to Fort Smith, and operating under the ruse that he was a relative of McBroom's aunt who lived in Texas, told McBroom he would get him out of jail if he told a straight story about the murder in Gainesville. "McBroom finally told a disjointed story about how he went to the house with two men who did the killing, but totally failed to describe the premises or the manner in which the girls were killed. Mr. Johnson is satisfied that McBroom knows nothing about the matter, but is simply a weak-minded idiot that can be led into telling anything but cannot tell the same story twice." McBroom's father lived near Gainesville and said that the younger McBroom had not been in that area for about a year. People and officials in Gainesville had no reason to believe McBroom was the guilty party, and the Fort Worth reporter again sounded a thought eerily similar to the Austin investigation.

> The officers say that the circumstances of the case show that the deed was coolly and deliberately planned and skillfully executed, and that it seems altogether improbable, in fact impossible, that the act could have been done by a lunatic. The announcement of the fact that a man had been arrested for the murder of Miss Watkins and has confessed the crime is getting so common that the people here have become very incredulous and pay but little attention to the reports. In the meantime, however, our local officers, assisted by the best detective skill in the country, are doing all they can to track down the murderer; but as yet they have met with scarcely anything to encourage them.

Meanwhile, two Cooke County officers had gone to Grapevine, in Tarrant County, to check out a story George Spaniard had told about working there. A widow lady in Grapevine verified that Spaniard had worked for her and had been in Grapevine the morning of the murder in Gainesville. The case against Spaniard was dismissed. Allen Ward was also able to produce a valid alibi. Work journals and officials of the East Line division of the Missouri Pacific railroad confirmed that Ward had been working on a construction train near Pittsburg from July 1 through July 15, proving that Ward was over 150 miles from Gainesville on the day of the murder.[26]

"The Beason Case"

One of the most troubling arrests was of a young man who apparently had no connection to the murder but died as a result anyway. William L. Beason was a vagabond of sorts. He was born near Meridian, Mississippi, in the late 1850s. He did not have a good reputation in Mississippi, but was said to be "reputably connected." As a young man, Beason travelled to Texas and got in trouble on several accounts. Around the end of 1886 in the Fort Worth area, Beason was employed by Ben C. Evans, doing collection work for him. According to Evans, Beason embezzled some "twenty odd dollars" from him, and Evans filed a complaint against Beason. Beason, though, had disappeared. About a year later, in December 1887, Beason supposedly passed a forged $600 check on a jeweler in Luling, Texas, about 60 miles east of San Antonio. Evans wanted Beason for both crimes, but also because Evans "had received positive information that Beason had been in Fort Worth the day after the Gainesville killing and was suspicious after learning this." Of course, Evans had no idea where to find Beason.[27]

Then a break in the case occurred. Evans discovered that Beason had written letters to a young woman in Fort Worth, but she never answered the letters. Evans found that the letters had been mailed from Dale, in Caldwell County, about 35 miles southeast of Austin and 25 miles north of Luling. Evans followed the trail to Dale, where he learned that Beason had been living with a couple named Burris, who were regarded as "excellent people." Beason and Burris had married sisters. According to the Burris couple,

> Beason had made confidants of the couple, and told them of much of his wrong-doing. The last time he came down Beason seemed to be in great trouble. He was BORDERING ON MADNESS. At night he walked the floor of his room for hours at a time. He seemed to be pursued by some demon of imagination. He told his sister-in-law that if he could do it he would go into the woods and hang himself. Finally he told them he had MURDERED MISS WATKINS and detailed the crime. He had determined to enter the house and steal what jewelry or valuables he could lay his hands on. With a hatchet he opened the window and entered the room. He approached the bed and Miss Watkins awoke. He used his hatchet. Miss Bostick awoke and again he used the hatchet.

By the time Evans reached Dale, though, Beason had fled.[28]

Evans learned that Beason had returned to Mississippi and was living near Meridian. On February 9, 1888, Evans received a requisition from Texas Governor Sul Ross. The requisition asked the governor of Mississippi to turn over Beason to Evans, who was appointed an agent of the state of Texas, to be conveyed to the Tarrant County jail on charges of forgery. Telegrams were sent to Mississippi, and Beason was arrested there. Armed with the requisition, Evans went to Mississippi, had the requisition signed by the governor of Mississippi on February 25, and started back to Texas with Beason. According to Evans, on the way back to Texas, Beason talked about the Gainesville murder and confessed fully to it.

> No one had been connected with him in the crime in any way. He could not tell why he had selected the Bostick house above others. When he went into the room through the window and got near the bed, Miss Watkins, or the young lady nearest the wall, raised herself in the bed and looked at him. He said he would never forget that look. For a second he didn't know what to do, and then a feeling rushed over him to kill her and he used the hatchet. He would have given his head the next minute if he had not done it.

Police officers theorized about Beason's movements that led to his being at the scene of the crime.

> The officers say that there is hardly a question but that Beason, after his murderous work, went out by way of the window and the bloody finger marks on the window sill show that he must have had his hands covered with blood. The south bound Santa Fe train on July 13, arrived in Fort Worth at 8:30 in the morning and left Gainesville about 5 o'clock. Beason was probably a passenger on that train to Fort Worth, or he may have come down on a freight train. The officers say there is no question of his being in this city on July 15.

When arrested, Beason was about 30 years old, under six feet tall, slim, with brown hair and mustache. "He was not well-educated, gambled, and drank." He seemed to be a fitting suspect.[29]

A more thorough questioning awaited Beason on his return to Tarrant County, but that questioning never occurred. After the train arrived in Texas, on a stretch of track between Bellville and Sealy, near the small town of Millheim, Beason leapt from the train in an apparent escape attempt. The attempt occurred on the morning of March 1. According to Evans,

> "It was about 10 o'clock this morning when the train was near Milheim going at the rate of about forty miles an hour that Beason rushed out the back door of the car to the platform and without a second's hesitation sprang to the ground. The train was stopped and backed and Beason was taken on board. Dr. A. B. Gardner of Belleville was telegraphed to and when the train reached there got on board and dressed Beason's wounds. All this time the prisoner was unconscious and so remained at the hour he was placed in jail. It was a fearful jump he made for freedom and we all expected to find him dead when the train was backed up."

But Beason was not dead. He was placed back on the train, which continued to Fort Worth. Upon its arrival there, a dozen officers and reporters quickly boarded the train.

> LYING ON A MATTRESS with his head hanging back, his lower jaw dropped, and the sound of labored breathing coming from his throat lay the man who had been arrested on a charge of crime against property, but who was also accused of the most terrible crime ever recorded in Texas. His hands were crossed on his breast and the face, badly discolored on the right side by the bruises received in coming in contact with the ground, bore no expression of any kind. Neither pain or remorse were recorded there, no expression of fear or anger, the face was a blank.

Nearly dead, Beason was transported to the jail.[30]

Beason's family did not abandon him. A Dallas attorney was hired to represent Beason, but upon arriving in Fort Worth and learning of Beason's woeful condition, the lawyer conceded that little could be done. One of Beason's sisters, Mrs. Julia Letellier, soon arrived to be with her dying brother.

> The lady at once went to the jail and before she reached the cot on which her brother was lying broke down and wept. Throwing herself down beside the dying man the poor woman gave vent to her grief. All present except one of the guards withdrew. After a time Mrs. Letellier was asked if her brother had given any sign of recognition, and answered sadly, "no." Never for a moment did she leave him until about 10:40 the angel of death came and settled forever as far as W. L. Beason was concerned his guilt or innocence. Death came quietly and within five minutes from the time the first spasmodic shiver came, all was over. A clean white sheet was brought and the corpse hidden from sight, and for a time the sister, the sole mourner, was left alone with her dead. That sister was as devoted to the brother she loved as if he had been the mightiest man in the land; as if he had died on a couch of elegance instead of on a mattress laid on the stone floor of a jail. That sister had all faith in the brother's innocence.

One rumor claimed that Beason had lived with Mrs. Letellier in Gainesville for a while, and was there at the time of the murder, but Mrs. Letellier said she was not living in Gainesville in July 1887 and that her brother had never lived with her in Gainesville. She did not move to Gainesville until October 1887. By that time she had lost track of her brother until she read about his arrest in the paper. When asked why she thought her brother jumped from the train, she said that he likely knew he would be jailed and could not make bond, that he could not afford lawyers to argue his case, and that "rather than be disgraced by being put in jail he made up his mind to take any chances and so jumped off the train." Mrs. Letellier also defended her brother, pledging his innocence.

> "Talk about my brother killing a girl for the little jewelry he would get, no one but a mean spirited person would do that, and he was never mean. He didn't seem to care much for anything after his wife died, and he had had a pretty hard time in Texas. He wrote to me that he had a sister-in-law in Texas, and that he loved her as a sister, but I never knew the lady, and, unless her first husband died and she married Burris, her name is Adams. I more sinned against than sinning. They never heard anything about my brother's last marriage until I saw it in the papers."

Beason had married his second wife in Mississippi about two weeks before he was arrested there.[31]

William L. Beason was buried in Fort Worth on March 3, 1888. Was he the guilty party? As it turned out, Beason was "the sixth man who has been arrested and made a confession of the tragedy, claiming to be the perpetrator." One wonders how many of these men actually confessed to the murder, especially in light of the reward money awaiting the captor of the murderer. Over $9000 in reward money had been raised, and arguments quickly arose about who should receive the money, and if Ben Evans should get his share for bringing in Beason. Just as in the Austin murders, authorities repeatedly claimed they had positive proof to demonstrate the guilt of the confessors, but no person was ever tried for the crime. Many people in Fort Worth and Gainesville, in fact, believed that Beason was not the guilty party, and soon others began to speak in his defense. On February 29, even before Beason's death, a man arrived from Luling, claiming to have known Beason well. According to this man, the forgery report was an exaggeration.

> Some ten or twelve months ago Beason circulated around Luling and pretended to have a railroad contract near that place. While at Luling he purchased a gold watch and chain from W. H. Nance & Co., jewelers, for $110. In payment for this Beason handed them a check for $600 drawn on the First National Bank of Fort Worth and signed by Joseph H. Brown. The jeweler would not pay the difference in cash, but agreed to take the check as security for the watch. Beason agreed to this and soon thereafter disappeared. Nance & Co. telegraphed to Joseph H. Brown, inquiring if the check was genuine. Brown replied that it was a forgery.

Certain parts of Beason's confession were also considered false.

> Beason's alleged statement that he entered the room by opening the window with a hatchet is not true, as all the windows were open when the young ladies retired. Besides, the character of the wounds were such that they could not have been inflicted with a hatchet. It is also doubted if it can be proved that Beason was here at the time of the tragedy, as no one has yet been found who saw him here. Major Bostick, father of one of the young ladies, is of the opinion that Beason is not the murderer.

Upon his arrest in Mississippi in March 1888, Beason had claimed he had not been in Texas for 11 months. If his statement was true, he could not have been in Gainesville in July 1887.[32]

However, other evidence placed Beason near Bastrop, Texas, east of Austin in early July 1887. At first, two letters were published saying Beason was at work on the railroad near Bastrop on the day of the Gainesville murder. However, one man, J.M. Whitehead of Smithville, near Bastrop, qualified his statement, saying that Beason left the railroad work on July 7. Whitehead did not know where Beason went. Beason returned August 1 to visit Whitehead. Beason stayed for about two hours. Whitehead claimed that Beason "did not look as he used to and seemed to be in trouble." Beason did not say where he was going when he left. Another man named Lynch also qualified his statement, saying that the published information was not as he had said it. He claimed that he might have seen Beason on July 19, not July 12. A picnic was held on July 21, and Beason had come to Lynch's house on a Tuesday before the picnic, but Lynch was not sure if Beason was there three days before the picnic or ten days. A third man who was willing to swear he had been with Beason in the Bastrop area on July 12 could not be found.[33]

Was William Beason the Gainesville murderer? Probably not. As noted, he was the sixth man who had confessed to the crime, and his recollection of the events of the crime was flawed. The popular belief, even unto the father of the injured Bostick girl, was that Beason was innocent of the crime. Nevertheless, Ben Evans, trying to uphold his reputation, continued on the case, and had been able to secure the "strongest possible affidavits placing Beason in Gainesville as late as 10 or 11 o'clock on the night of July 12, in which the house he was at and the words he spoke are given." Again, though, could the hefty reward money be at the root of these affidavits?[34]

"A Black Fiend"

William Beason was not the last man arrested for suspicion in the Gainesville murder. A black man named William Woods was arrested in Sherman, Texas, about 35 miles east of Gainesville. Woods was charged with the assault and outrage of Mrs. Maggie Miles, a white servant woman who worked for the family of J.R. Cole in Sherman. Like most servants, Mrs. Miles occupied a room in the rear of the main residence. The room was located just inside a fence bordering on an alley, with a window on the alley side. The window was open, and early in the morning of June 7, 1888, Mrs. Miles awoke to find herself in the grasp of a black man who told her his name was Sam. He said that if she screamed or made any kind of resistance, he would kill her.

> She made one effort to disengage herself from him, striking her hand against a sharp knife or razor which he held, and suddenly remembering the fate of Miss Genie Watkins, who was murdered by a demon in the same manner at Gainesville last year, ceased to make any resistance. After performing his brutal deed the black demon quickly made his escape by leaping out of the window. Mrs. Miles positively affirms that the negro William Woods is the one who committed the deed, though he left here for Dallas on Tuesday, and the negroes at the boarding house where he stopped state that he lodged there on the night that the deed was committed.

When Woods was brought back to town, the sheriff took a circuitous route to the jail because the talk of lynching was swirling around town. The possibility of a satisfactory alibi for Woods also prevented the populace from taking a rash action.[35]

The Sherman case had a very curious twist relating to the Gainesville murder. Maggie Miles worked for Mrs. J.C. Watkins in Dallas at the time Mrs. Watkins' daughter, Genie Watkins, was murdered in the Bostick home in Gainesville eleven months earlier. Whether Woods had any involvement in the Gainesville murder was unclear, but various conjectures arose nonetheless. Mrs. Miles was to visit the jail on June 9 to identify Woods, and a lynching was considered inevitable if the identification proved positive.[36]

"The Whitley Murder"

One final affair made many fear that the awful Austin murders had not really ended. During the afternoon of September 16, 1890, Henretta Whitley, the wife of James Whitley, "a very worthy citizen," was murdered in the Austin area. She was last seen picking cotton. "In the evening her husband went to the field and found her lying in one of the cotton rows dead. Her skull was crushed in a terrible manner as if done with a large stone or rock. On examining the body it was found Mrs. Whitley had been criminally assaulted, and then, to cover up the crime and prevent her evidence from being used against him, the fiend murdered her." The prints of the murderer's fingernails were left on her throat and elsewhere on her body, and the scene suggested a fearful struggle between the young woman and her attacker. Mrs. Whitley was only 23 years old at the time of her death, having been born in November 1867, and she had three young children. She was buried in Greenwood Cemetery in Travis County. Like the Blanton murder, the attack occurred during the day. The moon was two days past new moon.[37]

As usual, few clues were left behind. Big footprints were found in the vicinity, and because of the size of the prints, the murderer was believed to be a black man. Many feared he would not be caught. The murder caused great excitement, "as the people, especially the women, have not forgotten the series of terrible assassinations of women and servant girls in this city in 1885." Lo and behold, in May 1891, the grand jury returned an indictment against Sam Turner, who lived at the corner of East Third Street and Comal Street in East Austin. Turner had been arrested on suspicion at the time of the murder but had been released for lack of evidence. At that time, he had "sued the sheriff for $2000 for false imprisonment," a case still pending in district court at the time of his indictment. New evidence connecting him to the murder recently was uncovered, leading to his indictment and arrest. Turner was tried in November 1891 for the murder, but the jury was unable to agree on a verdict, and Turner was ultimately released. As with all the earlier servant girl murders in Austin, the case was never solved.[38]

"A Strong Reminder"

Were the San Antonio murder, the Blanton and Whitley murders, and the Gainesville murder committed by the servant girl annihilators? Not very likely. One can't really imagine that the annihilators would travel hundred of miles to commit single murders. The servant girl murders seemed to have a single controlling motive, whereas the other assorted murders seemed to have differing motives, probably jealousy or robbery or outrage. Marshal Lucy and Sheriff Hornsby were probably correct in their assessment that the servant girl murders ended with the death of Nathan Elgin and the imprisonment of Oliver Townsend. But the servant girl murders had certainly left a legacy: a blueprint for murder in "the approved capital city style" and a reign of terror that did not dissipate for years to come.

Notes

Title: *Fort Worth Daily Gazette*, 1/31/1886.

1. *San Antonio Daily Light*, 1/30/1886; *Fort Worth Daily Gazette*, 1/31/1886; *Trenton Times*, 2/1/1886; 1880 Federal Census.
2. *San Antonio Daily Light*, 1/30/1886; *Fort Worth Daily Gazette*, 1/31/1886; *Trenton Times*, 2/1/1886.
3. *San Antonio Daily Light*, 1/30/1886; *Fort Worth Daily Gazette*, 1/31/1886; "Moon Chart."
4. *Fort Worth Daily Gazette*, 1/31/1886; *San Antonio Daily Light*, 1/30/1886; *Fort Worth Daily Gazette*, 2/2/1886; *Fort Worth Daily Gazette*, 2/27/1886.
5. *Fort Worth Daily Gazette*, 3/8/1887.
6. *Fort Worth Daily Gazette*, 3/8/1887; *Fort Worth Daily Gazette*, 3/9/1887.
7. *Fort Worth Daily Gazette*, 3/9/1887; *Fort Worth Daily Gazette*, 3/8/1887; "Moon Chart."
8. *Fort Worth Daily Gazette*, 7/15/1887; *Gonzales Inquirer* 8/16/1887; 1880 Federal Census; "Moon Chart" (The news reports identified the Bostick girl as Mamie, though in the 1880 Federal Census she was identified as Mary Bostick.)
9. *Fort Worth Daily Gazette*, 7/15/1887; *Fort Worth Daily Gazette*, 7/22/1887 (Two names were given for the boyfriend of Miss Watkins, Abe Purdette and Abe Norwood. The latter was likely correct.)
10. *Fort Worth Daily Gazette*, 7/15/1887.
11. *Fort Worth Daily Gazette*, 7/15/1887.
12. *Fort Worth Daily Gazette*, 7/15/1887.
13. *Fort Worth Daily Gazette*, 7/15/1887; *Gonzales Daily Inquirer* 8/16/1887.
14. *Fort Worth Daily Gazette*, 7/22/1887.
15. *Fort Worth Daily Gazette*, 7/17/1887; *Fort Worth Daily Gazette*, 7/15/1887.
16. *Fort Worth Daily Gazette*, 7/15/1887; *Fort Worth Daily Gazette*, 7/17/1887.
17. *Fort Worth Daily Gazette*, 7/17/1887; *Fort Worth Daily Gazette*, 7/18/1887; Spitzka, E. C. "The Whitechapel Murders: Their Medico-Legal and Historical Aspects": 765-778; *Fort Worth Daily Gazette*, 7/22/1887.
18. *Fort Worth Daily Gazette*, 7/18/1887; *Fort Worth Daily Gazette*, 7/15/1887; *Fort Worth Daily Gazette*, 7/22/1887.
19. *Fort Worth Daily Gazette*, 7/22/1887; *Fort Worth Daily Gazette*, 7/15/1887.
20. *Fort Worth Daily Gazette*, 7/22/1887; *Fort Worth Daily Gazette*, 7/17/1887.
21. *Fort Worth Daily Gazette*, 7/18/1887; *Fort Worth Daily Gazette*, 7/22/1887.
22. *Fort Worth Daily Gazette*, 7/29/1887; *Fort Worth Daily Gazette*, 7/30/1887; *Fort Worth Daily Gazette*, 7/31/1887.
23. *Fort Worth Daily Gazette*, 8/4/1887; *Fort Worth Daily Gazette*, 8/5/1887; *Fort Worth Daily Gazette*, 8/6/1887.
24. *Fort Worth Daily Gazette*, 8/4/1887.
25. *Fort Worth Daily Gazette*, 8/4/1887.
26. *Fort Worth Daily Gazette*, 8/8/1887; *Fort Worth Daily Gazette*, 8/9/1887.
27. *Fort Worth Daily Gazette*, 3/2/1888; *Fort Worth Daily Gazette*, 3/1/1888.
28. *Fort Worth Daily Gazette*, 3/1/1888.

29. *Fort Worth Daily Gazette*, 3/1/1888.
30. *Fort Worth Daily Gazette*, 3/1/1888.
31. *Fort Worth Daily Gazette*, 3/9/1888; *Fort Worth Daily Gazette*, 3/2/1888.
32. *Fort Worth Daily Gazette*, 3/9/1888; *Fort Worth Daily Gazette*, 3/1/1888; *Fort Worth Daily Gazette*, 3/2/1888 (The news report in the March 2, 1888, edition of the *Fort Worth Daily Gazette* said the forged check was in the amount of $100, but that amount must have been incorrect. Why would a jeweler give a refund from a $110 purchase if the payment was only $100? Beason had been charged with passing a forged $600 check.)
33. *Fort Worth Daily Gazette*, 4/11/1888.
34. *Fort Worth Daily Gazette*, 4/11/1888.
35. *Fort Worth Daily Gazette*, 6/9/1888.
36. *Fort Worth Daily Gazette*, 6/9/1888.
37. *Fort Worth Daily Gazette*, 9/17/1890; *Fort Worth Daily Gazette*, 9/17/1890; "Henretta Whitley"; "Moon Chart."
38. *Fort Worth Daily Gazette*, 9/17/1890; *Fort Worth Daily Gazette*, 9/17/1890; *Fort Worth Daily Gazette*, 5/20/1891; *Fort Worth Daily Gazette*, 11/21/1891.

Chapter 31

"Villainy Which the Law Makes Possible and Permits"

What It All Seems to Mean

In a speech to the U.S. House of Representatives on January 25, 1877, John Hancock made an unusual statement that seemed to prophesy the potential for a future conspiracy and cover-up. Hancock noted that "There is no limit to the amount of villainy which the law makes possible and permits." The murders in the servant girl annihilator case were pure villainy, and villainy that the local politicos apparently chose to ignore. Either the local officials made no true effort to solve the murders and turned a blind eye to the perpetrators, or else they were indeed monumentally incompetent. A man with political influence and lots of money could easily get away with murder, and probably did.[1]

J.R. Galloway concluded that the murders were likely committed by Nathan Elgin, because after Elgin's death the murders apparently stopped. Galloway's conclusion is not unreasonable, but it is likely incomplete. Elgin's killing by a policeman in East Austin a week after the Philp article appeared seemed a bit too coincidental. After his death, Elgin's footprint was cast, and the cast matched the bare footprint found on the gallery of the Phillips home, even down to the missing toe, a key clue that was not revealed through much of the investigation. The link between Elgin and the key clue is too difficult to dismiss, meaning that Elgin almost certainly was involved in the murders.[2]

But the evidence and common sense suggest that Elgin, if indeed he was one of the killers, did not act alone. At several of the murders, the simultaneous subduing of victims was necessary to prevent an alarm, and one person could not have succeeded in subduing multiple people at the same time. The evidence suggested that at least two people were present at many of the murders, either through the logistics necessary to commit the murders or the reports of witnesses. Likely other members of the Thug Gang were involved, primarily Oliver Townsend and Glenn Drummer. Elgin and Drummer were impressionable young incorrigibles, still teenagers. Townsend was older, in his mid-20s. But did the Thug Gang act on its own, and were the murders random?[3]

A common theory during most of the year was that the murders were simply the result of jealousy or domestic trouble. This theory might have had limited validity, but it certainly did not cover all the murders. The theory that the murders were committed during robbery attempts also fell flat because very little was taken during the murders and much more wealth could be found in the homes of the white people only a few feet from the cabins in which the servants were murdered. The theory that the murders were committed during the act of rape, or simply for the thrill of murder itself, held some water, but some of the victims were not raped, and why would the perpetrator hack the sex object to bits? Prostitutes were readily available in Guy Town for a pittance, so why was brutal annihilation required to complete a rape or to conceal evidence?

As Philp suggested, the only "human passion devilish enough" to substantiate the murders was revenge. The only question remains then: revenge for what? As noted earlier, records to verify the trial Philp indicated could not be found, but that lack of records does not mean the trial did not take place. Many records have been lost over the century and more since the murders. The last two murders of the white women, though, did not seem to fit Philp's juror theory. Still, revenge seemed to be the most viable motive, and the one that is most acceptable in these quarters.[4]

"Brain Work of a Higher Order"

What follows is a breakdown of each murder and a likely explanation of it. Of course, each explanation is only speculation and could be completely incorrect. But the multitude of evidence pointed in the direction the explanations go. First, the conclusion here is that the murders were committed by Nathan Elgin and other members of the Thug Gang, at least Oliver Townsend, and probably also Glenn Drummer and Alex Mack, under the orders of a wealthy and influential white man, possibly John Hancock. That said, here's what the evidence suggested.

Mollie Smith's murder on December 31, 1884, did not seem to fit Philp's juror theory. Smith had only recently moved to Austin from Waco, and any relatives of hers in the Austin area could not be established. However, her employer, William K. Hall, was an insurance agent and a land agent, and his dealings as a land agent might have been the motive for the murder. Why wasn't Hall murdered instead of Smith? The object of the attack seemed to be revenge and retaliation, so a fright could certainly be sent through Hall if his servant was murdered only a few feet from his home, his wife, and his newborn child. Indeed, Hall and his family apparently left town not long after the murders.

Walter Spencer and William "Lem" Brooks did not seem likely suspects. The prosecution of Spencer late in the year was an insincere attempt to appease the black citizens of Austin that something was being done to solve the servant girl murders, and the jury quickly saw through that ploy by acquitting Spencer. Richard Walton in *Cold Case Homicides* mentioned bare footprints leading to Shoal Creek, but local reports did not support that statement. Galloway indicated that such bare footprints first appeared at the Shelly murder scene.[5]

The murder of Mollie Smith could have been the result of jealousy, but the mutilation of her body seemed too drastic for a simple case of jealousy. Nothing was stolen from her cabin, so robbery could not have been the motive. Rape and murder were possible motives, and both were achieved, but why was Mollie Smith chosen? Common sense keeps saying that something more must be involved, and that something was likely revenge, retaliation, or retribution.

Between the murders of Mollie Smith and Eliza Shelly, numerous homes were attacked. Black servant girls were often the target, but so were German and Swedish servant girls. But a more pertinent fact, perhaps, was that most of the homes that were attacked included residents that were involved in land, law, or finance. Many of the residents were land agents or worked for the General Land Office. Others were lawyers or employees in the Attorney General's office. Some were bankers. Most of the attacks were ineffectual, though some injuries occurred. However, little property was stolen, suggesting that robbery was not really a motive. Again, revenge or retribution seemed the most likely explanation, as most all those whose homes were attacked had at one point or another had dealings with John Hancock.

Eliza Shelly's murder on May 7, 1885, did not seem to fit the jealousy theory. Her husband was apparently in prison, and she had no male visitors while working at Dr. Lucien Johnson's home. But later, a young black man named Andrew Rogers cast a shroud of guilt over Ike Plummer, a simple-minded black man who knew Eliza Shelly. Plummer was not charged with the crime, and his involvement seemed unlikely because one of Shelly's sons saw the killer and did not recognize him as Plummer. However, Lucien Johnson, a medical doctor, had recently become a land agent in partnership with Dennis Corwin. Corwin had been the county sheriff in the late 1870s, and one of his deputies was Horatio Grooms Lee, the city marshal during most of 1885. Corwin had been involved in the Ake trial in 1878. At the Shelly murder scene, local reports noted the bare footprints for the first time, but the missing toe, a key consideration, was not mentioned. If the footprints did indicate a missing toe, then Nathan Elgin would seem to be the killer of Eliza Shelly. If Elgin was the killer, then jealousy certainly would not be a motive, and robbery would not, either. Revenge or retaliation again seemed the most likely motive, once more revolving around land or perhaps the Ake trial.

The next murder was of Irene Cross on May 22, 1885, on the property of Sophie Wittman. This murder differed from the first two murders because in this murder, the weapon seemed to be a knife or razor, whereas an ax or a hatchet, and perhaps a spike, were used in the first two murders. None of the white people on the property had any dealings in land, law, or finance. The nephew of Irene Cross, who was in the cabin at the time of the murder, saw the murderer and described him as a chunky, barefooted negro. The news reports, however, did not mention any footprints left at the scene. Was the killer again Nathan Elgin, this time using a knife or razor on his victim, or was the killer one of the other members of the Thug Gang? Jealousy, robbery, and rape did not seem to be viable motives in this murder. Murder itself could have been the motive, but as indicated earlier, Sophie Wittman was the widow of August Wittman, the hackman who was mysteriously killed in 1878, in keeping with Kenward Philp's story of revenge.

A few more home attacks occurred in early summer, but for the most part, Austin gained a reprieve from the violence during the summer. That reprieve ended on August 30, 1885, when Rebecca Ramey was attacked. Though Rebecca survived the attack, her young daughter, Mary Ramey, was carried off, raped, and murdered. As in the first two murders, the weapons used were an ax or a hatchet and a spike. Bare footprints were also found at the scene. For the first time, bloodhounds were used to pursue the killer, but they turned up only a man that doctors ruled incapable of rape. Alex Mack was also introduced as a suspect. Jealousy and robbery did not seem viable motives, but rape and murder certainly were. The man on whose property the murder occurred, Valentine O. Weed, was a prosperous businessman who owned a livery and had a few land dealings. Rebecca Ramey, though, was the older sister of Albert Carrington, a city councilman. And for the first time, the local newspapers began to hint that the murders could not have been conceived by ignorant negroes, but that they required a "superior intelligence, and brain work of a higher order," which would mean a white person. Even Philp claimed that "the white man dominated all through. The colored man's cunning baffled the bloodhounds, the white man's intelligence befogged the police." And William Hannibal Thomas, in *The American Negro*, suggested that a black man was himself incapable of a crime requiring forethought.

> There is good ground for believing that, were the negro once convincingly assured of personal security, all the malignity of his slumbering savagery would immediately find expression in the most revolting acts of physical lawlessness. His passions are easily excited, and his feelings readily inflamed to the point of reckless vindictiveness, though a natural unsteadiness of character renders him fickle and unstable in purpose. For the commission of crime requiring forethought, coolness, sagacity, and persistency, the negro would be entirely wanting in the requisite courage. He can and does commit offences of horrible atrociousness, but rather as the sequence of impulse than as the outcome of deliberate preparation. At every step in his criminal career he is timid and cowardly, and, whether his victims be human or animal, he is never generous in treatment nor magnanimous in forbearance so long as he occupies the vantage ground.

Of course, Thomas, born of free black parents, was labeled a Black Judas for his uncomplimentary views of his own race.[6]

The next murders had to involve more than one person because four people were subdued almost simultaneously. On September 27, 1885, Gracie Vance and Orange Washington were murdered on the property of William B. Dunham, and Lucinda Boddy and Patsy Gibson were seriously injured. Jealousy and robbery again did not seem to be viable motives, but rape and murder could have been. The murders were similar to most of the earlier murders. The heads of three of the victims were severely gashed, as if struck with a hatchet or an ax, and the two survivors were likely sandbagged. Gracie Vance was dragged outside and raped, and then her head was bashed in with a rock or brick, much like August Wittman had been killed. Two new suspects were introduced after this murder, Oliver Townsend and Dock Woods, both members of the Thug Gang. Oliver Townsend was chiefly implicated in a story concocted by Johnson Trigg, a story later recanted and suspected to be promulgated by the Houston detectives. William B. Dunham, the man on whose property the murders occurred, had been a state attorney in the late 1870s and had faced off against John Hancock in at least one case before the Texas Court of Appeals. Dunham was also the editor of the *Texas Court Reporter*. Could Dunham's legal standing have something to do with the murders? Was Dunham the target of the revenge? The possibility seems likely.

And then the murders abated for a while, but turmoil in Austin continued. The citizens were in an uproar, fearful to go out at night. The city marshal, Grooms Lee, was embattled for his failure to produce a viable suspect after 400 arrests. When Marshal Lee decided to get tough and strong-arm evidence from Alex Mack, he was roundly condemned and soon fired, The city government was undergoing constant criticism both locally and from around the state for its inability to stop or solve the murders. The citizens of Austin finally decided a change was necessary. In early December 1885, an election was held. Almost half of the sitting councilmen were ousted, among them Lewis Hancock, John Hancock's nephew, and Albert Carrington, the brother of Rebecca Ramey and uncle of the murdered Mary Ramey. As indicated, Grooms Lee was replaced as marshal by James E. Lucy, a former U.S. marshal and Texas Ranger. District Attorney James H. Robertson also made a lame attempt to try a suspect, Walter Spencer, for the murder of Mollie Smith months earlier, but that effort failed miserably, and Spencer was quickly acquitted. The Houston detectives who had been called in to solve the case had made no real progress, and the investigation had sputtered throughout the year. The detectives, consequently, were fired. As 1885 drew toward its end, all the murders remained unsolved, but at least they seemed to have halted.

But on Christmas Eve and early Christmas day, the murders resumed with a vengeance, and this time the victims were not poor black servant girls but reputable white women. The first victim was Sue Hancock, the 40-year-old wife of a carpenter who lived on Water Street. Moses Hancock, her husband, awoke late Christmas Eve with the feeling something was amiss in the house. When he went to investigate, he discovered that his wife, who slept in a separate room, was missing, and blood had been spilled in the room. He heard noises outside and found his wife in the backyard, mortally wounded with a gash in her head and a spike driven in her ear. He claimed he saw a man jumping the fence, and he later said another man with a pistol threatened him. Another witness saw four men running from the property. Not long afterwards, another murder occurred on West Hickory Street, about a half mile away. There, a 17-year-old woman named Eula Phillips had been bludgeoned and dragged outside, where she had been raped and had her head smashed in. Her husband was also seriously injured in the attack. As in most of the other attacks, the weapon this time was an ax or a hatchet.

Though these attacks used the same weapons, the victims were markedly different. One can assume that the motive might have been related to the trial Kenward Philp indicated, but that link was harder to establish this time. The Hancocks had not lived in Austin long, having moved there from San Antonio after also living in Waco. As a poor carpenter, Moses Hancock had little to do with land dealings, law, and finance. Eula Phillips and her husband, Jimmy, lived with Jimmy's parents. His father was a well-known architect and builder in Austin. Though somewhat well-to-do, the elder Phillips was not politically influential or wealthy. The two murders were harder to explain, but they may have served as the culmination of the series of murders.

On Christmas morning, a citizens meeting was held at the capitol. White people in Austin were now sincerely interested in ending the murders because the color line had been crossed. At the meeting, many favored the establishment of a vigilance committee to root out the murderers. Instead, a Citizens' Committee for Public Safety was formed, with 40 members and A.P. Wooldridge, an old colleague of John Hancock, as the chairman. A reward fund to find the murderers of the white women was quickly instituted, and rewards for the murderers of the black women were also created later. The white people in Austin were now truly afraid, as the black people of Austin had been all the year.

The murders of the two white women, especially the murder of Eula Phillips, created social turmoil. Rumors began to circulate that Eula Phillips, just a teenager but already a mother, had frequented assignation houses in Guy Town with prominent male citizens of Austin. One rumor had her riding in a carriage with a man on the night of her murder. That man was later rumored to be William Swain, the current comptroller of Texas and also a candidate for governor. But Swain's involvement seemed to be the product of political slander.

Just what did happen on that bloody night before Christmas? Strange as it seems, the murder of Moses Hancock's wife may have been a case of mistaken identity. At the time of the murder, at least six women in Austin had the name Sue Hancock. One of these women was married to John Hancock, and another was married to Hugh Hancock, proprietor of the Black Elephant saloon and the son of John Hancock by a mulatto mother. One was the black mother of Payton Hancock by John Hancock's father. One was the teenaged daughter of Aron Hancock, a black farmer. Another was the 20-year-old daughter of Rubin Hancock, John Hancock's mulatto half-brother. And one was the unfortunate wife of Moses Hancock. Was the murdered woman the intended victim? Or had the wife of John Hancock or Hugh Hancock perhaps discovered what was going on and threatened to tell the authorities? One cannot tell, but mistaken identity seemed the only reasonable explanation for the murder of Sue Hancock, the wife of Moses.

The murder of Eula Phillips may actually draw the whole picture together. Eula was a flirtatious young teenager, likely drawn to power and wealth. The three men explicitly mentioned in the Jimmy Phillips trial as companions of Eula were the secretary of the State Capitol Building Commission, the state superintendent of public instruction, and a clerk in the office of William Swain, the comptroller. The clerk was also the son of John Hancock's law partner. But she may also have been drawn to a man with much more influence and wealth than the ones mentioned in the trial. Who was the man seen in the carriage with Eula the night she was killed? One rumor mostly disproved was that the man was William J. Swain, the state comptroller. That rumor was seen as political slander meant to derail Swain's run for governor. Another rumor was that the man was a rich politician. Could that rich politician have been John Hancock? Philp contended that the carriage was the "hack of a white man, driven by a negro," and that its "tracks were followed for some miles from the scene of the murder, and were found to lead back precisely to the scene of the crime." Philp also claimed to have seen a private carriage being washed by a "villainous looking" gigantic black man at the home of his John Doe, the gentleman farmer.[7]

Was John Hancock the man in the carriage with Eula Phillips? Was she killed because she had learned something about him she should not know? Was she killed because of her relation to the Eanes brothers, who had killed C.D. McMillan in 1880? During the Jimmy Phillips trial, the rumor spread that May Tobin had blackmailed some of the prominent men of Austin who had visited her assignation house at the foot of Congress Avenue, and that those men had paid her handsomely to keep their name out of her testimony. Could John Hancock have been one of those men? The murder of Eula Phillips was as vicious as the murders of Mollie Smith and Gracie Vance, so the same parties seemed to have been the murderers. In addition, the bloody footprint on the gallery of the Phillips home matched the foot of Nathan Elgin, further galvanizing the belief that Nathan Elgin was one of the killers throughout the series of servant girl murders. Eula Phillips was only a few years older than Mary Ramey, so Eula's murder seemed as senseless as the murder of that poor black girl.

Within 24 hours after the last murders, at least six black men were arrested on suspicion, among them Oliver Townsend and Dock Woods. Several white men were also arrested because they had blood on their clothes, or their clothes appeared to be bloody. These white men were quickly exonerated. A Mexican named Anastacio Martinez was arrested several days after the murders, but he too proved to be an unreliable suspect, though he was eventually committed to the state asylum as a lunatic. The governor offered a reward of $300, and the Citizens' Committee for Public Safety formed on Christmas morning put up a $1000 reward. Despite the handsome rewards, no new evidence and no solid suspects were produced.

After the Christmas Eve murders, the string of crimes seemingly ended. Throughout the year, hundreds of black men had been arrested, but no creditable suspect was ever identified. Then, out of the blue, on New Years Day, Jimmy Phillips, who had been seriously injured during the attack, was charged with the murder of his wife, Eula Phillips. The evidence against Phillips was promoted by Thomas Bailes, a fired Austin policeman turned detective. Though Justice William Von Rosenberg, Jr., believed there was no evidence to support such a charge, he nevertheless went along with Bailes and had Phillips jailed. Could Von Rosenberg also have been intimidated by John Hancock? Von Rosenberg's father was a land agent, and likely John Hancock had dealings with him. Regardless, Jimmy Phillips was charged with murdering his wife, though few in Austin believed him capable of the deed. And before long, Moses Hancock was also charged with the murder of his wife. Again, the evidence seemed to come from Thomas Bailes, and again, the arrest warrant was issued by Justice William Von Rosenberg, Jr.

And then the Kenward Philp article was published near the end of January 1886, and of course no arrest of a gentleman farmer took place, but coincidentally, mysteriously a week later a prime black suspect was accidentally shot and killed in a scuffle with a white policeman in East Austin. That suspect's footprint matched the ones found at several of the murders, including the missing toe. And then Kenward Philp died mysteriously of blood poisoning just eleven days after Elgin was shot and killed. In the Philp article, the coroner became aware of Philp's evidence before the end of January 1886. Yet the trial of Jimmy Phillips continued. It was a tumultuous trial that included ax murder, rape, prostitution, and abortion. Moses Hancock's trial was more subdued but included alcoholism, wife abuse, and an explosive secret letter that, when revealed, proved to be a dud. And John Hancock defended Moses Hancock for free! The prosecution of Jimmy Phillips and Moses Hancock was simply an attempt by city officials to deflect criticism, just as the prosecution of Walter Spencer had been. Jimmy Phillips and Moses Hancock were, plain and simple, fall guys. If Philp was correct, then Justice William Von Rosenberg, Jr., knew that Phillips and Hancock were not guilty, but he let their prosecution continue. Even if Philp's article is not considered, the killing of Nathan Elgin, with his missing toe, was a clear signal that Jimmy Phillips was not the right defendant. As it turned out, though, after Phillips was initially convicted, his conviction was overturned by the Texas Court of Appeals. Moses Hancock was never convicted, his trial ending with a hung jury.

Travis County Sheriff Malcolm Hornsby seemed to be the only one at the time who really had a handle on the case, and he had little involvement in the investigation. Hornsby noted that "since the death of the colored man, Elgin, and the sending to the penitentiary of Oliver Townsend, there had been no mysterious murders in the city." Townsend had been sent to prison in 1886 on a burglary charge. Sheriff Hornsby was also the one who took the plaster cast of Elgin's foot and confirmed that it matched the footprint on the Phillips gallery. As far as Hornsby was concerned, he did not believe that the husbands were guilty of murdering their wives, but he did believe that members of the Thug Gang had physically committed the murders.[8]

"The White Man Dominated"

For over a hundred years, various researchers have tried to solve the murders, and most have come up short. This book is not meant as a solution to the case, but as a starting point so that others may verify or disprove the theory advanced in these pages. Some conclusions seem obvious, though. The Malay cook Maurice—who is said by some to be the murderer because he worked at the Pearl House, a location near some of the murders—was very likely not the killer, and his later presence in Whitechapel was also debatable. Nor was Jack the Ripper in any of his incarnations the servant girl annihilator. The means by which the murders in Austin and Whitechapel were committed varied so drastically that one cannot sensibly claim that the same hand was responsible for the murders oceans apart.

Why were these murders committed? Were they committed by the same person or the same group of people? Were the murders random, or were they orchestrated by a "superior intelligence"? Were the murders of people related to the jurors in a particular trial, as Kenward Philp suggested? Were they the result of jealousy and domestic disputes? Were the victims only tools whose murders were used to intimidate their employers? Were the murders indirect attacks on Grooms Lee and his family, the city officials, the white citizens of Austin for their southern allegiance, the black or mulatto community of Austin . . . or were they just random cases of rape and murder? In any case, officially, the servant girl murders were never solved.

In essence, then: The murders were likely committed, and probably for pay, by members of the Thug Gang, notably Nathan Elgin, Glenn Drummer, and Oliver Townsend. But the murders were orchestrated by a white man, possibly John Hancock, for revenge or retribution. The city officials and police were likely aware of Hancock's involvement but did nothing to stop it. Even after the killing of Nathan Elgin, the cover-up continued, resulting in the unwarranted prosecution of Jimmy Phillips and Moses Hancock. Again, the murders were most likely committed by black puppets whose strings were pulled by an influential white man, and local city officials conspired in a cover-up of the white man's involvement.

Notes

Title: Lynch, *The Bench and Bar of Texas*: 429.

1. Lynch, *The Bench and Bar of Texas*: 429.
2. Galloway, *The Servant Girl Murders*: 315-317.
3. *Austin Weekly Statesman*, 7/30/1884; "Convict Record, Texas State Penitentiary," 1886 (Townsend was known as a notorious chicken thief, but in 1884 he had been fined for carrying a dagger and later escaped from the chain gang.)
4. *Omaha Daily Bee*, 1/30/1886.
5. Walton, *Cold Case Homicides*: 555.
6. *Omaha Daily Bee*, 1/30/1886; Thomas, *The American Negro: What He Was, What He Is, and What He May Become*: 209, xi-xii. (See, for example, *Black Judas: William Hannibal Thomas and the American Negro*, by John David Smith.)
7. *Omaha Daily Bee*, 1/30/1886.
8. *Austin Daily Statesman*, 6/3/1887; *Austin Weekly Statesman*, 4/22/1886.

Chapter 32

"The Stain of Blood"

Aftermath

Even before the Moses Hancock trial concluded without a conviction in June 1887, the specter of the servant girl murders had reared its horrid head again. In February 1887, a new scandal arose involving the hiring of the Houston detectives. Somehow, several thousand dollars supposedly disappeared.

> It will be remembered that to ferret out the infamous devils who perpetrated these dreadful assassinations the City Council of Austin and the people of Austin furnished many thousands of dollars to solve the bloody problem, but without success. The Evening Call contains a communication this evening from citizens charging that whereas Mayor Robertson of Austin in a communication to the City Council last May stated that he had applied to the Pinkertons for detectives and over four thousand dollars had been expended on detectives, but Pinkerton denies having had any business whatever with the Mayor of Austin. A letter from W. A. Pinkerton himself is published . . . saying he had not been employed to work up the Austin murder cases.

Of course, the city council assured the citizens that nothing was awry. One council member said that nothing was wrong because the detectives had been in Austin. Friends of the mayor claimed he could show vouchers for all the expenses related to the detectives, and they vouched for the mayor's "honesty and integrity." Later, the mayor made a statement completely clearing himself of any wrongdoing.

> He said immediately after the murder of Mrs. Eula Phillips and Mrs. Hancock he had telegraphed the Pinkerton agency. They first sent one detective to Austin. Two days later two more arrived and the third and fourth a few days afterwards. These Pinkerton detectives remained in Austin investigating the servant girl murders till the middle of March, eighty-six days, during which time he paid out $1500. Mayor Robertson showed receipts from Matt W. Pinkerton that he had expended the $4000 in detective service, whereupon the Council unanimously passed a resolution fully and honorably exonerating Mayor Robertson from any suspicion whatever.

As it turned out, the confusion arose because there were two Pinkerton agencies involved. But the mayor wasted no time in denouncing the newspaper and the reporter who wrote the critical article.[1]

And then the Blanton murder occurred on March 7, 1887. After a successful appeal of Jimmy Phillips' murder conviction, at the end of March 1887 his case was revisited in the District court and dismissed. A mistrial was declared in the trial of Moses Hancock in June 1887, and he was not retried. In late 1890 came the rather fishy affair concerning the new dam. Initial estimates of its cost were about $150,000, but the final cost of construction was $1.3 million dollars, nine times the original amount. And when the first installment of the bonds went out, the winning bidder was a local syndicate consisting of John Hancock, his nephew Lewis Hancock, J. T. Brackenridge, George W. Breckinridge, A. P. Wooldridge, and James H. Raymond. All these men had dealings with John Hancock, some rather shady.

The Moonlight Towers

Construction on the new dam, called the Granite Dam, began in May 1891 and was completed in May 1893. Construction of the powerhouse, however, took another two years. As part of a bond election for $1.4 million in May 1890, the city council decided to construct a lighting system for Austin. The lighting system, though, was different from current street lights that concentrate light in a small area. Instead, the adopted lighting system included 31 towers, topped by six carbon-arc lamps each, that would throw dim light over an area stretching 1500 feet from each tower, or a circle of light 3000 feet in diameter. The light was supposed to be adequate for a person to read a pocket watch at midnight. These towers, affectionately called moonlight towers or moon towers in Austin, were common across the United States at the time.[2]

The acquisition of the towers, however, got the city embroiled in another controversy. The towers were purchased from the Fort Wayne Electric Company in Fort Wayne, Indiana, in 1894. At the time, the president of the Fort Wayne Electric Company, Ronald T. McDonald, was enmeshed in a stock and banking scandal. In addition, General Electric Company claimed in 1894 that it was owed over a $1 million by Fort Wayne Electric Company, and stock in the Fort Wayne company was placed in receivership. By 1899, Fort Wayne Electric Company plunged into bankruptcy after McDonald "left the place in a crippled financial condition." McDonald died in December 1898 while on a trip to Texas.[3]

The towers themselves also aroused controversy in Austin. The moonlight towers were constructed as a direct response to the servant girl murders in 1885. Yet some people feared the light from the towers would cause crops to grow 24 hours a day. Others believed that chickens would become confused, causing them to lay eggs 24 hours a day. When the towers were first lighted in May 1895, neither fear was valid, of course. There was a fallacy associated with the moonlight towers, however. The towers were built to illuminate Austin neighborhoods to prevent attacks such as those that occurred in the servant girl murders. But most of those murders were committed on bright, moonlit nights. The natural moonlight was equivalent to what the moonlight towers could produce, yet the natural moonlight had not prevented the murders, so how could the moonlight towers be expected to prevent such murders?[4]

The towers were 150 feet tall and were mounted on smooth, 15-foot tall poles to prevent people from climbing the towers. The carbon-arc lamps on the top of the towers were 165 feet from the ground. Each tower weighed about two tons and was supported by guy wires. The carbon-arc lamps had to be lit daily. A worker would ride a cable-driven elevator inside the vertical truss assembly to the top of each tower. There, he would light the six 2000-candlepower carbon-arc lamps that pointed straight down. The carbon-arc lamps were replaced by incandescent lamps in 1925, and those were replaced by mercury vapor lamps in 1936. The towers themselves were somewhat dangerous in their early days. One tower collapsed soon after its installation. Only a few weeks after the towers began operating, a worker named Gilbert Searight fell from atop one of the towers to his death. Over the years, several of the towers fell victim to automobile accidents, construction, and decay. Today, only 17 of the original 31 towers remain. Austin is the only city that has retained these holdovers from the 19th century.[5]

Then, on April 7, 1900, the dam collapsed during a flood, and the moonlight towers went dark from April 1900 until January 1901 because of the destruction of the dam's powerhouse. By 1900, segregation began to take hold in Austin. Prior to that time, black residences were scattered across town, with some blacks living in such neighborhoods as Wheatville, Clarksville, and Masontown, but by 1930, most blacks lived in east Austin. In 1928, a city plan designated the east side as "the Negro district." In 1903, Grooms Lee was elected the city engineer, and by 1906 he was the Travis County surveyor. In 1905, a few blocks of Congress Avenue were paved, with bricks, to accommodate the increasing number of automobiles in the city, but it was the only street in the city that was paved. And the city still had few sewers and no parks or playgrounds. Twenty years after the servant girl murders, the city of Austin had a population of just over 25,000 people, and it had electricity and water service, but in many regards, it had not changed much from 1885, and in a racial sense, it had become worse.[6]

They're All Dead Now

The servant girl murder victims were buried in Oakwood Cemetery in Austin.

> >**Mollie Smith** was buried in Colored Ground in Oakwood
> Cemetery on January 3, 1885. Cause of death: broken skull.
> She had been in the city one year. Her murder scene is now the
> Whole Foods corporate headquarters parking garage.
> >**Eliza Shelly** was buried at the age of 30 in Colored Ground in
> Oakwood Cemetery on May 10, 1885. Cause of death: wound
> on the throat. She was identified in cemetery records as Eliza
> Shelley. She had been in the city three years. Her murder
> scene is now the Vince Young Steakhouse.

>**Irene Cross** was buried in Colored Ground in Oakwood Cemetery on May 24, 1885. Cause of death: wounds. She was identified in cemetery records as Irina Cross. Her murder scene is now a Texas State Comptroller field office parking lot.
>**Mary Ramey** was buried in Colored Ground in Oakwood Cemetery on August 31, 1885 at age 11. Cause of death: murdered. She was identified in burial records as Mary Raney (Ramey). Her murder scene is now the Residence Inn hotel.
>**Grace Vance** was buried at the age of 22 in Colored Ground in Oakwood Cemetery on September 29, 1885. Cause of death: murdered. Her murder scene is now an Urban Outfitters store.
>**Orange Washington** was buried at the age of 21 in Colored Ground in Oakwood Cemetery on September 29, 1885. Cause of death: murdered. He was identified in cemetery records as O. Wasington.
>**Susan Hancock** was buried at the age of 44 in Lot 459 in Oakwood Cemetery on December 29, 1885. Cause of death: murdered. She was identified in cemetery records as S.C. Hancock, and they also indicated she had been in the city seven months. Her murder scene is now the San Jacinto Center building and the Four Seasons hotel.
>**Eula Phillips** was buried in the Old Graveyard in Oakwood Cemetery on December 25, 1885 at age 17. Cause of death: murdered. She was identified in burial records as Luly Philipps. Her murder scene is now the Jake Pickle Federal Building.[7]

Many other people who figured prominently in the murders were also buried in Oakwood Cemetery.

>**Dr. William J. Burt**, the city physician, died of dysentery in July 1886 at age 48. He was buried in Oakwood Cemetery.
>**Mrs. Sophia Phillips**, the mother of Jimmy Phillips, died of diarrhea in May 1888 at the age of 62. She was buried in Oakwood Cemetery.
>**Dr. Lucien B. Johnson**, at whose home Eliza Shelly was murdered, died of a heart attack in April 1889 at the age of 58. He was buried in Oakwood Cemetery.
>**Judge Joseph Lee**, an early Austin resident and the father of Grooms Lee, died of neuralgia of the heart in February 1891 at the age of 81. He was buried in Oakwood Cemetery.
>**Colonel John W. Robertson**, the mayor of Austin during the murders, died in June 1892 at the age of 52. He was first buried in Highland Park Cemetery in Austin and later reinterred in Oakwood Cemetery in February 1893.
>**Malcolm M. Hornsby**, who was Travis County sheriff during the murders, died in September 1892 at the age of 50. He was buried in Hornsby Bend Cemetery in Travis County, Texas.
>**Judge John Hancock**, who defended Jimmy Phillips and Moses Hancock in their trials, and who may have been involved in the murders himself, died of brain disease in July 1893 at the age of 69. He was buried in Oakwood Cemetery.

>**Justice Thomas F. Purnell**, who conducted some of the inquests for the murder victims, died from the effects of morphine in December 1894 at the age of 74. He was buried in Oakwood Cemetery.
>**William Walton**, who served as one of the defense lawyers for Jimmy Phillips, died of cancer of the face in July 1897 at the age of 76. He was buried in Oakwood Cemetery.
>**Dr. Richard M. Swearingen**, a doctor who treated several of the victims, died of chronic nephritis in August 1898 at the age of 60. He was buried in Oakwood Cemetery.
>**William Jesse Swain**, who was implicated as the man in the carriage with Eula Phillips, died in Houston in February 1904 at age 64. He was buried in the Texas State Cemetery in Austin.
>**Bethel Coopwood**, who was one of the defense lawyers for Moses Hancock, died of dengue fever in December 1907 at the age of 83. He was buried in Oakwood Cemetery.
>**Rebecca Ramey**, the mother of Mary Ramey who herself was attacked in August 1885, died of Bright's disease in February 1909 at the age of 73. She was buried in Oakwood Cemetery.
>**Mollie Eanes**, whose son was found dead and being eaten by hogs on Christmas Day 1885, apparently died of stomach cancer in May 1909 at the age of 63. She was buried in Bexar County, Texas.
>**James Phillips**, the father of Jimmy Phillips, died from the exhaustion of age in December 1909 at the age of 88. He was buried in Oakwood Cemetery.
>**Hugh Berry Hancock**, the mulatto son of John Hancock and the proprietor of the Black Elephant Saloon, died in January 1910 at the age of 55. He was buried in Pocatello, Idaho and was identified as Hugh P. Hancock in the death records.
>**District Attorney James Harvey Robertson,** the brother of the mayor and the prosecutor of Walter Spencer, Jimmy Phillips, and Moses Hancock, died in March 1912 at the age of 58. He was buried in Oakwood Cemetery, but he was listed as James H. Robinson in the burial records.
>**William B. Dunham**, at whose home Gracie Vance and Orange Washington were killed, died in December 1912 at the age of 64. He was buried in Oakwood Cemetery.
>**Sophie Wittman (Witman)**, at whose home Irene Cross was killed and whose husband, August Wittman, was mysteriously killed in 1878, died in September 1918 at the age of 80. She was buried in Oakwood Cemetery.
>**Justice William Von Rosenberg, Jr.**, who served as coroner and judge for several of the inquests and trials, died in January 1919 at the age of 59. He was buried in Oakwood Cemetery.
>**Moses H. Hancock**, who was charged with the murder of his wife, Sue, died in March 1919 at the age of 86. He was buried in Waco, Texas.
>**Edward Taylor Moore**, one of the lawyers that prosecuted Jimmy Phillips and Moses Hancock, died in March 1919 at the age of 72. He was buried in Oakwood Cemetery.

>**Horatio Grooms Lee**, who served as the city marshal during most of the murders, died in November 1923 at the age of 75. He was buried in Oakwood Cemetery.
>**James E. Lucy**, who replaced Grooms Lee as the city marshal near the end of 1885, died in 1927 at the age of 73. He was buried in Oakwood Cemetery.
>**Thomas Phillips**, the baby boy whose mother, Eula, was murdered, apparently died in 1928 at the age of 44. He was buried in Cedar Knob Cemetery in Salado, Texas.
>**May Tobin**, who provided incriminating evidence in the Phillips trial against several prominent Austin men, may have died in Bee County, Texas, in July 1928.
>**James O. (Jimmy) Phillips**, who was charged with the murder of his wife, Eula, died in January 1929 at the age of 67. He was buried in Odd Fellows Cemetery in Georgetown, Texas.
>**Alexander P. Wooldridge**, who was the chairman of the Citizens' Committee for Public Safety formed after the Christmas murders, died in September 1930 at the age of 83. He was buried in Oakwood Cemetery.
>**George A. McCutcheon**, who some believed was the real murderer of Eula Phillips, died in 1931 at the age of 82. He was buried in Shiloh-McCutcheon Cemetery in Hutto, Texas.
>**Valentine O. Weed**, at whose home Mary Ramey was killed, died in August 1935 at the age of 85. He was buried in Oakwood Cemetery.
>**Bella Brush Weed**, the wife of Valentine Weed whose brother was a city councilman during the murders, died at age 90 in February 1944. She was buried in Oakwood Cemetery.
>**Kenward Philp**, who wrote a provocative article about the murders, died mysteriously of blood poisoning at the age of 42 in Brooklyn, New York, on February 21, 1886, just three weeks after the article was published.[8]

Some of the people involved in the murders, such as the William K. Hall family, simply left town. Hall and his family were living in St. Louis, Missouri, in 1900. After that, they seemed to disappear from public records.[9]

What happened to the black suspects in the murders is for the most part unknown. Nathan Elgin was buried at the age of 24 in Colored Ground in Oakwood Cemetery on February 11, 1886. His cause of death was listed as a shotgun wound. What became of Oliver Townsend, Glenn Drummer, and Alex Mack is unclear. Oliver Townsend was sent to state prison in 1886 on a ten-year sentence for burglary. He escaped from prison in July 1895. Dock Woods may have married Dora Ates in December 1888. This couple appeared with four children in the 1910 census, living in Tyler, Texas. By 1920, Dock Woods had married Kathrine Furgersen and was living with her two children, still in Tyler. He was a farmer who died in August 1957 at the age of 95.[10]

As all these people faded into the past, so did the servant girl murders. Little was said of them for over a hundred years. The last twenty years, though, have brought a resurgence in interest. Unfortunately, the resurgence in interest has also prompted a wealth of incorrect information. One goal of this book is to try to correct some of that errant information.

Conclusion

In the scheme of things, 1885 proved to be a watershed year in Austin history. Austin went from a rowdy young frontier town with outlaws killing lawmen and gunfire in Guy Town and on Congress Avenue to the crass commercialism and vulgarity of a modern American city. The virgin had met the dynamo, and the dynamo had torn away the last shreds of innocence that clung to the "Athens of the West." The new century would be founded on money, not art or letters. Austin "progressed" from a frontier town with a gunslinger marshal to a modern city with its own enigmatic serial killer on the loose. Years before the 20th century's advancements had reached Austin's doorstep, the malevolent side of the coming century had been awakened early. Gunfights in the streets of Austin were at least a somewhat fair way of resolving a dispute or killing someone, but the tactics of the servant girl annihilators were decidedly more vicious. A glee seemed to be had in the act of murder, as well as a sense of revenge. Worse, the serial killer might have been protected from the law, even if his minions eventually were not. The year of 1885 was one the likes of which Austin would never see again.

Notes

Title: *Fort Worth Daily Gazette*, 11/8/1885.

1. *Fort Worth Daily Gazette*, 2/22/1887.
2. Humphrey, *Austin: An Illustrated History*: 135-139; Long, "Moonlight Towers," *Handbook of Texas Online*; "Moonlight Towers guide Austin through 110 years of history" 9/23/2005.
3. *New York Times*, 2/17/1894; *New York Times*, 7/27/1894; *New York Times*, 2/17/1899.
4. "The hush-hush history of the Moonlight Towers"; "What are the moonlight towers?"; "Moonlight Towers-1895."
5. "Moonlight Towers guide Austin through 110 years of history," 9/23/2005; "The Moonlight Towers Of Austin, Texas, USA"; Long, "Moonlight Towers," *Handbook of Texas Online*; Humphrey, *Austin: An Illustrated History*: 139; "Moonlight Towers-1895"; "What are the moonlight towers?"
6. Humphrey, "Austin, TX (Travis County)," *Handbook of Texas Online*; "The Moonlight Towers Of Austin, Texas, USA"; "Congress Avenue"; "City of Austin Population History, 1840 to 2013"; *Shiner Gazette*, 3/3/1903; *City Directory of Austin With Street Directory of Residents, 1906-7*.
7. This information comes from the Oakwood Cemetery Database.
8. This information comes from the Oakwood Cemetery Database; <www.findagrave.com>; "Texas Deaths, 1890-1976"; "Texas, Deaths (New Index, New Images), 1890-1976"; "Texas, Death Index, 1903-2000."
9. 1900 Federal Census.
10. Oakwood Cemetery Database; 1900 Federal Census; 1910 Federal Census; 1920 Federal Census; "Convict Record, Texas State Penitentiary," 1886; "Texas Deaths, 1890-1976"; "Dock S Woods" (Dock Woods was identified as Dock Wood in the census of 1900 and 1910, Dock Woods in the 1920 census, and Dock S. Woods in his death record.)

Sources and Resources

Alexander, Bob, and James R. Alexander. *Winchester Warriors: Texas Rangers of Company D, 1874-1901*. Denton, Texas: University of North Texas Press, 2011.

"Al Lackey Still Rides the Night." <http://www.flickr.com/photos/billstrain/56466798/in/set-72157600077209291>.

Anderson, H. Allen. "BAKER, BENJAMIN M." Handbook of Texas Online <http://www.tshaonline.org/handbook/online/articles/fba21>. Published by the Texas State Historical Association.

"The Archives War." <https://www.tsl.state.tx.us/treasures/republic/archwar/archwar.html>.

"Ardry 'Aubry' McCutcheon." < http://www.findagrave.com/cgi-bin/fg.cgi?page=gr&GRid=50413227>.

Atchison Daily Globe (Atchison, Kansas). Various dates. Retrieved at <http://www.casebook.org/press_reports/atchison_daily_globe/850930.html>; <http://www.casebook.org/press_reports/atchison_daily_globe/881006.html>; <http://www.casebook.org/press_reports/atchison_daily_globe/881119.html>.

The Austin Almanac. Edited by Will and Carol Howard. Austin: Winter Wheat House Publications, 1981.

"Austin City Council Minutes, 5/6/1975." <http://www.austintexas.gov/edims/document.cfm?id=32311>.

Austin Daily Dispatch, 10/14/1885.

Austin Daily Statesman. Various dates. Retrieved at Austin History Center and J.R. Galloway's *The Servant Girl Murders* and <http://www.casebook.org/press_reports/austin_statesman/as880905.html>.

"Austin's Guy Town." <http://www.historyhouse.com/in_history/guy_town/>.

"Austin's Guy Town 1870-1913." <http://www.texasescapes.com/AustinTexas/Guy-Town-Texas.htm>.

Austin Record, 5/29/1886. Retrieved at J.R. Galloway's *The Servant Girl Murders*.

Austin Weekly Statesman. Various dates. Retrieved at the Portal to Texas History, University of North Texas. <http://texashistory.unt.edu/>.

Baker, De Witt Clinton. *A Texas Scrap-book*. New York: A.S. Barnes & Co., 1875. Retrieved at Google Books.

Barker, Nancy N. "PIG WAR." *Handbook of Texas Online*. <http://www.tshaonline.org/handbook/online/articles/mgp01>. Published by the Texas State Historical Association.

Barkley, Mary Starr. *History of Travis County and Austin 1839-1899*. Austin: Austin Printing Company, 1963. Retrieved at Google Books.

Bartholomew, Eugene. *Bartholomew Diary*. Retrieved at Austin History Center. Austin Public Library.

Bastrop Advertiser (Bastrop, Texas). Various dates. Retrieved at the Portal to Texas History, University of North Texas. <http://texashistory.unt.edu/>.

Begg, Paul, Martin Fido, and Keith Skinner. *The Complete Jack the Ripper A-Z*. London: John Blake Publishing, 2010.

Bentley, H.L., and Thomas Pilgrim. *Texas Legal Directory for 1876-1877*. Austin: Democratic Statesman Office, 1877. Retrieved at Google Books.

Bicknell, Tom. "The Notorious Ben Thompson Becomes a Peace Officer." <http://www.imagesofyorkshire.co.uk/famous_people/ben_thompson/ben_thompson_marshall.htm>;<http://www.imagesofyorkshire.co.uk/famous_people/ben_thompsn/marshall_election.htm>.

Bicknell, Tom, and Anne Beck. "THOMPSON, BEN." *Handbook of Texas Online* <http://www.tshaonline.org/handbook/online/articles/fth16>.Published by the Texas State Historical Association.

Biographical Encyclopedia of Texas. New York: Southern Publishing Company, 1880. Retrieved at the Portal to Texas History, University of North Texas. <http://texashistory.unt.edu/ark:/67531/metapth5827/>.

"Biographies of Oakwood Cemetery Residents." <http://www.sachome.org/cemeteries/Oakwood/Oakwood%20Bios%20M.html>.

"BRACKENRIDGE, JOHN THOMAS." *Handbook of Texas Online* <http://www.tshaonline.org/handbook/online/articles/fbr03>. Published by the Texas State Historical Association.

Bree, Palin. "Austin's Bloody Murder Spree, 1884-1885." *Austin Genealogical Society Quarterly*, Volume 46, Number 3/4, September/December 2005: 117-118. Retrieved at <http://austintxgensoc.org/wp-content/uploads/2012/04/2005.3-4.pdf>.

Brenham Weekly Banner. Various dates. Retrieved at Chronicling America, Library of Congress newspaper collection. <http://chroniclingamerica.loc.gov/newspapers/>.

"Bridging the Colorado, an Iffy Proposition." <http://www.austinpost.org/history/bridging-colorado-iffy-proposition>.

"Brigham, Benjamin Rice." <http://www.sanjacinto-museum.org/Herzstein_Library/Veteran_Biographies/San_Jacinto_Bios/biographies/default.asp?action=bio&id=2936>.

"Brown Bowen of Florida and Texas." <http://freepages.history.rootsweb.ancestry.com/~bown/brown.html>.

Brown, John Henry. *Indian Wars and Pioneers of Texas*. Austin,
    Texas: L.E. Daniell, 1890. Retrieved at <http://archive.org/>.

Brown, Lee. "The Lackey Tragedy In Blanco County." *Frontier Times Magazine*, Vol. 13,
    No.7, April 1936.

Brownsville Daily Herald, 9/5/1895. Retrieved at Chronicling America, Library of Congress
    newspaper collection. <http://chroniclingamerica.loc.gov/newspapers/>.

"BULLOCK HOUSE." *Handbook of Texas Online*
    <http://www.tshaonline.org/handbook/online/articles/dfb03>.
    Published by the Texas State Historical Association.

"Central Austin Combined Neighborhood Plan." <ftp://ftp.ci.austin.tx.us/npzd/Austingo/ca-
    combined-np.pdf>.

Chambers's Encyclopedia: A Dictionary of Universal Knowledge for the People. Philadelphia:
    J. B. Lippincott & Co., 1883. Retrieved at Google Books.

Chester Times (Chester, Pennsylvania), 2/23/1886. Retrieved at Chronicling America,
    Library of Congress newspaper collection.
    <http://chroniclingamerica.loc.gov/newspapers/>.

Chicago Tribune, 10/6/1888. Retrieved at <http://www.casebook.org/
    press_reports/chicago_tribune/18881006.html>.

Childs, Allen. *Images of America: Sixth Street*. Charleston, SC: Arcadia Publishing, 2010.

City Directory of Austin With Street Directory of Residents, 1906-7. Retrieved at the Portal
    to Texas History, University of North Texas. <http://texashistory.unt.edu/explore/
    collections/CIT/browse/?fq=str_location_county%3ATravis+County%2C+TX>.

"City of Austin Population History 1840 to 2013." City of Austin.
    <http://www.austintexas.gov/sites/default/files/files/Planning/
    Demographics/population_history_pub.pdf>.

Colorado Citizen (Columbus, Texas). Various dates. Retrieved at the Portal to Texas History,
    University of North Texas.<http://texashistory.unt.edu/>.

"Commissioners Historical Bios." Texas General Land Office. <http://www.glo.texas.gov/
    GLO/history-of-the-Land-Office/commissioners-historical-bios.html>.

"Congress Avenue." <http://www.austinpostcard.com/congress.html>.

Connor, Seymour V. "ROBERTSON, JAMES HARVEY." *Handbook of Texas Online*
    <http://www.tshaonline.org/handbook/online/articles/fro27>.
    Published by the Texas State Historical Association.

"Convict Record, Texas State Penitentiary at Huntsville, Walker County, Texas" 1886.
    Thanks to J.R. Galloway.

Csida, Joseph, and June Bundy Csida. *American entertainment: a unique history of popular
    show business*. New York: Watson-Guptill Publications, 1978.

Cumberland Times-News, 7/31/2011. <http://times-news.com/local/x1443110454/LOOKING-BACK-1880-Will-the-real-Richard-Lindsay-please-testify>.

Custer, Elizabeth Bacon. *Tenting on the Plains, or General Custer in Kansas and Texas*. Williamstown, MA: Corner House Publishers, 1973 (reprint of revised 1895 edition).

Cutrer, Thomas W. "HANCOCK, GEORGE DUNCAN." *Handbook of Texas Online* <http://www.tshaonline.org/handbook/online/articles/fha45>. Published by the Texas State Historical Association.

Cutrer, Thomas W. "LEE, JOSEPH." *Handbook of Texas Online* <http://www.tshaonline.org/handbook/online/articles/fle15>. Published by the Texas State Historical Association.

Cutrer, Thomas W. "MCCALL, JOHN DODD." *Handbook of Texas Online* <http://www.tshaonline.org/handbook/online/articles/fmc05>. Published by the Texas State Historical Association.

Cutrer, Thomas W. "ROBERTSON, JOSEPH WILLIAM." *Handbook of Texas Online* <http://www.tshaonline.org/handbook/online/articles/fro30>. Published by the Texas State Historical Association.

The Daily Telegraph (London), 10/6/1888. Retrieved at <http://www.casebook.org/press_reports/daily_telegraph/dt881008.html>.

Dallas Morning News, 5/8/1892. Retrieved at <http://lackeymurders.blogspot.com/search/label/newspaper%20articles>.

Dallas Daily Herald, 10/2/1885. Retrieved at the Portal to Texas History, University of North Texas. <http://texashistory.unt.edu/ark:/67531/metapth287540/?q=%22october%204%2C%201885%22>.

Daniell, L.E. *Successful Men of Texas*. Austin, Texas: published by author, 1890. Retrieved at <http://archive.org/>.

Dante's *Inferno*, Canto XII < http://www.fullbooks.com/Dante-s-Inferno5.html>.

Decatur Saturday Herald, 8/29/1885. Retrieved at <http://lackeymurders.blogspot.com/search/label/newspaper%20articles>.

Deseret News (Deseret, Utah), 9/1/1885. Retrieved at Chronicling America, Library of Congress newspaper collection. <http://chroniclingamerica.loc.gov/newspapers/>.

"The Diary of Judge John Hancock." 1864-1865. <http://roborant42.appspot.com/show/entry/3043>.

"Dock S Woods." <http://www.findagrave.com/cgibin/fg.cgi?page=gr&GRid=94422678>.

Dodge City Times (Dodge City, Kansas), 9/3/1885. Retrieved at Chronicling America, Library of Congress newspaper collection. <http://chroniclingamerica.loc.gov/newspapers/>.

Dunn, Roy Sylvan. "DROUGHTS." *Handbook of Texas Online* <http://www.tshaonline.org/handbook/online/articles/ybd01>. Published by the Texas State Historical Association.

"Edwin B. Hancock." <http://www.findagrave.com/cgibin/fg.cgi?page=gr&GRid=39817111>.

The Eclectic Magazine of Foreign Literature, Science and Art, New Series, Volume 1, January-June 1865. Retrieved at <http://archive.org/>.

"Executions in the U.S. 1608-2002." <http://www.deathpenaltyinfo.org/documents/ESPYstate.pdf>.

"FBI—Serial Murder." <http://www.fbi.gov/stats-services/publications/serial-murder>.

Federal Census, 1860. Retrieved at Heritage Quest Online Database.
Federal Census, 1870. Retrieved at Heritage Quest Online Database.
Federal Census, 1880. Retrieved at Heritage Quest Online Database.
Federal Census, 1900. Retrieved at Heritage Quest Online Database.
Federal Census, 1910. Retrieved at Heritage Quest Online Database.
Federal Census, 1920. Retrieved at Heritage Quest Online Database.

Ford, Reuben W. *Austin Plat Map, 1872*. Retrieved at Texas State Library and Archives Commission. <https://www.tsl.state.tx.us/arc/maps/images/map0929b.jpg>.

Fort Worth Daily Gazette. Various dates. Retrieved at Chronicling America, Library of Congress newspaper collection. <http://chroniclingamerica.loc.gov/newspapers/>.

Frederick News (Frederick, Maryland), 11/20/1888. Retrieved at <http://www.casebook.org/press_reports/frederick_news/18881120.html>.

Freeman's Journal-Daily Commercial Advertiser (Dublin, Ireland),10/6/1888. Retrieved at <http://www.casebook.org/press_reports/freemans_journal_and_daily_commercial_advertiser/18881006.html>.

"Frontier Feudists Were True to Friends." *Frontier Times*, Vol. 4, No. 8, May 1927.

"Frontier serial killers: The Harpes." <http://www.illinoishistory.com/harpes.html>.

Galloway, J.R. *The Servant Girl Murders*. Booklocker.com, Inc., 2010. (This author currently has a website about the murders at <http://www.servantgirlmurders.com/>.)

Galveston Daily News (Galveston, Texas). Various dates. Retrieved at <http://newspaperarchive.com/>.

Gard, Wayne. "FENCE CUTTING." *Handbook of Texas Online* <http://www.tshaonline.org/handbook/online/articles/auf01>. Published by the Texas State Historical Association.

General Laws of the Twelfth Legislature of the State of Texas, First Session—1871. Austin: J.G. Tracy, 1871. Retrieved at Google Books.

Gilman, Virginia Roberts. "WALSH, WILLIAM C." *Handbook of Texas Online* <http://www.tshaonline.org/handbook/online/articles/fwa44>. Published by the Texas State Historical Association.

Gonzales Daily Inquirer. Various dates. Retrieved at the Portal to Texas History, University of North Texas. <http://texashistory.unt.edu/>.

"The Gregory Family." PBS. <http://www.pbs.org/wgbh/pages/frontline/shows/secret/readings/gregory.html>.

Guttery, Ben R. *Representing Texas*. Self-published: 2008. Retrieved at Google Books.

Haley, James L. "RED RIVER WAR." *Handbook of Texas Online* <http://www.tshaonline.org/handbook/online/articles/qdr02>. Published by the Texas State Historical Association.

"Hancock Creek/Arroyo Seco, Part 1." Voices of the Violet Crown. <http://www.violetcrownvoices.com/2011/history-hancock-creek-part-1>.

Hardin, Stephen L. "WOOD, DAVID L." *Handbook of Texas Online* <http://www.tshaonline.org/handbook/online/articles/fwo06>. Published by the Texas State Historical Association.

Harrison, Shirley. "Dear Diary." <http://www.casebook.org/dissertations/maybrick_diary/deardiary2004.html>.

Hazlewood, Claudia. "SWAIN, WILLIAM JESSE." *Handbook of Texas Online* <http://www.tshaonline.org/handbook/online/articles/fsw01>. Published by the Texas State Historical Association.

Hendrix, Don. "JOHNSON, FRANCIS WHITE," *Handbook of Texas Online* <http://www.tshaonline.org/handbook/online/articles/fjo10>. Published by the Texas State Historical Association.

"Henretta Whitley." <http://www.findagrave.com/cgibin/fg.cgi?page=gr&GRid=19027152>.

"Historic Austin, Texas street names of trees." <http://www.city-data.com/forum/austin/922264-historic-austin-texas-street-names-trees.html>.

"Historic Resources Survey of East Austin, City of Austin, Texas." September 2000. <http://soa.utexas.edu/files/hp/eastaustinreport_opt.pdf>.

"History of the French Legation." <http://frenchlegationmuseum.org/about/history-2/>.

"History of Weed-Corley-Fish." <http://www.wcfish.com/_mgxroot/page_10720.php>.

"H.L. McCutcheon." < http://www.findagrave.com/cgibin/fg.cgi?page=gr&GRid=47235613>.

Hollandsworth, Skip. "Capital Murders." *Texas Monthly*, July 2000.

Hooker, Anne W. "HANCOCK, JOHN." *Handbook of Texas Online* <http://www.tshaonline.org/handbook/online/articles/fha46>. Published by the Texas State Historical Association.

Horton, Louise. *Samuel Bell Maxey: A Biography*. Austin: University of Texas Press, 1974.

Humeston New Era (Humeston, Iowa), 9/3/1885. Retrieved at Chronicling America, Library of Congress newspaper collection. <http://chroniclingamerica.loc.gov/newspapers/>.

Humphrey, David C. *Austin: A History of the Capital City*. Austin: Texas State Historical Association, 1997.

Humphrey, David C. *Austin: An Illustrated History*. Northridge, California: Windsor Publications, Inc., 1985.

Humphrey, David C. "Prostitution and Public Policy in Austin, Texas, 1870-1915." *Southwestern Historical Quarterly* 86 (April 1983).

Humphrey, David C. "AUSTIN, TX (TRAVIS COUNTY)." *Handbook of Texas Online* <http://www.tshaonline.org/handbook/online/articles/hda03>. Published by the Texas State Historical Association.

"The hush-hush history of the Moonlight Towers." <http://www.examiner.com/article/the-hush-hush-history-of-the-moonlight-towers>.

"Idaho, Deaths and Burials, 1907-1965." FamilySearch.org. <https://familysearch.org/pal:/MM9.1.1/FWDM-7LC>.

"Ida M. Phillips." <http://www.findagrave.com/cgi-bin/fg.cgi?page=gr&GRid=8446218>.

"Ida Mae Hart." <http://records.ancestry.com/Ida_Mae_Hart_records.ashx?pid=20925242>.

"Jack the Ripper 1888." <www.jack-the-ripper.org>.

"Jack the Ripper—Suspects"
<http://www.casebook.org/suspects/>;
<http://www.casebook.org/suspects/carroll.html>;
<http://www.casebook.org/suspects/cream.html>;
<http://www.casebook.org/dissertations/dst-pamandsickert.html>;
<http://www.casebook.org/suspects/eddy.html>;
<http://www.casebook.org/suspects/ft.html>;
<http://www.casebook.org/suspects/james_maybrick/maybrick.html>;
<http://www.casebook.org/dissertations/rip-thirdman.html>;
<http://www.casebook.org/suspects/tumblety.html>.

"James O. Phillips." <http://www.findagrave.com/cgi-bin/fg.cgi?page=gr&GRid=8446222>.

"Jesse Pomeroy, The Boy Fiend." <http://www.celebrateboston.com/crime/jesse-pomeroy-serial-killer.htm>.

"J.L. McCutcheon." <http://www.findagrave.com/cgibin/fg.cgi?page=gr&GRid=47242513>.

Johnson, Francis W. *A History of Texas and Texans*. Chicago: American Historical Society, 1914. Retrieved at Google Books.

Johnson, John G. "CAPITOL BOYCOTT." *Handbook of Texas Online* <http://www.tshaonline.org/handbook/online/articles/oec01>. Published by the Texas State Historical Association.

"Judge's Hill History." <http://www.judgeshill.org/history/history.html>.

Kemp, L. W. "BRIGHAM, ASA." *Handbook of Texas Online* <http://www.tshaonline.org/handbook/online/articles/fbr49>. Published by the Texas State Historical Association.

Kerr, Jeffrey. *The Republic of Austin*. Austin: Waterloo Press, 2010.

Koch, Augustus. *Austin Bird's-Eye Map, 1887*. Retrieved at Texas State Library and Archives Commission < https://www.tsl.state.tx.us/cgi-bin/aris/maps/maplookup.php?mapnum=2341>.

"The Lackey Murders." <http://lackeymurders.blogspot.com/2007_09_01_archive.html>.

London Star, 10/12/1888. Retrieved at <http://www.casebook.org/press_reports/star/s881012.html>.

Long, Christopher. "ANDREWARTHA, JOHN." *Handbook of Texas Online* <http://www.tshaonline.org/handbook/online/articles/fanxd>. Published by the Texas State Historical Association.

Long, Christopher. "MOONLIGHT TOWERS." *Handbook of Texas Online* <http://www.tshaonline.org/handbook/online/articles/chmrx>. Published by the Texas State Historical Association.

Los Angeles Herald, 11/18/1880. Retrieved at Chronicling America, Library of Congress newspaper collection. <http://chroniclingamerica.loc.gov/newspapers/>.

"The Lost Valley Fight," *Frontier Times*, Vol. 3, No. 3, December 1929.

Lotto, Frank. *Fayette County, Her History and Her People*. Schulenburg, Texas: published by the author, 1902. Retrieved at <http://archive.org/details/fayettecountyher00lott>.

"Lovey S. McCutcheon." <http://www.findagrave.com/cgibin/fg.cgi?page=gr&GRid=50413126>.

"Lunar calendar." <http://www.rodurago.net/en/index.php?site=details&link=calendar>.

Lynch, James D. *The Bench and Bar of Texas*. St. Louis: Nixon-Jones Printing Company, 1885. Retrieved at Google Books.

"Marie Fiset Hancock." <http://www.findagrave.com/cgibin/fg.cgi?page=gr&GRid=39817395>.

"Marriage Records of St. John Lutheran Church at Ross Prairie & Ellinger 1861–1963." Entry 29. <http://www.fayettecountyhistory.org/st_john_lutheran_marriages.htm>.

Marten, James A. "RIO GRANDE CAMPAIGN." *Handbook of Texas Online* <http://www.tshaonline.org/handbook/online/articles/qdr04>. Published by the Texas State Historical Association.

"Mayors of Austin, Texas." <http://politicalgraveyard.com/geo/TX/ofc/austin.html>.

Maysville Daily Evening Bulletin (Maysville, Kentucky). Various dates. Retrieved at Chronicling America, Library of Congress newspaper collection. <http://chroniclingamerica.loc.gov/newspapers/>.

McComb, David G. "HOUSTON, TX." *Handbook of Texas Online* <http://www.tshaonline.org/handbook/online/articles/hdh03>. Published by the Texas State Historical Association.

McCook Weekly Tribune (McCook, Nebraska), 10/8/1885. Retrieved at Chronicling America, Library of Congress collection.<http://chroniclingamerica.loc.gov/newspapers/>.

Mead, Daniel. *Report on the Dam and Water Power Development at Austin, Texas*. Madison, Wisconsin: 1917. Retrieved at Google Books.

The Medical News, volume 50 January-June 1887: 718.

The Medico-Legal Journal, Volume 39, 1922.

Mercantile and General City Directory of Austin, Texas—1872-1873. Retrieved at the Portal to Texas History, University of North Texas. <http://texashistory.unt.edu/explore/collections/CIT/browse/?fq=str_location_county%3ATravis+County%2C+TX>.

Miller, Aragorn Storm. "DENTON, ASHLEY NEWTON." *Handbook of Texas Online* <http://www.tshaonline.org/handbook/online/articles/fdeal>. Published by the Texas State Historical Association.

"Milwood History." <http://milwoodna.com/the-neighborhood/history/>.

"Missouri Project." <http://www.usgennet.org/usa/mo/topic/afroamer/upperla/pafg309.htm#10389>.

"Monthly Record of Observations Taken at Stations in the Cotton Region." Signal Service, USA. Austin: June, August, October 1885.

"Moon Chart." <http://www.life-cycles-destiny.com/dw/18811890.htm>.

Mooney & Morrison's General Directory of the City of Austin, 1877-1878. Retrieved at the Portal to Texas History, University of North Texas. <http://texashistory.unt.edu/explore/collections/CIT/browse/?fq=str_location_county%3ATravis+County%2C+TX>.

"Moonlight Towers-1895." <http://www.austinpostcard.com/moontower.php>.

"Moonlight Towers guide Austin through 110 years of history." *The Daily Texan*, 9/23/2005. <http://www.dailytexanonline.com/2.8461/moonlight-towers-guide-austin-through-110-years-of-history-1.975370>.

"The Moonlight Towers Of Austin, Texas, USA."
<http://www.bbc.co.uk/dna/h2g2/A830378>.

Morrison & Fourmy's General Directory of the City of Austin, 1881-1882.
Retrieved at the Portal to Texas History, University of North Texas.
<http://texashistory.unt.edu/explore/collections/CIT/
browse/?fq=str_location_county%3ATravis+County%2C+TX>.

Morrison & Fourmy's General Directory of the City of Austin, 1885-1886.
Retrieved at the Portal to Texas History, University of North Texas.
<http://texashistory.unt.edu/explore/collections/CIT/
browse/?fq=str_location_county%3ATravis+County%2C+TX>.

Morrison & Fourmy's General Directory of the City of Austin, 1889-1890.
Retrieved at the Portal to Texas History, University of North Texas.
<http://texashistory.unt.edu/explore/collections/CIT/
browse/?fq=str_location_county%3ATravis+County%2C+TX>.

Morrison & Fourmy's General Directory of the City of Austin, 1897-1898.
Retrieved at the Portal to Texas History, University of North
Texas.<http://texashistory.unt.edu/explore/collections/CIT/
browse/?fq=str_location_county%3ATravis+County%2C+TX>.

Morrison & Fourmy's General Directory of the City of Galveston, 1882-1883.
Retrieved at <www.natchezbelle.org>.

"Mostly Blanco County Families."
<http://wc.rootsweb.ancestry.com/cgibin/igm.cgi?op=GET&db=nanaj&id=I10814>;
<http://wc.rootsweb.ancestry.com/cgi-bin/igm.cgi?op=GET&db=nanaj&id=I10755>;
<http://wc.rootsweb.ancestry.com/cgi-bin/igm.cgi?op=GET&db=nanaj&id=I10766>;
<http://wc.rootsweb.ancestry.com/cgi-bin/igm.cgi?op=GET&db=nanaj&id=I10851>;
<http://wc.rootsweb.ancestry.com/cgi-bin/igm.cgi?op=GET&db=nanaj&id=I18483>;
<http://wc.rootsweb.ancestry.com/cgi-bin/igm.cgi? op=GET&db=nanaj&id=I10770>.

The National Tribune (Washington, D. C.), 9/3/1885. Retrieved at Chronicling America,
Library of Congress newspaper collection.
<http://chroniclingamerica.loc.gov/newspapers/>.

Nicklas, Linda Cheves. "ROBINSON, RICHARD P." *Handbook of Texas Online*
<http://www.tshaonline.org/handbook/online/articles/frobx>.
Published by the Texas State Historical Association.

New York Sun, 9/30/1885. Retrieved at Chronicling America, Library of Congress
newspaper collection.<http://chroniclingamerica.loc.gov/newspapers/>.

New York Times. Various dates. Retrieved at
<http://www.nytimes.com/ref/membercenter/nytarchive.html>.

O. Henry. "Law and Order," chapter 21 in *Sixes and Sevens.* New York:
Doubleday, Page & Company, 1920. Retrieved at Google Books.

O. Henry. *Rolling Stones*. New York: Doubleday, Page & Co., 1912.
Retrieved at Google Books.

Oakwood Cemetery Database, Austin History Center. Austin Public Library.
    <http://www.austinlibrary.com/oakwood/>.

Omaha Daily Bee. Various dates. Retrieved at Chronicling America, Library of Congress
    newspaper collection. <http://chroniclingamerica.loc.gov/newspapers/>.

"Our Campaigns." <http://www.ourcampaigns.com/RaceDetail.html?RaceID=264393>.

"Past Sheriffs." Travis County Sheriff's Office. <https://www.tcsheriff.org/about/agency-
    history/past-sheriffs>.

Pennebaker, James W. Professor of Psychology, UT. Personal interview.12/24/2011.

Photographs of John Hancock. Library of Congress Prints and Photographs Division. Brady-
    Handy Photograph Collection
    <http://www.loc.gov/pictures/item/brh2003001275/PP/>;
    <http://www.loc.gov/pictures/item/brh2003001725/PP/>.

Pike, L.J. *Austin Plat Map, 1839*. Retrieved at Texas State Library and Archives Commission.
    <https://www.tsl.state.tx.us/arc/maps/images/map0926d.jpg>.

"A Plot For A Million: Or, the Minister and the Penny Paper." <http://www.
    thevirtualdimemuseum.com/2009/06/plot-for-million-or-minister-and-penny.html>.

Ramsland, Katherine. *Inside the Minds of Serial Killers: Why They Kill*.
    Westport, Connecticutt: Praeger Publishers, 2006.

Ramsland, Katherine. "Servant Girl Annihilator." <http://www.trutv.com/
    library/crime/serial_killers/history/servant_girl/>.

Reno Evening Gazette (Reno, Nevada), 12/26/1885. Retrieved at Chronicling America,
    Library of Congress newspaper collection.
    <http://chroniclingamerica.loc.gov/newspapers/>.

Report of the Register of the State Land Office for the Year 1866. New Orleans: J.O. Nixon,
    State Printer, 1867. Retrieved at Google Books.

*Reports of cases argued and adjudged in the Court of Appeals of the State of Texas,
    Volume 4*. St. Louis: F.H. Thomas and Company, 1879. Retrieved at Google Books.

*Reports of cases argued and adjudged in the Court of Appeals of the State of Texas,
    Volume 6*. St. Louis: F.H. Thomas and Company, 1879. Retrieved at Google Books.

*Reports of cases argued and adjudged in the Court of Appeals of the State of Texas,
    Volume 10*. St. Louis: Gilbert Book Company, 1881. Retrieved at Google Books.

*Reports of cases argued and adjudged in the Court of Appeals of the State of Texas,
    Volume 21*. Austin, Texas: Triplett and Hutchings, Printers, 1886. Retrieved at
    Google Books.

Reports of cases argued and adjudged in the Court of Appeals of the State of Texas, 1886:
    Case no. 2271, James O. Phillips v. the State. (This source was retrieved at J.R.

Galloway's defunct utexas.edu web site, but the case information should be available in Volume 22.)

Reports of cases argued and adjudged in the Court of Appeals of the State of Texas, Volume 23. Austin, Texas: Hutchings Printing House, 1887. Retrieved at Google Books.

Richmond Dispatch (Richmond, Virginia), 9/30/1885. Retrieved at Chronicling America, Library of Congress collection.<http://chroniclingamerica.loc.gov/newspapers/>.

"Robert Headen Eanes (1854-1918)." <http://records.ancestry.com/Robert_Headen_Eanes_records.ashx?pid=65250531>.

Roberts, R. L. "MCGARY, AUSTIN." *Handbook of Texas Online* <http://www.tshaonline.org/handbook/online/articles/fmccg>. Published by the Texas State Historical Association.

"Robertson Genealogy Exchange." <http://robertson-ancestry.com/>; <http://robertson-ancestry.com/sitemap.htm>.

"Robertson-L Archives." <http://archiver.rootsweb.ancestry.com/th/read/ROBERTSON/1999-11/0942262805>.

Robinson, Charles F. *Dangerous Liaisons: Sex and Love in the Segregated South*. Fayetteville: University of Arkansas Press, 2003.

Rochester Democrat and Chronicle, 2/28/1886. Retrieved at <http://www.fultonhistory.com/Fulton.html>.

"Rubin Hancock Farmstead." <http://www.texasbeyondhistory.net/rubin/index.html>.

"Rubin Hancock Homestead." <http://milwoodna.com/the-neighborhood/history/>.

Sacramento Daily Record-Union. Various dates. Retrieved at Chronicling America, Library of Congress newspaper collection. <http://chroniclingamerica.loc.gov/newspapers/>.

St. Paul Daily Globe. Various dates. Retrieved at Chronicling America, Library of Congress newspaper collection. <http://chroniclingamerica.loc.gov/newspapers/>.

Saline County Journal (Salina, Kansas), 8/29/1879. Retrieved at Chronicling America, Library of Congress newspaper collection. <http://chroniclingamerica.loc.gov/newspapers/>.

Salt Lake Daily Herald. Various dates. Retrieved at Chronicling America, Library of Congress newspaper collection. <http://chroniclingamerica.loc.gov/newspapers/>.

San Antonio Daily Express. Various dates. Retrieved at<http://newspaperarchive.com/>.

San Antonio Daily Light. Various dates. Retrieved at Chronicling America, Library of Congress newspaper collection. <http://chroniclingamerica.loc.gov/newspapers/>.

Sanborn Fire Insurance Maps. Austin, Texas, June 1885. Geography and Map Division, Library of Congress. Retrieved at <http://www.lib.utexas.edu/maps/sanborn/texas.html>.

San Saba News. Various dates. Retrieved at Chronicling America, Library of Congress newspaper collection. <http://chroniclingamerica.loc.gov/newspapers/>.

Saylor, Steven. *A Twist at the End*. New York: Simon & Schuster, 2000.

"Servant Girl Annihilator." <http://www.serialkillercalendar.com/Brief_Bio_of_SERVANT_GIRL_ANNIHILATOR.html>.

Shiner Gazette, 3/3/1903. Retrieved at Chronicling America, Library of Congress newspaper collection. <http://chroniclingamerica.loc.gov/newspapers/>.

Simpson, Carolyn. qtd. in O'Connor, Lona. "Two Suns in the Sky." *Palm Beach Post*, 1/27/2011 <http://www.palmbeachpost.com/news/news/two-suns-in-the-sky-in-2012-maybe/nLpdM/>.

Smithwick, Noah. *The Evolution of a State, or Recollections of Old Texas Days.* Austin: Steck-Vaughn Company, 1968. Reprint of 1900 edition.

Smyrl, Vivian Elizabeth. "MASONTOWN, TX." *Handbook of Texas Online* <http://www.tshaonline.org/handbook/online/articles/hrm80>. Published by the Texas State Historical Association.

Spitzka, E. C. "The Whitechapel Murders: Their Medico-Legal and Historical Aspects." *Journal of Nervous and Mental Disease*, Volume 13, issue 12, Dec. 1888: 765-778.

Stephens, Robert W. *Texas Ranger Indian War Pensions*. Quanah, Texas: Nortex Press, 1975. Retrieved at <http://www.texasranger.org/EBooks/Texas_Rangers_Indian_War_Pensions.pdf>.

"Susan E. Richardson Hancock." <http://www.findagrave.com/cgi-bin/fg.cgi?page=gr&GRid=39816954>.

"SWEARINGEN, RICHARD MONTGOMERY." *Handbook of Texas Online* <http://www.tshaonline.org/handbook/online/articles/fsw06>. Published by the Texas State Historical Association.

Tarpy, Pat. "Burditt family." <http://www.mochaonline.org/Burdittfamily.pdf>.

Terrell, Alex W. "The City of Austin from 1839 to 1865." *The Quarterly of the Texas State Historical Association*, October 1910: 113-128. Retrieved at the Portal to Texas History, University of North Texas. <http://texashistory.unt.edu/>.

Testimony Taken by the Committee on Expenditures in the Department of Justice. Washington, D.C.: U.S. Government Printing Office, 1884. Retrieved at Google Books.

"Texas Deaths, 1890-1976." Retrieved at <www.familysearch.org>.

"Texas, Deaths (New Index, New Images), 1890-1976." Retrieved at <www.familysearch.org>.

"Texas, Death Index, 1903-2000." Retrieved at <www.familysearch.org>.

"Texas Marriages, 1837-1973." Retrieved at <www.familysearch.org>.

"The Texas Trail." <http://cdrh.unl.edu/diggingin/trailsummaries/di.sum.0004.html>.

"Texas Trails: Big Boom of 1882."<http://www.countryworldnews.com/news/texas-trails/1040-texas-trails-big-boom-of-1882.html>.

"Texas Trails: Venturing into Hell's Half Acre." <http://www.countryworldnews.com/news/texas-trails/978-texas-trails-venturing-into-hells-half-acre.html>.

"Thomas Montgomery Gregory—The Black Renaissance in Washington, D.C." PBS. <http://www.pbs.org/wgbh/pages/frontline/shows/secret/readings/gregory.html>.

"Thomas Phillips." <http://www.findagrave.com/cgi-bin/fg.cgi?page=gr&GRid=15560471>.

Thomas, William H. *The American Negro: What He Was, What He Is, and What He May Become*. New York: Macmillan Co., 1901. Retrieved at Google Books.

Thompson, Nolan. "CLARKSVILLE, TX (TRAVIS COUNTY)." *Handbook of Texas Online* <http://www.tshaonline.org/handbook/online/articles/hpc01>. Published by the Texas State Historical Association.

Thompson, Nolan. "WHEATVILLE, TX (TRAVIS COUNTY)." *Handbook of Texas Online* <http://www.tshaonline.org/handbook/online/articles/hpw01>. Published by the Texas State Historical Association.

Thrall, Homer S. *A Pictorial History of Texas*. New York: N.D. Thompson Publishing Co., 1885. Retrieved at Google Books.

Todd IV, William N., and Gerald Knape. "SPENCE, JOSEPH." *Handbook of Texas Online* <http://www.tshaonline.org/handbook/online/articles/fsp09>. Published by the Texas State Historical Association.

"Travis County Court Criminal Minutes 1876-1886." Microfilm Reel 987174. Austin History Center. Austin Public Library.

Trenton Times (Trenton, NJ), 2/1/1886. Retrieved at <http://www.casebook.org>.

The Twentieth Century Biographical Dictionary of Notable Americans, vol. 5. Boston: Biographical Society, 1904. Retrieved at Google Books.

A Twentieth Century History of Southwest Texas, vol. 1. Chicago: Lewis Publishing Company, 1907. Retrieved at Google Books.

"United States, Civil War Soldiers Index." Retrieved at <www.familysearch.org>.

Waco Daily Examiner (Waco, Texas). Various dates. Retrieved at Chronicling America, Library of Congress newspaper collection. <http://chroniclingamerica.loc.gov/newspapers/>.

Wallenstein, Peter. *Tell the Court I Love My Wife: Race, Marriage, and Law: an American History*. New York: Palgrave Macmillan, 2002.

Walling, George W. *Recollections of a New York Chief of Police*. New York: Caxton Book Concern, 1887.

Walsh, Mary Jayne. "DRISKILL, JESSE LINCOLN." *Handbook of Texas Online* <http://www.tshaonline.org/handbook/online/articles/fdr06>. Published by the Texas State Historical Association.

Walton, Richard H. *Cold Case Homicides: Practical Investigative Techniques*. Boca Raton: CRC Press, 2006.

The War of the Rebellion: A Compilation of the Official Records of the Union and Confederate Armies, Series 3, Vol. 4. Washington, D.C.: Government Printing Office, 1900.

Warren, Lewis S. *Buffalo Bill's America*. New York: Alfred A. Knopf, 2005.

Weekly Colorado Citizen (Columbus, Texas). Various dates. Retrieved at the Portal to Texas History, University of North Texas. <http://texashistory.unt.edu/>.

"What are the moonlight towers?" Austin Public Library. Austin, Texas. <http://www.austinlibrary.com/ahc/faq4.htm>.

"William Howell Eanes." <http://www.findagrave.com/cgibin/fg.cgi?page=gr&GRid=8297982>.

"William Howell Eanes (1848-1914)." <http://records.ancestry.com/William_Howell_Eanes_records.ashx?pid=34267286>.

Williamson, Ron. *The Texas Pistoleers: Ben Thompson and King Fisher*. Charleston, SC: History Press, 2010.

Woodford Times (Essex, England), 10/12/1888. Retrieved at <http://www.casebook.org/press_reports/woodford_times/881012.html>.

Worcester, Donald E. "CHISHOLM TRAIL." *Handbook of Texas Online* <http://www.tshaonline.org/handbook/online/articles/ayc02>. Published by the Texas State Historical Association.

Notice: Given the transitory nature of the World Wide Web, some of the Internet addresses given in this list of sources may no longer be active when access is attempted.

Index

Abortion 140, 257, 258, 274, 400
Ake, Burke (alias Bunk Ake, Tobe Williams, Taylor Ake, John Williams) 363, 364, 395
Allen, George 213, 214, 245, 250, 259, 260, 265-267, 269, 270
Allen, Tom 83, 85-87, 197
Andrewartha, John 342, 344
Archives War 6, 71
Assignation House 10, 173, 174, 214-216, 223, 225, 246-248, 252, 276, 281, 398, 399
"Athens of the West" 5, 26, 162, 168, 408
Austin City Council 10, 12, 54, 67, 69, 84, 87, 99, 113-115, 118, 119, 122-127, 129, 132, 133, 147, 148, 151, 153, 177, 180, 198, 202, 345, 402, 403
Ax, axes 5, 13-16, 18-20, 22-24, 52, 53, 56, 57, 63, 82, 86, 94, 96, 106, 114, 120, 130, 137-139, 141, 143, 144, 150, 154, 160, 161, 171, 172, 182, 183, 185, 189, 190, 192-194, 196, 216, 227, 234, 242, 243, 246, 251, 255, 268, 279-282, 309, 310, 312, 313, 320-322, 325, 333, 334, 336, 338, 344, 360, 371, 395-397, 400

Bacon, Richard 129, 202
Bailes, Thomas O. 62, 174, 179, 210, 224, 289, 294, 298-300, 302, 303, 305-308, 399, 400
Baker, Benjamin M. 222, 223, 247, 248, 255, 277
Beason, William L. 384-389, 392
Behnke, Mrs. Edward 44, 61
Bennett, Dr. T.J. 56, 119
Black Elephant Saloon 9, 20, 61, 74, 102, 115, 116, 123, 147, 156, 191, 198, 201, 355, 357, 359, 398, 406
Blake, Mrs. 165, 203, 204
Blanton, Mollie 373, 374, 390, 403
Bloodhounds 82-84, 137, 158, 179, 197, 214, 255, 260, 261, 263, 279, 334, 337, 338, 376, 379, 380, 396
Bob the bloodhound 255, 261, 263, 279
Boddy, Lucinda 91-93, 95-99, 108-111, 159, 199, 200, 396

Bostick, Mamie 375-380, 382, 383, 385, 388-391
Boyce, Richard A. 118, 275
Bracken, John 210-212
Brackenridge, John T. 47, 50, 342, 344, 353, 354, 370, 403
Bragg, Dr. Thomas H. 275, 319
Breckinridge, George W. 353, 403
Brigham, Asa 6, 355
Brooks, William "Lem" 19-22, 26, 41, 55, 61, 129, 191, 193, 194, 196, 197, 394
Brown, Douglas 59, 60
Brown, George 314, 319, 323, 325
Brown, Henry 60, 70, 117, 158, 246
Brown, Rosie 20, 21
Brown, Sydney 176, 177
Brown, William M. 105, 148, 220, 343
Brunet, Joseph 296, 318, 323
Bullock, Richard 6, 12
Bundick, Tom 76-80
Burdett, Thomas A. 110, 140, 145
Burditt, Alice Missouri (Eanes) 140, 142, 145, 366
Burditt, Alma M. 140, 249, 250, 255
Burditt, Thomas P. 140, 145, 174, 208, 256, 257, 259, 262, 263, 271
Burglaries 28-30, 66, 68, 97, 100, 114, 177, 200, 212, 378, 400
Burleson, Albert S. 267, 269
Burt, Dr. William J. 18, 20, 22, 52, 67, 83, 85, 137, 143, 171, 192, 197, 211, 291, 296, 312, 313, 321, 405
Burt, Horace Roscoe 312-314, 321, 322
Butler, Michael 61, 92

Callaway, John I. 44, 45, 63
Campbell, Delia (Adelia Phillips) 214, 215, 222, 244, 246, 249, 253-255, 257-259, 265, 273-275, 278, 281, 283, 284, 287
Campbell, Evan 272, 273, 278, 291
Campbell, Lum 278, 287
Capitol 5, 6, 8, 29, 31-33, 36-38, 40, 41, 44, 46, 50, 59, 66, 71, 72, 74, 100, 105, 146, 154, 159, 183, 194, 195, 205, 220, 247, 342-344, 398
Carrington, Albert 84, 132, 396, 397
Carrington, Edward H. 84

Carrollton House 101, 111, 121, 200
Casanova, J.M. 320, 322
Chalmers, Thomas 16, 17, 20
Chamomile 140, 258, 274
Chenneville, John 47, 82, 94, 99, 100, 291
Chloroform 30, 49, 56, 57, 95, 99
Clarksville 9, 12, 141, 142, 219, 260, 404
Colorado River 5, 6, 8, 9, 34, 36, 44, 131, 157, 206, 342, 351, 352
Confederacy (Confederates) 41, 71, 72, 88, 110, 142, 147, 198, 219, 289, 342, 343, 346, 347, 356
Conner, James R. 59, 64, 94, 96, 116, 117, 121, 127-129, 164
Coombs, Jack 119, 177, 201, 202, 340
Coopwood, Bethel 209, 290, 298-300, 309, 328, 406
Coroner 18, 61, 78, 82, 97, 98, 143, 171, 172, 321, 332, 335-338, 340, 341, 361, 372, 400, 406
Corwin, Dennis 50, 70, 249, 364, 395
Creary, Edward 110, 249, 253, 258, 367
Creary, Kate (Phillips Deats) 244, 249, 253, 255, 258, 259, 269, 274, 367
Crockett, Cullen 129, 130, 202
Cross, Irene 59-61, 63, 64, 66, 86, 107, 160, 167, 170, 180, 183, 185, 237, 283, 333, 362, 374, 395, 405, 406; map 60
Cross, Washington 59, 60, 64
Cummings, Dr. Josephus 211, 251, 252, 267-269, 275, 327, 365
Custer, Elizabeth 7, 8
Custer, George Armstrong 7

Dallas, Texas 10, 28-30, 39, 49, 80, 109, 120, 121, 140, 147, 183, 236, 375-378, 380, 381, 387, 389
Dam 8, 343, 349, 352-354, 367, 403, 404
Daniels, L.E. 50, 281
Davis, Alice 119, 120, 177, 201, 332, 340
De Saligny, Alphonse Dubois 6, 9
Decordova, Phineas 148, 149
Deison brothers 306, 307
Dengue fever 91, 96, 406
Denton, Dr. Ashley N. 217, 218, 343, 344
Detectives 21, 22, 28, 29, 49. 50, 62, 81, 86, 99, 101, 105, 107, 108, 111-118, 122, 124, 130, 147, 148, 159-161, 165, 167, 173, 174, 178-180, 184, 190, 191, 193, 198, 199, 201, 204, 205, 209, 210, 221, 223, 224, 237, 238, 270, 276, 279, 282, 289, 295, 298-305, 307-310, 315, 320, 331, 334, 335, 379, 381, 384, 397, 399, 402
Dickinson, John T. (Dickerson) 247-249, 253, 254, 344
Dixon, Samuel H. 291, 292, 297, 324
Dodge, George M. 237, 238
Donnan, John K. 47, 85
Driskill Hotel 118, 204
Driskill, Jesse L. 118, 204
Driskill, John 118, 125, 126
Drummer, Glenn 108-111, 118, 131, 159, 198-201, 205, 393, 394, 401, 407
Duff, Harry H. 93, 94, 96, 100, 102, 110, 136
Dumont, Blanche 10
Dunham, William B. 91, 92-97, 99, 100, 103, 105, 109, 110, 362, 396, 397, 406
Duval, Thomas 7, 346, 358, 359, 369
Dyer, Annie 259, 263, 270

Eanes, Annie 364-366
Eanes, Claude 141-144, 146, 171, 172
Eanes, Hugh L. 142, 143, 145
Eanes, Mollie (Vess) 141-144, 146, 171, 172, 406
Eanes, Robert H. 364-367, 399
Eanes, William H. 364-367, 399
Eberly, Angelina 6
Echols, J.Q. 164, 203
Elgin, Nathan 205, 210-212, 215, 217, 218, 257, 287, 327-329, 340, 364, 368, 371, 379, 391, 393-395, 399-401, 407
Elgin, Texas 244, 253, 258, 259, 262, 310
Evans, Ben C. 384-386, 388, 389
Evans, Ira 147, 149
Evans, Jack 289, 328, 359

Fallwell, M.J. 179, 299, 300, 302, 303, 316
Felder, G.S. 130, 131
Femgerichte 26, 39, 40, 41, 239
Fence-cutting 66, 261, 350
Finley, Richard W. 46, 47
Finnin, Mary A. 62, 63
Fisher, Dr. C.E. 245, 268, 269, 275
Footprints 15, 19, 52, 53, 84, 86, 139, 144, 165, 166, 183, 190 196, 197, 202-204, 212, 215, 216, 234, 245, 257, 267, 269-272, 279, 282, 283,

425

287, 327, 329, 340, 378, 379, 390, 393-396, 399, 400
Francois, Emile 204, 205, 358, 359

Gainesville, Texas 234, 364, 374-378, 380-390
Galveston, Texas 7, 16, 19, 69, 84, 159, 236, 280, 359, 363
Gangs 26-29, 31, 54, 56, 63, 73, 106, 159, 165, 168, 180-184, 186, 191, 194, 195, 200, 204-206, 250, 280, 355, 357, 368, 393-395, 397, 400, 401
Gassaway, Joseph W. 292, 298, 299, 303-306, 314, 315, 319, 320
Georgetown, Texas 287, 288, 351, 355, 366, 407
Gibson, Patsy 92, 94-99, 108, 159, 333, 396
Glass, Lena (Steiner) 313, 314, 318, 319
Glass, Thomas 292-294, 297, 313, 314, 317-319, 322-325, 328
Glover, Jim 110, 111, 115, 131, 198
Gosling, Marshal Hal 26-28, 30, 36, 42
Government 6, 7, 32, 41, 44, 57, 64, 66, 67, 72, 73, 88, 89, 111, 112, 120, 122, 124, 128, 132, 133, 135, 146, 148-151, 154, 156, 168, 183, 219, 220, 222, 247, 330, 342-344, 346-349, 353, 397
Governor 91, 147, 167, 205, 219, 221-223, 225, 226, 255, 343, 345, 346, 349, 350, 351, 359, 369, 377, 385, 398, 399
Gray, John (Gray Jo) 165, 204, 205
Green, Dr. Joseph G. 217, 218, 343
Gregory, Thomas Montgomery 356, 359, 368
Guy Town 5, 9, 10, 13, 37, 47, 48, 63, 73, 74, 101, 119, 158, 165, 191, 195, 203, 362, 367, 394, 398, 408

Haenelt, Paul 292, 294, 297, 313, 318, 321, 322, 325, 326, 328
Hagy, David 136, 203, 289-293, 295, 296, 299-302, 305-308, 311, 312, 314, 321, 324, 325
Hall, Charlotte 38, 47, 120
Hall, Lucy 46, 47, 120
Hall, Sarah 33, 38, 39, 47, 51, 120, 194
Hall, William K. 13-17, 19-21, 33, 47, 56, 120, 394, 407
Hamilton, J.E. 241, 253, 280
Hancock, Aron 398

Hancock, Edwin B. 355-357, 367, 368
Hancock, George Duncan 345, 346
Hancock, Hugh Berry 20, 61, 74, 115, 123, 191, 355-357, 359, 361, 363, 368, 398, 406
Hancock, Hugh Ella (Huella) 356, 357, 368
Hancock, Ida 136, 203, 289, 290, 292, 293, 298, 300, 301, 306, 307, 309, 312, 314, 316-320, 324, 325
Hancock, James 365, 367, 369
Hancock, John 7, 50, 147, 180, 209, 241, 248, 279, 280, 290, 308, 309, 328, 344-353, 355-359, 361-365, 367-369, 393-395, 397-401, 403, 405, 406; photo 348
Hancock, John Allen 345, 355
Hancock, Lena (Ramsey) 136, 203, 289, 290, 292, 293, 299-303, 306, 307, 309, 312, 314, 316-320, 324, 325
Hancock, Lewis 180, 345, 353, 397, 403
Hancock, Moses H. 59, 136, 137, 144, 158, 171, 178-182, 184, 192, 203, 206, 209, 210, 213, 217, 218, 224, 246, 287-306, 308-310, 312-329, 341, 358, 359, 368, 371, 374, 397, 398, 400-403, 405, 406
Hancock, Orange 355
Hancock, Payton 355, 398
Hancock, Rubin 352, 355, 368, 398
Hancock, Salem (Solom) 355
Hancock, Susan C. (Sue) (Mrs. Moses) 59, 136, 137, 139, 144, 146, 155-157, 159, 163, 165-168, 170-172, 174, 178-181, 192, 199, 200, 203, 206, 209, 210, 238, 246, 266, 280, 283, 289-306, 308-310, 312-329, 333, 374, 397, 398, 402, 405, 406; map 136
Hancock, Susan E. (Richardson) (Mrs. John) 355, 356, 398
Hancock, Susie E. (James O'Connor) (Mrs. Hugh) 356, 357, 398
Hancock, Thomas 140, 287, 407
Hanna, Detective 22, 99, 111, 116, 130, 193
Hatchet 5, 16, 23, 52, 53, 55-57, 63, 112, 124, 166, 172, 179, 182, 183, 185, 190, 197, 203, 310, 322, 344, 371, 372, 375, 385, 388, 395, 396, 397
Hennessey, Detective Mike 22, 99, 111, 116, 130, 159, 165, 193, 204, 205
Henry, O. (William S. Porter) 12, 18, 24, 26, 74, 80, 205, 206, 290, 294, 368

Highsmith, Albert 248, 256, 257, 286
Hopkins, Preston 117, 123
Hornsby, Malcolm M. 69, 97, 98, 110, 158, 164, 202, 310, 327, 329, 371, 390, 400, 405
Hornsby, W.W. 96, 97
Houston, Sam 5, 6, 71
Houston, Texas 6, 7, 10, 22, 71, 99, 116, 159, 180, 184, 193, 199, 201, 204, 205, 221, 226, 249, 265, 311, 368, 397, 402, 406
Huntsville, Texas 7, 51, 109, 342
Hutto, Texas 174, 262, 407

Indians 6, 112, 225, 349, 352
Inquests 3, 21, 22, 52, 53, 61, 78, 82, 92, 97, 98, 142, 170-173, 175, 178, 194, 199, 212, 301, 336, 372, 377, 406
Interracial marriage 357-359
Ireland, Governor John 91, 154, 167, 205, 221, 349, 350, 359
Iron Front Saloon 9, 13, 68, 93, 102, 110, 130, 131, 136, 292, 303, 318, 319, 325
Ivey, Henry 301, 306, 307, 325

Jack the Ripper 4, 5, 227-236, 238, 239, 400
Jackson, Andrew 48, 57, 195
Jaqua, Stephen 81-83, 89
Jekyll-Hyde 185, 188-190
Johnson City, Texas 75-77
Johnson, Isaiah W. 115-118, 320-322, 324
Johnson, Dr. Lucien B. 50-52, 55, 56, 82, 196, 197, 327, 364, 395, 405
Johnson, Nora 61-63
Johnson, R.W. 125, 127-129
Jones, Frank E. 265, 267, 270
Jones, George "Wash" 349-351

Kelley, Fannie 10
Kelly, John W. 37, 39
King, Rosa 293, 294, 297, 313, 314, 318, 325, 328
Kirk, John P. 249, 265, 267, 304, 315

Lackey, Albert Newton 75-79, 81, 186
Lamar, Mirabeau B. 5, 6
Lambert, Will 147, 316
Lawlessness 8, 38, 39, 88, 152, 152, 192, 362, 396
Lawrence, John W. 46, 47

Leader, William Y. 49, 50, 115, 281, 352
Ledbetter, Edwin J. 257, 262, 271
Lee, Horatio Grooms 5, 17, 50, 67-73, 87, 88, 96, 97, 115-118, 122-129, 132, 133, 149, 191, 198, 246, 249, 266, 345, 357, 364, 367, 395, 397, 401, 404, 405, 407
Lee, Joseph 6, 31, 71, 72, 345, 365, 367, 405
Lee, Lydia (Mrs. Joseph W. Robertson) 6, 70, 71
Litten, Dr. James M. 174, 214, 245, 250-252, 266-268, 271, 275
Luckie, William (Luckey) 119, 177, 201, 202
Lucy, James E. 9, 132, 133, 135-137, 149, 152, 175, 176, 246, 248, 249, 291, 302, 314-317, 320, 329, 332, 349, 364, 371, 390, 397, 407
Lunatics 8, 23, 41, 45, 119, 141, 159, 160, 166, 184, 195, 204, 206, 217, 229, 231, 235, 343, 384, 399
Lust 94, 159, 160, 179, 184, 187, 335, 360, 377
Lynching 30, 77, 78, 83, 85, 87, 98, 108, 115, 123, 147, 164, 170, 176, 177, 197, 202, 205, 364, 377, 389, 390

Mack, Alexander 83-85, 87, 108, 110, 111, 115-118, 123, 125, 127, 128, 133, 159, 191, 197, 198, 205, 211, 250, 357, 394, 396, 397, 407
Mack, Sallie (Cook) 83, 123, 198, 250
Maguire, Eugene (McGuire) 244, 249, 265
Manchaca (Manschac) 244, 248-250, 253
Martinez, Anastacio 165, 166, 203, 204, 399
Masontown 9, 74, 83, 84, 210, 404
Maurice the Malay cook 191, 237, 238, 400
McCall, John D. 343, 345, 354
McCormick, Moses 326, 327
McCutcheon, Beauregard 243, 253, 258, 274
McCutcheon, George 208, 213, 243, 244, 248-250, 253, 255-259, 262, 263, 271, 273, 274, 284, 286, 311, 407
McCutcheon, Jack 257, 258, 262
McDonald, John 352, 353
McDowell, Emma H. 290, 294
McDowell, Henry 294, 295
McGary, Austin 342, 344
McLaughlin, Dr. J.W. 266, 367

McMillan, C.D. 364, 365, 366, 367, 399
Metz Brothers 9, 118, 119
Miller, Joel 148, 223, 224
Miller, Mason C. 270, 278
Miller, Monroe 271
Miscegenation 205, 355, 357, 358, 359
Mitchell, Fred 257, 258, 259
Mitchell, R.B. (Bob) 258, 262
Montopolis 12, 342, 343
Moon, full 13, 38, 56, 75, 81, 118, 170, 190, 195, 232, 372, 375
Moonlight 13, 14, 15, 96, 111, 138, 150, 165, 170, 232, 260, 265, 283, 375,
Moonlight towers 403, 404
Moore, E. Taylor 106, 184, 209, 213, 214, 216, 224, 241, 276, 280, 289, 365, 367, 406
Moore, Luke 179, 302, 303
Moore, Maurice 364-366
Moore-Hancock Farmstead 351, 352, 359, 368; photo 360
Morphine 10, 283, 367, 406
Morris, Dr. Wade 31, 32, 36, 37, 39, 56, 97, 100, 101, 200
Mount Bonnell 141, 164, 206
Mulatto 18, 29, 33, 38, 41, 59, 61, 84, 106, 130, 141, 143, 154, 194, 205, 333, 355-357, 368, 371, 372, 398, 401, 406

Necrophilia 189
Nisbet, J. Alexander 300, 311
Norwood Brothers (J.P. and J.T.) 164, 174, 202, 308
Nude (Nudity) 18, 138, 154, 251, 266, 268, 272, 275, 281
Numerologists 185

Oakwood Cemetery 18, 56, 61, 62, 71, 73, 84, 85, 98, 103, 119, 137, 140, 144, 171, 271, 311, 342-344, 353, 355, 365, 367-369, 404-407
Old John 63, 195
Opium (Opiates) 5, 10, 228, 229, 367, 379
Outrage (or rape) 15, 16, 19, 20, 29, 30, 33, 36-39, 41, 44, 45, 47, 49, 51, 53, 56, 63, 74, 82, 83, 85-88, 94, 96-98, 106, 108, 110, 113, 114, 118, 120, 124, 139, 150, 151, 159, 161, 165, 166, 170, 172, 177, 182-185, 187-190, 193-198, 202-204, 206, 211, 212, 216, 227, 268, 280, 333, 336, 337, 344, 360-366, 372, 373, 377, 382, 389, 390, 394-397, 400, 401
Overton, Beverley 96, 99, 199

Panic 86, 87, 91, 122, 133, 135, 170, 171, 176
Parmalee, Richard {Robinson) 23, 24
Pearl House 191, 238, 400
Pearson, Abe 33, 39, 41, 47, 51, 194
Pearson, Tom and Bob 35, 36,
Penn, John 244, 249
Persinger, Atlas M. 137, 158, 292, 294-297, 304-306, 312-315, 318, 321-324
Persinger, Mary 290, 295, 297, 301, 302, 313, 319, 321, 323, 325
Persons, Sam 130, 131
Phillips, Eula (Burditt) 10, 138-140, 142, 144-146, 155-157, 159, 163, 165-168, 170-172, 174, 175, 179, 180, 192, 198-200, 202, 203, 206, 212-216, 218-226, 232, 238, 240-253, 255-263, 265-277, 279-283, 286-288, 291, 292, 308, 310, 324, 327, 329, 333, 343, 344, 366-368, 374, 379, 397-399, 402, 405-407; map 139
Phillips, James O., Jr. (Jimmy) 138-140, 145, 173-175, 178-182, 184, 192, 206, 209, 210, 212-214, 216, 217, 219, 221, 223, 224, 240-250, 252, 255, 256, 259, 261-263, 265-273, 275-277, 279-284, 286-289, 291, 292, 294, 310, 311, 329, 330, 341, 344, 358, 367, 368, 371, 379, 398-401, 403, 405-407
Phillips, James O., Sr. 138, 139, 166, 173-175, 198, 212, 214, 215, 217, 244, 246, 249, 250, 257-263, 265-267, 269-272, 274, 275, 279, 287, 301, 327, 367, 393, 398, 406
Phillips, Sophia 173, 213, 214, 241-246, 250, 255, 256, 258, 259, 262, 265, 266, 274, 287, 398, 405
Philp, Kenward 331-341, 342, 344, 345, 359-362, 368, 393, 394, 396, 398-401, 407
Pig War 6
Pinkerton 50, 107, 108, 221, 309, 402, 403
Pitts-Yeager-Scott-Brannon Gang 26-28, 36
Platt, Radcliff 113, 114, 118, 126, 132
Platting of Austin 6, 9, 10
Plummer, Ike 55, 56, 111, 183, 196, 197, 395

428

Poisoning 142, 143, 227, 236, 332, 341, 400, 407
Pope, John H. 36, 37, 39, 43, 55, 195, 196
Population of Austin 10, 122, 161, 404
Prostitution, prostitutes 5, 10, 12, 23, 106, 107, 119, 120, 184, 185, 189, 201, 202, 227, 394, 400
Purnell, Thomas F. 52, 82, 89, 96, 98, 101, 212, 246, 406

Ramey, Mary 82-87, 91, 94, 107-109, 115, 116, 118, 129, 130, 132, 163, 166, 167, 170, 180, 197, 198, 200-202, 212, 238, 283, 396, 397, 399, 405-407; map 82
Ramey, Rebecca (Becky) 81, 82, 84-86, 89, 91, 94, 102, 107, 116, 132, 201, 396, 397, 406
Ramsey, Jack 295, 305
Ramsey, Sallie 302, 303, 316
Rape (or outrage) 15, 16, 19, 20, 29, 30, 33, 36-39, 41, 44, 45, 47, 49, 51, 53, 56, 63, 74, 82, 83, 85-88, 94, 96-98, 106, 108, 110, 113, 114, 118, 120, 124, 139, 150, 151, 159, 161, 165, 166, 170, 172, 177, 182-185, 187-190, 193-198, 202-204, 206, 211, 212, 216, 227, 268, 280, 333, 336, 337, 344, 360-366, 372, 373, 377, 382, 389, 390, 394-397, 400, 401
Raymond, James H. 319, 349, 353, 403
Revenge 15, 19, 41, 49, 81, 107, 109, 155, 163, 168, 173, 185, 188, 235, 240, 331, 333, 335, 337, 355, 360, 361, 394-397, 401, 408
Reward 113, 114, 118, 124, 155, 167, 177, 180, 181, 202, 210, 221, 237, 299, 303, 377, 380, 388, 389, 398, 399
Robertson, James H. 22, 71-73, 98-100, 108, 118, 130, 193, 209, 213, 214, 216, 241, 248, 275, 276, 279, 280, 285, 287, 289, 290, 292, 300, 307, 327, 329, 330, 397, 406
Robertson, John W. 9, 10, 32, 71-73, 97, 113, 124, 125, 132, 146, 148, 241, 304, 329, 367, 402, 405
Robertson, Dr. Joseph W. 6, 9, 70, 71, 72
Robertson Hill 9, 53, 71, 74, 98
Robinson, Della 10
Rockdale, Texas 176, 177
Rogers, Andrew 55, 196, 197, 395

Rosenberg (See Von Rosenberg)
Ross, Sul 225, 226, 385
Rust, Ella 37, 38, 39, 128, 291, 297
Rutherford, Adolphus S. 38, 39, 43

Saloons 5, 6, 9, 13, 20, 28, 48, 53, 61, 66, 68, 73, 74, 84, 93, 102, 110, 115, 116, 119, 123, 130, 131, 136, 147-149, 151, 156, 173, 191, 193, 198, 201, 210, 211, 238, 292, 303, 307, 311, 318, 325, 355, 357, 359, 361, 398, 406
San Antonio, Texas 5, 6, 8, 23, 26, 27, 46, 67, 68, 70, 94, 100, 106, 108, 132, 141, 143, 152, 159, 165, 172, 178, 179, 186, 204, 209, 212, 221-224, 240, 289, 290, 299, 300, 302, 303, 308, 315, 316, 319, 342, 343, 371-373, 378, 385, 390, 398
Scaggs, William T. (Skaggs) 289, 291, 292, 297-300, 302-305, 308-310, 314, 319, 320, 323
Scaggs, M.A. 298-300, 302, 324
Scholz's Garden 9, 59
Scott, Patty 371-373
Sellers, Mattie 61-63
Shelley, Nathan G. 147, 248, 260
Shelley, William D. 247, 248
Shelly, Eliza (Shelley) 50-53, 55-57, 59, 63, 64, 66, 82, 86, 95, 107, 111, 167, 170, 180, 182, 183, 196, 197, 236-238, 248, 283, 327, 333, 364, 394, 395, 404, 405; map 51
Shoal Creek 8, 13, 16, 19, 44, 260, 394
Simon's Restaurant 68, 132, 211
Smith, Carrie 10
Smith, Mollie 13, 15-20, 22-24, 26, 30, 32, 33, 38, 41, 47, 52, 54-56, 61, 63, 66, 85, 86, 107, 120, 129, 130, 154, 167, 170, 180, 182, 183, 192-194, 196, 236, 283, 329, 333, 394, 395, 397, 399, 404; map 17
Snyder, Mary 327, 328, 330
Spanlard, George 383, 384
Spence, Joseph 343, 345
Spencer, Cynthia 20, 85, 225
Spencer, Walter 16-22, 24, 26, 41, 47, 52, 55, 85, 114, 130, 131, 182, 192-194, 196, 197, 206, 287, 329, 394, 397, 400, 406
Spitzka, Dr. E.C. 233, 234, 235, 239, 378
St. Louis, Missouri 19, 28, 29, 49, 52, 56, 183, 230, 407

Stewart, Joe H. 32, 33, 39, 62, 63, 148
Stoddard, Dr. Charles 48-50, 56, 57, 95
Stone-cutters Association 29, 31, 194
Stotts, Lottie 204, 205, 358
Stovall, Dr. James 34-36, 42
Strand, Clara 36
Street names 10, 11
Suares, Isaac 22, 61
Swain, William J. 32, 219-226, 241, 247, 252, 343, 398, 399, 406
Swearingen, Dr. Richard M. 17, 24, 35, 37, 82, 83, 130, 406
Swensen, Christine 36, 37, 43

Taylor, Henry 84, 197
Templeton, John D. 32, 36, 37, 195
Terrell, Alexander W. 147, 148, 217, 350, 351
Theories 15, 20, 74, 106-108, 130, 139, 157-163, 172, 173, 175, 179, 182-185, 187, 189, 193, 194, 215-217, 228, 229, 231, 234, 235, 238, 279, 280, 282, 283, 332-336, 340-343, 360-362, 368, 377, 393-395, 400
Thomas, Henry 129, 130, 202
Thompson, Ben 5, 8, 19, 20, 67-70, 132, 162, 163
Thompson, James 20, 129, 202
Thompson, Walter 19, 20, 129
Thornton, Alex 156, 326, 328, 330
Thug Gang 159, 165, 168, 180, 181, 184, 191, 199, 200, 204-206, 250, 355, 357, 368, 393-395, 397, 400, 401
Tobin, Doc 47, 195
Tobin, Dr. John 21, 135, 257, 258, 274
Tobin, May 10, 214, 215, 219, 246-249, 252-255, 276, 277, 281, 284, 399, 407
Toe, peculiar or missing 52, 84, 197, 212, 257, 258, 269, 327, 329, 340, 379, 393, 395, 400
Townsend, Oliver 97, 99-103, 105, 107-109, 111, 115, 129, 159, 163, 181, 198, 200, 201, 205, 326-328, 371, 391, 393, 394, 397, 399-401, 407
Travis County, Texas 19, 34, 49, 71, 73, 75, 97, 100, 106, 124, 145, 158, 159, 202, 224, 249, 253, 308, 310, 327, 328, 343, 363, 364, 366, 369, 390, 400, 401, 404, 405
Trigg, Johnson 101, 102, 105, 109, 111, 114, 115, 119, 121, 129, 199, 200, 201, 397
Turner, Sam 390

Vance, Grace (Gracie) 91-98, 100-103, 105-111, 113-115, 119, 159, 163, 167, 170, 180, 198-201, 283, 333, 337, 340, 362, 396, 397, 399, 405, 406; map 92
Von Rosenberg, William, Jr. 18, 21, 29, 35, 55, 61, 70, 92, 97, 173, 174, 178, 196, 209, 212-214, 216, 259-261, 265, 266, 272, 290, 298, 303, 305, 307, 314, 332, 399, 400, 406
Von Rosenberg, William, Sr. 352, 399
Voodoo 64, 74, 120, 183, 335, 360

Waco, Texas 7, 9, 19, 20, 24, 30, 39, 52, 53, 107, 154, 159, 160, 179, 193, 209, 221, 224, 225, 241, 289, 290, 299, 301-303, 316, 319, 394, 398, 406
Walker, Alexander S. 217, 240, 241, 284, 286, 307, 328, 358
Wallace, Henry 48, 195
Waller, Edwin 6, 10
Waller Creek 36, 44, 157
Walsh, William C. 343, 345
Walton, William 68, 213, 216, 217, 241, 272, 280, 284, 285, 287, 289, 330, 367, 406
Ward, Allen 381, 382, 384
Ware, Sheriff H.P. 377, 382, 383
Washington, George 23
Washington, Orange 91, 92, 94, 96-98, 101, 102, 106, 109, 167, 168, 170, 180, 199, 200, 333, 362, 396, 405, 406
Watkins, Genie 375-377, 379-385, 389-391
Weather 15, 16, 24, 26, 135, 347, 376
Weed, Bella Brush 85, 407
Weed, Daniel 300, 315
Weed, Valentine O. 81-87, 197, 300, 315, 316, 396, 407
Weller, Dr. Cyrus O. 97
Wheatville 9, 74, 404
Wheeless, Thomas H. 272
Whipple, Fannie 214, 215, 244, 246, 249, 253, 284
Whitechapel, London, England 227-239, 378, 391, 400, 401
Whitley, Henretta 390
Williams, Andrew 53, 55, 196
Williams, Ed. 363, 364
Williamson County, Texas 73, 134, 174,

208, 243, 244, 248, 250, 253, 255-258, 262, 263, 287, 311, 351, 364
Wittman, August 361, 362, 369, 395, 397, 406
Wittman (Whitman), Sophie 59, 64, 362, 369, 395, 406
Wood, David L. 357, 358
Woods, Dock (Doc) 95-101, 103-111, 115, 129, 159, 163, 165, 198-201, 204, 205, 397, 399, 407, 408
Woods, Douglas 98, 104, 111

Woods, William 389, 390
Wooldridge, A.D. 258, 262
Wooldridge, Alexander P. 10, 148, 149, 167, 262, 352, 353, 367, 398, 403, 407
Wooten, Dudley G. 37, 126, 127, 290, 363, 364
Wooten, Dr. Thomas 37, 62

Xenophobia 183

Thanks and Acknowledgments

Thanks, first, to my wife, Anne Souby, for her research and patience. Thanks to my friends and colleagues who have endured my ramblings about the topic. Thanks also to Austin History Center and Austin Community College Library for their help in securing materials for this project. Special kudos go to James R. Galloway, who has provided valuable information about the mystery via his transcription of Austin news reports on the murders. Other researchers provided useful information, as well. Several Web sites proved useful in the research, chief among them the Library of Congress with its Chronicling America newspaper archives and the Portal to Texas History at the University of North Texas, an online repository of items from historical centers across the state. Google Books and Archive.org also proved to be excellent sources of historical items.